# THE BERG–SCHOENBERG CORRESPONDENCE
*Selected Letters*

*Alban Berg and Arnold Schoenberg, ca. 1914*

# THE
# *Berg-Schoenberg*
## CORRESPONDENCE

———

## *Selected Letters*

———

*Edited by*

JULIANE BRAND

CHRISTOPHER HAILEY

*and*

DONALD HARRIS

W · W · NORTON & COMPANY

*New York · London*

Published simultaneously in Canada by Penguin Books Canada Ltd,
2801 John Street, Markham, Ontario L3R 1B4
Printed in the United States of America.

The text of this book is composed in Electra,
with display type set in Deepdene.
Composition and manufacturing by The Maple-Vail Book Manufacturing Group.
Book design by Jacques Chazaud.

First Edition

Library of Congress Cataloging-in-Publication Data

Berg, Alban, 1885–1935.
The Berg-Schoenberg correspondence.

Includes index.
1. Berg, Alban, 1885–1935—Correspondence.
2. Schoenberg, Arnold, 1874–1951—Correspondence.
3. Composers—Austria—Correspondence.    4. Composers—
Correspondence.    5. Music—20th century—History and
criticism.    I. Schoenberg, Arnold, 1874–1951.
II. Brand, Juliane.    III. Hailey, Christopher.
IV. Harris, Donald.    V. Title.
ML410.B47A4    1987      780'.92'2      86–8346

ISBN 0-393-01919-5

W. W. Norton & Company, Inc., 500 Fifth Avenue, New York, N. Y. 10110
W. W. Norton & Company Ltd., 37 Great Russell Street, London WC1B 3Nu

1 2 3 4 5 6 7 8 9 0

# Contents

# List of Illustrations

# Introduction

Given the importance of Arnold Schoenberg and Alban Berg, it may seen irreverent to begin this publication on a somewhat whimsical note. Nonetheless, the history of this volume began unceremoniously in 1963 with a chance encounter. I was a young composer living in Paris when I met François-Regis Bastide, the director of a collection of monographs called Solfèges, published by the Editions du Seuil. Most of the well-known composers of the eighteenth and nineteenth centuries were already covered in his series, and he was beginning to branch out into the twentieth. I suggested that he consider a volume on George Gershwin, an appropriate subject, thought I, for a struggling American musician seeking recognition and in need of remuneration. Bastide mulled over my proposal for a few weeks and then responded: "What about a Berg? I don't need a Gershwin."

My reaction was astonishment. Why should an American write in French about a Viennese composer? It seemed an exercise doomed to failure even with the best of credentials, and mine, at the time, were modest indeed. Nevertheless my interest was piqued. I began to look into what had been written about Berg and discovered that although there was beginning to be a considerable body of literature concerning his works, very little had been written about his life. Redlich's very important critical study, extremely sketchy in biographical detail, had been published in 1957.[1] Willi Reich's biography, somewhat less sketchy but also less reliable, had only just appeared in 1963.[2]

I had heard that the Schoenberg Collection, which included his correspondence, had been deposited in the Library of Congress. The following summer I went to Washington and, thanks to Edward N. Waters, then Assistant Chief of the Music Division, received permission to look the collection over. I read through a vast number of letters and cards which Berg had written to Schoenberg and immediately understood how important they were for a biography. But before I could use them, I had to receive written permission from Gertrud Schoenberg, the composer's widow, to gain legitimate access to the collection, and then similar permission from the other widow in question, Helene Berg, to reprint any of the letters or use their contents in my proposed biography. I was warned that these permissions were dif-

1. H. F. Redlich, *Alban Berg: The Man and His Music* (London: John Calder, 1957).
2. Willi Reich, *Alban Berg* (Zurich: Atlantis Verlag, 1963; English trans., Cornelius Cardew, London: Thames & Hudson, 1965).

ficult, if not impossible to obtain. Evidently others had tried unsuccessfully before me.

It may have been impudence on my part, or naiveté, but I wrote directly to Mrs. Schoenberg outlining my request. Her surprising response came in November:

Dear Sir,

I am sorry that I could not give you permission until now, because I am waiting for an O.K. from Berg's widow who resides in Vienna, Trauttmannsdorff-gasse 27, Wien XIII, Austria. It is, of course, her decision to which I abide. Please write her a letter asking her permission and I will of course grant you mine after that. If you can, please write her in German and also send her an envelope with your address. This will hurry up things.

I am sorry to cause this delay but you must understand my point of view, being also a widow.

With kindest regards and best wishes,

Sincerely,
Gertrud Schoenberg

The path to Mrs. Berg proved only marginally more difficult. I opted not to accept Mrs. Schoenberg's advice, and did not write to Mrs. Berg in German. Instead I sought counsel from the Austrian Institute in Paris. Frau Marie-Edith Eberle, a member of the staff, was most helpful. Some months later, after I had met Mrs. Berg and established contact, Frau Eberle would help me write such letters. For the moment she wrote to Universal Edition, Berg's publishers, on my behalf, and to the Ministry of Culture in Vienna, enlisting their support. Early in December I was notified that Mrs. Berg would see me. We were to meet in Vienna later in the month before the holiday season.

For various reasons my trip was twice delayed. Our meeting did not take place until late January 1965. In the meantime I read everything I could get my hands on about Berg's life and informed myself as much as possible about his widow. I had been told that she was distant, elusive, not in good health, and fiercely protective of an incredibly pure image of her husband's life which she wished to maintain for posterity. Her opposition to the completion of the third act of *Lulu* was already well known. Needless to say, those facts about Berg's life which were to come to light twenty years later, such as the existence of an illegitimate daughter, Albine, or the secret agenda in the Lyric Suite, which described an illicit liaison with another woman, Hannah Fuchs-Robettin, were events which his widow wished to conceal. Neither was known then, nor were the reasons why Mrs. Berg had opposed the completion of *Lulu*, which proved to be a surprisingly uncomplicated task once Berg's *particell* became available upon her death in 1976.

That first meeting was very productive. I explained my project to Mrs. Berg and found her to be neither elusive nor distant, but most interested and supportive. I also found her in excellent health—a tall, striking, statuesque woman. Mrs. Berg took great pains to describe to me the lengths to which she had gone to protect the bulk of Berg's oeuvre from the Nazis. It was later confirmed that she had hidden his scores under the floorboards of the garage at their summer home on the Worth-ersee in Kärnten. She also described the foundation she had set up to protect Berg's work for the future and to aid young musicians upon her death. The Alban Berg Stiftung is today a functioning body. Among its many projects, it has greatly supported the publication of the Berg–Schoenberg correspondence. At the conclusion of our visit, when I asked for permission to quote from the letters, she responded without hesitation that if Trude (Mrs. Schoenberg) was willing to do so, then she would certainly do the same. A letter, dated January 27, 1965, formalized this arrangement.

In May of that year I received from the Library of Congress photocopies of all the letters from Berg to Schoenberg in its collection. I began to work on the transcription and translation of the letters with the first of my collaborators, an Austrian living in Paris, Frau Gi Veit, who was particularly adept in deciphering the handwriting styles of the period. The task proved to be monumental, but, unfortunately, the results were less than satisfactory.

We are taught as children that half a loaf is better than none. As far as this project was concerned, it was not long before I decided that half a loaf was hardly acceptable. To be sure, Berg had written to Schoenberg more frequently and at greater length than Schoenberg wrote to Berg. But to have the responses of one without the questions of the other, and vice versa, left too many gaps in the narrative. Even though at the time I was only attempting a biography of Berg, it became clear that what Schoenberg had written to his student—and later colleague—was as critical for an understanding of Berg's life as what Berg himself had written to his teacher. My French connection, Bastide, with whom I consulted, agreed, proposing an edition of the complete correspondence.

This project ran aground almost immediately. Mrs. Schoenberg resisted. She wrote in February 1966 that she intended to publish her husband's correspondence herself. Helene Berg also objected and said that she would approve the use of Berg's letters for biographical purposes but did not want the correspondence published in its entirety. During the next few years, I attempted to complete the biography, in vain. In the back of my mind, I never forgot how important it would have been to publish the correspondence. I had given the project up as unrealizable, but it was a continual preoccupation which hindered and ultimately prevented the progress of my research.

I returned to the United States in 1968. In 1975, I ran into Claire Brook, music editor at W. W. Norton, who suggested that I look into the publication of the letters once again. Perhaps the time was now ripe. It wasn't, but we were getting closer. It took another five years—until 1980—before rights had been secured and a contract issued. During the intervening years, I made several trips to Vienna, sent and received many telegrams, and had one precious but fleeting glimpse of the Schoenberg letters while visiting Mrs. Berg a few months before her death, when permission was *almost* obtained. By 1976, all rights to the materials in the Schoenberg Collection had been transferred to the Schoenberg estate, which was administered in this country by the composer's two sons, Ronald and Lawrence. They were not interested in publishing the letters themselves, as their mother had been, and were supportive of my project. Likewise, through the good offices of Claire Brook, I was placed in contact with Franz Eckert, one of the founding members of the Alban Berg Stiftung. The collaboration of this foundation was to prove decisive. It would have seemed then that with the support of the copyright holders on both sides, permission to photocopy the letters of Schoenberg to Berg, which had been deposited in the Austrian National Library upon Mrs. Berg's death, ought to have been relatively simple. However, it took another two years before these copies were obtained and another two before preliminary permission to publish was secured. Final clearance from the Alban Berg Stiftung was not obtained until 1985!

In the meantime, I had found another collaborator, Dr. Laurence Lyon, a recent Ph.D. in German literature from Harvard, who proved extremely helpful in the early negotiations until he gave up in despair at the incredible delays. Finally, I met Christopher Hailey and Juliane Brand, two young musicologists who were vitally interested in the period and conversant in German and colloquial Viennese. Their expertise in transcribing, translating, and annotating the correspondence has enabled the three of us to bring this volume to completion. In addition, Hailey and Brand were able to uncover a number of letters which had gotten lost or gone astray.

Why is the first publication of the letters in English? One reason lies in the intense interest of American scholars in the period and in the composers. With respect to Berg–Schoenberg scholarship in particular, Americans have been most persistent in their quest for historical accuracy. The work of George Perle is a striking example. He was the first to bring forth the truth about the third act of *Lulu*, almost twenty years before the opera was ultimately completed. It was through his efforts, along with those of Douglass Green, another American, that the hidden agenda of the Lyric Suite was first brought to light. Another example of this quest is the publication of this correspondence. It reveals two individuals who were as human and frail as the best and the worst of us. Our opinions of their music will not be changed, but our understanding of their times and the issues with which they were confronted will be significantly illuminated. Another level of perception will have been uncovered, and if the revelations are not as sensational as some may have presumed, neither are they mundane or prosaic. A probing biography of Berg, as well as further and more substantive studies on Schoenberg, are now almost possible. Still lacking are the published collections of the Berg–Webern and the Webern–Schoenberg correspondences. Perhaps the appearance of this volume will help spur on the other two.

Throughout the correspondence virtually every figure of musical importance in Vienna, indeed in most of Europe, along with those prominent in the worlds of fine arts or arts and letters, pass in review. We learn less about these others, though, than about Berg and Schoenberg themselves. Advocacy for Schoenberg's doctrines and beliefs is the single most important leitmotif in the correspondence. Almost everyone mentioned, however prominent in his or her own right, is seen as a believer or a detractor. Even Webern appears less as an individual than as a protagonist for Schoenberg's ideas. Many of the letters, particularly in the early years, discuss these issues of advocacy in great detail. In these instances Webern was as faithful a lieutenant as Berg.

Not surprisingly Berg's attitude toward Schoenberg was one of hero-worship. His total commitment to Schoenberg's ideas, as well as his astonishingly servile behavior in nonmusical matters will seem, however, surprising by today's standards. What Schoenberg expected of any student went far beyond what we would expect of students today. But the importance of his teaching in the evolution of his students, which in the case of Berg and Webern is virtually unparalleled given the value history has placed on their music, has been shown to have been decisive. Berg sensed this from the outset of his studies with Schoenberg in 1904. He willingly played by his teacher's rules, which were, to a large extent, the rules of the day. The subservient tone of Berg's early letters reveals characteristics of a traditional Central European teacher–student relationship which were not uncommon at the turn of the century. Berg was convinced that Schoenberg was as important a musical giant as J. S. Bach, to whom he happily compared him in an article written twenty-five years after he had completed his studies.[3] By the same token Berg's obsequious turn of phrase could lead one to believe that he was as intimidated by Schoenberg as he was in awe of him. He was rarely forthright. Almost always, particularly in the early years, his reasonings were circuitous, designed not to annoy or anger his master.

If Berg was the faithful disciple, willing and eager to prepare the index of the *Harmonielehre*, or to rehearse the chorus for the premiere of the *Gurrelieder*,[4] he was also the handyman, agreeing to oversee the moving of Schoenberg's personal effects to Berlin, negotiate with the movers, and generally tend to matters of no artistic worth, tasks which teachers today would hardly assign to their pupils.[5] Was this a sign of weakness, or, rather, of fear? After all, one did not cross the master without danger of excommunication. There is more than one occasion in the letters when Schoenberg's ruffled sensibilities require soothing.

Berg did fear Schoenberg and considered him a prophet, the bearer of truth from on high. Like many prophets, Schoenberg could be tyrannical, or at least perceived as such. His word, like that of Moses, was law, whether in the studio, the classroom, or in rehearsal. Berg hung on his every word, often would beg forgiveness when he felt, rightly or wrongly, that he had been mistaken, and never would question the wisdom of the elder without taking extreme precaution. A case could be made that Berg went too far in the direction of subservience, certainly at the beginning of their relationship. But one must never forget the correctness of Schoenberg's assessments, particularly insofar as Berg's music was concerned. Schoenberg's implied criticism of Berg's Altenberg Songs or the Clarinet Pieces, both of which were composed after he had left Schoenberg's direct tutelage, led to Berg's reexamination of his own style and objectives.[6] The result was first noticeable in the final movement of the Three Pieces for Orchestra, and ultimately in *Wozzeck*, his longest and most substantial composition reflecting the major innovative

3. A. Berg, "Credo," *Die Musik*, XXIV/5, (Berlin; January, 1930).
4. Both the *Harmonielehre* and the *Gurrelieder* are discussed in letters exchanged between 1911 and 1913.
5. See letters of 1911–13.
6. Compare the letter of 17 January 1913, Berg to Schoenberg, with that of 22 November 1915, Berg to Schoenberg, for an understanding of Schoenberg's implied criticism.

changes in compositional style that Schoenberg had brought about both before and after the First World War.

During the course of the correspondence, Berg's tone changes more than Schoenberg's. He ultimately made the giant leap from student to colleague, but it was painful, as painful as the maladies from which he suffered and to which he so often referred. The moving letter of 1918 in which Berg first used the familiar form of address is a milestone in their changing relationship.[7] But it was years before Berg would truly think of his teacher as a friend more than as a father figure. During the interim, the younger man gained some of the self-assurance he so badly needed. Certainly, after the success of the Lyric Suite and *Wozzeck*, Berg became known in his own right and not merely as Schoenberg's student. Important too in his development was the fact that the older man was increasingly absent from Berg's life; their meetings were less frequent, and consequently, Schoenberg's influence less overbearing. Needless to say, there were always remnants of the servile relationship, which Berg could never consciously give up in spite of Schoenberg's apparent willingness to do so.

Schoenberg's compositional advances were initially out of Berg's reach. The latter's concern, for example, that he would never understand *Pierrot Lunaire*[8] is not unlike his first experience with the twelve-tone system and his initial attempts to use it.[9] The idea that bound the two men together was their unwavering belief that Schoenberg's was the path to the future. Added to this was their common ambivalence about Vienna, the city of inherited traditions which had failed to recognize their talents and give them their due. Berg kept Schoenberg informed of what was happening in their native city. Sometimes the accounts were positive, like the description of Ravel's visit to the *Verein*.[10] More often than not they were critical, either of the press or of Hertzka and the Universal Edition over financial and artistic matters.

The Viennese musical establishment has always been essentially conservative and rigid. This is by now a fact accepted by all who are familiar with the vicissitudes suffered by Mozart, Beethoven, Schubert, or Mahler. It is therefore not surprising that Vienna did not play host to *Wozzeck* until it had become a success throughout Europe, and Schoenberg was denied major performances following the premier of the *Gurrelieder* in 1913 until well after the Second World War. However critical of Vienna both composers were, they were nonetheless always "Viennese" composers. They never ceased to hope for the approbation of their native city, and were always pained when it never came.

Two events described in ample detail in the correspondence will substantiate this point. Schoenberg had composed his monumental oratorio for chorus, soloists, and extra large orchestra, the *Gurrelieder*, in 1900. It was not orchestrated, however, until 1911, and only performed two years later when the composer Franz Schreker agreed to conduct the premiere. Since Schoenberg was living in Berlin at the time,

7. See letter of 24 June 1918, Berg to Schoenberg.
8. See letter of 20 July 1914, Berg to Schoenberg.
9. See letter of 13 July 1926, Berg to Schoenberg.
10. See letter of 28 October 1920, Berg to Schoenberg.

rehearsals were held without his participation. There were many problems attendant upon this gigantic undertaking, documented in many letters written between February 1912 and February 1913. Besides preparing the Guide to the *Gurrelieder*, a one-hundred-page analysis which Universal Edition published to coincide with the premiere, Berg prepared the piano reduction, corrected the proofs of the orchestral score, conducted choral rehearsals, and helped organize and promote the concert. The event was an unmitigated success: Schoenberg received a fifteen-minute ovation from the Viennese public, an exceedingly rare occurrence for him.

Such was not the case with the *Skandalkonzert*, which took place only months later. The program was to have included premieres of works by Webern and Berg along with performances of Schoenberg's Chamber Symphony, Opus 9, Four Orchestral Songs of Zemlinsky, Mahler's *Kindertotenlieder*, and the *Prelude and Liebestod* from *Tristan and Isolde*. Schoenberg was to have conducted the entire program. A critic for the Boston Evening Transcript recounted the event on 17 April 1913. "On the last day of March, Arnold Schoenberg conducted his 'Kammersymphonie' and pieces of two of his pupils of the 'Ultrists' in the Grosser Musikvereinsaal in Vienna. . . . The result was a commotion such as has never occurred in a Vienna concert hall. Hisses, laughter, and applause made a bedlam. Between numbers little groups of disputants came within an inch of blows; one of the composers shouted remarks and entered into the row; the conductor went on strike; an official boxed the ears of a man who had publicly assaulted him; the police commissioner ordered the hall cleared, and the concert was stopped before the final number. All because some 'Ultrists' or 'musical cubists' insisted upon going a little further than even an advanced musical public would tolerate."

The critic, known only by his initials, H. K. N., goes on to describe Schoenberg's reactions. "Out in the 'artists' room was Schoenberg, wildly talking to whomever was within hearing distance, or to the surrounding space. He would not conduct before such an audience. It was unbelievable. His arms waved, his bald head rolled about and his little figure jerked this way and that. The manager and some members of the orchestra gathered around to calm or persuade him. He grew momentarilly more excited. Then in a flash, he ducked through the door and was gone."

Berg's contribution to the program consisted of two of the Altenberg Songs. It was the last time he was to hear any of this composition during his lifetime. The next performances of this work did not take place until 1952, seventeen years after his death. This concert program of 1913, however, viewed in retrospect, represented the quintessence of contemporary music in the early part of this century for which Vienna is now remembered. Along with the works of its three most important protagonists, Schoenberg, Berg, and Webern, were compositions by Zemlinsky, who was almost their equal in stature and unquestionably their equal in conviction, plus works by Wagner and Mahler, from whom all four drew their inspiration. Nevertheless the Viennese public turned its back on them and their future endeavors. The events leading up to the *Skandalkonzert*, and in particular Berg's reactions, are well documented in the correspondence. The concert undoubtedly provided an important impetus for Schoenberg's creation of the Verein immediately following the First World War.

When the armistice was signed, Vienna was a destitute city. Whatever part of its musical life Schoenberg and his entourage might have laid claim to was virtually eliminated by the all-pervading poverty. Schoenberg's answer was to create his own musical environment: he founded the *Verein für musikalische Privataüffuhrungen*, literally Society for Private Musical Performance. The Viennese public would no longer figure in their considerations. The audience was invited through subscriptions and only those with membership passes could enter the concert hall. Later on, in 1920, there were special propaganda concerts, such as the one mentioned earlier when Ravel was invited to perform. But in 1918, when the Verein was founded, only the informed were participants. Schoenberg described the Verein's premises: there would be clear, well-prepared performances, with frequent rehearsals. The performances must not be touched by the corrupting influence of publicity. There must be neither applause nor expressions of disapproval.

Even though the performances were private, as Schoenberg had stipulated, and had little impact on the public side of Viennese musical life, the Verein concerts were important in that they brought together musicians with common interests to explore and study artistic issues of the day and to familiarize themselves with the musical developments of other nations. It was a learning experience not as public as the Bauhaus, for example, but with similar goals. Much of the activity of the Verein is chronicled in the correspondence. Berg was an officer. He drew a small salary and tended to many of the organizational details, often at the expense of his own composition.

As the activities of the Verein came to a close in 1922, the relevance of Vienna to the musical livelihoods of Berg and Schoenberg began to diminish in importance. This had been gradually taking place during preceding years in any event, but during the following years subsequent to Schoenberg's move to Berlin in 1926, Vienna almost ceased to play any activity whatsoever as a backdrop for their activities. In the case of Berg, for example, who did continue to reside in Vienna, the Lyric Suite was first performed there by the Kolisch Quartet in 1927. It was but one of numerous performances of this work that would take place throughout Europe during the following years, thereby insuring an international success for which Vienna could hardly be held responsible. On the other hand both the Chamber Concerto and *Wozzeck* received their premieres in Berlin, a city far more receptive to new music. The Verein would be the last important activity of the Schoenberg circle in which Berg would actively collaborate. His international career had begun in earnest with the success of *Wozzeck* in 1925; it would rival Schoenberg's. Little by little the collaboration between the two lessened. Opportunities for interaction between them grew fewer and fewer.

The tone of the correspondence began to change as it began to wind down. The intensity of communication preceding the First World War and during the Verein years was never to be recaptured. There was no need for it. After 1925 few letters were exchanged, and those that were are by and large less agitated, less polemical, and less engaged. More often than not they consist of simple exchanges of information, of reports on what one or the other has been doing. References to their own music, however, becomes much less detailed.

There is a passing reference to *Moses and Aron*, as well as a few other compositions on which Schoenberg was working, but little or no understanding of his compositional process is gained. Beyond Berg's groping for permutations of the row to
satisfy structural needs in *Lulu*, he, too, became less communicative about his
music as his career progressed. More lighthearted comments now appear, such as
the description of the 1930 Ford cabriolet which Berg purchased, and which is still
in good working order in the garage of the Berg summer home on the Worthersee,
or the amusing Schoenberg letter-newspaper of September 22, 1928.

The mood changes when Schoenberg converts to Judaism in Paris, before emi-
grating to the United States. The specter of Nazi Germany is at hand. Not only
does Schoenberg express his fears about whether he would be able to retain his
appointment at the Academy in Berlin, the reality of a hostile Europe in which he
would have no place begins to set in. His first months in the United States are
described in several letters, one of which is a rather graphic representation of the
problems he encountered in this country and his bitter disappointment.[11]

Berg's final letters and Schoenberg's responses cannot fail to touch the reader.
The former's concern for his teacher's comfort and happiness never wavered from
those first moments when he began to serve his master in just about every way
possible. At the end, as in the beginning, the correspondence is initiated by Berg.
Schoenberg's responses are almost always replies, for that was the nature of the
relationship. But, finally, it is Schoenberg who writes to Helene Berg when he
learned of Berg's death. His letter and her response reflect a sadness and grief which
we cannot but share.[12] Whatever his reasons for not completing the third act of
*Lulu*, he remained faithful to his pupil and friend. The friendship between them
had begun in 1904 when Berg became his student. It was to end with the two men
separated by thousands of miles and two continents, so there could be no final
adieu. During their lifetimes each wrote much of the century's most important
music. Through their letters they have left a moving testimonial to their lives, their
times, their music, and their relationship; in view of the technological advances of
the last half-century, in which letter writing has almost become a thing of the past,
this may well be one of the last times in which so much of history will have been
recorded by the protagonists themselves.

Donald Harris

11. See letter of 25 November 1934, Schoenberg to Berg.
12. See letters of December 1935, Schoenberg to Helene Berg, and her reply, 14 January 1936.

# Translators' Preface

With a self-acknowledged propensity for looking gift horses in the mouth, Arnold Schoenberg once wrote to Alban Berg concerning the latter's gift of Wagner's autobiography, *Mein Leben*:

> Actually the book isn't what I had hoped for, since I had above all expected: insight into the inner experiences that led him to his works. Instead he writes almost entirely—obviously intentionally—about external events. [13 January 1912]

Those approaching the Berg–Schoenberg correspondence for the first time may be similarly disappointed. One could expect a correspondence between two of this century's most significant composers, numbering approximately eight hundred items and spanning nearly all of the thirty-one years of their relationship, to be a documentary source of unparalleled richness. Riches there are, but "insight into inner experiences," or, indeed, the subject of their own compositional development, are rarely among them.

One must approach the correspondence between Berg and Schoenberg with a clear awareness of the limits of the relationship. Theirs was less a meeting of the minds than a coincidence of needs, a kind of intellectual, spiritual, and psychological dependency. While each man no doubt held the other in genuine esteem and affection, each maintained a lifelong reserve that—certainly on paper—prevented any truly candid exchange of ideas. In that regard the contrast between the Berg–Schoenberg correspondence and that of Berg and Webern or Webern and Schoenberg is particularly striking, for both Berg and Schoenberg were much readier to share personal feelings and artistic motivation with Anton von Webern.

The often mundane nature of a working correspondence like this one demonstrates how crucially important letter writing was in the time before telephones had become the common means of communication. Though obvious, this statement deserves elaboration. The postal system, representing as it did the one and practically only method of long-distance communication, offered rather more differentiated and more efficient services than it does today. A letter posted in Vienna by midday might well be delivered in Berlin by the afternoon of the next day and an express letter might arrive in as little as twelve hours, possibly that same day. In large cities mail was delivered up to three times a day—in 1912 Berg actually complains that there was but one daily delivery in the remote mountain village of Tra-hütten. Furthermore, many larger cities had elaborate pneumatic systems, whereby communications from one section of town to another could be expedited within the hour; more valuable intracity packages, money drafts, etc., could be sent by private messenger.

As a matter of fact, the efficiency of the postal system can be seen as a reflection of the quickening pace of contemporary life, where writing long and thoughtful letters was becoming a vanishing art. By the early twentieth century correspondence editions had acquired their place as a literary genre that they continue to enjoy today. Interest in and publication of composers' letters, which began in earnest in the 1860s, was to some degree an outgrowth of the subjective sensibilities of the nineteenth century. If an artwork was a reflection of personality—indeed, if the artist's *personality* was his ultimate creation—then those products of intimate communication offered an insight into that personality which could be as revealing as the artworks themselves. In the last third of the nineteenth century musicology under the pioneering leadership of Gustav Nottebohm lent scholarly legitimacy to this preoccupation with the by-products of the artistic mind by emphasizing the importance of manuscripts, drafts, sketches, and letters as source material. It is not surprising that artists became aware of their debt to posterity and soon self-consciously began to preserve the tangential papers of their creative lives. By the twentieth century this concern had become obsessive—in 1926, for instance, Richard Strauss and Hugo von Hofmannsthal authorized the publication of their correspondence in their own lifetime.

Self-consciousness came early to members of the Schoenberg circle. By 1911 Schoenberg was sufficiently convinced of his historical importance that he began saving most of his sketches and correspondence, as well as making carbon copies of his own important letters. Moreover, there is no doubt that the copious marginalia in his books and letters were penned for posterity, like so many bottled messages tossed into the seas of time. Berg's habits of preservation, on the other hand, might be better classified as simply compulsive. When, for instance, Schoenberg expressed anxiety regarding the fate of his papers during his 1911 move from Vienna to Berlin, which Berg, Webern, and Polnauer were overseeing, Berg reassured him:

> There can be no question of "throwing anything away." How could I throw away so much as a piece of paper bearing a word of yours or a brushstroke or even just one note. Before I'd do that I'd take it home myself, for it goes without saying that I save everything of yours, be it only an envelope for printed matter or the like. [26–27 September 1911]

Though Berg and Schoenberg no doubt wrote certain of their letters to each other with future readers in mind, the substance of the correspondence is a natural reflection of the needs of the day—and of their different attitudes toward letter writing. Berg enjoyed correspondence as a form of self-expression and for the discursive freedom it allowed him. (The fact that he made and then preserved so many drafts—now in the Berg Archive—attests to the importance he accorded the activity.) It is consequently not surprising that he was particularly fond of published letter editions; in the early years many of his Christmas and birthday gifts to Schoenberg took just that form: Christmas 1910 the five-volume collection of Beethoven letters, Christmas 1912 the two-volume Balzac's *Letters to a Stranger*, 1916 the Wagner–Liszt correspondence. Schoenberg became increasingly annoyed, as it turned out, for he suspected that the gifts were a broad hint regarding his own letter-writing style (and so he told Berg in a September 1916 letter).

Schoenberg's antipathy toward reading letters reflected his dislike of writing them. For him, letters were more often than not a time-consuming and tedious chore, and in a letter to Webern of 31 October 1927 he articulated what apparently was a deep-seated frustration with the form itself: "I find it increasingly difficult to write something as incomplete and as improvised in form and content as a letter."

Their attitudes toward correspondence reflect something of the essential dichotomy between Schoenberg and Berg as personalities. Indeed, one is tempted at every turn to draw analogies between the form and content of their letters and their creative processes and compositional styles. Schoenberg, especially in the early years, is brief and to the point. He writes for the sole purpose of transmitting or requesting information and he likewise exhorts Berg to organize his thoughts, number or underline key points, write more legibly, and in general simplify his prose. Berg, on the other hand, who sent at least three letters to Schoenberg for every *one* he got in return, appears to have written as the thought occurred to him and reveals at times a fairly astonishing convolution of logic. As in his piano reductions and analytic guides, he revels in detail, and his attempts to take every conceivable factor, real or imagined, into account result in complex and often confusing perorations.

From the myriad of unequal parts that make up the Berg–Schoenberg correspondence there emerges a richly textured whole that cannot easily be summarized or abridged. In their entirety the letters conjure up a picture of nearly three decades of European cultural history, most particularly that of Vienna. We learn to appreciate the importance of the café as a meeting place and as a branch library for the plethora of local newspapers. We begin to grasp just how far Berg's thirteenth-district home in Hietzing must have seemed from central Vienna when many of his longest—and least legible—letters are written on the hour-long trip. We get a feeling for the rigid hierarchy of Viennese society, for the system of "contacts" and "influential acquaintances" by which things were accomplished, and for the geographic concentricity of Vienna's cultural life, focused as it was on the central first district. Most important, we are introduced to a range of personalities, known and unknown, who populated the intersection of Berg's and Schoenberg's lives—an imposing cast of supporting characters, many of whom are no less important to an understanding of the period than the two correspondents themselves.

The value of the Berg–Schoenberg correspondence lies less in its merits as a source for future Berg and Schoenberg biographies than in the perspective it gives us on these men and in the way it places the Schoenberg School in a larger cultural setting. The history of early twentieth-century music history has for the most part yet to be written and where it has been writ large, it must be rewritten. Berg–Schoenberg research is a case in point. Postwar publication on the so-called Second Viennese School was a chummy sort of undertaking, more reliant upon fond recollection, and on random, self-serving source selection than historical scholarship. The sloppy editorial practices and haphazard selection of some earlier letter editions typify the worst excesses of a-historical hero worship. Yet at a time when the sources were still guarded as jealously as the grail, these works permitted a vicarious peek into an inner sanctum. Only in the past twenty years or so have the availability of important primary sources and new standards of accuracy imposed upon scholars the responsibility to air out that musty sanctum and to assign its relics their appropriate place among the artifacts of our culture. Today, we have entered a period of demythologizing and revisionism. One can no longer discuss Berg's operas without knowledge of the works of Franz Schreker, one cannot trace the origins of Schoenberg's "system" without studying analogous contemporary experiments, or consider Webern's conducting style without a familiarity with turn-of-the-century Viennese performance practice. We must recognize that no historical edifice—sanctum or otherwise—can be allowed to stand without a factual and contextual foundation.

Careful and objective research must be the cornerstone of that foundation. With regard to the Schoenberg circle it is fortunate that so many sources have survived two wars and the emigration of most of its principal figures. Among the most important sources are not only the correspondences among Schoenberg, Webern, and Berg, but the dozens of equally vital exchanges with fellow composers, students, performers, friends, and relatives. Today most of these sources are readily available in public research institutions, but the task of sifting through them has only begun. Our present needs call less for a cult of personality than for the illumination of an era. The Berg–Schoenberg correspondence is therefore first and foremost a document of the period, not a sacred relic from the founding saints of a sect.

The political and economic turmoil of this century has not encouraged a sense of historical continuity or organic growth. Posterity has tended to confuse the fragments salvaged from the wreckage of an era with the era itself. It is our hope that this edition will enable the reader to read between the lines, to read critically, to read objectively, and to discern that one perspective is valuable only to the degree it informs a vision of the whole. If part of the historian's painstaking task is to reconstruct the past from the artifacts of its culture, then the Berg–Schoenberg correspondence can provide a source whose sum is greater than its unequal parts.

## Selection

Reference has been made to the comprehensiveness and bulk of this correspondence. However, gaps do exist. During the past four years of collecting, transcribing, translating, and annotating, it was possible to supplement the main body of letters in the Library of Congress and Vienna National Library by about three dozen additional items from a variety of archives and private possession; in addition, a number of letter fragments could be completed from drafts found in Washington and Vienna, bringing the total to 725 cards and letters and 37 telegrams. Unfortunately, a number of letters are in the hands of private collectors, who, despite the intercession of the Alban Berg Stiftung, have refused to provide copies for publication. Obstructive practices by dealers and collectors, often in collusion with librarians, are an unsavory but very real curse upon scholarship. Seven letters from Berg to Schoenberg from the years 1934–35 were entirely unavailable for purposes of this edition, while in the case of six letters that are included we had to rely upon the sometimes abridged published transcriptions in Josef Rufer's article "Dokumente einer Freundschaft," in *Melos* (February 1955).

The correspondence between Berg and Schoenberg falls easily into three decade-long periods: 1906–15, 1916–25, and 1926–35, each corresponding to Schoenberg's moves to and from Berlin. These are likewise the rough demarcation points of the evolution of Berg's relationship to Schoenberg, from that of the student (which climaxes in the wrenching letter of November 1915), to that of the friend (Berg was offered the German farmiliar *Du* in 1918), and finally to that of the colleague and peer (after the 1925 premiere of *Wozzeck*). In our selection process we have adhered roughly to the proportions of the complete correspondence. Thus well over half of the items fall into the first decade, and the more equal balance of Berg and Schoenberg letters emerges only in the later years.

In the course of our work we have transcribed, translated, and annotated the complete Berg-Schoenberg correspondence—only limitations of space prevent publication of the whole. In this edition 296 letters appear complete; a further 45 were subjected to internal cuts and in those, summaries are given in square brackets [. . . .]. Telegrams and vacation postcards have generally been excised, although they are often subsumed into the footnotes, and letters that merely contain repetition or document a continuing misunderstanding have been omitted altogether. However, this is precisely the point at which selection became difficult. Until roughly 1922 the correspondence is characterized by a painstaking and often agonizing accumulation of detail, some more properly the preserve of the specialist. We have, for instance, chosen to summarize the minutiae of Schoenberg's financial affairs. Similarly, many details concerning the activities of the *Verein für musikalische Privataufführungen* have been excised, particularly those dealing with operational or organizational questions, where the Berg and Schoenberg letters give only a frustratingly incomplete picture; this, too, is rightfully a concern for the specialist with time and space to explore the massive body of correspondence exchanged among the dozens of Verein participants. However, no major topic of conversation has been omitted without being summarized or alluded to in the annotations, and we have tried to retain sufficient detail so as not to misrepresent either the relationship, the personalities of the correspondents, or indeed the sometimes stifling nature of the correspondence itself.

On topics of musical substance the letters are virtually uncut. It is particularly important to place the music of the Schoenberg circle in a cultural framework, to take note of the context in which their works were (or were not) performed, and to have their comments on the music of their contemporaries, both known and forgotten. While Berg's readily preferred critical judgments are all too often colored by his eagerness to please Schoenberg, they are a revealing expression of that garrison mentality and snobbishness that belong to the less appetizing legacies of the Schoenberg circle. On the other hand, observations on contemporary performance and performing practice can be quite revealing and useful guides for modern-day interpretation.

## Translation and Editorial Practice

No edition of letters can impart the many nuances of the original document. The printed page cannot reproduce the appearance of the original, the nature or quality of the stationery, the degree of haste or care exhibited in the handwriting, or idiosyncratic errors and misspellings that usually find editorial correction. Translation further obscures and even distorts the form and content of the original. It is difficult to find English equivalents for colloquiallisms without becoming too slangy, or to render a play on words without sounding academic. Those frequently used and often untranslatable words of emphasis, such as *doch* and *ja*, have sometimes been approximated through an editorial use of italics to suggest the proper "reading" of the sentence. Stylistic differences involve a further set of problems: Schoenberg's taut style has many similarities with English usage, but the actual turn of phrase is often difficult to capture concisely, while Berg, who delighted in the Baroque splendor of his native language, is sometimes impossible to translate satisfactorily. This has frequently meant focusing our translator's ambition on coming up with an English sentence that reads as awkwardly as Berg's German original while yet conveying the meaning. In a few rare cases we have succumbed to the necessity of breaking up an especially unwieldy sentence with a semicolon. It was challenging to try to reflect the evolution from the tentative, turgid prose of Berg's early letters toward the self-assured and often witty style of his later years, and from the acerbic edge of Schoenberg's prewar letters to the lighter, more open style of the Twenties and Thirties, particularly after his marriage in 1924 to Gertrude Kolisch.

In our editorial decisions we have tried to reflect the idiosyncracies of the originals. Berg deploys dashes, parentheses, colons, semicolons, and ellipses with virtuosic abandon, like so many road signs left to guide the wary reader through the maze of his prose. To the extent these do not represent specifically German usage or do not actually obscure understanding we have retained some of the punctuational irregularities. Berg's and Schoenberg's underlinings (from one to three) have been rendered as simple <u>underline</u>, **<u>boldface and underlined,</u>** and ***<u>boldface italics and underlined</u>*** respectively. Likewise their irregular use of cardinal and ordinal Roman and arabic numbers has been retained. However, the frequent misspellings of proper names have been corrected, except where intentional or revealing, as when Berg refers to his opera in progress as *Woyzeck* instead of *Wozzeck*, or when Schoenberg writes about *Mose und Aaron* before settling on *Moses und Aron*. Both Berg and Schoenberg are very inconsistent in their treatment of work titles and usually do not set them apart by quotation marks or any other device. To avoid confusion and for easier reference we have normalized all titles with quotation marks or italics; newspapers and periodical titles likewise appear in italics in the body of the letters.

All dates have been normalized in the European fashion, with the day preceding the month and year. This was necessary in order not to lose what for the numero-logically conscious Berg and Schoenberg are often significant orderings of numbers. Most undated items have been dated either by postmark (though these, too, can prove unreliable) and / or context. Postmark dates are given in square brackets, half brackets reflect dating by context. All editorial information appears within square brackets. *Everything else*, even where it may seem editorial, is by Berg and Schoen-berg and a faithful translation of the original. One final note concerns the spelling of Schoenberg's name. It was not until 1933 that Schoenberg replaced the umlaut ö in his name with oe. That shift is reflected in the text of the letters, though all editorial references have been normalized to comply with today's usual spelling, Schoenberg.

## Annotation

An edition of the Berg–Schoenberg correspondence cannot aspire to give the reader a biographical overview of either man, for it is but one of many sources informing a comprehensive view. The more limited objectives of this edition are to give as accurate a reflection as possible of the relationship and to provide the reader the necessary information for an informed understanding of the topics at hand. While our manuscript annotations are frequently quite lengthy and detailed it proved necessary to abridge them for publication. We have sought to identify succinctly all individuals and organizations (always at their first appearance in the body of the text), to document relevant concerts and events (giving complete programs where possible), give appropriate bibliographic references, and provide essential back-ground information. We have not attempted to give biographical or historical infor-mation that goes beyond the scope of the subject at hand and is in any event readily available in biographical and lexicographical reference works. Further, we have reluctantly omitted information identifying correspondence to or from third parties.

In our own research we soon became wary of the completeness and accuracy of the available secondary literature and sought where possible to examine the relevant original sources in over two dozen archives. Our annotation research ranged from other unpublished correspondences to contemporary newspapers, military reports, and municipal and parliamentary records. Where questions remain we have felt it better to point them out than to let the reader wonder about an oversight; oversights no doubt remain, but the acknowledged lacunae will be filled all the sooner for being made apparent. While we have attempted to give an indication of primary sources that might be fruitful avenues of future research, our references to secon-dary literature have been limited to those books and articles that deal directly with primary sources or contain information not found elsewhere.

Juliane Brand
Christopher Hailey

# Acknowledgments

A project that has taken over twenty years to complete owes a great many debts to a great many people. First and foremost the editors acknowledge the support of the late Mrs. Gertrud Schoenberg and the late Mrs. Helene Berg, without whose interest the project would never have been able to begin. Subsequently their support was continued by Schoenberg's two sons, Ronald and Lawrence, and by the Alban Berg Stiftung. Without their backing, the project could never have been completed. Special mention must be made of Dr. Franz Eckert, a member of the Stiftung, whose support was critical.

We also wish to acknowledge Claire Brook of W. W. Norton. Not only was she helpful and understanding, she was patient through the long, arduous months of negotiations to secure the rights, and during the ensuing years when the translation was being prepared for publication. Our thanks also to her husband, Dr. Barry Brook.

Generous grants-in-aid were received from the National Endowment for the Humanities, the Alban Berg Stiftung, the Rockefeller Foundation, and the Chapelbrook Foundation.

During the course of our research many libraries were consulted. They are listed below along with selected members of their staffs.

The music division of the Library of Congress, Edward N. Waters, the late Donald Leavitt, Wayne Shirley.

The Arnold Schoenberg Institute of the University of Southern California, Leonard Stein, the late Clara Steuermann, Jerry McBride.

The music division of the Austrian National Library, Franz Grasberger, Günter Brosche, Rosemary Hilmar.

The Vienna City Library, Ernst Hilmar; the Morgan Library, Rigby Turner; the Archive of the Berlin Academy of the Arts, Dagmar Wünsche; the Prussian State Library, Rudolf Elvers; the City Library of Winterthur, Harry Joeson-Stronback; the Mengelberg Archive, Gemeentemuseum in the Hague, Fritz Zwart; the Saxon State Library of Dresden, Dr. Ritschel, the archives of the Chicago Symphony Orchestra, R. H. Kular and of the Boston Symphony Orchestra, Joyce Spinney.

Additional research was conducted at the Bavarian State Library, Munich; the German State Library, Berlin; the City and University Library, Frankfurt; the Austrian National Library, the Vienna Urania; the Gesellschaft der Musikfreunde, Vienna; the Vienna Musikhochschule Library; the British Library; the libraries of Yale and Harvard Universities; and the New York Public Library.

Throughout the years the staff at Universal Edition, Vienna, was always most cooperative, in particular Alfred Schlee, Stephan G. Harpner, Trygve Nordwall, Margherita Kalmus, Elena Hift, and Friedrich Saathen.

We are grateful to many friends, colleagues, and correspondents, both in this country and abroad, for their assistance and insights, in particular: Lisa Jalowetz Aronson, Erich Alban Berg, Magda Breisach, Gertrude and Josef Barth, Inge and Gerhard Brand, Regina Busch, Joan Beadling, Steffi Dopler, Michael Friedmann, Harald Goertz, Susan and Paul Hawkshaw, Andrea and Hans Hammerschmied, Elizabeth Johnston, the late Rudolf Kolisch, Maria Kolisch, the late Hans Keller, Felix Khuner, Louis Krasner, Ernst Krenek, Eva Keresztes, Lisa Lieberman, Anna Maria Morazzoni, Gösta Neuwirth, James and Miriam Niederman, Paul A. Pisk, George Perle, Cathy Potter, Josef Rufer, Barbara Schoenberg, Randol Schoenberg, Joan Allen Smith, Rudolf Stephan, Fritzi Schlesinger, Haidy Schreker-Bures, Eric Simon, Hans Heinz Stuckenschmidt, Edward Tufte, James and Anne Weber, Emmy Wellesz, Imanuel Willheim, Horst Weber, and Harry Zohn. A very special note of thanks to Mark DeVoto and Douglas Jarman for their careful reading of and comments on the translations and annotations.

Juliane Brand
Christopher Hailey
Donald Harris

# Austrian Currency Conversion Table

100 heller = 1 krone

|  | KRONE TO $1 | KRONE TO £1 |
|---|---|---|
| Pre-war parity | 4.935 | 24.02 |
| 1916–Jan | 7.60 | — |
| 1917–Jan | 8.60 | — |
| 1919–May | 23.2 | 110 |
| Aug | 38.5 | 170 |
| Sep | 42–68 | 190–270 |
| Nov | 99–130 | 400–500 |
| 1920–Jan | 180–260 | 690–960 |
| Jun | 140–150 | 580–610 |
| Oct | 270–405 | 940–1400 |
| Dec | 513–670 | 1785–2350 |
| 1921–Jan | 670–786 | 2352–3130 |
| Jun | 610–727 | 2325–2720 |
| Sep | 1103–2585 | 4115–9600 |
| Nov | 4600–8600 | 18,000–34,500 |
| 1922–Jan | 5825–10,200 | 24,550–43,800 |
| Jun | 11,250–19,025 | 50,325–84,400 |
| Aug | 51,075–77,600 | 226,000–346,000 |
| Oct | 73,800–74,300 | 325,000–330,000 |
| 1923–Jan | 66,700–75,300 | 310,000–350,000 |
| Jun | 67,750–72,004 | 315,000–335,000 |
| 1924–Jan | 70,600 | 300,000 |
| Jun | 70,500 | 306,000 |
| 1925–Jan | 79,700 | 338,000 |

*New currency introduced—100 groschen–1 schilling*

|  | SCHILLING TO $1 | SCHILLING TO £1 |
|---|---|---|
| 1925–May | 7.08 | 34.4 |
| 1926–Jan | 7.08 | 34.4 |
| 1927–Jan | 7.08 | 34.4 |
| 1928–Jan | 7.08 | 34.4 |
| 1929–Jan | 7.11 | 34.5 |
| 1930–Jan | 7.11 | 34.5 |
| 1931–Jan | 7.11 | 34.5 |
| Oct | 7.7 | 30 |
| 1932–Jan | 8.93 | 30 |
| 1933–Jan | 8.57 | 28.5 |

Blue Self Portrait, *ca. 1910 by Arnold Schoenberg (Arnold Schoenberg Institute 26)*

# 1906-1915

Berg studied with Schoenberg from 1904 to 1911. These were the years during which Schoenberg made the dramatic and revolutionary transition from the highly chromatic late-Romantic style of *Pelleas und Melisande* and the D-minor String Quartet, Op. 7, to the "atonal" world of the Second String Quartet in F♯ minor, Op. 10, the Five Orchestra Pieces, Op. 16, and perhaps most significant, *Erwartung*, Op. 17. Berg himself matured from a self-taught musical dilettante with a gift for lyric compositions to a highly sophisticated master of the modern idiom in works such as his Piano Sonata, Op. 1, the Op. 2 songs, and especially his String Quartet, Op. 3, which marked the end of his formal studies with Schoenberg. These years of fermentation, undoubtedly central to an understanding of both Berg's and Schoenberg's artistic development, pass all but unregistered in the extant correspondence.

In a significant passage from a letter of 1 September 1909 to Helene Nahowski, Berg reflected upon the idea of writing to Schoenberg: ". . . I was really looking forward to a correspondence with Schoenberg; but when I started the first letter I realized that I couldn't write conventional letters to him, to whom I am attached with more than 'deep and sincere devotion.' I realize that they would have to be letters like those I write to you, not as often, but just as profound and as revealing of the depths of my soul." If Berg did indeed pen such letters to Schoenberg they have not survived, for Schoenberg did not begin saving Berg's correspondence until mid-1911. In any case, to judge from Schoenberg's extant communications, which begin in 1906, such energy as Berg may have lavished upon the correspondence at this time was not reciprocated. There is only a series of curt cards and notes regarding lessons, rehearsals, and performance dates and times.

The correspondence proper begins in the spring of 1911, shortly after Berg's marriage to Helene Nahowski and just prior to Schoenberg's second move to Berlin. Schoenberg was on the brink of becoming an international celebrity, or at least a cause célèbre. His music was beginning to receive an international hearing with performances (several of which he conducted) in England, Holland, America, and Russia; his writings, above all his 1911 *Harmonielehre*, were widely disseminated and discussed; and his students were beginning to make their mark upon the music world as composers and conductors. Throughout these years Berg remained completely caught up in the vortex of Schoenberg's life. He and various fellow students served as Schoenberg's "eyes and ears" in Vienna, and the correspondence focuses accordingly on Schoenberg's activities and financial interests, and on performances of his works. The resulting disruption of Berg's creative life, as well as his difficulties in defining both his style and professional identity, laid the foundation for the tensions and dissatisfaction that would seriously undermine the two men's relationship by the time Schoenberg returned to Vienna at the end of 1915.

*Portrait of Alban Berg, ca. 1910 by Arnold Schoenberg (Historisches Museum der Stadt Wien)*

# 1911

*Berg to Schoenberg*

Friday
[Trahütten, 16 June 1911]

For some time now, dear, esteemed Herr Schönberg, I have been meaning to write to you. Unfortunately something always interfered.

As you know, we left Prein[1] after a 2-day stay to come here,[2] where I felt pretty well at first until my asthma got very bad again; there were a couple of frightful days and nights. Once it became somewhat more bearable, we meant to return to Vienna, when a new misfortune detained us. Helene struck her head so violently one day that she was overcome by severe dizziness and developed a terrible headache. Since then she can't bear the slightest movement, such as walking, standing up, sitting down; the spot on her head is very painful both externally and internally, which is why Helene is condemned to absolute quiet and immobility.— My initial concern, which was tremendous, *has* been somewhat alleviated, as on the whole one can detect extremely slow but steady improvement; but the absolute lack of doctors here, and the impossibility of energetic intervention in case of emergency, does make me very uneasy and is, apart from my own suffering, very worrisome.—

We live here with Helene's father and brother[3] in a small house at circa 1,000 meters' altitude, from where it takes 2 hours down a completely impossible road to get to Deutsch-Landsberg, the nearest town, and from there another 2 hours by local train to Graz, the nearest town where one might find a doctor.

On the other hand it is out of the question to subject my wife to the jolting of such a 2-hour journey in an uncushioned coach, so we are forced to wait until she can be moved and therefore postpone our departure from day to day. Having done so every day this week, we now hope that things will perhaps be far enough along by Monday the 19th to allow our undertaking the trip in stages.

In any event I will let you know, dear Herr Schönberg.— Once in Vienna we

---

1. After Berg and Helene Nahowski were married on 3 May 1911, they spent a short honeymoon in Prein near Payerbach, a small town south of Vienna.

2. Helene Berg's parents owned a country home and property in Trahütten, about 35 kilometers south-southwest of Graz.

3. The railroad official Franz Nahowski and Helene Berg's brother Franz (also nicknamed Frank).

would be staying with Helene's parents on Maxinggasse.

One bright spot during these sad days has been reading Wagner's autobiography,[4] which we bought in Graz. Out of the completely straightforward, unadorned enumeration of experiences there emerges a monument to the most unbelievable artistic suffering, which in its simplicity and intensity often reminds me of Strindberg (indeed, some things could have been written by him)—which is, I believe, unprecedented; here one individual is writing for all, and that should be a warning, a lesson for all centuries to come! But critics, publishers, theater directors and actors, and various other "artists" continue undisturbed in their destructive work and the true artists must suffer and suffer until they can suffer no more. Oh, dear Herr Schönberg, while reading this I have to think repeatedly and often of you and of— —Mahler.[5]— — — — — — — — — — — — — — — — — — — — — — — — —

I wonder what you, esteemed Herr Schönberg, are working on now? Has the *Harmonielehre* progressed very far?[6]—

Webern[7] and Jalowetz[8] are probably back in Vienna by now. Please give them my best.

To you yourself, Herr Schönberg, the best and sincerest regards from your devoted and ever grateful

Alban Berg

My wife also sends you and your esteemed wife all the best.

---

4. Wagner's autobiography, *Mein Leben*, was published privately during his lifetime. The first commercial edition appeared in an abridged version in 1911.

5. Gustav Mahler had died in Vienna only one month earlier, on 18 May 1911. Both Berg and Schoenberg attended the funeral on 21 May.

6. Schoenberg had largely completed his *Harmonielehre* in 1910; work on the publication with Universal Edition was beginning at this time.

7. Anton von Webern studied with Schoenberg 1904–08.

8. The Austrian conductor Heinrich Jalowetz studied with Schoenberg 1904–08.

*Berg to Schoenberg*

[Vienna, end of June 1911]

Esteemed Herr Schönberg,

I've been back in Vienna for a few days now.

Of course I wanted to come see you immediately, Herr Schönberg, but had to keep putting it off as a result of continual upheavals. The administrative work[1] that had piled up during my absence, errands, etc., concerning our new apartment,[2] and not least of all the continuing indisposition of my wife, kept me in a daze. Added to all this there is a most unpleasant family matter concerning my sister

---

1. Berg received financial support from his mother for overseeing various family real estate properties in Vienna.

2. Alban and Helene Berg moved into their own home that fall, the first-floor apartment on 27 Trauttmansdorffgasse in Vienna's thirteenth district of Hietzing; they remained there for the rest of their lives.

Smaragda, which requires my complete attention and repeated intervention, and which absolutely must be settled in the next few days.[3]

That's why so far I've been unable to spare the few hours to visit you, dear Herr Schönberg. Apart from all of this I still hope to arrange things so as to be able to get away very soon.—I am presently living with my parents-in-law in Hietzing XIII, Maxinggasse 46, where I don't even have a telephone.[4]

I was very, very pleased with many things in the *Merker*; your contributions naturally made me very happy and the whole thing gave me renewed hope.[5]

But nothing of that in this letter, just my warmest and most sincere regards

from your devoted and grateful Alban Berg

---

3. The precise nature of the family matter concerning Berg's sister Smaragda is unknown. However, after a brief marriage to Adolf von Eger during 1907 (21 April–23 December) she had become increasingly open about her lesbianism, which led to some friction within the family. Her long relationship with May Keller began in 1911.

4. Helene Berg's family home on Maxinggasse was just around the corner from the Trauttmansdorff-gasse apartment.

5. *Der Merker* was a biweekly Viennese cultural journal, published 1909–23. Its first June 1911 issue (II/17) was dedicated to Schoenberg; contributions included articles by Richard Specht, Karl Linke, Rudolf Reti, and Paul Stefan, as well as an excerpt from Schoenberg's *Harmonielehre*, "Ästhetische Bewertung sechs- und mehrtöniger Klänge" (Aesthetic Evaluation of Chords with Six or More Tones), the text of *Die glückliche Hand*, and a reprint of the song "Waldsonne," Op. 2, No. 4.

## Berg to Schoenberg (letterhead: Berghof am Ossiachersee)

Tuesday

Berghof,[1][18 July 1911]

I meant, dear, most esteemed Herr Schönberg, to send my first note from here together with the promised copies.[2] But as usual the photographer is taking his time, so this is to tell you briefly that we have been here since Sunday afternoon and that for the time being I'm doing preparatory work for the index;[3] a task that is actually a battle between my great love for the work and the desire to remain strictly businesslike. Or am I displaying the former when I yield to the latter? At any rate I have come to the conclusion that I must regard the index from 2 standpoints. First, that it must be easy for anyone to find the individual "subjects" according to their most important aspects, and second, that looking up and locating things must be especially easy even for those who have read the book, so that I cannot bring myself to omit things that someone not familiar with the book would not look for, such as, for example, "voice leading event" or "repetitions of pitch patterns or sequences." But I assure you, dear esteemed Herr Schönberg, that I will keep the index within the limits of length and moderation you desire, so that you will be satisfied.

---

1. Berghof, located on the Ossiachersee in Carinthia, was the Berg family's summer property, and included both lodging facilities for paying guests as well as dairy and farming operations.

2. Berg had taken snapshots of Schoenberg during his recent stay in Vienna.

3. Berg prepared the indexes for both the first edition and the 1921 revision of Schoenberg's *Harmonielehre*.

Otherwise there is nothing worth telling. We don't feel all that comfortable here. The matter I told you about in Vienna is still unresolved and we suffer from continual and above all pointless squabbling. Add to that my asthma, despite the attempt to convince myself that the whole thing is, as you said, based on autosuggestion, hasn't improved at all and torments me every night, thus merely giving me, the insomniac, more time to dwell on the unhappy thought that I had to leave Vienna still conscious that I am not back in your favor, at least not as much as I was before my trip.[4] The thought, too, that I can never succeed in explaining my odd behavior in not coming to see you right away (were it only for a brief moment), can never succeed in convincing you that there was no coldness, no indifference in this apparent negligence, since I suffered so terribly at being unable to visit you immediately, that this suffering alone would have done more to convince you of my absolute and unbounded loyalty than the joy I always experience when permitted to visit you— — —. So that thought too, the impossibility of making oneself completely understood, is clouding my mood here and I, who had so passionately longed for the spring and summer, now long only for the fall.

But until then there are still 6 long weeks.— — — — —

Forgive me, dear, esteemed Herr Schönberg, for my interminable, cumbersome sentences, and for mentioning a matter that can only annoy you in your busy life. But the pain which I had anticipated even before I had the opportunity to visit you and which, after having been mute before, erupted, loud and screaming, when you received me with so much disdain—and when you grew scarcely more cordial during the 2 weeks than you are, for instance, with someone from the seminar[5]—that pain does not subside—and has forced me to write, despite the wish not to burden you.

Please, beloved Herr Schönberg, accept my most devoted and sincerest regards.

In unchanging love Alban Berg

Warmest regards, your devoted Helene Berg

---

4. Schoenberg, who had learned of Berg's return to Vienna from Webern, was deeply offended that Berg had not visited him immediately.

5. Schoenberg taught a private course in harmony and counterpoint at the Vienna Academy of Music 1910–11.

*Berg to Schoenberg (letterhead: Berghof am Ossiachersee)*

Thursday

Berghof, [3 August 1911]

I have now received the conclusion of the *Harmonielehre* as well as the beginning: the divine foreword—and the dedication.[1] This wonderful book has now received

1. Schoenberg had been dissatisfied with his first foreword to the *Harmonielehre* and had written a new one in July. He addresses himself to the dangers of complacency and the importance of continual struggle. He opens with the sentence, "I learned this book from my students" (Arnold Schoenberg, *Theory of Harmony*, translated by Roy Carter, New York, 1979).

Schoenberg dedicated his *Harmonielehre* to the memory of Gustav Mahler.

its final consecration: before entering the sanctuary one kneels devoutly and crosses oneself in profoundest humility. The appropriate words of composure, a heartfelt sigh from a believer's breast before commencement of the holy service.

And that this work was written in the service of the deity becomes ever clearer and more certain to me, the more I read it, the deeper I delve into it. And that we poor mortals may partake of it—that is our highest joy:

For that, we thank you, beloved Herr Schönberg. ——————————

I'm so overwhelmed from reading the *Harmonielehre*, so completely engrossed, that I would like to discuss each and every item, but I think it is more important that I use the time to get on with the index. (It went relatively slowly the last 2 days, since the many—(wonderful!) examples took a great deal of time, in addition to which the incredible heat made it impossible for me to read "attentively" for more than 5–6 hours a day, but I hope that it will go more briskly now: I have reached "Nonharmonic Tones").

*[Berg criticizes the design of the title page.]*

And now my regards to you, esteemed Herr Schönberg, in devotion and eternal gratitude

Alban Berg

(I am so exhausted from the heat that I can't write any more, i.e., not legibly. Be so kind as to excuse that, too.)


*Berg to Schoenberg (letterhead: Berghof am Ossiachersee)*

Berghof, [13 August 1911]

About 3–4 days ago I wrote you a note, my dear Herr Schönberg, which I sent to Munich (care of general delivery).[1] I had just heard from Webern of your sudden departure, after the cessation of daily notes to which I had become pleasantly accustomed, which, though not addressed to me, were nevertheless from your hand and occasionally included a personal greeting, and which always made me very happy . . . . . I repeat: when your notes ceased and the new chapter (on the chromatic scale)—for which I was waiting in vain—broke off abruptly, I became very apprehensive. But the news of your departure seemed sufficient explanation of the above and I allowed myself to interpret it as a promising turn of events in your destiny. Such was the substance of the brief note I sent off to Munich, uncertain whether it would reach you, but continuing to entertain the brightest hopes and bidding Webern to forward any information to me at once.

And it came! Last night I received the dreadful news.[2] But is it really news? When

---

1. Schoenberg apparently never received this letter.

2. During the preceding weeks there had been a series of altercations between Schoenberg and another tenant in his apartment building in Hietzing. When on 4 August these tensions erupted into a violent confrontation, Schoenberg left precipitately for the Starnbergersee near Munich, where his brother-in-law Alexander Zemlinsky was spending the summer while conducting during the Munich summer operetta season. The experience contributed to Schoenberg's decision to leave Vienna and resettle in Berlin in September. For more information, see footnote 1 of Schoenberg's letter, postmarked 16 September 1911.

you, esteemed Herr Schönberg, had anticipated and feared it for months? Is it not rather fulfillment of the fate of genius? Regardless whether manifested negatively, in the incomprehension of a thousand "sensible" people, or positively, in the hatred of a madman! I only know that this hatred, this diabolic madness, which ordinarily lies concealed, was revealed on this occasion in a crime against your holy person—of course the details are unknown to me—but I *do* know (—with the sublime conviction born of unerring hope and expectation—) that the world, which heretofore passed by your deeds with a "shrug of the shoulders"—must pause before the misdeed of a fiend—if only to come to its senses. And this moment of reflection—which beneficently intervenes in the lives of all great men—has surely interceded now in your distress—or in any event cannot be long in coming, for it is high time. — — — —

But!! What meaning can time or things temporal have for you, dearest Herr Schönberg——even sublime moments of suffering—since you have been granted the "deep deep eternity of all joy"?![3]

We mortals can only bow before your destiny, must realize that even our most fervent hopes are insignificant: somewhere there *must* be a sublime Judgment, a divine Will. And surely that is infallible—even if it appears all too enigmatic to us. — — — —

And now I shall end this letter, or rather: shall interrupt it until I hear more (from Webern, who plans to visit soon) to solve—or deepen?—the enigma. Until then my most respectful regards in devoted gratitude and veneration:

Alban Berg

---

3. A quotation from Friedrich Nietzsche's "Das trunkne Lied" from *Also sprach Zarathustra*: "Doch alle Lust will tiefe Ewigkeit— / will tiefe, tiefe Ewigkeit."

## Schoenberg to Berg

Schloss Berg am Starnbergersee, 18 August 1911

Dear Berg,

You wrote me with such warmth that what stood between us is completely forgotten. I'm convinced it was not as I had interpreted it. One thing, though: I fear being overrated! Try not to do it. It weighs upon me a little. And perhaps it is partly the fear of being overrated that makes me so suspicious. Perhaps because I fear: the impending backlash, the moment I am no longer overrated, perhaps because I continually fear the inevitable moment when people will actually begin to underrate me, perhaps that's why I detect a hint of defection in the slightest negligence. That is certainly unjust. But I can't help it.—Quite candidly: I took offense. You know I'm very fond of you. That I take a great interest in you. That I strive wherever possible to secure a future for you. And then you never came to see me, though you had been in Vienna for some time. Please don't misunderstand me: I am not implying ingratitude. Of course not; gratitude is a most wearisome obligation, which I myself avoid whenever I can. And I don't wish to impose such an obligation on others. If I *did* want to, then only by means of the <u>Good</u> and the <u>True</u>. Only that and friendship—you understand what I mean!

And though I still don't understand why you avoided me back then, I am now convinced it wasn't in bad faith! Perhaps negligence—but I don't want to be angry about that any longer and I'm not.

Now one question: Webern sent me a large sum of money today without indicating the source.[1] Please tell me whether you participated. I believe so, as I infer it from the fact that no name is given. That is very kind of you; but I would much rather know who the friend is, who helps me. I'd like to thank him. So for now, please accept my thanks. I was very happy to hear from you and Webern. And it also did me good that Horwitz[2] and Jalowetz were so ready to help me, as I was very depressed at the time.

When you're back in Vienna, I'll tell you all about this incredible incident. It is unbelievable that one should have to undergo such an experience, and the thought that it might be retribution is, by contrast, actually a consolation.

So, dear Berg, even without being certain that you were the one who sent this large sum: everything as before. I would have written that in answer to your letter even if this matter (which unfortunately entwined the two) hadn't interfered. Now I must do so despite the connection. But nonetheless I do it gladly. Because I am sure: that we won't let matters come to such a pass again! And I consider that important and worthwhile! So, my warmest regards in true friendship to you (and your wife)

from your Arnold Schönberg

---

1. Webern collected 1,000 kronen for Schoenberg, consisting of five 200-kronen contributions from Webern, Berg, Jalowetz, Erwin Stein, and Karl Horwitz.
2. Karl Horwitz studied with Schoenberg 1904–08.


## Berg to Schoenberg (letterhead: Berghof am Ossiachersee)

Monday

Berghof [21 August 1911]

I have just returned from taking Webern to the train station, as you, esteemed Herr Schönberg will have gathered from the picture postcard we sent from there.[1] These were lovely days. They were spent in thoughts of you. But when your wonderful letter to me arrived, my happiness was almost too much for me: for they were the first kind words from you, dear Herr Schönberg, in more than two months. And with your forgiveness I feel reborn, purified, and today, 2 days after receiving your letter, your anger seems to lie far, far away—indeed, <u>as if I</u> had not actually experienced it <u>myself</u>, just dreamt it, perhaps. And what seems inexplicable to me in the matter is perhaps only the inadequacy of the human mind to interpret dreams. And even if Prof. Freud hasn't succeeded there,[2] he is at any rate correct that it is a peculiarly human trait to view unpleasantness and past suffering as if through a

1. Webern visited Berg in Berghof from 17–21 August.
2. Sigmund Freud's *Traumdeutung* (Interpretation of Dreams) first appeared in 1900.

veil so that the past soon appears in a milder light—and one can face the future with confidence. In this respect I, too, feel that everything experienced during these months was a preparation, a requisite first step toward the forthcoming bliss of your unchanging goodwill; the fact that you yourself, Herr Schönberg, believe you won't ever need to withhold that goodwill from me again, that is the crowning glory of your letter.

Given such circumstances and knowing my recent grief as you do, you can imagine how happy and hopeful we have been these past few days. Every day we spent many enthusiastic hours playing from all of Mahler's symphonies and from your orchestral songs and piano pieces[3] and up to the hour of Webern's departure we were still at the piano, playing (4-hands!) the last piano piece, and my wife sang songs from Opp. 2 and 6.—But throughout these days of wonderful storms on the lake, throughout these moonlit nights, there has loomed horrifyingly sublime, distressingly terrifying, like the forest fire that has been raging on the hill across the lake for 3 days now: your tragic fate with its horrendous suffering, and the inexhaustible source of all imaginable human troubles. That we, Herr Schönberg, who love and appreciate you—and it can never be a case of overrating—all our efforts can be directed only toward that one end, to underrate you as little as possible, given our subordinate natures (as if glass could overrate a diamond)— — —anyway, that it isn't granted us to help you as regally as our love for you would wish, to clear all these repulsive things from your path, that is the saddest aspect of the whole thing and merely reinforces our wish and hope that decisive assistance will come at last—I don't know: from outside or, as it were—above—from God, like the sudden cloudburst that just broke and completely extinguished the forest fire.

But those are merely glimpses into the future—which almost lead me to forget the present!: How is the *Harmonielehre* coming along? According to my calculations the proofs of the final book form ought to be ready by now, and nothing should stand in the way of completing the index. Right now and during the coming 2–3 weeks I could easily spare the time for it (as it only requires 1–2 days!), whereas during the first days back in Vienna (around 12 September) it would be more difficult, as I'll be moving and arranging the apartment then. I only ask when I'll receive the copy of the *Harmonielehre* so that I can budget my time, either adding a few days to my stay here in order to finish the index in peace, or returning to Vienna earlier in order to be finished with the apartment by the time I'm able to start the work. I believe I have expressed myself clearly, and a card with the information as to when I'll be able to have your *Harmonielehre* would determine all my plans for the coming 2 weeks. May I ask you, dear Herr Schönberg, for that information? Also news of how you are doing at the Starnbergersee and whether your wife is already completely recovered from her illness[4]— — —and all the other questions I would like to ask— — — — — ?

The letter must be sent off, I close in haste and with the warmest devotion,

Your Alban Berg

---

3. Schoenberg's Six Orchestral Songs, Op. 8, and the Three Piano Pieces, Op. 11.
4. Mathilde Schönberg was suffering from a mild case of pneumonia.

## Schoenberg to Berg (postcard)

Berg am Starnbergersee [25 August 1911]

Many thanks, dear Berg, for your very kind letter, which made me very happy. I, too, am very impatient for the final proofs, but to date have received only the beginning (pages 1–32), which are of no use to you, so I won't send them until there are more. I firmly believe that the entire manuscript will arrive before the end of August, but I don't know for sure. At any rate: I hope the book will be printed by 15 September. So it should arrive the first week of September at the latest.—I'm presently working a little on *Die glückliche Hand* and am very curious to know "*wie man Schmuck schafft*" [how one makes jewels].[1] I am working remarkably slowly this time, more slowly than ever before. Although the "material" interests me very much. As yet I have no idea why that is. Are you composing anything? See that you do.

Many warm regards, also to your wife, also from my wife

Your Arnold Schönberg

---

1. From the text of *Die glückliche Hand*, Op. 18.

## Schoenberg to Berg (postcard)

Berg bei Starnberg [16 September 1911]

Dear Berg,

I accidentally sent a copy of my "deposition" against Wouwermans to Dr. Rosenfeld, I, 21 Wipplingerstrasse.[1] He will probably send it to you tomorrow. Please read it so that you will be informed and can keep an eye on things a bit. My impression is that Dr. R. doesn't consider this trial lucrative enough and is expecting only a lean settlement. So I would like to know whether you think he is exerting himself sufficiently in the matter. That's why I ask that you look him up and find out from him exactly what W.'s statements and charges against me were (in the 1st hearing), and write them to me in detail so I can refute them.

What are you up to? Have you recovered by now? How is your wife? (Please give her my best, also from my wife!) My *Harmonielehre* probably won't appear any time this century!!

Best regards

Your Arnold Schönberg

1. Viktor Rosenfeld was one of Vienna's leading trial lawyers. In his deposition, a 19–page document now located in the Berg Archive (Austrian National Library) Schoenberg explains at length the background and his interpretation of the altercation with his neighbor, the engineer Philipp Josef von Wouwermans, who lived at 113 Hietzinger Hauptstrasse 1911–12.

On 19 July Wouwermans had had the first of several temperamental outbursts, directed in part toward Schoenberg and his family. Over the course of the following two weeks Wouwermans forced his way into a neighbor's apartment, struck that neighbor's maid, and cursed and threatened Schoenberg (calling him, among other things, an immoral swine). On the basis of several complaints Wouwermans was given two weeks' notice on his apartment on 4 August and, assuming Schoenberg to have been the principal instigator (which, according to Schoenberg, was not the case), Wouwermans resumed his threats. These led to a confrontation in which Wouwermans demanded to see Schoenberg, while Schoenberg, fearing physical violence, refused to open his door and threatened to use a pistol should Wouwermans attempt to enter. At the heart of the affair was Wouwerman's claim that through indecent behaviour the then nine-year-old Gertrud Schoenberg was corrupting his five- and eleven-year-old sons; Schoenberg insisted that it was more likely that Wouwerman's older son was the corrupting influence.

## Schoenberg to Berg

Berg am Starnbergersee [19 September 1911]

Dear Berg, a favor.

I shall probably move to Berlin after all. Of course I'm terribly sorry with regard to you and my other friends, whom I will see only infrequently, and about Königer[1] and Linke;[2] and I had very much looked forward to our socializing often in Hietzing. To our spending several evenings a week together and your wife and mine would certainly have become friends. All of that is a real pity and I regret it very much. But it's high time I leave Vienna. You know I've always wanted to. It just won't work. My works suffer and it's almost impossible for me to make a living in Vienna. But since there may well be such an opportunity for me in Berlin, I must take advantage of it! Naturally Bahr's campaign [Aktion] is to continue.[3] I hope Viennese patrons will do what they do for me even if I am not in Vienna. In any case, for the time being you must not spread reports of my plan to move.

Now for the favor I want to ask of you.

I have to keep my apartment and also pay rent until February. Perhaps you know how one can rent it out as early as November.—But even more important, I want to ask you to locate a mover for me who will undertake the move to Berlin for the lowest price. I've inquired into a few and received an estimate from one (Knauer and Rosin) that was insanely <u>steep.</u> About twice what I had figured!!

The man simply regards me as "prey."

[Schoenberg gives details pertinent to the selection of a moving company.]

The actual packing is a problem. Unfortunately I will have to have it done by strangers.

But my books, scores, and manuscripts: I would appreciate if you could be there to oversee it. You and Polnauer.[4] You'll do that for me, won't you?

Couldn't you come to Berlin too? Life is cheaper here. You'd get more for your money. Could start a career more easily! Think about it!

Pan (15 September) had an appeal, "for Arnold Sch."[5] by Kerr,[6] signed by Busoni,[7] Fried,[8] Schnabel,[9] and Clark.[10] Also I'm negotiating with Reinhardt[11] about his performing my two stage works and engaging me to conduct these and possibly

---

1. Paul Königer studied with Schoenberg during 1911.
2. The Austrian grammarian Karl Linke studied with Schoenberg 1909–12.
3. Schoenberg had asked the Austrian writer Hermann Bahr, whom he had met in 1909 through Bahr's wife, the dramatic soprano Anna Bahr-Mildenburg, to start a collection drive. The campaign was initially intended as an appeal to a small number of wealthy patrons to establish a yearly stipend of 6,000 kronen for Schoenberg. That plan was not fully realized and the resulting Schoenberg Fund (Schönberg Fond), which Berg administered, eventually included many smaller one-time donations.
4. Josef Polnauer studied with Schoenberg 1909–11.
5. An appeal for funds for Schoenberg appeared in the Berlin cultural periodical Pan I/22 (16 September 1911), 741.
6. Alfred Kerr, Berlin's leading drama critic, was an editor of Pan.
7. Schoenberg had known and corresponded with the Italian-German composer Ferruccio Busoni since 1903.
8. The German conductor and composer Oskar Fried, who had performed Schoenberg's Pelleas und Melisande in Berlin in 1910, had long sought to further Schoenberg's music and career.
9. Schoenberg had known the Viennese pianist Artur Schnabel since his youth.
10. Edward Clark was the Berlin correspondent for the Musical Times of London.
11. Oskar Fried introduced Schoenberg to Max Reinhardt in Munich on 31 August.

other things that he will stage this winter. Furthermore, Gutmann[12] is trying to secure engagements for me for concerts (in which I'm to conduct *Pelleas*). I hope that works out. In Prague I will be conducting an entire subscription concert on 29 February with *Pelleas* and works of Bach, Mozart, etc.[13] Surely you'll come to that. Could you send me the Mozart symphonies (score) from among my things? I want to study the G minor.

As you see there are a number of things being planned, which will, I hope, advance me and my cause. Perhaps I may yet manage to extricate myself from these disgusting money problems that are plaguing me again just now.

How are you? Are you already composing something? How is your wife doing? Has she quite recovered? Please give her our best regards!

Write soon.

I am sorry to have to trouble you. But I hope to be of use to you again, soon.

Tell me, would you like to write 5–8 printed pages about me right away for a music periodical?[14] I have been asked to suggest someone. Above all it is to be a clear characterization of my musical personality (my origins, development, and present style). I'll also ask Webern? Discuss it with him and decide between you who is to do it.

Many warm regards

Your Arnold Schönberg

---

12. The Munich concert agent Emil Gutmann. At the beginning of 1912 he opened a second office in Berlin and moved his headquarters there.

13. At the invitation of Alexander von Zemlinsky, who had recently become General Music Director of the Neues Deutsches Theater in Prague.

14. Gerhard Tischer, publisher and editor of the *Rheinische Musik- und Theaterzeitung*, had approached Schoenberg about the article.

## Schoenberg to Berg

Berg am Starnbergersee, 22 September 1911

Dear Berg,

Finally another installment of the 3<sup>rd</sup> set of proofs. I am sending you the beginning. You will have to ask Universal Edition[1] for one sheet (pages 33–48). I hope the whole thing will arrive soon now. It would be best to tell U.E. always to send one set <u>directly</u> to you (the other two to me!).

You can pick up the picture of your wife with the enclosed note.[2] I would appreciate it if either you or Webern would also pick up two pictures that are in the attic (one of me, one depicting my wife and Trudi)[3] and if you or Webern could do that, place them in safekeeping somewhere. But that can wait until our things are packed.

1. The Viennese music publishing firm, founded 1901.

2. Schoenberg had painted portraits of both Alban and Helene Berg, now located in the Historical Museum of the City of Vienna (see pp. xxvii and 14). In a letter postmarked 17 September 1911 Berg asked permission to pick up the portrait of his wife.

3. Trudi was the nickname of Schoenberg's daughter Gertrud Schönberg.

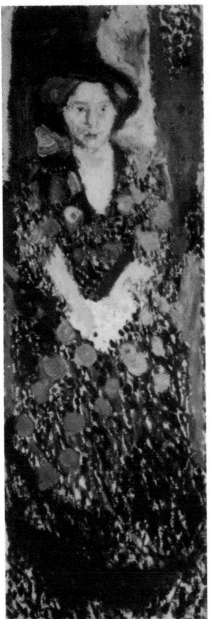

*(Left) Portrait of Mathilde Schönberg,
ca. 1908 by Richard Gerstl*

*(Right) Portrait of Helene Nahowski,
ca. 1910 by Arnold Schoenberg
(Historisches Museum der Stadt Wien)*

14

Dear Berg, I very much count on having you and Linke or Polnauer pack the things in my room. My books, manuscripts, scores, etc. Of course if necessary I will employ a packer to help. But it has to be done with intelligence and love. So that absolutely nothing gets lost! Unfortunately I am terribly pedantic in this regard. You know I can't throw away an old pen without "a quiver of the heart!" That's why I am very anxious.

I shall probably travel to Berlin in the next few days. But for the present go on writing to me here. I will let you know my address in time. I plan to arrange my moving affairs there myself. I hope you will soon have some information in Vienna, too. On the one hand I'd prefer not to return to Vienna! But possibly, if I were able to live there. On the other hand I can get ahead more quickly in Berlin. Have you seen Löwe's programs yet?[4] What are Nedbal's like?[5] Should I return to Vienna??? Whenever I see that I get so furious I'd like to lash out. That fat pig, Löwe—he's an animal in any case, a pig in lion's clothing, he and his Boehe.[6] And of course: Graener![7] Tell me what Nedbal is going to perform. I haven't seen it. Could you send me a Vienna paper sometime (Sunday edition)?

At any rate, send me everything that is written about me. I saw that the *Zeit* published a notice of alarm: "A. Schbg's Emigration Plans."[8] Perhaps there are other things elsewhere.

Couldn't you come to Berlin, too?

But if you stay in Vienna, I will recommend you to my students. Certainly you could take over the new harmony students at the Academy. You should stop by and ask what's up. If you think it necessary I would write to these students myself. Also the counterpoint seminar. You could hold these courses at your home or in a rented hall in the city (at Schwarzwald's,[9] for instance!!). As my substitute! You would also have to take over Königer and Linke and Polnauer. Königer pays, but you would have to teach Linke and Polnauer for nothing, just as I do. Fräulein Rethi also pays.[10] Winkler too![11] You would have to charge less than I do (5–6 kronen), but it would be a good beginning!

I suppose you know that I am to conduct a concert in Prague! On 29 February (leap year!); you must come.

4. The Austrian conductor Ferdinand Löwe was the director of the Vienna Konzertverein Orchestra from its founding in 1900 until 1924, as well as the principal conductor of the Munich Konzertverein 1908–14.

5. The violist and operetta composer Oskar Nedbal was a founder and principal conductor of the Vienna Tonkünstler Orchestra 1906–19.

6. The German word *Löwe* means lion. The German composer and conductor Ernst Boehe was associated with the so-called Munich school of composers.

7. The German composer Paul Graener was director of the Mozarteum in Salzburg 1910–13.

8. In a 17 September article entitled "Auswanderungspläne Arnold Schönbergs" the Viennese newspaper *Die Zeit* reprinted the *Pan* appeal and commented: "It would be interesting to know why Arnold Schönberg is fleeing Vienna. This city, which according to the appeal bears him a grudge, offered him a position at the Academy, has given him a publisher and many friends and students, and his works are repeatedly performed by outstanding Viennese musicians in Vienna and abroad."

9. Dr. Eugenie Nussbaum Schwarzwald ran a progressive private girl's school, which provided facilities for adult lecture series and special courses. Schoenberg taught harmony and counterpoint there 1903–05.

10. Elizabeth (Else) Rethi studied with Schoenberg during 1911.

11. The cellist Wilhelm Winkler studied with Schoenberg 1910–11 and thereafter with Berg.

Perhaps the others will come, too. It would be lovely if I could see everyone there.—But for the present I'm not even in Berlin yet. I just very much hope to be.

In Paris a certain Lejeune Quartet is doing an entire evening of my works: sextet, songs, and II[nd] Quartet.[12] That's nice!!

Write to me soon. Good news, I hope. Tell me more about Bahr sometime. What does he say? What does he think of me? Was he angry at my presumption?

Has a *Fackel* appeared? Could you send it to me. Kraus will probably attack me now, because of Kerr.[13] But I don't even know Kerr.

Oh yes: a song! I almost forgot.[14] I have absolutely nothing here!—I'd have to use something from the *Gurrelieder* again. Perhaps the Waldemar song: "Es ist Mitternachts-Zeit"—or "Du wunderliche Tove." You decide, ask Hertzka[15] for his permission, have it copied quickly (at Hertzka's expense), and send it directly to Kerr, with my regards. I believe that's the best way. Then, while you're in my apartment, you could take the manuscript paper with five new piano pieces[16] out of the "folder" that serves as a writing pad on my desk and send them to me. You will find the *Gurrelieder* on the bottom shelf of the bookshelf between the windows. Though maybe Webern has it!

Please, for the time being you are not to pack my manuscripts. I want to send some of them by parcel post and will let you know about that in more detail soon.

Enough for now!

Don't be angry at all the errands! Many warm regards to you and your wife,

Your Arnold Schönberg

Give my best to Linke, Königer, and Polnauer. I shall write to them very soon. And tell Königer that if he is really successful with wishes, I'd very much like him to wish hard that I get to Berlin! I could use that!

---

12. The Parisian concert agent Nestor Lejeune first wrote to Schoenberg on 17 September 1911 of his interest in arranging a concert of *Verklärte Nacht*, Op. 4, the Second String Quartet, Op. 10, and various songs, possibly including the George Songs. This concert did not take place; only the Sextet was performed on a concert in the Salle Pleyel on 20 March.

13. The Viennese satirical journal *Die Fackel* was edited and largely written by Karl Kraus from 1899 to 1936. The next issue (XIII/331–32) appeared on 30 September 1911. Alfred Kerr was a frequent target of Kraus's ire and during the spring and summer the two had been feuding in print.

14. In a letter dated 20 September, Berg referred to Kerr's request for a short song by Schoenberg to be reprinted in *Pan*.

15. Emil Hertzka, director of Univeral Edition 1909–32.

16. Five of the Six Piano Pieces, Op. 19.

*Berg to Schoenberg*

Friday morning

[Vienna, 22 September 1911]

Forgive me, dear Herr Schönberg, for writing in pencil; but I have much to tell you and it takes too long with ink, and as you yourself once said, pencil is perfectly adequate for a letter.

I went to see Dr. Rosenfeld yesterday. You have probably received <u>his</u> detailed report in the meantime, so there is nothing for me to tell you but the impression he made on me and my own opinion about the progress of the lawsuit. Then on the way home I met Hermann Bahr at the Neuer Markt and rode with him as far as St. Veit. It goes without saying that the hour-long ride was spent talking only about you, esteemed Herr Schönberg. And also about the suit. And to the extent I can now assess the matter I am forced to the highly painful conclusion that the suit should be dropped. Because it is—in a word—nearly impossible to obtain true justice in Austria. This cur Wouwermans knows how to twist the facts so as to give the impression of a calm, peace-loving man; the witnesses in the I$^{st}$ hearing aren't perceptive enough to grasp what I see as your unbelievably serene nature (—for I would have pitched the fellow down the stairs) as absolute self-defense and not as a "threat"————so that the judge and it seems to me even Rosenfeld himself think that you called W. upstairs (!) simply in reaction his cursing and threatened him with the revolver. Even though these idiots have read your concise, magnificent deposition from which just the opposite emerges. From it I see the whole matter so clearly before me, feel your righteous indignation and the urge to obtain satisfaction just as strongly, and consequently suffer most intensely in having to conclude that there is no justice to be found here. In my opinion it would not have been excessive had you pitched the fellow down the stairs. You were so completely in the right that such fury would have been justified. The gentlemen forget that even He, by whose cross they swear, wielded the whip over the money changers in "holy rage" and chased them from the temple. But these gentlemen, this Herr Rosenfeld and consorts, actually look like the mob that once screamed: "To the cross with him! Give us Barrabas!" Things don't change. Geniuses must suffer, are betrayed and defamed, and the criminals (the Wouwermanses) have it good. I can no longer see the entire matter from any other point of view. It is simply one more bit of suffering that you've had to undergo here; so I will dare to repeat it: put the matter behind you, dear, good Herr Schönberg. The moral injustice you have suffered cannot be made good even with the best civil judgment you could possibly achieve. And, as it seems to me as well as to Bahr, it is by no means certain that Wouwermans would be convicted. As I said above, his gentle demeanor makes the best impression, the witnesses (your maids, I believe) have in their blindness possibly even strengthened W.'s credibility; the lawyer, one of the most cunning, who loves to make a splash and only takes cases that are a sure thing, is only concerned with expanding his reputation as a defense lawyer and would never risk an uncertain case, especially one that, being connected with you, will undoubtedly make all the papers; even if he does succeed in obtaining justice for you he wouldn't have much to show for it, whereas, according to Bahr, if he doesn't succeed he will be eternally disgraced. And I have to be the one to tell you all this, I, for whom your justice is my own, I who read your deposition, which I consider irrefutable. As it was (even before I went to Dr. Rosenfeld), Webern and Königer, too, were considering letting the matter drop—primarily because of the "business with the children". This consideration also confirmed Bahr in the same opinion, preconceived if only because of the impossibility of obtaining justice in Vienna. Indeed, wouldn't it be for the best, since you're leaving Vienna anyway!? For then you needn't give a hang and would be spared much time-consuming unpleasantness. Of course these are only my unsolicited ideas. But I know, even if they contradict your ideas, that you won't be angry with me. I simply <u>wrote</u> as if I were standing before you, <u>telling</u> you my opinion, always ready to bow to your superior understanding. And of course I also know that whatever you now choose to do will be the only right and only possible solution.————

And with that I have already broached the topic of your move to Berlin. When I entered your apartment yesterday and went into your study to pick up the Mozart symphonies (I assume you have received them by now), I was overcome by the magnitude of your decision and by the sadness and emptiness ahead once your decision becomes final and irrevocable. But I won't let my heavy heart interfere where only my head should rule. Naturally I understand and know this to be the only right decision (—indeed the only possible one, as Bahr says) that you <u>take advantage</u> of the prospects in Berlin, even if at first they're not *that* bright. In Bahr's opinion, even if our campaign helps you for a while, it would be for only a relatively short time and <u>after that</u> even a campaign such as that would no longer be feasible. He is firmly convinced that <u>Vienna</u> is the least favorable place for you and Moll[1] said the same thing about this "Balkan nest" when I spoke with him not too long ago about you and your affairs. For—as far as I can predict the results—our campaign is sure to be successful, indeed, very successful I believe. But I rather doubt— and so do Bahr and Moll—that we can find a <u>number</u> of patrons to declare themselves willing to do something over (3) <u>years</u>. Perhaps one or two! But in general the Viennese aren't good for that sort of thing, more likely the Berliners! <u>But that</u> which we can expect to achieve will be, I confidently hope, a significant one-time sum, which can perhaps help you over several years. Nevertheless, in keeping with your wish, we are placing most of the emphasis on an annual subsidy and the first results should be apparent by the 1st to middle of next week. I don't wish to speak of the smaller sums collected so far, nor can I yet do so. More about that tomorrow, perhaps.

Tomorrow, esteemed Herr Schönberg, I'll also let you know about moving your things to Berlin. *[Berg informs Schoenberg about the results of his inquiries into moving firms.]*

Now just a few answers to your very dear letter which, being from you, made me very happy, but which also caused me great pain—because you are moving away from Vienna. That I move to Berlin is completely out of the question, at least for the present. Only the prospect of a terrific position, of which there is of course none, could justify my leaving the administrative work <u>here.</u> For from that moment on I would receive nothing more from my mother. Moreover, I also think it would be impossible for my wife to be completely separated from her family. Those are the major reasons. As for the minor ones: the completely refurbished apartment, for instance, which cost a great deal of money, and other such considerations. The more I think of it, the more certain I am that it is impossible!—Webern is lucky; he can follow you everywhere. <u>He</u> is going to write the article you wrote me about.[2]

1. The Austrian Seccessionist painter Carl Moll was the stepfather of Alma Mahler.
2. Webern's article, "Über Arnold Schönberg," was published in the *Rheinische Musik- und Theaterzeitung* XIII / 7 (17 February 1912), 99–103 and XIII / 8 (24 February 1912), 118–122.

The topic was a great temptation for me, but given my terrible ponderousness in writing I either wouldn't bring it off as it should be done, or else much too slowly. I know that from my contribution to the little book about you.[3] Despite the enormous amount of material I had and which I intended to deal with, ultimately, after working long and hard, I wrote something very short, which didn't exhaust so much as a millionth of the essence of your pedagogical gifts. It's the same with composing. Even <u>here</u> I haven't written anything yet. Granted, I've hardly had any time until now. Apart from other things there was the apartment to set up, which has, I think, turned out very beautifully. Will you be able to see it soon? We haven't rented out the apartment on the Hauptstrasse, either,[4] so you can see, dear Herr Schönberg, that I have no advice on how you could rent out yours. I have racked my brains and asked for advice. Without success. Perhaps some of the lost money could be recovered only through a <u>very</u> reduced rent.

It goes without saying that I will oversee the packing once things reach that stage. That will be sad work.—

The appeal in *Pan* was reprinted in the *Zeit* with an idiotic commentary. I am very eager to hear the results. And what did Reinhardt say, and Gutmann. Of course I will come to Prague, that will be a festive day!

With that I have discussed everything of importance. This afternoon Linke will accompany Webern to see Bahr. Since that was planned for yesterday and I had to go see the lawyer, it was necessary to announce Linke in my place (with Webern), and since Bahr postponed it until today I can't take it away from Linke now, although I do have time today. But, as I told you, I already met Bahr yesterday afternoon anyway and discussed in detail everything concerning the campaign. Then tonight or tomorrow morning Webern will come see me, so I'll have more and I hope better news to tell you by then.

My regards to you, dear esteemed Herr Schönberg, in profoundest veneration.

Your devotedly grateful Alban Berg

May I, Herr Schönberg, pick up my wife's picture at some point? Also, if you are really leaving Hietzing, could I have your telephone. Otherwise I won't get one for a whole year, whereas this could be done in a week. Of course I would relieve you of all the paper work.

My wife sends her very best to you and your esteemed wife. She is very well.

I also went to see Hertzka. He was unavailable all day. I think he's afraid I may say something to him about the *Harmonielehre*. But at least I found out that *Pelleas* is coming out in a few days (also the piano reduction of Schreker's *Ferne Klang* of which I'd naturally like a free copy,[5] something Hertzka is trying to avoid.) I wasn't able to find out anything about the *Harmonielehre*.—

Again many, many warm regards from your Alban Berg

3. In response to poor reviews of a 24 April 1911 concert of works by Berg, Webern, and Horwitz, Schoenberg had suggested that his students write a brochure on his activities as a teacher. The project eventually reached book-length proportions and was published in 1912 under the title *Arnold Schönberg*. Berg contributed a brief essay on Schoenberg the teacher.

4. One of the Berg family properties in Vienna, at 6 Hietzinger Hauptstrasse.

5. Berg prepared the vocal score of the second and third acts of Franz Schreker's first opera, *Der ferne Klang*. Schreker was director of the Vienna Philharmonic Chorus, which he had founded in 1907.

## Berg to Schoenberg

[Vienna, 26–27 September 1911]

Above all, dear esteemed Herr Schönberg, I want to answer your kind letter again.[1] I've indexed the first 32 pages now and am awaiting Hertzka's reply and the next installment of proofs. I'm also setting up a names index, which you can incorporate if you wish.—

Should your move be definite, I only await word as to when we should begin packing. I foresee that either Polnauer or I (Linke has school and probably won't have too much time) will supervise the packer sent by the moving firm and that we ourselves will pack the most important things: books, scores, manuscripts. There can be no question of "throwing anything away." How could I throw away so much as a piece of paper bearing a word of yours or a brushstroke or even just one note. Before I'd do that I'd take it home myself, for it goes without saying that I save everything of yours, be it only an envelope for printed matter or the like. So you need not be in the least anxious that anything will get lost. *[Berg suggests that Schoenberg nevertheless take out insurance for his move.]*

Likewise I would prefer to wait and see whether you are definitely going to Berlin before I make inquiries at the Academy. Were I to do so <u>now</u>, it would look very prearranged and calculating of me if you then actually canceled the course and I took over some of those students. Were I to go there now and ask, they would naturally ply me with questions; and of course I wouldn't be able to tell them that most likely you will <u>not</u> be returning to Vienna, but would have to declare just the opposite. How would it look if your definite decision to leave Vienna and the course became known perhaps 1–2 days later and I, who had made such urgent inquiries, then stepped forward as your "substitute." Oh, dear, esteemed Herr Schönberg, how deeply you have honored and pleased me with your choice of this word. I know only too well that there can be no question of substitution. Who could substitute for you?——But that you should permit me to represent myself as your substitute——not outwardly, no!, but inwardly—that is a great joy for me in this time of gloomy foreboding. For there is something so wonderful in being the chosen one, the champion and comrade-in-arms for your ideas, your ideals, your artistic intentions——even if it is only in this God-forsaken city. May my joy over this priestly function (for so I should like to call it) be your guarantee, dear esteemed Herr Schönberg, that I will administer it to the best of my ability. Perhaps I shall even succeed in accomplishing something in this very restricted sphere of activity for the great and holy cause for which you, surrounded by an ever-growing body of followers, will be fighting in the world outside. To be a constant assurance that even at a distance there is someone who acts as if he stood under the protection of your immediate presence.———

These thoughts also give me the strength and opportunity, even the joyous responsibility, to benefit from something as sad as your move and to fulfill in deed your incredibly provident desire that I take over your students . . . that is: if they

1. Berg had already answered Schoenberg's letter of 22 September 1911 in a postcard postmarked 25 September 1911, in which he also announced that he was sending a *Fackel* and a Sunday copy of the *Neues Wiener Journal*.

(the students) are willing . . . !— — — —

I interrupted this letter yesterday when Webern came and told me that you were in Berlin. He heard it from your mother-in-law[2] when he went to the apartment yesterday to get the 5 (incredibly beautiful) piano pieces out of the folder. He also brought me the *Gurrelieder*, which were in his possession, and we 4, Webern, Königer, Linke, and I, immediately sat down to play part of the wonderful 3<sup>rd</sup> part. The melodrama and the last chorus, unspeakably beautiful!!

As I didn't know the address, I have <u>not</u> yet sent the newspaper and *Fackel!* I sent a detailed card to "Berg" [am Starnbergersee] earlier.

Your card from Steglitz with the Berlin address arrived just now.[3]

In response to my letter yesterday, Hertzka sent me the next installment of the III<sup>rd</sup> set of proofs. Not <u>one</u> word as to whether he will <u>permit</u> publication of the song. Since I am first of all not sure he'll permit it and secondly, a great deal of the *Harmonielehre* arrived (up to and including page 144), which means that I have a great deal to do, <u>I</u> won't be able to copy the song at present and will therefore send Part I of the *Gurrelieder* off to Hertzka this afternoon, together with a detailed note and the request that he have it (Du wunderliche Tove) copied <u>at once</u> and sent directly to Kerr. I will also write briefly to Kerr and you will of course see him in Berlin.

*[Berg discusses estimates from two Viennese moving firms.]*

I'll close now, as I must do some work on the index. My card, in which I answered the most important questions, will probably be forwarded.

And so you are really in Berlin now!!! And as you want it so much—and really need it . . . it simply must be so, and I too wish it with all my heart, though it is so sad for me.

I wish you all the very, very, very best in Berlin, dear, good Herr Schönberg.

With warmest devotion and admiration,

> Your ever grateful Alban Berg

Tuesday

---

2. Clara Semo von Zemlinsky.

3. Schoenberg sent a postcard from Berlin, postmarked 25 September 1911, announcing his arrival in Berlin; initially the family lived in a pension near Edward Clark's apartment, whose address Schoenberg included.

## Schoenberg to Berg

Berlin-Steglitz [29 September 1911]

Dear Berg,

I just received 424 marks. I am tremendously surprised? From whom is it?[1] Of course it comes in very handy.—I am really happy to have such friends. Yet it is curious: I should feel very important as a result of these things. But, instead of

1. Independent of the Bahr campaign, Berg, Webern, Linke, and Königer had drawn up an appeal for donations on Schoenberg's behalf, to which 48 prospective contributors responded. This collection was soon subsumed in the larger Bahr fund drive which was administered by Berg.

raising my self-esteem, it lowers it. I can't stop wondering whether I am worth all this. And though while I'm working my ego says "yes," this here is something else. I'm happy, but depressed. I'm pleased and worried—whether I am the person I thought I was and would have to be, to deserve so much effort.

A good deal has been happening in Berlin too. The matter with Reinhardt will lead to something. Not what I expected, but at any rate something similar.[2] Yes, and the concert agency Wolff wants to take charge of my affairs in order to "establish" me in Berlin.[3] No doubt that means performances.

I wish I could be a powerful man soon, so as to carry out that which I consider good, and to be of service to my friends who want to work with me. I hope I can do that soon. And perhaps one day we will constitute a power, but one in the service of moral ends!

My warm regards to you, dear friend, and to Webern, Linke, Königer, and all other friends.

Please tell Königer, to whom I'll write soon: I am <u>tremendously</u> pleased that he intends to come here.[4] And it confirms what I already believed earlier, namely that in him I shall have a new and worthy friend.

Many warm regards to all my dear friends.

Your Arnold Schönberg

---

2. Nothing came of the negotiations with Max Reinhardt.

3. The concert agency Hermann Wolff, run by Louise Schwarz Wolff.

4. Königer had written to Schoenberg on 22 September 1911, but nothing came of his plan to continue his studies in Berlin.

## Berg to Schoenberg

Early Saturday

[Vienna, 30 September 1911]

Dear Herr Schönberg,

No doubt you have received telegram, express letter, and clipping from the *Wiener Journal*.[1] With regard to the last-named, the 4 of us (W[ebern], L[inke], K[öniger], and I) debated for a long time whether the *Wiener Journal* shouldn't be forced to

---

1. On 29 September the *Neues Wiener Journal* reprinted the *Pan* appeal with the following commentary:

"Arnold Schönberg is moving to Berlin for the second time now. It has been divulged by those who are close to him that grinding poverty forced him to leave Vienna. The total lack of recognition and the brusqueness with which this is publicly manifested have cost him his last students. Despite strenuous attempts on the part of his friends, it was impossible to find him a position capable of supporting him. So what could he do but emigrate. To that extent his decision is understandable and certainly regrettable. But that doesn't give the gentlemen who signed the appeal in *Pan* the right to shake their heads over Vienna so piously! Beethoven and Mozart lived in Vienna without starving to death. Besides! "Apparently" Berlin is also not the city "to which musicians flee." Herr Schönberg was in Berlin once before and was forced to draw that conclusion. Now he is making another attempt. We hope his experiences will not give the lie to his aphorisms in *Pan*."

No aphorisms by Schoenberg had appeared in *Pan*. The unsigned writer of the above commentary may have been thinking of the aphorisms that appeared in the Berlin publication of the Gutmann *Konzertkalender, Konzert-Taschenbuch* (IV, 1911 / 12), 104–06.

print a correction. Particularly because of the passage about supposedly "costing you your last students." Ultimately, despite unanimity of opinion (regarding the base deceitfulness of this insult), we couldn't agree on what action to take. Probably because everything is up in the air just now—your Berlin ventures and our campaign. This is not the right moment for decisive action. Besides, I have probably assigned the matter too much significance and the world in which all injustices remain unatoned will not be improved by justice done in one solitary case. Indeed, I think that would merely afford an opportunity for 1,000 new injustices to arise from that one instance of justice.

The main purpose of our meeting was of course the campaign, for which we have now done our part. If those on whom results now depend would act with a dispatch equal to the urgency with which we implored them, we could celebrate our success by tonight. But since they won't, our patience will again be tried for several days to come. But as I said: by early next week (in other words, as of about 3 or 4 October) I should be able to answer your telegraphed question satisfactorily and to indicate tentative results. In my opinion the final outcome won't take too much longer either (a few days). And will, I hope, be favorable!

*[Berg encloses a mover's estimate.]*

———————————

I'm off to meet Webern now, we are going to your apartment to pick out 6–8 pictures to send Kandinsky.[2] He wrote to me yesterday.

He also wants a "short composition" from me for a "book about art."[3] No doubt you arranged that, dear Herr Schönberg, and I am very pleased. What should I send? Probably one of the 4 published songs. Would you recommend, in case you recall it, the last one, which is "very modern," or one of the first, which still bear traces of tonality?[4]

Yesterday I finally had an opportunity to see Nedbal's program. Stöhr, Sinigaglia, Gernsheim, J. B. Förster, J. Lauber, Sibelius, Schreker *(Phantastische Ouvertüre)*——and to top it off, **Oberleithner.**[5]

A great selection, one worthy to stand beside Löwe's.

And with that I must close in haste, as Webern is already waiting for me; I have mentioned the most important matters——but of course the most important thing

2. Schoenberg had met the Russian painter Wassily Kandinsky on 14 September, after they had been in correspondence since January. Kandinsky invited Schoenberg to participate in the *Blaue Reiter* exhibition to contribute to the group's first (and only) almanac. Of the eight paintings by Schoenberg that Webern and Berg sent to Kandinsky, four were shown in the first exhibit of the *Blaue Reiter* which opened in Munich on 19 December 1911 (a landscape, a self-portrait, and two "visions").

3. The almanac of the *Blaue Reiter* appeared in May 1912 with compositions by Schoenberg, Berg, and Webern, as well as reproductions of two of Schoenberg's paintings (a self-portrait and a vision) and his article "Das Verhältnis zum Text" (The Relationship to the Text).

4. Berg contributed the fourth of his Op. 2 songs, "Warm die Lüfte" (Mombert), which had been composed about 1909 and published at Berg's own expense in 1910. Schoenberg had cited a passage from this song in his *Harmonielehre* as an example of quartal harmony.

5. Nedbal's programs included premieres and / or Viennese first performances of Richard Stöhr's Phantasy for Organ, String Orchestra, and Brass, Leone Sinigaglia's Two Pieces for String Orchestra, Friedrich Gernsheim's *Zu einem Drama*, Op. 82, Josef Bohuslav Förster's *Legende von Glück*, a violin concerto by Joseph Lauber, Jean Sibelius' *Karelia* Overture, Franz Schreker's *Phantastische Ouvertüre*, and Max Oberleithner's Third Symphony.

is now up to **you**): we are awaiting your plans with bated breath; what Berlin will decide to do. Your last communications (telegram and express card)[6] weren't very auspicious, but perhaps something good will come of it after all. We wish that for you so passionately and fervently that it must happen.

Many, many regards, dear Herr Schönberg, in veneration and gratitude

Alban Berg

6. An express postcard of 27 September and telegram of 28 September.

*Schoenberg Self Portrait, dated 1911, shown in the* Blaue Reiter *exhibition (Arnold Schoenberg Institute)*

## Schoenberg to Berg

Berlin-Zehlendorf [c. 4 October 1911]

Dear Berg,

Two urgent requests.

1) Withdraw my suit against Wouwermans. Surely you can find someone who will do that at no great cost. But it must be done quickly. Before 7 October, which is when a hearing is scheduled.

2) It is most urgent that you promptly tell me the unvarnished truth about the state of your Vienna campaign. It's my impression that to date you haven't achieved any tangible results. And that your continued hope is only wishful thinking.

But I don't like to rely on something that will probably never materialize. I prefer an unpleasant certainty right now to a big disappointment later.

So tell me straight out

1) What is absolutely assured to date? How much and when will it be available?
2) Are there assured prospects and why do you think these prospects assured?
3) What has gone awry so far?
4) What are you still hoping for and why?

Please do this promptly.

Should you know of any favorable partial result, I would be grateful if you could wire me the information immediately.

In haste!

Best regards

Arnold Schönberg


## Berg to Schoenberg (postcard)

[Vienna] [6 October 1911]

Dear Herr Schönberg,

Your moving van left yesterday. I think everything is all right. You won't find anything missing. Webern, who is presumably leaving for Berlin tonight as well, will tell you, dear Herr Schönberg, everything about it that may interest you.[1] Also everything about the nature and results of the campaign. There's nothing left for me but to give you the last details about the apartment and to reassure you that everything is being well taken care of. There's even a prospect of renting it.— —

——

Today I shall find out who the 4 newly registered harmony students are, whereupon I'll ask you, dear Herr Schönberg, what I can charge if these 4 or 3 or 2 want to take lessons with me simultaneously (together). And what I can charge Blau[2] and Fräulein Steiner,[3] should they come to me with Polnauer. At any rate I want to

1. Webern had left his Danzig theater position in the spring and accepted Zemlinsky's offer of a position in Prague, only to return to Vienna five days later. He had now made a rather sudden decision to follow Schoenberg to Berlin, where he and his family remained until May 1912.
2. Karl Blau studied with Schoenberg in 1911.
3. It has not been determined how long Jenny Steiner studied with Schoenberg or Berg.

thank you very, very much right now, dear esteemed Herr Schönberg, for having taken the trouble to write to Wiener.[4] It would make me happy if I were successful. As happy as I can be, so far away from you. Oh! dear Herr Schönberg . . . . . . .

Now I'm awaiting Webern to say good-bye.

Most warmly your Berg

I heard from Hertzka that he will not allow the publication in *Pan!*[5] It would undermine the work's success!!!! Have received *Harmonielehre* up to page 192.

Forgive me, Herr Schönberg, that this hasn't turned out to be a letter, but for a week now I have had the time-consuming job of settling the rent accounts (in other words have been uninterruptedly doing sums!).

---

4. Karl von Wiener, president of the Vienna Academy of Music 1909–19.

5. Instead of an excerpt from *Gurrelieder*, *Pan* (I / 4, 16 November 1911, between 114 and 115) published Schoenberg's "Aus: Waller im Schnee" (Stefan George).

*Berg to Schoenberg*

Saturday
[Vienna, 7 October 1911]

Esteemed Herr Schönberg,

I have just come from your apartment. It's completely empty. Horrible!— — — Frau Zemlinsky is still there, presumably until Tuesday. No doubt you have heard that Herr Zemlinsky did not conduct *La Belle Hélène* in Vienna. He arrived to find impossible singers and a still more impossible orchestra, and conducted the rehearsals, but not the premiere. Huge row between him and Reinhardt's assistant, which might end in a lawsuit.[1]—I also spoke with Gutheil,[2] after she had written asking me to do so. I got the impression that her feelings were hurt in connection with you. Because of Kerr's appeal! Of course I explained to her that, first, you knew nothing about the wording of Kerr's appeal, and second, that your bitterness against Vienna couldn't be mitigated by the fact that 2 people, Rosé[3] and she (Gutheil), have done so very much on your behalf. Everything else: the various orchestras and their conductors (Loewe, Nedbal, Schalk[4]), the 2 opera houses in Vienna, and finally the press have made any performance of your works impossible. The result being a threat to your very existence . . . etc. Naturally all of that calmed her and she couldn't say enough about her "devotion and love for you." It almost seemed to me, though no names were mentioned, that the Rosé Quartet[5] also share her hurt feelings. It seemed as if she wanted it to appear that she was not the only one

---

1. Zemlinsky was scheduled to conduct the 6 October performance of Max Reinhardt's production of Offenbach's *La Belle Hélène*; his cancelation did not result in a lawsuit.

2. Marie Gutheil-Schoder sang the soprano solo in the premiere of Schoenberg's Second String Quartet.

3. Arnold Rosé was concertmaster of the Vienna Philharmonic Orchestra, founder of the Rosé Quartet, and brother-in-law of Gustav Mahler. His ensemble premiered Schoenberg's sextet, *Verklärte Nacht*, as well as the First and Second String Quartets.

4. Franz Schalk was a conductor of the Court Opera and concert director of the Gesellschaft der Musikfreunde.

5. At this time the other members of the Rosé Quartet were Paul Fischer, Anton Ruzitska, and Friedrich Buxbaum.

who felt personally wounded by Kerr's criticism of Vienna, but that others who had worked with equal enthusiasm for the propagation of your music felt the same. But I may be mistaken. You, who presumably exchange letters with Rosé now and then, will certainly be able to assess the situation properly.

Since you are now informed regarding the campaign, dear esteemed Herr Schönberg, I can tell you the following and add that Gutheil acted on her own initiative and will send the sum to the "Schönberg Fund." I don't as yet know how much it is, probably won't know until the day after tomorrow.

But I did hear from Bahr just now that he is going to transfer to this fund the sum of 940 kronen, received from some donors who wish to remain anonymous, and that it will presumably arrive the day after tomorrow. Enclosed a list of what has been achieved so far.

Now one great favor, dear Herr Schönberg, which I already mentioned in yesterday's card.

It concerns the students!

At the conservatory there are only 2 gentlemen desiring harmony lessons who remain a possibility:

Mikoliesch, Arthur, II, 8 Fugbachgasse

Brunner, Egon, VI, 6 Magdalenenstrasse, apt. 11.

Should I write to them? or would you prefer to send them a short note, dear Herr Schönberg, telling them to contact me. And what can I charge if, for instance, these 2 come to me in one lesson, or each separately?

You also wrote once that among the paying students a Fräulein Rethi and a certain Winkler were possibilities, neither of whom I know. Nor their addresses. Are they to be taken individually; and in what. Probably not harmony. It goes without saying that I will teach Königer, Linke, and Polnauer for nothing if they wish to study (though Königer is leaving.) Should I take Polnauer together with Fräulein Steiner. For she wrote to me on her own that she would like to study composition with me. What can I charge? Polnauer thinks that Dr. Blau will certainly be there too.—? Should I write to Dr. Ernst Kraus.[6]

Please, dear Herr Schönberg, don't be annoyed that I ask you all this, particularly when you yourself aren't settled yet. But I rather think I shouldn't postpone the matter or these few students will get away, and I would be very glad to earn a little, since there apparently aren't any piano reductions to be done just now. So you won't think my many questions presumptuous and importunate, will you, Herr Schönberg. If I were lucky enough to be able to speak with you, like Webern, the matter would be settled in 2–3 sentences. But under these circumstances the result is a letter with many questions and annoyances. Forgive me.

I am so alone now.—————You can't imagine how I felt yesterday when I saw the huge furniture van drive off across the Hietzinger Platz ———————
Many, many warmest regards, dear, kind Herr Schönberg

Ever your Berg

Please excuse the careless form, dear Herr Schönberg, but I still have letters to write and moreover up to page 240 of the *Harmonielehre* arrived today.

6. Ernst Kraus, vice-president of the Gesellschaft der Musikfreunde, studied with Schoenberg 1910–11.

## Berg to Schoenberg

[Vienna, 14 October 1911]

Again, dear Herr Schönberg, I've come to bother you with my affairs. About a week ago I wrote to you with regard to students I could perhaps take over. I still haven't answered Fräulein Steiner, the only one who contacted me on her own, since I don't know what I can reasonably ask her to pay. I think she could come with Polnauer (perhaps with Blau as well?), but don't have the slightest idea what I could charge in that case. You once mentioned 5–6 kronen. Isn't that too much? I heard from Botstiber[1] that in addition to Blau, Kraus and Weishut also want to continue studying. But I imagine they will naturally be interested only in your personal lectures and that there's no hope for me there.

*[Berg continues to discuss the student question.]*

Incidentally, I'm supposed to give you Botstiber's regards, dear esteemed Herr Schönberg, and to tell you that he was very "exasperated" by your move to Berlin. You should have had more "patience." You have no idea how repulsive I found the man. The impression he made on me when I visited you once while you were painting him,[2] that of a cocky fool, was only reinforced and confirmed by a rather long discussion with him about you. —————————

So you will be so kind as to drop me a hint as to what I should do with regard to the students, won't you, dear Herr Schönberg: who else could be considered, what I can charge, whether to take them separately or in the form of a small seminar, etc.? . . . Perhaps you could discuss it with Webern, who is so fortunate and enviable in always being with you, and he could let me know what you advise (on a card, for instance).[3]* By the way, please give him my best regards and thanks for his kind letter. I will write to him again soon, also about *Elektra*.[4] Maybe I'll wait for the 1st Mahler memorial concert on Thursday (Symphonies I and IV, Orchestral Songs, Nedbal)[5] because I am sure that by then I will be able to see clearly what now I perceive only dimly. No doubt it is all perfectly clear to you, but I have to work my way through it slowly in order to find an explanation for the fact that that which once provided me with such joyous and enthusiastic hours can under certain circumstances rebound without effect—*Elektra*, for instance.—Why does that never happen with one of your works or Mahler's or Beethoven's—or even, for instance, Schumann's works? —————————

I shall take some renewed steps in the campaign now. First I'll write to ask Bahr when I can see him. For the project is progressing extremely listlessly, as Webern will have told you. So far the following has been accomplished:

*[Berg itemizes a campaign total of 4,620 kronen.]*

1. Hugo Botstiber became secretary of the Gesellschaft der Musikfreunde in 1905 and was Kanzleidirektor of the Vienna Conservatory (which became the Academy in January 1909) 1905–14. Berg had gone to Botstiber to obtain information for Webern concerning the Academy's *Staatspreis* (State prize), for which Webern was considering applying.

2. Schoenberg's portrait of Botstiber, probably painted around 1910, is privately owned in Vienna.

3. Webern and his family had been the Schoenbergs' first houseguests in Berlin (6–12 October), until they found an apartment close by.

4. Berg had attended a Vienna Court Opera performance of Richard Strauss's *Elektra* on 9 October.

5. On 19 October with the Tonkünstler Orchestra.

That is much less than I had expected. I had imagined at least twice that. But more will _have_ to be accomplished.—

Enough for today, dear Herr Schönberg, and forgive my importunateness concerning the students, but you will understand that it is important for me to earn at least _something_ and this is the only way, I think!

Many, many regards, dear Herr Schönberg, also from my wife, and regards to your esteemed wife

from your completely devoted Alban Berg

_Harmonielehre_ has arrived up to page 400.


*For I really don't want _you_, who must surely be preoccupied with your own affairs just now, to have to waste _your_ precious time on _mine_, too.


## Schoenberg to Berg

Berlin-Zehlendorf [16 October 1911]

Dear Berg,

I wrote you a letter on the 9th that answered your questions. I don't remember exactly what was in it and at the moment your letter—I'm busy packing—is not within reach! Maybe you'll still get it!

At the same time I wrote to 5 students,[1] telling them to go to you. One of them—Kolisko[2]—has already answered: he's going to Schreker. But the others, the two from the course, Fräulein Rethi and Winkler, both of whom paid 40 kronen each for one lesson a week (you can probably give 2 lessons a week) will probably write to you. I think you should ask for 5–6 kronen per lesson. In the beginning you will have to be a bit flexible. Possibly less for talented ones. But not for dilettantes, [in that case] 5 kronen!

I also asked you to send me some of the available funds. But now I think it would be best if you sent me—as soon as possible, if you can—1,000 kronen or 1,000 marks, a round sum.

I mentioned a number of other things. Anything I remember I'll add later.

Warmest thanks, my dear Berg, for the great trouble you took with my move. Please: pass that on to the others too. I am _very grateful_ to you all! You did a lot of work for me and relieved me of a great worry. So again: heartiest thanks.

One thing I'm very sorry about: that you aren't here, too. I must say that even if I'm happy here I would still miss my dear friends, you, Königer, Linke, and Polnauer, too (who was very nice). But cheer up: I probably won't be happy—so I'll miss you all the more!

One more word regarding the "campaign."

Where does it stand now—by and large, no details: they depress me; especially the "small" details. The "big ones" much less, of course. On the contrary!

I still think: one shouldn't neglect making personal calls, for instance to Dr.

1. Probably Karl Blau, Robert Kolisko, Else Rethi, Jenny Steiner, and Wilhelm Winkler.
2. Robert Kolisko studied with Schoenberg in 1911.

Lemberger,[3] *Baurat* Carl Redlich,[4] Theodor Hämmerle,[5] Wittgenstein,[6] Gutmann,[7] etc.!

Concerning Gutheil-Rosé, I wrote: that I had nothing to do with Kerr's appeal. I wasn't very pleased with it and I still haven't met Kerr, as I am avoiding his acquaintance.

Many warm regards to you and your wife, also from my wife.

Your Arnold Schönberg

---

3. The textile businessman Emil Lemberger had given Schoenberg money in 1908 and again in 1910, for which he had received a painting in return.

4. *Oberbaurat* (Construction Councillor) Carl Redlich was a patron of the arts.

5. *Kommerzialrat* (Commerce Councillor) Theodor Hämmerle was a wealthy Austrian industrialist particularly interested in chamber music; evidence of his support of Schoenberg goes back to 1902.

6. The wealthy Viennese Wittgenstein family was generous in its support of the arts. Leopoldine and Karl Wittgenstein, parents of the pianist Paul Wittgenstein and the philosopher Ludwig Wittgenstein, were benefactors of the Schoenberg Fund, along with other members of the family.

7. Max Gutmann, a prominent Viennese banker.


*Berg to Schoenberg (letterhead: Berg / IX., Fuchsthallergasse 2[1] [crossed out])*

Wednesday
Vienna [18 October 1911]

Dear, good Herr Schönberg,

I was very happy about the dear letter you wrote me and would have answered right away if I hadn't shortly before cut my thumb half open and thus been <u>unable</u> to write. Even <u>today</u> it's still very difficult and I beg you in advance to excuse both pencil and handwriting. Meanwhile you will have received the money, 1,000 marks, by transfer from the Anglo-Austrian Bank; I took care of that yesterday. (It would have cost about 5 kronen by postal money order, but almost nothing this way)—

The whole letter affair has been cleared up now, too. For the telegram I received from you Saturday evening was <u>distorted</u>. It asked whether I had received the letter from g (G). You can imagine my perplexity, dear Herr Schönberg, and I was about to telegraph back that I didn't even know who **G.** is. (Perhaps Gärtner,[2] Gregor???[3]) Luckily I went to the post office that evening <u>myself</u> and asked whether the g. was correct, upon which I was told that it was supposed to be a nine. Everything then fell into place, though it was unfortunately also clear that one of your letters to me must have gone astray. Next day I was told at the post office that there was no letter to Berg (say with a wrong address) and I consequently waited most impatiently for new word from you. I was sure the lost letter would have made me very happy and

---

1. Fuchsthallergasse in Vienna's ninth district had been Berg's address before his marriage, when he still lived with his family. He also used stationery bearing the letterhead "Berg/III, Vordere Zollamstr.," where the Bergs had lived from May 1908 to May 1910.

2. The noted concert singer Eduard Gärtner had sung Schoenberg's Op. 1 songs as early as 1898.

3. Hans Gregor was director of the Vienna Court Opera 1911–18.

was on the other hand afraid that in it you might have given me some important task. If you should still find it—for I gather from your last letter that you merely mislaid it and that it didn't get lost in the post—I beg you to send it to me even if it's no longer "relevant"—after all it was intended for me—and I dare not lose a single one of those words (especially at a time when I have so few of them). For after all, what is a letter compared to a conversation from the Karlsplatz station to Schwarzenbergplatz and back![4] And then the lessons twice a week and other times when I was fortunate enough to speak with you, no:—to hang on your words!!!——However, you must not think that it could "console" me in my isolation to know that you "are not happy" in Berlin, either. Only the thought that you have found there, if not happiness, then at least the prospect of happiness, or at least a chance of being able to find it and indeed finding it—that alone can reconcile me to the fate of having to be without you—because I can then perceive it as a necessity beneficial to you———though detrimental to me!

But as it is——? To go about here, unhappy myself, —knowing, what is more, that you aren't happy either——— and conscious on top of that of the pathetic lack of success to date of the campaign for you———! As you already know from my last letter on Saturday, it has almost ground to a halt and as you yourself wrote and as Webern wrote earlier, something has to be done now. Unfortunately Bahr is out of town for a few days,* but as soon as I find out when he returns I will call on him. Perhaps he is even going to Berlin, I forgot to ask. But you would surely hear of that.

On the afternoon of the day after tomorrow I'm meeting with Linke, Königer, and possibly Stefan, to whom I wrote, since he is giving a lecture in Vienna "About Mahler and the Younger Generation."[5] At that time we will "confabulate" (as Hertzka would say) about advancing our campaign. Who else could be approached. And what could still offer hope of success. Probably first and foremost the individuals you suggested, but also others, I think! But what's the good of my thinking? I don't put much stock in it any more myself, since all my hopes and endeavors regarding the campaign have been so cruelly disappointed.

I also hope to hear something from Stefan about the booklet.[6] Do you know anything about it, dear Herr Schönberg?

And now after all this, above all many warm thanks for your kind answers to my questions (about the "students") which I unfortunately repeated in my last letter, before receipt of the telegram. I have now invited Fräulein Steiner to a meeting— she will be starting composition lessons either alone or with Polnauer. I also wrote to ask Galitzenstein[7] whether he wouldn't like to go on studying, since he wrote to me not long ago that his brother, the virtuoso Gottfried Galston(!) wants to play my sonata.

4. During the time Schoenberg taught his private course at the Vienna Academy, Berg was in the habit of accompanying him from the Karlsplatz Stadtbahn (city railway) station to his classroom at the Academy and back.
5. The critic Paul Stefan held his lecture at the University of Vienna on 18 October 1911.
6. Paul Stefan was serving as an advisor in finding a publisher for the book on Schoenberg that was being compiled by his students.
7. Ernst Galitzenstein studied with Schoenberg 1910–11.

No one else has contacted me—not even one of the 5 you were so kind and good as to write immediately. Maybe something will still happen. In any case many, many thanks!—

*[Berg gives further details relating to Schoenberg's former Vienna apartment.]*

But now I don't know what else to say and will therefore close, since I've already been too hard on my throbbing thumb.

Please give your wife and the dear little ones my devoted best. Also from my wife. And also to Webern, to whom I will write soon.

And to you, dear kind Herr Schönberg. All the best and warmest regards

from your grateful, devoted Alban Berg

* Yesterday when I could have spoken with him, I did this thing to my thumb, in consequence of which I was overcome by dizzy spells and forced to cancel at the last minute; and today he is already gone.

*Schoenberg to Berg (postcard)*

Berlin-Zehlendorf, 22 October 1911

Dear Berg,

The index is <u>absolutely outstanding!</u>[1] I'm immensely pleased with it. It must have been a great deal of work. There is a great deal of diligence invested in it and it is done with real "economy." Really fantastic!—I shall have two copies of the proofs sent to you and 1 to myself. The one as a supplement for your copy; the other for entering your corrections. The latter you are to send to Universal Edition for printing. Make some arrangement with them. For I will keep my copy here; in other words won't read any more proofs.—So this correction depends entirely on you! Is that clear?

One more favor, dear friend; namely, would you please give immediate notice on my apartment for 1 February 1912. Otherwise I might have to pay rent again. Take the amount out of the 200 kronen you mentioned (minus fees).[2] Likewise I'd like you to use this money to pay Polnauer, who paid for some ads for the apartment. Write to him that he should study with you.—Has Fräulein Rethi contacted you? Or Herr Winkler? Write to both of them. I'd like to know whether they didn't receive my letters either.

Warmest regards and thanks

Your Arnold Schönberg

1. Berg had sent Schoenberg the completed indexes for the *Harmonielehre* c. 21 October, along with a short note.

2. On 14 October Berg sent Schoenberg an itemization of the fund, in which 200 kronen cash was listed as being in Berg's possession.

## Berg to Schoenberg

Tuesday
[Vienna, 24 October 1911]

Dear, kind Herr Schönberg,

Yesterday and today I experienced a very, very great joy; first your dear card, which told me how satisfied you are with the index; the knowledge of that and my pleasure in the work and its success would alone have been sufficient recompense for my trouble. But then I also received a totally unexpected "honorarium" from Hertzka, who summoned me to him today, for which I'm sure I have only you to thank, dear Herr Schönberg. 100 kronen; 50 of that in cash and—this is the best of it—: the score of *Pelleas* (which costs 48 kronen retail).[1] That's really wonderful! The work looks splendid and I believe you too will be pleased with it. Today Hertzka seemed slightly more agreeable than usual, I had the feeling he spoke of you with more warmth, not so businesslike. It seemed to me that he is concerned that your cause—which of course is ours as well—be successful. As for instance in the Tonkünstlerverein,[2] of which he spoke and with regard to which you yourself once had all sorts of plans. He thinks I should definitely join, that in this way modern influences could infiltrate slowly, since it's not possible as quickly or overnight as you had imagined. Although the entire matter is highly repugnant to me, I am considering whether it might not after all be the way to go about it! At least to **prepare** the way so that if you really did return to Vienna some of the groundwork would already be laid and you could take immediate charge of the whole thing, since by then the Stöhrs and Graeners would no longer be so firmly entrenched and in control of the best positions![3]

I must ask you something about another matter as well. Wymetal, who is presently secretary of the Urania, organizes concerts and therefore asked me to come by. There will be a Mahler memorial concert—a Reger concert, a Pfitzner concert—a——"**Stöhr concert**," a modern piano music recital by Busoni—and also a concert of modern Viennese composers, where you "and your group" (instead of giving you 100 concerts of your own would be in the company of Weigl, Walter, Streicher, etc.[4] Naturally I explained how ridiculous it was, but he said that it

---

1. In a 24 October letter Schoenberg told Berg he had suggested that Hertzka pay Berg 100 kronen for his *Harmonielehre* index. The full score of Schoenberg's *Pelleas und Melisande* had just appeared that month.

2. The Vienna Tonkünstlerverein, a composers' organization, was founded in 1885. Schoenberg, whose connection with the organization came about through Zemlinsky, was a member 1894–1900, and elected into the central committee during his last year.

3. Both the Austrian composer Richard Stöhr, who taught at the Vienna Conservatory 1903–38, and Paul Graener belonged to the central committee of the Tonkünstlerverein.

4. In 1911–12 Wilhelm von Wymetal was secretary of the Urania, a cultural organization founded in 1910, which specialized in adult education. In February and March 1912 the Urania sponsored four concerts of works by the Austrian composers Stöhr, Theodor Streicher, the "Jungwiener" composers (Friedrich Mayer, Egon Wellesz, and Franz Mittler), and Rudolf Braun. Nothing came of plans to devote concerts to the music of Max Reger, Hans Pfitzner, or Ferruccio Busoni.

The Austrian composer Karl Weigl studied composition with Zemlinsky and musicology with Guido Adler.

Bruno Walter, protégé of Mahler and conductor at the Vienna Court Opera 1901–11, was at this time the director of the Vienna Singakademie.

would be merely a preliminary step for later concerts in the coming years. He has to establish himself first and make the concerts palatable and after some financial success he would have more artistic leeway later. That's why your contributions and ours would have to be of the tamer variety, for instance your 1$^{st}$ quartet, older songs, *Gurrelieder,*\* sextet.\*\* Naturally he would also be pleased with an entire concert of you and "your group," as long as we could find people who would do it for nothing. For that is the main thing about all these performances: the participants must do it without fee. Thus Stöhr, for instance, is doing his concert because he found a group who will play his quartet. A violinist who has already played his sonata in Berlin (very successfully!) will also play it gratis in Vienna, likewise songs. So if I could tell Wymetal that, for instance, we had a program (of your works and ours), as well as performers, the matter would be settled! Essentially it would mean that he places the hall at our disposal. Later one might be able to persuade him to do a separate Schönberg concert. But whom could we use? Again only Gutheil and Rosé, and I don't know whether they'll do it. Until now I guess they've always done it for nothing. Haven't they?— — —

It would be possible that our works, "your group," could then be included elsewhere, if Wymetal wants to perform them and if something tame enough can be found. But I doubt it, just as I rather doubt the sincerity of the entire thing. Basically the Urania wants to make a nice profit and Wymetal has to help them do so, which will doubtless succeed if, for instance, he has Grünfeld[6] play Stöhr's piano pieces. But a concert failure would simultaneously be a failure for Wymetal the secretary. And though we can take that risk, the secretary can't!

But at any rate I have told you about it, dear Herr Schönberg, and if you think anything of the matter you can take appropriate steps.

Otherwise there's not much news. Since Königer suddenly developed a very severe sore throat, we had to postpone our calls to the patrons. There doesn't seem to be much sense in my going alone, as I don't have what it takes to accomplish anything with people like that. I would return home empty-handed. Stefan won't go. Linke is too busy with school, so I have to wait until Königer is well again. I'm also expecting a letter from Bahr any day. But everything in this world takes so long. No word from any students yet either. Granted it hasn't been that long since I wrote and I expect something may arrive tomorrow.

*[Berg discusses remaining issues concerning Schoenberg's Vienna apartment, his own students, and a point of grammar in the* Harmonielehre.*]*

Naturally I will do the corrections for the index as quickly as possible.—

And now adieu, dear, esteemed Herr Schönberg; as soon as I have accomplished anything—with regard to the campaign—I will write immediately. It is dreadful that I keep having to postpone it.

Please give my best to Webern too. But particularly to you, my dear Herr Schönberg and your esteemed wife from me and my wife.

I thank you once more for putting in a kind word for me with Hertzka.

5. This performance took place on 14 March 1912.
6. The Viennese pianist and composer Alfred Grünfeld.

The 50 kronen come in very handy——but the score makes me truly happy! In continually renewed gratitude,

Your Alban Berg

\* Have you already finished orchestrating it, Herr Schönberg. I think that would be very important for your cause. If only it were already engraved. Or even performed!! In my opinion that would do more than all of our campaigns!

\*\* will be performed in Munich, as I hear from my sister, who saw posters for it (Heyde Quartet)[5]

## Berg to Schoenberg

Saturday
[Vienna, 28 October 1911]

Dear, esteemed Herr Schönberg,

It has now become clear to me why our campaign was so unsuccessful. Apparently there is a counter-committee intent on frustrating our attempts, which it is doing quite simply by proclaiming that your financial situation is excellent anyhow, and the results of the campaign very satisfactory.[1] I have heard from various sources now that not only is our campaign believed to have made very favorable progress (though no one but me could possibly know that), but the Berlin patrons are believed to have raised 6,000 marks, etc., etc. . . .

That's why some people who might otherwise have given something felt exonerated, just as others who might have made an effort to raise something failed to do so.

Above all Frau Mahler,[2] for example. To date she has done absolutely nothing, since first she was waiting to be contacted again, although I had not only done so by letter long since, but had also discussed **everything** down to the smallest detail with Moll (about 3 weeks ago). However, she heard in the meantime that the matter had been brought to a successful conclusion and thought the campaign over. My visit yesterday with Moll cleared up this misconception. Above all he is now going to take a hand in the matter himself; then see to it that Frau Mahler goes to the Rothschilds, etc. I also wrote to her yesterday to this effect. But the matter is complicated by the fact that everyone in question has to a great extent already been involved: many gave 5,000 kronen apiece to the Mahler stipend[3] and won't want to do still more for art. Furthermore they all supported Walter to bring about the performance of Mahler's VIII[th] Symphony.[4]

1. The counter-committee seems to have been no more than some passing remarks made by Paul Stefan, Karl Linke, and others about the success of efforts on Schoenberg's behalf.

2. Alma Schindler Mahler, Gustav Mahler's widow, met Schoenberg about 1900 through Zemlinsky, with whom she had studied composition.

3. The Gustav Mahler Trust Fund was established with 55,000 kronen, the interest of which was set aside as an annual stipend for a needy and deserving composer. The fund's central committee included Alma Mahler, Busoni, Strauss, Walter, and the *Kommerzialrat* Friedrich Redlich; Schoenberg received the stipend in 1913, 1914, and again in 1918.

4. Bruno Walter led the Vienna Philharmonic in the first Viennese performance of Mahler's Eighth Symphony on 14 March 1912.

But in any case you will at least have the benefit of the Mahler stipend. Today it amounts to 50,000 kronen, but once the American contributions arrive it should be at least twice that. Naturally the first installment of interest on this capital is intended for you and it may even be possible to transfer this sum to you earlier (that is before 1 January 1912). Should the capital continue to grow, the interest would naturally be added, whereby at least 4,000 kronen would be at your disposal for 1912. Perhaps even more.

Surely Frau Mahler will also accomplish something in person, so in about 2–3 weeks, I will ask Moll.

What I accomplished at Bahr's amounted more to advice than results, but at any rate, I think—coming as it does from a man who knows how to get along so well in a world he professes to improve and who is so well loved and understood in a town he hates and curses . . . in other words I think that the advice of such a "philosopher" [Lebenskünstler], of someone so "knowledgeable in the ways of the world and men(!)" [Welt- und Menschen-Kenner] can't be all bad. He thinks that success is certain as long as you succeed in making your way in Berlin for a while. But that is absolutely essential before you return to Vienna. If, on the contrary, you should return earlier, that is, without proof that you were well treated in Berlin and that performances of your works had been successful, then you will have lost all chances in Vienna and he would advise you rather to live in a smaller city and try to make advances from there.

Of course that's really nothing new. I myself regard your Berlin stay as an intermediate stage only. I imagine that in the course of the 1st or 2nd year your name will become ever more prominent through successes out there in the "Reich" and that the city that is at present playing the insulted, basely deserted beauty will soon grow ashamed of her own inadequacy and "call" you back to Vienna. That will certainly happen one of these days! But in order for it to happen it is, in Bahr's opinion, crucial that the Viennese understand how very highly esteemed you are abroad.— — —

Concerning the students here, the matter is as follows. Dr. Kraus has canceled; I had enclosed your letter and he regrets very much that his profession is so time-consuming. He would not have been able to come even if you had continued the seminar. Perhaps he will be able to come next year . . . "he regrets the canceled course very much, not only for personal reasons but also for the sake of modern music."—

For the present Fräulein Rethi merely has "plans for the future", "at the moment she isn't mistress of her own time" as she has become "engaged."[5]—

With that, aside from Polnauer, Steiner, and Königer, whom I have already mentioned, I am left with Herr Winkler who has an appointment tomorrow, and Galitzenstein, who has one the day after.

Oh yes: A certain Schmid from Kalksburg is also coming to me once a week for counterpoint (for free).[6] He is the one who came specially from Salzburg to study

5. Else Rethi was engaged to the caricaturist and former Schoenberg student, Benedict Fred Dolbin. They were married 1912–17.

6. Josef Schmid, who was then teaching piano at a convent school in Kalksburg near Vienna, had initially written to Schoenberg, asking to study with him.

with you. Webern knows about it.

Back to the campaign. Bahr advises calling only on certain people. Namely calling on those where using his name might help. He is totally against going to others, such as Köchert,[7] who is said to be a very rich man. Rather one should send them the appeal again by registered mail, with a reference to Bahr in a cover letter. If that doesn't work, then going there wouldn't help either. Since Königer is well now, thank heavens, we'll be able to make various calls. Granted, there is nothing more to be expected from the main people, just smaller sums! With the 940 kronen Bahr got out of them, the Wittgensteins are finished. The 2nd Redlich[8] has promised something and Bahr will speak to him about it in the next few days. But that's all Bahr has accomplished. In person, that is!—

With that I have told you everything of importance, dear Herr Schönberg, and can only hope that—when I write again, I'll have more favorable news to report. Enclosed the [apartment] termination notice. Oh yes, both Rethi and Winkler received your letters.

My very warmest regards to you, dear, esteemed Herr Schönberg,

from your ever devoted Alban Berg

Something else: Naturally I am in agreement with the teaching fees you suggested. To Winkler I will suggest 40 kronen a month for 2 hours a week, as you advised. The same for Galitzenstein, if he comes alone. Or perhaps Weishut will come with him; then of course half.—

Once again many warm regards, dear Herr Schönberg,

from your grateful Alban Berg

My wife, too, sends her very best to you and your esteemed wife.

---

7. The jeweler and banker Theodor Köchert was a talented amateur musician and patron of the arts.
8. *Kommerzialrat* Friedrich Redlich.

## Schoenberg to Berg

Berlin-Zehlendorf, 31 October 1911

Dear Berg,

First of all, heartiest thanks for your dear letter. Concerning the counter-committee you suspect, its head can probably be found there where our "dear" Dr. Stefan lacks his. I really must publicly and definitively dissociate myself from this person. He leaves me no other choice. His good will is so repugnant to me that I must somehow inspire his hate. Since he has only hurt me to date, maybe then he'd be useful.

As far as the facts are concerned around which Herr Dr. Stefan, who is after all "Prof.," has painted pretty pictures, I have the following to say and beg you to tell or read it to all concerned.

1). The sum raised by Berlin patrons was barely sufficient to cover the enormous costs of my move here.[1] Moreover, since I came here in the hope that I would be given enough to live on for half a year and had been told that I would find students right away, neither of which has happened, my situation here is not only not splendid, but on the contrary **_highly_ precarious**! Of course I myself hope that students will turn up, once concerts and the lectures I will be giving in Stern's Conservatory (on aesthetics and composition) have made my presence here generally known. So far, however, that has not been the case!![2]

2). However, and this is the more important portion of this letter:

This whole collection drive is not what I had in mind. I had turned to Bahr in a certain matter. Namely, I had requested that he induce several rich people to give me an annual salary of at least 6,000 kronen for several years, so that I might finally find time to compose. In other words I never insisted that I was starving, something millionaires prefer to see even in lesser artists before deciding to do something for art. I don't at all see why millionaires should demand something of me that they themselves are so careful to avoid. I should think it would suffice that an artist of my stature is, despite great diligence, unable to earn enough money to devote himself to his work halfway free of worries. I should think it would suffice that I have worries—and that in order to earn money I have to do work that is beneath me and that is the cause for my having for two years now found no time to compose.

Therefore if these millionaries do not comprehend my right to their help although I am not yet dying of typhus, then as far as I'm concerned they can keep their wallets shut.

But I must state: I have never begged. And have never asked for money because I was starving. I merely want to lead a calm and modest life, much more modest than that of millionaires, though I accomplish much more! And I want to offer my family that modicum of comfort that millionaires would consider depressing poverty if they had to live like that themselves.

Further:

I expressly declared what I wanted the money for: in order to live well!

Even if the Berlin campaign had gone splendidly (though 6,000 marks is a far cry from being splendid, millionaires could convince themselves of that easily enough if they ever tried to get by on it), there's still no need for annoyance on the part of these millionaires, who no doubt all have an income commensurate with their individual merit. For didn't they themselves want to do something for me so I would be better off.

But not even half of that has been collected. And all of that went for the move!

So, dear Berg, tell them that!

———

And now I would appreciate it if you would have everything presently available transferred to my account at the Dresdner Bank.

1. Schoenberg received a total of 2,000 marks from various patrons, as well as the support of numerous musicians and influential personalities who were trying to establish his career in the German capital.

2. Schoenberg began his Monday afternoon lecture series on 20 November. During his first stay in Berlin 1901–03 he had taught harmony at the Stern Conservatory.

for Arnold Schönberg, deposit account U II, **Zehlendorf**, 7 Hauptstrasse of the Dresdner Bank in Berlin.

And then you will be so kind as to send me a concise statement of all the money I can still count on, in other words what has already been secured, but won't be paid in until later. Write down the total sum. Deduct the amount I have already received and tell me what I will still get and when.——————

I hope you can still accomplish something. I remind you again of Dr. Emil Lemberger and Theodor Hämmerle, who will **most** certainly do something. Be sure to try there!! At least 1,000 kronen each!! The idea for an annual salary was Hämmerle's. And Lemberger has always helped me out; so he will this time, too. Likewise the *Oberbaurat* Redlich. Tell Bahr that the latter has to give at least 2,000 kronen. He can do more and will do so, too.

Don't give up yet.

That I am to receive the Mahler stipend is an unbelievable honor for me. And very touching. It almost seems as if Mahler is giving me a sign from the grave. A sign that he liked me and is concerned about me even after his death. I am very happy about it. That is something one can accept with pleasure!

————

Now tell me, dear Berg, what do your lessons bring in? Is it a significant amount yet? If not, just be patient, things will work out. At least it's a beginning. And under different circumstances you would have had to wait a long time for such a beginning. I believe it will work. At any rate people know now that I recommend you. And admittedly that isn't much, but it's something. Visit Wiener and Bopp[3] sometime, too.——————

Now as for Wymetal: He's scum. A fitting colleague for Herr Dr. Stefan. Tell him: I forbid so much as one note of mine to be performed in the Urania. If Herr von Wymetal, this shoepolish as Polgar quite correctly discovered in no time, wants to shine at any price, then he's not to do it at my expense, but on my shoes.[4] Though I consider even the dust on my shoes too good to be replaced by Wymetal's brilliance. Given that I shake that dust off my shoes—and I do just that—what possible use would I have for Wymetal?

But that should in no way keep you from arranging a concert at the Urania of your things and Webern's. Just keep me out of it. This time anyway. I would be **proud** and happy to present myself with both of you! But Herr von Wymetal has something else in mind!! And I reject that!

Besides: Pfitzner concert, Reger concert, Stöhr concert!

It's low-down and too idiotic for words!

Enough. Many warm regards

Your Arnold Schönberg

3. The German conductor Wilhelm Bopp, director of the Vienna Academy of Music 1907–19.
4. The Austrian theater critic and satirist Alfred Polgar wrote for the *Wiener Allgemeine Zeitung.*

*Berg to Schoenberg (letterhead: Berg/IX., Fuchsthallergasse 2)*

Vienna [3 November 1911]

Thank you very much, dear, kind Herr Schönberg, for your dear, long letter. As I was teaching when the letter arrived yesterday and was too exhausted, I postponed answering until today, when I could attend to the money matter at the same time. Statement of same is enclosed. But concerning the other matter I must tell you the following: Our calls on various rich people have so far produced no results at all, that is, one of them may perhaps contribute a trifle to the Schönberg Fund, but hasn't done so yet. But we weren't even able to see the others, though we inquired at offices and homes. We hadn't announced ourselves in order not to be turned down at the outset, had gone there on the off chance and simply sent in a letter of recommendation from Herr Bahr, but still they wouldn't see us. Apparently they suspected what it was about, since all of these patrons had already been sent the appeal along with a few words from Bahr. So we have resolved to announce ourselves in writing to the principal people. That was done with Hämmerle the day before yesterday. I wrote at length and hope he will indicate a day when I can speak with him. Then I will tell him everything you wrote. I won't rest until I have been allowed to see him. Likewise Lemberger, to whom I will write immediately. I'll also write to Bahr with reference to *Oberbaurat* Redlich. However, that's just the sticking point.

I reread your 1$^{st}$ letter to Bahr and immediately realized that Bahr hadn't taken the matter in hand as he should have and as you had intended. I am positive that he could have come up with what you wanted (6,000 kronen a year). But to do that he would have had to go to 5–10 millionaires whom he knows sufficiently well and who would have done it for his sake and because of his standing, and pressured them until the desired result was achieved. As it was, however, he only wrote to a few, did a little telephoning, and we were forced, since the generous sums were not forthcoming (and I realized this from the first visit to Bahr, as Webern can confirm), to pursue the matter on a small scale, for which a campaign in the form of appeals seemed to us the most suitable. On his own Bahr thus achieved only the 2 times 500 kronen from Redlich and the 940 kronen from all 5–6(!) Wittgensteins together. He certainly didn't exert all his influence on these people. But when I reproached him with that he gave me these people's excuses and explained that they had in any event contributed more than anyone else and more would be out of the question, etc., etc. That explains why the contributions were so small. Apparently Bahr never expected more and now I'm at a loss whether there really are patrons who'd give 1,000 kronen or more since not even the Wittgensteins, Hammerschlag,[1] etc., gave anything worth mentioning. Well, in any case I will pester Bahr again about Redlich and will insist on speaking with Hämmerle and Lemberger (perhaps also Director Hammerschlag, Dr. Spitzer, Fritz Hamburger, who isn't in Vienna at the moment, Schenker, Artaria, Kuffner,[2] Köchert, all of whom are very wealthy people and

---

1. Dr. Paul Hammerschlag was the director of the Austrian Credit-Anstalt bank.

2. The lawyer Dr. Hugo Spitzer, Fritz Hamburger, the shipping agent August Schenker-Angerer, the art dealer Karl August Artaria, and the brewer Moritz Kuffner were all prominent Viennese art patrons.

could perhaps do something, but though able to give thousands they give maybe 50 or 100 kronen, which, considering the cause, is of course ludicrous. However, I have had even more ludicrous experiences—but I'll spare you. That's why I'm not sending you the complete list of contributions but only the sums. Anyway, by now my only real hopes are for Frau Mahler's efforts. Rothschild and others to whom she will turn or has already turned will have to do <u>more</u>.— — — — — — — — — —

I have the following gratifying news about my teaching: I have 7 students, 2 of whom are nonpaying: Polnauer and Schmid from Salzburg (who isn't very talented) so that I earn 125 kronen a month. Circa! For I still don't know what's up with Weishut, who is, however, coming to see me on Monday and who will probably come for 2 lessons a week together with Galitzenstein, for which each would pay me 20 kronen. In that case I would be getting 125 kronen a month. In addition I have Königer twice a week, Winkler once a week, Fräulein Steiner once a week, which makes 9 lessons a week. Naturally I enjoy that very much, and now that I myself am reviewing so much counterpoint and composition I realize how much I learned from you, dear Herr Schönberg, indeed, that I owe <u>everything</u> to you. But I also realize how exhausting it is and how much effort and energy you lavished in teaching 2–3 lessons in succession. The <u>millionaires</u> should just think of <u>that</u>! But of course they don't realize the difference between your teaching and that of (say) a Stöhr! Don't realize what it means when for a couple of kronen you have to sacrifice your time and effort to an untalented, ungrateful student, time and effort that you ought to devote to your own work, indeed owe your work. Time may be money, but the stock marketeers never think of "eternity."

Well, that's certainly what I'll tell the millionaires I approach in the matter. In any case I know your letter by heart, as I do all your letters for a few days.

Thank you very much for your last long, kind letter and my regards to you in never-ending veneration and gratitude

Your Alban Berg

[Berg details the contributions and expenditures of the Schoenberg account, which then totals 4,760 kronen.]

*Schoenberg to Berg (postcard)*

[Zehlendorf] 4 November 1911

Dear Berg,

Did you get my letter of 31 October? I expected your reply by today!—Would you have time to finish the piano reduction of *Gurrelieder*.[1] Hertzka wants to publish it now. I could send you the rest of the score and the piano reductions in approximately 5–6 days. Could you do it quickly?

Best regards

Your Arnold Schönberg

1. Berg had completed a reduction of Parts I and II of the *Gurrelieder* in the spring of 1911. Schoenberg completed the score of Part III on 7 November 1911.

*Berg to Schoenberg (letterhead: Berg/IX., Fuchsthallergasse 2)*

Monday

Vienna [6 November 1911]

You mustn't be angry, dear, kind Herr Schönberg, if the reply that you will meanwhile have received came later than you expected. When that happens it's not from disinclination to write, or negligence in your concerns, rather I often hesitate to write because I don't like to tell you anything negative, i.e., because I keep hoping that if I wait another day I'll finally be able to give you some good news for a change. I can't do so today either. On the contrary, so far the only results of my meetings with various millionaries, when, by referring to Bahr, I have been able to speak to them about you, has been that 2 of them have definitely refused: Hämmerle and Köchert. The others haven't even answered yet. As to the answers I got from those two, I will spare you, dear Herr Schönberg, you can ask Webern if it really interests you. I am writing to him at the same time. Perhaps you can think of something else, which might at least bring Hämmerle to his senses. If only I had the opportunity to tell him what you wrote me not long ago, if I could give him that it might be effective. If you were to approach him personally in this way you would surely be successful. After all, the man simply needs to be enlightened and to realize that it is base not to do anything more for you. But they don't pay any attention to me, these millionaries, or to Bahr either, apparently. Perhaps he wasn't forceful enough. I'm curious to know what he accomplished with *Oberbaurat* Redlich. As you know I wrote Bahr about this with great urgency and conviction, 8 full pages, preferring that to a meeting where he never lets one get a word in, that is to say, has an answer for everything. This way, without being able to object, he is virtually forced to put everything on the line to achieve a success with Redlich. In case he doesn't answer me himself I shall inquire in a few days, likewise at Moll's. Oh, if only I could hear some good news for once: as it is I can only write you letters full of bad news and doubts, and I find that so dreadful that I always prefer to postpone it one more day, hoping with every postal delivery that at least one of these patrons has invited me to visit him. But nothing comes. Only your card, dear esteemed Herr Schönberg, telling me that you have been waiting for a reply. . . . But——at least containing something wonderful, that I am to complete the piano reduction of the *Gurrelieder*. Oh, that's something I'm looking forward to. Do please send it at once, dear Herr Schönberg, I'll do a good job on the conclusion. Clearly all good things come from you and other truly great men. Yesterday Mahler's V[th] with the Philharmonic[1]—and I finally received the Liszt article[2]——these are obviously life's highpoints, everything else is stupidity and baseness. I thank you, Herr Schönberg, for such words, since the world is ungrateful for all your immeasurable works. I'll write again soon, dear Herr Schönberg; today just briefly because I want you to have my answer regarding the *Gurrelieder* as soon as possible and because I have students coming now, after which I still want to write Webern about

1. Under Felix Weingartner.
2. The Liszt issue of the *Allgemeine Deutsche Musik-Zeitung* XXXVIII/42 (20 October 1911) included Schoenberg's article "Franz Liszt's Werk und Wesen," 1008–10.

the 2 refusals.

In eternal veneration

Your grateful Alban Berg

Here, dear Herr Schönberg, is the accounting of my expenses for which you had asked and the present state of the 200 kronen:

*[The expenses Berg itemizes leave a remainder of 86.90 kronen.]*

P.S.

Have you received the song recital program, dear Herr Schönberg.[3] I also met Stefan there, that pest. Never before have I treated anyone so rudely, I confidently expected that would be the end of it; the next day, at the Philharmonic concert, he was the first who crept up to me again,—and asked me whether I knew the latest sonata by the little Korngold[4] and assured me that he liked your article in the Liszt issue very much: "there's a great deal in it!" was his judgment, to which I would have liked to respond, whether he shouldn't perhaps take the comment about life's strivers *[Lebenstüchtigen]*[5] personally. But what's the use? I don't even know why I'm telling you all this, dear Herr Schönberg, you know it as well as I do, indeed better.

Again many, many regards

Your Berg

---

3. Berg had written a short note on the back of a program of a 4 November recital by the singer Rudolf Ritter, accompanied by Karl Severin. The program included songs by Mahler, Zemlinsky, Schoenberg, Joseph Marx, and Max Reger, as well as a number of lesser known Viennese composers. Berg crossed through the names of the composers he particularly disliked and placed an exclamation mark by the first grouping of composers (Mahler, Friedrich Mayer, Robert Gound, and Camillo Horn). Helene Berg and Josef Polnauer also signed the note to Schoenberg.

4. The Austrian composer Erich Wolfgang Korngold, son of the influential Viennese music critic Julius Korngold, attained early fame as a child prodigy. Korngold's Second Piano Sonata, Op. 2, was written and published in 1910, when he was 13.

5. The last sentence of Schoenberg's Liszt article refers to the *Lebenstüchtigen* as people who honor the names of those whose spirit they choose not to comprehend.

## Schoenberg to Berg

Berlin-Zehlendorf, 17 November 1911

Dear Berg,

Only now am I writing the letter I promised you together with the *Gurrelieder*.[1] I hope you have meanwhile completed the reduction. If so, please send me the score and reduction immediately. It still has to be copied. I'd like Hertzka to have it engraved soon!

Where the campaign is concerned, you mustn't give up hope yet of achieving something. Lemberger hasn't refused yet, nor *Oberbaurat* Redlich. What that ass Köchert replied is so stupid and irrelevant that it didn't even upset me. For his logic goes as follows: "I don't understand Schönberg's things, therefore let him starve." What a cretin!

1. In a postcard, postmarked 8 November 1911, Schoenberg informed Berg that a portion of the *Gurrelieder* score and a copy of the piano reduction were being sent off.

However, since, with the exception of the two who are still outstanding, the matter seems to be at an end, I ask you to tell Redlich and Mauthner[2] what has happened, and that there is unfortunatley no longer any possibility of an annual salary and they had better give the entire sum they intended to contribute right away so that I can hold out in Berlin until I have established myself here. Unfortunately I shall need the money all too soon! And therefore it would be very convenient if I could have it by early December. Also I beg you to see to the following with respect to the Mahler stipend: I. that I receive an official notification. II. that the promised sum be made available to me as early as January.

I would be glad of some reassurance that I will be secure at least during this period, so I can wait calmly until it's possible for me to make a living here.

I have a terrible writer's cramp and cannot write any more. So I must close.

What are you doing?

Are you very busy?

Are you composing anything?!?!

Oh yes: Schreker would like me to ask whether you (and Linke and Polnauer) would check the parts of the orchestral accompaniment to my chorus.[3] Would you please do that? Ask Hertzka whether they are ready yet.

What's happening with the *Harmonielehre?*

When did *you* finish with it?

Do you go to many concerts?

Will something come of your Urania concert?

Have you mentioned me to Wymetal? If not, then tell him the following:

I forbid that so much as a single note of mine be performed in the Urania!

How is your wife? Why doesn't she write herself sometime? Give her my regards. Also from my wife.

Will you be hearing a rehearsal of my chorus soon? I asked Schreker to allow it. Has he notified you? If not, then write him.

Have you sent Kandinsky any of your songs? Which one will he use?

Enough. Best regards

Your Arnold Schönberg

---

2. In the documents of the Schoenberg campaign both Magda Mauthner-Markhof and Edith Mauthner-Markhof appear as donors.

3. Schreker had asked Schoenberg to provide a discreet orchestral accompaniment to his a cappella chorus *Friede auf Erden* to aid the intonation of the amateur singers of the Philharmonic Chorus.

## Berg to Schoenberg

Monday morning
[in the train, 20 November 1911][1]

I'm finally getting around to writing you, dear esteemed Herr Schönberg, as well as to answering your kind letter of the 17th. As you can tell from the handwritting,

1. Berg wrote this letter on his way to Munich to hear the world premiere of Mahler's *Das Lied von der Erde* and a performance of the Second Symphony under Bruno Walter; Schoenberg had considered attending, for which purpose funds had been collected, but the beginning of his lecture series at the Stern Conservatory coincided with the performance and prevented his attendance.

I'm doing so in the train, which is jolting horribly.—I'm on my way to Munich: only today. Bad luck interfered even with this pleasure. My health, poor of late with respect to the respiratory organs, failed completely these last few days. Maybe it was due to the continually mounting joy, which finally broke into exaltation when I heard that you might be coming to Munich, too, maybe it was the incredible change of weather—indeed, maybe even the earthquake[2]—in any case I suffered a dreadful asthma attack the night before my planned departure for Munich, from which I was unable to recover until last night, so that not until today—but *at least* by today—have I been halfway able to travel. I will arrive at 6 o'clock, meet Webern there, which I'm looking forward to immensely, and will attend the concert in the evening, although I don't yet know how I'll manage to get in. And travel home again tomorrow morning. My illness is also the reason why I didn't answer immediately and haven't sent the *Gurrelieder* off yet, although it was finished before the trip. More about that later. Now first to answer your letter. My despair over the failure of the campaign is justified insofar as I had, as you know, set the highest hopes on it and was able to accomplish only a fraction of what I had been certain of accomplishing. It is not the first nor the last disappointment, my illness now, above all the shattered hope of seeing you in Munich, rob me of all capacity for hope, and anything I can say about further chances for the campaign is merely in keeping with my pessimism: naturally I went to see Lemberger, he was very nice, but all I was able to accomplish was his promise to give you 50 kronen every quarter year over a period of 2 years, that is 400 kronen all told, which in accordance with your letter I'll try to induce him to give in one sum, preferably at once. Likewise the 4 times 200 kronen from Mauthner and the 2 times 500 kronen from Redlich. There's still no news about what *Oberbaurat* Redlich will decide to do, and lately Bahr's opinion has been that he cannot press him any further without jeopardizing everything. But he has promised to give something and I will simply keep asking until I have his decision. Nor have I heard anything about the results of Moll's and Frau Mahler's efforts. I fear even this last hope will be shattered. I had hoped to be able to speak with both of them in Munich, but there probably won't be time today. Perhaps Webern said something, after all he was at 2 rehearsals and the dress rehearsal and presumably at the song recital.[3] In any case I'll look up Moll again in Vienna right away. Above all with respect to the Mahler stipend, of course. That is absolutely certain. I also believe it will be possible for you to get the interest of the capital, which, as I hear already amounts to 60–70,000 kronen, earlier, that is, on 1 January. And I shall see to it that you are officially notified.

I only spoke with Schreker once and he, too, mentioned the matter regarding the parts for the orchestral accompaniment for the chorus. But at the time (about 2 weeks ago) he was embroiled in a feud with Hertzka* with regard to having the parts copied, which Hertzka originally balked at, but which has probably been done by now. On Saturday I will see Schreker at my place and then we'll certainly make

2. A minute-long tremor was registered at 10:25 pm on 16 November in Austria and southern Germany, but was actually noticeable for only about six seconds.

3. Bruno Walter accompanied Madame Charles Cahier in a Munich recital of Mahler songs on 19 November.

some arrangements for the corrections (also for my attending rehearsals), so you needn't be uneasy about that. I'll also let Polnauer know. And now the most important matter: Is it true you're coming to Vienna? To the performance of the chorus?! Schreker says: yes!—It would make me unbelievably happy!! To be able to see you again, hear you speak— — — — —!! Perhaps Webern will know something!

I believe the concert will be on the 9th. Mahler's III[rd] under Schalk is on the 8th!— —

I also spoke to Schreker about the placement of your chorus on the program. He wants to open with it. It's to be followed by something "very gentle" by an Englishwoman (!)[5] which can't be done first, and the 2 other works by Braunfels[6] and Fried can't be done before your chorus out of dynamic considerations. For which reason they have to be last. And your chorus first. Schreker assures me that he won't begin until a quarter of an hour after the announced concert time. Is that all right with you? Of course I can't possibly decide. Generally I myself love to hear a beloved composition with pure, unsullied ears, the impression is, if I may say so, virginal, and many others will feel that way too, but I rather doubt whether that's the proper point of view when a popular success is at stake. In that case, other factors are involved. Above all experience. Which I don't have, but you certainly do, dear Herr Schönberg! — — — — — — —

I shall speak to Webern about the Urania.—Likewise about Dr. Pollak (Hofrat? or the like) from the Railway Ministry,[7] whom I met just now in the train completely by chance; he's traveling to Munich in the same train (1st class, naturally) and paid me a visit in the III[rd] class and spoke very warmly of you. Also about a matter that, as I say, I'll tell Webern, or write to you sometime. It's **not important** and yet it is something you ought to know: For today just this, that you have in him an extremely well-meaning and admiring friend, who belong to the better sort of human being. He's the one who persuaded Mahler to do the Chinese poems.[8] He also thinks the Mahler stipend could be awarded you over several years. I discussed all that with him after already having written the first part of this letter. — — — —

I sent Kandinsky the published volume of songs and recommended the last one.[9]

My wife isn't feeling very well either and understandably I'm very worried about it: if I were to succeed in building up her strength, her nerves and anemia would improve quickly, but that's just the difficulty. She would also very much like to continue singing and on good days sings really very beautifully— —but then there will be 2 weeks where it's impossible.[10] Those are so-called small worries, but, when

4. Universal Edition moved its offices from 32 Wipplingerstrasse to 9 Reichsratstrasse in 1911. In 1914 the firm found its final home in the Musikverein building on Karlsplatz.

5. Berg was possibly confusing the Austrian composer Johanna Müller-Hermann with the English composer Ethel Smyth, whose works were not performed on the concert in question.

6. The German composer Walter Braunfels was active in Munich.

7. Hofrat (Privy Councillor) Theobald Pollak was a director in the Austrian Railroad Ministry.

8. Mahler drew his texts for Das Lied von der Erde from the collection of free translations by Hans Bethge, Die chinesische Flöte, published in Leipzig, 1907.

9. Opus 2, No. 4 ("Warm die Lüfte," Mombert).

10. Helene Berg had studied voice and before her marriage sang in student recitals.

one's close to them (which is a matter of course in a marriage), they take on gigantic proportions. I am very happy that you, dear Herr Schönberg, and your wife take an interest in my wife and thank you very much for the kind inquiry. She asked me just before my departure to send her very best regards to you and your esteemed wife. And now finally to the *Gurrelieder*.

Naturally the reduction is finished and I have it and the score with me so as to give it to Webern to bring back with him. That is safer than the post and just as quick. With the conclusion of the reduction I was of course attempting above all to present **that** which isn't already in the choral reduction, that is either the complex accompaniment, or: the harmony of new, additional voices, as for example the many entrances at the end. In the case of one passage I'm not sure it's good. Of course it's good when played **together** with the choral reduction; but **alone** it's unclear; perhaps one should leave out the 16^ths (which I transformed into triplets to make them more playable). I'm referring to the piano reduction p. 243–45, in that case only the following would remain:

 etc.

But in general I was very surprised that contrary to your first instructions (about 10 days ago), you wanted the piano reduction **back.** I thought I was to proofread it!? As it is, I naturally haven't done it; to do so I would above all need **my** original reduction. The copy is full of mistakes. In fact I don't know whether it wouldn't be best to give the engraver my piano reduction, at least of Parts II and III, after I have looked it over again very carefully and made the necessary simplifications, which you will please indicate to me. My mistakes could at most be accidentals. But those of the copyist could be **all** sorts: all the way from staccato dots to omitted measures. In any case, I find that copying is something mechanical, whereas the engraver thinks, at least re-thinks. My experience, though slight, confirms this! The reduction of Act III of *Ferne Klang*, done in a tearing hurry completely in pencil, where I went ahead and cut things, added altered measures in the margins, then handed the whole thing over in loose sheets that were often nothing but corrections of the 1^st failed piano reduction, and in all different colors; in short, a dreadful sight:** this reduction had comparatively few mistakes in the 1^st engraving, at most those I had perpetrated myself (due to haste). But such mistakes wouldn't be a problem in the *Gurrelieder* reduction, because as I said, I would proofread my own reduction with immense care. Thus at least the additional copyist's mistakes could be **avoided,** for if chances are that one can find 99 out of 100 of one's own mistakes, that number remains constant in the 100 mistakes of another, thus doubling the **remaining** mistakes. And now I gather from your letter that you want to have the whole thing copied again, using the doubly flawed copy for that purpose!?—But of course I'm just as ready to proofread and prepare the new copy for printing, if you think that would be better. For I really don't remember if my original reduction is written clearly enough. Well, I've given you my opinion on this. Of course your decision alone will be decisive.—

Enough for today, dear Herr Schönberg. I'm traveling through the wonderful Salzburg region now, which gave Mahler so much pleasure when he returned home dying. So I want to look out.

Many, many warm and devoted regards

from your grateful Alban Berg

(You can imagine how curiously moved I was when I prepared the piano reduction for the <u>conclusion</u> of the *Gurrelieder* and on the same day got to know the conclusion of *Das Lied von der Erde* for the first time.)[11]

* U. E. has been terribly disorganized since the move.[4] I <u>presume</u> that's the reason for the delay with the *Harmonielehre*. <u>I</u> sent off the correction of the index one day after receipt of the proofs. That must have been 4–6 weeks ago now.

** by which I merely wish to point out that so-called <u>beautiful</u> appearance doesn't mean anything to the engraver.

---

11. Berg had been working on the piano reduction for the conclusion of the *Gurrelieder* when he acquired the newly published score of *Das Lied von der Erde*. The final measures of both works are dominated by the same sonority, a C-major triad with an added major sixth.

## Berg to Schoenberg

Tuesday
Vienna [28 November 1911]

I still don't have anything definite to tell you, dear Herr Schönberg, about the transformation of annual payments into a lump sum. *[Berg gives details of the complications.]*

You are <u>absolutely assured</u> of the Mahler stipend, Herr Schönberg, and I hope that as a result of Moll's efforts abroad this has now grown to 100,000 kronen, or <u>will</u> at any rate reach that level in the near future, then the available interest might amount to 4,000 kronen. Not that that's very much! — — — —

I <u>must</u> tell you, albeit very reluctantly, of a small contribution for you: it's from *Hofrat* Dr. Theobald Pollak, <u>whom I met</u>, as I wrote you in the train. Without the <u>least</u> prompting from me (naturally) and without the slightest expectations on my part, simply upon mentioning the campaign, about which naturally he knew through Moll, he gave me a sum (admittedly very small) which, however, he wants to continue in monthly installments, and for which he asked for deposit slips for the Schönberg Fund.[1] Considering people like Lemberger, etc., who have at least 20 times the income, this small contribution by Pollak is thoroughly decent and almost touching. It truly springs from his admiration for you as well as from this strange man's incredibly upright, indeed almost pedantic sense and understanding of honor; that's why I couldn't reject it—although it can hardly be of much use to you, Herr Schönberg, and you never envisaged assistance of this kind and are less than enthu-

---

1. According to bank statements in the Berg archive, Theodor Pollak's first contribution to the campaign amounted to 10 kronen, which, however, did not continue long, as Pollak died the following March.

siastic about it. Perhaps it's just a sign that the Schönberg Fund in the Hietzing Exchange, though quite shrunken, won't ever dry up completely and we'll at least be forced to keep it open, as it may yet be predestined for something great.

This Dr. Pollak is a strange fellow in every sense, however, if one can speak thus of a man whose life began with the most unparalleled deprivations and who has now, thanks to his diligence and his longing for something higher—in an inner as well as external sense—worked his way up so far. Such a man becomes so singular in some things that he can appear strange—indeed petty—(without necessarily being so). That is proven by the following incident, which unfortunately I must relate to you. One of his first remarks in the train was an inquiry about you, Herr Schönberg, whereupon he told me with great agitation that you had insulted him deeply. He had procured a reduced fare for you not long ago, something he would be very happy to do for you at any time and something you can always count on; and as a condition for being allowed to continue to be of assistance to you in such matters he had begged you not to refund him the 2 kronen the transaction had cost him (just as one doesn't enclose a stamp for a reply in a letter to a good friend of whom one is asking a favor). I can well understand Herr Schönberg, that—in ignorance of the singular character of this man, you felt this kind of condition, seeming almost like alms to you, to be very unpleasant and that you sent him this small fee. But he was deeply insulted, carefully saved the 2 kronen with the slip for the deposit in "a little box" in his desk, and constantly wondered how he could get rid of it again. Seizing the opportunity of that moment, he gave me 2 kronen from his wallet (no doubt disappointed that they weren't the 2 kronen he was keeping at home in the little box) with the urgent request that I return it to you with this examplanation! Acceptance of this sum is his condition if he is to continue to serve you, which he confidently hopes to do.

I would have liked to spare you this boring tale, dear, kind Herr Schönberg, but the above-named condition compels me to do so and since it is easily possible that he could, that is to say would procure a reduction for you, the 2 kronen affair would surely come out, and I would be placed in an awkward light, and—this is the crux of it—you would learn of the matter anyway.

For it seems to me that you could already take advantage of Dr. Pollak's services in the very near future, Herr Schönberg, if only you were to come to Vienna for *Friede auf Erden*. Surely Webern has already spoken to you about it. I discussed it with him at length. At first Mahler's III[rd] was to be on Friday the 8th and your chorus on the 9th. Meanwhile the Philharmonic canceled, so Schalk has do the III[rd] with the Tonkünstler Orchestra; however, that endangers Schreker's concert, which is also using the Tonkünstler Orchestra, but which nonetheless is still to take place on the 9th.[2] How can they possibly accomplish that: 12 rehearsals for the III[rd], 5 for Schreker. 17 rehearsals in about 10 days. Of course your chorus isn't threatened, the orchestral parts (which, by the way, I have finished correcting) are really simple compared to the Braunfels, etc.

2. Schalk's planned 8 December concert of Mahler's Third Symphony was canceled due to lack of rehearsal time with the Vienna Philharmonic Orchestra. Instead, the work was performed on that date by Oskar Nedbal and the Tonkünstler Orchestra.

The program is posted as follows:

Fried
Schönberg
the Englishwoman (?)
Braunfels[3]

I've been waiting every day for word that the chorus will finally be <u>rehearsed</u> in its entirety, <u>in order that I</u> can go. Polnauer was there already, apparently it is going well. Perhaps I'll go on Thursday (with Königer).

Enough for today, dear esteemed Herr Schönberg. I'll write as soon as I know anything about any of these matters (concert, campaign, etc.). And I'll also tell you about my teaching, which I enjoy very, very much; I'm already very involved. And also about concerts I've attended, operas, etc. (Mahler's VI[th] today, *Bergsee*).[4]

My very, very warmest and most devoted regards, dear Herr Schönberg

from your beholden Alban Berg

(Also from my wife the very best greetings and regards to you and your esteemed wife.)

Oh! Do come to Vienna for *Friede auf Erden*.

---

3. The program of the Philharmonic Chorus comprised Oskar Fried's *Erntelied*, Schoenberg's *Friede auf Erden*, Johanna Müller-Hermann's *Im Garten des Serail*, and Walter Braunfels' *Offenbarung Johannis*.

4. Ferdinand Löwe performed Mahler's Sixth Symphony with the Konzertverein Orchestra on 28 November.

The premiere of Julius Bittner's opera *Bergsee* took place at the Vienna Court Opera on 22 November under Bruno Walter.

*Schoenberg to Berg*

Berlin-Zehlendorf, 5 [4!] December 1911

Dear Berg,

I'll send you the piano reduction today (or tomorrow). I had to change some things in the new part. (That is, you'll have to change them; I just made suggestions) because the sound of the piano texture just doesn't correspond to the orchestration. And as you know, <u>one judges tempo by the sound</u>!! So that's very important. I don't think it will be much work for you. The rest of it is <u>very good</u>! I'd like to persuade you to revise the entire piano reduction a bit, to simplify everything that seems too difficult to you. But particularly: the many unimportant figures in small notes on extra lines! You'll have to delete a lot of that. Above all, everything that's merely there to indicate sonority. Only those notes should remain that represent important voices that had to be left out.

I am in favor of using the copied reduction for engraving. I looked through it a bit and find that in general it is <u>well</u> copied. I don't think there are that many mistakes and they are easily found. Polnauer, Linke, and perhaps Galitzenstein will surely help you. I will then proofread the first and second proofs of the engraving as well! After you have read them. So I'll get them from you.

I don't get around to writing very often because I'm very absorbed in my lectures. Even though I don't spend all my time preparing, in fact, postpone preparation until the last days so as not to tire myself, I nonetheless continually catch myself thinking about it. Or at other times I'm burdened by the thought that I ought to be dealing with it. It is rather inconvenient, but gives me pleasure nonetheless. And I believe it's turning out to be worthwhile. I find it rather useful to have to present in an organized form all these things I've thought about for so long. Otherwise I would have continued just to think them instead of ever writing them down. I think I'll begin a book when I've finished the series.[1]

On the other hand, I'd rather compose just now. But working with so much theoretical material makes it impossible for me to open up there. I'll have to take a long break from it soon. Otherwise it might spell the end of my composing. Perhaps that's why at present I feel no inclination to paint, either.

From the fact that, though inwardly very preoccupied, I am at present not working on anything—at least to the extent one considers that to mean deskwork—it's clear to me how very much I am a musician and how much less satisfying I find theories than composing. It's a pity about all the free time. Who knows when that will be the case again.

I hope to hear news of your final campaign efforts soon. What do Moll and Bahr say? Have they let the matter drop altogether? I'd like to hear something definite soon.

For now many warm regards, also to your wife (also from my wife)

Your Arnold Schönberg

---

1. Among other things Schoenberg was at this time planning a counterpoint book as a companion to his *Harmonielehre*.

## Berg to Schoenberg (letterhead: Berg/IX., Fuchsthallergasse 2)

Vienna, 6 December 1911

Excuse the pencil, dear, kind Herr Schönberg. It is late and I am already in bed due to my (20th) cold. And since I plan to attend the rehearsal of *Friede auf Erden* tomorrow morning, I would have no time to write unless I do so now, for tomorrow afternoon I have to give 3 lessons: that's why—I thought—better to write this letter right now in pencil—than one in ink later!—

In town today, I met Loos,[1] who advised me to do the following: to publish a compilation of all projected performances of your works abroad (Germany, Prague, Paris) in the Viennese papers. (Naturally under Cultural News.) So I'd like to ask you, Herr Schönberg, to let me know the place and date of all performances; then I'll put it together, have it typed up, and sent to all the papers: I'll let you know which ones take it. It's no great loss if one or two papers do not print it, but I'll see to it that it appears in the *Presse, Tagblatt, Neues Wiener Journal, Arbeiter-Zeitung,*

---

1. The Viennese architect Adolf Loos was a leading theorist of the movement away from historicism and ornament and toward functional design.

possibly *Fremdenblatt*.—I don't know whether the *"Zeit"* will take it.—Since the whole thing is—we'll say—<u>my</u> idea—<u>you</u> can't be accused of seeking publicity, whereas on the other hand such notices, if they go to all the papers, will help you a little, at least they'll open people's eyes here in Vienna.—Were those notices later to be followed by reports of favorable reception of the works abroad, that would definitely make an impression. So once more, a list of planned performances please!

Loos is going to give a lecture soon on his house on Michaelerplatz. The following poster can be seen all over Vienna

Akademischer Verband für Kunst
und Literatur

"A horror of a building"
(from the city council)
A lecture given by
Architect Adolf Loos
Tickets @ 5 and 20 kronen
Sofiensaal

Naturally I'll go.[2]

By the way, one Viennese paper implied that Loos had gone mad as a result of the building and was seeking treatment in an institution. That's typically Viennese!

———————

Now as to the campaign. *[Details regarding contributions by Magda Mauthner von Markof, Emil Lemberger, Kommerzialrat Fritz Redlich, and Oberbaurat Carl Redlich follow.]* You will understand from all this, esteemed Herr Schönberg, why I haven't written for some time; apart from the 1st [of the month], with its attendant real estate affairs, I continued to wait, hoping finally to hear something definitive. But now I'm writing to you despite that. For you already know pretty much what I

2. Adolf Loos's lecture was a defense of his building on Michaelerplatz, which was built that year amid a storm of controversy. The phrase *"Ein Scheusal von einem Haus"* (a horror of a building) was the 1910 denunciation of the building by the sculptor and city council representative Karl Rykl.

finally heard from Moll. It is practically certain that you are to receive the Mahler stipend, in January at that, at least a portion of it, and should the capital grow, the balance of the interest would naturally follow. Moll cannot send you a written declaration yet. For as long as the foundation's charter has not been drawn up, the committee (Frau Mahler, Strauss, Walter, Busoni), which of course doesn't exist yet, cannot make any decisions. Still less just one member of it (Frau Mahler). But it's a matter of course that as soon as the committee has been organized (which happens when the foundation's charter, drawn up by a lawyer, is approved by the authorities), Frau Mahler's recommendation will be decisive—apart from the fact that from the outset the committee will be in favor of the same award, namely to you. As soon as the concerts in New York, Paris, etc., on behalf of the Mahler stipend are over, the capital will doubtless amount to 100,000 kronen. The foundation charter will still be drawn up in December and the 1st interest payments will be available as of 1 January. I wasn't able to find out or accomplish any more. But I do believe you can rest assured, at least with regard to this matter.

7 December, morning

I had to interrupt my letter yesterday because my 2 styes, which have tormented me again the past 2–3 days, began to swell up so painfully and to press upon the eye so much that I couldn't continue writing. Now they are, if possible, still worse and more unbearable. I can't do anything but sit for hours with closed eyes, waiting for it to pass. I hope that will happen today still, so I can attend Mahler's III$^{rd}$ tomorrow and *Friede auf Erden* the day after; going out today (to the orchestra rehearsal for it) is out of the question. I am very curious to hear how the performance will go. When I asked Schreker when the chorus and orchestra would rehearse together, he answered laconically: "at the performance!"— — —

Immediately after the concert I'll write again, should something unusual happen I'll even telegraph, for surely you will be very interested. Oh, that you yourself aren't coming to Vienna!! You will be thinking of Vienna a great deal tomorrow evening, but we will be thinking of you much much more during the performance of that divine chorus. I'm so glad I copied out the chorus for myself a while ago, that way I can prepare myself for it properly. Have actually already done so. And every time I properly assimilate something of yours, the longing for you to compose something new reawakens, a longing most certainly rooted in my egotism. But the fact that, as you say, you don't get around to it as a result of too much theorizing is completely understandable and reminds one of the period in Wagner's life (after *Lohengrin*) when he, too, was so busy with musical aesthetics and theory that he didn't get around to composing for years. He complained about it in letters to Liszt, which I am presently dipping into.—To take this analogy further, what cause for our rejoicing when you create your *Ring*, your *Tristan*, *Meistersinger*, your *Parsifal*. . . . . .

I'll write again soon, dear esteemed Herr Schönberg! Many, many admiring regards

from your devoted, grateful Alban Berg

I assume you received the letter detailing the Dr. Pollak matter?!

*Berg to Schoenberg (postcard)*

Vienna [9 December 1911]

Dear Herr Schönberg,

I made the changes today and am deeply ashamed at the flawed first version. Apparently I had an *idée fixe* while completing the remainder of the reduction, or was it perhaps the illness that broke out right before the Munich trip and lay dormant even then. In short: it was, as I now realize, abysmal, and I sincerely beg your forgiveness, dear Herr Schönberg, first that I did a poor job, and 2nd that I caused you inconvenience. Then I thank you most sincerely for the precious words about preparation of piano reductions in general, which you interspersed among the various corrections. I have taken them very much to heart and think it may be quite good now.

I have already begun to make corrections, i.e., revisions. That is crucial (accidentals!!!!) But I very much miss my original (I suppose it's out of the question that I have recourse to the full score! It would be too inconvenient and risky to send it here.) But I believe my original reduction would be helpful here and there in clearing up mistakes when I'm in doubt. But it will be all right without it, too. At worst I'll turn to you, dear Herr Schönberg, in a questionable passage.

And now— — —I'm off to the concert in which *Friede auf Erden* will resound: I tremble with anticipation.— — —I'll write directly afterwards.

Most, most warmly

Your Berg

*Berg to Schoenberg (postcard)*

Vienna [10 December 1911]

Dear Herr Schönberg,

*Friede auf Erden* enjoyed a unanimous, very nice, warm success. All critics present. Of the respectable people present, Loos, *Hofrat* Pollak, etc. The other things: Braunfels, Frau Müller, Fried were, in that order: horrible, more horrible and most horrible! In such company your *Friede auf Erden* sounded like the voice of an innocent child among old debauchees. And that was also the impression made on the audience and above all on him who reveres you completely and for all time,

your Berg

Performance quite good!

*The Villa Lepcke in Berlin-Zehlendorf, where Schoenberg and his family lived from October, 1911 to May, 1913 (Arnold Schoenberg Institute 1701)*

*Schoenberg to Berg (picture postcard: Villa Lepcke)*[1]

Berlin-Zehlendorf, 12 December 1911

Dear Berg,

Many thanks for your letter; it certainly didn't contain anything to make me very happy.[2] And I couldn't decipher it all, either. Has Hertzka sent you my *Harmonielehre* yet?—Rosé didn't play my quartet yesterday. It won't be done now until 5 March!![3] I'm not pleased.—On the other hand I am getting a grand piano from the Ibach firm free of charge (on loan, of course).[4] I appreciate that very much. Only I need a photograph of myself. The manager of the firm made a special request for one. So could you send me one or two of the recent pictures? If you don't happen to have any it would be best if you simply sent me the plate (which I'd like in any event). I think I could get prints more quickly here. Let me hear from you soon. How is your teaching going. Webern tells me you wanted to ask me something in that connection. Do it soon! But if you have questions you want me to answer, then do it as I have of late: add large numbers in blue to the appropriate questions and underline the passage in question in color. That way it's immediately apparent upon consulting the letter again.

Many warm regards.

Your Arnold Schönberg

I just noticed that I have pictures as well as the plates. I will do it.

1. From October 1911 to May 1913 Schoenberg rented for a nominal fee an entire floor of a villa owned by the sculptor Ferdinand Lepcke.
2. Schoenberg is presumably referring to Berg's letter of 6–7 December.
3. The Rosé Quartet had been scheduled to play Schoenberg's First String Quartet, Op. 7, in Berlin on 12 December. The rescheduled concert took place on 5 March.
4. The loan of the Ibach piano was arranged through the American pianist Richard Buhlig.

## Berg to Schoenberg

Tuesday

Vienna [12 December 1911]

In great haste, dear Herr Schönberg, as I'm in the middle of correcting the reduction. I must read and play through it very, very carefully, not so much, as I said, for mistakes, as for omission of accidentals, extraneous accidentals, choral text, and the chorus itself. Once I've revised it, Polnauer will go through it, too, so that it will go to the engraver with as few mistakes as possible; please tell me, Herr Schönberg, am I to take the reduction straight to Hertzka after finishing the corrections? I imagine so! But I'd like a word from you.

In my card I told you what's most important about the performance and for the present I haven't much to add. The performance was really very good, the orchestra could scarcely be heard, only the horns came out a bit too loudly in a few passages. But it's impossible to tell you what a profound and joyous impression the work made on me: only you can speak that way of peace on earth [*Friede auf Erden*], you who have known all its torments. But we who went through them with you can understand your longing for it. Which is how I explain to myself why this work will never have a so-called public success or failure, just like the 1ˢᵗ movement of the IIⁿᵈ quartet, for instance——or like so many middle movements of Mahler symphonies, or even *Das Lied von der Erde*: all that is nothing for the masses, who after all long only for their petty but overrated passions, for which they themselves aren't even responsible—in other words, who long to hear those passions stirred or want to fancy they hear them where they don't exist. That's impossible with this chorus— and so they're mystified and applaud out of a sense of shame.

Publicly the success of the chorus* stood between the things of the lady composer, which were fairly well liked, and the Braunfels Hymn, which was tremendously successful. Fried's chorus amazed everyone with its unspeakable inanity and loathesomeness (1 chord, above that a rough men's chorus melody in unison, hurried through from *p* to *fff*. Quite simply: trash!!)

And now to the money matters. [*Berg itemizes 800 kronen in the bank, which he promises to send, as well as an additional 100 kronen and 100 marks in cash, for which he asks instructions.*]

As soon as I know more about that I'll write at once; I'm off to the bank now and after that to the café to look for reviews.

Today your quartet will be played in Berlin!!!!!—

Oh, to be there, what joy——

Your, <u>your</u> Berg

* I know that Dr. Pollak liked your chorus very much. I concluded the same about Loos on the basis of his impassioned applause. I don't know about anyone else. Aside from your enthusiastic students. I read all the papers every day and will send you clippings when something appears.—

## Berg to Schoenberg (postcard)

Vienna, 16 December [1911]

Dear Herr Schönberg,

Your dear card with the picture of the wonderful Villa Lepcke arrived yesterday; I'm very glad that you are so beautifully situated, and about the Ibach grand piano. I'm very indignant about the canceled concert. I can't explain it either!

The parcel with my original *Gurrelieder* reduction arrived only this morning, and I'm very happy at now being able to compare it once again with the copy, which is already largely corrected, and to correct dubious passages. I have corrected a great deal in Part III, i.e., simplified a lot, particularly in the melodrama, without, however, impairing the sound or completeness. Once Polnauer and I are completely finished, I'll write in greater detail, hoping that by then I will have heard from Bahr and found out about the rest of the campaign: and about the "journalistic" success of *Friede auf Erden*. So far only Batka is said to have written 2 lines about it,[1] which eluded me in my search for reviews, but I'll get them. In addition, in a lecture on style (which must have been the most idiotic nonsense) that preceded the recently inaugurated Young People's Concerts, that pig Hirschfeld mentioned, for instance, that he had just heard a chorus that is only singable with orchestral accompaniment, hence a stylistic anomaly.[2] No mention of names, of course. And that's the sort of thing Vienna's young people are told. Luckily once they're of an age to understand (and despise) that lecture, your works will be heard frequently and such idiots silenced for ever . . . but until then. . . . . . . !

Have I already thanked you, dear Herr Schönberg, for the *Harmonielehre* that Hertzka gave me? I'm overjoyed!!!

Your ever more grateful Alban Berg

1. Richard Batka wrote for the *Fremdenblatt*; his review appeared on 11 December 1911.
2. Robert Hirschfeld, critic for the *Wiener Zeitung/Abendpost*, gave his lecture on 13 December at the second of three youth concerts.

## Berg to Schoenberg (letterhead: Berg/III. Vordere Zollamtstr. 11)

Wednesday and Thursday
Vienna [20–21 December 1911]

Esteemed Herr Schönberg,

There's not much news, but at least I'll tell you what little there is: *[Berg discusses a contribution to the Schoenberg Fund from Fritz Redlich, a cousin of the Kommerzialrat Friedrich Redlich.]*

That's one thing.

Then I wanted to tell you that there still haven't been any reviews. I still don't have the 2 lines in the *Fremdenblatt*; I was sent the wrong issue of the paper. But I wasn't able to find a single word about the concert in any of the other papers, although I go to the café every day to look—I did read, though, Kalbeck's review of

Mahler's III[rd].[1] Incredible; the first movement is the music of a conductor who recalls 1,000 melodies from the most diverse compositions, etc.; with his usual idiocy Korngold offered up his Prater comparison again, etc.[2]—

I went to the Tonkünstlerverein the day before yesterday; upon Hertzka's urging I became a member. But I regret it immensely. It was horrible. 2 full-bearded levantines [Morgenländer] played their compositions at the piano until one was bored senseless.[3] You simply can't imagine it. And an audience to match. Nothing but females and those who would like to be. I haven't the slightest hope that anything will come of this, even though Wellesz[4] and Hertzka are recruiting new elements and want to see to it that it changes. By the way, the latter wants to introduce a pension fund, an idea Hertzka claims as his, but one that you told me about ½ year ago in strict confidence. Didn't Hertzka get the idea from you?!

As to the other elements knocking about in the Verein. The visages of Stöhr and Spörr,[5] Wöss[6], etc.—

By the way, Herr Schönberg, what do you think of the article in the Wage?![7] Hertzka is incensed, he told me. Actually it's funny: the Germans: Konta,[8] this Ur-German, Wöss, Horn,[9] etc. . . .

By the way, Wellesz told me that Gutheil is to perform your quartet with Bartók in Budapest and to sing songs, too![10] That's very, very good news. If only she gets time off from Gregor. That gentleman **never,** or only very rarely, allows the opera singers to concertize any more.

A wonderful review of the sextet is said to have appeared in Frankfurt.[11] Also I just heard that the Monday paper Der Morgen mentions the performance of your

1. Max Kalbeck's review appeared in the Neues Wiener Tagblatt on 8 December 1911.

2. Julius Korngold had succeeded Eduard Hanslick as chief music critic of the Neue Freie Presse in 1902. In his review, which appeared on 9 December 1911, Korngold wrote of the first movement of Mahler's Third Symphony: "Once again we were estranged by the Prater-like bustle of the development section, shocked by the reckless use of elements alien to art music." The Prater is a popular park in Vienna's second district, which also includes a large amusement park.

3. The Tonkünstlerverein concert of 18 December, which was held at the Neuer Wiener Frauen-klub (New Viennese Ladies' Club), presented songs by Jakob Fischer and Leon Erdstein and a violin sonata by Benno Sachs.

4. The Austrian composer and musicologist Egon Wellesz, who studied with Schoenberg 1904–05, was a member of the central committee of the Tonkünstlerverein.

5. Martin Spörr was one of the three conductors of the Vienna Konzertverein Orchestra.

6. The Viennese composer Josef Venantius von Wöss.

7. The article, entitled "Die 'Universal-Edition'," which appeared in the Viennese weekly Die Wage on 9 December 1911, praised U.E. for its comprehensive publishing program; however, the author, who signed himself with the initial b., expressed the opinion that sound, healthy "Ur-German" talents such as Julius Bittner, Wilhelm Kienzl, Robert Konta, Friedrich Mayer, and von Wöss, were being neglected in favor of ultra-moderns who were neither German nor healthy. Schoenberg's Harmonielehre is cited as an example of a modern work that would soon be an obscure curiosity.

8. The Viennese composer Robert Konta.

9. The Viennese composer Camillo Horn.

10. Under the auspices of an Hungarian New Music Society, with which the Hungarian composer Béla Bartók was associated, Marie Gutheil-Schoder was scheduled to sing Schoenberg songs and the Second Quartet with the Waldbauer-Kerpely Quartet in Budapest on 26 March 1912. Before the Schoenberg concert could take place, the organization was disbanded on 15 March, due to lack of public interest.

11. The Frankfurt-based Rebner Quartet performed Schoenberg's Verklärte Nacht in Leipzig on 8 December. The review to which Berg refers has not been identified.

"dissonant-happy Chorus."[12] I'll try to get hold of this review.

But the very, very best news I've heard is what Webern told me, that you, dear Herr Schönberg, have composed a song by Maeterlinck. God! How sublime that must be! If I weren't already convinced that everything you write, no, everything you do, think, intend, plan, is most sublime: Webern's description, his incredible enthusiasm would be proof that this song is the "pinnacle of music."[13]

To be able to see it, to get to know it . . . let alone to be able to **hear** it!! If Winternitz[14] really signs it!! And the piano pieces, the new ones! I am eagerly awaiting Webern's news as to whether the concert will actually take place. After Rosé canceled so disgracefully!—

I'm working hard on the *Gurrelieder*. It's a very complicated matter. Especially the third part. The practice of placing accidentals before every note, whether ♭, ♯, or ♮, now means I have to delete all unnecessary accidentals, so that about ⅔ of all accidentals must go. There probably aren't any musical errors in all 3 parts, but I as well as Polnauer have to look at it again for extraneous accidentals. Likewise with respect to the text, which I must check against the poem. But at least this way I hope to be able to send a copy to the engravers with as few mistakes as possible. That's right, isn't it: I am then to take it straight to Hertzka. Any mistakes that might be left can still be found in the proofs, which will arrive in small installments, thus being easier to correct. First I'll go through it thoroughly, then Polnauer (possibly Galitzenstein) and then I'll send it to you, Herr Schönberg. The same procedure with the II^{nd} set of proofs. The way you wanted it anyway.— I tell you, dear, dear Herr Schönberg, the work is beautiful, **beautiful**, *beautiful* beyond all measure. I regard it as a supreme joy to be able to occupy myself with it, even if only more or less mechanically.

I won't write any more. I'm so terribly nervous again that I can't write legibly, which I hope you'll be so kind as to excuse. I have so much to do (all of the administrative work, since my mother is out of town on account of a sick brother), *Gurrelieder*, Christmas shopping—and last but not least, lessons, about which I really will write you an entire letter soon.

Many, many warmest and most sincere regards

from your eternally grateful Alban Berg

12. The review, signed "dt", appeared in the weekly *Der Morgen* on 18 December 1911.

13. Schoenberg's Maeterlinck song, "Herzgewächse," Op. 20, was completed on 9 December. In a letter to Berg of 17 December, Webern had written that Schoenberg's song represented the "pinnacle of music."

14. The Austrian soprano Martha Winternitz-Dorda was engaged at the Hamburg Opera 1910–33.


## Schoenberg to Berg

Berlin-Zehlendorf, 21 December 1911

Dear Berg,

I didn't get around to answering right away. But: I thank you and the others very much for your idea of using the money in question for my song recital and I accept gladly, because I sense that it is given gladly. I don't know yet whether I'll give the song recital.[1] At the moment I am not very interested in doing so, for I am unusually depressed. Perhaps it's because of the revolting news I hear from Vienna about my works, etc. But perhaps only because I'm not composing anything at all right now. At any rate: I've lost all interest in my works. I'm not satisfied with anything any more. I see mistakes and inadequacies in everything. Enough of that; I can't begin to tell you how I feel at such times. It's not ambition. Otherwise, I would be satisfied that there are some people who think better of it than I do.—

Some time ago I gave your piano sonata and songs to a pianist who is going to play my piano pieces in London and Berlin.[2] But now I have no more copies. Would you please send me a few. Especially of the sonata (I still have 2 volumes of the songs). I don't consider it at all impossible that he play the sonata.

Keep the funds for the concert for the time being. But I would appreciate it if you could arrange to have the other funds[3] available by 1 January. Of course I still have a bit. But it makes me very uneasy not to know whether the remaining funds will be available on time.—Hasn't Königer heard from Mauthner yet? And how will the matter with the *Handelskammerrat* Redlich be settled? And the other Redlich? What does Bahr say to all this?—Do you think I should send Bahr my book?— Now in closing I wish you a very Merry Christmas. Also your wife. Best regards from my wife and me

Your Arnold Schönberg

---

1. Berg heard from Webern in a letter of 13 December that Schoenberg was planning a song recital in Berlin with Winternitz. At Webern's suggestion, he wrote to Schoenberg on 14 December 1911 and offered 150 marks to help finance the concert; of that sum 110 marks had originally been collected to finance Schoenberg's trip to Munich to hear the 20 November premiere of *Das Lied von der Erde*, and Berg, Webern, and Königer were ready to contribute the remaining 40 marks.

2. The pianist to whom Schoenberg refers has not been definietly identified, though it may have been Eduard Steuermann or Richard Buhlig, who performed Schoenberg's Op. 11 in Berlin on 16 February 1912.

3. 76 kronen in cash still in Berg's possession, which he mentions in his letter of 14 December 1911.

## Berg to Schoenberg

[Vienna, c. 22 December 1911]

Reading this book[1] aroused two emotions in me: solace and enlightenment. Solace, because I realized once again that greatness is inseparable from suffering, indeed that without suffering there can be no true artist; enlightenment because that which is inexplicable, mysterious in greatness, is made self-evident here, those phenomena of every artist's soul that the masses interpret as "contradictions" are reconciled here, in that, to use a beautiful phrase from Karl Kraus, "they must meet somewhere in a higher sphere, and be it where God resides."[2]

We who are fortunate enough to take part in your life need such comfort and enlightenment. But to you this book and its inner meaning will be nothing new. May it at least afford you a few beautiful hours!

1. Berg's Christmas gift to Schoenberg was Wagner's autobiography.

2. Berg quotes one of Karl Kraus' "Pro Domo" aphorisms, which appeared in the *Fackel* XIII/338 (6 December 1911), 17.

With the utmost veneration and gratitude we wish you, dear esteemed Herr Schönberg, and your worthy wife and the dear little ones a very, very Merry Christmas and pleasant holidays

Your Alban and Helene Berg


## Berg to Schoenberg

Vienna, 23 December 1911

Dear kind Herr Schönberg,

Your letter made me very unhappy. What you say about your divine works is dreadful! Oh, believe me, Herr Schönberg, you can no longer judge what they signify, they are already too far removed from you; something magnificent is growing within you, your gaze is so fixed on the future that you can no longer see the past, indeed, perhaps no longer the present. But you must believe us, who live in your works, me above all, as I'm now experiencing the unique joy of immersing myself in the *Gurrelieder,* indeed of being engulfed by it, staggering from one treasure to another like a drunken man—you must believe me, when I swear to you that your works belong to the very, very highest, that they can only be considered in company with those of Beethoven, Mozart, Wagner, and Mahler and that all others are beneath them. They really are, as Webern wrote to me yesterday: "emanations from God *[Ausstrahlungen Gottes]*:

Beethoven—Kant
Wagner—Schopenhauer
Schönberg—Strindberg"[1]

Now that I have received this letter of yours I am actually glad I was able to give you Wagner's Life. What I got out of it (as from the life of any one of those 6 great men above)—I called it "solace and enlightenment"——you too, my dear, esteemed Herr Schönberg, will experience. I wrote at the time that you weren't in need of such, and of course that is true. But the solace and enlightenment that we receive through our reverential understanding will do your anxious heart and your doubts good by way of comparison. Even if only for the moment; for I know only too well that your depression is just a matter of time and must soon give way to a more sublime, a most sublime confidence.

However, if the description of Wagner's struggles and myriad sufferings, and his never pure, always clouded joys raises even a momentary spark of confidence in you, if our unswerving worship of you is able to contribute to that, then that would be the greatest happiness this Christmas could bring me.

Perhaps the enclosed reviews will accomplish that by way of negation: namely that you perceive the true and eternal value of your works by the very distance between their wise message and the stupid, monotonous drivel of the base,

*Your* Berg

1. Berg's analogy between composers and thinker/writers was suggested to him in Webern's letter of 17 December.

## Schoenberg to Berg

Berlin-Zehlendorf, 28 December 1911

Dear Berg,

Your present arrived early this morning. It's unbelievable how long the post takes!—Heartiest thanks for it and for the very, very dear letter. If it were possible to find a cure for what I wrote you about through encouragement and friendly concern from without, through friends and through examples, then your lovely letter and your intention in presenting me Wagner's Life as solace would no doubt be successful. But this is an inner matter I have to deal with—or not—by myself. I have experienced it very, very often before and it was always followed by periods of self-delusion (as I must call it now) that made life easier for me. That has nothing to do with success and failure. It's a kind of persecution complex; an insight can persecute one too.

"But enough of that." Christmas was so lovely that I hope soon to be "discharged fully cured." Many, many regards

Your very affectionate Arnold Schönberg

## Berg to Schoenberg

[Vienna] 30 December 1911

Again only briefly, dear kind Herr Schönberg. Many thanks for the dear card[1] and now also for the letter card that arrived today. I was very unhappy about the delay of the book package. I had seen to it myself on the morning of the 22nd had even asked when the book would arrive, whereupon I had received the answer early on the 24th or in the evening, which was exactly what I wanted.

As it was it didn't arrive until 4 days later. The reason I can't write more, dear Herr Schönberg, is that I have a so-called rush job at the moment. Hertzka gave me a small portion of the 4-hand piano reduction of Mahler's VIIIth, done wretchedly by a certain Neufeld, to revise, i.e., practically to redo.[2] As it's only 50 pages, which I will have completed in a few days and for which he has to pay me well—since that's the only reason I'm doing it—I won't fall behind with the Gurrelieder. First because: all 3 parts are presently in Polnauer's and Linke's hands, who are proofreading it once more, and 2nd, I have already done it thoroughly myself.

My only question: once the Guerrelieder are back in my possession, should I take it straight to Hertzka? In my opinion there's no reason not to. It is ready for engraving! I shall discuss it with Hertzka when I bring him the piano reduction of the VIIIth.

Any day now I hope at last to get a reply from Bahr. He's returning to Vienna. As you know it concerns the two Redlichs.

And now I thank you many times, my dear, kind Herr Schönberg, for your kind words and for the New Year's wishes for myself and my wife. It is such a matter of

---

1. Postmarked 27 December 1911.
2. Berg's revisions are not credited in the score. The pianist was Albert Neufeld.

course that I return them most, most warmly, sincerely, and affectionately, that it's almost unnecessary for me to say so.

But since it is after all the only <u>visible</u>, that is <u>external</u> sign of an <u>inner</u> matter, I think it's wonderful to have the chance to <u>say</u> it again sometimes. Therefore all the very, very best good fortune—indeed, what's almost more important: no further misfortune in the <u>New Year.</u>

To you and your esteemed wife and the dear children.

Unfortunately my wife is ill with a slight case of pleurisy, which is why she doesn't send her very warmest New Year's wishes <u>herself</u>, but only through me.

In this and <u>**all**</u> the coming years

Your Berg

# 1912

*Berg to Schoenberg*

Thursday morning
[Vienna, 11 January 1912]

I meant to write you a long letter today, dear Herr Schönberg, but since I have to go into town in the morning and give lessons in the afternoon, I can only report the most important things. I saw Hertzka yesterday, after waiting 1½ hours. Most important, I dropped off the *Gurrelieder*, which seemed to please him very much. Of course the engravers are supposedly all overworked, so the *Gurrelieder* will not be done right away; he thought it could be finished in the summer, at which I naturally protested and categorically demanded that the *Gurrelieder* be engraved immediately. I don't know whether that will happen, but in any case, dear Herr Schönberg, please insist at some point that it be engraved at once. Very likely Gutmann will want to do the *Gurrelieder* soon,[1] and surely the piano score is absolutely indispensable for rehearsing. For copying out the choral parts, etc., etc. Considering how long it takes to publish a work long after it has been completed, one cannot be too insistent, especially with a publishing house and a director as disorganized as U.E. and Hertzka. (His desk even looks like a Viennese dung collector's cart. Right down to the bell! Ancient memoranda and rubbish are piled in confused layers and the only thing missing is a prod to poke around with, to see if there's something useful there after all. And just as dung collectors aren't connoisseurs of art, he generally hits on the wrong things, too, e.g., symphonies by Weigl, Konta, etc.— —). Joking aside, it is unfortunately all too serious. So, dear Herr Schönberg, you will be so kind, won't you, as to pressure him now and again. I shall read the proofs most carefully, will have Polnauer and Linke recheck them, and then send them to you!—

I met Specht there, too. He told me that he will write a detailed review of the *Harmonielehre* in the *Merker*.[2] Incidentally, Hertzka expects many, also positive, reviews in the near future.

I have finally implemented the idea advanced by Loos, which I had mentioned

---

1. The concert impresario Emil Gutmann had assured Schoenberg of his intention to promote a Berlin performance of the *Gurrelieder*, but the performance did not take place.
2. The Viennese music critic Richard Specht had founded the cultural periodical *Der Merker* in 1909; the *Merker* review of Schoenberg's *Harmonielehre* (III / 6, March 1912, 209–11) was written by Walter Klein.

to you, of sending a notice to all the papers about coming performances of your works: in a few days U.E. will place a long notice to this effect in about 60 papers.

Unfortunately, my dearest Herr Schönberg, I don't have any other good news to report. *Kommerzialrat* Redlich still hasn't answered. I'll wait a while longer and then contact Bahr again. I also have to meet with Moll again.

I hope to have good news soon, at least from that quarter.

But I must be off now, dear Herr Schönberg, I'll write again soon and ask only that you forgive my long silence. My wife's illness and my own (which are, thank heavens, past), finishing the piano score of Mahler's VIII$^{th}$, and the *Gurrelieder* kept me fully occupied.

With the very warmest regards to you, esteemed Herr Schönberg, and the most devoted regards to your gracious wife from me and my wife

Your ever grateful Alban Berg

## Schoenberg to Berg

Berlin-Zehlendorf, 13 January 1912

Dear Berg,

I was very sorry to hear that you and your wife had been ill. I simply don't understand what ails you, so I really don't know what to advise. In any case I think you should consult several doctors. It is definitely some sort of nervous disorder. But surely there's a remedy for that. Some rigorous course of treatment. You should do whatever is necessary to rid yourselves of it once and for all. That's important.

I received your scores and was very happy to see the sonata again. It really is a very beautiful and original piece. Why aren't you composing anything! You shouldn't let your talent rest so long. Write a few songs, at least. It's a good idea to let poetry lead one back into music. After that: something for orchestra.

I'm very glad you delivered the *Gurrelieder* reduction. Of course Universal Edition will deal with it shoddily as usual. But: you need have no fear that the *Gurrelieder* be performed before it's printed. What I mean is: neither [event] is about to happen soon, if it happens at all, then later rather than sooner. Gutmann has plans, yes; but will he actually do it? It's all just talk. With all the patronage I don't know which end is up. On all sides I have to be careful not to upset one of these protectors, patrons, and sponsors. It made me so nervous that I'm back to upsetting things with complete abandon. Of course that way some patrons may fall by the wayside, but it doesn't matter!

At present I'm reading Wagner's Life straight through, with mixed impressions. Actually the book isn't what I had hoped for, since I had above all expected: insight into the inner experiences which led him to his works. Instead he writes almost entirely—obviously intentionally—about external events. Still even that is so fascinating that while sitting here writing letters I can't wait to get back to reading.

As regards your work on the piano score of Mahler's VIII$^{th}$ Symphony, I recommend that in the future you only undertake complete works. If Hertzka doesn't have sufficient faith in you, you can only achieve it that way. Why does he give a job like that to someone nobody has ever heard of? Why not to you from the outset?

I'm convinced Mahler would not have agreed to it. Such patchwork! Did Hertzka pay you decently for it?

Incidentally, I'm negotiating with him at present and am very interested to see how it will turn out. He has to decide either to publish 6 of my works right away, or to return the rights to me. I have very significant offers for these works from a very large publishing house!! and another smaller one. I am curious to see what he'll do![1]

Now to the money matters. Please intervene energetically now. Above all with Bahr. Once and for all he is to do something. The affair with Redlich seems most unsavory. And he should finally persuade the other Redlich to do what he promised.

And then: what's the situation with the Mahler stipend. I had very much counted on this matter being settled by the beginning of January. Please try to see Moll right away.[2] And Frau Mahler too (do you know her address? Send it to me).

I sent my book to Moll, but he hasn't written a word about it. Ask him if he received it.

If Mauthner's money is there, please send it to me immediately. I am getting very concerned!!! Please **expedite** it.

What is Königer doing. He no longer writes!

Have you seen any reviews of my chorus? Korngold, Bienenfeld, Graf, Stauber, or Liebstöckl, the Zeit, etc. Specht?[3] Send me everything in this regard. Also anything you see about the Harmonielehre. And anything on my Budapest exhibit![4]— Enough for now.

Many warm regards

Your Arnold Schönberg

1. Schoenberg was in contact with several publishers at this time. The large one he mentions is no doubt the Leipzig firm of Peters, which was to publish his Orchestra Pieces, Op. 16, later that spring. The smaller one was the Cologne firm Tischer and Jagenberg, which published Friede auf Erden that summer. During the first half of 1912 there is also correspondence with the Berlin publishers Bote and Bock, Adolf Fürstner, and of course the Dreililienverlag, which had already published several early Schoenberg works. In a letter of 18 January 1912 Schoenberg informs Berg that his negotiations with Hertzka had broken down and that as a result he is desperately in need of money.

2. In two letters postmarked 15 and 18 January 1912, respectively, Berg tells Schoenberg that Moll is out of town and that his meeting with Bahr produced no concrete results; further that Königer had told Magda Mauthner to transfer the remaining 400 kronen directly to Schoenberg's account in Berlin.

3. No Korngold review has been found.

A short mention by Dr. Elsa Bienenfeld appeared in the 10 December 1911 issue of the Neues Wiener Journal (a promised longer review did not appear).

Max Graf's review appeared in the 6 January issue of Die Zeit and was positive, although harsh criticism was leveled at Schoenberg's later works.

Paul Stauber's review appeared in the Illustrirtes Wiener Extrablatt on 27 December 1911.

Hans Liebstöckl reviewed concerts for the Neues Wiener Tagblatt, but the 20 December 1911 review of Schoenberg's chorus was signed "rp".

Richard Specht's favorable review of the work appeared in Der Merker III / 3 (first February issue 1912), 112–13.

It is quite likely that Berg had seen and collected all these reviews, but in a letter of 28 December Webern had urged Berg not to send negative reviews for fear they might upset Schoenberg.

4. The Austrian painter Max Oppenheimer had suggested Schoenberg's participation in an exhibit of Viennese painters ("Neukunst-Wien") in Budapest. The exhibit, arranged by Anton Faistauer, ran from 6–27 January and included works by Faistauer, Paris von Gütersloh, Anton Kolig, Robin Chr. Andersen, and Egon Schiele. Paintings by Schoenberg (23 in all) and Oskar Kokoschka joined the exhibit on 20 January and were given a special opening.

## Schoenberg to Berg

Berlin-Zehlendorf, 20 January 1912

Dear Berg,

My concert here is on 28 January. Winternitz will sing 5–6 older songs (Op. 6), the George Songs, and the new song with harmonium, celesta, and harp, Petri is playing the new piano pieces, and I will probably perform the Orchestra Pieces in Stein's 8-hand arrangement.[1] Couldn't you come. Ask Königer, too!—but surely you'll come to Prague.

Please send the 150 marks immediately that you and your friends set aside for this concert, by postal order <u>directly</u> to me (not to the bank, that takes too long).— Please hurry the Bahr matters along. Pressure him a little if need be! It won't hurt. He shouldn't be so terribly slipshod! Otherwise I'll forbid him to criticize Vienna. I sent him my book.

Many warm regards

Your Arnold Schönberg

1. Due to scheduling conflicts, the concert was not held until 4 February. The Austrian soprano Martha Winternitz-Dorda sang five early songs and the George Songs, Op. 15, but not "Herzgewächse." She was accompanied by Eduard Steuermann; Louis Closson played the Piano Pieces, Op. 19, in place of fellow Busoni student Egon Petri. The matinee program closed with Erwin Stein's eight-hand, two-piano arrangement of three of the Orchestra Pieces, Op. 16. The pianists in the Op. 16 performance were Steuermann, Closson, Webern, and yet another Busoni student, Louis Grünberg.

## Berg to Schoenberg

Vienna [c. 26 January 1912]

Since I want to write to you before the concert, dear Herr Schönberg, but have to spend the entire day in the tax offices, at the lawyer's, and at the postal savings bank, etc., I can only find time for my letter while using various means of public transportation— —for which reason I ask you to excuse the form and content of this letter—above all the pencil.

It's such a marvelous spring day here today that I'm inclined to regard it as a positive symbol and to view life, heretofore so gloomy, almost rosily. Of course that's primarily due to the news of publication of the Orchestra Pieces by Peters. Quite apart from the fact that I'll soon have these enigmatically beautiful works with me at all times, I'm very happy about the publication <u>in light of</u> the impression on the **world**, that such a famous publisher should "scramble" for your works and want to publish them. That can, that <u>must</u> be of great <u>practical</u> value to you and your work. Performances will soon follow; the fact that such an old and respected, even conservative publisher is interested in you will impress even your "opponents" and "adversaries" and this seemingly small matter can be more decisive than might at first glance be expected. (Naturally I'm only speaking in <u>practical</u> terms here.) It's delightful to observe Hertzka's reaction (for whom, of course, it is the greatest embarrassment). He received me not long ago by conveying a greeting from you and telling me that he had an interesting bit of good news; taking the precaution of asking whether I had already heard it from you, which I could readily deny (having heard it from Webern), he told me about releasing the Orchestra Pieces. He had been very happy to do this, intending thereby to serve you and get your work out, as well as to see you promoted by this publisher (Peters) (since he was, *nota bene*, not able to publish the work at the moment!). Instead of saying straight out: "I am no artist and don't understand Schönberg, can therefore be of no service to him. But I'm not a good businessman either, which is why I undermine my own publishing house!!" One should tear the bearded mask off the face of this old prattler! Then the whole world would know what we have known all along!— — —

Naturally I consider the concert on the 28th another favorable event of the past few days. In any event it will be a memorable day. Winternitz will sing divinely, Webern will accompany, and sounds of unprecendented beauty will be revealed— for the very first time—even to you—and to the whole world through that portion of humanity allowed to be present. While I (I am thinking of the Maeterlinck song) have to stay in Vienna, consumed with longing and most sacred curiosity, and seek consolation in a Dehmel matinee which will also include songs of yours (to Dehmel poems).[1] A few days later Pazeller will sing "Verlassen" and "Natur,"[2] and a few days after that Dr. Reti will play the 2nd of your 3 piano pieces in an historical concert. It will be a Piano-Song Recital, beginning with Buxtehude, Couperin, etc.—Part II, the *Appassionata*. III.—Schönberg, Debussy—and Reti ( a sonata with two obbligato voices).[3]

Even these small events seem positive to me. It may not be raining but it's sprinkling. Of course this is all merely preparation for Prague. Already I live wholly in anticipation. I have begun to immerse myself in *Pelleas* and of course am completely captivated. More than ever I sense an unprecedented miracle of instrumentation here—both as regards sound (as far as I can imagine it) and voice leading. I would say: here there are no longer chords, what we hear as such—as you yourself say—are "voice leading events." Something that occurs much less in Mahler, for example. In general I am led ever more to the comparison:

> Beethoven—Mozart
> Mahler—Schönberg

One could continue the list, but nowhere does it seem so marvelously accurate as with these 2 grandiose pairs.

— — — — —

On returning home I found a letter from Webern, who tells me that the concert has been postponed! No doubt you are very upset, Herr Schönberg!! I, too, am terribly depressed! This morning's rosy mood has pretty well dissipated by now! This

---

1. The Akademischer Verband für Literatur und Musik (Academic Association for Literature and Music) sponsored the event, in which Richard Dehmel gave a lecture "über poetische und musikalische Lyrik" (On Literary and Musical Poetry) and read several poems, and Thea von Marmont sang Dehmel settings by Schoenberg, Reger, Conrad Ansorge, and Oscar Posa.

2. On 4 February Elsa Weigl-Pazeller, accompanied by her husband, Karl Weigl, sang a recital of songs by Mahler, Zemlinsky, Schoenberg, Weigl, Konta, Graener, Walter, Richard Mandl, and Josef Marx.

3. The Austrian pianist and theorist Rudolf Reti gave a recital on 4 February under the auspices of the Akademischer Verband, which featured Buxtehude's Passacaglia in D minor, Couperin's *Les folies françaises*, Handel's *Harmonious Blacksmith*, Beethoven's *Appassionata* Sonata, Schoenberg's Piano Piece, Op. 11, No. 2, Reti's own piano sonata with 2 obbligato voices, and Debussy's *Children's Corner* Suite.

*Anton Webern, portrait given to Schoenberg, Christmas 1911 (Arnold Schoenberg Institute)*

letter, too, has now failed its purpose; it was supposed to reach you, dear Herr Schönberg, on a day on which by rights I should have been present, so as at least to assure you of my participation in spirit. And that is <u>still</u> so, but no longer joyfully, rather with increasingly overwhelming melancholy.

Your entirely, entirely devoted
and most grateful Alban Berg

*Berg to Schoenberg*

Tuesday
Vienna [6 February 1912]

Dear, esteemed Herr Schönberg,

I haven't written you for a long time because of the February quarterly. Anyway, I wanted to wait to hear whether your song recital had finally taken place. According to a notice I read Sunday in a Saturday newspaper from Berlin, the song recital, or matinee, was scheduled for Sunday the 4th. I am immensely curious to know whether it took place and how it went. At the very same hour I was at Dr. Reti's piano recital in the Bösendorfersaal. I was very, very disappointed. His very physiognomy boded ill. He is a poor pianist! Doesn't understand the works on his program! Naturally least of all your piano piece, which he played too fast rhythmically, always agitated and distorted, and unclear due to excessive use of pedal. Judging by the applause it was received just like the other numbers on the concert. Except for his own composition, of course, which was more successful because it was atrocious. It was an attempt to imitate you, but as the style is foreign to him, led inevitably to the worst banalities. It was pitiful. Hertzka wants to publish it!![1]

The Pazeller song recital was in the evening. Another disappointment. She sang the lesser songs (Marx,[2] Graener) and the very bad ones (Mandl,[3] Konta, Walter) very well. Best of all, of course, Weigl's horrible things. The Zemlinsky was not as good. But worst of all, a worthy counterpart to Weigl's completely cold accompaniment, was her rendition of Mahler's—and your—songs. Obviously people like Weigl and consorts don't have the slightest affinity for your art—or for art at all, otherwise it wouldn't be possible to mutilate a song as divine as "Verlassen." Here again, a hurried tempo entirely spoiled the mood of the song. Not to mention 2 actual mistakes Weigl made in accompanying and 3 wrong notes by Pazeller. There was nonetheless some measure of success, evident after each song.

That's how you are performed in Vienna, dear Herr Schönberg! It would be better if it didn't take place at all. It doesn't do justice to your work and the public gets the wrong impression. They (the Viennese) ought to stick to their kindred spirits, Stöhr, Scherber,[4] etc., to whom, according to the enclosed programs, entire concerts are devoted. (Of course I won't go!)—

Forgive me, dear Herr Schönberg, that despite your request I didn't send you any newspapers; at that time I was without a subscription for 2 months and almost never read newspapers, which is why—to be honest—I forgot. Later, when I remembered, I thought it was too late—and perhaps even unnecessary, until Webern reminded me of it, which is why I will naturally do my best to make it up.

I heard from Bahr today (from Prague, where he is on tour) that *Kommerzialrat* Redlich finally answered him. He must be a vulgar sort of person: first, he was unable to do anything for you with his relative, *Oberbaurat* Redlich. He gave no reason. 2nd, he (the *Kommerzialrat*) would naturally be happy to pay the remainder (700), but only in the manner initially pledged, in 2 installments, therefore he will transfer another 200 kronen to me now; he will transfer the 2nd installment (500 kronen) at the end of the year! Redlich's letter closes with the remark: "After that Schönberg's friends and students must see to raising funds elsewhere and give something themselves, not just write letters!"

Although it was directed at Bahr and not at me, I have decided to answer the letter, that is, this remark myself. Bahr is naturally outraged, uses it to carry on about Vienna again and further writes that he has spoken to Gutmann in Munich, "who has the highest hopes for you in Berlin, where you will surely establish yourself yet," and that he had promised him (Bahr) "to do everything in his power for you there." If only I could see some action— —I have already heard so many words of this sort!!! I have great hopes for the song recital, for *Pelleas*,—but above all for

---

1. Reti's sonata remained unpublished.
2. The Austrian composer and pedagogue Joseph Marx.
3. The Austrian composer Richard Mandl studied with Leo Delibes.
4. The Austrian lawyer, composer, and music journalist Ferdinand Scherber was director of the music collection of the Vienna Court Library.

the *Gurrelieder!* I haven't received any proofs from Hertzka yet. Should I urge him again to send the thing to the engravers?! It would really be very advantageous if it were published!!— —

Again, dear Herr Schönberg, I've been unable to give you any good news, so that I'm losing all desire to write letters. I am very eager to hear about the success of the song recital, perhaps that will be good, hopeful news! Otherwise I shall hope for the future: for 29 February! My anticipation is frantic!! How marvelous it would be if you were to come back to Vienna with us afterwards! At least for a couple of weeks!!! On 14 and 15 March Walter is doing Mahler's VIII[th]![5] Stefan tells me he asked you to give a lecture in Vienna.[6] That would be wonderful, wonderful!! I can't even imagine the splendor of this thought!! Perhaps something will come of it!!!— — —— — — — — —

Many, many warm and affectionate regards from your completely, completely devoted and grateful

Alban Berg

---

5. Bruno Walter conducted the first Viennese performances of Mahler's Eighth Symphony in a concert by the Vienna Singakademie, of which he was the director.

6. Paul Stefan, who belonged to the central committee of the Akademischer Verband für Literatur und Musik, apparently initiated the idea of asking Schoenberg to deliver a lecture on Mahler in Vienna.

## *Berg to Schoenberg*

Vienna, 14 February 1912

It has been a long time since I last wrote, dear, kind Herr Schönberg. When I heard the marvelous news from Webern about your coming to Vienna, your giving a lecture (on Mahler!!!— —), about the planned concert, I was overcome by such rapturous joy that I wrote you a letter, Herr Schönberg,—that—thank heavens—I did not send. I guess I went a bit crazy for a moment with so much joy so <u>suddenly,</u> after so many deprivations, anxieties, and worries, and when I reread the unfinished letter next day, I had to tear it up with a laugh, it was so foolish. And then I waited (since I, too, was terribly busy) until I heard of your definitive plans from Webern, waited also until I myself had achieved some tangible results with regard to the concert. So, dear Herr Schönberg, you have decided to live in the Hotel über den Pilsenetzern during your Vienna stay. I find your decision to stay in town very "practical," since my own experience has taught me how time-consuming it is to live in Hietzing. (The so-called Z-cars scarcely run at all any more.) Of course from <u>my</u> point of view it's very sad that you won't be staying with me or Königer, but 1st, you will probably be more comfortable in a hotel and 2nd, there is nothing to prevent my being with you in town, dear Herr Schönberg. But you will be so kind, won't you, and allow us the small pleasure of providing for you in every way during your Vienna stay, if not with us (which would be a great pleasure) then at least at the hotel. That is merely an insignificant sign of hospitality from a city that was so tactless as to let you leave!

I hope arrangements for the planned concerts will go smoothly! The Akademischer Verband[1] has suggested 11 March for the lecture; yesterday we decided on that day because the dress rehearsal is on the 13th and the two performances of the VIII[th] on the 14th and 15th, so this way the audience has a one-day break (namely the 12th). I think you will agree with that. The Ehrbarsaal would be a possibility, perhaps the Kleine Bühne, which is said to be very nice (Oerley).[2] You will probably turn to the Akademischer Verband in this matter (Ullmann[3] or Buschbeck[4]), with whom I'm in constant contact. Nothing definite has been decided about the concert yet. Since Winternitz is definitely coming to Vienna for the VIII[th], she will be the first to be considered. The only question is whether she'll already be in Vienna by the 9th, when the concert is planned. But she'll be there on the 11th for sure!! The Akademischer Verband is asking her by express post, and as soon as we have an answer we can decide whether it's possible to have the concert before or not until after the VIII[th]! Only then can I get in touch with Rosé. Unfortunately he is out of town until 1 March (will then be playing, I believe Webern said, in Prague and Berlin, but I don't know when) so it may be that he can't be reached. In that case only the Hungarian String Quartet (Waldbauer-Kerpely)[5] would be available. But it's questionable whether they would do it for a small fee, for the Akademischer Verband is a "nonprofit organization!" At worst, if there were no quartet available, it would have to be just a song recital (Winternitz, older songs, George Songs, and "Herzgewächse"), in between the 3 older piano pieces (Werndorff)[6] and the 6 new ones (Webern). That too would be a very beautiful concert!

I hope Winternitz answers soon, so that this concert, too, can be scheduled soon. Do you really plan to return to Berlin after Prague and only then travel to Vienna? That's what Ullmann said. Are you going to turn over your lecture to the Akademischer Verband? It is sure to be fantastic!! I can't conceive of anything more beautiful, dear Herr Schönberg, than your speaking on Mahler.———

And the exquisite aphorisms in *Ruf.*[7] They are really incredible, it always seems a mystery to me how such golden words can appear in the company of such spirit- and humorlessness. Those essays by Bahr![8] And the poems!! And the other things might just as well be in the *Neues Wiener Journal!*—But since it is at least an opportunity to publish you, esteemed Herr Schönberg, to make your marvelous

1. The Akademischer Verband für Literatur und Musik (The Academic Association for Literature and Music), founded in 1908, sponsored a wide range of progressive musical and literary events.

2. The 1910 piano performance of Part I of the *Gurrelieder* took place at the Ehrbar Hall. The architect Robert Oerley designed the interior of the Kleine Bühne.

3. Ludwig Ullmann was the first chairman of the Akademischer Verband.

4. The Austrian dramaturg and theater director Erhard Buschbeck had been elected to the central committee of the Akademischer Verband in 1911 and initiated the organization's contact with Schoenberg.

5. The Waldbauer-Kerpely Quartet was founded in 1909 by the violinist Emerich Waldbauer and the cellist Eugen Kerpely.

6. The pianist Marietta (Etta) Jonasz Werndorff premiered Schoenberg's Piano Pieces, Op. 11, on 14 January 1910.

7. *Der Ruf*, the literary organ of the Akademischer Verband, was edited by Paul Stefan, Erhard Buschbeck, and Ludwig Ullmann. Schoenberg was represented in its first issue by six aphorisms. He was disturbed that his contribution had been abridged and that his name was not more prominently displayed on the cover.

8. Hermann Bahr's contribution was entitled "Eipeldauer 'Elektra'."

words a little better known, I'll tolerate the setting. I was most pleased with the sentence about overrating, about the critic-bailiff, and about dramatic music.[9]

What do you say to Stefan's essay? How well he "captures" the Kraus style.[10]

Were there reviews of the Berlin concert? How were the pieces reviewed?

The other things I hear from Webern about you give me renewed hope: the commission by the Viennese lady to set some poems as a melodrama![11] The Parisian quartet concert. The Orchestra Pieces in Paris!!! Will something come of that?[12] Finally Moscow! (*Pelleas* and the D-minor Quartet!!!)[13]— — —it's wonderful how things are beginning to stir out in the world. It seems as if recognition is slowly taking shape and will begin to surround Vienna from all sides until, taken captive by it, she can hold out no longer and will be forced to give you what is surely the very least due you, a professorship at the Vienna Academy.[14]

But until then we will still have to endure much suffering, which, however, we will gladly bear if only this goal were finally achieved.

Always and eternally, your, your Berg

---

9. The aphorisms in question read:

A poor devil must be careful not to spend more on a thing than it's worth. That's why those who are as economical with their tastes and opinions as with their money, fear nothing so much as the possibility of overrating someone.

A critic, as judge of art, ought to be satisfied with having pronounced judgment. But since he usually insists upon also personally carrying out the execution, I suggest the official garb and other prerogatives of the hangman. Above all: that he be excluded from society and that every self-respecting man shun him. To be sure, our culture will continue to condemn geniuses to starvation. But it would be a sign of progress, at least things wouldn't be worse than they were before and present-day culture would make, if not finer distinctions, then at least *as* fine a distinction as the culture of earlier ages, when the criminal was less despised than the bailiff.

Dramatic music: I find it more trouble than it's worth to immerse myself in the inner motivation of people indifferent to me, in order to portray them through their actions.

10. Paul Stefan's "Geheimbericht eines chinesischen Revolutionärs über seine Reise nach Österreich" (Secret Report of a Chinese Revolutionary on his Trip to Austria).

11. Early in February Schoenberg had met the Viennese-born singer and actress Albertine Aman Zehme, who commissioned him to write a series of melodramas on Albert Giraud's *Pierrot lunaire*.

12. Schoenberg's Orchestra Pieces, Op. 16, were not performed in Paris.

13. Nothing has been found on the Moscow performance of Schoenberg's First String Quartet in D minor, though Webern may have been referring to a February performance of Schoenberg's Second String Quartet, Op. 10, in St. Petersburg with Sandra Belling as the soloist. The planned performance of *Pelleas und Melisande* in Moscow under Serge Koussevitzky was later postponed for the 1913 / 1914 season and finally canceled altogether.

14. In February 1912 Schoenberg, was among those being considered to replace the theory and composition professors Robert Fuchs and Hermann Graedener, who were retiring from the Vienna Academy.

## Schoenberg to Berg

Berlin-Zehlendorf, 14 February 1912

Dear Berg,

I was so busy I was unable to answer. I don't have much time now either, so only briefly. Anyway, we will see each other in Prague, then we can talk.

We almost saw each other in Vienna at a Mahler lecture I was going to give at the Akademischer Verband. But I turned it down. For reasons the Akademischer Verband can tell you from my letter: I don't want to have anything to do with Vienna. I don't want to contract any new depressions there.

Webern probably told you about the outcome of my concert here. I am very satisfied with the impression it made. At any rate a great deal is being written about it, some of it even positive. However, the sum you placed at my disposal was almost entirely used up—thanks to the intervention of a 2$^{nd}$ concert agency.[1] It would have been cheaper to do it alone, but I couldn't ward off the patronage forced upon me and must pay for it now. In any case, my heartiest thanks to you and the other friends who made it possible.

Reti: tell me, aren't you perhaps being a little too harsh in your judgment. He made quite a good impression on me. Of course he seems to have quite "a mind of his own" and that is probably where he is weakest. But in the more "accessible" areas, where he is more dependent, he seems fantastic to me.

Why haven't you sent me any more reviews of my chorus? Surely there were more? And of the *Harmonielehre?* Hasn't anything been written about that yet?— Do you ever see Linke? What is he doing? You should take care to keep in touch with one another so as to stay abreast of possible developments. How is your teaching going. Is Königer making progress? And Polnauer and little Steiner? Tell me all about it sometime; I'm extremely interested, even if I can't answer "by return post."

Then: How's your composing? You never mention it. You should see to it. Perhaps a few songs for the time being!! Perhaps orchestral songs!

You told me once that your ailments were giving you a lot of trouble. How is it now? Are you better again. I was very worried about it at the time. Couldn't you find out something from a good doctor?

I must close, dear Berg, I have things to do. So: Warmest regards, also to your dear wife

Your Arnold Schönberg

---

1. Schoenberg's concert was co-sponsored by the Hermann Wolff and Emil Gutmann concert agencies.

## Berg to Schoenberg

Vienna, 17 February 1912

Dear, esteemed Herr Schönberg,

Your letter made me very sad. I had so very much looked forward to your coming and to the lecture . . . what an understatement!! I was in a sea of happiness! Just now I meant to write to beseech you to abandon your decision which at first seemed so mysterious to me, to give your lecture as planned, when I received the gloomy news from Ullmann as well, who said in reference to your letter to Buschbeck, "the substance of which is gripping in its embittered logic," that he "doesn't believe a change of heart probable." And now I hear the same from Webern, too! That is very, very sad for me and you can imagine how I feel, my dear, good Herr Schönberg, since the news hits me simultaneously with another most agonizing event: my wife is ill again. It's an inflammation of the appendix and in the next few hours or perhaps tomorrow it must be decided whether an <u>operation</u> is necessary. You will understand, dear Herr Schönberg, that I can't find time to write at the moment, or to answer your dear letter in full.

Only this, that the Akademischer Verband is organizing only one concert. Since I'm in contact with the group I will see to the necessary arrangements as soon as Winternitz has answered, so that we will have at least one good and very beautiful concert.

I am too agitated to write more, dear Herr Schönberg, the next few days will probably be decisive and I will keep you informed.

In the face of all this sadness, my happiness over Prague already so enormous, has again receded into the background. Soon I won't be capable of any but anxious, trembling happiness!

Thanks again, many, many thanks for your <u>dear</u> letter and many kind and reverential regards

from your gratefully devoted Alban Berg

The Paris concert has been announced in the *Münchner Neueste Nachrichten!*


*Berg to Schoenberg*

Sunday

Vienna, 10 March 1912

Dear, esteemed Herr Schönberg,

I meant to write immediately upon my return home;[1] but I was so terribly depressed after those wonderful days in Prague that I thought it better to remain silent. I always go through this when thrown back into the workaday world from the heights of human experience, which is what it means to me to be together with you and to revel in the sounds of *Pelleas.*

Other time-consuming matters detained me as well. I've finally composed something again, a short orchestral song on a picture postcard text by Altenberg,* to which I will add several more as soon as the concerts here are over.[2] I will give the completed one to Webern, whom I see often, to take along for you. For after this long period of stagnation I am completely incapable of judging my work and really can't say whether it's any good or the greatest rubbish. And so I ask you, dear Herr Schönberg, as soon as you have time, to look at what I've composed and tell me, or let me know through Webern, what you think of it, that is to say, whether it is

---

1. In the fall of 1911 Zemlinsky had invited Schoenberg to participate in a Deutsches Landestheater concert in Prague on 29 February 1912. Schoenberg conducted the first half of the program, comprising Mahler's Bach orchestral suite arrangement and his own *Pelleas and Melisande*; in the second half Zemlinsky conducted cello concertos by Haydn and Saint-Saens with Pablo Casals as the featured soloist. Schoenberg had traveled to Prague on 21 February, accompanied by Webern. Berg arrived in Prague on 25 February, on which day Webern presented Schoenberg with the book of essays, *Arnold Schönberg* (Munich, 1912).

2. Berg and his wife knew the Viennese essayist Peter Altenberg. Berg drew the postcard texts of his Altenberg Songs, Op. 4, from Altenberg's book, *Neues Altes* (Berlin, 1911), which also contains three items ("H.N.," "Bekanntschaft," and "Besuch im einsamen Park") inspired by Helene Berg.

*Alexander Zemlinsky,
Arnold Schoenberg, and
Franz Schreker in Prague,
March 1912 (Österreichische
Nationalbibliothek)*

good or bad, and what it is that's bad. I must get on the right track again so that at the very least I'll be able to apply what I already knew, namely the infinite number of things I learned from you, Herr Schönberg. Moreover, considering my limited talent for orchestral writing, this will no doubt turn out badly, at least at first. Perhaps I could learn something more in this regard, too, particularly if you'll be so very kind as to make corrections, i.e., criticize some of it—all of it would no doubt be asking too much.

I've also had a lot of correspondence these days with Hertzka and the directors of the Tonkünstlerverein, whom I have notified of my resignation. The behavior of the members and the executive committee during and after the performance of your 2 piano pieces (by Werndorff) led me to take this step.[3] It wasn't a scandal, which quite frankly I would have preferred,—but a kind of malicious, secretively triumphant smugness, expressed partly with chattering and laughter during the performance, partly with silent contempt—indeed indifference—finally even with insults. In short I got the impression that the great majority thought: "Oh well, let it be; we'll soon return to our Kontas, Kleins, Scholzes, Szudolskys, Petyreks, Mittlers, Stöhrs, Drdlas, and company."[4]

Hertzka—who, by the way, was not present—sent me a letter of regret with the request that I not make my resignation official; I had, however, already done so, in response to which Bopp asked me to present my grievances in person, which I shall do on Tuesday.

3. On 4 March the Tokünstlerverein sponsored a concert that included two of Schoenberg's Piano Pieces, Op. 11, as well as works by Wellesz and Debussy.

4. The Viennese composer Walter Klein was the secretary of the Tonkünstlerverein. The others mentioned are the composers Arthur Johannes Scholz, Marius Szudolsky, Felix Petyrek, Franz Mittler, and Franz Drdla.

All of that took a lot of time, and I just didn't get around to writing, especially as I also had errands to run, though *these* were of the pleasant variety. For I succeeded in arranging a concert for the "Akademischer Verband," to take place 16 April in the Bösendorfersaal. Rosé will play your Sextet and the D-minor Quartet! Rosé, whom I naturally went to see, told me a lot about Berlin, and read me the Rotterdam reviews.[5] He was very nice and obliging (he didn't ask anything for himself, just for the members of the Quartet, that is to say sextet, 400 kronen in all). My idea is to have songs between the two pieces, this time with a male singer who would do, say, Op. 1, then "Frundsberg," "Warnung," "Wanderer," etc. But that will probably remain a dream, for the kind of singer capable of doing that (Weidemann)[6] and a virtuoso to accompany him would cost a great deal of money and the Verband has none at all, indeed is in debt. And something of that kind must be done with style. But I shall make every conceivable attempt. Of course the Rosé Quartet is the most important thing, anyway—and, funny as it may sound, the Bösendorfersaal. I'm pleased that I was able to get it and that I rejected the Ehrbarsaal and others. This was primarily at Rosé's urging!

Webern[7] and I also went to see Walter, who received us very kindly, spoke much of you and the *Gurrelieder*[8] and gave us permission to attend rehearsals.[9] Unfortunately there will only be 2. We already heard one choral rehearsal; the last ensemble rehearsal is tomorrow in Weigl's Dreherhalle[10] and Tuesday there is another Cahier-Mahler recital.[11] We won't be allowed to attend the dress rehearsal on Wednesday. The 2 performances are Thursday and Friday———! That you, dear, dear Herr Schönberg, won't be present is terrible. How much more wonderful it would be if you were there. These days, with dear Webern telling me such good and wonderful things about you every day, it's "as if" I were only now beginning to feel the great loss in your being so far from Vienna.

Will that ever change!!!—

Sending my regards to you with all my heart, dear, good Herr Schönberg, and to your esteemed wife and the lovely children, I remain

your eternally grateful and loyal Alban Berg

*from his most recent book

5. The Rosé Quartet gave first performances of Schoenberg's First String Quartet in Rotterdam on 22 February and in Berlin on 5 March.

6. The baritone Friedrich Weidemann sang at the Vienna Court Opera 1903–19.

7. Webern had arrived in Vienna on 6 March for a two-week stay.

8. Bruno Walter was at that time planning a performance of *Gurrelieder* in Munich.

9. For the performance of Mahler's Eighth Symphony.

10. The Katharinen Hall of Weigl's Dreher Park, an amusement park located in Vienna's Meidling district, had a capacity of 7,000.

11. On 12 March the American alto Madame Charles Cahier and Bruno Walter gave a Vienna reprise of their 19 November 1911 Munich recital of Mahler songs.

*Berg to Schoenberg*

Vienna [18 March 1912]

On Saturday, my dear Herr Schönberg, I had a rather long talk with Bopp! It went pretty much as expected. Bopp is a diplomat, which is readily apparent from the fact that he holds such a position despite his lack of talent. And he acted the diplomat: he pretended indignation and promised that the matter would not go unavenged. He would take it up at the next executive committee meeting, would declare that such impropriety must never occur again, etc., etc. On the other hand he declared that he was personally very sorry I was leaving, not only on my account but also with regard to the principle that the younger generation—above all the Schönberg School—be represented in the Verein.

Thus he exonerated both himself and the Verein. Now one can no longer say that the Verein resisted modern developments or had acted improperly. On the contrary: on one such occasion the president of the Verein took immediate action and forbade a recurrence in the "strongest" terms!!

On the other hand, he didn't hurt his standing in the Verein!! Since he didn't want to hear any names from me, he couldn't proceed against anyone individually, only in general! Not one of those swine Dittrich,[1] Stöhr, Drdla, Duesberg,[2] etc., etc., will come forward! On the contrary, the only lesson for them is to be more circumspect in their agitation against modern music (whether in connection with you, Herr Schönberg, or even just Debussy (or Wellesz, for instance), who were similarly harassed and suppressed at that concert).

How could the outcome have been any different! I can't comprehend how I could have fancied that my action, my compelling evidence, and my detailed account would lead to these swine, above all Stöhr, being thrown out of the Verein, to our (you and your students) being received with open arms, and to my being admitted into the executive committee, thus advancing our cause.

I think: the Verein members are basically relieved that I'm out again, but I'm left with <u>one</u> consolation: all of them put together couldn't be <u>as relieved as I am</u>!!

I can breathe again!!—My experiences at the <u>previous</u> concerts, where lack of talent, impotence, and affectation reigned supreme, were possibly even more depressing than those at the performance of your piano pieces. The first concerts reduced me to painful lethargy, the last gave me the strength to shake myself free of it.

Thank heavens it's over.

———————

I finally heard from Piper,[3] dear Herr Schönberg, whom I had asked to send you free copies of your book. He writes that he is sending you 5, but that he <u>won't</u> send one to the head of Peters Edition. As the publisher he is not concerned with pub-

---

1. The organist Rudolf Dittrich was a member of the central committee of the Tonkünstlerverein.

2. The Viennese violinist August Duesberg was the founder of the Duesberg Quartet and a prominent member of the Tonkünstlerverein, though Berg may be referring here to the composer and violinist Natalie Duesberg, who had recently appeared on a 19 February Tonkünstlerverein concert with Szudolsky and Petyrek.

3. The Munich publisher Reinhard Piper had published the Schönberg book as well as the *Blaue Reiter* Almanac.

licity for you and your works, but only with publicity for the <u>book,</u> which, however, wouldn't be served by <u>giving</u> it away to all who are interested. After all, he writes, Peters Edition doesn't give him any scores, and U.E. was petty and let him down. I don't understand this last point! He probably wanted Hertzka to take some books off his hands! "which would have been in his [Hertzka's] interest."

Will <u>you</u> send a copy to Peters Edition, Herr Schönberg, or should we do so?! We have already sent away all of our free copies,* but are entitled to copies at 1 mark 40 pfennigs (instead of 3 marks)! At the time I also asked Piper to send free copies to Moll, Frau Mahler, Bahr, Loos, Kraus, but I don't know whether he did so! —————————

Tomorrow I'm meeting with the Akademischer Verband again. The printed items, posters, etc., are already being ordered! But I still have <u>no idea</u> who is to sing the songs! I simply don't know anyone! Of course, if the organization had money we would ask either Gutheil or Weidemann. Perhaps the organization will turn a profit soon (Karl May is to lecture in the Sophiensaal),[5] in that case we could ask someone. But even if we don't find anyone suitable, the concert will be very nice the way it is! I think the following order would be most advantageous:

I. Quartet
(possibly songs)
Sextet!

Do you approve of that, dear Herr Schönberg?? —————

We've just had some magnificent days here, all under the banner of Mahler's VIII[th]. It was heavenly!! The work is so wonderful I really didn't even notice that the performance wasn't particularly good. But it was nonetheless an unprecedented success! And yet: next day the critics dared to let loose their abuse. It's obviously too late to housetrain these old curs.

By contrast your lines in the *Merker* made me all the happier!![6] Oh, how divine that it has finally been said; so that all the blasphemers can now recognize themselves!! That should take them aback!! What one man, who is worth more than all of them put together (from Liebstöckl all the way up to Loos-Kraus), thinks of Mahler!! <u>That</u> was my <u>superficial</u> satisfaction! Of the inner joy I felt when I read your words, I cannot speak—for that there are only tears!——

And then Mahler's wonderful letters!!—And the death mask[7]——!——

Enough for today! Thinking of such sad-beautiful things always incapacitates me for hours—days; anyway there's nothing more to tell! Webern, whom I see every

---

4. The Austrian musicologist Guido Adler was the director of the musicological institute at the University of Vienna. Adler was a childhood friend of Gustav Mahler and in sympathy with the progressive elements of Vienna's musical life.

5. On 22 March, shortly before his death on the 30th of that month, Karl May, German author of popular novels of the American West, spoke in Vienna's Sophien Hall in Vienna's third district.

6. Schoenberg's article "Gustav Mahler: In Memoriam" was published in the *Merker* III / 5 (March 1912), 182–83 and appears in translation in *Style and Idea* (1975).

7. The same issue of *Merker* included a selection of letters, "Gustav Mahler: Ein Selbstporträt in Briefen" (Gustav Mahler: A Self Portrait in Letters) 172–81, as well as a number of photographs and a reproduction of the death mask taken by Carl Moll.

day, will tell you all the other little bits of news in person.

The very warmest regards from my wife and me to you and your highly esteemed wife

Always your grateful Berg

Has the mix-up with Riegl's widow been resolved yet?[8]

* mine to: Wiener, Bopp, Walter, Guido Adler,[4] Rosé.

8. Concerning an electrician's bill Berg had been asked to pay.

## Schoenberg to Berg

Berlin-Zehlendorf [3 April 1912]

Dear Berg,

I'm busy, so this will be brief. I'm sorry, but I must remain adamant in my refusal to allow the performance of my manuscript piano pieces. You should not have disposed over a manuscript without asking my permission. I would have given you the name of an excellent pianist who would have come in return for travel expenses (100 marks).[1] I am definitely no longer satisfied with Werndorff now that I know it's actually possible to play my piano pieces. I am not one bit interested in having her represent me with a new work. Anyway, I don't want a new work done in Vienna. At least at present.

To extricate yourselves from the situation it will probably be best to tell Werndorff the following: I am not allowing any new works to be performed in Vienna at the moment, as I find that Vienna hurts me abroad. For that reason I want you to return my manuscript to me as soon as possible.

You will probably be angry with me, but I have no choice.

For now warmest regards

Your Arnold Schönberg

1. Either Eduard Steuermann or Louis Closson, who had premiered the Op. 19 pieces at the 4 February concert in Berlin.

## Berg to Schoenberg

Wednesday
[Vienna, 3 April 1912]

Again, dear Herr Schönberg, I am forced to write in haste, partly in the streetcar, partly in the café, etc.—and therefore in pencil. It concerns performance of the 6 new piano pieces. Assuming that you would agree to the performance, we included them on the program (minus the opus number), likewise on the poster; both of which will appear any day now. After we were unable to find a singer (we turned among others to Steiner,[1] who is unfortunately unable to do it, and Förstel,[2] who didn't reply), we hit upon the piano pieces. Naturally the new ones as well. For through Webern I am thoroughly acquainted with these, have practiced them a little myself and believe I've mastered them—if not technically, then at least musically. Therefore (encouraged by Webern) we decided that I should rehearse them with Werndorff. And that is the way I arranged it with Werndorff on the telephone, sending her the piano pieces at the same time so that she is presumably learning them now. Granted, we should have asked you beforehand, but since I was certain that you would permit it for the first piano pieces, and since I was firmly convinced that, after my going through them with her—, Frau Werndorff would manage the new piano pieces very well, indeed dynamically even better than the old ones, in which, after all, certain passages do require a man's strength (—I would even say not just the physical but also the spiritual strength) which women lack———All these assumptions led to the carelessness of making a decision I had no right to make.

Wouldn't it perhaps be possible that I tell Frau Werndorff that you wish her to study the pieces with you in Berlin, to which she very possibly might not agree.

Wouldn't it I. be very insulting if we were to take the pieces away from her?! Perhaps we could bring off a good performance with united forces. II. I'm concerned less for Werndorff than for the poster and programs, which have already been printed.—Of course, one could announce at the concert that the pieces had to be canceled.

But would that suit you, dear Herr Schönberg??! And what "reason" would one give. One couldn't very well give the real reason, that would disgrace Werndorff!!

In the end one could make up some other reason!

I'm only writing this crazy letter because I'm thinking that, considering the circumstances, you might perhaps agree to let Werndorff play the new pieces after all, even if she doesn't come to Berlin!!!

Of course I would nevertheless try to persuade her to make the trip, and perhaps she'll do it!! But in case she won't, are we then, dear Herr Schönberg, to refrain from doing the new piano pieces after all!!* If you don't permit it, I would naturally tell her, emphasizing above all that the mistake was mine for having arranged something I had no right to do without your permission. Until now I haven't told Werndorff anything, having myself just found out about it from Buschbeck, who is largely responsible for my writing you this letter. Please, dear Herr Schönberg, perhaps you will let me know your final decision through Webern again. No doubt you yourself have no spare time just now!!

Oh, that I wasn't in Prague, I read about your great success in the *"Prager Tagblatt"!!*[3] How wonderful that must have been!!! If only I could at least read it, given

1. The Hungarian baritone Franz Steiner lived in Vienna.

2. The soprano Gertrude Förstel sang at the Vienna Court Opera 1906–12.

3. Schoenberg was asked to give a Mahler lecture in conjunction with the Prague performance of Mahler's Eighth Symphony under Zemlinsky. There were reviews in the *Prager Tagblatt* of 29 March 1912 and 30 March 1912.

that I wasn't able to <u>hear</u> it!!

Excuse my haste!! In a few minutes I'm due at the doctor's, who will decide whether my wife needs an operation after all.[4] In any case I haven't the time or peace of mind for quiet letter writing!

In this letter I just wanted to straighten out the matter with Werndorff.

More soon about other things, my dear, good Herr Schönberg!

Your completely devoted Alban Berg

\* For I am sure that the <u>new</u> piano pieces would be very successful. Perhaps even <u>more so</u> than the <u>old</u>!

---

4. Helene Berg was still suffering from an inflamed appendix, but an operation was not necessary.

*Berg to Schoenberg*

Vienna [12 April 1912]

Again in pencil, dear esteemed Herr Schönberg. I find time to write only in the streetcar, as I'm busy all day, and in the little time remaining to me—have done a bit of composing again. But I want to tell you about the concert. It's finally settled now that <u>only</u> the quartet and sextet will be performed. I managed to induce Werndorff to bow out—without hurting her feelings. So neither the old nor the new piano pieces will be performed. I went to see Rosé again, who was very nice. I also met Whitfield[1] there, whom Rosé is preparing for the state board examinations. Apparently the poor fellow is going completely blind and is trying to get a teaching position (violin) in an institution for the blind. It is terrible!—

I have a new student. Schreker sent me his brother-in-law, an 18-year-old business school graduate who wants to become a conductor.[2] I'll give him a 1-hour lesson 2 times a week for 40 kronen a month. I'm very pleased. Particularly because I'll finally have a chance to teach harmony again. I feel much more secure there than with counterpoint. I'm also very pleased that you, dear Herr Schönberg, looked at Königer's work, and I learned a great deal that way. And I also found all the other things Königer had to report immensely interesting.[3] Above all <u>our</u> June music festival.[4] As soon as anything decisive occurs in this regard, Königer will report to you. For the present we have discussed it only with the Akademischer Verband, which would naturally be glad to participate. Königer has already written to Prague

---

1. The English violinist Ernst Whitfield.

2. Karl Binder, brother of Schreker's wife, Maria Binder Schreker.

3. Paul Königer, who had shortly before married Maria Mörtl Commerlohr, the sister of Webern's wife, Wilhelmine Mörtl Webern, had just returned from a Berlin visit with the Weberns.

4. Schoenberg's plan for a music festival, developed in conversations with Webern after their return from Prague, was to provide a forum for progressive living composers not represented in the concerts of the first Vienna Musikfestwoche, which was scheduled for 21 June–1 July.

and to Strasser regarding Pest.[5] Of course the best thing about it is that you will then give your lecture in Vienna, too![6]—

A while back I went to see Hertzka, who wanted to speak to me about the *Gurrelieder*. A subscription drive is being planned for the performance under Schreker in the fall.[7] A committee of 25 is to collect pledges for ticket purchases. If every one were to buy 40 tickets averaging 10 kronen, that would already (!) raise 10,000 kronen! But knowing my beloved Vienna as I do, it would probably be the same 40 people!—The piano reduction is finally going to be engraved. Again Hertzka set himself up as your most enthusiastic admirer and patron and I could only think of the "fog" of which you speak in the Gutmann calendar.*[8] He's also publishing the George Songs now ("granted, only the piano reduction," as he said[9]).

I am at present wholly engrossed in your 2 works: I$^{st}$ quartet and sextet. They are divine works; I am incredibly excited about hearing them Tuesday. Of course I'll give you a complete report right away and will collect reviews. (A week from Monday Schreker will conduct *Das klagende Lied* and Zemlinsky's 23$^{rd}$ Psalm.)

I think I've mentioned everything now and close this scribble with the request that you excuse the handwriting: the tram jolts terribly.

Most warmly and affectionately

Your always devoted Berg

With the greatest joy and a curiosity bordering on longing I hear from Webern that you, dear Herr Schönberg, are working on the melodramas. I'm also overjoyed about the score of the Orchestra Pieces.[10] — — — — — —

---

*Gutmann sent it to me, no doubt at your kind instigation. Upon rereading it, the article struck me as still more wonderful!

---

5. Schoenberg's plan included inviting representatives of contemporary Czech and Hungarian music. Istvan (Stefan) Strasser, a young Hungarian conductor at the Prague Deutsches Landestheater, had greatly impressed Schoenberg during his recent Prague visit.

The Hungarian capital city Budapest had originally comprised the twin cities, Buda and Pest, which were joined in 1872.

6. Schoenberg did not give his Mahler lecture in Vienna until the following fall.

7. Franz Schreker had long planned to perform the *Gurrelieder* with his Philharmonic Chorus and wrote to Schoenberg in March that he had set a date for the following November. The idea for a subscription campaign most likely originated with Schreker. The first meeting of the subscription committee, which comprised Hertzka, Schreker, Berg, Linke, Paul Stefan, Richard Specht, Wilhelm von Wymetal, and Johanna Müller-Hermann, took place on 24 May.

8. In his article "Parsifal und Urheberrecht" (Parsifal and Copyright) in the Gutmann *Konzert-Taschenbuch für die Saison* 1911/12, V (Berlin, 1912), 84–90, Schoenberg wrote of the mental "fog" spread by those who confuse moral principles with financial interests.

9. Hertzka apparently thought the George Songs had an orchestral accompaniment, which of course was not the case.

10. The Peters publication of the Orchestra Pieces, Op. 16.

*Berg to Schoenberg*

[Vienna, 16 April 1912]
at night

I have to write, dear, dear Herr Schönberg, though I'm already in bed. But I am so drunk with the beauty of the music, with the unprecedented, unanimous success, that I simply have to tell you a bit more about it:

The hall was jam-packed: one could sense incredible excitement. In attendance were the Molls, Frau Mahler, Frau Rosé,[1] Roller,[2] Loos, Kokoschka,[3] Bahr, Mildenburg,[4] Schreker, etc., etc. Korngold, even the little one, Batka, Hoffmann,[5] Specht (Bienenfeld couldn't come because of her father's death), Graf was <u>not</u> there, then many others, whom I only know by sight and who must also be artists or people of stature (Lemberger too).—The performance was fabulous, especially the sextet. In the quartet it took them a bit longer to get over their initial nervousness, i.e., until they hit their stride. But that didn't hurt the work's reception any. The success, unparalleled in its warmth, was enthusiastic, indeed ecstatic, everyone stood up, waved, shouted bravo; Rosé had to take 8–10 bows. * There was incredible animation during the intermission, it seemed as if people wanted to embrace one another from sheer emotion and joy. Following the sextet the jubilation was, if anything, even greater. ¾ of the hall remained seated and refused to move until Rosé had again taken 10–15 bows and lights had been turned off. And this general mood was evident among all those individuals named above: (the Bahrs, the Molls, Frau Mahler, etc., applauded like crazy). Rosé beamed. At the end, I had to thank him on behalf of the Verband, he was in an absolutely ebullient mood. Kokoschka was extremely enthusiastic and moved. Loos too. Moll even told me he thought it a pity the piano pieces weren't played. Everyone was wildly pleased: many people even bought scores at the box office and followed along. Hertzka beamed constantly and gestured to me as if to say: "Well, wasn't I right!" Stefan too was swimming in bliss and I forgave him many of his villainies: for I was in a state closer to tears of emotion than anything else, my heart very nearly stopped when confronted by the beauty of these works. In my delirium I wrote the telegram to you, dear, idolized Herr Schönberg—which everyone signed: and now I'm afraid that in the end it may have awakened you. I hope the post office will wait with the delivery. The concert was over about 9:30. I enclose the notice that was distributed during the intermission.[6] I hope it will be effective.

Of course today's concert was just a prelude to the incredible success the *Gurrelieder* will have. But we're not talking about concerts, these are events that can only be compared with natural phenomena:

---

1. Justine Rosé was Gustav Mahler's younger sister and Arnold Rosé's wife.
2. Alfred Roller, a central figure in the Secessionist movement, was the chief stage designer of the Court Opera.
3. The Austrian painter and writer Oskar Kokoschka was just beginning to be internationally known.
4. The Austrian soprano Anna Bahr-Mildenburg sang at the Vienna Court Opera 1898–1923. She married Hermann Bahr in 1909.
5. Rudolf Stefan Hoffmann was a medical doctor and critic for the weekly *Wiener Montags-Revue*.
6. This note concerned plans for the performance of *Gurrelieder*.

the leap year in Prague this year.
tomorrow's solar eclipse[7]— — —

But I'm beginning to fantasize and had better do that in my thoughts, dear, best Herr Schönberg, than bore you with it— — —only once again:

It was a heavenly evening— —and we have you to thank for it. Thank you! A thousand thanks.

In deep reverence and sublime love,

Your devoted Alban Berg

\* Not a single sign of opposition!

7. Vienna experienced a partial solar eclipse on 17 April 1912 at 1:29 P.M.

## Schoenberg to Berg

Berlin-Zehlendorf, 19 April 1912

Dear Berg,

I thank you very, very (!!) much for your exceptionally warm letter. Truly, I sensed how devoted you are to me and my works and that gives me an extraordinarily good feeling. As you describe it, it must really have been wonderful—and that made me particularly sorry not to have been there: I would for once have liked to hear these things in peace, indeed, perhaps even in the proper mood. Something that is never possible. Usually one senses only the audience's antipathy and resistance. Perhaps this once I would have caught something of the mood of the audience, perhaps people's backs would once again have pleased me. Which hasn't been the case for a long time! Almost since the time I wrote them. Your letter and the concert made me very happy and I thank you very much. It was better that the piano pieces weren't done. That would definitely have been too much. Now I am very curious how the subscription drive for the *Gurrelieder* will go. That was certainly a good idea. I am—frankly—very hopeful.—What about the unofficial music festival? Are you making any headway?

Many warm regards

Your Arnold Schönberg

## Berg to Schoenberg

Vienna [23 April 1912]

Dear, good Herr Schönberg,

Your letter made me very, very happy. It was happiness enough that I had the privilege of arranging such a wonderfully, wonderfully successful concert, one I myself was able to attend, and since that evening I have been in a truly ebullient mood such as I haven't felt for a long time. But now your dear words of thanks have absolutely overwhelmed me with joy, so that I scarcely feel the shame, since it is actually I who should thank you for being permitted, as it were, to participate in a concert which provided such great satisfaction and resulted in such a richly reward-ing evening not only for others but above all for myself. The Akademischer Ver-band, too, is so proud and happy at the moral success of the concert that they have turned to me to act, so to speak, as musical adviser for the organization and to decide what should and should not be performed. The most important concerts the organization is planning for the fall are the following: a Schönberg song recital (with a fine singer (probably Steiner) and Winternitz), where primarily the older songs and ballads would be done, then a concert of *Pelleas*, the Orchestra Pieces, possibly the Orchestral Songs (under your direction, of course) with the Tonkünstler Orchestra. They also want to do a concert with the F♯-minor Quartet, all the piano pieces . . . possibly the Chamber Symphony (?)!

They are also participating in the *Gurrelieder* performance. And they want to do a modern concert with things by Webern and me, etc., which I am to select. So there are bright prospects for next season, which are almost certain to materialize, naturally only if you agree to it. This makes me all the happier, since my hopes of doing something for your cause, which is of course *our* cause, failed so miserably in the wretched Tonkünstlerverein, while here in the Akademischer Verband we really have found a broad and willing forum. My principal goal is now above all to educate the audience systematically to your music. The quartet concert was the beginning. There will be ever more people who are both willing and understanding, so that soon the great circle of your unconditional supporters will enable the per-formance and success of each of your existing as well as future works. Perhaps then it will be possible for the Verband to realize its highest goal, that of producing your 2 operas. That would surely be an incredible event and I virtually shudder in ecstasy when I think of it.

Königer will tell you about the music festival in detail, I don't want to anticipate him. The main issue is, of course, finances, and that simply takes time in Vienna. But since Königer has already raised 250 kronen and has hopes of raising more, we hope to get something from the Prague gentlemen[1] as well. My inquiries—without revealing the purpose—at the Bösendorfersaal and Tonkünstler Orchestra unfortu-nately bore no results. Neither is available after 1 May. But the main problem is still money!

I hope we'll soon have good news to report and will close for now, thanking you again most warmly for your dear, kind letter. Please give your esteemed wife my most devoted regards; also from my wife; who is, thank heavens, feeling better.

Your devoted and most grateful Alban Berg

Excuse the inverted stationery, dear Herr Schönberg, I had begun backwards and had to tear it apart.

I was at Schreker's concert yesterday, which, like all of those concerts, was too

1. The Czech composers Josef Suk and Vitězslav Novák.

long by half.[2] That half being the overture for chorus, organ, and orchestra by Scott: never-ending mush, no doubt modern, but it almost made me nauseated. Nonetheless. Colossal success. Zemlinsky's magnificent work, on the other hand, fell flat; most of the audience can't appreciate such chaste beauty, such slightly understated warmth. Even the Molls, Rosés, Frau Mahler, Kokoschka (who now belongs to this circle![3]), Rollers didn't lift a hand, which I thought very odd. Naturally the success of *Das klagende Lied* was all the more sensational! It was also a very successful performance!! A magnificent work!!!! It was my first Mahler experience!![4]

Once again 10,000 warm, devoted regards

from your Berg

---

2. The Philharmonic Chorus concert presented the overture to *Princess Maleine* by Cyril Scott, Zemlinsky's 23rd Psalm, and Mahler's *Das klagende Lied*.

3. Oskar Kokoschka's presence in the Mahler circle came about through his affair with Alma Mahler, which had begun shortly before.

4. Berg had attended the 17 February 1901 Vienna premiere of *Das klagende Lied*, conducted by Mahler himself.

## Schoenberg to Berg (postcard)

Zehlendorf [30 April 1912]

Dear Berg,

Hertzka wants to print a piano reduction (2-hand) of the 3rd and 4th movements of the F♯-minor Quartet, suitable for rehearsing (etc.). If you would care to prepare it very quickly, go to Frau Gutheil (give her my very warmest regards) and pick up the reduction I made.[1] It is unplayable. *This* reduction must be absolutely easy to play. That's the main objective!! I don't know whether Hertzka will pay much for it. But certainly something (100 to 150 kronen, I hope), and maybe you can get more out of him. Please reply at once.—

The unofficial music festival must not be organized as a demonstration against the official Vienna Musikfestwoche. That would backfire. But it is possible as a supplement, as Specht suggests![2]

Warm regards

Schönberg

---

1. Schoenberg's piano reduction of the last two movements of his Second String Quartet, Op. 10, has not been located.

2. Independent of Schoenberg's plan, Richard Specht had been planning an alternative concert in the Music Festival which was to include works of Schoenberg.

## Berg to Schoenberg

[Vienna, 1 and 8 May 1912]

I began this letter about a week ago, but interrupted it because of the piano reduction. That's why I'm only resuming it today:

Dear Herr Schönberg,

Enclosed the program of a concert I attended out of curiosity.[1] It was dreadful! Again and again I fancy I've experienced the worst, but there's always something still worse. However, it can't possibly get any worse than these things by Walter Klein, Hertzka's newest protégé.[2] He is a young, totally untalented member of the Tonkünstlerverein, who's being enthusiastically promoted in Vienna just now. All the better sort of people, who attended the concert partly because of Rosé, partly because of Walter, were shocked. Buxbaum,[3] Bittner[4]—above all Schreker, who demanded testily: "Say, where are we anyway? In the loo.?——"

Reti, too, disappointed me anew—and more than ever! I'm sure that you, too, dear Herr Schönberg, would have been extremely disappointed with his performance.

I believe you already know Walter's violin sonata. With the exception of the beginning of the II[nd] movement, which I found mildly interesting because of its resemblances to Mahler, I was terribly bored by the whole thing. But at least one was reminded again—this in contrast to Klein's composition—that there are also augmented triads and not just diminished triads and 7th chords, that the violin has a mute, that there are ways of bowing other than a steady sawing back and forth as in the first violin sonata. (That Rosé consented to play something like Klein's sonata! I believe he played it *prima vista* and without **any** enthusiasm.)

I was very disappointed by Zweig's[5] compositions. One movement, a scherzo, seemed a bit better: it was at any rate carefully worked out, which is probably what he retained from your teaching. But the other movement is pure swindle and clumsy to boot. Imagine, dear Herr Schönberg: a kind of rondo with a decided polka rhythm (à la *Walzertraum*, only much more vulgar): following that a singer begins to howl a popular song, accompanied by arpeggios and passage work, upon which the brilliant polka again follows in conclusion. And all that as accompaniment to words which I remember so well from Webern's song![6] I'm deeply outraged by the swindle of appropriating what you first did in a quartet and copying it in a sonata movement, and, what's more, taking a poem by the same poet, when Roda Roda[7] would have suited him much better!—

This, dear Herr Schönberg, is where I continue my letter:

8 May

The last movement of the quartet is finished. I found the job relatively difficult. I think it's easy enough. In very difficult passages I was sometimes forced to disfigure

1. An Akademischer Verband concert on 27 April presented the first performance of Walter Klein's Violin Sonata, a Gavotte with Variations by Rameau, a Chopin Prelude, Debussy's *La neige danse*, Reger's *Tagebuchblatt*, Bruno Walter's Violin Sonata, and two movements of a Sonata with vocal obbligato by Fritz Zweig. Among the performers were Etta Werndorff, Rudolf Reti, Arnold Rosé, Bruno Walter, and Fritz Zweig.
2. Walter Klein's works were never published by Universal Edition. The sonata in question was printed by the composer.
3. Friedrich Buxbaum was a cellist in the Vienna Court Opera and a member of the Rosé Quartet.
4. The Austrian judge and composer Julius Bittner.
5. Fritz Zweig had studied with Schoenberg 1910–11. His sonata remained unpublished.
6. Zweig's text has not been identified.
7. Pen name for the Austrian satirist Sandor Friedrich Rosenfeld.

your work. Forgive me. That was hard enough for me—above all in my heart! Despite your dislike of them, I found I had to use a number of additional staves, not that the player should try to play them, but to provide orientation for the singer, or better said, to avoid potential confusion (when for instance the I$^{st}$ violin begins a run which the singer might otherwise look for in vain in the reduction (measure 86)). For the same reason I sometimes indicated the instrument, viola, cello, — — —*

I'm beginning the other movement now, which strikes me as even more difficult, particularly making it easy to play! Unfortunately I don't have your reduction of this (III$^{rd}$) movement, Gutheil doesn't have it! Perhaps you have it. In that case maybe Webern would be so kind as to bring it along or send it.

Also enclosed is Korngold's "witty(!)" review.[8] He's as great an idiot as the others, only wittier! It's telling how cleverly the lack of understanding is concealed. But in the end he falls into his own trap when he pretends outrage that one "passes judgment on substantial works after a few unusual harmonies." For what does he do but just that. And it doesn't make his opinions better—as I said, just wittier—if he then takes really insignificant works like Cyril Scott's overture and writes mush about it that matches the overture itself, music which doesn't have the least resemblance to yours and only a few whole-tone chords in common with Debussy! It's a priceless lie that the D-minor Quartet never encountered any resistance to speak of: or the sextet none at all. And that same lie will resurface with every performance from now on (the F♯-minor Quartet in June—if you agree to the performance— *Pelleas* next year, Chamber Symphony, etc.). Until the tables are finally turned completely: and then we'll hear: "What! this quartet is modern?! This motive bizarre?! Those are new harmonies?!"— — — —Just as already today Korngold considers Mahler's handling of orchestra and chorus "tentative," whereas 10 years ago at the premiere of this wonderful work people couldn't say enough about such "daring," etc. . . . .

Incidentally, the performance was not very good. The whole concert endlessly long. I find Zemlinsky's chorus wonderfully beautiful, especially toward the end. But it wasn't well received. (But I think I already told you about that, dear Herr Schönberg. Excuse the repetition!)

Not long ago I heard Schreker give a reading of his III$^{rd}$ drama,[9] parts of which I liked very much and which is incredibly effective, powerful, and skillfully done— granted, also a bit kitschy. Next year Gregor wants to perform Schreker's II$^{nd}$ opera, *Die Prinzessin und die Spieluhr* [sic], not *Ferne Klang*.[10]

The *Gurrelieder* drive isn't going very well at the moment. We'll have to organize a committee, to which I will belong. Each member has to commit himself to taking at least 200 kronen worth of tickets. It's a good idea, but very difficult for the mem-

8. Julius Korngold's review of both the Schoenberg concert of 16 April and the Philharmonic Chorus concert of 22 April appeared in the *Neue Freie Presse* on 8 May 1912; Korngold drew parallels between the music of Scott, Schoenberg, and Debussy.

9. Schreker's reading of his libretto for *Die Gezeichneten* on 30 April was sponsored by the Akademischer Verband.

10. In 1910 *Der ferne Klang* had been accepted for performance at the Vienna Court Opera by Felix Weingartner. His successor, Hans Gregor, decided instead upon *Das Spielwerk und die Prinzessin*.

bers! Schreker wants an additional chorus (perhaps off-stage) for the *Gurrelieder.* Are you going to write one?

I have nothing else of interest to relate. You've been informed about the Music Festival and we are awaiting your answer (to Königer) with great longing, as well as that of the Czechs, so that we can proceed in selecting a hall. You already know that Rosé readily agreed. But he wants Winternitz for the quartet and will check to see whether Gutheil is <u>not</u> in Vienna, so that she won't be insulted if she's not asked. We await Winternitz's answer daily.—

Enough, my dear kind Herr Schönberg. I'm already looking forward to Webern, he'll have a great deal to tell me about you again.[11] Oh, that I could be with you! These are bleak times, what's more, it seems like spring will never come.—And Strindberg lies dying.[12] — — — — — — — — —

As soon as I've finished the III$^{rd}$ movement of the quartet I'll send you that, too. Then it's up to you, whether you want to send it back to <u>me</u> or directly to Hertzka. I don't think I'll get more than 70–90 kronen out of him for it, since his rate is 3 kronen per page (engraved). But maybe that's payment enough!

My regards to you, dear, esteemed Herr Schönberg, with my customary and everlasting love and gratitude

Your Berg

Please greet your esteemed wife from me and my wife. We hope that she and the dear little ones are well.— — —

\* Incidentally, please delete whatever seems superfluous to you.

---

11. Webern traveled to Vienna on 12 May for a brief vacation before taking up his new duties at the Stettin Stadttheater on 22 June.

12. August Strindberg died on 14 May 1912.

## Berg to Schoenberg

[Vienna, 25 May 1912]

My dear Herr Schönberg,

We've had a couple of terribly nerve-racking days here! The letter you wrote to Webern about half a week ago concerning the Academy situation led us to fear the worst—(that you would turn it down—). But thank heavens the spell has been broken. I'll never forget that moment yesterday when Webern brought along your short note to Jarno's Strindberg festival *(Dance of Death).*[1] Now everything is all right again— —Indeed, I would say—better than ever! Through the sudden imposition of a barrier the course of events has become—yet more powerful and inexorable! I see the coming fall as a resurrection after a long period of torment.

Yesterday brought other gratifying events, too. In the afternoon there was a meet-

---

1. The Austrian actor and theater director Joseph Jarno starred as Edgar in a performance of Strindberg's *Dance of Death* at the Josefstadt Theater on 24 May.

ing at Hertzka's about the campaign for the *Gurrelieder* performance. Present, aside from myself, were Schreker, Linke, Stefan, and Frau Müller-Hermann. *[Berg outlines a plan to expand the number of committee members from about forty to one hundred, who are each to sell five ten-kronen tickets.]* I am certain the required sum of 4–5,000 kronen can be raised this way. I think Schreker will have 3–4,000 kronen at his disposal in any case: i.e., 2,000 kronen cash, and they are ready to accept a deficit of 2,000 kronen. I assume that you have been informed about the performance itself. The expanded Tonkünstler Orchestra with 10 rehearsals. And definitely Winternitz!

Schreker said you were thinking of Slezak,[2] which would certainly be wonderful, but they're afraid they can't afford him. Burrian[3] is also being considered, which wouldn't be bad either (he's enjoying great triumphs here in the *Ring*, by the way). But I strenuously opposed Schreker's suggestion of using "Maikl."[4] That's impossible!!! It would be dreadful. Webern, to whom I mentioned it, was also very much against it. Do you know him? I heard him in Mahler's VIII[th] as well as in the *Klagende Lied* and the Requiem. Granted he's musical and sings effortlessly, but the timbre of his voice is horrible. A real necktie tenor! I've been thinking that if we can't get Slezak we should consider Miller,[5] whom we heard in *Das Lied von der Erde* and who is also quite musical and has a very pleasant, if not overpowering voice. (Webern is in favor of that too.) I'll sound them out about it at the next meeting at Hertzka's (29 May 1912), but will insist on Slezak for the time being!!

————————

I finally saw——just think, Herr Schönberg,—the nearly completed engraved proofs of Part I of the *Gurrelieder!!* At last, at last!! It is now being proofread at Hertzka's, whereupon I will get it. Should I send it to you as well, dear Herr Schönberg? Or would you rather see the 2nd set of proofs. That is, will a 2nd set even be necessary?————What about the (II[nd]) Quartet song reductions. You probably haven't had time, dear Herr Schönberg, to look through it again, after all, it probably isn't as urgent as many other things. By the way, Bien is bringing me her beautifully copied reduction of your 1st Quartet today, which she prepared at the time.[6]

(Afternoon) I just played through the reduction together with Bien. I think it's quite good, some passages, in fact, are very good, and it's almost always easy to play. I fancied I could even see where you repeatedly intervened and found ingenious solutions for particularly difficult passages. How wonderful if the reduction could be published very soon, the work would find rapid dissemination, which isn't so easy with full scores. I must admit that the magnificence of the work often led me to forget to judge the reduction, but maybe that, too, speaks well for the reduc-

2. The heldentenor Leo Slezak was engaged at the Vienna Court Opera 1901–34.
3. The Czech opera tenor Karl Burrian sang at both the Vienna Court Opera and the New York Metropolitan Opera.
4. The Austrian tenor Georg Maikl joined the Vienna Court Opera in 1904, where he remained for the next forty years.
5. The American tenor William Miller sang at the Vienna Court Opera.
6. The Viennese pianist Irene Bien had studied with Schoenberg; her piano reduction of the Schoenberg's D–minor Quartet has not been located.

tion. Bien said she has already written to you about it and spoken with Hertzka. But it's a matter for the Dreililienverlag. That's why she will send you a copy of the piano score very soon and I hope you will find 2 people in Berlin to play it for you, so you can assess it and either permit or forbid its publication. No doubt the Dreililienverlag will be happy to engrave it, which would be lovely because then in perhaps 3–4 months it would be possible to play the work (at least the reduction) by oneself whenever one wished, which after all isn't as easy from the full score.

Bien asked me to speak to you about the piano score, dear Herr Schönberg, since she's very depressed that you haven't written and thinks you are angry with her, though I consoled her with the fact that you simply don't have time to answer every unimportant letter.

Otherwise there's nothing new. Webern tells me that he has informed you about the music festival, Herr Schönberg. I discussed it with Schreker on Wednesday. My piano sonata will be played by a Viennese virtuoso, Richard Goldschmied,[7] who is said to play very well and is interested in everything modern. We haven't settled on the program order yet; in a few days I'll discuss with Rosé whether he wants to play Webern's violin pieces on the same concert with your and Zemlinsky's quartet, in which case the program would be: I$^{st}$ [concert] Zemlinsky, possibly me, Webern's violin pieces, your F♯-minor Quartet. II$^{nd}$ concert, the Czechs (piano) and songs by Zemlinsky, Schreker (Bittner?)[8] and your George Songs. (Of course the order will be different in the actual concerts and hasn't been determined yet. But if Rosé wants to perform Webern's violin pieces alone on the II$^{nd}$ concert the programs would be I.) F♯-minor Quartet, George Songs, Zemlinsky quartet. II.) Czechs, Schreker, (Bittner), Webern's violin pieces, my sonata.) Perhaps you'll let us know how you feel about this ordering. As soon as the question of the hall has been settled (if there are no rehearsals in the large Musikvereinsaal, the 2 concerts are to take place in the small hall), we want to publish programs and posters, but for that we need the program order.

But I shan't weary you any longer, dear, kind Herr Schönberg, and will close. I am to send you and your esteemed wife and the dear little ones my wife's warmest regards. She shares my happiness that the coming fall holds such bright prospects for you.

Your grateful, devoted Alban Berg

---

7. The pianist Richard Goldschmied taught at the New Vienna Conservatory; he was the second husband of Martha Winternitz-Dorda.

8. In a letter of 13 April Berg had mentioned Paul Königer's idea of including a composition by Bittner in the unofficial festival concerts.

## Berg to Schoenberg

Wednesday
Vienna, 5 June [1912]

Again in haste, dear Herr Schönberg, since the concert arrangements, proofreading, etc., don't leave me a minute.

Yesterday we had the meeting in the small Musikvereinsaal, which was poorly attended but nonetheless successful. Those present signed for about 1,700 kronen of tickets (among them Loos for 500 kronen). We will print new circulars with the signatures of all those present yesterday (about 20–30) and all the subscriptions gathered to date, with a call for _further_ pledges. So that in my opinion the thing is already assured. Considering that potential ticket sales in the large hall amount to 8,000 kronen anyway, and that the concert will _surely be sold out,_ all these measures are probably superfluous. But they can't hurt!—

So _our_ concerts are assured. Steuermann[1] has written me and I him. Frau Winternitz, who is presently not in Hamburg, will be advised to travel via Berlin. I hope she'll be able to do so. Posters[2] go up in the next few days; I'll send you one! I am very sad indeed that you, my dear, kind Herr Schönberg, won't come to Vienna in June—that means I probably won't see you until fall. I must leave for the country soon, since my health is again completely shattered. Now I'm even getting asthma in Hietzing!—But I mustn't be ungrateful: after all it's almost too overwhelming that you'll be returning to Vienna for good in the fall!!—

Yesterday I attended a private Strindberg lecture by Kraus.[3] I was extremely distressed and disappointed——and embittered!! 2 pages, without any warmth—though I didn't fully understand them after just one hearing—and criticizing Strindberg's relationship to women, preceded the reading of excerpts _from the Fackel_ (of course). Of course they were declamatory achievements of the 1st order, but nothing _more!_ It may well be that Kraus knows no _more_ of Strindberg than the excerpts in the _Fackel!_ It's shameful!!

Naturally for Nestroy 30 pages aren't enough and excerpts from his _complete_ works.[4]—I'm fed up with Kraus!!

———————————————

The 1st set of _Gurrelieder_ piano score proofs is out now! 238 pages! Proofreading at U.E. is going slowly, Hertzka now has an "assistant" for Wöss! Polnauer has been left high and dry. Likewise an excellent copyist, Kornfeld,[5] whom Mahler particularly liked and whom Hertzka swindled so badly on a big job that over the summer he had to take up hauling bricks! He's the one who copied Bien's piano reduction. Now he's copying a gigantic score of Mandl's. Magnificent, as if engraved.——None of that is relevant here, but I was so moved when he told me this not long ago (he copied the Zemlinsky songs for me), that I had to tell you! —

1. The pianist Eduard Steuermann studied in Berlin with Busoni 1911–14 and with Schoenberg 1912–14. He had agreed to travel to Vienna to accompany Schoenberg's George Songs in the unofficial music festival.

2. Designed by Egon Schiele.

3. Karl Kraus gave a lecture in Strindberg's memory under the auspices of the Akademischer Verband on 4 June. His introduction was subsequently reprinted in the _Fackel_ XIV / 351–53 (21 June 1912), 1–3, along with a listing of the Strindberg excerpts read at the lecture as well as all the Strindberg selections which had ever appeared in the _Fackel._

4. On 2 May Kraus delivered a lecture, likewise sponsored by the Akademischer Verband, in commemoration of the fiftieth anniversary of the death of the Austrian playwright and satirist Johann Nestroy. The lecture was reprinted in the _Fackel_ XIV / 349–350 (13 May 1912), 1–23.

5. Josef Kornfeld.

*The* Blaue Reiter Almanac, *edited by Wassily Kandinsky and Franz Marc, published by Piper Verlag in May 1912*

---

I heard privately that the *Merker* is sponsoring a <u>matinee</u> during the Music Festival: Rosé will play a Beethoven quartet—and, of all the tasteless things: Walter will play *Das Lied von der Erde* <u>on the piano</u> with Weidemann and Miller—the Vienna first performance— — —: on the piano!![6] That goes to show! Now we only need the Thern brothers[7] to follow it up with a 4-hand "execution" of Beethoven's IXth. — — — — —

I'm reveling in the *Gurrelieder* just now. (Still in Part I!) Truly, it's unbelievably magnificent, this is condensed music, as all great works are distinguished from the lesser ones in that they are saturated with music, like full, ripened fruit, ever ready to be savored in complete freshness. That's my yardstick: for example, I just took a look at Schreker's 5 Songs,[8] which Drill-Orridge[9] will sing—when I heard them at your place in Ober St. Veit I thought they weren't bad. Today they meant <u>absolutely nothing</u> to me! It, <u>too,</u> is music, but not music in the above sense. Not only do I feel this in my soul, but I could explain it theoretically as well!!

As to the "Herzgewächse," which I got a while ago in the *Blauer Reiter*[10] . . . words fail me! Absolutely godlike—God-inspired— — —

Yours in devoted reverence Alban Berg

---

6. The matinee concert planned by the *Merker* did not take place. However, a concert series under the periodical's auspices was inaugurated the following season.

7. Willy and Louis Thern were renowned duo-pianists. Louis Thern taught at the Academy; Willy Thern had died in April of the previous year.

8. Schreker's "Fünf Gesänge für tiefe Stimme," completed in May 1909.

9. The English alto Theo Drill-Orridge.

10. Schoenberg's "Herzgewächse" was first published in the *Blaue Reiter* Almanac.

## Berg to Schoenberg

[Vienna] 22 June 1912

Just briefly, dear Herr Schönberg, as I am really so busy (the concerts, *Gurre-lieder* score, and subscription drive), that I only find time, that is, <u>must</u> find time for the unpleasant letters and simply <u>don't</u> have time for the pleasant ones, letters to you, my dear Herr Schönberg.

There was another *Gurrelieder* meeting yesterday: poorly attended as usual, but we reached a pretty firm decision. The performance is to be 12 December 1912 (that's something to interpret: 12.XII.12) Open dress rehearsal possibly 11 December. Tickets for the performance 20, 15, 10, 8, 6, 4, 3, 2 kronen. As to the participants: The Akademischer Gesangsverein, which is to sing the II[nd] and III[rd] men's choruses (the men from the Philharmonic Chorus will sing the I[st]), has not yet agreed: some of them resist "collaborating" on a concert! What nonsense! I think they'll come around!

Winternitz is definitely singing <u>Tove,</u> although Schreker thinks one won't be able to hear her! Of course I contradicted him! The reason it was hard to hear her in the Delius Mass[1] was due to the dreadful orchestration of the work!

They don't want Winternitz as Waldtaube, it would be anticlimactic. Your wishes regarding Cahier, Kittel,[2] Wenger,[3] which Webern conveyed, were not sufficiently respected, they seem set on Mildenburg. Not only because of the drawing power, but also because she probably wouldn't ask a fee. It is also <u>my,</u> of course insignificant, opinion that Mildenburg would be very fine artistically as well, an incredible crowning touch to Part II. And she only has a guest contract at the Opera and is therefore <u>easily</u> available. Generally it's risky to try and get opera singers for 2 concerts! But Schreker thinks the Volksoper is riskier still! So for the time being he won't contact Ritter[4] for the Klaus-Narr role (he doesn't think him suitable anyway), but will ask Preuss,[5] who is at least musical and has a beautiful voice: for the Bauer they're considering Wyss,[6] who has an extremely large range and is musical.

Finally, Waldemar. Piccaver[7] cannot be located, doesn't seem to be in Prague any longer, although I wrote there (to Zemlinsky). Anyway, Schreker heard that he's very unmusical. "Burrian" was considered! Now they're going to wire Slezak to see whether he will be in Vienna on 12 December. Loos will mediate. Maybe he'll take the part! But Schreker is also going to contact Miller.

I'm telling you this in such detail, dear Herr Schönberg, because I take it that you want to be able to veto one or the other decision before it's too late, which is something <u>I</u> of course can't do, partly because I'm not sure whom you want and partly because no one would agree with <u>me,</u> or take <u>my</u> advice!—

1. Frederick Delius' *Mass of Life* was first performed in Vienna on 18 February 1911 by the Philharmonic Chorus under Schreker.
2. The Austrian actress and alto Hermine Kittel was engaged at the Vienna Court Opera 1900–30.
3. The alto Clothilde Wenger was engaged at the Vienna Volksoper.
4. The German tenor Rudolf Ritter was engaged at the Vienna Volksoper 1910–13.
5. The German tenor Arthur Preuss was engaged at the Vienna Court Opera 1908–15, after which he went to the Vienna Volksoper until 1930.
6. The bass Robert Wyss taught voice privately in Vienna.
7. The English tenor Alfred Piccaver was engaged at the Vienna Court Opera 1912–37.

We're in the middle of the Musikfestwoche now, though my contact with it is pretty much limited to the silly drivel I read in the papers. I have completely immersed myself in Mahler's IX[th], which has appeared in a 4-hand arrangement.[8] This is music no longer of this world. <u>Mysteriously</u> beautiful and magnificent. I shudder at the thought of being able to hear this music on Wednesday. It is a mysterious miracle of nature.——Our I[st] concert is Tuesday: Suk, Zemlinsky, your George Songs,* Schreker songs, Novák.

Winternitz arrived in Vienna the day before yesterday and has already consulted with Rosé. I assume Steuermann is coming Sunday?!

> The II[nd] concert is Saturday the 29th:
> Zemlinsky Quartet
> my Sonata
> Webern's Violin Pieces
> <u>your</u> Quartet.

I'm already quite satisfied with Goldschmied. I think he'll do it very well.

He would very much like to learn your piano things, too, to rehearse with you and, if you're satisfied, perform them!

—Have you, dear Herr Schönberg, seen the Akademischer Verband booklet. I think it's called "Das festliche Wien," or something like that. Stefan in the forefront, of course! But there's an unknown picture of Mahler in it and Kokoschka's portrait drawing of Webern, which is splendid. There's also said to be a very enthusiastic article by Linke about Webern and me. Then there's a funny, telling juxtaposition by Polnauer of reviews of Mozart's C-major, Beethoven's F-major, and your F♯-minor Quartet. And some other things.[9]

As soon as it's out I'll sen you one, dear Herr Schönberg.—

Our concert will be announced in the next *Fackel*.[10]—

I must close, Buschbeck is waiting for me in the café[11] and after that the *Gurrelieder* proofs (incredibly faulty) await me.

In most profound gratitude and devotion,

Your Berg

* the George Songs arrived 2 hours after Königer's telegram.

---

8. The four-hand arrangement of Mahler's Ninth Symphony was published by Universal Edition. The world premiere of the work took place on 26 June with the Vienna Philharmonic Orchestra under Bruno Walter, as part of the Vienna Music Festival.

9. The brochure published by the Akademischer Verband, *Das Musikfestliche Wien* (June 1912), included contributions by Paul Stefan, Schreker, Stefan Zweig, and Ludwig Ullmann. Linke's article on Webern and Berg was the first study on either composer. Polnauer's contribution, "Der Künstler und die Zeitgenossen" (The Artist and his Contemporaries), was unsigned.

10. The concert was advertised on the back flyleaf of the *Fackel* XIV / 351–53 (21 June 1912).

11. Berg and Buschbeck, who both lived in Vienna's thirteenth district of Hietzing, most likely met in the Café Gröpl on Hietzinger Platz, a favorite meeting place of members of the Akademischer Verband (so much so, that they were known as the "Café Gröpl Circle").

*Poster by Egon Schiele for the concert of Living Austrian Composers, June 1912 (Musiksammlung der Österreichischen Nationalbibliothek)*

## Berg to Schoenberg

Vienna [25 June 1912]

Dear Herr Schönberg,

This time just a short hasty report: I'm so tired after 2 rehearsals of Mahler's IX[th], a rehearsal with Winternitz in the Beethovensaal, and finally now the I[st] concert, that I can't report fully. Our I[st] concert was very beautiful.[1] Your George Songs were unquestionably the high point (everyone said so). It was apparent even super-ficially. They received the loudest, longest, and most enthusiastic applause. After-wards Frau Winternitz had to take 3 bows (Steuermann 1 or 2 as well), whereas the other numbers received at most 1 or 2, even Schreker, the only composer present, who appeared on stage twice. Frau Winternitz sang beautifully; Steuermann is a splendid pianist and a very dear fellow (he'll have a lot to tell you about Vienna, especially about a piano which couldn't be located until 4 o'clock that afternoon). I had 2 rehearsals with Frau Winternitz, the first a three-hour one at my place, during which I believe many rhythmic and dynamic details became clearer. We also rehearsed Zemlinsky's songs (which none of us knew) until we were able to form an opinion of these fine works. They weren't terribly successful. Nor were the Suk pieces, which I liked pretty well and which are very fine (though really quite French!). Novák's were more successful; they were real virtuoso piano pieces, bril-liant, rippling (as you once remarked to me) but, it seemed to me, **real music** notwithstanding! Štěpán played these fairly melancholy works very well. And with

1. The program of the first concert of the unofficial music festival, which took place on 25 June in the Beethoven Hall, consisted of:

| | |
|---|---|
| Suk: | Two selections from "Vom Mütterchen," Op. 28; Three selections from *Erlebtes und Erträumtes*, Op. 30 (Václav Štěpán, piano) |
| Zemlinsky: | Maeterlinck Songs, Nos. 1, 2, 3, and 5 (Martha Winternitz-Dorda, alto; Eduard Steuermann, piano) |
| Schreker: | *Fünf Gesänge* (Theo Drill-Orridge, alto; Clemens Krauss, piano) |
| Schoenberg: | George Songs, Op. 15 (Winternitz-Dorda, soprano, Eduard Steuermann, piano) |
| Novák: | Two selections from *Pan*, Op. 42 (Václav Štěpán, piano) |

97

a vocal beauty more <u>conscious</u> than real, Drill-Orridge sang the Schreker songs, which owe their success, it now seems to me, more to a superficial than an inner radiance.

The concert was not very well attended. The hall is too large. But one saw many important people. The Rosés, Loos, Fried, Gutmann;[2] of the critics: Korngold, Specht, Bach, Bienenfeld, Rudolf Stefan Hoffmann, Konta, and probably others whom I don't know as well and didn't notice. (Gütersloh,[3] the poet of *Glaube und Heimat*,[4] my pianist Goldschmied, who is a **very sincere** admirer of yours, and probably many more.)

The concert lasted until 10 o'clock, almost everyone stayed to the end (when Novák's pieces were played). (Rosé liked everything very much, strangely enough the piano things most of all, apart from the George Songs which seem to have moved him deeply.)

There is even greater interest in the II$^{nd}$ concert in the important social circles (Mahler clique, etc.), though at the moment the prospects for ticket sales aren't very good (probably because of the 2 holidays, the 29$^{th}$ and 30$^{th}$).[5] Already I'm very much looking forward to your Quartet and Webern's Violin Pieces.

I liked the George Songs more than ever; I always thought them the most wonderful things and had fancied I understood them, but I now realize I still have a long way to go for a deeper understanding of these enchantingly beautiful pieces. And there are no doubt many who feel the same way. Our understanding and our hearts are almost too limited for the grandeur of such art!—

All in all a successful evening, and even outwardly, socially, something of an event that didn't pass unnoticed, but definitely left an impression on the music world.—

9:30 tomorrow morning, dress rehearsal for Mahler's 9$^{th}$, which is <u>not</u> open to the public; thanks to Frau Mahler's and Rosé's thoughtfulness we can attend all the rehearsals. But we also got Walter's permission. It's impossible for me to write about the work itself. Even in the so-called lighter movements (II$^{nd}$, III$^{rd}$) it represents the deepest, most unfathomable emotion for me. The performance is this evening!

Many, many warm and devoted regards in highest esteem,

from your grateful Berg

(Piano score of the quartet movements has arrived.) Rosé is presently rehearsing with Frau Winternitz.

---

2. The banker Max Gutmann.
3. The Austrian artist Albert Paris von Gütersloh.
4. The author of this 1910 historical drama was Karl Schönherr.
5. In 1912 the double holiday of the Feast of Saints Peter and Paul on 29 June fell on a Saturday.

*Berg to Schoenberg (postcard)*

Saturday night
[Vienna] [29 June 1912]

It's so frightfully late, dear, kind Herr Schönberg, that I can't tell you fully about the concert. Just this much: The success grew from piece to piece. First the Zemlinsky Quartet, then my Sonata, then Webern's Violin Pieces, which were **very** effective despite some stupid opposition (laughers, whom Rosé immediately reprimanded and Loos actually expelled from the hall), finally your Quartet, which was unanimously successful, the response growing more fervent with every movement and finally becoming absolutely frenetic.[1] You will get the card with the signatures of the best of those in attendance[2] and Webern will soon tell you everything else in person, dear Herr Schönberg! Of the critics I saw Specht, Konta, Hoffmann; also present were Schreker, Frau Mahler, Kokoschka, etc. Fabulous performance, especially the 2nd movement!— —

Now 10,000 heartfelt and devoted regards

Your Berg

1. The program of the second concert of the unofficial music festival consisted of:
Zemlinsky: String Quartet in A major, Op. 4 (Rosé Quartet)
Berg: Piano Sonata, Op. 1 (Richard Goldschmied, piano)
Webern: Four Pieces for Violin and Piano (Arnold Rosé, violin; Anton Webern, piano)
Schoenberg: Second String Quartet, Op. 10 (Rosé Quartet with Martha Winternitz-Dorda, soprano).
2. The card, dated 29 June, included greetings and signatures of Webern, Alma Mahler, Arnold Rosé, Justine Rosé, Martha Winternitz-Dorda, Paul and Gretta Stefan, Erwin Stein, Alban and Helene Berg, Heinrich and Johanna Jalowetz, Irene Bien, Paul and Maria Königer, Josef Polnauer, Carl von Webern, Ernst Dietz, and Oskar Kokoschka.

*Schoenberg to Berg (picture postcard: Ostseebad Carlshagen)*

Carlshagen,[1] [c. 4 July 1912]

Warm regards, dear Berg, to you and your wife.—I'm returning *Gurre* to you uncorrected![2]—Hertzka is behaving basely![3]—I shall not come to Vienna. I turned it down on Sunday.[4] There were interpellations in Parliament, I understand. What happened after that? Newspapers, etc.? I hope next time you send me a card it won't contain something as boorish as what Kokoschka wrote on the last one.[5] I was annoyed all day!

Warm regards

Your Arnold Schönberg

Who has the George Songs? I need them!!

1. Schoenberg spent six weeks of his vacation in Carlshagen, on the island of Usedom in the Baltic Sea.
2. Berg informed Schoenberg in a letter of 2 July 1912, that Universal Edition had mistakenly sent the second set of proofs for Part I of the *Gurrelieder* to Schoenberg before he had a chance to correct them.
3. Schoenberg's correspondence with Hertzka at this time concerns his insistence that the George Songs, Op. 15, be printed and a decision reached on the Chamber Symphony.
4. Schoenberg had been approached about a position at the Vienna Academy in June, which he declined in a 29 June letter to Karl von Wiener. The question of Schoenberg's appointment had become entwined with the internal politics of the Academy and the effects of a general reorganization undertaken by Director Wilhelm Bopp and President Karl von Wiener. The affair was the subject of heated discussion in the newspapers and led to a 27 June interpellation in the Austrian Parliament.
5. On the 29 June postcard following the second festival concert Kokoschka had written, "Today I believed in you for the first time!"

*Berg to Schoenberg*

Vienna, 5 July 1912

I herewith return the newly corrected piano score to you dear Herr Schönberg. Of course I corrected the passages you indicated, and in places calling for a major change, where I wasn't sure I had hit on the right solution, I either corrected in pencil or merely pasted it on in such a way that it can be torn off again. For the most part these are passages you yourself corrected, dear Herr Schönberg, among them the fabulous solution at (30) in the III^rd movement.

Steuermann's solutions, which were enclosed with the piano scores, I treated differently. Since I'm not sure these solutions of various passages are good, and, in fact, don't even know whether you, dear Herr Schönberg, approved of them, I couldn't make up my mind to incorporate them into the score as the final solution in place of my own. That's why I merely pasted them in and permitted myself a critique of each solution. So it remains for you to decide, dear Herr Schönberg, since in some cases it really is impossible for me to do so on my own. In my opinion none of Steuermann's solutions immediately amazes one with its simplicity and obviousness (Columbus and the egg) as does your solution, e.g. at measure (30) in the III^rd movement, they are merely more or less successful attempts to deal with difficult passages. Of course I unfortunately have to admit the inadequacy of many of my solutions, too, and couldn't come up with anything better this time, either, despite hours (truly) of trying. I'm all the more pained, dear kind Herr Schönberg, as it has meant and will mean so much aggravation for you. But this is due in part to an excusable misunderstanding in the beginning when you commissioned the scores from me. At that time you defined as the "main objective of the score" that it be "absolutely easy to play," leading me to assume that the difficulties should not be kept in even relative proportion to the difficulties of the work, but that the result was to be an absolutely simple piano score—which I consider the Wagner piano scores to be, e.g., or of the newer ones: the Debussy, even the Strauss scores, all of which are easier to play than the quartet reduction Steuermann has in mind. I thoroughly understand that it's not to be an easy score of that kind, but rather a transcription of the quartet song into a piano song, and that it is no matter if there are piano passages that only a first rate pianist can play,* as long as they sound good, i.e., are idiomatic for the piano. My initial misunderstanding of your intentions was the reason for both the faulty score and the enormous annoyance caused you before the result could correspond with your wishes. I hope it's not far off now. Next time I'll do better from the outset; after all, I've learned so much from this.—

—

Also enclosed the George Songs and 2 reviews of our concerts.

My departure is imminent and as soon as you have decided one way or the other with regard to the piano scores, please be so kind as to let me know at "Berghof," Post Annenheim, Ossiachersee, Carinthia. I assume you will also have come to a decision regarding the proofs of the *Gurrelieder* score.

Excuse my great haste and accept my very warmest regards in devotion and gratitude

Your Berg

Please convey my best regards to your esteemed wife and the dear little ones. Likewise my wife's very warmest regards to you and your wife! *[in Schoenberg's handwriting:]* must answer about score

* as for example the VIII^th George song or passages in the XV^th

## Schoenberg to Berg *(postcard)*

Carlshagen [6 July 1912]

Dear Berg,

I'm sending you the *Gurrelieder* uncorrected. I did glance at it. There seem to be incredibly many errors. However, much of it seems incorrectly copied from the full score!! I think you'll definitely have to check it once more against the full score, which is presently in Vienna!! I think you frequently misread transposing instruments and various other things. Perhaps prior to the last set of proofs! Did I already tell you that I have refused the Academy?

Warm regards

Schönberg

## Berg to Schoenberg

Berghof, 9 July 1912

Arrived here yesterday to find your 2 kind cards from Carlshagen. The news that you are not coming to Vienna plunged me into complete inner turmoil. Is it really final? Didn't Wiener answer immediately and convince you anew that all these interpellations and other attempts by various idiots have absolutely no meaning in the face of so much as one person's and Bopp's and all sensible people's wishes and decisions!?! Surely Webern or Jalowetz told you how completely insignificant the matter is (the interpellation), how Rosé doesn't attribute the slightest significance to it, that such interpellations generally have no effect whatsoever, as has already become apparent: since the report in the papers (which, by the way, named no names, but spoke only of representatives of a modern movement), there hasn't been another word, clearest proof that it was only the pitiful attempt of one person to sabotage something solid. Please, dear Herr Schönberg, let me know somehow, preferably through Jalowetz,[1] whose address I don't know (or I would have asked him myself), how the matter with the Academy now stands. I still can't believe that nothing has come of this most cherished hope of recent years, the disappointment would be too

1. Heinrich Jalowetz had just completed the conducting season in Danzig and was vacationing with Schoenberg in Carlshagen.

overwhelming. I'm in frantic distress!!——You must not consider me so selfish that, having once realized your decision is irrevocable, I, too, wouldn't realize that what you think and decide and do is for the best; but my great sorrow at the very thought that you won't be in Vienna next year—meaning I'll continue to live separated from you—has already seized hold of me and plunged me into a state of utter distress. Perhaps Webern already knows more, then no doubt he'll let me know. And add to that this great distance: I believe it takes 3–4 days for a letter to traverse the length of Europe.—

I'm most impatiently awaiting the *Gurrelieder* score you were going to send me. I'm very unhappy that there are still so many errors. The engraver must have left in half of the ones I had corrected. Well, I have the first proofs here with my corrections and can compare them as soon as I receive your copy. But I can hardly believe that there are also major mistakes of mine. Not that I doubt that I may occasionally have erred in transposing, but how could this have happened of all places in Part I, which is based so heavily on your own reduction and surely can't contain that sort of error. Of course most of the errors stem from Hertzka's dreadful copyist, whose mistakes are simply multiplied in the engraving process. That's why I compared the 1st proofs with your score of Part I. At most there may be a few mistakes in the complicated preludes and interludes, for which I would need the full score. I didn't know it was in Vienna——I'll now proofread it again very thoroughly, mark the questionable passages, then send you the reduction, and while you go through it you can mark the errors I missed and send it to Wöss, who will be the last to look at these IInd proofs anyway, with the note, "check full score, Schönberg." I believe this entire mix-up has been caused by Hertzka's tight-fistedness, since he obviously wanted to "cut corners" again. And I gather from your card that he has again been (not just stupid, but also) "base." Now I understand his wary demeanor when I was last there to see him: his guilty conscience!! From your card I can imagine how vilely he must have treated you. It concerns the publication of the "George Songs" which "you need," doesn't it? This, along with the reduction of the quartet songs, were sent to Zehlendorf on 5 July as a registered package, I have the receipt. It was Winternitz's copy. Didn't Steuermann send his copy?!

I must close, the postman is waiting. I don't think I left out anything important. As to the most important thing: I hope I'll soon hear your decision on your coming to Vienna. This uncertainty is frightful.

I wish you a wonderful summer at the seaside, dear, kind Herr Schönberg, and send many, many regards.

Always with you in my thoughts,

Your Berg

*Schoenberg to Berg (postcard)*

Carlshagen, 11 July 1912

Dear Berg,

I wrote to the president explaining in great detail that it was my irrevocable(!) decision not to come to Vienna, so he had no alternative but to accept it. He wrote to me politely and not uncordially.—It goes without saying that I am sorry I won't be able to see my friends. Very sorry in fact! But I had no choice. That business with the interpellations was only of minor importance. The main reason is: my aversion to Vienna. I still don't know whether I did the right thing, for I'm certainly in no way provided for here. But at any rate I immediately felt much better.—

Why do you write so infrequently. Do write, even if I don't answer right away. I'm working on a number of projects, so I don't have much spare time. You must know that I always enjoy hearing from you!!!—

Best regards to your wife, also from my wife.

Your Arnold Schönberg

*Berg to Schoenberg (picture postcard: "Berghof" am Ossiachersee)*

[Berghof, 16 July 1912]

Dear Herr Schönberg,

It just occurred to me: the piano score <u>must</u> be numbered. ☐ to ☐. I think each part should begin with 1! But how??! Every 10 measures would be easiest but senseless! U.E. could easily do that. But perhaps I should do it as in Mahler's VIII$^{th}$? According to the music! Regardless of whether it's 9 or only 7 measures sometimes, or even just 3 or 4?! Simply according to the practical considerations of studying and rehearsing, i.e., with entrances, rests, cadences, and phrase beginnings, etc., in mind. It goes without saying that I myself would undertake numbering of <u>this</u> kind; I could incorporate it into Parts II and III right now, which I'll have corrected in 2–3 days and will then send you. I'm waiting to get Part I from you, anyway, and would add the numbering there, too. Please be so kind as to let me know what you decide, dear Herr Schönberg.

Many warm, devoted regards

from your Berg

## Schoenberg to Berg (postcard)

[Carlshagen, 23 July 1912]

Dear Berg,

I forgot: please enter rehearsal numbers as follows: a number every $10^{th}$ measure (thereby representing multiples of ten), thus at the $10^{th}$ measure 1

| at the | | | |
|--------|------------------|------------|-----------|
| at the | $20^{th}$ measure | | 2 |
| " | $30^{th}$ | " | 3 |
| " | $40^{th}$ | " | 4 |
| | — | | |
| | — | | |
| | — | | |
| " | $240^{th}$ | " | 24 |
| " | $1,280^{th}$ | " | 128 |
| " | $34,270^{th}$ | " | 3,427 |
| " | $928,790^{th}$ | " | 92,879 |
| " | $4,635,220^{th}$ | " | 463,522 |
| " | $82,756,930^{th}$ | " | 8,275,693 |

etc.—I hope that's clear. I consider this system of numbering practical because then it's easy to see whether a measure is missing in any part! Now: I sent you the proofs of Part I long ago. I shall demand reclamation myself. You do the same and wire me. Perhaps you should ask U.E. for a new copy right away. Incidentally, the choral parts are to be copied from the full score! That's much more reliable!! Also, Hertzka told me they would be engraved!! What a. . . .! I am really very sorry that you are so unwell.[1] Maybe you should take better care of yourself! I hope with all my heart that you feel better very soon.

Your Arnold Schönberg

---

1. In a letter of 20 July 1912 and again on 23 July Berg wrote of his "complete physical breakdown," caused by asthma, jaundice, and exhaustion.

## Schoenberg to Berg (postcard)

Stettin, 10 August 1912

Dear Berg,

As you see I have already left Carlshagen: beginning of term. I'm a slave to the Prussian school year. At present I'm visiting Webern (until tomorrow evening) and am very pleased with how lovely his place is.[1]—I received Gurre proofs. I won't be able to finish them until Zehlendorf. I'll be there Monday (12 August).

Warm regards

Schönberg

1. Webern had accepted a conducting position at the Stettin Stadttheater as of 22 June 1912. Between 10 and 12 August the Schoenbergs stopped off in Stettin on their way back to Berlin. While there, Schoenberg heard Webern conduct Leo Fall's operetta, Dollar Prinzessin.

## Berg to Schoenberg

Berghof, 12 August [1912]

Dear esteemed Herr Schönberg,

I thank you very much and most warmly for your 2 dear cards (on the high seas and from Rügen), the outing must have been wonderful![1] I would have answered right away, dear Herr Schönberg, if there hadn't been so many time-consuming and health-robbing vexations here recently. Without warning I found myself embroiled in a morass of the most repugnant family matters and can't wait to get away from it all. We leave here tomorrow and then my address will be:

> Alban Berg c/o Nahowski
> Trahütten in Styria
> Post: Deutsch Landsberg
> on the Graz-Köflach Rail Line

Apart from the quarrels, these last days here have been more pleasant to the extent that my health has been much better than at first and I was able to enjoy something of "country life;" of course I didn't find the peace to work, but hope to be able to compose something in Trahütten.

I've been doing some kite flying here. I was sent a wonderful and very unusually designed kite about 3 meters high and 3 meters wide that can do amazing things. I find this activity so interesting because I believe it helps one understand the problems of flying. Because it's my opinion that today's airplanes, despite their incredible achievements, are based on the wrong principle. The fact alone that progress is gauged only in terms of ever greater speed and altitude records and increased carrying capacity, while the airplane itself is no more stable today than the first ones were, in other words the fact that there is not the slightest safety in that regard— that storms, indeed any small, unforeseen, or even expected gust makes flying impossible, so that most of the great pilots who haven't gotten themselves killed prefer to retire from flying—Bleriot,[2] for example, only builds planes now (as a business) and leaves flying to those who do it either out of adventurousness or because their profession (officers) requires proof of courage (which in this case amounts to foolhardiness): for me that fact alone is sufficient proof of the above. But I've always noticed that birds not only do not fly worse in strong wind and storm, but on the contrary much better, just as a piece of wood loses none of its buoyancy in turbulent seas. If our pilots could really fly the way the piece of wood floats, indeed like the swimmer who swims more effortlessly in waves than in still water, then they would never run the risk of crashing, but at worst that of not being able to fight against the storm; but of course our technology is so far advanced that if the machine were stable—which it's not, that's something that's just simulated by the pilots'

---

1. Schoenberg had sent Berg two picture postcards from Rügen, both with the postmark 7 August 1912. The first card was signed by Mathilde Schoenberg, Stein, Heinrich and Johanna Jalowetz, and Ite and Erna Liebenthal; the second card bore the same signatures, as well as those of Karl Horwitz and Irene Bien.

2. The French engineer Louis Bleriot was the first to fly over the English Channel in 1909 in an airplane of his own design.

acrobatics—it would surely be possible to fly against a strong wind, just as our steamships travel against the current.

Now the kite, which is also heavier than air, proves to me that it is possible to fly—(of course, since it's without a propeller: not in the desired direction, but only as the wind blows)—despite, indeed because of the wind, and despite the weight of the heavy string it's dragging behind it, indeed despite the opposing force of this taut string, which actually seems necessary, for without such an opposing force the kite wouldn't fly at all: in other words it not only transcends gravity but also a force operating—not against the force of gravity (as in the case of balloons—but with gravity, in fact an even stronger force, since I need all my strength to keep the kite at an altitude of about 200 meters. A child would have been lifted up by it. But when it tore itself from my wind-torn fingers, instead of flying higher it sank slowly in the direction of the wind. Therefore I conclude, without quite knowing why, that rather than having to overcome gravity, flying requires a force external to the flying object (perhaps external to ourselves, for which reason it may never be possible to fly). On the other hand it's possible for forces to operate on objects external to ourselves, that is, without a direct connection like the kite's string: electricity, magnetism, light and heat rays or waves— — —indeed, as the ultimate ideal: transmission of will, powers of attraction—telepathy.— —Causing an empathetic being to fly toward one through the power of one's innermost thoughts: Seraphita and Minna on the insurmountable peak of the Fallberg.[3]

I'm so deeply involved in this matter that I have unintentionally introduced and thoroughly discussed something without knowing whether you, dear Herr Schönberg, are even interested in it at the moment. But I'm sure you won't take these remarks ill, born as they are of the need to share my thoughts with you. I almost feel transported back to the times I took walks with you in the Karlsplatz and discussed everything that preoccupied me. Actually only the distance has changed and as ever I feel myself walking at your side, even if the sound of your words doesn't reach me. But what sort of consolation is that when you're in Berlin and I'm in Vienna?!

I'm very eager to know what's happening with the *Gurrelieder*. Have you gone through it? Were there still many errors? When will it be sent to U.E.?

A word from you would be very reassuring!

And now many very warm and devoted regards, also to your esteemed wife, also all the best from my wife.

from your grateful and always faithful Alban Berg

3. Berg's reference is to the second section of Balzac's *Seraphita*. Berg had recently learned from Webern of Schoenberg's plan to use the Balzac text for a major stage work.

## Schoenberg to Berg

Berlin-Zehlendorf, 15 August 1912

Dear Berg,

I have received *Gurrelieder*, Part I. I'll finish proofreading and will probably send it to U.E. today still.—From now on send all manuscripts, packages, etc., with a declared value of 1,000 kronen. Otherwise there's no assurance they'll arrive. I am missing a certified letter that contained money and a package in which I had sent the manuscript of *Pierrot lunaire* to Frau Zehme! Packages valued at less than 600 marks get treated differently and could easily get stolen.

—Your conclusion about the flight of kites is wrong. Flight is not caused by your pulling on the string, but by the position of the kite in relation to the wind. As soon as you let go, the kite positions itself in such a way that it no longer catches the wind and then naturally it falls. It only gains altitude against the resistance of the air. It's just the same in sailing: if you let go of the rope that regulates the position of the sail, the sail will turn. Of course you are absolutely right in what you say about the stability of airplanes and about the flight of birds. But in the case of birds, stability is probably achieved because adjustment to every change of air pressure is made not by a machine but by a sensitive living organism. This almost unconscious adjustment is more effective than the most finely tuned machine. You can observe that in many similar instances. For example when singing, or still better: when whistling. Do you have any idea how you manage to produce exactly the desired pitch? And yet with such certainty! We cannot give our machines a soul, and only the soul, emotion can: maintain equilibrium. Reason fails. Capsizes. Only the immaterial possesses stability.—

—You did an excellent job of proofreading the *Gurrelieder*. There were only a few errors left. In fact I'm extremely pleased with the reduction, though it's very difficult. It is often very imaginative and ingenious. So is the one of the quartet. Only that one is <u>intentionally</u> too easy.—I have to proofread now; enough for today and warm regards

Your Arnold Schönberg

## Berg to Schoenberg

Trahütten, 19 August 1912

Thank you very much, dear Herr Schönberg, for your dear letter. I'm very happy that you are satisfied with the proofs and the reduction, I'm already very much looking forward to its publication. (Just to prevent any misunderstanding, I repeat that I sent off Parts II and III about 4 weeks ago and you, dear Herr Schönberg, probably corrected these 2 parts before Part I; I only mention this: because in your letter you mention only Part I!)

From now on I'll never send manuscripts, etc., without a value declaration of at least 1,000 marks. *[Berg discusses postal insurance.]* Have your missing things been found: the certified letter and *Pierrot lunaire?* I assume you have a copy of the latter!

Otherwise it would be terrible!! I hope you were at least well compensated! I mean for the certified letter and the copy of *Pierrot lunaire*, as well as for the package sent to me with the *Gurrelieder* (Part I). The possibility that your only copy of the melodrama was lost is absolutely unthinkable! I can't even imagine such a thing, it's as if I saw someone sitting at an open window in a 5th floor apartment; I get dizzy at the thought!

Naturally I understand my error with regard to kite flying. What you said about the adjustments birds make in flight, about living organisms in general, is wonderful! Particularly the sentence: "Only the immaterial possesses stability"; I consider that one of the greatest truths, from which many others can be derived.—

I've become acclimated to this place now, too, and feel very fit physically and emotionally. The countryside here is uniquely beautiful, the air heavenly! I hope to compose something soon, since there's plenty of peace and quiet! Otherwise there's nothing to tell, dear Herr Schönberg. I myself get much of what I know of the musical world from the papers and then pass it on to you. For instance the news of Schreker's appointment as professor, which I must amend to the extent that it's only provisional:

> The Minister of Education has provisionally appointed the conductor of the Vienna Philharmonic Chorus, Franz Schreker, to a position teaching music theory and composition at the Academy for Music and Art.
>
> Personal News, *Neue Freie Presse*[1]

By the way, the premiere of the *Ferne Klang* took place yesterday in Frankfurt, and I'm curious to know how it went. Or was it postponed again?[2]

Enclosed I'm also sending you, dear Herr Schönberg, 2 feuilletons that may interest you. Particularly the one about Strauss! All of the other *Parsifal* articles are impossible once one has read your essay.[3] It should be printed in some newspaper! So it could be read more widely than in the calendar.

I found something else in the *Neue Freie Presse* that will confirm you, dear Herr Schönberg, (and of course me as well) in the feeling that you were right not to have accepted the appointment in Vienna:

> The Vienna Konzertverein has concluded a new contract with its conductor, Ferdinand Löwe, which commits the artist to further activities for Vienna and

---

1. Of 15 August 1912.

2. The Frankfurt premiere of *Der ferne Klang*, originally scheduled for the previous spring, took place on 18 August.

3. Richard Wagner had stipulated that *Parsifal* never be performed outside Bayreuth. On 1 January 1914 the copyright was due to expire and a debate arose whether a special law should be enacted to protect the opera from performances elsewhere. The two feuilletons Berg sent were most likely Hermann Bahr's "Parsifalschutz" (Protection for *Parsifal*), *Neue Freie Presse* of 15 August and Felix Weingartner's "Der freie '*Parsifal*'" (The Free *Parsifal*), *Neue Freie Presse* of 18 August, both of which supported the Bayreuth monopoly. The Strauss reference appears in Bahr's article, where he cites an appeal in favor of restricting *Parsifal* performances, "Aufruf zum Parsifalschutz" (Appeal For Protection for *Parsifal*), signed by a number of prominent artists, including Richard Strauss. Schoenberg's own *Parsifal* article, cited above (see footnote 8 to Berg's letter of 12 April 1912), gave conditional support to open performance of the work.

the Konzertverein. In consideration of Löwe's conducting activities abroad and in order to relieve him, the well-known composer and Royal Prussian conductor Paul Scheinpflug was engaged to conduct some of the regular and auxiliary concerts.[4]

Scheinpflug,[5] of course! What about Boehe?

I must close now, dear, kind Herr Schönberg, as the postman is coming and the letter would otherwise lie around one more day; besides, I really don't have anything interesting to say.

Please give my most devoted regards to your wife, also on my wife's behalf, and to you yourself our very best and warmest regards.

Your grateful and devoted Alban Berg

---

4. *Neue Freie Presse* of 18 August 1912.
5. The German conductor and composer Paul Scheinpflug.

*Berg to Schoenberg*

Trahütten, 27 August 1912

Dear Herr Schönberg,

I just received a package from the post office with Part I of the *Gurrelieder*. I assume it's the part that went astray. It was sent from Carlshagen (no date), was at the Vienna Staatsbahnhof, then at Ossiachersee (24 August 1912), from where it was forwarded to me here. Since there are still errors in it that I can remember having corrected, I can't imagine that it is a new (III$^{rd}$) set of proofs, so for now I'll keep this Part I here so as not to cause confusion at U.E., where I hope they'll soon have completed the final version. In addition to a few trivial corrections there are 2 remarks in your hand on the first page, which I assume you've already sent to U.E. The translator's correct name! (which I don't know)[1] and the remark: "without opus!." No doubt you added that to the corrected proofs I sent you!— —

Regarding myself I can tell you, dear Herr Schönberg, that my health is very good now, and that I have finally found the strength and peace of mind to work, and compose every day now. I've completed a 3$^{rd}$ orchestral song and am beginning a IV$^{th}$! In fact, I feel that my stay here marks the real beginning of my recuperation; the time at Berghof wasn't pleasant, either physically or emotionally. Here there is a wonderful sense of peace, heavenly clear air, and a region that no picture, no description can approximate. Imagine, dear Herr Schönberg, a rolling plateau, on one side inclining toward the Koralps; this chain of wonderful mountains is about 20–30 kilometers away and about 2,000 meters high and is covered with snow even now. On the other side, this plateau, on which Trahütten lies, dips down rather sharply into the plain where the small villages of the Köflach rail line lie, which

---

1. Schoenberg used the German translation of Jacobsen's poems by Robert Franz Arnold, *Jens Peter Jacobsen. Gedichte* (Leipzig, 1897).

*The Villa Nahowski in Tra-hütten*

extends all the way to Graz—at the very distant horizon one can even see Semmering. On both sides the plateau descends into dark, thickly forested valleys, indeed ravines, on whose opposite sides mountains again ascend, which incline toward the Koralps just as the plateau does. That gives an idea of the territory. It's impossible to describe the vegetation, the overflowing richness of forests and alpine pastures. In general everything here is much more vivid than in the valley, more aromatic, veritably magnified. A thunderstorm up here is the most grandiose sight imaginable. Not long ago a bolt of lightning struck a huge fir tree and the forest within a radius of at least 100 meters was covered with splinters and remnants of the tree, all buried halfway into the ground from the force of the fall. Among them were 2–hundred-pound pieces that—to use a common but telling comparison—simply lay strewn about like matchsticks, better yet: toothpicks; the tree itself had been torn off above the root and hurled against another tree, which it half uprooted.

Such are the pastoral events here, which are by God more beautiful than those in the city and I don't even want to be reminded that I'll have to return to the city.——and to Vienna at that!! What could possibly draw me there?!—There's only one pleasant thought when I think of Vienna: the *Gurrelieder*. But already today I dread the moment when the last note has sounded; then the only pleasant thing will be "PAST." But no doubt there will be a few other pleasant events! The Akademischer Verband will see to that.

Many warm regards to you, dear Herr Schönberg, and your honored family, also From my wife.

From your eternally grateful, loyally devoted
Alban Berg

I just heard from Polnauer that he's in Vienna and I am to ask you to think of him in case there's anything you need or want to know.

Please excuse the smudges, the blotting paper is terrible!

*Schoenberg to Berg (postcard)*

Berlin-Zehlendorf [30 August 1912]

Dear Berg,

Today I am sending you the manuscript of your piano score of my II$^{nd}$ Quartet in two registered packages (acknowledge receipt). I made many more annotations. Look at it and use your own judgment! I almost fear I'm harassing you unnecessarily. The minute I see something, I immediately feel the urge to contradict. So don't take it too seriously—maybe just a bit here and there. At any rate don't send it back to me, for safety's sake. Otherwise I'll start harassing you all over again.—

I'm very pleased that your health is good and that you're working. Wouldn't you like to visit Berlin some time?—

Warm regards

Your Schönberg

The package is presumably the one from July!!! In other words, superfluous! Send it to U.E.

*Berg to Schoenberg*

Trahütten, 5 September 1912

Dear Herr Schönberg,

I sent the piano reductions to U.E. last night; I took all your comments into account and followed your suggestions.\* I also wrote Hertzka a detailed letter and explained why I was asking for more than he usually pays (I asked for 150 kronen, whereas by his rate, 3 kronen per page, I figure I would get about 80 kronen. I'm curious how far he'll barter me down). I also wrote that these scores should be sent to the engraver immediately, as they will be needed shortly. And asked if the *Gurre* score isn't finished by now. And I really let him know what I thought about the "difficulties" of my reductions. For he continually reproaches me that my reductions are so difficult as to be unplayable. Of course he himself doesn't know anything about it and doubtless gets his opinion from Schreker. And Schreker naturally can't play my reductions, as he plays and sightreads very poorly himself, but after having given me daily assurances when I did the score of the *Ferne Klang* that "it was not to be a reduction for children"—he was incensed over "Scholz,"[1] who wanted to turn his opera into "Diabelli Exercises"—after even writing me that Walter found the reduction outstanding[2]— — —, after all that he now grumbles about the reduction's difficulties every time I see him, also about the *Gurre* reduction, and Hertzka right along, of course. I dare say my letter, which wasn't particularly friendly, will cure the latter of his error. But I won't even try with Schreker, especially now that his success will soon be giving him delusions of grandeur. Inciden-

---

1. Arthur Johannes Scholz prepared a number of piano reductions for Universal Edition. Though Josef Venantius von Wöss is credited with having prepared the first act of *Der ferne Klang*, Berg's reference here suggests that it was Scholz' work.

2. Bruno Walter, to whom *Der ferne Klang* is dedicated, was instrumental in getting the work accepted at the Vienna Court Opera by Felix Weingartner in 1910.

tally, I haven't had a personal word from him for months.

There's nothing new in my life just now, tomorrow I begin to compose again, after having left off for a few days. I hope my wife will be better soon so I can work peacefully; she is habitually plagued by terrible nightmares that cause her to leap out of bed in absolute panic. Only last night she leaped over the headboard, head first behind the bed, and landed hard on her head and body. She inflicted terrible injuries on herself and at first we even feared a concussion and internal injuries. As it turned out, there's no danger of that, but she is in great pain and has to rest and I want to go back to her now, so I'll close. I hope to have better news for you soon! Give my devoted regards to your wife, also on my wife's behalf, and the warmest regards to you yourself from both of us, but especially ·

from your grateful and reverent Alban Berg

My student Josef Schmid (whom you met during your Vienna visit) is in Königsberg for the summer at an Ansorge piano master class. He just wrote that he played my Sonata for Ansorge,[3] who was apparently very interested, calling it "linear art"[4] and incidentally recognizing it immediately as Schönberg School; Schmid will play it at the conclusion of the seminar at a concert of the master class students on 16 September. —I am, by the way, very concerned about Schmid's future. Last year he taught at the Kalksburg convent, but now he's out of work and completely without funds and wants to join a salon orchestra in order to continue his studies. He's thinking of Vienna or Berlin.—But will he be able to find anything??!——

*I certainly don't need to repeat how absolutely inspired I thought the various solutions. From the major passages down to the smallest: e.g., dividing the figure between the left and right hands.

---

3. The pianist and composer Conrad Ansorge studied with Liszt and was for a time closely associated with the circle around Stefan George.

4. The term "linear music" (Linienkunst) was generally used at the time to describe music in which voice leading considerations seemed to be breaking down traditional harmonic language. The term was widely applied to Viennese music and in particular to that of Mahler, Schoenberg, and even Schreker.

## Berg to Schoenberg

Trahütten, 13 September 1912

I got a letter from Webern yesterday, dear Herr Schönberg, who gave me so much interesting and heartening news. Above all the new U.E. publications: Chamber Symphony, new piano pieces[1] (which I had copied out for myself, not knowing they would appear so soon), the *Gurrelieder* full score for only 20 marks. It's all so marvelous. But the prospect of performing the *Gurrelieder* during the II[nd] Vienna Musikfestwoche is the best! But we don't want to give up the performance on 12 December and the one in Berlin, which I'll naturally attend!! It must be possible to perform the work during the Musikfestwoche with the Philharmonic, the Männer-

---

1. Schoenberg's Chamber Symphony and the Piano Pieces, Op. 19, appeared in October 1913.

gesangsverein, and first-rate soloists and narrator without having to cancel those 2 performances.

Webern also wrote that the tour with your new work,[2] presumably also with you, will be in Vienna in November; that *Glückliche Hand* will be finished soon[3]— — —all news of the most wonderful expectations and hopes!!—

I was deeply moved by your suggestion, dear Herr Schönberg, that I stay in the country for good, particularly as this wish has completely preoccupied and consumed me these past 4–6 weeks—but also because the utter impossibility of fulfilling this wish—now or in the near future—has been weighing me down. Of course you know, dear Herr Schönberg, under what conditions I was permitted by my family to count on the steady income that made it possible for me to marry. First, that I take over a great deal of the administration of the houses, which thus chains me to Vienna, and 2nd that in my actual profession I try to secure for myself if not a livelihood, then at least a source of income, something I could begin to do last year with the piano reductions and teaching. To give that up now—apart from the first reason—is completely impossible, without running the risk of endangering my existence—insofar as it depends on my support from home. Already the preferential treatment from home is an indirect cause for something of a falling out with my siblings.

So for now I guess I'm condemned to remain in Vienna and await the time when I can at least live and work farther out in the country, if not at an altitude of 1,000 meters! As it is, I can be grateful that I'm not in the city proper, but live out in Hietzing, where I have the wonderful garden of my parents-in-law in close proximity—almost completely to myself. Granted, I have plenty to put up with from my family about living out here "at the end of the world." But that doesn't really matter!

But I don't want to keep talking about Vienna, when I can stay here another week. We go back to Vienna on Thursday, the 19th, XIII / 1, 27 Trauttmansdorff-gasse. I'll still try to finish the 5th orchestra song I started here, thus completing the projected cycle. Only it's a pity the weather is so bad that one can hardly go outdoors. For how right you are in this, dear Herr Schönberg, as in everything, everything, that one works best on walks—in the country, naturally—and the reason I didn't work for so long may have been because I didn't get out. Of course I also need great emotional peace and complete mental and physical equilibrium, which I found here—with the obvious exception of my wife's illness, though thank heavens it ran its course much faster than could initially have been expected. She is completely well again and sends you, dear Herr Schönberg, and your wife, who we hope is very well, her very best regards! Please convey my most devoted regards to her as well and to you my warmest and best greetings

from your Berg

An endearing document of our time: This tasteful program for the first concert cannot even be justified with the need to do choral works.

2. Following the Berlin premiere of *Pierrot lunaire*, a tour of several German and Austrian cities was planned. See footnote 4 to Schoenberg's letter of 3 October 1912.

3. *Die glückliche Hand* was not completed until 18 November 1913.

The *Wiener Singakademie*, which is entering its 55<sup>th</sup> year in the coming season, has notified us that they will perform the following works under the direction of the Royal and Imperial Court Opera conductor Bruno Walter: 1<sup>st</sup> concert: First performance of Gustav Mahler's *Lied von der Erde* and two choral works with orchestra by **Ethel Smith** [sic]. 2<sup>nd</sup> concert: Missa solemnis by L. Beethoven. 3<sup>rd</sup> concert: The Verdi Requiem. 4<sup>th</sup> concert: *The Seasons* by Haydn.[4]

And these kind words of old "Hans Richter": (also addressed to Karpath.)

There's only one solution: German women must take *Parsifal* under their protection; at the forefront an idealistic, noble lady from powerful, influential circles, who could lend her words the necessary emphasis. But where is such a woman? Your old Hans *Richter,* former Hofkapellmeister and conductor of the Festspiel."[5]

Please excuse the torn sheet! I didn't notice until I had almost finished writing.

---

4. From the *Neue Freie Presse* of 10 September 1912.
5. From an interview with Hans Richter that appeared in the *Neues Wiener Tagblatt* on 10 September 1912.

## Berg to Schoenberg

[Vienna] 21 September 1912

Dear Herr Schönberg,

Your card from Rheingold, forwarded first to Trahütten and then here, made me very happy, except for the news of your birthday, which I didn't know until now and therefore—as perhaps the only one among your students—didn't honor. But as you well know, dear Herr Schönberg, it's not mentioned in any work about you, not even in our little book, so I hope you won't be angry that I have never congratulated you on this occasion. Nor do I dare make up for it now, 10 days late, in any case you must know that my wishes for your birthday and every day are the very, very best and most fervent of which I am capable! But at least I'm glad I've found out about this wonderful day, the 12<sup>th</sup> of September, and to know that you spent it so pleasantly and agreeably.[1] Thanks again for your greeting!

I arrived here the day before yesterday and am certain that it will take a long time for me to become acclimated spiritually—and even physically, for the strangest thing happened—now I can't tolerate the Viennese air, I got a touch of asthma the first night. I actually regard it as a good sign, as it seems to confirm my aversion to large cities, but regarded dispassionately it simply means that I can't tolerate any change of locale, i.e., climate, particularly when the change is to lower elevations: which is essentially the same as saying: Away from the lowlands! Up into the mountains![2]

---

1. Berg had confused the date of Schoenberg's postcard with that of his birthday, which is actually 13 September.
2. "Away from the Lowlands . . ." ("Fort aus den Niederungen! Hinauf in die Berge!") is a paraphrase of the conclusion of Eugen d'Albert's opera *Tiefland* (Prague, 1903; 2<sup>nd</sup> version Magdeburg, 1905).

Of course, I cannot yet tell you anything about Vienna that might interest you, annoyances with the transportation system and with ridiculously high income taxes, which again necessitate a great many errands—that's the sum of my first delightful experiences!

Oh yes, apropos delightful! *[Berg encloses a clipping[3]detailing the programs of the Vienna Philharmonic Orchestra subscription concerts under Felix Weingartner for the coming season, which were to include first performances of works by the Austrian composer Alfred Arbter, the French composer Alfred Bruneau, Karl Goldmark, Erich Wolfgang Korngold, Ferdinand Scherber, Jean Sibelius, and Felix Weingartner.]* What a collection of names!!

A card just arrived from Schmid, who was in Berlin.[4] The lucky fellow will hear the melodramas! I'll probably see him today and am eager to hear all about it! Also about the reception my sonata was given in Königsberg!

I'll close now with a thousand very warm regards

your Berg

---

3. From the *Neue Freie Presse* of 21 September 1912).
4. Josef Schmid stopped in Berlin on his way back from Königsberg to hear a rehearsal of *Pierrot lunaire.*

## Schoenberg to Berg

Berlin-Zehlendorf, 3 October 1912

Dear friend,

I am very busy with rehearsals for *Pierrot lunaire.*[1] In addition, I'm reading proofs for the full score of the Chamber Symphony and have to revise my Mahler lecture, which I'm giving in Berlin on the 13th (on the occasion of *Lied von der Erde*).[2] In between I have orchestrated four Schubert songs for Frau Culp,[3] some of which were fairly long. And then there are so many people who come by. I usually have more visitors here in a week than in Vienna in 3 months. Truly! There are far more people interested in me here than in Vienna.—The *Pierrot* rehearsals are almost over (20 so far!). The last are on the 5th, 7th, and 8th, on the 9th there is an open dress rehearsal (to which I also invited your sister, who just wrote to me). Then there are at most another one or 2 rehearsals for the II[nd] set of performers. Then the performance on the 16th, which I hope will be excellent. Then comes the tour.

1. The first performance of *Pierrot lunaire* received 25 rehearsals.
2. Mahler's *Das Lied von der Erde* was given its first Berlin performance on 18 October with the Berlin Philharmonic Orchestra under Oscar Fried. Emil Gutmann handled the arrangements for Schoenberg's Mahler lecture on 13 October in the Harmonium Hall.
3. Julia Culp was a Dutch concert mezzo-soprano who toured Europe and America 1900–19. In February 1912 Schoenberg had orchestrated Beethoven's "Adelaide" for her. His arrangements of Schubert songs ("Suleika," "Suleika's zweiter Gesang," "Ständchen," as well as a fourth unidentified song) were completed in September. Culp had sole performance rights for two years, after which Schoenberg intended to publish the arrangements. Nothing came of that plan and the manuscripts of the arrangements have now been lost.

I myself will participate in the following cities: Hamburg 19 / X, Dresden 24 / X, Stettin 25 / X, Breslau 31 / X, Vienna 2 / XI, Leipzig 23 / XI. In addition there are Danzig, Munich, Stuttgart, Karlsruhe, Mannheim, Frankfurt, and Graz![4] (For the present!) Those will be conducted by Herr Scherchen.[5] I'll be away a lot for other reasons, too. On 28 and 30 November I'm conducting *Pelleas* in Amsterdam and the Hague, on 21 December in Petersburg. (Bodanzky is doing it in Mannheim[6] and Mengelberg in Frankfurt.[7] On top of that, Specht wants to do *Pelleas* or the Chamber Symphony in Vienna.[8] But I don't know what's happening with my chamber music this year. For the moment it seems to be in hibernation. Likewise the songs. Strange, that no quartet other than Rosé has played both of my quartets. Apparently they are too difficult for everyone.—I already have a few students here, too.[9] On the whole, I'm not at all dissatisfied.—

Now let me hear some time what you're up to! Do you already have students! Do you have any other work? I hear you had a falling out with Hertzka about the Schreker piano score. Unfortunately that is the fate of all piano scores: the first are always too difficult. A few years later, when it is easier to prepare a less difficult one, no one minds any more. I had the same experience with the piano scores I did for Zemlinsky.[10] And Zemlinsky got an unusable(?) one from Bodanzky,[11] after which Zemlinsky prepared an unusable(?) one for himself.[12] Cheer up, dear Berg! Your score really is too difficult. You remember I warned you. The *Gurrelieder* score is also too difficult. But that doesn't matter. You'll make a simpler one next time.—A pity though that you yourself didn't offer to prepare the simplified score for Schreker.[13] But that's no great misfortune. Hertzka will give you other jobs.—

What about your compositions? Have you finished anything? Wouldn't you like to show it to me? Wouldn't you like to visit me with it?—I was horrified at your wife's misfortune this summer. Stupidly enough, I kept forgetting to ask you how she was. I hope she has completely recovered by now.—I'm not working—that is

---

4. Following the 16 October premiere of *Pierrot lunaire*, the tour took place as scheduled, with the exception of Stettin and Leipzig. Subsequent performances took place in Munich (5 November), Stuttgart (11 November), Mannheim (15 November), Frankfurt (17 November), with repeat performances in Berlin (1 and 8 December). Performances in Danzig, Karlsruhe, and Graz did not take place.

5. Hermann Scherchen began his conducting career freelancing in Berlin in 1912, about the time he met Schoenberg.

6. The Austrian Artur Bodanzky was principal conductor at the Mannheim Court Theater 1909–15 and later conductor of German repertoire of the Metropolitan Opera. His friendship with Schoenberg dated back to childhood.

7. Willem Mengelberg was the permanent conductor of the Amsterdam Concertgebouw 1895–1945. He also directed the Frankfurt Museum Concerts 1907–20.

8. Under the auspices of the *Merker* concerts. Nothing came of the plan.

9. In a letter to Berg of 5 October, Webern speaks of Schoenberg having five students: these would have included Edward Clark, Leo Perelmann, Eduard Steuermann, and Fritz Zweig.

10. Of the opera *Sarema* (1895), prepared in the summer of 1897. Nothing is known of other piano scores Schoenberg prepared for Zemlinsky.

11. Artur Bodanzky studied composition with Zemlinsky and prepared a reduction of Zemlinsky's *Traumgörge* in 1906.

12. Unidentified. Schoenberg may be referring to Zemlinsky's vocal score for *Kleider machen Leute* (1911).

13. The simplified score to Schreker's *Der ferne Klang* was prepared by Ferdinand Rebay and appeared in 1912.

to say, composing—at all. I probably won't get to it this winter. It seems that my intention to conduct more frequently is to become reality. I hope so! But don't spread it around!!—Wouldn't you like to get back to composing? Have you ever thought of writing something for the theater? I sometimes think you would be good at that! In any case it could be very stimulating for you. Just see that you don't take the *Dream Plays* away from me, for I'm considering them myself.[14] But some other Strindberg work! I consider that very feasible! Let me hear from you soon and warmest regards to you and your wife—

from your Arnold Schönberg

Warm regards also from my wife!

N.B.: Are you absolutely sure you can't come to Berlin for the 14th? *Das Lied von der Erde* is on the 18th. You and your wife could stay with us, as well as the Weberns and Jalowetz. We have plenty of room!

N.B. Another thing: I've long been wanting to ask you, since I can't remember: don't I have another 500 kronen "coming" from this *Kommerzialrat* Redlich? Or from Frau Mauthner? If so, then surely this would be the time to "sue for it"!! I could use it. Perhaps you'll take care of it right away—

Warm regards

Schönberg

---

14. Nothing came of Schoenberg's plans to set Strindberg's *Dream Play* (1901) or the three-part *The Road to Damascus* (1898–1901).

*Berg to Schoenberg*

Vienna, 6 October 1912

P.S. This letter isn't as important as it is long! So please read it only when you have a lot of spare time, dear Herr Schönberg!!

Many thanks, dear kind Herr Schönberg, for your dear, long letter. Everything you write affects me so deeply that I would have liked to answer right away, but though I couldn't find time until now, I did write a registered letter to <u>Redlich</u> immediately and hope to hear soon!

How gladly I'd come to Berlin!! Just the prospect of seeing you, of being able to talk with you at length, is so tempting—not to mention hearing the dress rehearsal and performance of your *Pierrot lunaire*, your lecture on Mahler, *Das Lied von der Erde*—that it almost seems sinful not to take up your kind invitation! But it can't be done! At least not at present! My current financial situation makes it impossible. Of course you know, dear Herr Schönberg, that I (as well as my wife) do get a steady income from home, but this barely suffices to get by on, and faced with the relatively high cost of living here—(I mean: the apartment, related expenses, insurance, an overly high income tax, etc., etc.—) faced with insanely inflated prices for everything, faced with the accumulation of small expenses like public transportation, etc., etc.—anyway, faced with all that, every additional expense—and there always are some (doctors this year, for instance)—takes a heavy toll, indeed, such expenses are at times (now, for instance) impossible. In order to live halfway free of anxiety, constant calculation, economy, and frugality are required, and still one can't get ahead. With no prospect of increasing my income just now, I can't alter my present lifestyle at all and can only hope that it will soon be possible for me to visit you in Berlin, dear Herr Schönberg, and to take advantage of your kind offer to stay with you. It really will happen this season still; it must!! After all I must see how you live now, dear Herr Schönberg, must feel at home again in your study, which right now I can only imagine, I want to sit at the piano with you again, be allowed to look at your new works,— —finally to impose on you with my orchestra songs, which I shall bring along (I'm presently finishing the 5th, the last, and then would like to start something else right away,— —if only I had a suitable text: for the theater. I was already considering Strindberg's *Chamber Plays*,[1] and now that you suggest Strindberg that of course seems all the more compelling). But to get back to my visit with you, dear Herr Schönberg: though I cannot come now, I console myself (as far as possible) with the thought that I shall see you in Vienna in 3–4 weeks, dear Herr Schönberg, when you conduct your new work and perhaps also take up Specht's idea (Chamber Symphony or *Pelleas*) and we will, I *hope*, finally hear the Mahler lecture. The opportunity, coming as it does before *Das Lied von der Erde*, which is on 4 November[2] (your melodramas are on 2 November), is ideal and Buschbeck, whom I see once a week, tells me that it will probably come off. Please, dear Herr Schönberg, do give the lecture, that is not just my fervent wish, but that of everyone I know, all of whom are dying for it, and over and above that: it is vitally important that in Vienna, where Mahler is slowly beginning to be forgotten (no performance in 1912 / 1913 apart from the IVth and *Das Lied von der Erde*), where, as I saw not long ago, his grave is allowed to fall into disrepair, that here words be spoken just once about Mahler's greatness and holiness—and who should do so, who can do so but you, Herr Schönberg?! That would be a wonderful week in Vienna, if it were all to come true! Only by keeping that in mind can I resign myself to the thought of not visiting you right away; besides, it would also entail something unpleasant, which we thereby avoid. Of the flood of spitefulness that fell to our lot (to my wife and me) this summer, a good portion was due to my sister and her girlfriend[3] (who is actually responsible for everything) and, as I told you, that finally led to a break between us, which is why it would be extremely unpleasant to meet her just now, after such a short time:—let alone this girlfriend—, and as it would be unavoidable at dress rehearsals, performances, etc., I circumvent it by not coming to Berlin just now. When more time has passed, once the unpleasant causes for the break are no longer so fresh in our memory, a meeting won't be as awkward! But now it almost seems as if that were an additional reason for our not coming now! Certainly not!! Naturally it wouldn't be a consideration if my financial situation permitted the trip; it's only meant to be a sort of consolation I hold out to myself—perhaps delude myself with: "as long as it's impossible anyway, at least I'll

1. Strindberg's four *Chamber Plays*, the best known of which is the *Ghost Sonata*, were written in 1907.
2. First Vienna performance under Bruno Walter.
3. May Keller.

avoid this bit of unpleasantness!" Basically it's as if, for instance, I were prevented from accepting a wonderful gift, and sought to console myself with the fact that at least I was spared the trouble of reaching out my hand.—

Now finally to something else. To turn to your dear letter: my teaching! There's little to tell about the few students I do have, but that little is good news. Above all Königer, who plans to resign from the office in 2 months and wants to devote himself entirely to music.[4] Since his most recent things, especially the songs he did over the summer, are quite good and definitely show great progress, I'm very pleased with his decision and now we'll be able to do a lot of work together in counterpoint and composition. I am very satisfied with Schmid, who has reached 3–part fugues! Unfortunately he's unemployed, indeed completely without resources, and if nothing turns up here (he would take <u>anything</u> that turned up) he'd have to return to his people, who are poor village schoolteachers!—Polnauer is preparing for his doctoral exams and can't possibly work. He just <u>comes by</u> and we look at various things together, mainly your works (not long ago the chorus and the Orchestra Pieces). In addition the young fellow is coming to me again, the one who took harmony with me for several months last year, who is already composing at the early age of 12, 13.[5] Lighter music, of course: waltzes, marches, also songs and piano pieces, but he's very talented. Since his parents are very poor it's a matter of course that I teach him gratis, like all of them except Königer, who pays. "Binder," who also took from me last year and was my 2<sup>nd</sup> paying student, didn't come back this year; he's probably taking from his brother-in-law Schreker at the Academy.[6] That's all. But here, too, I console myself about the financial situation with the fact that at least I have a lot of time to compose. I probably won't get any commissions from Hertzka either; on the contrary, it's much more likely he'll pinch something off work already delivered: he's only giving me 100 kronen for the piano score of the quartet songs, where I had asked 150 kronen. Anyway—knowing him as I do—I hadn't expected <u>more.</u>

Of course I thoroughly appreciate what <u>you</u>, dear Herr Schönberg say about the difficulty of my reductions; only that's not quite what <u>Hertzka</u> thinks. I wrote to him that I didn't think it would be necessary to pulp <u>my</u> reduction of the *Ferne Klang* just because a II<sup>nd</sup> simplified one is called for. Rather, the necessity for this merely proves to me that the *Ferne Klang* will be the kind of "hit" that even children and amateurs want to play; my score is too difficult for that, just like Singer's[7] I<sup>st</sup> *Elektra* score, say, where a simplified version was likewise required. Nevertheless, these first reductions are not <u>unplayable</u>, as Hertzka insists, but merely <u>very difficult</u> (yet pianistic, therefore playable). After all, Hertzka will consider the reductions to "Litanei" and "Entrückung" unplayable, too; as you know, that was the reason I erred <u>initially</u>, i.e., compromised by drafting something <u>easy</u>—in other words poor—from which, thank heavens, <u>you</u> saved me, so that these 2 reductions turned out no easier than that of the *Ferne Klang*, though they are still easier than

4. Königer never did act on this plan.
5. Probably Karl Sluzansky.
6. Karl Binder studied with Schreker 1912–15.
7. The German composer Otto Singer prepared piano reductions for the Fürstner publishing house, including a number of Strauss operas.

Webern's reduction of the Orchestra Pieces, for instance, which I consider simply marvelous, unsurpassed in sound and pianistic in all respects, though also very difficult; in my opinion there's no comparison with the Orchestra Song reductions,[8] which aren't nearly as pianistic. But that's probably due also to the differences between the works, from which I project—no doubt incorrectly—onto the reductions!

In order to answer everything in your letter: will the scores of the Schubert songs be published. Is Culp going to sing them in Vienna? Are they set for large modern orchestra or for Schubert's orchestra (I mean historical!).

I'm happy that Berlin is treating you more decently than Vienna; everything proves it: the many visitors, the tour, all of the conducting this year, the performances in Mannheim and Frankfurt. That probably wouldn't have been possible from Vienna. Though even here in Vienna, apart from the ever growing community of enthusiasts, it seems to me that the stupidity and baseness and maliciousness of the others has turned into a kind of respect, which in the case of many has even led to a recognition of their error. Only, like everything else in Vienna, the change is nice and slow. But all the more sure! I'm pinning all my hopes on the *Gurrelieder*. It will be decided on the 9th whether it is to be performed in the Musikfestwoche; it's not definite there'll be another festival, but if there is, then it's 90% certain that your work will be accepted. But in that case what about Schreker's performance and the one in Berlin? Will they be canceled after all? Granted, if it's for the sake of a performance with the Philharmonic, the Männergesangverein, first-class forces—under your (?) direction!! Two forces, better said two weaknesses, have already been secured for Schreker's performance: Wyss (for the Bauer, who lisps) and Drill-Orridge (as Waldtaube). I beg you, dear Herr Schönberg, try to prevent the latter at all costs. Drill is the most unrefined, brutal, soulless singer I know. Her voice, as it has developed of late, lacks any hint of refined nobility, of beauty, it is at best an expression of coarse sensuality, sensuousness—the polar opposite of Waldtaube, who has something of the Holy Spirit! At least the same symbol, if not more!

Have you read the insignificant nonsense Wellesz wrote about the *Gurrelieder* in Hertzka's music-educational journal.[9] The "place of honor in choral literature" is priceless. And the comparison with the Sextet![10] One could say the same thing about Delius's *Mass of Life* and the like, then at least the place of honor in choral literature, actually a grave of honor, would apply. Shouldn't it be said above all— and I would have said it if Hertzka had asked me to write the article (that he didn't do so is typically Hertzka–esque)—that the *Gurrelieder* have absolutely nothing to do with literature, nor with choral literature (after all one could just as well call it a

8. Webern had prepared piano reductions of Schoenberg's Six Orchestra Songs, Op. 8, in the summer of 1910, which appeared with U.E. in 1911.

9. Egon Wellesz's article, *"Gurrelieder von Arnold Schönberg,"* appeared in the *Modernes Musikleben* (1 October 1912), 36–37.

10. In his article, Wellesz made the following comparison: "In this work Schoenberg has written melodies of a warmth and beauty that could only be compared with the climaxes of the sextet *Verklärte Nacht.*" The article concludes with the sentence: "And despite the technical difficulties arising from the large forces needed for performance, the *Gurrelieder* are assured a place of honor in choral literature."

song book!!), but that it is as sublime and elevated a work as any, including Beethoven's IX^th or Mahler's VIII^th, which don't have places of honor either; thank God!— —

So Reti is to play the piano pieces after all.[11] Buschbeck told me. Our initial reluctance was based on the not very accurate interpretation of one of your piano pieces and on his "unappealing" appearance. It isn't his "Jewishness," as you wrote,[12] for Steuermann has that to the same extent, perhaps even more strongly, more pronounced. Rather it is the oily, un-<u>forthright</u>, wavy, snakelike, unconvincing quality of his bearing, of his interpretation, whereas Steuermann makes an agreeable and convincing impression with his calm, assured bearing alone. But, as you say, that has probably changed. Reti's positive attitude toward your work, his earnestness and enthusiasm will surely show him the right way, so that you—not to mention we—will be satisfied!—

Another thing: Fleischmann's biographical sketch of you (also in the *Musikpädagogische Zeitung*)[13] gives all the names of those "who have championed your works." No one's missing; not even Reti, Werndorff, Schreker, ! <u>Only</u> Gutheil! Isn't that extremely tactless! It was probably just an oversight, but how would Gutheil feel if she were to see it. Wouldn't it be possible to "correct it"? Demand a small notice of rectification!?!

But enough for now: I have taken up enough of your time with trivia, dear Herr Schönberg, and will therefore append a <u>P.S.</u> to the <u>beginning</u> of this letter to warn you of possibly wasting your valuable time reading it!

I thank you again for asking about my wife's condition. Thank heavens she is well again now.—

We hope the same is true for you, dear Herr Schönberg, and your wife and the dear children, whom we send our very warmest regards.

But especially to you, dear, esteemed Herr Schönberg,

from your grateful and devoted Alban Berg

7 October 1912

11. Reti performed Schoenberg's Op. 11 and gave the Vienna first performance of Op. 19 in a concert of the Akademischer Verband on 20 November 1912.

12. In a letter to Erhard Buschbeck of 2 October, Schoenberg had written of Reti: "Denn er sieht ja mehr jüdisch als unsympatisch aus und das ist ja schliesslich doch nicht dasselbe" (For his looks are more Jewish than unpleasant, which is, after all, not really the same thing).

13. Hugo Fleischmann's article on Schoenberg was the sixth in a series of "Biographical Sketches of Modern Musicians." His Schoenberg article appeared in *Modernes Musikleben* (1 October 1912), 33–35.

## Berg to Schoenberg

[Vienna] 18 October 1912

Dear Herr Schönberg,

I just received the card with all the signatures![1] You can imagine how I feel at not having been there, in general how I've felt these past few days. Only the thought that I will soon hear this work, will see and talk to you in Vienna, as well as my interest in how the work was received in Berlin and the other cities, only this helped me occasionally to forget my anguish at not having been there. Now the premiere is over and I am poorer by one beautiful memory! I hope my longing for it will be satisfied by actually hearing the work itself in all its dreamed-of splendor. There are still 2 weeks until then!

And then you'll also speak on Mahler! That has always been one of my greatest desires! And that of many others! Of course the song recital will take place too:[2] without the George Songs or piano pieces! The program is long enough! A wonderful program! We'll discuss the order when you come to Vienna, dear Herr Schönberg.

Redlich still hasn't answered. Either he is out of town again or he's trying to get out of it! In any case I'll write to him once more (again registered)!

From Hertzka, whom I told that the reduced fee did not in fact "seem appropriate," as he had assumed, but that I accepted it "because I had no alternative," I received a letter that "it certainly was possible to do something other than accept, namely, to withdraw my piano reductions of the 2 quartet movements"!

Maddening!

Incidentally, he invited me to come by, as he wants to propose something "for which you, dear Herr Schönberg, had recommended me." My debt to you, which has long since exceeded infinity, continues to grow and grow with each of your actions, your works—your thoughts. Again and again I have to thank you.

You're probably in Hamburg now and will return to Zehlendorf where these few lines will reach you. Many, many regards (also from my wife) to you and your esteemed wife

from your Berg

---

1. Following the premiere of *Pierrot lunaire*, Webern sent Berg a card signed by the Schoenbergs and many of the performers and friends who were present.

2. A recital of Schoenberg songs by Martha Winternitz-Dorda, planned by the Akademischer Verband at this time, never took place.

## Berg to Schoenberg

Tuesday
[Vienna] 22 October 1912

Dear Herr Schönberg,

Yesterday Hertzka told me of your proposal for the work on the *Gurrelieder*, but he himself knew so little about it that it's not clear from what he said how this so-called short score (?) [*Particell*] is to be done[1]—so I told him I would write to you in the matter and if—as I assume—you don't have time to write back at length, I would have to wait to discuss it with you in Vienna. Naturally I have given it some thought myself, so I'll tell you, dear Herr Schönberg, how I envision it. A score reduction with the usual 𝄞 and 𝄢 clefs, which would at times have 2 staves like a piano score (for the simple passages), and at times require 1 or 2 or 3–4 extra staves. Thus 3–6 staves or more. So that, for example, the principal material would be in the 2 middle staves (as in a piano reduction), but with indication of the instruments, regardless of playability. And above and below that various accompanimental figures, those passages in which thematic material is presented in a number of instruments that play only part of the theme, or enter earlier or break off later than the primary instrument carrying the theme. I forgot to ask Hertzka whether this short score (?) is to be engraved or just copied, or whether just my manuscript would be used. In the last instance one could make it clearer with colors. But it boils down to the fact that Hertzka is too cheap to have a proper score engraved, there being no large usable score (to conduct from) available (other than yours, which, again, is too large).

Surely it would be much easier if one (—that is, I—) were to reduce, as best I could, this large score of perhaps 40 staves (yours probably has that many) to one of 25–30 staves. Often that would be merely a case of consolidating the multistaffed instruments (for instance the 8 horns) into 1–2–3 staves, and possibly of notating just once those figures, themes, etc., played by <u>a number of</u> instruments

e.g. 3 flutes    2 clarinets    1 oboe

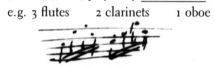

finally, that one separate those places in your score with 2 or more systems on <u>one</u> page and write them not on <u>one</u> but on 2 or more pages, which would make them large and easy to read, in which case a format with fewer staves would suffice. Thus

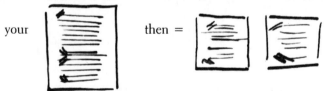

It would also be easier to work from, i.e., conduct and rehearse from such a score, whereas it would be much more difficult from the so-called orchestral reduction I outlined earlier—indeed, Schreker thinks it would be quite impossible (at least for rehearsing, possibly serviceable only for the performance (18 January)).

I don't dare ask you to write me in this matter, dear Herr Schönberg; I'm sure you're much too busy now, so I'll wait until you come to Vienna! That day is already fast approaching! Thank Heavens!! Are you already coming on the 1st, as

---

1. In a letter to Hertzka of 10 October, Schoenberg had suggested that Berg prepare an orchestral short score such as Berg describes, since the printed score would not be suitable for conducting, and large-format handwritten copies of the score too costly and too subject to error.

you wrote Buschbeck. Will you stay in Vienna longer, even though the *Pelleas* concert can't take place?[2] That would be wonderful!! All the more so, as it is once again my misfortune that these days, the most wonderful in months, happen to coincide with the quarterly rent, and this time of all times I have to manage <u>all alone</u> since my brother—who could conceivably have relieved me of the work during the first days of November—was laid low with stomach ulcers 2 weeks ago! All my energies are now directed toward arranging and preparing my work so as to save as much time as possible so I can be with you often during your days here.

Surely you'll stay for *Das Lied von der Erde*. Will you be coming alone or with your family, or will you travel with the entire company doing the tour? I just can't wait for all of these things; talking about it, asking questions, is already a <u>part</u> of the great, heavenly joy of being able to hear your work. We already have wonderful tickets, way up front! (for *Pierrot*). I still have to get some for the lecture.

You are probably in Stettin now, which is why I write to Webern, who will give you the letter. I'm enormously eager to hear how the work was received in the other German cities!

Enough now, dear Herr Schönberg. I won't say *auf Wiedersehen* yet, since I'll probably write again before I see you. Of course, the main purpose of this letter was to write you about the *Gurre* matter. Hertzka has now given me a very easy job— one I'll definitely accept: to collate and compare the orchestra parts of *Gurrelieder* with the full score. He was, by the way, very unctuous, good-humored, and funny— —the last unintentionally.

Many, many regards, also from my wife

Your grateful Berg

Should your esteemed wife also be in Stettin, please convey our most devoted regards.

---

2. When the *Merker* concert did not materialize, Schoenberg initially planned to conduct *Pelleas und Melisande* and the Chamber Symphony in a concert sponsored by the Akademischer Verband. This concert, originally scheduled for November, was by this time rescheduled for February.

## Berg to Schoenberg

Sunday evening
[Vienna, 3 November 1912]

I'm very unhappy, dear Herr Schönberg, that I wasn't able to accompany you to the station. Not only did I miss a few more quarter hours of your short stay here, but I'm also very worried that you might take it ill. But I must tell you that it was <u>not</u> for reasons of **convenience** that I said adieu right after your lecture, but <u>only</u> because I was so concerned for my wife's well-being.

In her present condition, my wife isn't used to being **up**, that is to say, her weakness usually requires that she remain recumbent and she just wasn't quite up to the strain, so I <u>couldn't permit</u> her to <u>go to the station</u>, though **she** did **not** want to inflict on me the pain of not being with you. To allow her to leave <u>alone</u>—was impossible, because I feared a possible fainting spell, of which I have unfortunately witnessed several, and because I knew that our maid, who had the evening out, would not be home by the time my wife arrived there alone.

And when I, that is we, finally arrived home by taxi it was already too late for me to return to the station, where I could at least have seen you again.

Thus: everything conspired against me, against the happiness of spending more time with you. From the administrative work to my wife's indisposition. If only I could be certain that you and your wife didn't think ill of me, or us! If that were so, I would have to give up: my great sentimentality, now completely overpowering me, could at least become sorrow. Your lecture! That was too wonderful! Please, please publish it, I must have something like that about me, be able to read it a thousand times! I'll write again soon, dear, kind Herr Schönberg, right now I'm too restless at the misfortune of not having been able to accompany you to the station. I can think or speak of nothing else.

Your distraught Berg

Again we thank you and your esteemed wife very much for giving us so many hours of your precious time when you came to see us. That was too much kindness and honor for us!

I hope you found the dear little ones well upon your return and that you had a good trip and have recovered from your cold! Your hoarseness was hardly noticeable during the lecture. I heard every word!


## Berg to Schoenberg

[Vienna, 5 November 1912]

In haste I send you, dear Herr Schönberg, a review from the *Tagblatt*,[1] stupid of course! Yesterday I heard *Das Lied von der Erde*.[2] It was wonderful, even though I didn't particularly care for the performance, and Weidemann was vocally inadequate. I also met Moll there, who had been at your lecture and was very enthusiastic, strongly urging me to see to it that the Akademischer Verband publish this lecture.[3] Naturally I am all in favor of that since it coincides with my desire to have these words about me always. I'll discuss it with Buschbeck.

Your lecture left an excellent and persuasive impression in Vienna. From what I've heard. Despite having been poorly attended! It turned out there were 4 lectures the same day. Including Specht's Strauss lecture, which had to be canceled for lack of interest.

All this in great haste, but with the very, very warmest regards

from your Berg

Oh yes: Ethel Smyth![4] That was the stupidest, most revolting thing you can

1. An unsigned review of the *Pierrot lunaire* performance and Schoenberg's Mahler lecture appeared in the *Neues Wiener Tagblatt* on 4 November 1912.
2. In a Singakademie concert under Bruno Walter. Friedrich Weidemann and William Miller were the soloists.
3. Portions of Schoenberg's lecture appeared for the first time in *Arnold Schoenberg zum 60. Geburtstag, 13. September 1934* (Vienna, 1934).
4. The concert included three choruses with orchestra by Ethel Smyth ("Auf den Klippen von Cornwall," "Sleepless dreams," and "Hey, nonny no!").

imagine. I actually longed for Wottawa![5] Nor would it have been successful if she hadn't taken a bow at the end. It was incredibly insulting to perform it at all, let alone preceding Mahler!

Please be so kind as to excuse the smudges!

--------

5. The Austrian composer and pianist Heinrich Wottawa had died on 7 February 1912.

*Berg to Schoenberg (postcard)*

Tuesday
[Vienna, 12 November 1912]
In the café

I must ask you something important, dear Herr Schönberg, about the concert on the 20th. Should Reti play your piano pieces, the old and the new, in succession, or should there be an intermission between them—or, finally, should something else be played in between. In that case the program suggested by the Akademischer Verband would be: 1) Wellesz (!): piano pieces, 2) your 3 old piano pieces, 3) Webern's violin pieces, 4) my 4 old published songs, 5) your new piano pieces, 6) Bartók piano pieces! The order of the Wellesz and Bartók is certainly good. But the others are questionable, so please let me or Buschbeck know your decision soon.

Many thanks, dear Herr Schönberg, for your portrait postcard. With the exception of the left cheek I consider it very good. But the one Königer has is even nicer.

Many, many thanks, dear Herr Schönberg,

Your Berg

*Schoenberg to Berg*

Berlin-Zehlendorf, 16 November 1912

Dear friend,

It is difficult to judge a program from afar. I think one has to be emotionally involved somehow. But I can't be emotionally involved in anything taking place in Vienna. I'm sorry, if only because of the interest I take in your and Webern's compositions; but unfortunately that's the way it is. But the program order seems all right. Is Dr. Reti playing all of it?—In any case let me know how it turns out. Who is singing your songs? Who is playing Webern's violin pieces? Will the things be well performed?—You were supposed to get a picture like Königer's in Vienna. But I forgot. There are much better pictures of me now. One by this person Schenker,[1] then 3 by a Dresden photographer Erfurth.[2] But they are very expensive.—I leave for Amsterdam in a week!

For now the warmest regards

Your Schönberg

1. The Viennese photographer Karl Schenker.
2. Hugo Erfurth.

*Portrait photograph of Arnold Schoenberg by Hugo Erfurth of Dresden, 1912 (Arnold Schoenberg Institute 1480)*

## Berg to Schoenberg

Saturday
[Vienna] 23 November 1912

Dear Herr Schönberg,

Yesterday I returned from my trip[1] and heard of what has been happening meanwhile with the *Gurrelieder* parts. About 2 weeks ago, and frequently thereafter, I asked Hertzka when I would finally be able to check the parts, but he always answered evasively; during my absence he finally bade me by pneumatic post to come see him, whereupon my wife went and gave him the addresses of Königer and Polnauer; she also met Schreker there, who was still complaining that he doesn't have a chorus. Unfortunately Schmid, who could have been used as a copyist, is out of town until the middle of next week (until about the 26th–28th). Heller[2] is probably unusable, possibly another student,[3] who, however, doesn't have much time, as he's in high school. But Hertzka has apparently found a copyist and if worse comes to worse I myself know of an excellent copyist. In other words, what with our (Königer's, Polnauer's, and my) help (copying, checking, numbering the full score (!!)) the matter will be settled somehow; Polnauer, who spoke with Englisch[4] or Hertzka yesterday (unfortunately the latter is sick), is coming to see me this afternoon together with Königer, and then I'll add a note as to how the work was par-

1. In mid-November a fire at Berghof that destroyed the barn and killed some of the livestock made it necessary for Berg to travel there.
2. Rudolf Heller, originally a student of Schoenberg, studied with Berg intermittently in 1912/13 and again in 1922.
3. Gottfried Kassowitz.
4. Office manager at Universal Edition.

celed out and what we'll do to see that it's completed on time. From what I understand, the 1ˢᵗ rehearsals start on 5 December. Another possibility is that the performance be postponed from January to February, so that instead of <u>dividing</u> the rehearsals between January and December, <u>all</u> of them will be in January (or February). It isn't altogether clear to me (for instance that you yourself, dear Herr Schönberg, are said to have copied some of the orchestral parts of Part I!!), so I won't write more about it until I know more. Anyway, it was another case of Hertzka's incredible carelessness and a great pity that I was away just then.

I was in Carinthia for almost a week—amidst the deepest snow, fighting it out with the insurance people so as to keep the loss caused by the fire to a minimum. The loss is nonetheless substantial and I realize that so-called "insurance" doesn't protect one from loss. Unless one is <u>dishonest</u>. For insurance is calculated according to the monetary, not the ideal value of an object, not, for instance, according to its usefulness. But as far as I'm concerned the value of a machine, say, resides in the fact that it threshes all of my grain, and I can only consider myself fully insured if, in case I lose this machine, I'm given a replacement that will continue to thresh my grain. But the insurance companies calculate: the machine costs, say 200 kronen when new. With 5 years' use there's a deduction of 25% (even though the machine does the work for me today <u>just</u> as it did 5 years ago), making 150 kronen, whereby I suffer a loss of at least 50 kronen! And above all: the 150 kronen I get back don't put me in a position to purchase a machine that will perform the same work for me.

And the same applies to the larger things, buildings, feed supplies, etc.

In other words a very unpleasant, unproductive matter, to which I was forced to devote a great deal of valuable time. I didn't even find time to think about the job Hertzka has offered me, of preparing a "thematic analysis of the *Gurrelieder.*" I would really like to know what you think about that, dear Herr Schönberg, and about thematic analyses in general!! Basically I am very reluctant to do such work and have always been contemptuous of such things (for instance, those by Specht or Wöss). Now I <u>myself</u> am to do that sort of thing, and for such a beloved work, at that!! I don't even know what <u>purpose</u> such a project serves, whether it increases understanding of the work itself. Whether, for instance—to be quite clear about it—the reader of such an analysis, approaching the work with no initial understanding, can get to know it through the analysis—indeed can learn to love it—which would at least be something! (Or is that unimportant?) If one took one of these analyses (e.g., for Mahler's VIIIᵗʰ) and left out the musical examples,* then the text could just as easily apply to a work by Delius, or the like. I quote:

> At [73] the orchestra joins in a <u>powerful cadence</u> over an E♭ pedal (contrabasses, bassoon, bass clarinet, contrabassoon, drumroll)—<u>which sinks to D</u> after 12 measures and remains there for the next 32—and the <u>trumpets</u>, example 29, blare triumphantly into the <u>vigorous figures</u> of example 40. Gradual calm—and in a measured rhythm—but with <u>undiminished strength</u>—a reminiscence of the Iˢᵗ theme enters: the <u>astringent harmonies</u> of [9] <u>soar</u> in the woodwinds and strings and <u>lead to a literal recapitulation</u> of 10 ([76] 5).—

Completely at random I have here taken a passage from Specht's analysis of the VIII[th],[5] but it's a perfect example of the dreadfulness and *irrelevance* of such analyses. I don't know upon which passage from the VIII[th] this—parody—was coined, nor do I wish to know, so as not to spoil the passage for me; rather I'll assume that it concerns a work by Delius, to which it could apply just as easily. I cannot believe that such details, such measure-counting, where the trumpets blare triumphantly and where the astringent melodies soar—aside from Specht's style—(for how else is one to formulate it if one wants to say—or is to say—a ***single word***—about a long succession of harmonies of which, after all, only music is capable), I therefore cannot believe that someone who already knows the work anyway (that is, after all, a prerequisite) could get anything out of such an analysis. Surely it has absolutely no scholarly, music-theoretical value (at best "literary" value, exploring "spiritual relationships"[6] (!!!), etc.). For if one were really going to analyze, then it shouldn't be just thematically: the theme itself, all developmental, variational, formal aspects, etc. But also harmonic, contrapuntal, and finally orchestrational aspects——: that way one would end up with four entire volumes on one work, indeed for every symphony, comprising all of theory, indeed one couldn't get by with less (harmony, counterpoint, form, orchestration). I still remember only too well the time of my great good fortune when I could listen to you, dear Herr Schönberg, "analyze"; when you would discuss the orchestration of the *I*[st] measure of a Beethoven symphony for an hour——or, as now in the Mahler lecture, the melody (ten measures) of just the slow movement of Mahler's VI[th]! That is analysis, *that's* worth doing—that enriches the knowledgeable and enlightens the ignorant! Everything else is drivel. At first I thought that such a project (for the *Gurrelieder*)—if it were not to be something à la Specht—would only work if one pointed out the beauties (which would, of course, result in citing the entire piano reduction, and occasionally analyzing a passage thoroughly (now harmonically, now thematically, formally, orchestrationally), in other words merely pointing out features and bringing many, many musical examples. (ultimately—the entire piano score(!))). But either the result would be terribly spotty (since it couldn't be complete) or (if I possessed the requisite literary qualifications) a mere essay or the like———Neither corresponds to Hertzka's commission, nor, as Hertzka would insist, would there be much of an audience. As you see, dear Herr Schönberg, I'm very uncertain whether I should, can—must accept this commission of Hertzka's! Of course, if it's possible to do something like this well, if it needs to be done——then I would consider it my duty to try. That's why I'm writing at such length, dear Herr Schönberg—to ask whether you would be so kind as to let me know at some point whether I should take on this project. In my state of complete uncertainty it's impossible for me to decide one way or the other, so a simple "Yes" or "No" from you would suffice! That—as always—would be decisive!!

5. Specht's analysis was published by Universal Edition in 1912. Berg quoted from a passage (34) dealing with Part II of the Symphony. The underlinings are Berg's.

6. The very next sentence in Specht's analysis begins: "Der geistige Zusammenhang ist klar: . . ." (The spiritual relationship is clear: . . .).

Many thanks for your kind lettercard, which was awaiting me in Vienna. As you know, Webern's violin pieces and my songs were dropped from the program[7] because of Werndorff's illness, who was to have accompanied them (a certain "Sembach" from the Volksoper[8] would have sung them). Königer probably told you about the rest. Because of my absence I naturally wasn't at the concert!

Now I'll wait for Polnauer and Königer with regard to the *Gurrelieder* parts, after which I'll finish the letter!——

24 November 1912

Well, dear Herr Schönberg. The *Gurrelieder* are in the hands of various copyists and will certainly be completely finished in a week. Whereupon we, Königer, Polnauer, possibly also several students, and I will collate all the parts and enter the rehearsal numbers, which were forgotten in the full score (they *are* in the piano reduction), so that the rehearsals can begin without delay in early December (the 5th, I believe). To be sure, Hertzka is still babbling about postponing the performance. But that doesn't affect writing out the parts.

Now I really will close, dear Herr Schönberg, with the very warmest regards to you and your dear family, also on my wife's behalf, and remaining in immutable loyalty and gratitude

Your Berg

(I think it's better to have the parts written out by copyists than by those who are unpracticed in notation (Polnauer, for example). The orchestra will be able to read the former more easily and it will be more consistent!)

\* after all, they aren't decisive, for if the listener doesn't like them, then neither will the reader. So he doesn't need them. And if the listener likes it, then he doesn't need an analysis, he could do the same with the score itself.

---

7. The 20 November concert of the Akademischer Verband included the Ravel Sonatina, Five Piano Pieces by Egon Wellesz, Schoenberg's Opp. 11 and 19, and a Bartók Burlesque and Rumanian Dance (given as Op. 8 and Op. 8c in the program). Rudolf Reti performed the Schoenberg work and Norah Drewett the remaininder of the program.
8. Erwin Sembach.

*Berg to Schoenberg*

[Vienna] 27 November 1912

Dear Herr Schönberg,

I was just at Hertzka's, who told me of the probable postponement of the *Gurrelieder* performance from 18 January to 23 February. I just want to tell you, as I also told Hertzka, that this postponement is not on account of the parts not being finished, but for **other** reasons, which Hertzka admits. The parts given to us from a portion of Part III will certainly be finished by 5 December, when the 1st rehearsal was to have taken place, and are guaranteed flawless. So that's not the reason. The parts Hertzka himself gave to copyists may be incorrect and in need of spot checking: but not ours! The real reason for the postponement, and one I can appreciate, is simply the following: there would be an interruption of 1 month between the first 5 rehearsals in early December and the last ones: in the middle of January, which would surely be extremely disadvantageous!, while in February all 10 rehearsals could take place in succession. On top of that, Schreker's Court Opera premiere is at the end of January,[1] so throughout January he will be overburdened with rehearsals there, which also would not be the case in February!

Of course the delay will cause the following: *Pelleas* was to have taken place midday on 23 February, which is impossible if the *Gurrelieder* are in the evening. So the Akademischer Verband would <u>have</u> to cancel (they wouldn't have any choice, since Hertzka could refuse them the parts.) For the eventuality that the *Gurrelieder* actually are postponed, I advised Buschbeck to take 18 January, the day originally set aside for the *Gurrelieder*, for *Pelleas!* Buschbeck is going to discuss that with Höllering,[2] Schreker, and Hertzka, and will let you know.

Finally an error turned up in Part I of the *Gurrelieder* piano score! While the parts were being copied out and rehearsal numbers entered, **one missing measure** was discovered in the piano score. This measure can be added very easily, and since the score isn't engraved yet, it's no disaster. Naturally Hertzka is triumphant that he delayed the publication of the score so long! If he hadn't, as we had wished, the score would have been flawed. <u>Now</u> it will be flawless! The missing measure is the enclosed. The same measure is missing in your first reduction of Part I, which I merely revised, and the mistake arose because I didn't notice the discrepancy between it and the full score, as both cases are possible. And here I would like to pass right on to a favor I have long wanted to ask of you, dear Herr Schönberg. You see, I have the reduction you made of Part I here with me and would very, very much like to ask you whether I could keep a few pages of it. Not only would it be a wonderful memento of this project and of a time when I learned so much from you about preparing piano reductions . . . , but it would also be the wonderful fulfillment of a long cherished wish: to possess a manuscript of yours, dear Herr Schönberg. I don't dare ask you for the <u>whole thing</u>——that would be **too wonderful**! But a portion, perhaps the prelude or an interlude——! In that case I would have the portion given me copied and inserted as replacement, and return your manuscript of Part I minus the portion given me.

I also discussed the thematic analysis with Hertzka, and my indecisiveness about accepting the job. Which he appreciated, and he thought a so-called thematic <u>table</u> would suffice. Now I am even more undecided whether that would be possible for the *Gurrelieder*, i.e., whether you would approve of it, all the more, since one would have to name the individual themes. And the thought of: Love motive, etc., is abhorrent to me. Well, the matter isn't urgent and perhaps you'll be so kind as to let me know your opinion regarding a thematic analysis, that is a thematic table, which would be the only relevant and decisive opinion for me. I won't begin such a project <u>until</u> I hear from you.

---

1. The Frankfurt and Vienna double premiere of *Das Spielwerk und die Prinzessin* did not take place until 15 March 1913.
2. Georg Höllering, secretary of the Tonkünstler Orchestra.

Many regards, dear kind Herr Schönberg! I presume you are now in Amsterdam and I'm already enormously eager to hear all about it.[3]

In unchanging devotion and gratitude

Your Berg

_____

3. On 25 November, Schoenberg arrived in Amsterdam where he had three rehearsals with the Concertgebouw Orchestra for performances of *Pelleas und Melisande* on the 28th and 30th in Amsterdam and the Hague. The program also included the Dvorak Cello Concerto (with the soloist Serge Barjanski) and Wagner's *Tristan Vorspiel und Liebestod*, both conducted by Willem Mengelberg.

## Schoenberg to Berg

Berlin-Zehlendorf, 4 December 1912

Dear friend,

The performances in Amsterdam and the Hague were lovely. Especially in the Hague. I was able to make music with the orchestra with absolute freedom. I took completely different tempos than in Amsterdam. The right tempos. I summoned the courage to take everything as slowly as it ought to go. Whereas I used to hurry over certain passages as quickly as possible so as not to be disturbed by the audience. For instance, the $^{12}/_{8}$ measure beginning at rehearsal number 50. The sound was therefore very beautiful and for once the whole passage with its apprehensive, morbid, raw and yet subconscious mood came out very beautifully. And the beginning and many other things finally worked, too. Perhaps I should have rehearsed some things more. Some polyphonic passages, for instance, weren't clear enough for my taste. But one can't have everything all at once. The orchestra is wonderful. Above all the winds: extremely refined sound and phrasing!

Now as for the *Gurrelieder* analysis. I don't think it would hurt if you were to do it. I myself don't see what good it can do. I find it downright abominable in concerts. But perhaps for those who wish to prepare themselves beforehand. However, the main point seems to me: that Hertzka apparently wants it at all costs and in that case it would be a pity if just anybody did it. Perhaps you can think of an alternative. Something like this, for instance:

A list of the most important themes, in the order of the individual sections. And then an indication of the principal points at which these themes recur. Perhaps including some of the most characteristic forms they take on. Perhaps the attempt to describe certain characteristic moods in a simple, unbombastic (i.e., somewhat detached) style. Now and again at some characteristic passage perhaps mention of the structure. In other words, not a thorough treatment in which everything has to be said, but only things one happens particularly to note **and** about which one has something to say. So on no account mention everything simply under force of the succession of events. Nothing philosophical. Rather, aphoristic, unforced, unrelated, short discussions in loosely constructed paragraphs on things that occur to one. So: in a loose aphoristic form! That would certainly be something new.

I'd very much like to know how things stand with the *Gurrelieder* performance. And what the Akademischer Verband will do now!—Not only do I not find the idea of 5 rehearsals in December and 5 in January unfavorable, but on the contrary very advantageous. Another instance of Hertzka's high-handedness. I think the intervening break would be as enlightening for the orchestra as 2–3 rehearsals.

As for the error of which you wrote, that's an error in the full score. One extra measure. The piano score is correct!! So Hertzka could have published it long ago.—Incidentally, you should still have the original manuscript—no you don't, I just found it. There it says:

in den Tod

You may keep the piano score to *Gurrelieder*. All of it. Otherwise there's no point.

———

Don't name the motives. That's not necessary. The vocal text is usually there anyway. So in heaven's name what more could one possibly need! 2 texts?!? And music? Perhaps pictures and a thermometer as well!

Warm regards

Your Schönberg

*Berg to Schoenberg*

[Vienna] 6 December 1912

Again, dear Herr Schönberg, I can only write with pencil (in the streetcar), since checking the parts takes all day,[1] but I did want to answer your dear, long letter right away and my only opportunity is during the time I'm forced to spend on public transportation on interminable trips to the tax offices, etc. What you wrote about the *Pelleas* performances only intensified my already keen longing for this work, which grew even more when I thereupon looked at the score a bit with Königer during his lesson. That reawakened my great resentment against a world order that denies me such treasures. For the present I can't tell you anything about the Vienna performance of *Pelleas*, either. Apparently the switch (*Gurre* 23 February instead of 18 January; *Pelleas* 18 January instead of 23 February) will not work. It's impossible to get a decision out of this Höllering character. Everyone keeps "passing the buck" to someone else. Höllering to Schreker, Schreker to Hertzka, Hertzka to Höllering, and so on. So it's conceivable that 18 January won't be free even if *Gurrelieder* isn't done until 23 February. Which means *Pelleas* won't be done until after the *Gurrelieder*, which would have much, indeed everything in its favor, except for our longing to hear the work as soon as possible and to have you back in Vienna! I hope this matter will be resolved soon, I expect it daily. I'll probably see Schreker in the

1. In an intervening postcard of 3 December, Berg described his work checking *Gurrelieder* parts, in which there were many errors.

next few days at a rehearsal for the 12 December concert (Schumann-Pfitzner, Reger, Schillings)[2] and can find out more about the *Gurrelieder* performance then; where he is to find the enormous forces, <u>why</u> the postponement was even necessary?! Because the divided rehearsals can't have been the only reason! I don't even know which <u>men's chorus</u> will be participating. I'll write fully after talking to him.

I'm very grateful for the stimulating ideas about the *Gurrelieder* analysis. I had begun to envision the project similarly, but lacked the courage! But what you say confirms that it's possible after all, so I look forward to the work with pleasure and hope to come up with something halfway useful. As soon as I've finished my work on the parts, which will probably take until the end of next week, I'll start on the thematic analysis.

And now, dear, best Herr Schönberg, thank you for your *Gurrelieder* score. I am overjoyed and as soon as I can do without it I'll have it nicely bound and will treasure it as the most valuable of keepsakes. I thank you for it a thousand times, dear Herr Schönberg.

Warmest regards to you and your esteemed wife, also on my wife's behalf, and, thanking you once again for the great kindness of your dear letter, I am <u>as always</u>

Your Berg

---

2. The Philharmonic Chorus concert presented Pfitzner's arrangement of Schumann's women's choruses, two works by Delius, *In Meerestreiben* for baritone, mixed chorus, and orchestra, and the orchestral piece *Paris*, as well the *Hochzeitslied* for soprano, baritone, mixed chorus, and orchestra by the German composer and conductor Max von Schillings.

## Berg to Schoenberg

[Vienna] 21 December 1912

I haven't written for a long time, dear Herr Schönberg. The reason was the enormous task of the *Gurrelieder* parts, I have turned over that portion for which I was responsible (woodwinds, brass, and percussion from page 123 to the end of the score, 750 pages in all) to Hertzka. Because the full score turned out to have so many mistakes, I am now supposed to look through all the other parts as well, including the handwritten string parts, but only spot checking, since these parts have been checked often and are from Berlin. Besides, these are the parts from the portion of the *Gurrelieder* that had been copied into the full score at the time of composition,——which surely contains far fewer copying mistakes, small transposing errors, missing dynamic and rhythmic signs, slurs, dots, etc., than the portion from page 123 on, where you didn't take as much time and were doing the new orchestration incidentally, as it were. If I were to look through all of the other parts and portions of the full score as carefully as I did the parts from page 123 on, I would be checking at least 5 hours a day for 6–8 weeks, which would scarcely be worth the relatively few mistakes in this portion, and these will be found much more quickly in the course of the 1st rehearsals. From glancing at these parts it does seem that they are much more accurate than those of the last portion, not only because the copyists' errors have already been corrected but because, as I said, the full score of those portions is so much more correct, perhaps even flawless. After that I could finally turn to the thematic analysis, which will doubtless take me quite a long time in order halfway to accomplish what I have in mind and you suggested. Finally, Hertzka doesn't want to spend one more heller on the parts, which have apparently cost him 1,000–1,200 kronen already; he was furious when I asked for 200 kronen for the work I've delivered to date, at least 100 hours' worth.

His explanation is that he can't expect to have his expenses for the parts reimbursed either by Gutmann in Berlin or by the Philharmonic Chorus. The latter, it turns out, sustained heavy losses from its last concert.* And the Philharmonic Chorus is in financial straits. Rehearsals have begun with the chorus itself, although there's still no men's chorus! All the larger choruses have declined and now they're looking among the smaller choruses: Kaufmännischer Gesangverein as reinforcement for the Philharmonic Chorus' own forces for the men's choruses. Schreker is incredibly busy. He leaves after Christmas for premieres,[1] his Vienna premiere is early February. During his absence, I am to conduct 2 rehearsals of the mixed chorus and several with the men's choruses. I'm not at all sure I can handle this! But have to decide soon. What speaks **for** it is that I don't wish to leave anything undone to help bring about this performance, which is being prepared so laxly, and that I'm immensely eager to make music in this way, above all with this work.** And you, dear Herr Schönberg, know what speaks **against** it: my doubts as to my abilities and the thought that my confidence in undertaking it may perhaps be overconfidence, which I would come to regret. A word from you, dear Herr Schönberg, would be most valuable. It would be (if it arrived in time) decisive, as always! After all I could participate in preparations for the performance in other ways as well, for instance, in coaching the narrator's role, Klaus-Narr, etc. . . . , since Schreker, considering the time constraints he is under, would be happy to have assistance. By the way, Schreker tells me there's apparently still no narrator! Onno[2] apparently considers the range too high and yet he's the only one I consider suitable. I don't know of anyone else and neither does Schreker!—As you see, dear Herr Schönberg, I'm giving you nothing but partial facts, so I had better wait for a thorough discussion with Schreker in the next few days, after which I'll know more. For now, my very best wishes for Christmas and the coming holidays to you, my dear, kind Herr Schönberg, and your dear family. Also on behalf of my wife. We hope that you returned from your trip to Russia successful and in good health, and thank you very much for your card from Petersburg. I'm immensely eager for news of the performance and reception! Very satisfactory, I'm sure! (I know that Buschbeck wrote you at length about the prospects for the Vienna concert. I'm delighted with your idea of performing the *Eroica* and Webern as well as the Chamber Symphony.[3] Nedbal did the *Eroica* yesterday.)

I have taken the liberty, dear Herr Schönberg, of sending you a few volumes of

1. *Der ferne Klang* received its first Leipzig performance on 9 February 1913.
2. The Austrian actor Ferdinand Onno.
3. On 13 December Schoenberg wrote to Buschbeck of his plans to perform the orchestral version of his Chamber Symphony and possibly "Natur" and "Sehnsucht" from the Six Orchestral Songs, Op. 8, as well as Webern's Orchestra Pieces, Op. 6, and either Beethoven's *Eroica*, or a coupling of Wagner's *Tristan und Isolde* prelude with Brahms's *Haydn Variations*.

Balzac—(directly from the bookstore, as that was most convenient—) of which I myself am familiar with the *Letters to a Stranger*,[4] which I liked <u>very</u> much (particularly the I$^{st}$ volume), as they are very informative, especially about <u>Seraphita</u>, *Lambert*, etc., and while reading I kept thinking that they might interest you; the other works, which I know only in part, appear to belong to the most beautiful things Balzac wrote, judging by what's in the "Letters" about them, and I hope I haven't gone completely wrong in my choice; for now that I'm so far away from you and don't even know what music, books, etc., you have, it was enormously difficult to find something that might give you, dear Herr Schönberg, a little pleasure—and something you don't already have. I hope you don't also receive these books from someone else and I hope you won't take it ill that I wasted <u>so many</u> <u>words</u> on a trifle that isn't worth <u>mentioning</u>.

Again a thousand Christmas greetings, my dear, esteemed Herr Schönberg, from one who is almost always with you in spirit,

Your Berg

*That included new works by Delius, who has gone over to the French, and Schillings, who is continuing the compositional style between *Don Juan* and *Elektra*, which Richard Strauss has abandoned—also the Schumann-Pfitzner choruses. Performance <u>very poor</u> both vocally and instrumentally.

**I should probably rehearse the men's and women's choruses——<u>separately</u>.

---

4. The two-volume set *Briefe an die Fremde*, translated by Eugenie Faber (Leipzig, 1911).

*Arnold and Mathilde Schoenberg with their children, Gertrud and Georg, Berlin, 1913 (Arnold Schoenberg Institute 1763)*

## Schoenberg to Berg

Berlin-Zehlendorf, 28 December 1912

Dear friend,

My warmest thanks for the beautiful Christmas gift. I'm looking forward to reading it. It is very gratifying to me that my friends go to such trouble to give me pleasure. That they rack their brains until they find something that appeals both to their tastes and mine, and that they concern themselves so intensely with my tastes is something that always moves me very deeply. Again, warmest thanks.

Now to your letter: It goes without saying that you should take advantage of this opportunity to get involved in practical music making and should definitely conduct the rehearsals for *Gurrelieder* choruses and solos. Of course it won't be easy for you to do something like that for the first time. Therefore, in haste, I'd like to tell you the most important things experience has taught me. Namely: when you break off (and you must break off whenever you 1) <u>hear</u> a mistake and 2) know how to correct it) you must express yourself as **clearly** and **concisely** as possible. Talk as little as possible. Never try to be witty. Most important: there are only the following kinds of mistakes.

1. wrong notes (possibly faulty intonation)
2. wrong rhythm (possibly faulty declamation, pronunciation!)
3. wrong dynamics (*p, f*)
4. wrong phrasing

Thus there are no corrections or explanations other than:

1) g instead of g♯; too sharp, too flat
2) demonstrating the correct rhythm! (stronger, weaker)
3) demanding more or less *p* and *f*
4) correcting breathing, accents(*p, f*), phrase endings and entrances.

The last (4) already comprises finer interpretation. If one understands something about singing one can also make various technical points. And one can pay attention to accurate pronunciation, but <u>everything</u> else, particularly: mood, ideas, beauty, character, and everything poetic is bad!! That's for us, not for the chorus! Believe me and take what I say to heart as soon as possible. I, too, had to learn that. And the skill lies in asking for *p* and *f* in such a way that everything else follows just from that. That is not just my advice, but that of all conductors; but it's true nonetheless!

So: Good luck! Let me know how it goes!

It's a real shame, though, that Hertzka pays you so wretchedly for your work on *Gurrelieder*. I made a particular point of telling him he should pay well. But it's impossible to prevail against him. Anyway you needn't put up with it. Simply demand the equivalent of whatever time it takes you. Arrange for him to pay you a certain hourly rate. If it's too expensive for him, he should organize his office better!

The mistakes in the *Gurre* full score: [*Schoenberg details various errors such as misplaced performance indications and wrong accidentals.*] It certainly doesn't bode well! Never before have I made so many mistakes!

A quick word about Petersburg: the performance was good but not as good as Amsterdam. Not enough rehearsals! Very enthusiastic reception!

Now many warm regards to you and your wife

Your Arnold Schönberg

*Berg to Schoenberg*

New Year's Eve 1912
[Vienna, 31 December 1912]

My dear Herr Schönberg,

Many thanks for your dear letter. It made me incredibly happy, particularly because you encouraged me to conduct the chorus rehearsals, which, as a result of Schreker's urging, I had already agreed to do prior to your advice, since otherwise Weigl would have undertaken it. But as a result of your letter I am now convinced I did the right thing—also because I had the first rehearsal shortly after receipt of your letter with its wonderful conducting tips, and, as far as I could tell, it went quite well. Unfortunately the rehearsal wasn't well attended, maybe 50–60 sopranos and altos, but only 6–8 men. So I worked mostly with the women. We went through the final chorus, first individually, then in groups, finally all the women from "Seht die Sonne" to Bewegter (full score page 172). In contrast to Schreker, who always takes individual voices as well as choruses with piano accompaniment, I rehearsed only a capella, so that the passages rehearsed to date are already secure and going well.* The chorus, particularly the women, is not as poor as I had expected, nonetheless I naturally had to correct and also frequently to repeat a great deal (mainly rhythmic, but also melodic and dynamic things). I not only had your kind advice, but also the memory of your own choral rehearsals and I stuck to that. Finally Webern, too, to whom I had written of my intention, reminded me of the choral rehearsals with the chorus you founded,[1] and gave me a few tips from his own experience, so that it's hardly my doing that the matter went well. Unfortunately, I could hardly rehearse anything with those few men, only the measures: "Seht die Sonne." An additional men's chorus rehearsal will be held soon. By then the problem with the men's choruses for the "Wilde Jagd" should be resolved. So far, aside from their own men, they have the Kaufmännischer Gesangverein, said to be only 120 men strong, which is why they are also counting on a Czech chorus,[2] so there would actually be 3 choruses. For the present the first few rehearsals of the Kaufmännischer Gesangverein are being led by their conductor Henriquez,[3] after which I'll probably take over. I'm already looking forward to it, for now that my initial fear of the purely technical aspect of conducting, for which, as you'll surely remember, I've always displayed great awkwardness, has, in my immodest opinion, been transformed into **somewhat** of a routine (through practice at home)——now that, as I said, I'm at least no longer afraid of that and can really hear, meaning I can also make demands, in a word can really make music, the activity gives me a great deal of satisfaction! I do hope the expectations I have of my own abilities are not too optimistic and that my rehearsals really will have positive results (not just for me but also for the chorus—and for the work).

---

1. Schoenberg conducted the Chormusikverein during the 1906/07 season. Berg sang in the bass section.

2. This chorus may have been either the Prague Deutscher Singverein or the Prague Deutscher Männergesangverein; both had participated in the first Prague performance of Mahler's Eighth Symphony in 1912. The choruses in the 1913 Vienna *Gurrelieder* premiere were all Viennese.

3. Artur von Henriquez, director of the Kaufmännischer Gesangverein.

I'm also working on the thematic analysis, which is going very slowly, as well as continuing to check parts. And am still finding mistakes in the engraved choral parts, but unfortunately also some small ones in the piano score. Now Hertzka can gloat again that he delayed publication.—I shall make a note of the corrections in the full score you gave me and copy them into the parts.—

And now, my dear, kind Herr Schönberg, my wife and I wish you and your esteemed wife the very, very best for the New Year, and I surely don't need to add that these wishes aren't just restricted to 1 January, but are equally valid <u>throughout</u> the year, <u>and life long</u>. As is my gratitude,

Your Berg.

Please, dear Herr Schönberg, excuse the form of this letter, solely a result of my great haste since I've had to take over all of the administrative work for the houses, now that my mother is out of town (in <u>Berlin</u>!).

\*I had the impression that the chorus is very enthusiastic about the work and that everyone is pleased with his part. (Of course that's understandable!!)

*Berg to Schoenberg (picture postcard: Gustav Mahler and his birth house in Kalischt, Bohemia)*

[End of 1912?[1]]

Doesn't this resemble the shelter in which Christ was born?

Berg

1. Berg's undated postcard of Mahler's birthplace has a printing date of 1912 and, given the allusion to Christ's birth, may well have been sent around Christmas 1912.

*The postcard illustration of Mahler's birthplace which Berg sent to Schoenberg (Library of Congress)*

# 1913

*Schoenberg to Berg (postcard)*

Berlin-Zehlendorf, 7 January 1913

Dear friend,

Do you have 1–2 fairly short (fairly easy?) orchestra songs for mezzo soprano? I may do them in the Akademischer Verband orchestra concert if it's on 30 March. For on that day Frau Freund[1] would participate (for free!). The program would include: Webern's Orchestra Pieces, your Orchestra Songs, Mahler's *Kindertoten-lieder*, my Chamber Symphony.—Ask Buschbeck about the date. I wrote to him a while ago!—I hope to be able to do the Berlin *Gurrelieder* performance on 25 March. 4/5 of the guarantee fund has already been collected.[2]—Have copies of the orchestra songs prepared right away if you can (piano reductions for Frau Freund and me and full score for me). Likewise: parts, as soon as possible. But it must require at most half a rehearsal? Or perhaps the Akademischer Verband will grant an additional one.

Warm regards

Your Arnold Schönberg

1. The German soprano Marya Freund toured widely as a recitalist and oratorio singer. Schoenberg first met her in 1908.
2. When the financial arrangements for the Vienna premiere of the *Gurrelieder* became threatened in 1912, Schoenberg began plans for a Berlin premiere, which at this time was scheduled for late May, as Schoenberg tells Berg in a postcard of 10 January 1913. By the end of January, 6,000 marks had been collected toward the estimated cost of 10,000 marks.

*Berg to Schoenberg*

[Vienna] 9 January 1913

My dear, good Herr Schönberg.

Your card made me happier than I can say. Your intention alone makes me so happy, moves, touches me so deeply that I cannot begin to tell you! The intention alone is so beautiful, so enriching to me personally, that even were nothing to come of it, it would have given me an overabundance of happiness. Of course, I don't know whether you, dear Herr Schönberg, will consider the songs any good or worth performing. I myself won't know until I have shown them to you. And then I'm not sure whether they might not be too difficult after all. In any case I'll immediately send you a copy of the full score, which I had had prepared just in case, but which turned out very ostentatious, as the copyist[1] chose an excessively large format and drew in the titles, scoring, etc. (apparently he wanted to surprise me), all of which would have been deserving of a worthier object. I only mention this, dear Herr Schönberg, so that you won't be put off from the outset by the flashy format. On the other hand, being so beautifully copied it's splendidly suited for performance purposes. The pieces are the 5 Altenberg Songs I finished this summer, i.e., this fall, which are conceived cyclically, though they can easily be performed singly. They are all short. Some (II, III, and IV) extremely short. If I were to advise you, dear Herr Schönberg, I would suggest—considering above all the musical simplicity of the vocal line (i.e., the pitches are easy to "hit")—the V$^{th}$ song (a passacaglia). Nor would it be difficult to rehearse with the orchestra (though it is the longest of the songs, it can still be considered short, 55 measures). Naturally this song can be performed alone. But as you are so kind and write: 1–2, I shall be so immodest as to suggest yet another: namely the III$^{rd}$ or IV$^{th}$. The III$^{rd}$ is easier for the singer and has only one difficult passage for the orchestra, the tempo transition (over a long ritardando) from $\frac{3}{4}$—over $\frac{9}{8} = 3$ times $\frac{3}{8}$—to $\frac{3}{8}$, so that the last $\frac{3}{8}$'s are equal to the initial $\frac{3}{4}$. Overall the IV$^{th}$ song (voice and orchestra) is more difficult. On the other hand it is decidedly a woman's song. So that, if two songs are possible, I would suggest the combination: III and V or IV and V. Of course the II$^{nd}$ is very easy, too; but too short, perhaps, to stand alone beside another song (possibly the V$^{th}$). The I$^{st}$ is too difficult! In every respect! So I won't even suggest it! Of course the scoring, which you will find noted at the beginning of each song, may also be crucial for your decision. And then: whichever one you consider good, whichever one you wish to perform! My suggestions mainly concerned ease of performance and comprehensibility. But it could just as well be the combinations I–V or II–III or III–IV, or the like! As regards range, the songs are all suited for mezzo-soprano. So that wouldn't be an obstacle! But of course I don't know what can be expected of the singer's musicality (accuracy), therefore, solely with regard to the difficulty of the vocal part, I have set up the following order: V easiest. II also easy. III middling. IV and I most difficult!—

So, dear, kind Herr Schönberg! I'll send the full score of all 5 right away. I'll be able to prepare piano reductions quickly from some sketches and have them copied. But only of the last four; a reduction of the first is impossible. Possibly the vocal line together with the most important orchestral parts (I dare say that's all that matters!). But most important, I shall prepare the 4 reductions, have them copied and then send you both copies of the 4 last songs as well as, possibly, something makeshift for the I$^{st}$ song. But maybe you will already have decided on which 1–2 songs before I'm finished with the reductions, so that I need send you only 2 copies of the 1–2 songs in question. In any case I'll hold off on writing out the parts until you have decided on which 1–2 songs. My copyist could do that very quickly; he

---

1. Probably Josef Kornfeld.

could have all the parts of the 5 songs done in 1–2 weeks, thus for 2 songs at most 5–8 days. And a good job, too! So, dear Herr Schönberg, with regard to the parts I'll await your decision, you'll receive the reductions in a few days.[2]

By the way I just read that Freund is giving a song recital in the Bösendorfersaal on Sunday the 19th: Schumann, Brahms, Mahler, etc. Why no Schönberg!!! But we'll go hear her anyway.

I personally don't know when your concert is scheduled! Buschbeck is away! Should return to Vienna any day, though. I'll write to him at once in Salzburg (9 Ernest Thunstrasse). Apparently 2 March was under consideration before Christmas—but not definitely, perhaps the end of March! Didn't he tell you about that?! (2 March would suit you, wouldn't it?! Exactly 1 week after 23 February, which is practically certain for the *Gurrelieder*.) I'll write as soon as I hear more.[3] And will tell Buschbeck to write.

And now, dear Herr Schönberg, I'll get right to work (piano scores), so as not to interrupt my other project too long: the thematic analysis. That is going slowly but not too badly, I think. Though it will be very long!

Again I thank you many, many times, dear Herr Schönberg, for your kind intention. We, my wife too, are really moved by it and overjoyed at the thought that it might come true.

I'm also really excited about the program! Mahler's *Kindertotenlieder* conducted by you!!!

But not enough by you!! Couldn't you include a couple of orchestra songs after all?—Or are yours too high for Freund? Perhaps *Pelleas*; or would that be too much?— Surely all of that would take at most 2½ hours!—

Enough! I must close! Again a thousand thanks and many regards to you and your esteemed wife, also from my wife

from your Berg

Given the difficulty of the passage, the 2nd choral rehearsal didn't go as well as the first. Now Schreker is back and will probably resume rehearsing with the mixed chorus; I am waiting for the men's chorus, which I will conduct soon. Perhaps I'll also hear more regarding the soloists. I'm very apprehensive about the speaker. Klitsch[4] from the Volkstheater has been asked to do it. I'm looking forward to the Berlin performance like crazy, then my old wish to visit you in Berlin will finally come true, i.e., it must come true, though the "How" is still unclear (financially speaking, of course). But I don't care! "It must be!"[5]

Again a thousand regards and thanks

Your Berg

2. Schoenberg received the full score of the *Altenberg Songs* by 13 January, as he acknowledges in a postcard of that date.

3. In a postcard of 10 January Berg informs Schoenberg that Buschbeck had returned to Vienna and the date of 30 March had been reserved for the Akademischer Verband concert.

4. The Austrian actor and director Wilhelm Klitsch.

5. "Es muss sein" is a quotation from "Der schwergefasste Entschluss" (the difficult decision), the motto Beethoven gave the bridge section between the third and fourth movements of his String Quartet, Op. 135.

## Schoenberg to Berg

Berlin-Zehlendorf, 14 January 1913

Dear friend,

Please number your questions so I can find them more easily when I answer you.[1]

I. For the present I won't need the piano score of the 1st song. I'll be able to study it quite well from the full score. And I rather believe the others are more likely candidates. A pity, by the way, that you chose such a large format and always used whole pages for so small an orchestra, which could almost always have fit comfortably on 24 staves (frequently even less). It makes it unnecessarily difficult to get an overview.—I don't know the things very well yet (time!!), but they seem (at first glance) remarkably well and beautifully orchestrated. I find some things disturbing at first; namely the rather too obvious desire to use new means. Perhaps I'll come to understand the organic interrelationship between these means and the requirements of expression. But right now it troubles me.—On the other hand I already have a clear impression of a number of passages, which I definitely like. We shall see.

II. Regarding the melodramas in the *Gurrelieder*: pitch is by no means to be taken as literally here as in the *Pierrot* melodramas. By no means should a similar songlike *Sprechmelodie* be created here. It is important that (depending on the accompaniment) rhythm and dynamics be maintained throughout. In a few passages where it's almost melodic, one could speak in a **somewhat**(!!) more musical manner. The pitches are to be regarded only as "registral differences" *[Lagenunterschiede]*; i.e., the particular passage (!!! not the individual note) is to be spoken higher or lower as the case may be. But not intervallic proportions! Is that enough for you? If not, I'll be happy to tell you more.

III. Roller: that's excellent. Please convey my deepest esteem to him! Perhaps with slight alterations it would also be possible to use the same poster for Berlin and later everywhere. Would you please ask him?

I must close. Many warm regards

Your Arnold Schönberg

---

1. Schoenberg is responding to a letter of 13 January 1913, in which Berg discussed piano scores of his songs, funding and soloists for the performance of *Gurrelieder*, the performance requirements of the speaker's part, and the poster for the *Gurrelieder* being prepared by Alfred Roller. (See p. 144.)

## Berg to Schoenberg (express letter)

[Vienna] 17 January 1913
early

Dear Herr Schönberg,

I reproach myself dreadfully for not having answered your letter right away, but you will forgive my delay when I tell you that I work on the guide from 6 in the morning until evening. Now, 5:30, still sitting in bed, I'll hurry to make up for the omission and tell you how happy I am that you don't consider the songs completely

*Poster designed by Alfred Roller for the* Gurrelieder *premiere on 23 February 1913*

bad. Particularly with regard to the orchestration—where, remembering my inauspicious beginnings,[1] I feared I had done something idiotic in every measure, no matter how intensely I heard it. Even Webern's assurances to the contrary (he only saw 2 songs) couldn't reassure me. Only your kind words in the letter! And here I'd just like to say a word about the "new means"; afterwards, when I saw them heaped in such profusion (though while composing they came about very naturally), they bothered me too, not because I thought them superfluous, but because I feared the somewhat pretentious impression (well, "we've got it," "as long as it's good and extravagant," etc.), especially the obtrusive red boxes into which the copyist stuck the most harmless markings. But perhaps—no, certainly—my use of so many new means can be explained as follows. It hasn't been very long since I first began to hear the sounds of the orchestra with real understanding, and to understand scores. And because it was always the newest compositions, since in recent years I have scarcely held a score of Wagner, let alone the classics in my hand (surely a great mistake!), I'm more receptive to the new sounds created by precisely these new means, hear them everywhere, even where it might be possible without them, and thus I employ them because I don't know anything else! Perhaps my mode of expression is like that of a child who hears so many foreign words at home that he uses them all the time, even when he hasn't quite mastered German yet. But at least I cherish the hope that the child uses the foreign words correctly. Or: does the witticism apply here!? "Better not use new means, you never know how they'll sound!"?

1. With regard to Berg's earliest attempts at orchestration, see his letter of 16 February 1932.

I had nothing to do with the ridiculous format of the score. I told you right from the start that it was the choice of my somewhat high-handed copyist. I wrote my manuscript on perfectly ordinary Eberle-paper with fewer or more staves, depending on the scoring!

We still don't know (unless perhaps you have just written to Buschbeck) whether 30 March will suit you for the concert or whether you are considering 2 March (the Sunday after the *Gurrelieder*, 23 February), Buschbeck wants to negotiate with the Konzertverein and told me that he had also suggested the *Lieder eines fahrenden Gesellen* to you. They would certainly <u>draw</u> more than the frequently performed *Kindertotenlieder!* I understand regarding the speaker's part. Thank you <u>very much</u>. Zehme wrote that she wants to do the speaker's part in Vienna too. Is that your wish? Perhaps it would be possible to rescind the agreement with Klitsch, who hasn't begun yet. In that case you, dear Herr Schönberg, would have to write to Schreker immediately!! Supposedly Klitsch isn't particularly good, though he has a beautiful voice!—For that reason I'll send this letter express, so it won't be too late should you wish to undertake something in the Zehme matter.

I'm going to Freund's recital tomorrow, Saturday. Am very curious!

I saw Altenberg in Steinhof not long ago.[2] His brother[3] asked me to visit him. He's doing very poorly. The doctors call it paranoia. But it's an "inferno." He suffers dreadfully! Nonetheless, I hope he'll improve and will be able to work again.

Do you have the original full score of the *Gurrelieder*, Herr Schönberg? Schreker wrote that he wasn't to get it until 31 January, the day of the 1st rehearsal, and he considers that too late. And that Part III has to be copied! But don't worry, Herr Schönberg, I shall settle the matter with Hertzka! After all, Schreker can study the work at home from the engraved full score[4] and get to know it through the reduction!

I must close, hope I haven't forgotten anything. Work awaits me. Again many thanks, dear Herr Schönberg, for your kind letter and the kind words

from your Berg

I assume the piano scores arrived?!

My mother writes that she's going to see you. Oh! Would that I were in her place!!

---

2. Peter Altenberg suffered from periodic bouts of mental instability. He committed himself to the Steinhof sanatorium from 10 December 1912 to 28 April 1913.

3. Georg Engländer.

4. The full score of the *Gurrelieder* was not engraved until 1920. Berg is referring to the 1912 facsimile edition.


## Schoenberg to Berg

Berlin-Zehlendorf, 20 January 1913

Dear friend,

If you think Klitsch would not be good you shouldn't take him. I am not at all pleased that Frau Zehme contacted you. I'm not necessarily in favor of her speaking the role in Vienna because I think a man's voice would be more be more effective.

Also (for subsequent performances) I'd rather that people associate the part with a man's voice than with a woman's. However, one must take into consideration that Zehme does the thing very musically and is extremely enthusiastic and diligent. Then again she has other defects. But she also has merits. If Klitsch isn't musical enough one ought to take the part away from him and if no musical man can be found, Zehme must be called upon.

_____

For the Vienna concert: 30 March
  of yours: 2–3 songs (numbers 2, 3, and 4). Frau Freund will make the selection.
  I will do _Kindertotenlieder._
  Hertzka has the original full score of the _Gurrelieder._
  Warmest regards

Your Arnold Schönberg

Let Buschbeck know the scoring of your songs.


_Berg to Schoenberg (postcard and letter)_

[Vienna, 22 January 1913]

Esteemed Herr Schönberg,
  I just made the horrifying discovery that there are measure discrepancies between the full score and the just published piano vocal score of the _Gurrelieder_ .
  _[Berg details two discrepancies.]_ If these passages are wrong in the full score, please inform Hertzka,* who is at this moment putting the finishing touches to the parts, so he can insert the missing measure or cut the superfluous one (the 1st rehearsal is on the 31st). But what if the full score is right and the piano score wrong!!! That would be terrible for me!
  (continuation of the card)
  I'd also like to ask you the following, dear Herr Schönberg: I'm not entirely certain whether you orchestrated all of Part III in 1911 or only from page 117 on.—
  Then: Whether the complete composition existed and how much of the orchestration had been completed?!
  I think it's important for me to mention that in the guide so that the facts are established in an appropriate place. Because there's a rumor that you didn't compose Part III until 1910/1911. Specht once wrote something like that[1] and very likely the wildest and most idiotic ideas will be spread about unless it's spelled out clearly once and for all.
  So should I discuss it or just indicate the dates in the beginning, and is there anything else you'd like mentioned in the analysis, dear Herr Schönberg?!
  I still have 2 weeks' work on it; the guide will be very long, certainly 3–4 times as long as Specht's guide to Mahler's VIII[th] Symphony. I do hope it will be good.

_____

1. Possibly a reference to "Die Jungwiener Tondichter" (published in two parts in _Die Musik_ IX / 7, first January issue 1910, 1–16 and IX / 8, second January issue 1910, 80–85), in which Specht stated (p. 14) that only Part I of _Gurrelieder_ had been completed.

I've just come from a wretchedly bad performance of Mahler's IV[th] under Löwe.[2] Schreker's *Phantastische Ouvertüre*, which preceded it, is a very poor, patchwork thing.—It was a general failure, too.

Many thanks, dear Herr Schönberg, for your last letter. I can hardly believe that you're even talking about 2–3 songs now, and have made a selection already, in other words that the performance is really going to take place! I couldn't believe such great good fortune! And now it's to come true?!

My scoring is much smaller than Webern's, so it won't require anything <u>extra</u> beyond 1 player for the harmonium and piano (and xylophone, I forgot that!). I spoke with Buschbeck, he's dreadfully upset that you didn't mention the Chamber Symphony. I reassured him that it would surely be done! You just forgot to mention it again! Isn't that right!! He's writing you, too!

Schreker has already rehearsed with Klitsch, <u>apparently it's going very well!</u> He already knows his part! Zehme didn't write to me, but to Buschbeck, though of course all that is superfluous now! Klitsch will narrate!

I close, dear, kind Herr Schönberg, by telling you once more how happy I am about the performance of my songs! That's absolutely the most wonderful thing!!! I must stop <u>thanking</u> you, it sounds so silly in the face of this wealth of kindness!!!

your Berg

(Oh yes: I heard Freund (in a ¼-filled Bösendorfersaal), I liked her very much, as did the audience—and the critics, too!)[3]

*who doesn't know about these new errors yet

---

2. This concert took place on 22 January, hence the dating of this letter.

3. On her 18 January recital Marya Freund, accompanied by Georg Göhler, performed songs by Debussy, Schumann, Brahms, Mahler, Richard Halm, and Delibes.

## Schoenberg to Berg

Berlin-Zehlendorf, 24 January 1913

Dear friend,

I have long intended to write down *Gurrelieder* facts. You probably know most of it. Write without any polemics, without style, purely "statistically" or "histori-cally" or whatever you want to call it.

I. So: March–April 1900 I composed the first and 2nd Parts and much of the 3rd Part. After that a long interruption, filled with operetta instrumentation. **Completed the rest** in March (thus early in 1901)!! Then began orchestration in August 1901 (again interrupted by other jobs, as I have always been prevented from composing). Resumed in Berlin mid-1902. Then prolonged interruption due to operetta instru-mentation. Last worked on it in 1903 and finished up to about page 118. Then put it aside and gave up on it entirely! Took it up again July 1910. Orchestrated every-thing except for the final chorus. Completed that in Zehlendorf, 1911.

So the entire composition was, I think, completed in April or May of 1901. Only the final chorus existed merely as a sketch, which did, however, include all the most important voices and the entire form. While finishing the score I merely reworked a few passages. This applied only to passages of 8–20 measures; particularly for example in the piece "Klaus Narr," and in the final chorus.* Everything else (even some things I would have liked to have changed) remained as they were. I could no longer have duplicated the style, and a halfway knowledgeable person should have no trouble finding the corrected passages anyway. <u>These corrections caused me more trouble than the entire orchestration had earlier.</u>

If you like you may quote a sentence or two from this account.[1]

II. Now to the missing measures:

Unfortunately the piano score is correct in both cases. I have written out the missing measure of page 71 [full score]. It's enclosed.—The 5th measure on page 115 of the full score, in other words the measure preceding the trombone theme, must be cut. **Tell Hertzka.** He must <u>print an errata sheet</u>. Maybe in the guide?[2] But would that suffice? For conductors?

It's not a good idea to let the guide get too long. Cut as much as you can. Most important: no poetry. No Spechtian "flowery adjectives" (he includes at least 3–4 uncharacteristic adjectives in every sentence).

III. Now to something that concerns you. I'm not sure Freund will be able to sing your songs. She writes—she doesn't have time to learn them.[3] Could you find another singer, male or female? Possibly someone suited for singing the *Kindertotenlieder* as well. Because if Freund is going to make a fuss I'll break with her. But I hope to bring her around yet. In any event you'll have to think of alternatives.

IV. Of course I'll do the Chamber Symphony, too. You know the scoring: 12 I$^{st}$ violins, 10 II$^{nd}$ violins, 6–8 violas, 6–8 cellos, 6–8 basses, 1 flute, 1 oboe, 1 English horn, 1 E♭ (and D) clarinet, 1 A (B♭) clarinet, 1 bass clarinet, 1 bassoon, 1 contrabassoon, 2 horns.[4]———

Warmest regards

Your Arnold Schönberg

*The original composition contained only a very few orchestrational notes. I didn't make note of such things back then since one naturally knows what sound one wants. But apart from that: it must be obvious that what was orchestrated in 1910 and 11 has a completely different orchestrational style than that of Parts I and II. I never meant to deny that. On the contrary. It's obvious that I would orchestrate differently 10 years later. Specht is a liar!

---

1. In his guide (p. 18) Berg quotes nearly verbatim the passages in Schoenberg's letter concerning the genesis of the *Gurrelieder*, adding only a few explanatory remarks and omitting Schoenberg's reference to Richard Specht. In the last sentence, however, he replaced the word "orchestration" with "composition" ("These corrections caused me more trouble than the entire composition had earlier").

2. A footnote on p. 19 of the guide explains the redundant and missing measures.

3. Schoenberg was trying to spare Berg's feelings; in reality Freund had refused because she did not like the songs, as Schoeberg told Buschbeck in confidence.

4. The instrumentation of the full orchestral version of the Chamber Symphony.

## Berg to Schoenberg

[Vienna] 1 February 1913

Dear Herr Schönberg,

I wanted to wait until after the first reading rehearsals before writing and can now report: it's going very slowly. So far there have been 4 rehearsals: 2 with strings, in which we got all the way through Parts I and II, hence both are now flawless. 1 brass / percussion rehearsal, where we got as far as the song of the Waldtaube, and 1 woodwind rehearsal, which only got to the song: "So tanzen die Engel vor Gottes Thron nicht." Now there is still one rehearsal each for: woodwinds and brass (4 and 5 February), in which Schreker intends to get as far as Part II, inclusive, then he leaves town for a week, should be back in Vienna on the 12th, after which 7 more rehearsals are scheduled. But that won't be enough. There will have to be additional rehearsals. Searching out the errors, particularly in the woodwinds, but also in the brass, slows things down immensely. Of course Part III, which I corrected, will presumably be much more accurate than Parts I and II, which weren't checked at all or only insufficiently. One or two days before the first rehearsal it was unbelievably hectic and it's not much calmer now. Rehearsal numbers had either not been entered at all, or else incorrectly. Parts partially unusable. For instance, the parts for the 4 Wagner tubas had been written out separately, rather than into those of the horns 7–10. After I had more or less settled that for the 1st rehearsal, it turned out that the horn players in the orchestra couldn't play because, as they insist, there's no such thing as a tenor tuba in E♭ or bass tuba in B♭. So that will have to be transposed. (Just as in Bruckner).[1] A lot of other things went wrong too, but with Königer's and Schmid's help and that of another student of mine, a young high school student,[2] it was possible for the rehearsals to take place without further delay. Now we're checking woodwinds and brass further. I'm looking for the errors in the full score, since it's impossible, particularly in soft passages and in the brass, to hear who's playing incorrectly, and whether it's just the part that's incorrect or the full score as well. So: if Schreker really did write to you, dear Herr Schönberg, that you have to check parts and score yourself, that's not true! Given the short time remaining that would be such an enormous and almost useless job, since the errors can be detected in the rehearsals. Either immediately, since I know the work so well that in most cases I can make the decision and have the error corrected immediately (for I sit next to Schreker), or in unclear cases I take it home with me and study it, and then I always figure it out! In other words removing all the wrong notes from the work is only a matter of *time*. But another, even more important question is how, apart from that, Schreker is to bring it off. I don't think Schreker knows the right tempos. When I point that out to him he says it's because of the reading rehearsals. But it's apparent to me from certain nuances that our interpretations do differ; completely when it comes to dynamics! Neither in the rehearsals nor anywhere else have I ever heard a *pp* from Schreker. Once the soloists join in, it will be impossible to keep the orchestra down and it certainly would be a very good idea if you, dear Herr Schönberg, were present at a good many rehearsals. He doesn't take my word for it and when he does he doesn't want to admit I'm right! But on several occasions I've noticed that it serves some purpose when I give my opinion, and it still won't be too late by the time you come. I have to conduct the mixed choruses 2 more

1. The tenor tuba is usually in B♭ and the bass and contrabass tubas in F and C (and hence non-transposing). Schoenberg's use of E♭ and B♭ in the *Gurrelieder* follows Wagner's practice in his last three *Ring* operas, though, unlike, Wagner, Schoenberg neglected to provide for re-transposition in the parts themselves. Bruckner writes his tuba parts in B♭ and F from the outset.

2. Probably Gottfried Kassowitz.

times. Apparently they're already going very well, and the men's choruses, too.

I haven't answered your last kind letter yet because I <u>simply do not</u> have the time. I've even had to stop work on the guide for 4 days now and am so tired that, as you see, I can't even write simple sentences.

But I must hurry now! I still have all of Part III (guide) to do—must keep it much shorter than in the I<sup>st</sup>. Don't worry about my writing too effusively, dear Herr Schönberg!! Completely matter-of-fact, <u>without</u> any flowery adjectives, nothing psychological—Spechtian! Perhaps without once using the word "<u>beautiful</u>," the beauty of the work and how much I love it will be **better** expressed than with all of Specht's adjectives.

Not that even those descriptions could suffice, especially now that I've heard so much of it in the orchestra. I wish I could tell you of my specific impressions, of the fabulous sounds, etc., but it's too much and I have too little time. I sometimes sit there entranced by the sound of the strings—the winds (especially in the beginning). Oh, that you aren't here!!! Just please do come soon, dear Herr Schönberg!! I'm very unhappy that Königer and Schmid aren't permitted to attend the rehearsals. Schreker doesn't tolerate anyone at the sectionals but me (whom he <u>needs</u>)—

———————————————————

Webern told me that he saw you the day after you wrote to me[3] and that you indicated that Freund's singing my songs was <u>not</u> in question. Was she persuaded after all?! Webern indicated it was quite settled! He also thought the <u>last</u> song (V) would be the easiest vocally, which is of course why I suggested it to you at the outset. Perhaps she would <u>rather</u> sing that one. And it isn't <u>long</u>, either, (about 4– 5 minutes) and more rewarding! But maybe she has already turned it down <u>absolutely</u> and all my suggestions are superfluous. If so, then <u>besides</u> the pain of disappointment I will at least have the indelible joy that <u>you</u>, dear Herr Schönberg, <u>wanted to perform it</u>, and I will always be infinitely grateful to you for that!!——[4]

*[margin note:]* (Excuse the extra space! I'm not quite well!!)

———————

3. Webern visited Schoenberg on 25 January en route from Stettin to the Semmering, where he spent a sick leave granted him by the Stettin Stadttheater.

4. There is no signature at the conclusion of this letter, though it would appear that the letter is complete.

## Schoenberg to Berg

Berlin-Zehlendorf, 3 February 1913

Dear friend,

Enclosed my answers to your questions about errors—

Hertzka wrote about your analysis today, he's shocked at the length.

Frankly: so am I!

Not on my account, for you know where I stand on such matters. But on Hertzka's account. There's not much he can do with it; as a publisher.

Of course I tried to reassure him. But that's not going to help much. I'm afraid you will have to cut it.

At least the musical examples!!

That seems a bit much to me, too!

Perhaps you didn't quite heed my advice after all: to discuss only things about which something occurred to you!! Perhaps you gave in too much to the temptation to *have* something occur to you (past perfect and future tense) for everything.

Another thing, of which I am, as a matter of fact, quite certain:

You have **no doubt** expressed many things awkwardly. Out of a desire to say it beautifully and effectively!! I know the feeling and can tell you: almost everything I have written to date I would do differently today. Above all: shorter! As short as my music.

See if you can't cut about 15–30 pages!

Take care not to cut any ideas!

But definitely anything that's merely an anticipation or afterthought of those ideas.

But I don't wish to pester you. Perhaps your work is such that you cannot find anything to change. Then leave it as it stands!! No half measures: either cut, in which case cut extensively because it's necessary; or don't cut anything!

But see if there isn't a great deal that could be omitted!

Incidentally: don't let me influence your decision in any way. As far as I'm concerned, you have a completely free hand.

Many warmest regards

Your Arnold Schönberg

*Berg to Schoenberg (express letter; letterhead: J. Berg / VI., Linke Wienzeile 118)*[1]

Wednesday
Vienna, 5 February [1913]

Dear Herr Schönberg,

You have received Hertzka's telegram! I've just come from the 2$^{nd}$ woodwind rehearsal, after which Schreker saw only one way out, namely that you come to Vienna as soon as possible. In this rehearsal we only reached ⑨⓪ in Part I, still without being certain that what we had rehearsed is free of error, particularly in some passages (orchestral interlude). Schreker has to leave town now.[2] He thinks that during the time until 14 February the score should be checked for mistakes and these mistakes then corrected in the parts. That's why you are to come to Vienna, because no one can detect the mistakes in the full score. Now: **I believe** that I might be able to find them, but because I would have to compare each part with the others as well as with the harmony, etc., I would need about 1–2 months for Parts I and II, just as I did for Part 3.* And there still wouldn't be any guarantee!! Besides,

---

1. The address of Johanna Berg.
2. For the final rehearsals and Leipzig first performance of *Der ferne Klang* on 9 February.

there are so few rehearsals left that they would have to be divided; during the rehearsal on the 14<sup>th</sup> you could, for instance, do winds and brass, while Schreker (at the same time) did strings, that way we would at least get through all 3 parts during the so-called reading rehearsals. For the ensemble rehearsals begin on the 17th; 6 in all (with the one on the 14<sup>th</sup> making 7 rehearsals), which together with the 6 preceding ones would be: *[Berg details the nature of the thirteen rehearsals, culminating with seven ensemble rehearsals 17–22 February.]*

Perhaps it could be arranged that you conduct one or 2 divided rehearsals during Schreker's absence, which would be a very good idea. But Hertzka would have to pay for that and Schreker thinks it would amount to 600–1,000 kronen.

Naturally I told Hertzka (on the telephone) that you, Herr Schönberg, would have to be reimbursed for your trip, whereupon he immediately said you could stay with him. But I don't think it would be that simple! For if you came to Vienna now you would miss so many lessons, for which you would certainly have to be reimbursed! I'm sure Hertzka will understand—because he must! Schreker practically made it a condition that Hertzka see to it that you come to Vienna soon, otherwise he wouldn't be able to perform the work. So we are now awaiting your decision. You won't be able to write to Schreker, since he's leaving for Leipzig today and returns around the 12<sup>th</sup>. In case you don't write to me in the matter I'll inquire at Hertzka's on Friday the 7<sup>th</sup>.—

———————————

I shall cut some things in the guide and maybe try to leave out some examples. In any case, keep it short for the remainder of Part III so there won't be too much more. Forgive the brevity, dear Herr Schönberg, but there's another rehearsal in half an hour (brass). I just used the lunch break for this letter.

For now many warm regards and thanks for your kind letter

from your Berg

(It would certainly be a good idea if you took a hand in the rehearsals! Schreker isn't good, doesn't know the work well enough!——)

\* and then I'm working constantly on the guide!

*Schoenberg to Berg (special delivery letter)*

Berlin-Zehlendorf, 6 February 1913

Dear Berg,

The enclosed letter was intended—before your express letter came—for Hertzka. It contains my opinion, though in a very mild form. Notwithstanding, I restrained myself and didn't send the letter to Hertzka. I'm sending it to you now for your information.—Since Schreker refused my offer (that I conduct), I won't come to Vienna. May he prosper and be happy! Perhaps I'll come to Vienna for the last rehearsals. But Hertzka will probably cancel now. That will be the 2<sup>nd</sup> time the scoundrel has caused a cancelation.

—Should the performance take place, Frau Zehme is only to be called upon in an emergency, i.e.: if no <u>man</u> can be found to do the role.

Warm regards

Your Arnold Schönberg

## Schoenberg to Hertzka[1]

Berlin-Zehlendorf, 6 February 1913

Dear Herr Director,

Berg's announced letter has not come yet. Should it cause me to change my opinion, I will gladly take back everything I am forced to say here.

First: in response to the telegram from you and the Philharmonic Chorus I have just sent the following telegraph reply:

If Schreker cannot find the time, I will be glad to come and conduct; but not to correct. Bad parts not my fault. Don't hesitate to cancel.

The purpose of my letter is to explain this telegram, to show you why you were wrong, and to convince you that my coming is completely unnecessary.

I. Above all I consider "Schreker urgently **requires**(!!) your immediate presence" a bit strong. I would have expected a little more politeness even if I had committed a crime.

II. I am expected to shoulder travel expenses of perhaps 150–200 marks, while not even 10 kronen were spent to give detailed reasons for my incurring such expenses.

I shall demonstrate below that the reasons stated in the telegram are no reasons at all.

III. I'm expected to shoulder the expense, but no one asks <u>whether I'm in a position to do so</u>!!

IV. If something is requested of me, someone should first have declared himself willing to shoulder all expenses.

V. But now the main point: I, the composer, am expected to run errands for the conductor because he doesn't have the time to devote to this matter, as his artistic responsibility demands: his responsibility to me and to himself!!

For: if Schreker had studied the score properly, <u>as is his responsibility</u>, it would be quite impossible that he only now discover how flawed it is. (An aside: it's not my fault if the score is so faulty! The orchestral parts ought to have been <u>corrected in plenty of time</u>!!) He should have noticed that long ago! But I have long since deduced from Berg's naive reports that he doesn't know the score: "it is so difficult <u>to detect</u>(!!) the errors in the brass and woodwinds(!!)" Of course, if one doesn't know the score!

I can appreciate that Schreker doesn't have time to study the thing. I can even

---

1. Schoenberg's letter was written after an exchange of telegrams with Schreker and Hertzka regarding the possibility that Schoenberg help correct the parts. This letter was abridged in Erwin Stein's edition of selected Schoenberg letters and Stein neglected to note that the letter remained unsent.

understand and excuse it. What I cannot understand or excuse is that he nonetheless insists on conducting the work himself. Not only would it be nobler of him to invite me to do so; it would be more decent from the artistic standpoint!!

VI. Anyway: why should I come to Vienna? I simply can't understand it. You all seem to have lost your heads and now I'm supposed to jump in and help. Gladly; but only insofar as necessary. And above all in a capacity for which one needs the composer (to conduct), certainly not to do copyists' work! One doesn't undertake such a trip for that!!

You telegraphed about "deciphering" the score. What does that mean. Surely the score is not illegible, unclear? There are errors; but surely 2 musicians should be capable of correcting those by themselves! Or if not: what about the post? Surely they can ask me? Detach the pages in question from the printed score, mark it in red (?X) and send it to me express. I'd answer express! Or ask me to check through the score and send all the errors I find to Vienna every day. Or send me another 3 scores so I can have them checked by friends here in Berlin!! And: one gets a couple of good musicians to do the same in Vienna. Pays them a fee. Then you'd find some! That would be just as quick and more dependable and cheaper. And that way it wouldn't be the innocent party who has to **shoulder all the costs and trouble by himself**. Surely my score doesn't contain more errors than any other. It's just the dimensions of the work (in all respects) that make it seem like so many. And of course: the uncorrected parts!!

People greatly overestimate the importance this performance has for me. It may very well be advantageous for me. But I don't allow anyone to bully me. And above all I won't be threatened: "otherwise performance canceled." I'm not that desperate for success. And above all: I'm not that eager for a performance, just for a good one. And there's no way this can be a good one. Only 10 rehearsals with the mediocre Tonkünstler Orchestra!! I'll have 9–11 with the excellent Berlin Philharmonic!!

In conclusion then: I'll be happy to give you all the advice that occurs to me. I'll be happy to conduct the performance myself for expenses. I'll be happy to come to Vienna around 18 February so as to shape the last rehearsals. But anyone who thinks I can be intimidated by threats underestimates me. For that I have just one answer: don't hesitate to cancel.

Of course it would be a great pity for you if you had to cancel.—but I'll manage on my own.

You will find this letter rather testy, but I can't help that. I'm fed up with having people from Vienna continually slap me on the back. Why else do you think I turned my back on Vienna. Everywhere else I go to perform my works, that is regarded and treated as what it is: I'm thanked for allowing my work to be performed. In Vienna I'm trapped by everyone's various business complications, which they claim are meant to further my cause. But I refuse to lend my neck for such a noose any longer, or my shoulders for such patronage, and prefer to retain the position I assumed towards Vienna when I left it.

———

As far as Klitsch's cancelation goes, Frau Zehme is to be considered only as a last resort. I want a man for the premiere!

No hard feelings, I hope.

Warm regards

Your Arnold Schönberg

*Schoenberg to Berg (postcard)*

Berlin-Zehlendorf [8 February 1913]

Dear friend,

Frau Zehme is not to be the speaker. Not only because she isn't up to it vocally. But because the role doesn't suit her. And above all: because it must be a <u>speaker</u> [*Sprecher*] (masculinum). Only as a last resort can it be a woman. Should this necessity arise, I will suggest someone. But it is my wish that a man be found!! Please be forceful in representing my interests.

Warm regards

Schönberg

*Berg to Schoenberg*

Monday
Vienna [10 February 1913]

Dear Herr Schönberg,

Your last card (Zehme) reassured me somewhat, indicated that you weren't angry with me, since from your last letter I had deduced displeasure not only with Vienna but also with me. All the more as the letter intended for Hertzka stopped with <u>me</u> and I couldn't even pass it on. That hurt me very much, and if I hadn't had to finish the "guide" these past 2 days, I would have written right away to try to shift the weight burdening me. Your dear card helped a bit: and I can now discuss the matter more calmly.

The situation is as follows: I had not <u>allied</u> myself with Hertzka and Schreker when I told you in my express letter of the "desire" of these two fine gentlemen. Rather it was my intention to prevent Hertzka from wiring and to ask <u>you</u> what we should do. But when I called Hertzka he had already heard from Schreker and had—as he stated—already had a very long <u>detailed</u> telegram prepared and just wanted to add that I would be writing you in the matter. So my letter was on the one hand an explanation of the telegram (—whose wording I <u>didn't know</u>)—on the other hand it did occur to me that it would be a good idea if you came, not to correct parts, but to make a halfway decent performance possible. (The corrections would have resulted as a matter of course during the rehearsals. ¾ has already been corrected, anyway.) And in order to bring about a halfway decent performance it would have become clear, not that the errors need correcting, but that <u>several addi-</u>

tional rehearsals are necessary. And I hoped that your coming might have made that possible. I cannot convince Hertzka, it was hard enough to add one rehearsal (the 13th). And since your intervention would make a good performance out of this one, which is certain to be a bad one, I just thought—and therefore told you—that it would surely be a good idea if you came soon. After all, I had just that one choice: either you come too late to salvage the inadequate rehearsing in the few rehearsals that you would attend—or you come earlier and make good, proper rehearsing possible. Naturally I chose the latter, knowing that the III[rd] possibility: that you perform the entire work was not a possibility—I know Schreker too well for that. He's not performing the work so that it gets performed, but only in order that he perform something. I laughed in their faces when the people at U.E. informed me that they had telegraphed your offer to Schreker. I knew too well, could have sworn that Schreker would immediately refuse this—one chance for a good Gurrelieder performance. Because then he wouldn't be named, because his filthy ambition is so overpowering that he would rather conduct—no, beat time—wrong time—to a work he doesn't know—than forgo the opportunity to appear before an audience, to bow (he telegraphed that he had 47 curtain calls at the Leipzig premiere!), to being mentioned in the papers, etc. But you, dear Herr Schönberg, don't know Schreker's character well enough yet, so you can't understand that I could be more certain than anyone—including his Du–friend Hertzka[1]—that the performance could now take place only under Schreker, who would never ever step down, not even if due to paralysis of the arms he had to conduct with his feet. That's why I could and did consider only one of the other possibilities when I indicated it would be a good idea if you were to come soon—so you could influence the performance as much as possible. Not to "run errands" for Schreker— —

To be sure, I didn't know the wording of the telegram sent to you. I thought they had asked for your advice in a long, detailed telegram—had informed you that it would very much facilitate the rehearsals if you came now. Of course, when they told me the wording I was shocked. I immediately told them at U.E and also let Hertzka know, who wasn't present, that it was like a threat—and that to speak of an indecipherable score clearly compromises me—as if I didn't understand it. (To say nothing of Schreker—who really doesn't understand it). Königer, who was present, very correctly pointed out that it sounded like criticism— —And in fact this piece of madness has resulted in your wondering, dear Herr Schönberg, how it is that 2 musicians cannot manage on their own. I have always managed, have pointed things out to Schreker probably 1,000 times, have straightened out the orchestra members and their parts and have cleared up ambiguous passages, but my ear is not so finely tuned, perhaps I also have too little practical experience—you yourself expressed surprise—to hear which instrument is causing the muddiness in ff passages with 20–30 instruments playing all sorts of runs, trills, syncopations. Of course Schreker ought to be able to do that—but I usually hit on it sooner. Especially if I go through the passages at home— —

---

1. Schreker and Hertzka were on familiar Du terms from the end of 1912 (following the premiere of Der ferne Klang) to approximately the middle of 1914.

Just returned home, I find your 2<sup>nd</sup> card,[2] in which you ask why I don't write anything about the G. performance. So my intuition that you, dear Herr Schönberg, are angry with me about the whole thing has been confirmed: it is terrible! But at least hear me out as to why I haven't written. Naturally I meant to tell you right away how things stand, but was and still am so insanely busy that I had to keep postponing the letter, which, after all, had to be a detailed account. I couldn't send the foregoing one either, which I began earlier today, because it wasn't finished. I'll complete it now, though of course in a most melancholy mood: You will ask, dear Herr Schönberg, what it is I have to do and will not think it much, since you accomplish everything so quickly, but I work so slowly: In the last 3 days I completed the guide. Began to read through the full score of *Gurrelieder*, checking for copying errors and transferring the corrections into the parts, conducted 2 chorus rehearsals, for which of course I had to prepare—I've just now returned from a rehearsal, but had already been in town earlier this morning to see Löwy[3] about Zehme-Gregori[4] and was tied up for almost 2 hours at Univeral Edition with arrangements for the guide and corrections for the parts, then to see Roller about the poster (to rectify a blunder the Philharmonic Chorus had made). He sends you many regards, dear Herr Schönberg, and is pleased that you also want to use his posters for Berlin. Then in the afternoon I had to give 4 lessons—finally from 7–9:30 chorus—That's just one day; the preceding ones were similar! Just remember that I live at the back of beyond—in Hietzing, have no telephone, impossible transportation, and finally that 3 days ago my wife had the misfortune to injure her eye, couldn't see *anything* the first 2 days, was never without pain except for a few hours at a time through cocaine injections—and still isn't much better, so that the doctor isn't sure whether it may not be a case of retinitis?——Not only did that take up a lot of time—but my capacity to work was likewise affected by my anxiety, as well as by my fear, ever since your last letter with the enclosed one to Hertzka, that you might be angry with me————Perhaps then, dear Herr Schönberg, you will be less annoyed that I didn't find time for a detailed letter.

To be sure, I could at least have sent you a few words as to whether the G.*lieder* had been canceled. But there was never any question of that! It didn't occur to anyone to cancel or postpone, neither to Hertzka nor Schreker. Nor would it have been possible. If it had been possible, they would have postponed it and not have felt it necessary to ask you to come to "correct parts." Only Hertzka and Schreker thought that might be a way out!!—And I was so absolutely convinced that a cancelation would never be considered that I never even assumed you might think so—though, of course, you had to think so after that stupid telegram. (You are right, Herr Schönberg—I, too, "lost my head"—that I should have been so incapable of comprehending your present position). On the other hand I assumed with certainty that Hertzka would have telephoned you from Leipzig.[5] He promised to do so in

2. In this card, postmarked 9 February 1913, Schoenberg had asked briefly and rather testily for news of the performance.

3. Robert Löwy, secretary of the Philharmonic Chorus.

4. The Hofburgtheater actor Ferdinand Gregori had been tentatively engaged for the speaker's part.

5. Hertzka had traveled to Leipzig for the Schreker premiere.

Vienna, before his departure, and right up to this hour I assumed you were thoroughly informed—also through Löwy, who surely wrote you a few days ago—so he told me today.

The *Gurrelieder* will be performed on 23 February. It is frequently announced in all the papers, soon Roller's large new posters will be up, ticket sales are going very well (over 6,000 kronen have come in so far, only about 3,000 kronen are still outstanding). Gregori has already rehearsed once. Friday is another orchestra rehearsal, by then I will have to finish checking the score, so I probably won't be able to write until after the rehearsal, dear Herr Schönberg, which I hope you won't take ill, likewise my dreadful handwriting, but I began the letter in the streetcar—and am now finishing it in bed—and also have a corn on my forefinger from writing, which hurts.

Very early tomorrow I'll send off a telegram, so that you'll at least be informed regarding the suspected cancelation (I repeat: there was never any question of canceling—only the fear—of **having** to postpone—and not being **able** to do so!)

Please also excuse the style of this letter, dear Herr Schönberg. —But, apart from the fact that I've been up almost 20 hours—I'm in such a depressed state of mind—in such a frenzied state, that I'm incapable of anything better.—

Many, many regards, dear Herr Schönberg, in unswerving grateful attachment and love

from your devoted Berg

### Berg to Schoenberg

Vienna, 1 March 1913

I finally have time to write, dear Herr Schönberg. The "administrative work" these past few days has been never-ending and I'm still not finished, but my urge to write to you again is too strong! You can have no idea of the feeling of emptiness, hollowness, dear Herr Schönberg, of the emotional hangover that overcame me once you were gone, and the joy of these past days—with its high point, the performance[1]—was suddenly over! What wonderful days they were! It was life lived with doubled, tripled intensity. Real life, as opposed to the usual state of vegetating.

The only thing enabling me to endure the present emptiness is the thought that these days will return, that the *Gurrelieder* will be repeated in March, that the Chamber Symphony will come to life on 30 March—when I leafed through the score a bit my longing for it grew to infinite proportions——and that you, dear Herr Schönberg, will return to Vienna for all of that. But after that?!—Of course in May we will be in Berlin!!—: The only recourse for one whose misfortune it is to be Viennese and to have to live in Vienna, is to concentrate life into a few weeks

---

1. The *Gurrelieder* premiere on 23 February enjoyed an overwhelming popular and critical success. The soloists were Martha Winternitz-Dorda (Tove), Marya Freund (Waldtaube), Hans Nachod (Waldemar), Alfred Boruttau (Klaus Narr), Alexander Nosalewicz (Bauer), and Ferdinand Gregori (Speaker). The Philharmonic Chorus, Vienna Kaufmännischer Gesangverein, and Vienna Tonkünstler Orchestra were conducted by Franz Schreker.

of the year and the rest of the time to live from those joys or in anticipation of them. Of course! There is one way to make life here worth living: if you were here!! But you probably won't ever return, not any time soon anyway, I felt only too clearly how much you hate Vienna!——Back to the present: the date for the *Gurrelieder* reprise will presumably be set tomorrow. 19 March was mentioned; the Wednesday before Maundy Thursday, which certainly isn't ideal; probably it will be set for a day after Easter, which would be pretty good, since you would already be here for your concert on the 30th and could combine the two. In any case the Philharmonic Chorus has already received many requests for tickets for the reprise (among others from Schnitzler[2]), and essentially it's just a question of a date. The reprise will take place with normal prices and should therefore sell quite well. There will have to be a refresher rehearsal beforehand!

I spoke with Hertzka about the fee for the guide and am quite satisfied with the arrangement. I received 300 kronen on the spot and am to receive another 300 kronen when 5,000 copies have been sold. Almost 1,000 were sold at the first performance, so I'll get the additional 300 kronen after the 4th to 6th performance, which will take place next season. Naturally that includes payment for all the other work with the parts, etc., etc. Hertzka gave Specht only 120 kronen and an honorararium (I don't know how large) for a subsequent printing.[3] As you saw in the various reviews, the guide was also mentioned a few times—admittedly not very favorably (Batka[4] Hirschfeld[5]). But that probably doesn't matter! Anyway I don't think Batka is right. Nonetheless my doubts regarding the quality of the guide, initially aroused during proofreading, have not subsided. Have you already leafed through it a little, dear Herr Schönberg? When you return to Vienna you must please tell me what its deficiencies are—both as regards specifics, if you can remember them—and overall concept. You alone can tell me, from you alone can I learn something—even here. And then I could hope that where this time there were perhaps only good intentions, someday I may achieve something **really** good. Just as I hope in the case of piano scores, if ever I'm given the chance to prepare another one.—

I'll see Buschbeck tomorrow and am wondering whether he has found a singer for Zemlinsky's and my songs.[6] Tell me, Herr Schönberg: **if** Förstel doesn't sing could Boruttau be considered? Buschbeck says you don't want him!! But I think he's much better than Gürtler, who admittedly is musical, but doesn't sing beautifully.[7] Of course it's still a thousand times better to have him sing than to have the

2. The Austrian physician and writer Arthur Schnitzler was peripherally associated with the Mahler circle.

3. For Specht's recently published thematic analysis to Mahler's Eighth Symphony.

4. In his review of the *Gurrelieder* performance, which appeared in the *Fremdenblatt* (26 February 1913), 15, Richard Batka said of Berg's guide that it was too long, technical, and uninformative.

5. Robert Hirschfeld reviewed the *Gurrelieder* in the *Wiener Zeitung / Abendpost* (25 February 1913), 1–3, and referred to Berg's guide only in passing. No reference to the guide was found in any of the other reviews.

6. Zemlinsky's 1910 Maeterlinck Songs, Op. 13, numbers 1, 2, 3, and 5.

7. The tenors Alfred J. Boruttau and Hermann Gürtler were both concert recitalists and taught voice in Vienna.

songs dropped. No doubt under <u>your</u> direction Gürtler will sing so beautifully that no one will recognize him! I only ask about Boruttau because I find him more agreeable than Gürtler and because I don't know whether you <u>really</u> don't care for him or whether Buschbeck is mistaken![8] In any case, dear Herr Schönberg, I'll send you a card tomorrow to let you know <u>whether</u> or not Förstel is going to sing![9]

I have to go back to adding sums now—and owning up to income tax! so I close this—most uninteresting letter, which originated solely in the desire to talk with you a bit.

Please convey my regards to your esteemed wife, also from my wife. She begs that your wife please remember the promised picture of you with the children! We would <u>very much</u> like to have it. My wife's very warmest regards to you too, dear Herr Schönberg, and from both of us thanks, infinite thanks for your *Gurrelieder* and for the happiness that I was permitted a small part in the performance.

Your Berg

---

8. In his postcard reply of 3 March Schoenberg tells Berg that he has no objections to Boruttau for Berg's songs, but that Zemlinsky's songs require a mezzo-soprano.

9. Berg did indeed send a postcard on the following day, postmarked 2 March 1912, but it was not until a postcard of 4 March that he was able to inform Schoenberg of Gertrud Förstel's refusal.

## Berg to Schoenberg

Vienna, 9 March 1913

My dear Herr Schönberg,

Naturally I wouldn't dare keep pestering you with details about the performance of my songs. But since <u>you</u> are so kind and infinitely good as to want to perform something of mine, <u>I</u> should leave nothing undone to promote your plan, even at the risk of pestering you again.

It turns out a new complication has arisen: the copyist[1] whom I commissioned to copy out the parts for the 3 songs (II, III, and IV) has skipped—that is to say <u>disappeared</u>—with the scores, a portion of the string parts written by me, an advance of 20 kronen, and the music paper! He registered his move with the police—and, according to the records, moved to <u>Mödling</u>, where, however, he is not to be found—as the police told me. Of course I'll do my best to find him, will even ask little Korngold, whose favorite copyist he is—, and various other composers for whom I know he works. And have the police look for him. But: even <u>if</u> I get the scores back, it would be too late for the concert. So now I have the following options: since I don't have a copy here, the parts to the 3 songs (II, III, and IV) can only be written out in Berlin from the <u>copy</u> of the score. I can't possibly impose on you, dear Herr Schönberg, to see to <u>that</u>! Proofreading the parts can only be done here by me, since after a hasty comparison with the original score—which of course I no longer have—I'm not sure there aren't still mistakes left in the copied score. And here I

1. Joseph Kornfeld.

had intended to give you parts with as few mistakes as possible (—since my *Gurre-lieder* debacle I no longer believe in the possibility of guaranteed flawless parts—). So as not to hold up rehearsals with that! But I think all that would be too complicated; perhaps the second possibility, which I humbly proffer, would be better: namely that instead of the 3 songs (II, III, and IV), one of the other 2, I or V, be done (both would probably be too much for half a rehearsal); I still have these original scores and I could copy out the parts, i.e., have them copied out. In that case, since the I<sup>st</sup> song is in every respect, technically and rhythmically, the most difficult for voice and orchestra—that would leave—as I originally suggested—the V<sup>th</sup> song (the Passacaglia). This is certainly shorter than the other 3 (II, III, and IV) together and because it is, as you say, more difficult for the orchestra than those 3, but easier for the voice, since there's almost always an instrument accompanying the voice—and since the harmony is still almost tonal— —it shouldn't require more rehearsal time than the other 3 songs.

But of course you, dear Herr Schönberg, may have still other reasons for deciding against this suggestion. It is—as I said—just a suggestion, a possibility I crystallized out of the various obstructive circumstances.

If these various possibilities—turn out to be impossibilities—I would naturally understand, dear Herr Schönberg, if you were to reconsider your intention of performing something of mine. You know, Herr Schönberg, what immense joy it would be for me if such a performance (and were it only of one song) came about—through you, but you also know that I'm not so presumptuous as to regard this joy as something to be taken for granted, nor am I incapable of renouncing such joy—if you think it necessary—in which case I would regard your kind **intention** alone as a greater joy than I deserve!

So please be so kind, dear Herr Schönberg, as to let me know. It will be decided soon whether or not Boruttau will sing. If he doesn't sing, then surely Bum[2] will! She is so musical that she could certainly learn the last song (V) very quickly. I can't decide yet whether she could bring off II, III, and IV, or the I<sup>st</sup>. But I rather think so!

Should she also sing the Zemlinsky songs? I have the Maeterlinck songs here (copies). Are they the ones?—Or will Freund sing them?

You will meanwhile have written to Buschbeck about the rehearsal schedule! Again a typically Viennese "mess" [*Pallawatsch*]! No doubt you were extremely annoyed; tomorrow, Monday, I'll see Buschbeck; maybe he will already have heard from you, dear Herr Schönberg! It is characteristic of such things in Vienna that one never knows who is responsible for a muddle [*Schlamperei*]! I don't know this time either: whether it's Buschbeck, the Konzertverein, Easter vacation— —? Probably a combination of everything: in one word: Vienna.

Please forgive this latest disturbance, dear, kind Herr Schönberg!

My wife has been meaning to thank you and your esteemed wife for the dear picture, which made us immensely happy and which we find splendid! But it's washday—so everything's topsy-turvy— —: probably nowhere but in Vienna!

2. The Viennese alto Margarethe Bum.

Many, many regards to you, dear Herr Schönberg, and your esteemed wife from your <u>eternally grateful and devoted</u>

Berg

Tomorrow or the day after I'll know more about Boruttau or Bum (with whom I will go through <u>all</u> 5 songs) and will let you know immediately!—

## Schoenberg to Berg (postcard)

Berlin-Zehlendorf, 10 March 1913

D[ear] f[riend]

What a pity!—I'll try to find copyists here. If I don't, you'll have to have it done in Vienna. In any case it would be a good idea if you were to prepare the 5th piece. I may have to send you the score. <u>In any case,</u> the parts must be perfect. You might consider autography. Perhaps Eberle[1] could do it. Ask Hertzka for advice (Webern should do so, too). I would almost prefer Bum to Boruttau. She is to sing the Zemlinsky songs, too <u>(the Maeterlinck songs that you have!). She is to learn them as quickly as possible!!</u> She will almost certainly sing them. Rehearse them with her. Does she have a large and beautiful voice?— I shall do your orchestra songs for sure. I only hope nothing goes wrong. Anyway, your copyist is sure to turn up again?—I still haven't finished reading the Berg guide. But I have been very pleased with everything I read. Sometimes you overstate the case a bit. And I'm afraid you often claim something is new when that can scarcely be proved!! But it's definitely a very interesting piece of work. More some other time.

For today, many warm regards

Your Arnold Schönberg

Tell Buschbeck to insist on 6 successive rehearsals.

The Konzertverein just offered me a Tuesday morning rehearsal. That would be fine with me.

---

1. R. v. Waldheim-Josef Eberle & Co., the principal engraver for Universal Edition.

## Berg to Schoenberg

[Vienna] 11 March 1913

Dear Herr Schönberg,

Many thanks for your dear card, which made me very happy in every respect. Meantime your telegram[1] arrived before I had a chance to answer your card, so I can answer both now. You must not think, dear Herr Schönberg, that my wiring meant I was or ever could be impatient, but I had to know your decision on Boruttau, who is very *nice*, but understandably doesn't want to learn all 5 songs on the off chance, only to find himself singing one or two. For that he's too lazy. Besides,

---

1. Schoenberg's telegram of 11 March 1913 informed Berg that Boruttau was to learn only the second and third Altenberg Songs.

I was firmly convinced from what Buschbeck said that at least two of your orchestra songs would be done and I wanted to be sure of that, too, so I'd be able to rehearse them with Boruttau before he leaves town (for a few days). That's the only reason I telegraphed without waiting for an answer to my last letter. I now assume, dear Herr Schönberg, that the concert will bring my 2$^{nd}$ and 3$^{rd}$ songs and nothing of yours; I've already begun rehearsing with Boruttau. The only question is who will see to the parts! Have you found a copyist in Berlin, dear Herr Schönberg, or have you sent the scores to me so I can quickly have them copied out here. I believe a portion of your card has been superseded by the telegram, and the suggestion that I have the parts for the V$^{th}$ and I$^{st}$ song written out is thus no longer valid. For I hardly think Boruttau (—or any singer—), much as he might like to sing more, is capable of learning such difficult songs in 4–5 days. But I'll try to hunt up a decent copyist and—if you still think it necessary—or as a precaution—will, together with the copyist, copy out the parts for these 2 songs, I and V. It probably won't be possible to have them autographed! I discussed it with U.E. and Waldheim and was told that it's not worth it, i.e., it's only cheaper than copying when one orders about 100 copies. In the case of single, double, or triple scoring (of the strings), copying would be cheaper. Since I could have only a portion of the parts (V and I) prepared in this way, I think I had better do without autography for the present (nice as it would be) and wait for a time when I can have all of the songs (I–V) prepared this way—autographed. I'd also like to wait until after the first performance. There may be a need for revisions in passages where you advise it!!! I don't know what the situation is with Webern's parts. I only know that the parts to his Orchestra Pieces are being copied out in Berlin and assume that holds true for all the string parts as well. Apparently it has become necessary to have them autographed?! I haven't been able to reach Webern yet, but am sure to see him tonight;[2] then I'll show him your card and he will probably write to you in the matter right away, dead Herr Schönberg. Maybe he'll talk to Waldheim again about his parts!

To return to my affairs, I'm sending you the enclosed sheet which you, dear Herr Schönberg, will perhaps fill out. Again, I'm not doing this out of impatience, but to save you at least some tedious letter writing.

I'm very sorry that, as you wrote, you would "almost prefer Bum to Boruttau." But I don't think anything can be done about it now. Boruttau has already agreed and is rehearsing diligently, and I have no excuse to take the songs away from him. But I think you'll be satisfied with him. Technically he knows them very well. Naturally they present him with some musical difficulties, but I believe he'll soon surmount the problems, all the more as he has perfect pitch. He is also very experienced when it comes to singing with orchestra and wouldn't get flustered easily in case of disturbances in the audience, which might not be the case with Bum! Finally, the Akademischer Verband was eager to have a soloist with a name, which Bum doesn't yet have (a purely superficial reason directed toward concert attendance). I still haven't heard Bum. She has a cold, but has the Zemlinsky songs,—is probably

2. On 9 March Webern had been discharged from Dr. Vecsey's sanatorium in the Semmering, from where he returned to Vienna to prepare for the concert.

already learning them and tomorrow I shall begin with her.

Judging by various reports she has a very beautiful voice, very reminiscent of Freund's. I'll let you know as soon as I have formed my <u>own</u> opinion.

And now thank you very much for your kind card, dear Herr Schönberg, for the dear words about the Berg guide, and for your firm intention, unswayed by all obstacles, to perform my orchestra songs—! That makes me ever so happy and is a ray of light during the dark days I'm once again experiencing: my wife had another of her nightmares—there was a new moon—and experienced the panic-stricken fear of being walled up, of having to break down the resistance of a wall that she ran into while sleepwalking—and again she injured herself terribly! I'm afraid there's no alternative—dubious as it seems—but to go to a neurologist! But to whom? I long to talk it over with you—when you come to Vienna, dear Herr Schönberg; but now I won't take any more of your time and shall close.

Many very warm regards to you and your wife, from my wife and

Your Berg

## Berg to Schönberg (postcard)

Vienna [13 March 1913]<br>in the streetcar

Dear Herr Schönberg,

I have just come from Frau Dr. Bum.[1] As far as I can tell—she doesn't have a very large voice, but it's a very pleasant one and she seems to be musical. I think she will do the Zemlinsky songs very well. I'm also writing to Zemlinsky to ask that he send me the manuscripts or duplicates of his songs because I want to study them <u>myself</u>, not having seen them since the music festival. The copies I mentioned aren't in my possession but in Pappenheim's,[2] who has placed them at Bum's disposal. Anyway, there are only 3 songs. One is missing. That's another reason I'm writing to Zemlinsky.

Many warm regards.

from your Berg

(Do you, dear Herr Schönberg, by any chance have extra copies of the songs)

1. Margarethe Bum was married to the Viennese dental surgeon Dr. Rudolf Bum and, according to European custom, was therefore referred to as "Frau Dr."

2. The dermatologist Dr. Marie Pappenheim had known Schoenberg since 1908; in 1909 she wrote the libretto of Schoenberg's *Erwartung*.

## Schoenberg to Berg (postcard)

Berlin-Zehlendorf, 15 March 1913

Dear Berg,

I hope things have been settled with Fräulein Bum. She is to study only the Zemlinsky songs. I'm sure she'll sing those! Wouldn't it be a good idea if you went through your two with her (something to fall back on)? I hope Boruttau is dependable!—Yesterday I sent you a copy of each of the 4 Zemlinsky songs. Please let me know if you got them.—Do send me the Korngold review.[1] I want to read it. One should know what "Father Korngold" has to say about one. I'm surprised he has the courage to take revenge!—I'll be in Vienna soon, then we can discuss many things in detail.—Oh yes: I'll have the copyist send the parts of your songs directly to you, C.O.D.[2] You'll have to correct them immediately, as well as you can (without score). Then later again with the score. I probably won't get to them until the 3rd rehearsal. But they must be ready on time.

Warm regards.

Your Arnold Schönberg

Ask Hertzka sometime about the piano score of the quartet.—

Buschbeck just telephoned to say that the concert has been changed to Monday evening.[3] That's fine with me. In that case couldn't the *Gurrelieder* be done on Sunday?

1. Julius Korngold's review of the *Gurrelieder* premiere appeared in the 1 March issue of the *Neue Freie Presse* and, though generally positive, stated that the *Gurrelieder* had little relevance to the Schoenberg style of 1913. He insinuated that Schoenberg refurbished this older work because he needed a popular success, especially after the poor reception of *Pierrot lunaire*.

2. In a postcard of 11 March Schoenberg informed Berg that he was having the parts for the second and third Altenberg Songs copied in Berlin; Berg received them on 21 March.

3. The concert was postponed to 31 March because Alfred Boruttau had a conflict.

## Berg to Schoenberg

[Vienna] 20 March 1913

Finally I can answer some of your questions, dear Herr Schönberg: I've learned (Hertzka told me) that the reductions of the two string quartet movements are to be published after Easter.[1] The *Gurre* reprise is definitely set for 29 April. 30 March is impossible, if only because the Tonkünstler Orchestra is on tour at that time.

Bum already knows the Zemlinsky songs pretty well, vocally, too—as far as we (Webern and I) can judge in a room. But it would have been impossible for her to sing my 2 songs, that is, learn them as backup, she isn't musical enough. Nor does she, I think, have the high range!

Unfortunately Boruttau is out of town now, but he took the songs with him and is learning them by himself.

Otherwise I can't think of anything new to report. On yes! Would you perhaps know, dear Herr Schönberg, where and whether the parts to Zemlinsky's songs are being prepared?! I asked Zemlinsky himself a while back and reminded him of the importance of having the parts ready on time; but he didn't answer. I'm going to write to him again today; but I think everything is all right!

Enclosed, dear Herr Schönberg, one of Korngold's typical reviews![2]—

1. Berg's piano reduction of the third and fourth movements of Schoenberg's Second String Quartet, Op. 10, was not published until 1921.

2. Probably Korngold's review of the 15 March premiere of Schreker's *Das Spielwerk und die Prinzessin*, in the *Neue Freie Presse* of 18 March 1913.

Schreker's opera was half empty at the 2<sup>nd</sup> performance, little success, no booing![3]—
Sales for the *Gurrelieder* reprise are said to be going splendidly.—

Excuse my haste, dear Herr Schönberg: I still have to write to Zemlinsky and a student will be here soon.

Many warm regards

from your Berg

When are you coming to Vienna, dear Herr Schönberg? Are you coming directly from Berlin, or will you be in Prague over Easter?[4] I'll write again soon, as soon as anything happens! — — —

---

3. Schreker's *Das Spielwerk und die Prinzessin*, premiered simultaneously at the Frankfurt City Opera and the Vienna Court Opera (with Maria Jeritza in the title role), provoked an unprecendented scandal in Vienna, precipitated as much by the extravagant staging by Court Opera director Hans Gregor as by the work itself. Julius Korngold's review was particularly harsh; he attacked the complexity and symbolism of Schreker's text, as well as his "impressionistic" music. Berg summarized his own opinion in a 17 March letter to Schoenberg: "It was a great disappointment. With the best intentions and highest expectations, I could scarcely muster any enthusiasm. I don't know why; perhaps I'm wrong, if only because the critics are abusing it and calling it a failure. But none of the critics object to what I miss in the music. On the contrary!" In 1915 Schreker revised the work, which received its second premiere as *Das Spielwerk* in 1920.

4. Schoenberg traveled to Vienna via Prague, where on 24 February, under the auspices of the Prague Kammermusikverein, he conducted a performance of *Pierrot lunaire* with the original performance forces; the concert provoked violent opposition. Schoenberg arrived in Vienna on 26 March.

## Berg to Schoenberg

[Vienna] 3[2] April 1913

Dear Herr Schönberg,

I hoped to write to you today in peace and quiet and—once again—to <u>thank</u> you. For even the various distortions in the papers—or the scandal in the Musikvereinsaal[1] have been unable to diminish my joy over your performance of my songs. My joy over your decision to do it, over the great trouble you went to, over the chance of hearing my things done by an orchestra—under <u>you</u>—the fact that they really were performed—and in the company of works by you and Mahler and Webern, at that—in short **over everything**!

But today, after reading the enclosed newspaper clipping,[2] I can't find the peace of mind to write about that. I would have liked to spare you this greatest of all

---

1. The concert Schoenberg conducted in Vienna on 31 March led to one of the best-known and best-documented scandals in twentieth-century music history. The program comprised the premiere of Webern's Six Orchestra Pieces, Op. 6, followed by four (numbers 1, 2, 3, and 5) of Zemlinsky's Maeterlinck Songs in their orchestral version, Schoenberg's Chamber Symphony, Op. 9, the premiere of numbers 2 and 3 of Berg's Altenberg Songs, and, scheduled to close the concert, Mahler's *Kindentoten-lieder*. The audience responded noisily to the Webern and again to the Schoenberg, but the two Berg songs completely unleashed a tumult, and the concert had to be curtailed. The Akademischer Verband never recovered from the aftereffects of this scandal; its membership declined radically and the organization was disbanded in April 1914.

2. Berg was particularly upset by the 2 April article in *Die Zeit*, in which it was hinted that Schoenberg had performed works by Webern and Berg to repay them for financial support in the past.

*Caricature from the 7 April 1913 issue of* Die Sonntags-Zeit *with the caption:* "The next Viennese Schönberg Concert"

indignities, but it won't do! This cannot remain uncorrected!

Above all I shall set right that which concerns me (about the financial support); that should appear tomorrow morning (3 April).

"On the basis of Paragraph 19 of the press law, I request that the following correction be printed: In the article, **Scandal in the Concert Hall**, in today's issue of the *Zeit* (morning edition), it says that I 'supported Schönberg financially over a long period of time.' That is completely untrue. I have never supported Schönberg financially. On the contrary: for years Schönberg instructed me gratis. Vienna, 3 April 1913 Alban Berg"

Königer is also sending the clipping to Webern, who will surely send in a similar correction. I have also spoken with Hertzka, who likewise intends to rectify the reference to him (presumably in tomorrow's *Zeit*), that you never advised him to publish the two of us and that you don't consider our things "entirely sound artistically"![3] And I shall try to meet a few people from the Konzertverein Orchestra

3. The same article in *Die Zeit* claimed that Schoenberg did not think much of the Webern and Berg works, and further that he had never recommended publication of his students' music to Emil Hertzka. (As a matter of fact Schoenberg had frequently urged Hertzka to publish Webern. There is no evidence of similar support for Berg.)

today!* Perhaps they will rectify the lie that your response when the orchestra refused to play Webern's things (not mine) was merely to say that the program had already been printed![5]

Of course I'll keep you informed, dear Herr Schönberg, will send you the printed retractions express, will wire if necessary, possibly telephone. Please let me know your telephone number. By the way, I'm meeting Buschbeck again tomorrow morning, who probably has it (your telephone number)! What are you going to do, dear Herr Schönberg? Are you going to refute the various statements in this article? We assume so! Indeed, I have even wondered whether one couldn't sue. But that may be very difficult—or even impossible!

Buschbeck has already been questioned by the police.[6] They're saying Webern will be sued for shouting "scum" [Bagage]. A kind of collective suit. Incidentally, Kokoschka's picture of Webern has been reprinted in the Extrablatt—without the permission of the Akademischer Verband.[7] They also wanted yours, mine, and Buschbeck's.

Buschbeck corrected a few little things! In today's Wiener Journal, for instance![8]— the Arbeiterzeitung did not print the retraction!

In short, the matter won't be settled for quite a while!! It certainly is awful!—Oh yes. Altenberg sent me a copy of his new book![9] Since I had already bought one I now have two copies and, if you don't yet have one, dear Herr Schönberg, and as that seems the ideal use for it, I would like to send it to you. May I? And now, thank you once again!!! Again and again, thank you!!!!

Your Berg

*Berla, principal concertmaster; Holger and Doktor, the 2 principal violists; Hasa, principal cellist.[4]

---

4. Karl Berla, Oskar Holger, Karl Doktor, and Josef Hasa.
5. This, too, appeared in the 2 April Die Zeit article, which claimed that Berg's compositions had motivated the musicians' refusal.
6. Buschbeck had an altercation with a member of the audience, Dr. Viktor Albert, who insulted him and whom Buschbeck had in turn struck. Charges and countercharges were lodged. For information on the outcome of the affair see Berg's letters of 24 April and 6 May 1913.
7. Oskar Kokoschka's 1912 pen and ink drawing of Webern, first published in the Akademischer Verband's Das musikfestliche Wien, was reproduced in the Extrablatt on 2 April.
8. In the Neues Wiener Journal of 2 April, Buschbeck corrected that newspaper's report that he had asked the audience to be quiet "at least" for Mahler's Kindentotenlieder. He had, instead, requested that the audience either listen quietly to the Mahler work or leave.
9. Semmering 1912 (Berlin, 1913).

---

## Berg to Schoenberg

[Vienna] 3 April 1913
in the afternoon

Dear Herr Schönberg,

In great haste and—between 2 lessons—I must tell you that the retraction I mentioned yesterday has not yet appeared. I went to see Hertzka this morning and presumably his correction will be in the Zeit tomorrow, Friday. Strangely enough,

I found none of the various Konzertverein members at home and regard that as an omen not to undertake anything on that front. It is conceivable that one or the other, or all of them, would refuse to do it and that would be even worse: it would be said that I had tried to persuade the gentlemen of the "Konzertverein" to demand a retraction, but that they didn't do so. Consequently there must be something to it! We assume that you, Herr Schönberg, will refute this lie! The enclosed interview[1] with you is an enormous relief to me and all of us. There are wonderful things in it!!

If a retraction doesn't appear in today's evening edition, I'll send it in again, again invoking Paragraph 19 and demanding that the correction appear in the same place in the morning edition!

Forgive my haste and brevity, dear Herr Schönberg, I just wanted you to know the most important things by early tomorrow.

Many, many warm regards

from your Berg

Please don't forget to let me know whether I may send you my extra Altenberg book!

---

1. In an interview, which appeared in *Die Zeit* on 3 April, Schoenberg defended those who arranged the concert, including Buschbeck, and affirmed his belief in the quality of Webern's and Berg's compositions; he states that noisy audience demonstrations ought to be considered an offense punishable by law. Schoenberg had granted his interview before the appearance of the 2 April article in *Die Zeit* that so incensed Berg. Schoenberg also sent a short letter, published in the *Neue Freie Presse* on 4 April, in which he responds to newspaper reports that the Akademischer Verband had programmed works with the intention of causing a scandal. Schoenberg replies that he alone was responsible for the programming of the concert.

## Berg to Schoenberg (express letter)

[Vienna] 4 April 1913

Dear Herr Schönberg,

Today brought no new developments. The *Zeit* still hasn't printed my retraction. Nor the one Hertzka sent off yesterday. I'm going to have mine sent in again today by a lawyer who's a friend of Buschbeck. Perhaps it will appear tomorrow. Hertzka is going to try to get his published by way of personal mediation. Otherwise the only alternative would be to sue, which I'd do in an instant with regard to my correction that I never supported you financially. But Hertzka, who—it seems to me—is much at fault in the matter—after all, he got into a conversation with various journalists after the concert and no doubt gave ambiguous answers to their question why he hadn't published anything of ours—Webern and me—etc., etc.— Hertzka certainly wouldn't sue for a retraction if the *Zeit* doesn't print one. He's too cowardly for that and besides, he's probably too guilt-ridden. Well, for the time being we can't do anything but wait! We're anxious to know what Webern has done[1] and whether you, dear Herr Schönberg, will do anything. And how that filthy rag will respond to that! Whether it's waiting to print all the retractions together,

---

1. After the concert Webern and his family left for Portorose, a spa on the Adriatic; he did not take any steps in the affair.

or whether it will suppress yours and Webern's as well. I wouldn't put it past the *Zeit*! Instead of printing my retraction they had the gall to send me a friendly pneumatic letter, politely requesting my photograph for purposes of a caricature! (Probably for the Sunday *Zeit*.) Otherwise the furor over the concert has settled down somewhat, except for the *Mittags Zeitung*, in which daily battles are still being waged between Ullmann*—who defends the Verband—and a certain "Veritas."[2] This "Veritas" is said to be a well-known Viennese critic; I suspect Stauber, but it could well be Hirschfeld, as he's the only one who hasn't written anything about the "Scandal in the Concert Hall." This "Veritas" reaches absolute depths of baseness. He calls Altenberg's poems "anal poetry" [*Afterpoesie*], my songs "a hoax" [*Ulk*], "hyper-modern *Gstanzel*,"[3] no, the other things he writes are simply too much, this is the least of it. Perhaps you have read it, I won't sent it to you but will save it for eternity. I can understand why he doesn't dare betray his incognito. Yes, he takes this opportunity to scoff at "Mahler's sanctification," to describe Loos merely as "the well-known deaf architect," for whom this music probably "represents music of the spheres," etc., etc.

Of the latest insults, the following is of interest and almost gratifying: Reitler (the 2nd music critic of the *Neue Freie Presse*)[4] said "that Korngold and he had decided not to attend any concerts that include the names Schönberg—Webern and Berg!" Thank Heavens!! (That reminds me of a scene in the concert: after my first song someone shouted into the uproar: "Quiet, here comes the 2nd picture postcard!" And after the words: "plötzlich ist alles aus!" [suddenly it is all over!] someone else shouted loudly: "Thank Heavens!"). By the way, it's interesting that the ushers sided with those who were hissing and laughing. Someone from the audience wanted to evict my student Kassowitz,[5] who was applauding heartily, and two ushers were actually about to do it! Many people threw small change at the people applauding in the standing room section—as payment for the claqueurs— Yes, that's Vienna! You are so right, dear Herr Schönberg! Your revulsion against Vienna has always been justified and I see—unfortunately too late—how wrong I was to have tried to reconcile you to Vienna, dear Herr Schönberg. It's true! One can't hate this "city of song" enough!!

I assume I'll hear from you soon, dear Herr Schönberg, and am already looking forward to it. I shall close now, to see whether there's anything in the evening papers. I cannot rest until these horrible lies in the *Zeit* from the day before yesterday have been eradicated! I can't even read a book, let alone work!

I hope to have good news for you soon, dear Herr Schönberg, and for the time being send my very, very warmest and most grateful regards

Your Berg

My wife also sends her very best to you and your esteemed wife.—

* he was president of the Akademischer Verband before Buschbeck.

2. The feud between Ludwig Ullmann and the self-styled Veritas was played out in three issues of the *Wiener Mittags-Zeitung* from 1, 2, and 3 April.
3. A *Gstanzel* is a bantering, four-line yodeling song.
4. Josef Reitler, who studied with Schoenberg in 1903, joined the *Neue Freie Presse* in 1907.
5. Gottfried Kassowitz became Berg's student sometime after April, 1912.

## Berg to Schoenberg

[Vienna] 7 April 1913

Many thanks, dear Herr Schönberg, for your kind card. I'm very happy to be able to give you the book.[1] I was at the Konzertverein today to pick up your parts and Zemlinsky's and sent the former to you, the others to Zemlinsky.

Regarding the retractions, the matter looks increasingly hopeless. Hertzka can't be persuaded to act energetically in the matter; he's trying to get a retraction published through personal means—amicably—through the editorial staff of the *Zeit*, where he knows various people; but should that fail—and it will—he'll let it drop, since he can't afford to make enemies at the *Zeit*—and he couldn't care less if people think he doesn't publish me because my things are bad! Webern's and my retractions weren't printed, even though we invoked Paragraph 19. I spoke with a lawyer and he thought that if I sued (I don't know what Webern will decide) I could manage to have a retraction printed! But I don't know whether it makes any sense for me to do it alone. For even if a retraction were printed, the *Zeit* would follow it with a comment. Something like: "Berg may not actually have supported Herr Schönberg, but we do know of the 'campaign' led by Berg in the fall of 1912, so we weren't far off the mark when we initially stated that Schönberg performed Berg's works (which he doesn't consider artistically sound and which he hasn't recommended to his publisher) to 'pay off his debt'!" etc., etc., etc.

8 April 1913

I had to interrupt the letter, dear Herr Schönberg. Meantime I received a letter from the Dreililienverlag,[2] citing a passage from a letter of yours in which you recommend Webern to him. I am to see to the retraction! But can I do that?! Should I send the letter to Webern? But surely he can't correct that either. Surely the Dreililienverlag would have to do that!! But as I see the present situation (no retraction appeared today either!), it's all the same who sends in the correction, whether Webern or I or the publisher: it won't be printed! The papers know that no one will sue anyway, or they're willing to take that chance! And yet this would be an opportunity for once to break the incredible power, the inviolate position of the press!

A pity that Kraus wasn't in Vienna, he would certainly have written about it, one could have given him this article in particular (and others as well) through Loos. Now it's already a bit late, has gone up in smoke, and maybe he won't hear of it.[3]—

As far as I can remember, dear Herr Schönberg, the works you performed were hardly discussed in the reviews. Buschbeck, who collected everything from the *Observer*,[4] will send you the ones in question!—

1. See footnote 9 of Berg's letter dated 3 [2] April 1913.

2. In a postcard of 3 April 1913, Schoenberg urged Berg to send the *Zeit* review to the publishing firms Simrock, Tischer and Jagenberg, and Dreililienverlag, and to ask them to set things straight; Schoenberg, who had had works published by the two last-named firms, had previously sent letters recommending Webern (but not Berg).

3. Karl Kraus had been in Munich to give a lecture on 29 March in honor of the 150th anniversary of Jean Paul's birth. In the next *Fackel* XV / 374–375 (8 May 1913), 24–25, he did in fact discuss the Schoenberg concert scandal, which, according to him, had nothing to do with response to new music, but how and when to express a negative response. Kraus berated the Viennese press for having sunk even below its previously registered depths.

4. The *Observer* is a newspaper clipping service in Vienna.

That's all there is to tell, dear Herr Schönberg. Should anything occur I'll write at once![5]

Many, many warm regards

from your grateful, devoted Berg

Please convey my wife's and my warmest regards to your wife. And my wife sends you, dear Herr Schönberg, her best regards.

---

5. Berg was never successful in getting a retraction printed, and from statements made years later it is apparent that he felt Schoenberg let him down on this occasion. In a letter to Berg of 9 October 1929, Theodor Adorno, writing in another matter, accused Schoenberg of ". . . the same disloyalty, which, according to you, he also displayed toward you when there was a scandal after the Altenberg Songs and he didn't say a word to identify himself with you."

*Berg to Schoenberg*

[Vienna] 16 April 1913

I haven't written for a long time, my dear Herr Schönberg. My wife was very ill: a serious sore throat, which turned into a completely mysterious inflammation of the entire throat and larynx—probably through infection. A specialist called in at a critical stage in the illness—(my wife couldn't even swallow any more)—saw no alternative but to make a huge incision in her palate. Presumably that speeded her improvement, thank Heavens my wife is on the way to recovery—and after all this excitement I can find the peace of mind and time to write you again, dear Herr Schönberg.

So both *Gurrelieder* performances have come to nothing. The Vienna reprise due to the baseness and intrigues of the Philharmonic Chorus and its director. For it simply isn't true that ticket sales were going poorly. I know that sales began splendidly, Dr. Löwy told me so repeatedly; also that there was continuing demand. For example, 500 kronen alone were sold at Kehlendorfer[1] (the least important ticket office), and there were only very few tickets left at Gutmann's when I bought mine there!

Besides, no one can be certain on the 8th or 10th of the month whether a concert on the 29th is going to be well attended! Performances of your works in particular demonstrate that the greatest demand isn't till the last minute. That's why I firmly believe there were other reasons for the cancelation! In certain circles it was welcomed that the *Gurre* success was "negated," as it were, by our concert. And that's how it is to remain! Another success—inevitable in the case of a *Gurre* reprise—was not desired! If it weren't for our loss in not hearing this work again, one would have to rejoice that this heavenly, pure music has escaped—it is to be hoped forever—those filthy fingers. In your hands—though not until winter—the *Gurrelieder* will celebrate a worthier resurrection. I found out about it from Königer yesterday, who in turn had it from Webern. Webern didn't give the reason for the Berlin

---

1. Karl Kehlendorfer, a concert ticket agency in Vienna's first district.

postponement.[2] I'm sure that's something you'll tell me, dear Herr Schönberg, when we come to Zehlendorf—no! to Schlachtensee[3]—at the end of May. I'm already looking forward to the days with you, to be able to spend time with you again, to discuss with you the things that move me—finally, to get away from here. Away from this air that threatens to choke me. (For my asthma attacks have become unbearable and keep me from sleeping at night, from working during the day.)

I have nothing new to relate, dear Herr Schönberg. We went to see Altenberg again in Steinhof. He's doing very well and was in very good spirits.—There's a Kraus lecture I'm going to tonight.[4] They say that Altenberg [sic] is going to read some of his sketches. I'm very curious!

I'll close now, dear Herr Schönberg. My very warmest regards—also on my wife's behalf—to you and your esteemed wife.

In gratitude and esteem,

Your devoted Alban Berg

(Oh, yes! I assume you have received the parts to the Chamber Symphony?! Also the Altenberg book! I only ask in case I have to file a claim due to some muddle in the postal system, something one always has to reckon with!—)

---

2. According to a contract Schoenberg signed on 12 April, the Berlin *Gurrelieder* performance was now set for 2 February 1914, after having earlier been tentatively set for 27 May 1913. The postponement seems to have been due to fund-raising difficulties.

3. When the Schoenbergs had to leave the Villa Lepcke in Zehlendorf they initially considered moving to Schlachtensee, also in the southwest outskirts of Berlin.

4. Karl Kraus's 16 April lecture in the small hall of the Musikverein included readings of sketches from Peter Altenberg's new book, *Semmering 1912*.

*Berg to Schoenberg*

[Vienna] 24 April 1913

Actually I have nothing new to tell you, my dear Herr Schönberg, but my desire to talk with you, my feeling of loneliness (—I can't call it anything else—) —which has been growing ever since you left—is so overpowering, that I take refuge in letter writing, not quite having the courage for the other alternative I kept considering these past few days—namely simply to telephone you, dear Herr Schönberg. For what would you think if in response to your obvious question "what's up" I had nothing to say—or merely: "I just wanted to hear your voice, Herr Schönberg, to ask you how you all are, what you are doing and about everything relating to you!"

During these last months, actually since the *Gurrelieder* events, my life has been so completely under your spell, I would almost say: that each of my actions was in some joyous way connected with you, dear Herr Schönberg; now that this has ceased, following the 31 March concert and its aftermath, now that for 3 weeks I really haven't heard anything concerning you, anything concerning you in a real and inner sense, —I consequently feel completely hollow, as if uprooted and— perhaps for the first time in my life—I'm bored, i.e., feel that these last weeks have been never-ending and I can't even imagine how I'm to get through the weeks to come before our Berlin trip! And all this: despite the fact that I'm composing again and don't have any spare time! I'm continuing the pieces for clarinet and piano.[1] There will probably be 4–6 short pieces, which I intend to finish in a few weeks in order—after the Berlin trip—to begin a symphony. I hope my asthma, which is already causing me a great deal of trouble and which I'm trying to fight in every possible way as regards my lifestyle—won't be an obstacle in the execution of these— as it seems to me—and as it will appear to you, too, dear Herr Schönberg—ambitious plans.—

My wife, thank God, is quite well again; but the illness left her very weak.—

On 16 April I was—as I already told you—at a Kraus lecture, where he gave a beautiful introduction to his readings of Altenberg's sketches. It will probably appear in the next *Fackel*.[2] In other respects, too, the evening was wonderful, * only somewhat tiring—and attended by a most disagreeable audience that laughed loudly in the most unseemly (most tragic) spots.—

You will probably have heard that Buschbeck was sentenced to a fine of 100 kronen for that box on the ear![4] Considering that we—and the lawyer—feared a prison sentence, that (the 100 kronen) isn't bad. In terms of justice, of course, outrageous!—

The enclosed clipping[5] may interest you.

Otherwise I really don't know of anything—without running the danger of telling you something you already know. And at least I have satisfied my urge to chat with you, dear Herr Schönberg—even if only one-sidedly (alas, alas!)—something for which you'll surely forgive me!

I hope you are well in all respects, dear Herr Schönberg, likewise your esteemed wife and the dear children. My wife and I send our warmest regards to all.

But to you, dear Herr Schönberg, the special regards of most grateful devotion and infinite esteem.

from your Berg

\* Among other things he read Pfleget den Fremdenverkehr, Sommerschlaftraum (Riedl Dangl),[3] Kinder der Zeit, Lehar in Tripolis!!! Mittheilungen aus unterrichteten Kreisen, etc.

---

1. The Four Pieces for Clarinet and Piano, Op. 5, were completed in May 1913.

2. *Die Fackel* XV / 374–375 (8 May 1913), 20.

3. Actually entitled "Fiebertraum im Sommerschlaf," which first appeared in the 1911 "Sommer-Revue" number of the *Fackel*; Ludwig Riedl was a leading Viennese cafe owner, Dangl a restaurateur. With the exception of "Die Kinder der Zeit," (1912), all the other items Berg mentions first appeared in the *Fackel* during 1913.

4. The hearing dealing with Dr. Viktor Albert's assault charges against Buschbeck took place on 21 April; Buschbeck did not dispute the charge. His fine was eventually reduced to 20 kronen, as Berg tells Schoenberg in a letter of 22 June 1913.

5. Possibly a report such as the one in the *Neue Freie Presse* of 22 April 1913 giving details of the hearing.

## Berg to Schoenberg

Vienna, 6 May 1913

Dear Herr Schönberg,

I didn't know your new address and couldn't get it from anyone in Vienna, and it wasn't until I asked Webern that I heard to my great astonishment that you, dear Herr Schönberg, have not moved. So, my dear Herr Schönberg, I will once again be able to write you—one of my many uninteresting letters.

As you probably know, the hearing concerning Buschbeck's suit against Dr. Albert, who was also fined 100 kronen,[1] is over. The judge[2] was very likable. Several witnesses testified so decidedly against Dr. Albert, that his claim to have said only *Büberei* [boyish mischief] utterly collapsed. Linke and Polnauer were among the witnesses. Also the critic Brandt,[3] who didn't hesitate to swear to a variety of lies on his word of honor. Well, everyone knows what honor means to this fellow, who has used the title Doctor for years, though he still has no right to it. If it were really to come to another hearing, it would probably be necessary to unmask this villain. Portions of the hearing were quite amusing. Of course it wasn't at all the way the papers reported it, where everything that spoke in favor of Buschbeck or exposed the baseness of Albert and the rest of the audience was suppressed!

6 May

I was interrupted. Meanwhile I spoke with Buschbeck. He has probably written to you that he is "on the outs" with the Verband. Nevertheless we're already planning various things for next year. Above all, Buschbeck has—what I consider—a splendid idea: that on the day after the *Gurrelieder* performance in Berlin a separate train take all the participants of the performance (chorus, orchestra, soloists) to Vienna,[4] there to repeat the performance—naturally with you in charge. Buschbeck figures that the costs would be relatively low and easily covered by ticket sales! I imagine Kehlendorfer would gladly take over the formal arrangements for the concert—on the other hand, it's likely that the Berlin agent (Wolff, I believe) would be interested in the idea!

Well! I had better discuss all of that with you in person, dear Herr Schönberg, when I come to Zehlendorf, assuming you aren't so sick of Vienna after these latest events that you won't want to hear of it.—

I saw a *Tristan* not long ago that led to another scandal, whistles in action, etc. The cause was Mildenburg's—I must admit—almost unbearable indisposition (fatigue) in the last act![5]

Otherwise the days pass rather monotonously. Unfortunately I'm suffering severely from asthma again. A new treatment based on the latest research (inhalation of

1. In his countersuit, Buschbeck stated that Viktor Albert had called him a scamp *(Lausbub)* when Buschbeck appeared on the stage to appeal for quiet. The hearing took place on 2 May.
2. Dr. Hermann Decker.
3. The composer and music journalist Johannes Brandt wrote for *Der Morgen* and *Der Merker*.
4. An idea first raised by Adolf Loos in a letter to Schoenberg of 7 February 1912; Schoenberg himself had mentioned the possibility to Buschbeck in a letter of 27 December 1912.
5. The Court Opera performed Wagner's *Tristan und Isolde* on 5 May 1913, with Erik Schmedes and Anna Bahr-Mildenburg in the title roles.

atropine, adrenaline, etc.) doesn't offer significant relief. Let alone cure the malady.

I feel a tremendous longing for news of you, dear Herr Schönberg—. Not that I am so presumptuous as to expect a letter or any sort of communication from you, particularly as there's nothing to answer or report: but I don't hear anything about you from anyone; even Webern could tell me only very little. I can't wait to hear more and am counting the days until we can begin our trip. I don't know the exact date yet, but once I do I'll be so bold as to ask you, dear Herr Schönberg, to reserve lodgings for us sometime when you're passing through Zehlendorf, preferably somewhere near you—of course, only if you think advance reservations are necessary for a suitable hotel and that we couldn't just take a room upon arrival. We'll probably leave around the 20th. Oh, how I'm looking forward to it!—

Enclosed one of Korngold's latest howlers.[6]—

I am reading Maeterlinck just now: *Death*.[7] So far I haven't worked up any real enthusiasm beyond a degree of interest. Actually Maeterlinck just reports what science knows about death, whereas I had expected something different on the subject, something more sublime. Indeed—almost contemptuously—he avoids anything of that kind (like the Catholic doctrine). But maybe I'm jumping to conclusions: I haven't finished the book yet.[8]

Enough for today.

My very warmest regards—also on my wife's behalf—to you, dear Herr Schönberg, and your esteemed wife. In unending gratitude and esteem I remain

Your devoted Berg

---

6. Berg is probably referring to something in Julius Korngold's feuilleton "Von der grossen und von einer kleinen Musikfestwoche. Der Bösendorfersaal" (About the Major and a Minor Music Festival Week. The Bösendorfer Hall) in the *Neue Freie Presse* of (3 May 1913).

7. Maurice Maeterlinck's *La Mort* (Paris, 1913) appeared that year in the German translation of Friedrich von Oppeln-Bronikowski, *Vom Tode*.

8. Webern was reading this book at about the same time and shared Berg's disappointment.

*Schoenberg to Berg*

Berlin-Zehlendorf, 9 May 1913

Dear friend,

I'm moving not to Schlachtensee but rather to:

Berlin-Südende, Berlinerstr, 17a.[1]

We'll probably be moving between the 20th and 25th and will be ready to receive guests about 5–6 days later.

That's why it would be a good idea if you postponed your visit until the end of May (circa 29th or 30th, I'll let you know the exact dates). We are very much looking forward to seeing you and your wife. Unfortunately we won't be able to put you up,

---

1. The Schoenbergs had been offered the second floor of a house that was partly owned by Albertine Zehme. During her stays in Berlin she occupied the ground floor.

since the Zemlinskys will be here at about the same time. But it won't be difficult to find something suitable for you, you'll just have to tell me precisely what you want: how many rooms (1 or 2), price, length of stay, floor, hotel or pension. I would advise a pension (if I find a good one). That's generally just as good and cheaper (particularly as regards tips!). But if you prefer a hotel, I'm sure we can find a good one.

I haven't seen anything about Buschbeck's trial. Send it to me.

Nor have I seen a single review of the concert. Wasn't there one anywhere? Could you send me something?

On 7 May Scherchen performed my Chamber Symphony here "privately" (except for press) in the Harmoniumsaal.[2] A few bad reviews have already appeared. Others will follow. The performance was quite good, though rather bourgeois in interpretation (temperamental and sweet). Scherchen had 5 rehearsals, causing me to realize that it was tantamount to suicide when I did it with 2.[3]

I consider Buschbeck's idea for the *Gurrelieder* impractical. The orchestra alone would cost at least 3–4,000 marks, not counting expenses. Add to that expenses of at least 2,500 marks. Then perhaps living expenses for many members of the chorus. And then travel for about 600 people; soloists' fees! etc. . . . Why, it would amount to 20,000 marks!!!

But maybe I'm wrong? I don't think so!

I hope your asthma is better again. In any case I'm glad you are treating it seriously now.

I'm very much looking forward to your visit and hope you'll be able to stay a **good long time.**

Many warm regards

Your Arnold Schönberg

---

2. Hermann Scherchen's concert consisted of two successive performances of Schoenberg's Chamber Symphony, Op. 9, with members of the Berlin Court Opera and Deutsches Opernhaus Orchestras.

3. For Schoenberg's 31 March concert in Vienna.

*Berg to Schoenberg*

[Vienna] 15 May 1913

Dear Herr Schönberg,

I intended to answer your dear letter immediately, which had made me immensely happy (I mean the fact that I again received a letter from you). But many things unexpectedly intervened,—the most time-consuming and upsetting being a serious dental problem of my wife's—and forced me to postpone my letter. And then I was unable to locate the newspaper clippings you wanted until yesterday. As you see, dear Herr Schönberg, apart from what Buschbeck sent you (which were for the most part mere reports), no real reviews appeared, with the exception of Bienenfeld's silly drivel[1] (which I enclose). I also found just this one enclosed review of Dr. Reti's miserable performance of the piano pieces.[2]—

Our trip to Berlin is approaching! So we are not to see Zehlendorf! But of course the important thing is not the place but the fact that I'll be able to be with you again for a long visit.

I'm not sure when we'll leave. It depends on whether I have to be here for the June rent (there's always a lot to do at the beginning of each month!) or whether I will after all be able to leave on the 29th or 30th, whichever you say! We would arrive on 3 or 4 June at the latest and could stay at least a week. Concerning lodgings, the most important thing for me would be to be very near you. If there is a pension, we would of course prefer that (if only for financial reasons). But most important is the greatest possible quiet for my wife, who sleeps very lightly. If, despite your move and all the work you always have, you are kindly prepared to trouble yourself about our lodgings, dear, kind Herr Schönberg, the following considerations would be the most important! What I have in mind, if there is such a thing, is: a pension close to you, possibly in one of the so-called Berlin "garden houses" (courtyard wing), which are supposedly very quiet! (I believe my sister lives like that in Berlin.) But if that's not possible we would of course take a hotel. We need 2 (small) single rooms, connected! Who knows if one could get that in a pension?! The floor doesn't matter! Possibly the higher up the quieter and cheaper it would be. But ground floor, II[nd] floor, or the like, is fine too! I can't judge the price. Do you think one could get something nice and decent for 3 marks a room?* Of course, we'll take our breakfast there. As you see, dear Herr Schönberg, I'm very presumptuous. Since it might really be difficult to find all that, it may also be possible—in order to spare you the trouble—that we move to a hotel first and then look for a pension ourselves.

I must repeat: Of course I would understand if it's impossible to get something like that for 3 marks a room. Maybe such a room would cost 4 or 5 marks in Südende. In that case the following would suit us, too: 1 nice room (by which I really just mean a clean room in a decent pension—connected to a very simple closet! A dark hole with a bed for all I care, since I'll really only be in the pension to sleep and I sleep very soundly, whereas for my wife, for whom it's more critical, I want a room that isn't exactly ugly or uncomfortable!—It's much more important that both rooms are adjoining than that both rooms are equally nice or large. In other words a nice, decent room (for my wife) and next to it (for me) any kind of

1. In her first review of 1 April, Elsa Bienenfeld, like all the other critics, had merely described the scandal, but in a second article (*Neues Wiener Journal* of 27 April) she wrote that she had been impressed by the orchestral version of Schoenberg's Op. 9, which she considered clearer and more intelligible than when she first heard it in its chamber version in 1908; she goes on to mention bizarre, ugly sound effects and the monotony of modern harmonies such as Schoenberg's, and closes with another attack on Berg's Altenberg Songs, which she describes as "totally unsuccessful attempts and a grotesque expression of complete artistic impotence."

2. Rudolf Reti had performed Schoenberg's Piano Pieces, Op. 19, and Op. 11, No. 1, in an afternoon concert of modern chamber music in the small hall of the Musikverein on 6 April. The program also included Walter Klein's "Fünf Gesänge" with string quartet accompaniment (performed by the Rosé Quartet and Eduard Gärtner), songs by Reti, and piano music by Ansorge, Reger, Zoltán Kodály, and Wellesz. The review Berg sent has not been preserved or identified.

room (be it ever so dark or unprepossessing). Of course I have no objection to beautiful rooms. I just mean in case 2 adjoining rooms aren't possible, the above combination would do, too!

Have I expressed myself clearly?! I've certainly used enough words!

Otherwise there's nothing worth telling. Tonight I'll see *Entführung*.[3] Wedekind is coming to Vienna at the end of May to perform *Franziska*, which we'll see before we leave for Berlin.[4]

My joy at seeing you soon—is boundless. I can't wait, and just thinking about it makes me so restless that I can't write calmly. Put the illegibility of this letter down to that restlessness, dear Herr Schönberg.

Many, many warm regards to you, dear Herr Schönberg, also from my wife and likewise to your esteemed wife

from your Berg.

I will know shortly whether we can come at the end of May (29th or 30th) or not until early June (3rd or 4th) and will let you know immediately!!

* of course the 3 marks isn't a limit or suggestion, just an idea. With all of the conditions I'm setting I'll simply have to pay what it costs. And of course that's not particularly important or significant.

---

3. At the Court Opera, featuring Selma Kurz as Constanze and Alfred Piccaver as Belmonte.
4. It was not until after Berg returned from Berlin that he and Webern attended a touring performance of Frank Wedekind's *Franziska* at the Vienna Volkstheater on 12 June. Wedekind himself appeared in this Munich Ensemble production.

## Berg to Schoenberg

[Vienna] 14 June 1913

My dear, kind Herr Schönberg,

I was prevented from succumbing to the urge to write you immediately, dear Herr Schönberg, by a multitude of urgent matters that greeted me upon my return (among other things, there was a fire in one of the houses). I've been back in Vienna for several days now, but all my thoughts are still with you in Berlin, in your dear, lovely home.[1] Perhaps these thoughts will express my gratitude better than my words can. For how can words encompass the wealth of gifts, impressions, memories that overwhelmed me. Truly I can only think of the infinity of beautiful details with deepest gratitude and tell you that it is so. Of your and your wife's overgenerous hospitality to us, of the many cozy hours spent with your family, at home or elsewhere, of the thousand conversations during walks, of the drives together into the outskirts, trips in the underground, elevated railway, streetcars, and auto, etc., of the theater[2] and concert visits together, etc. Up to the wonderful hours when I was allowed to study the score of *Pierrot* with you, dear Herr Schönberg—and when the following day I was able to attend the unforgettable *Pierrot* rehearsal and performance.

1. Berg and his wife were in Berlin 4–11 June.
2. Including a performance of Strauss' *Ariadne auf Naxos* (first version).

You will certainly understand, dear Herr Schönberg, that into these most beautiful memories of untroubled enjoyment, there intrude memories of the last afternoon with its depressing truths.[3] But I must **thank you** for your censure as for everything else I've received from you, knowing as I do that it is meant well—and for my own good. Nor do I need to tell you, dear Herr Schönberg, that my deep pain is assurance that I will take your censure to heart. And—if I succeed in this resolve—which admittedly I hope for with tremulous apprehension at best (for my self-doubt is so strong that the least criticism from you, who alone are qualified to give it, robs me of almost all hope)—as I said, if I succeed in my resolve, then my pain will also lose its bitterness and—as always when you appeal to my conscience with inexorable truths—will belong to those memories that are—despite their depressing aspects—full of profound, though sad and earnest beauty.

I hope I can soon prove to you in deed what I have scarcely been able to express here in words. Once I am in the country I intend to begin with the suite. Maybe I'll manage to write something cheerful for once!—We'll probably leave for the country the middle of next week (circa 18 June), from where I'll send you my address. Actually I'll do that from Vienna, when I give you the exact date of my departure.—

Included in the urgent matters mentioned at the outset was also the revision of the score and orchestra parts to the *Lied der Waldtaube*, which Polnauer and I undertook at U.E. As you know, Freund is to sing it in Paris on the 22nd,[4] so the dynamic revisions you noted a while back had to be entered. We also went through the preceding introduction very carefully.

I'm very happy about this performance. If only because it's taking place abroad, and is a wonderful confirmation of your assertion that your recognition isn't dependent on this country. How I wish I could be there! Are you going, dear Herr Schönberg? It should be very interesting to see how a piece like that works by itself! The performance should be excellent, as there will surely be enough rehearsals, considering that it's a relatively short piece (Hertzka is leaving for Paris today already (the 14th) and the concert isn't until the 22nd!)

Enclosed a clipping from an American newspaper[5] about your Vienna concert last March. My brother, who lives in America,[6] sent it to me. I had asked him for the *New York Times* issue with an article about you that included a number of pictures and musical examples, as well as your portrait.[7] I had promised several copies of it to Frau Zehme, too. But my brother writes that despite various attempts, he hasn't been able to get this issue. Would you please tell Frau Zehme!—The enclosed review is certainly idiotic!—

3. Schoenberg had expressed dissatisfaction with Berg's most recent compositions, the Altenberg Songs, Op. 4, and the Clarinet Pieces, Op. 5.
4. The concert, originally to have been conducted by Alfredo Casella, ultimately took place under Oskar Fried's direction.
5. The *Boston Evening Transcript* of 17 April 1913.
6. Hermann Berg was part owner of the import / export firm Georg Borgfeldt & Co. in New York.
7. James Huneker's article, "Schoenberg, Musical Anarchist who has upset Europe" in the *New York Times* on 19 January 1913, included a photograph of Schoenberg, reproductions of three of his paintings, and a page from the printed score of *Verklärte Nacht*.

Of course I saw Webern, who was in Vienna for 2 days,[8] and told him a great deal about you!—

Oh yes—I have told U.E. that a percussion score has to be taken out of the *Gurrelieder* to be autographed. It will be done. The wind parts will likewise be autographed. Presumably you'll be corresponding with Hertzka on the matter, since you still want to add some revisions!

Well, dear Herr Schönberg, again warmest thanks for our week in Berlin. Also to your very esteemed wife for the great trouble she went to during our visit. I hope your wife is quite well again, likewise the dear little ones, whom I greet warmly. Give my most devoted best to your wife, and to you, dear Herr Schönberg, my very, very warmest regards

always and forever in your debt,

Your Berg

---

8. Webern's summer stay in Mürzuschlag was interrupted by a short trip to Vienna 11–14 June.

## Berg to Schoenberg

Trahütten, 9 July 1913

Many thanks, dear Herr Schönberg, for your dear card.[1] Also for sending the address of the photographer Erfurth. Unfortunately I still haven't heard from him. But I'll wait a few more days.[2]

How are you, dear Herr Schönberg? I would love to know what Gautzsch looks like, how you live there, whether you, your gracious wife, and the dear little ones are comfortable there, go for many walks, and enjoy country life!?[3] Whether you have the leisure to work on *Glückliche Hand* or something else and what that might be!?![4] In short, I again find myself in need of a few days with you to find out all I'm permitted to know about you. These days I often think how wonderful it would have been if you had followed your initial plan of going to the Alps this year; then we wouldn't have been at all far apart and I, that is, my wife and I, could easily have spent one or two weeks at the same place with you. But as it is I probably won't see you again until fall or winter at one of the *Gurrelieder* performances in Amsterdam, Munich, or Berlin (that would be long overdue!)[5] Maybe something will come off in Vienna after all! I'll contact Buschbeck again about the Mahler concert (VI[th] and *Kindertotenlieder*).[6] It would be just too wonderful if that came

1. Dated 25 June 1913.
2. Berg received a print of Hugo Erfurth's Schoenberg portrait photograph shortly thereafter, as he tells Schoenberg in an undated picture postcard from mid-July.
3. Schoenberg had been invited to spend the summer with the Zehme family at their villa in Leipzig-Gautzsch.
4. That summer Schoenberg worked primarily on *Die glückliche Hand*, which he completed on 20 November.
5. The only *Gurrelieder* performance that took place in the 1913 / 14 season was in Amsterdam with the Concertgebouw under Schoenberg.
6. Although Buschbeck was no longer associated with the Akademischer Verband Berg hoped to enlist his help in organizing a concert to be conducted by Schoenberg.

off. By the way, I heard of the wonderful *Waldtaube* success in Paris from Hertzka (who turned to me about the *Gurre* score in which I had corrected errors),* and from Webern. Polnauer too, who has been commissioned to check the new parts, wrote to me that Hertzka had told him that none of the other numbers on the program, Debussy, Casals, etc., were nearly as successful as the *Waldtaube*.

Webern also told me that he is ill again.[7] It's terrible! But I wrote to him that I still believe his treatments and months in the country were not useless. The results won't be apparent until later. I myself have often experienced—and observed in my wife—that one sometimes feels even worse during treatment, and only months later does the malady suddenly improve or disappear. After all, the situation with my asthma is no different. The consequences of a careless, nerve-racking lifestyle torment me most now that I'm living very sensibly, abstaining almost entirely from alcohol, nicotine, coffee, and tea. Only now, for the first time this summer, am I experiencing the effects of all my efforts and privations. I'm free of all asthmatic complaints: shortness of breath, hayfever, etc., though I go for hour-long hikes and am much outside in all kinds of weather—and am working. Unfortunately I have to confess, dear Herr Schönberg, that I haven't made use of your various suggestions as to what I should compose next. Much as I was intrigued from the start by your suggestion to write an orchestral suite (with character pieces), and though I immediately began to think of it often and seriously, and did intend to work it out, nonetheless it didn't come about. Again and again I found myself giving into an older desire—namely to write a symphony. And when I intended to make a concession to this desire by beginning the suite with a prelude, I found (upon beginning the work) that it again merely turned into the opening of this symphony. So I simply decided to go ahead with it:—it is to be a large one-movement symphony, naturally including the requisite 4 movements, i.e., sections, with developments, etc. Similar in construction to the Chamber Symphony. Concurrently though, the plan for the suite is sure to mature to the point where I can actually begin writing it, and then your kind suggestion will be realized—though belatedly. I hope with all my heart that you won't be angry with me for postponing realization of your suggestion. Will not regard it as wilfullness! You yourself know, dear Herr Schönberg, that I am always conscious of, and never want to be conscious of anything but: being your student. To follow you in every respect, knowing that everything I do in opposition to your wishes is wrong. If during these last months I have thought so often and intensely about writing a symphony it is surely because I want to make up for what I would have composed under you, dear Herr Schönberg, had you stayed in Vienna and because I want to heed your words, "Each of your students should at some point have written a symphony."—

Many warmest regards, dear, kind Herr Schönberg, to your very esteemed wife—also from my wife—and our—but most especially my—very best to you

Your—student, Berg

Warm regards to Frau Zehme.

---

7. Webern had suffered from almost constant ill health since leaving the Stettin position earlier that year.

(It may be possible to omit Nahowski and Graz Köflach rail line from my address, i.e., write "near Graz" instead. But that could be dangerous and undependable! So I'll send you these 2 envelopes![8])

*You, dear Herr Schönberg, were probably asked about the parts, too. Hertzka wants to prepare scores for the winds as well, i.e., all the horns, all the trombones, etc. Surely that's impractical and would be understandable only for <u>reasons of economy</u>. But surely <u>that's</u> no reason! Maybe <u>pairs</u> of winds: for instance (1st and 2nd horn), (3rd and 4th horn), etc., (7th and 8th horn, i.e., 1st and 2nd Wagner tuba). I have written to U.E., i. e., inquired there about the <u>transposition</u> of the Wagner tubas!

---

8. Schoenberg had asked on two different occasions whether Berg's summer address could be shortened: he never used the two envelopes Berg enclosed.

## Schoenberg to Berg

[Gautzsch] 16 July 1913

Dear Berg,

I must tell you something important about the concert I am to conduct in Vienna. We initially spoke of the Mahler VI[th], but the following considerations have now led me to choose the V[th].

Mahler reorchestrated the V[th] almost entirely.[1] A while back Hinrichsen (he's the owner of Peters Edition) showed me this practically new score and asked whether I considered the symphony any good (!!!) (the idiot!).[2] He can't decide whether to have the orchestra material altered according to Mahler's directions. He doesn't think it would be worth it. Göhler has asked him about it, too, because he wants to perform it in January.[3] But that wasn't enough for him. That's when I realized the importance of performing the V[th] and told him so. Consequently he has now decided to have the parts prepared.

Maybe Buschbeck can bring it off. Just the V[th]. Nothing else. The question is whether one could get the Philharmonic. [Schoenberg discusses the relative cost and number of rehearsals required for the Philharmonic or Konzertverein Orchestras.]

Of course I don't know what Buschbeck can and / or is willing to venture.

But perhaps he can do it. Maybe he'll even venture a 2nd concert in which I would conduct only classical works. For instance the Eroica, Mozart G-minor, Brahms C-minor, or the like.

In any event, the first concert would be the more important one. But I almost think that if both concerts were announced together you could attract an audience. Perhaps a guarantee fund could be raised. Or: it might even be possible for the

---

1. Mahler's Fifth Symphony underwent numerous revisions after its 1904 premiere; the final stage of revision dates from 1910.

2. According to Schoenberg's published Berlin diary (Berliner Tagebuch, ed. Josef Rufer, Frankfurt, 1974; 16), Henri Hinrichsen first discussed Mahler's works with Schoenberg in January 1912.

3. The conductor Georg Göhler led the Winderstein Orchestra in the first performance of the revised version of Mahler's Fifth Symphony in Leipzig's Albert Hall on 9 January 1914. Peters did not publish the final version of the work until 1964.

Konzertverein to invite me! If that were properly mediated, it ought to be possible. Only you mustn't discuss it with this Herr Kaudela.[4] For he is doubtless one of my greatest enemies!

Oh yes: Buschbeck! Frau Freund wrote that she still hasn't received her concert fee (*Kindertotenlieder!*)!![5] Remind Buschbeck. Of course she must be paid.

You have probably heard from Webern by now that I had a falling-out with Ochs.[6] So much for the Berlin *Gurrelieder* performance, for now anyway. But there may be one in Leipzig instead.[7] Maybe with the same ensemble as in Berlin.

I've already given my opinion regarding the wind score (of *Gurrelieder*). I'm not opposed. But it will have to be tried out first, spot-checked.

I'll probably leave here on Saturday. It's not as comfortable as I could wish. Mostly because I feel somewhat constrained. Frau Zehme is not an overwhelmingly generous hostess. Her husband and son, on the other hand, are all too generous with their reserve. So it's not very comfortable. Then there are so terribly many mosquitoes here (how do you spell that?!) The river was drained, so there's no opportunity for swimming, either. In a word: things aren't quite right any more.

We want to go to Göhren on Rügen, where Jalowetz is.[8]

For the present write to me here. I'll send you my new address when I get there.

For now: warm regards to you and your wife, also from my wife

Your Arnold Schönberg

---

4. Julius Kaudela, secretary of the Vienna Konzertverein.

5. Marya Freund had, of course, been prevented from singing in the 31 March concert. In a letter to Schoenberg of 9 June 1914 Freund mentioned that the fee was still outstanding. It is unlikely that she was ever paid, since the Akademischer Verband had been disbanded in April of that year.

6. The German conductor and composer Siegfried Ochs was closely connected with plans for the Berlin *Gurrelieder*. The disagreement with Ochs arose when he told Schoenberg that the proceeds were likely to amount to no more than 2,000 marks. Schoenberg responded that had he known that from the outset, he would never have considered the performance.

7. Albertine Zehme's husband, the lawyer Felix Zehme, took care of the financial arrangements for the Leipzig *Gurrelieder* performance, which took place on 4 March 1914. The principal soloists were the same as in the Vienna premiere, with the exception of Albertine Zehme in the speaker's role.

8. Heinrich and Johanna Jalowetz were vacationing in the town of Göhren on the Baltic Sea island of Rügen, where the Schoenbergs did join them.

## Berg to Schoenberg

Trahütten, 19 July 1913

Your letter just came, dear Herr Schönberg, and I thank you very much. Webern indicated briefly on a card that Ochs was apparently unbelievably impertinent and the Berlin *Gurrelieder* therefore canceled. I don't know the background, nor do I understand it. I can only imagine that as a "famous" conductor he's accustomed to having all the composers he performs lick his backside and blindly agree with all of his opinions since he's such an experienced old hand and musician. I hope Webern will soon write more fully.[1]

1. In a letter of 24 July 1913 Berg writes that Webern told him more about the affair with Ochs, which apparently ended with an exchange of verbal insults.

I wrote to Buschbeck quite a while ago about the Mahler concert. I also mentioned a classical concert and even fantasized about an entire cycle: I Mahler—, II classical—, and III your own works (orchestra pieces, orchestra songs, *Pelleas*) and the *Gurrelieder* reprise by special train. (Which would now originate in Leipzig instead of Berlin.) I asked Buschbeck to get in touch with Kehlendorfer about these ideas. And at least to stress the Mahler and classical concerts, which would require fewer rehearsals and would be easier to do. Buschbeck hasn't answered yet, maybe he has already taken steps?! In any case I'll write to him at once about your new decision to conduct the V[th] instead of the VI[th], but I think that concert might be too short. The V[th] is a good deal shorter than the VI[th]. Surely that would be just half a rehearsal more, if Freund would rehearse diligently with you at the piano. (And—forgive my forwardness: in the other half-rehearsal a few of Mahler's Rückert songs (they aren't sung very often and would therefore, if only for practical reasons, draw well!))

I can't say anything at all about the choice of orchestra. That seems to be strictly a question of finances and I don't know if Buschbeck—who is of course no longer in the Akademischer Verband—can raise a guarantee fund. But I should think one could get a few thousand out of the Mahler Society (for instance from Frau Mahler's friend[2]), if it concerned the V[th] Symphony, not in the first, incorrect version (as is customary!), but with, for once, the orchestrational changes desired by Mahler.— No doubt Buschbeck will write to you about that himself.—

I'm very happy that you're going to the sea after all. How I envy you the air. There's nothing of the sort here! But then it's so cool here all summer, even on the warmest days, that one hardly ever misses it! But how much more do I envy Jalowetz the joy of being together with you; for such a long time at that! Please give him my regards; for this letter probably won't reach you any more in Gautzsch and will, I hope, be forwarded!

I take it, dear Herr Schönberg, that you received my previous letter (from the beginning of the month)? I only ask because you didn't mention it (though there's nothing in it to respond to); but if it had gone astray I wouldn't want you to think I hadn't written at all, dear Herr Schönberg, i.e., I wouldn't want to leave you thinking that! I suspect the loss of my letter because it's easily possible, given the barbaric postal service here (a drunken peasant coachman delivers letters whenever he happens to feel like it) and because you haven't used the enclosed addressed envelopes. (I wanted to spare you the boring address, which is hard to shorten.)

I'll also write to Buschbeck regarding Freund!

Otherwise there's no news. We (my wife and I) are fine. My work on the Symphony is going slowly. Apparently Webern has finished something. But he didn't say "what."[3]

And now many warm regards to you, dear Herr Schönberg, and your esteemed wife.

from your Berg

2. Most likely Lilly Lieser-Landau, the wife of the textile industrialist Adolf Lieser.

3. Probably the Three Pieces for String Quartet, the first and third movements of which were later to become the first and sixth Bagatelles, Op. 9.

Best regards from my wife to you and your wife and the dear little ones. Please let us know how the children are, especially Trudel with her feet?![4]—

Have you heard that a People's Music Library is to be founded in Vienna. Hertzka has generously made every one of his publications available.[5] Perhaps you could write to Tischer and Peters some time and ask that they send *Friede auf Erden* and the Orchestra Pieces.—

Should we, Webern and I, send our published things (Webern's Orchestra Pieces and my Sonata and songs) to this library? Or would that seem stupid or presumptuous?!—

---

4. Schoenberg's daughter Gertrud suffered from a recurrent skin infection on her feet.

5. U.E. was one of the principal organizations involved in the formation of the *musikalische Volksbibliothek*.

## Berg to Schoenberg

[Trahütten] 9 August 1913

The enclosed page from the most recent *Muskete* should interest you, dear Herr Schönberg.[1] That's Vienna in all its baseness! By comparison the caricature and review in the German periodical *Zeit im Bild*, which so annoyed Kraus that he even printed his own portrait in an issue of the *Fackel*,[2] is the purest paean. It really seems that Vienna is intent on surpassing every country, every nation in baseness, just as the unspeakable accusation that you performed Webern and me out of financial considerations probably couldn't be surpassed by any German or foreign newspaper.—

What do you say to poor Webern, dear Herr Schönberg. I thought he was long since in Prague; then today I received a letter telling me of his latest illness. He seems very distraught and perplexed. Do you think there's anything to be gained with a psychoanalyst.[3] What can *he* know, unless he happens to be a genius. No doubt you, dear Herr Schönberg, have written or will write to him at length, and that is sure to be decisive for him!

There's no news from here. I assume you received my letter of the 3rd (with the enclosed letter from Buschbeck)!

Have you heard of Vienna's new Konzerthaus-Quartet: Busch, Rothschild, Doktor, and Grümmer.[4] I once heard the concertmaster Busch, a very young man, play the solos of the *Missa solemnis* very beautifully. I don't know Rothschild. The reports of this quartet's debut in Salzburg[5] (music festival) have, incidentally, been

---

1. Berg enclosed a caricature by Fritz Scheinpflug depicting Karl Kraus, which appeared in the *Muskete* XVI / 410 (7 August 1913), 148.

2. *Die Fackel* XV / 374–75 (8 May 1913), 32.

3. Webern's new position as assistant conductor at the Prague Deutsches Landestheater was to have begun on 4 August. He went there at the end of July, but found himself unable to take up his duties and returned to Vienna. Shortly thereafter he began a three-month course of treatment with the psychiatrist Dr. Alfred Adler.

4. Adolf Busch, Fritz Rothschild, Karl Doktor, and Paul Grümmer.

5. On 3 August 1913.

unanimously enthusiastic.—

Will you stay in Rügen much longer, dear Herr Schönberg?[6] I thought the Berlin [school] vacation ended mid-August. In that case this letter could still just reach you!

Please give your esteemed wife the warmest regards from my wife and me. Likewise the dear children, Görgl[7] and Trude, who's surely looking forward to her Berlin. Our very warmest regards to you as well

Your Berg

---

6. The Schoenbergs returned to Berlin on 11 August, as Schoenberg mentions in a card of 13 August 1913.

7. Görgi and Görgl were both nicknames for Schoenberg's son Georg.

## Berg to Schoenberg

Trahütten, 10 September 1913

During my final days here I want to send you one more greeting, dear Herr Schönberg. Even though—as you can imagine—there's nothing much to tell. We return to Vienna on Sunday the 14th, and as always, leaving the country is very painful for me—indeed, perhaps more painful than ever before. The thought of having to live in a city—and in Vienna at that—depresses me already and I can't understand why one should have to spend one's life in such unwholesome circumstances—for both body and soul. I can well imagine spending my entire life in the country, visiting cities only when something is going on there: particularly, performances of your works. Naturally one would often remain in a city for weeks, perhaps months—but home would be in the midst of nature—not in the so-called cultural centers. Of course, the proximity of such a center—and it would have to be a real cultural center, like Berlin (particularly because you are there, dear Herr Schönberg)—not a pseudo-metropolis like Vienna———of course such proximity would be desirable. But not for the things that make up a city: millions of disagreeable people, houses, streets, etc., but only for a readier supply of all necessities, for better postal and rail connections, etc. I don't even miss Vienna, despite daily opera performances and concerts, for I can assure you, dear Herr Schönberg, that I'm more profoundly immersed in music here in the country than in the Vienna Opera or the Musikvereinsaal. When I sit here poring for hours and days at a time over your Orchestra Pieces, reveling in anticipation of these sounds, in the unprecedented formal and expressive concentration—then I have more music in me than I ever do during the regular run of Viennese performances. The experience could be surpassed only if this anticipated beauty were realized——this year in London![1] I wonder if I'll get there!!?! I have saved a little over the summer. Maybe it'll be possible. Of course I have to go to Leipzig, too.[2] As for Amsterdam?[3] And who

---

1. Schoenberg was scheduled to conduct his Orchestra Pieces, Op. 16, in London in January 1914.

2. The Leipzig performance of Gurrelieder was scheduled for early March 1914.

3. Schoenberg was to conduct his Orchestra Pieces, Op. 16, in Amsterdam in March 1914.

knows where else you may conduct your works?! In my last letter of 16 August, dear Herr Schönberg, I asked whether you'll be conducting anywhere else. (It was the letter in which I explained[4] why I hadn't sent the songs[5] to Herr Zemlinsky any earlier; I also asked about the proposed Mahler concert in Vienna, after having discussed this at length in the letter before that, of 3 August (with the enclosed Buschbeck letter)). At that time I also wrote about my work on the symphony[6] and about Webern, etc. I only mention this in case those letters got lost!

I suddenly realize, dear Herr Schönberg, that I haven't written for almost 4 weeks. I hope you aren't offended, since you very well know that I think of you every day with—yes, I can even say: with <u>longing</u> and that the only reason I didn't write was because there was absolutely no news.

But yes! There is something worth relating. Did you know that since autumn a so-called "phantom" [Bauernspuk] has been roaming around the forests in this very region in the Koralps, at whose foot we live. During this time about 3–400 head of cattle have been attacked on the surrounding alpine pastures (often only 2 hours away from us), some killed and devoured, others "mutilated." There have been repeated hunting parties. Battues, often with 500–1,000 hunters. But no result! At first wolves were suspected, then, after people saw <u>tracks,</u> a lioness or leopardess with young. Now that it has become known that during the time in question some animals in Deutsch Landsberg escaped from a traveling menagerie, whose owner skipped town, wolves as well as a large bobcat with young are suspected. Indeed, some people claim to have seen both! Now that the stock have been driven off the alm, there is growing fear for the safety of people—schoolchildren who often have long walks along lonely forest paths. Which is why some schools will be closed.

That's the kind of news we have here. But though it may be somewhat sensational and unpleasant, it can't counterbalance the deep and quiet joys of country life. Often there are days here of profoundest melancholy: wisps of fog on the surrounding mountains, below us the valley, with all its towns, appearing, if possible, to recede <u>still further.</u> And these alpine meadows with their infinitely soft covering of moss, clearings with their fields of currant berries and heather———and now's the time for the pungent odor of autumn gentian with their tiny violet blossoms. They're so similar to pasqueflowers—but how long until then———: an entire winter intervenes and that winter will be———in Vienna! Even the name of this city bodes ill!—

Our very best, dear Herr Schönberg, to your esteemed wife and the dear little ones—we'd love to hear a word or two as to how they're doing. And to you, dear Herr Schönberg, our warmest regards, particularly from your eternally devoted

Alban Berg

Forgive this foolish letter.—And the smudges: the blotting paper is at fault!

---

4. In response to Schoenberg's urgent postcard inquiry of 13 August.
5. Maeterlinck Songs.
6. Berg wrote that he had completed about one-fourth of the projected symphony.

## Berg to Schoenberg

Friday
Vienna, 3 October 1913

I haven't written since my return, dear Herr Schönberg—and that was over 2 weeks ago now. I hope you received my last letter from Trahütten (of 10 September) and the 2 preceding ones?! I found a mountain of work here related to administration of the houses and that consumed all of my time the first few days back; after that, and before writing to you, dear Herr Schönberg, I finally wanted to take some definitive steps regarding the Mahler concert. Unfortunately I haven't had much luck there, either. To start with, I initially intended—as I once told you—to try to procure an invitation from the Konzertverein, since at the moment that seems easier than collecting a 4–5,000 kronen guarantee fund for the concert. But my attempts to achieve this <u>directly</u> have failed to date. Like everything else in Vienna—it only works indirectly. But—it seems to me—there's a chance, dear Herr Schönberg, that you'll be invited to conduct a Mahler concert—if I undertake to cover <u>just a **portion**</u> of the costs with a guarantee fund. Botstiber, the secretary, could probably arrange it. And he would do it if Hertzka asked him, since he has close ties to U.E.[1] But in order to get Hertzka to give the matter his active support, Frau Mahler has to do her part. Unfortunately I haven't been able to talk to her yet, but she ought to be back in Vienna any day now, and then I'll get in touch with her at once.

As to the program! You, dear Herr Schönberg, want to conduct the V[th]. But Löwe himself is going to do Mahler's V[th] on 14 January 1914.[2] Don't you think, dear Herr Schönberg, that a 2nd performance might meet with difficulties from the Konzertverein, as well as in terms of concert attendance? If you concur, dear Herr Schönberg, then we could reconsider the VI[th] (and the *Kindertotenlieder?*)! At any rate, for the time being I won't mention which works are to be performed, but will simply speak of your plan to perform a symphony and possibly the *Kindertotenlieder*. I do hope I'll finally get somewhere in this matter! Then I'll write immediately.—In addition to Mahler's V[th] in the Konzertverein, Nedbal is doing Mahler's IX[th].[3] And <u>all of that</u> takes place this year!

You have probably heard everything else concerning our dear Vienna from Webern, who, on the other hand, has told me everything concerning you, dear Herr Schönberg. As did Stein![4] Naturally we're all completely engrossed in your projected idea of founding your own opera house! Tomorrow, that is Monday, Stein will find out more about his project, which gave rise to this splendid idea.[5]

1. The Konzertverein was closely linked to the Vienna Konzerthaus Society, in which Universal Edition had a financial interest.
2. This Konzertverein concert actually took place on 25 February 1914.
3. In a concert with the Tonkünstler Orchestra on 12 February 1914.
4. Erwin Stein had recently left a conducting position in Danzig and returned to Vienna.
5. Stein conceived of a plan to perform chamber operas at the Vienna Volksbühne, which had opened a theater in November 1912. However, nothing came of the plan, perhaps due to the financial difficulties that beset the organization from the start and which led to its demise with the outbreak of the First World War.

Apart from what I've already told you, there's nothing new with me. Only that the transition from country to city life was again very difficult—indeed, it brought on—conversely now—strong asthma attacks; and that I hope, once that and all the trouble with the houses is past, to resume work—the continuation of my symphony and teaching some of my old students; Königer is still in the country and another student hasn't begun yet. I intend to place an announcement in the so-called "artists' bulletin board" [Künstlertafel] in the Merker to see if I can't acquire one or 2 new students.[6] Maybe it'll help!

I spend a lot of time with Webern. We usually play music. Among other things some very fine music from Charpentier's Julien.[7] Webern apparently feels a great deal better; at any rate he's very pleased with his therapy. But I think—please, dear Herr Schönberg, don't mention this to him—that he doesn't look at all well: I even think he looks worse than after the treatment in the Semmering, and I don't mean his complexion, but rather the tired expression in his eyes. Perhaps this whole psychoanalytic therapy isn't quite the answer. On the other hand, much of what Webern reports seems very plausible and reasonable. It does seem to be completely different from what Kraus attacks!—

From the two different inks you can deduce, dear Herr Schönberg, that I had to interrupt this letter—and to finish writing it somewhere else. I was called away by the telephone—because the plaster was crumbling from a fire wall. That's typical!

I am to convey my wife's regards to you, dear Herr Schönberg, and to your gracious wife and the dear little ones. I hope you are all well—and that Trudl's feet are better!

Very warmest regards,

from your grateful Berg

Has Webern already written you, dear Herr Schönberg, that we are seriously considering the suggestion you made to him about giving a concert together in Berlin?![8] If he hasn't, he certainly will do so any day now. I don't want to anticipate him.—

---

6. Berg never placed an advertisement in the Merker.

7. Gustave Charpentier's second opera, Julien, ou la Vie du Poete, was completed in 1913 and first performed in Paris on 4 June of that year.

8. Webern wrote to Schoenberg on 7 October about a joint Schoenberg, Webern, and Berg concert in Berlin. Nothing came of the plan.

## Berg to Schoenberg

[Vienna] 31 October 1913

Would you please see to it, dear Herr Schönberg, that the enclosed letter somehow reaches Steuermann. Either in a lesson with you or—if you want to take the trouble of filling in the address—by post! I'm asking him whether he is going to play my sonata in the planned concert in Berlin.[1] That would make me very happy,

---

1. Eduard Steuermann gave a recital in Berlin in the Bechstein Hall on 7 January 1914. Berg's Sonata, Op. 1, was not included.

as I'm sure he would do it splendidly!—

Nothing definitive has happened with regard to the Mahler concert! So I learned from a conversation with Hertzka, who in turn had discussed our plan with Botstiber.[2] He said there's no chance of inviting you just now, dear Herr Schönberg. Apparently for purely administrative reasons. But Hertzka is confident that these can be dealt with, given time, and that it isn't necessary to bother with the collection of a guarantee fund to arrange such a concert. I hope those aren't merely empty promises and that the Konzerthaus Society will indeed invite you to give a Mahler concert with the Konzertverein this season still.

Nor do I know anything about the Vienna *Gurrelieder* performance!! I don't think any one knows anything!

Incidentally, yesterday we (Webern, Stein, and I) went to a concert of the Tonkünstler Orchestra that included an early Suite by Schreker—which was very well-received.[3] A totally insignificant work, which, where still indebted to the Fuchs School (Andante for string orchestra) had a certain polish, but the other movements didn't even have that,* due to his inability to write a longer melody—immediately after some fragmentary melodic beginnings it starts "building to a climax"! In other words, the title *Romantic Suite* is no designation, but rather an excuse and is true only insofar as it does not apply to the mood (otherwise it would have to be called "boring suite" or "bad-sounding suite"—)— and—as in the case of the *Romantic Overture*[4] performed last year—is true only insofar as it is perhaps romantic to write such music, but things like that can never become classic.—The funny thing is that people nonetheless like music like that and that such fragmentary melodic beginnings with their climaxes are perceived as melodies, whereas true (modern) melodies aren't recognized as such; it is when they're as logically constructed and as well-rounded as, for instance, your melodies, with not one note too many or too few—there of all places—that the audience and critics speak of "fragments"! And that reminds me, dear Herr Schönberg, that I haven't yet responded to your article "Why Modern Melodies are so Difficult to Understand."[5] It's the most wonderful thing ever written about melody, about the essence of melody. Those few lines contain absolutely everything that could ever be said about melodies in general. We're all completely overwhelmed by the wealth of ideas and by the incredibly succinct form given those ideas. It sounds like a magnificent modulation, so compelling, so concentrated! Oh, I can't find the words and the comparison is much too weak!—

There's no point in wasting a single word about the prize-winning *Frühlingsfeier* by Prohaska![6] It was nauseating. Never have I heard anything so ludicrous, indeed

2. Hugo Botstiber was general secretary of the Konzerthaus Society from 1913–37.

3. The concert, conducted by Oskar Nedbal, included Berlioz' *Symphony fantastique* and Chopin's E-minor Piano Concerto (with Moriz Rosenthal).

4. Actually *Phantastische Ouvertüre*.

5. Schoenberg's "Warum moderne Melodien so schwer verständlich sind" appeared in *Die Konzertwoche* (1 October 1913), n.p. [3–4], a publication of the Konzerthaus.

6. Karl Prohaska, who taught theory at the Vienna Conservatory, wrote his *Frühlingsfeier* for soloists, double chorus, large orchestra, and organ in 1913. It was awarded first prize (10,000 kronen) in a contest commemorating the centenary of the Gesellschaft der Musikfreunde and premiered under Franz Schalk on 29 October 1913 in the first Gesellschaft concert of the season.

horrible-sounding, so immeasurably boring.

The performance: worthy of the work! Aside from Schalk's customary brilliance: completely out-of-tune brass and a vocal solo quartet that sang completely out of tune.

After the II[nd] part we fled to the Café Capua, a new café on Johannesgasse decorated by Loos.[7] Completely paneled with huge, wonderfully veined agate plates (Africa). A plaster cast of an old Greek vase as a frieze (relief) closes off the walls at the top. Mahogany furniture upholstered in dark blue-green monochrome (!) velvet. One large completely uninterrupted room!— Lighting, the pleasantest imaginable. Not at all glaring; fragmented light (like daylight) created by a great number of small lights hanging on chains! And many mirrors!

brass

cloudy milk

glass

Now I must get back to work: copying out the parts of my Quartet,[8] which I'm doing myself for 2 reasons. I. economy, II. I believe I can write the parts out better, more clearly than the copyist, who doesn't understand anything about the symbols. I can see, by the way, that the old parts were and are completely unusable!

Many, many warm regards to you and your dear family, also from my wife,

from your Berg

* his feeling for form just barely suffices for 8-measure periods. As for a real 1st movement theme, Schreker is completely incapable of it!

---

7. The café, located on 3 Johannesgasse, had opened that fall.
8. Probably in connection with the planned concert mentioned in his letter of 3 October.

## Berg to Schoenberg

[Vienna] 26 November 1913

Dear Herr Schönberg,

As you probably know, the *Gurrelieder* reprise under Schreker is going to take place in March after all. The Philharmonic Chorus is sponsoring the concert together with the Tonkünstler Orchestra. I discussed various things with Dr. Löwy. Above all I wanted to persuade him—i.e., Schreker—**not** to use **Gregori** again as speaker. But to no avail. Perhaps a word from you, dear Herr Schönberg, is needed. I don't know whether you want to recommend Frau Zehme for the role, but I do know that you object to Gregori!—The Philharmonic Chorus concert scheduled for today had to be canceled 3 days ago. Because of unusable parts, it was said. Primarily for Weigl's piece; but those for the Delius were also poor.[1] But ticket sales for this

---

1. This concert finally took place on 29 November and included works by Jaroslav Kricka, Robert Fuchs, Johanna Müller-Hermann, and Friedrich Klose. The works by Karl Weigl (*Weltfeier*) and Frederick Delius (*Arabeske* for soloists, mixed chorus, and orchestra) were not included.

concert had been practically nil, which was probably an **additional** reason for the cancelation. I saw Delius, who had been especially invited to this concert, at Hertzka's (very attractive, but somewhat effeminate in appearance).* I had gone to Hertzka concerning another matter—which I'll tell you about later—and at the same time received the commission to prepare a thematic table based on my *Gurrelieder* guide, i.e., to list the most important themes and reduce the text to an **absolute** minimum—keeping it to telegraphic brevity—so as to result in a normal program booklet of about 40–50 pages (including the song texts). That won't be much work, since it consists almost entirely of cutting, which anyone else could do just as well. Since someone else would do it if I didn't—and I can't prevent it in any event, I shall prepare this thematic table myself, which may be more practical for concert purposes than my guide, though I know full well that it will severely encroach on dissemination of my work (the guide). For that is to go up in price. At the concerts everyone will naturally buy what's cheaper and elsewhere of course there's little demand for a purely musical text. And here it was my purpose and my joy all along that this guide, by virtue of its reaching almost everyone at the concerts, would be read by more people, that even if incomplete it would at least interest and stimulate and thus give the audience, in other words, the majority, some idea of the musical, i.e., high artistic significance of the *Gurrelieder*. And not just those few individuals who would now buy the guide even after there is a simpler and cheaper one available.

It's also clear that I am thus done out of the remainder of the fee promised me after the sale of the 3,000[th] copy[2]—which, as it now stands, might happen in 10 years, if I'm lucky. I will have to discuss that with Hertzka. Maybe I can find some alternative to the requirement of the sale of 3,000 "guides," such as the sale of 4–5,000 "thematic tables"!

Reading through the above I realize I haven't described the thematic table clearly enough. It's not a shortened, i.e., spoiled version of my guide by means of condensation, cuts, and excisions—something to which I would never consent (—unless I realized that what I had said was wrong—), it is rather simply a compendium of all important themes from *Gurrelieder* in the order of their appearance, and with reference to repeated appearances. *[Berg explains by citing several musical examples (by number) of Tove and Waldemar themes from his guide.]*

However, the reason for my visit to Hertzka was the projected Mahler concert under your direction. Until now it has been impossible to get any definite information, though I've called him any number of times and (at a concert) spoke with Frau Mahler, who, incidentally, is immensely interested in this Mahler concert and took that occasion to inquire after you. Finally Hertzka told me that an invitation from the Konzerthaus was out of the question this year. He was still hopeful, but because the Konzerthaus's financial situation at present appears so unfavorable, its directors couldn't possibly take on a further risk of loss—which is how they stupidly regard a concert with only Mahler works! Until now the entire Konzerthaus

---

2. Berg's contract specified that he receive the second half of his fee after the sale of 5,000 *Gurrelieder* guides; of the 2,000 copies of the first printing only 700 had been sold, as Berg writes in a letter of 27 November 1913.

affair has been the biggest fiasco.[3] Some of the halls remain unused as the demand in Vienna isn't so great, others remain half empty due to consistently substandard concerts. The papers rant about poor ventilation, acoustics, etc., etc., and Botstiber and Co. seem completely broken, Hertzka hinted, which is why they can't—or won't—risk anything more. According to its statutes, the Konzertverein isn't able to invite guest conductors (they're only allowed to give concerts with their own 3 conductors). Perhaps something can be arranged with the Tonkünstler Orchestra. They recently gave a Strauss concert under his direction.[4] Financially that was very successful. Only it's so terribly difficult to get to the powers that be. But it may work through Nedbal.—

The Konzerthaus really does beggar all description; there's no doubt: it is the ugliest, silliest thing ever built. By comparison the Volkstheater is a monument of classical architecture.[5] At the same time it is unbelievably impractical. Carpets and upholstery in a light color and of a material that already today looks dirty and worn. The main staircase so narrow that there's an indescribable crush after every concert. One can't go into details! You'll see yourself, dear Herr Schönberg, and despite the wish to judge mildly, will have to admit that you hadn't expected it to be so dreadful.

Yesterday I heard Ottilie Metzger in the small hall, whose poster, besides Mahler, Weingartner, Knab, and Brahms songs, had announced: Schönberg songs.[6] But in actuality she didn't sing any, and only the fact that she sang the Mahler songs badly, (though initially it **angered** me immeasurably) tempered my **regret** that she didn't sing **your** songs.

Among the loveliest evenings of this season was the last Kraus lecture,[7] in which, besides almost all the glosses from the last *Fackel*—"Der Neger," "Der Mord an der Prostituierten,"[8] "Der Biberpelz"—he read some of the letters he had received in the course of the last 15 years, of which he is publishing a selection of 300 in book form (in all there are about 30,000, mostly anonymous).[9] He read them in such an order that expression of most abusive invective alternated with most fervent enthusiasm. The latter also included some signed letters.

The small Musikvereinsaal was fuller than I had ever seen it. The audience's enthusiasm continued unabated to the end (10:45).

Enough for today. A student will be here any minute (in addition to Königer, Heller, Schmid, and Polnauer (who, however, still hasn't time to work yet, since he'll be finishing his doctorate shortly), I have a new student, who works in the

3. Vienna's second major concert building, the Konzerthaus, opened on 19 October 1913. The building was designed by Ludwig Baumann and Ferdinand Fellner and included one major concert hall and two smaller halls for solo and chamber recitals.

4. On 20 November.

5. Vienna's Volkstheater, built in 1889 by Ferdinand Fellner and Edmund Hellmer, was designed in a highly ornamented neo-Baroque style.

6. Also on the recital, in which Metzger was accompanied by Karl Gotthardt, were songs by Gustav Brecher.

7. 19 November.

8. Actually "Eine Prostituierte ist ermordet worden."

9. Kraus himself never published letters from readers of the *Fackel*, but a selection of such letters appeared posthumously under the title *Mit vorzüglicher Hochachtung* (Munich, 1962).

Music History Department.[10] Unfortunately I lost Kassowitz, since, much as he would have liked, he wasn't able to combine music study with high school. But he hopes to get away from school).

Otherwise I'm busier than ever with administration of the houses. For I'm once again suffering under sibling enmity stemming from the fact that I have to be supported by my mother; therefore I must see that I work off the support with these dreadful tasks. On such days there's no escape but to the score of your Orchestra Songs.[11] How wonderful it is to own something like that; I am clearly indebted to you for everything beautiful, dear Herr Schönberg!

Many warm regards (also from my wife)

from your Berg

(Please also give your gracious wife and the dear little ones our very best!).

*Obviously I'm referring to Delius and by God not to Hertzka.

---

10. Theodor Adam.

11. Berg was studying Schoenberg's Op. 8 songs in preparation for their performance under Zemlinsky in Prague.

## Schoenberg to Berg

Berlin-Südende, 28 November 1913

Dear friend,

I really don't know what to advise you. Maybe you should ask a lawyer. It almost seems necessary. After all, you're not married to Hertzka! Maybe he'll accede to your demands. Remind him that it wasn't only for the guide!!

It would be best if you could come to terms (lawyer or no lawyer). For instance: Hertzka could give you a small sum for preparing the thematic table, and expand the clause regarding 5,000 copies to include this table. Perhaps in such a way that you receive the rest of the fee as soon as the guide and table **together** have sold 5,000 (possibly 6, 7 . . .) copies. He can do that despite the fact that the thematic table is cheaper, since the price of the guide is going up and because you were promised the fee for the guide.—But discuss it with a lawyer in any case.

I'm not quite sure how one should go about making such a thematic table. It would probably be best if the poem came first (then perhaps the text) and afterwards the themes you mention, together (possibly!!!) with a designation indicating position in the piece, but only where absolutely necessary. At least you wouldn't have much to do in that case but cut, and wouldn't spoil your guide.

---

Gregori won't do. Please telephone Schreker. (possibly Zehme.) Possibly: Mildenburg! Or Gutheil? Or an intelligent singer (but not Boruttau, he's an "intelligent" singer.) Zehme would be best. He could take a chance with Moissi.[1] Perhaps

---

1. The Austrian actor Alexander Moissi.

Steuermann's sister, who's engaged at a Viennese theater.[2] Go hear her!

___

You asked Frau Zehme for the Leipzig **_Gurre-poster_**. Don't use it. It's dreadful. Better use Roller's again. Or a brand new one. Zehme "surprised" me again.—She got it for nothing. But it's not even worth that.— — —

Regarding the individual selections from the _Gurrelieder_.[3]

1) preludes and postludes as short as possible!!!

2) but complete phrases nonetheless!

3) Of course it doesn't have to begin with a triad, but perhaps it should close with one. You'll have to add that (I don't envy you that job); but it doesn't matter. I have absolutely no objections if you succeed in composing new conclusions. It won't always work without that.

4) possibly simplify the accompaniment, if Hertzka is going to engrave new plates.

___

___

I've long intended to write, but have so little time. I had to be unfaithful to you with the piano reductions to the monodrama and to _Glückliche Hand_. It wouldn't have worked at this distance. One has to be able to discuss things like that. As often as possible. And particularly here, where the task is so difficult, you wouldn't have been able to manage without my help. So I had Steuermann do it. But to make it up to you, I'll tell you now that you are definitely to do the 4-hand reduction of the Chamber Symphony. (N.B., the reductions of the monodrama and _Glückliche Hand_ won't be published just now, nor even remunerated.)[4] Would you like to do the Chamber Symphony on speculation. Perhaps Hertzka would publish it if you offered it to him!!

Something else, dear Berg. When you write to me, always underline the main points, particularly those I am to answer. It's hard for me to write to you, since to do so I'd have to read your letter 3–4 times and your handwriting is too illegible for that.

And something else: be more concise. You always write so many excuses, parenthetical asides, "developments," "extensions," and stylizations that it takes a long time to figure out what you're driving at. I think one should work on oneself in such matters. A letter must be kept in telegram style and a telegram must be of absolutely telegraphic brevity.

Don't be angry with me. I want to facilitate communication between Berlin and Vienna. Simplify! Then you will be able to write to me more often! And I'll answer everything. You have written infrequently of late. Of course your formalities take so much time. Break that habit!! Many regards to your wife, also from my wife.

___

2. Eduard Steuermann had two sisters who were actresses: Salome (Salka), who later married Berthold Viertel, and Rosa, who later married Josef Gielen. Schoenberg is referring here to Salome, who was at this time engaged at the Neue Wiener Bühne.

3. Four individual numbers from the _Gurrelieder_ ("So tanzen die Engel," "Nun sag ich dir zum letzten Mal," "Du wunderliche Tove," and "Tauben von Gurre") were published by U.E. in 1914.

4. Steuermann's reductions of _Erwartung_ and _Die glückliche Hand_ appeared in January and May 1923, respectively.

Warmest regards to you,

Your Arnold Schönberg

I was in Stettin:[5] Jalowetz is already a perfectly splendid conductor. They could use him in the Vienna Court Opera as principal conductor! I heard *Rheingold* and *Oberon*.[6] He does an excellent job rehearsing.

---

5. Schoenberg visited Stettin 22–26 November, where he gave his Mahler lecture on 25 November.

6. Jalowetz, now principal conductor at the Stettin Stadttheater, conducted Wagner's *Das Rheingold* on 23 November and Weber's *Oberon* on 26 November.

## Berg to Schoenberg

Vienna, 3 December 1913

Forgive me, dear Herr Schönberg, if I deviate one more time from my resolve to be concise. But again I *must* begin the letter with "apologies," which I cannot bring myself to suppress, even at the risk of seeming incorrigible. So please excuse me, dear Herr Schönberg, for not immediately answering your long kind letter, but I was so busy with meetings about various things like the "guide," publication of the individual *Gurrelieder* numbers, Vienna *Gurrelieder* performance, and then, of course, 1 December has just passed, my busiest time.

Second, I ask that you forgive me, dear Herr Schönberg, if I do not undertake the task: of preparing conclusions for the individual songs of the *Gurrelieder*. I did think about it intensely for 3–4 days and experimented with various solutions—but I have to admit that I cannot do it. In passages where it might be harmonically possible to add a cadential chord, I simply <u>cannot</u> bring myself to do so.

For instance

Or

But I'm simply <u>not **capable**</u> of composing a conclusion to one or the other of the songs. Maybe that's a sign of intellectual poverty. At any rate I lack the fantasy to rethink something, even partially, that has become so much a part of me as the *Gurrelieder!* Perhaps someone who doesn't know the work <u>as well</u> could do better! I'm very curious, but very apprehensive how Universal Ed. will handle this—but also unhappy at being incapable of finding a good solution and of doing something as important as assisting in bringing out the individual numbers of the *Gurrelieder* satisfactorily.—

There is no possibility of simplifying anything, since the old plates will be used and new ones made only where beginnings and cadences require it.

And now, after thanking you once again for your kind letter, my dear Herr Schönberg, above all for your good advice regarding a lawyer in the guide matter (which I won't fail to follow) and also for your affectionate admonition regarding my correspondence style, I shall finally take the last to heart and keep what follows concise and to the point:

The Leipzig posters will not be used.

I've spoken to Schreker about the role of narrator. He's not in favor of Zehme, for ridiculous, purely superficial reasons. They're going to try to get Onno. Mildenburg offered on her own to do "Waldtaube." She is firmly engaged. Do you agree with that, Herr Schönberg? Would it conceivably be possible to have Mildenburg not only sing Waldtaube but also do the "speaker"? Who's singing Waldemar in Leipzig? (Schreker wants to know that.) If it's someone other than Nachod,[1] Schreker would like him for Vienna as well. Schreker will keep Nachod for Vienna only if Nachod is also singing in Leipzig! Probably Boruttau for "Klaus Narr" (or won't he be singing in Leipzig?)

I shall begin the piano reduction of the Chamber Symphony as soon as I'm finished with the thematic table. Please may I borrow your piano reduction?[2] It would be helpful, the work would go faster, though I wouldn't misuse your reduction, but would try to prepare a completely independent arrangement—and one that's easily playable (as easy, for instance, as Zemlinsky's reduction of Mahler's VI[th])![3]

How wonderful that there are already piano reductions to the monodrama and *Glückliche Hand*. I'm sure they'll be very good!! Naturally it was out of the question that I do it—at such a distance. I know how difficult it was with the Quartet songs! (Why haven't they been published?)

The thematic table will be as follows: [*Berg discusses the format of the table and gives several examples, using the example numbers of his original guide.*]

And now very warm regards, dear Herr Schönberg, and thanks again for your kind, long letter

Your Berg

Many regards also from my wife and likewise our warm regards to your esteemed wife and the little ones.

1. Schoenberg's cousin, the tenor Hans Nachod.
2. In a picture postcard postmarked 14 December Schoenberg promises to bring his piano sketches for the Chamber Symphony to Leipzig, where the two were to meet on the occasion of the *Gurrelieder* performance.
3. Zemlinsky's reduction had appeared in October 1910.

*Schoenberg to Berg (postcard)*

Berlin-Südende, 4 December 1913

Dear friend,

Mildenburg is not to do the melodrama. It has to be done by a man. I just canceled my participation in the Leipzig performance because Frau Zehme is unusable, and it's quite clear to me now that it has to be a man. Even Gregori if necessary. Nachod is to sing Waldemar in Leipzig. I suggested Winkelmann[1] for Vienna. Boruttau was also engaged for Leipzig. I'll be happy to send you the piano reduction of the Chamber Symphony. Remind me again sometime.—It sounds like the thematic table will turn out quite well.—You should try to do the cadences for the *Gurre* selections yourself. If only to prevent someone else from doing it. It will work if you just give it some thought. One simply has to make use of the cadential feeling, which is there anyway. For instance the following seems quite possible.—

—In my letter to Hertzka I gave fairly detailed directions where it would be best to begin and end. Have him show you that letter. Go ahead and try it. It'll work. Write something down. The 2nd attempt will be better and the 3rd will be good. After that work on the 1st and 2nd again.

Now: many warm regards,

Your Arnold Schönberg

Why didn't anyone tell me of Rosé's 50th birthday? I just happened to read about it! Did you send congratulations![2]

---

1. The tenor Hans Winkelmann from the Deutsches Landestheater in Prague, was to be the soloist in the 29 January performance of Schoenberg's Op. 8 songs.

2. Arnold Rosé celebrated his fiftieth birthday on 24 October 1913. As Berg informs Schoenberg in a letter of 9 December, Rosé kept the event a secret from all but a few very close friends.

*Berg to Schoenberg (express letter)*

[Vienna] 15 December 1913

Dear Herr Schönberg,

This letter: express, so you'll get it before your departure, since I didn't have time to write the past few days.

I've now "come to terms" with Hertzka regarding the guide. After the sale of

6,000 copies of both guide <u>and</u> thematic table (originally it was 5,000 copies guide alone) I'll get the 2nd half of the fee = 300 kronen. For my work on the thematic table I'm getting 50 kronen straight off. So I'm quite satisfied with the financial settlement.

I have now prepared cadences to the 4 songs as you suggested. Of course it's best that way and prevents outside tampering. As I'm not sure you want Hertzka to know that the 3 cadences are yours, but can't say they're mine, I just dropped them off at Universal Edition without a word of explanation, where they are now going to the engraver.

Anyway, you'll see Hertzka yourself, dear Herr Schönberg. How I envy him and Stein for being able to attend the first rehearsals in Leipzig.[1] Well, we'll definitely come to the rehearsals before the March performance! And to Mannheim.[2] Maybe even to Prague![3]—What a pity there's nothing in Munich![4]—

The last of the *Gurrelieder* parts will arrive in Leipzig tomorrow, Tuesday. Either express from U.E. or Stein will bring them (these are only ⅔ of the parts). All the remaining new, uniformly beautifully copied parts are already in Leipzig. Incidentally, the <u>old</u> parts originally used in Vienna, which aren't nearly as beautiful due to the many cuts[5] and the work of 4–5 copyists, have been in Leipzig for a long time now.—

And now, many warm regards—also from my wife—to you and your esteemed wife,

Your Berg

P.S. The enclosed typewritten review was in an American newspaper. Here the (poor) translation![6]—

Max Graf's review (m.g.) of Schmidt's Symphony certainly reaches the <u>depths</u> of baseness.[7] I'm sending it to you to give you some idea of the level of Vienna's current musical life. It can't possibly get worse. (No need to say that this symphony is <u>totally</u> insignificant; it alternates between insincerity and immeasurable tedium.)

---

1. Schoenberg's refusal to participate in the Leipzig *Gurrelieder* was short lived. Rehearsals began on 10 December 1913.

2. For a planned performance of *Erwartung* under Arthur Bodanzky.

3. For the performance of Schoenberg's Op. 8 songs on 29 January 1914.

4. The Munich *Gurrelieder* performance was canceled because of a conflict with the first performance there of Schreker's *Der ferne Klang* (28 February 1914); as Bruno Walter explained to Schoenberg in a letter of 12 December, only one large work could be accommodated and preference had been given to the stage work.

5. Berg's reference to cuts (*Striche*) in the Vienna *Gurrelieder* premiere is unclear, as none have been documented. He may be referring to revisions in orchestration.

6. Has not been preserved or identified.

7. The review of the 3 December premiere of Franz Schmidt's Second Symphony, in which Graf called the work the "strongest symphonic creation in Austria since the death of Bruckner," appeared on 7 December in *Die Zeit*.

*Schoenberg to Berg*

Berlin-Südende, 27 December 1913

Dear friend,

Warmest thanks for your magnificent Christmas present.[1] I was very pleased and will soon have read it all. Until now I had only read *The Brothers Karamazov* (in a poor edition) and a few trifles, and I owned nothing else by Dostoyevsky. However, I now own two copies of *The Idiot*. Since Clark gave me that and *Poor Folk*. But he's going to exchange it for *Crime and Punishment*.

You and Webern don't seem to know that I canceled in Mannheim. I'll tell you the reason in person. Mainly it was because of several annoying incidents and the small orchestra (only 5 contrabasses!!)

I'm leaving for London in about 2 weeks. Weren't you planning to come along? What about it? Or would you rather come to Amsterdam?

Stein probably told you about the Leipzig rehearsals. Too bad you weren't there. I would have liked to know what you thought of the orchestra in comparison to the Vienna Tonkünstler Orchestra. Since you were at the first rehearsals back then.— Today I'm pretty certain that most of the really difficult passages weren't even played in Vienna. I suspected as much at the time, since one couldn't hear anything even in the strongly orchestrated passages. But since Schreker didn't rehearse them individually, I couldn't swear to it. I hope it will be different in Leipzig.

When will you come to visit us?

My best to your wife.

Many regards and again warmest thanks. Many regards also from my wife.

Your Arnold Schöenberg

---

[1] Two twin-volume editions of Dostoyevsky's *The Idiot* and *The Brothers Karamazov* in the translation of E. K. Rahsin (Munich, n.d.).

# 1914

*Schoenberg to Berg (postcard)*

[London] 15 [16] January 1914

Dear friend,

I'm sending you the continuation of my card to Webern. Wood is a very kind fellow.[1] I was very well received here. The orchestra is very willing. There is great interest in me here. Apparently there were articles about me in the papers all last week. My sextet was very well performed yesterday at the Music Club, which gave a "reception" in my honor.[2] Enormously enthusiastic applause. The songs were not as good, but numerous (about 10!). I shall send the continuation to Stein.

Many warm regards

Schönberg

---

1. Schoenberg was in London to conduct his Orchestra Pieces, Op. 16, at the inviation of Sir Henry Wood, who had a premiered the work on 3 September 1912.
2. The reception, held at the Grafton Galleries on the evening of 15 January, included performances of *Verklärte Nacht* by the London String Quartet with James Lockyer and Cedric Sharpe, and nine songs sung by Juliette Autran and Frederic Austin, accompanied by Arnold Bax.

*Schoenberg to Berg (postcard)*

[Osnabrück, 18 January 1914]

Dear friend,

I probably won't be able to write at all (here in the dining car), as it's jolting terribly. But I wanted to tell you: in London[1] just as in Amsterdam, the Hague, and Petersburg the audience greeted me with applause before I conducted. There was hardly any applause after the first piece. Pretty strong after the 2$^{nd}$. A bit less after the 3$^{rd}$. Very strong after the 4$^{th}$!! Strongest at the end. The 4$^{th}$ caused a sensation. I had to take a number of bows and in the end I asked the orchestra to stand. The

1. In the 17 January London concert Henry Wood conducted Brahms's Tragic Overture, Haydn's symphony *Le Midi*, Tchaikovsky's Piano Concerto (with the soloist Adela Verne); after the intermission Schoenberg conducted his Orchestra Pieces, Op. 16, which were followed by Charpentier's *Impressions d'Italie*, again conducted by Wood. Printed on the program was the note: "Herr Arnold Schönberg has promised his co-operation at to-day's concert on condition that during the performance of his Orchestral Pieces perfect silence is maintained."

pieces sound very beautiful. It's an entirely new sound. Extraordinarily elegant and refined. Very individual. I miscalculated a few dynamic things. Muted brass was often too weak! Or incorrectly marked. That can be very deceptive. But most of it was fine. Nonetheless, I shall revise the score.[2] The first piece is very difficult. It caused me the most trouble. I wasn't quite able to finish rehearsing the 3rd, 4th, and 5th. I was afraid I wouldn't finish. But they went fairly well notwithstanding. The 3rd least well. Give Stein and Webern my regards. I can't write to them. It's jolting too much.

Warm regards

Schönberg

---

2. Schoenberg's revisions of Op. 16 were undertaken over the next several years; a list of corrections and changes was printed in 1922.

## Berg to Schoenberg

[Vienna] 26 March 1914[1]

Dear Herr Schönberg,

The photographer kept me waiting so long for the copies, i.e., he put me off from day to day, that I, too, postponed writing from day to day. Then, ever since my return—excepting only a few mornings when I began composing (a suite, i.e., a series of character pieces, March, Waltz, etc.)[2] and a few afternoons when I gave lessons—I have been fully occupied with calculating my mother's income tax. With the new law that went into effect this year it's even more complicated, occasionally even incomprehensible, and takes all my time and energy. I hope to be finished in a week.—Attending Schreker's rehearsals for the *Gurrelieder*[3] has also taken time, as well as robbing me of the desire to write to you, dear Herr Schönberg. Of the new soloists I have so far heard only Förstel, who sings very beautifully and musically (she gives Schreker the right tempos), but whose middle range seems too weak. At 9:30 this morning there's a rehearsal with Mildenburg (the first and only one). I hope Nachod will be at this morning's open dress rehearsal. Gregori still isn't good, but rhythmically he's better than last year. The orchestra is coarse and inattentive as usual, and Schreker really does restrict himself only to "playing it through" [*Probieren*], though, as you have said, "studying [*Studieren*] is better."[4] For instance,

1. The long break in the correspondence can be explained by Berg's presence at concerts in Prague (performance on 29 January of three of Schoenberg's Orchestra Songs, Op. 8), Leipzig (rehearsals and performance on 6 March of the *Gurrelieder*), and Amsterdam (performance on 12 March of the Orchestra Pieces, Op. 16). Webern and Stein also attended the Leipzig and Amsterdam performances; Helene Berg accompanied her husband on the trips to Prague and Leipzig, but not to Amsterdam.
2. Schoenberg had encouraged Berg to write orchestral character pieces. Berg's work on a suite eventually led to the Three Orchestra Pieces, Op. 6.
3. The Vienna *Gurrelieder* reprise took place on 27 March, with Franz Schreker conducting the same orchestral and choral forces as in the previous year; new among the principals were Gertrud Förstel, who sang Tove and Anna Bahr-Mildenburg who sang the Waldtaube.
4. Schoenberg had apparently inverted the German saying "Probieren geht über Studieren" ("practical experience is better than theorizing") to make a point about rehearsal technique.

he plays a passage, it goes badly because some forgot to enter, others played out of tune, still others played unrhythmically. He breaks off and says in slang: gentlemen, it's dreadful, sounds awful. Again from rehearsal number . . . ! And so on for the entire rehearsal. If a halfway decent performance results, then only because the orchestra pulls itself together in the end, and because the work itself inspires both orchestra and conductor with the kind of grace that brings about an otherwise inexplicable clarity and beauty. I hope that will already be true tonight at the dress rehearsal!—Oh, when I think of the Leipzig rehearsals. To think of what must have been accomplished in the rehearsals I didn't attend, so that <u>every</u> figure was correctly phrased, every tempo change, every caesura correctly felt, every forte just right!! Even though the Leipzig orchestra[5] was worse than this one!! Even though resistance against a <u>new</u> work had to be overcome there, whereas here there is the pervasive awareness of a sure success with a <u>well-known</u> work!— —

As you can see, the pictures are very mediocre due to the poor weather, and some didn't turn out at all. Nonetheless they will be a lovely memento for me and I thank you very much, dear Herr Schönberg, for allowing me to photograph you so often. If you need more copies please just let me know of what and how many you'd like! I've sent copies of the relevant pictures to Frau Zehme, Hertzka (Stein and Webern), and my sister.—

This way I can relive with my eyes that precious time that continues to dominate my thoughts: Leipzig, Amsterdam, and Berlin. Without yet fully understanding or comprehending them, the scores of *Glückliche Hand* and *Seraphita* constantly hover before me.[6] And now Stein has brought some good news from Berlin.[7] That makes me very happy!—If only I could succeed in following your well-intentioned advice for my composing. I've been working toward that for almost a year now! I won't be satisfied until I achieve it. Perhaps it will be something decent this time!—I must close, to go to a rehearsal. Many, many warm regards and many eternal thanks for everything I learned and experienced anew,

from your eternally indebted Berg

—The handwriting is dreadful again after all, and a few blots fell on the paper from dipping too fast. Sorry, Herr Schönberg, but it happened in my haste, since I'm in a hurry to leave—for the rehearsal—where it wouldn't do to be late.— A Philharmonic concert under Rich. Strauss scheduled for yesterday (Beethoven's 5th Symphony and *[Symphonia] Domestica*) had to be canceled due to lack of audience interest.[8] Of course!: When Schönberg and Mahler are performed he must step aside!—

---

5. The Leipzig *Gurrelieder* had been performed by the Leipzig Winderstein Orchestra; Artur Nikisch had led premliminary rehearsals for Schoenberg.

6. In October / November 1913 Schoenberg had written two versions of the song "Seraphita" on a Stefan George translation of the Ernest Dowson poem.

7. It has not been determined what Stein's good news was, though it may have concerned the fact that Ernst von Schuch, music director of the Dresden Opera, was considering staging Schoenberg's two one-act operas. That spring Schoenberg and Steuermann traveled to Dresden to play through *Erwartung* for Schuch and theater director Count Nikolaus Seebach. As a result of these developments U.E. decided to publish *Erwartung*.

8. Strauss postponed the concert because of a scheduling conflict with the Berlin Court Opera.

*(From left to right): Paul Königer, Edward Clark, Erwin Stein, Edward Steuermann, Schoenberg, unidentified man, Heinrich Jalowitz, Anton Webern, and Josef Polnauer in Leipzig, March 1914 (Arnold Schoenberg Institute 2227)*

## Berg to Schoenberg

[Vienna] 28 March 1914

It was impossible, dear Herr Schönberg, to telephone you about the performance. I couldn't place a call the day before at the post office so I did it today at 8:30 this morning. I waited there until 11:15, then canceled and found out that due to a number of "urgent" calls (Saturday stock exchange!!) mine would be delayed another hour. I couldn't wait that long, as I had to be in the city before noon, so I telegraphed and am now writing in the Stadtbahn because I have students coming this afternoon at 2 o'clock. So at least I'll inform you briefly, though in a handwriting (in pencil!) made still worse by the jolting: naturally the performance can't be compared with the one in Leipzig, nonetheless it was full of spirit, seemed to be precise, and compensated for a lack of finer shadings through its enthusiasm and spirited musicality. Several songs, by the way, the Prelude, interlude in Part I, and much of Part III were absolutely outstanding. The choruses were particularly good, the men could be heard very well in the Wild Hunt and in the soft passages later really very *ppp* and in tune! Nachod was freer this time, more unfettered and confident than I have ever seen him: also very good in general; vocally in wonderful form, he could always be heard very well. Förstel was a bit weak in her middle range, but wonderful in the high range and sang very musically, only rather wilfully, too much the prima donna. Mildenburg interpreted her part too dramatically, too grandiosely, too much pathos, but in consequence of the consistency of her interpretation, her enormous voice, and self-possession with which she sang the Waldtaube completely from memory (stepping far forward without looking at the conductor!) made a grandiose impression. (Unfortunately she sang the two F♯'s very out of tune, but the G♭ and B♭ were fabulously strong and beautiful.)

Boruttau was the same as always, Nosalewicz pretty good,[1] Gregori indifferent, except for several passages where the slightly too deep timbre of his voice matched the orchestra sound very well. That's when I realized (though Zehme was of course much better than he), that a man's voice really is preferable for the speaker. Rhythmically, by the way, he was much better this year than last.—The audience response was wonderful. After both Parts I and III Schreker was called back at least 10–15 times (sometimes with, sometimes without soloists). The hall was filled to overflowing (certainly sold out, at least I didn't see a single empty seat; indeed, people were standing against the wall in the boxes). At the end about ¾ of the audience stayed in the hall for perhaps a ¼ hour—even though the lights were turned off—applauding madly. In the forefront Frau Mahler, who was deeply moved and affected. Frau Moll actually wept. Loos, too, who was at the dress rehearsal and performance, seems to have liked it very much. (The dress rehearsal, by the way, wasn't nearly as good, suffering from the lack of spirit with which Boruttau sang Waldemar in Parts I and II. Nachod, who had just arrived from the station, sang Part III.) Nonetheless the dress rehearsal went just as magnificently and was almost sold out (a few 5–kronen seats were empty, but all 2–4–kronen seats were taken!) The wonderful reception of the actual performance (yesterday) was reported today in the *Wiener Journal* (in a long, very enthusiastic article) and in the *Arbeiterzeitung* (more briefly).[2] At the dress rehearsal and performance there were many calls for you, Herr Schönberg, from the applauding audience!—The percussion complement was complete this year![3]—

Now, warmest regards, dear Herr Schönberg, also to your esteemed wife and the dear children. My wife's warmest and sincerest congratulations to you all on this renewed success!

Your Berg

The old refrain: forgive the form of this letter; but this was the only way I could manage to report to you.

(I'm going to Emmy Heim's song recital tonight. "Waldsonne" and "Erhebung"!—)[4]

---

1. Alfred Boruttau sang the role of Klaus Narr and Alexander Nosalewicz that of the Bauer.

2. E[lsa] B[ienenfeld] reviewed the *Gurrelieder* performance in the *Neues Wiener Journal* on 28 March 1914. The unsigned 28 March review in the *Arbeiterzeitung* may have been written by David Josef Bach.

3. This may be in connection with what Berg in his letter of 15 December 1913 had termed *Striche*, or cuts, in the *Gurrelieder* premiere.

4. In addition to the Schoenberg songs, the recital included songs by Reger, Weigl, Schoenberg, Wellesz, Mussorgsky, and Mahler, as well as Bohemian folk songs. The accompanist was Vacláv Štěpán.

*Berg to Schoenberg*

Vienna, Good Friday 1914
[10 April 1914]

Dear Herr Schönberg,

Best wishes to you and your dear family for very pleasant holidays. I hope the days in Gautzsch have been lovely so far and that you will be able to enjoy the countrylike visit for some time to come.[1] And perhaps compose something! I wonder what?? . . .

There's no interesting news from Vienna aside from the reactions to the performance of Mahler's VIII[th] Symphony.[2] So far only the *Fremdenblatt* has printed a review, which tore Schreker to shreds.[3] That seems to have hurt Schreker deeply, at least I got that impression from a very kind but depressed note in which he thanked me for some warm words I had written him on the occasion of the two performances (*Gurre* and VIII[th]) and his illness.[4] He also wrote that he was so very pleased by your letter. By association of ideas (display of letters received, carrying about of same: a typical Schreker trait) I am reminded that I met Buxbaum at Siegfried Ochs's concert, who told me how very pleased he was by your card from Amsterdam and that he always carries it around with him (and he actually had it in his wallet). Ochs himself had a great success here;[5] his manner, probably only superficial, of performing a work with utmost dynamic and rhythmic accuracy (incidentally this applies only to the chorus, not to the orchestra and soloists), impressed both the public and the critics. In point of fact, by following the signs on the **paper** so exactly, by focusing so completely on the work being performed and through the resultant attention to the purely musical events (such as exact observance of note values, function of the fermata ( $\frown$ ) within the chorales, preventing the chorus from fading on sustained notes, clarity in fugal and imitative entrances, etc.), Ochs achieves performances of rare precision. But that's all. He never even gets close to the spirit of a work, to the things that aren't on paper. Indeed, I even believe he inhibits that in those members of the chorus, soloists, and orchestra who, apart from musical precision, would be capable of grasping the soul of a work. Simply as a result of his superficial manner of rehearsing and conducting, which is both martial and affected (I was also present at a semi-open rehearsal). The tricks, which initially impress one, such as sharp commands and calls of encouragement, stamping of feet, actual breaking off in order to achieve an extreme diminuendo (a habit that

1. Schoenberg and his family accepted the invitation of Albertine Zehme to spend two weeks at her home in Gautzsch near Leipzig.

2. On 3 April, just one week after the *Gurrelieder* performance, Schreker led his Philharmonic Chorus and the Tonkünstler Orchestra in a performance of Mahler's Eighth Symphony.

3. By Ludwig Karpath on 4 April 1914.

4. As a result of over-work and over-exertion Schreker had suffered a fainting spell following the performance of Mahler's Eighth Symphony.

5. On 6 April the Berlin choral conductor Siegfried Ochs led a concert of the Schubertbund and Singakademie in a program of five Bach cantatas: *Du Hirte Israel*, BWV 104, *Es erhub sich ein Streit*, BMV 19, *Jesu, der du meine Seele*, BMV 78, *O Ewigkeit, du Donnerwort*, BWV 20 or 60, and *Nun ist das Heil*, BWV 50.

could mislead the orchestra, or at least confuse it), clenching of the fist, completely ceasing to conduct in the middle of the most spirited passage for the sake of dramatic resumption with the next entrance of a voice, etc., but no: not: etc.—I think the things I just listed are the extent of what's characteristic of his rehearsing———— —, one has grasped all these tricks in a few minutes, they become tiresome and one soon realizes that it's always the same, the same with every work, just as it probably has been for 20–30 years, or however long Ochs has been a choral conductor. I needn't add that the performance of these 5 cantatas nevertheless can't be compared with performances under Schalk or Löwe, where execution isn't even precise. Under Ochs these Bach works, which I didn't know, *did* make a powerful impression on me, whereas, for instance, I can no longer bear to hear the St. Matthew Passion under Schalk! But from my experience watching you, dear Herr Schönberg, rehearse and perform the Bach Orchestra Suite arranged by Mahler,[6] I do know that Ochs's is not the right approach to performing Bach's works: I'm sending you the program of his choral concert under separate cover.—

As of three days now I have finally been able to work, the plan for a fairly large movement, representing a march, is finished, as are a number of sections;[7] unfortunately my wife is ailing again. Her continually increasing rheumatic and neuralgic pains have brought on a high and prolonged fever, which still hasn't completely subsided. With the coming of spring my asthma, too, has reappeared. Sufficient prerequisites, as you see, for at last writing something cheerful. Maybe for once it will work in reverse!: If what I write doesn't represent what I have experienced, then perhaps my life will for once conform to my compositions, which would in that case be purest prophecy. But I think I lack that power as I lack so many others, and even if I'm absolutely determined for once to avoid "the tears" it will probably not be the march of an upright person marching cheerfully, but rather at best—in which case it would at least be a "character piece"—the "March of an Asthmatic," which I am and, it seems to me, will remain forever.—

Again, dear Herr Schönberg, a very happy Easter and many warm regards,

from your Berg

---

6. On 29 February 1912 Schoenberg had given a performance in Prague of Gustav Mahler's 1910 arrangement of individual movements from various Bach Orchestra Suites.

7. This was to be the third of Berg's Three Orchestra Pieces, Op. 6.

## Schoenberg to Berg (postcard)

Berlin-Südende, 28 May 1914

Dear Berg,

I *must* tell you that today, the 28th(!!), your [bank] transfer still has not arrived.[1]

1. Early in 1914 Schoenberg's financial situation was once again critical. Berg and Webern organized another drive to provide Schoenberg with a monthly stipend of 500 kronen, which they hoped would continue for at least two years. In addition to soliciting contributions from Schoenberg's students they approached Emil Hertzka for support. To reach wealthier patrons they drew Alma Mahler into their plans, who began to play a central role in the fund-raising activities. By way of immediate results she obtained a gift of 500 kronen from Frau Lilly Lieser, which was sent directly to Schoenberg in January 1914. The renewed Mahler stipend of 2,000 kronen was paid in full in May 1914.

I'm extremely annoyed, for I realize how irresponsibly you treated the matter. Since you went to the bank too late on the 23$^{rd}$, it would have been your duty to make up for it somehow. Particularly when doing someone a favor one must do it conscientiously. For the other person tends to be indiscriminate!—Luckily the matter wasn't so urgent this time because I received the Mahler stipend a few days ago. But now I know that I cannot depend on you.

Regards

Schönberg

*Berg to Schoenberg*

Vienna, 8 June 1914

Dear Herr Schönberg,

There were three reasons why I didn't finish several letters begun last week and why I didn't send a finished one: 1. because knowing that you, Herr Schönberg, are busy with an important new work,[1] I didn't wish to—dared not—bother you with endless explanations, excuses, pleas, etc., 2. because I know your aversion to reading long epistles containing thousands of words that could be expressed in one sentence, which in this case would be: Forgive me, I will do better. And 3. because I can't possibly attain such forgiveness with such a letter, but only through improvement, i.e., through actually righting my wrong.

I owe it to Webern that, unsuspecting until then, I was enlightened as to the wrong done you, dear Herr Schönberg, and thus also the wrong done him and the whole world and, finally, myself.[2] But now I also know how to right it and during these past few days, whenever my work didn't distract me from the enlightenment that came to me as in a trance, I have been setting up a program for conducting my life, in which all the failings, some unsuspected, some heretofore unavoidable, will be corrected. If in the foreseeable future I restrict this self-imposed task to my **habits**—that is, primarily to something external—it is because my wrong—I can swear to this with a clear conscious—didn't contain a single atom of transgression of thought or attitude; but [I realize] that the nexus of all my activities and omissions these last years couldn't help give the impression of "unreliable" friendship, "lack of self-discipline," and a slackening and "deterioration" of my person.

Whether I can ever obtain your forgiveness, Herr Schönberg, naturally depends on whether my resolve to improve—the only thing keeping me upright since this catastrophe—is carried out——. To expect that at this point would be sacrilege; but I do dare to ask, Herr Schönberg, that at some point you send me—whether directly or through Webern or Stein, when you happen to write them,—one word, to which I can cling in my helplessness and which would give me a little courage and the ability to hope . . . . . . , I dare ask you for that already today, dear Herr

---

1. During the summer of 1914 Schoenberg was working on a Symphony (which remained unfinished) and the text of his oratorio *Die Jakobsleiter*.

2. Schoenberg did not write to Berg for the next two-and-one-half months, and Berg had to rely solely on Webern and Erwin Stein for news of Schoenberg.

Schönberg, knowing your great kindness. That would also make it easier for me when I write to you to spare you emotional outpourings and to remain calm and matter-of-fact, as you desire in a correspondent—in other words in accordance with my resolution to improve in this respect as well.

My regards to you, dear Herr Schönberg, in complete devotion and love,

Your Berg

## Berg to Schoenberg

Vienna, 9 July 1914

Dear Herr Schönberg,

Stein told me you were wondering why I had not yet prepared a reduction of the Chamber Symphony. Here's my answer, dear Herr Schönberg: Upon your suggestion I immediately began to work on it. But I was interrupted by the more pressing work on the abridged version of the *Gurre*-guide. Then I heard that a new, revised score of the Chamber Symphony was to appear,[1] so for the time being I began to work on my own orchestra pieces. It was a good idea—I think—to wait for the revised edition for—as far as I can judge the changes in the score—they would have necessitated significant changes in the reduction as well. Mere cutting would probably not have sufficed, as demonstrated by a simple comparison of the proofs with my reduction, worked out to about ⑥, page 7 (old edition). *[Berg gives a number of examples.]* Now that nothing stands in the way, should I, dear Herr Schönberg, do the reduction right away or could it wait until mid-September when I will be finished with my orchestra pieces. Then it would probably take 5–7 weeks to complete.—

As you know, dear Herr Schönberg, I'm staying in Vienna until my wife returns from Karlsbad.[2] She just wrote that her doctor there, *Dozent* Dr. Kolisch,[3] who was recommended to us by Professor Ortner,[4] "has turned out to be a fervent Schönberg admirer. He has apparently read the *Harmonielehre* with great enthusiasm and his very musical (?) son would definitely be studying with you if you were in Vienna."[5] Now I know my wife is in good hands and my anxiety at having had to leave her in Karlsbad all by herself has lessened.—

I hope you and your dear family, whom I send many regards, are pleased with Murnau.[6] Perhaps Stein will write sometime and tell me what it's like there; I would very much like to know what the place is like where—in my thoughts—I spend so much time.

Many, many warm and devoted regards

from your Berg

1. The new edition of Schoenberg's Chamber Symphony, Op. 9, appeared in 1914.
2. As he informed Schoenberg in a letter of 28 June 1914, Berg brought his wife to Karlsbad on 29 June, where she underwent treatment until 21 July.
3. Dr. Rudolf Kolisch was a world-renowned diabetes and metabolism specialist, who was also interested in the pathology and treatment of arthritis.
4. Prof. Norbert Ortner taught at the Vienna University.
5. The violinist Rudolf Kolisch later studied with Schoenberg and a close friendship developed between them.
6. The Schoenbergs spent the summer from 4 July until 10 August in Murnau, Upper Bavaria, in a house by the Staffelsee which Wassily Kandinsky and Gabriele Münter found for them.

*Berg to Schoenberg*

Vienna, 20 July 1914

Dear Herr Schönberg.

Tomorrow we leave for Trahütten. The address is the old one; anyway it's on the back of the envelope. At long last I was granted that great joy: the George Songs. It was—for me—high time they were finally published[1]—as—for years now I have been longing in particular for them—I would say—more than for anything else. Now I'll be able to immerse myself completely in their incomparable glory and that doubles the pleasure of leaving for the country. Perhaps it will make me readier for *Pierrot*. By "readier" I mean that at this stage I'm still so terribly far from understanding it as I would like (knowing full well that at the point when I tell myself: now I finally understand it completely—I would be entirely <u>mistaken,</u> and that upon looking at the work again closely a year later—ever since the "guide" I can't help analyzing—I would realize that I hadn't understood it at all before). But right now I'm not even that far: I only know that on the 2 occasions I heard *Pierrot* I was conscious of the most profound impression I have <u>ever</u> experienced from a work of art, and that the enigmatic power of these pieces has left <u>indelible</u> traces on my innermost being. But when I look at the score it still remains completely enigmatic and mysterious and I can't imagine that I, with my modest ability (and great failings), will ever be able to get close to this work of art, which seems to me like a miracle of nature. No doubt that's partly because I haven't heard the music often enough. Twice is ridiculously little. And the short time I've been able to study the score is likewise nothing. After all, I know how long I needed for all the other things. Here, too, I'm hampered by not having a piano reduction that would allow me to play the music straight through. That's what enabled me to become relatively familiar with the monodrama. In fact, that's one of my most treasured memories: slowly practicing the piano reduction of the monodrama at home and being allowed to play from it at every "lesson," and your then telling me so much about it that in the end the results at the piano were halfway decent. So it is that I live more in my memories than in the present, am more with you than with myself, and perhaps that's what enables me to bear this excruciating period.—Why hasn't Stein sent me a <u>single word</u> since he has been with you in Murnau, dear Herr Schönberg? For weeks now I have been completely cut off from you; I don't even know whether you are in Murnau, whether this is the correct address. Nor of course do I know where Stein and Jalowetz live,[2] and since they presumably don't expect me to burden you, dear Herr Schönberg, with letters and messages to them, they show no apparent desire to get letters from me with urgent inquiries. So I must regard that, too, as part of the great punishment, which I am—next week it will be 2 months—suffering under——and must submit to for as long as I can endure it.—Perhaps I will hear something indirectly through Webern. He wrote to me very kindly not long ago, from which I gather that he hasn't yet dropped me entirely.

Otherwise the recent weeks have been spent working on the orchestra pieces,

1. Schoenberg's George Songs, Op. 15, were published by U.E. in November 1914 so that Berg must have had an advance copy.
2. Erwin Stein vacationed in Murnau during July and while there visited both Schoenberg and Jalowetz, who was likewise spending the summer there.

which keep me in a constant state of apprehension. After all, I continually have to ask myself whether what I'm expressing, measures over which I often brood for days on end—is any better than my most recent things. But how am I to judge? I hate those things so much that I came close to destroying them completely, but this I can't judge yet at all, because I'm in the middle of it.—

U.E. is going to publish an album of modern songs.[3] Dr. Kalmus[4] (Hertzka's assistant), whom I know quite well, had the idea—of his own accord—of including something of mine, i.e., of suggesting it to the director. Naturally I had no objection, but did stress that Webern must be considered for this album first and foremost. As I've now heard from Kalmus, Hertzka has asked for time to think it over. Should anything come of it at all, only one of the short songs—one page long—from my published song collection—would be a possibility. But Webern will be asked for a song in any case. I imagine he will send one of his George Songs.—

Now many regards to you, dear Herr Schönberg, and I remain in unchanging love and gratitude,

Your Berg

---

3. *Das moderne Lied*, published by U.E. in 1914, included 50 songs by 33 contemporary composers, including Schoenberg, Schreker, and Zemlinsky.

4. Alfred Kalmus joined Universal in 1909.

## Berg to Schoenberg

Trahütten, 2 August 1914

Dear Herr Schönberg,

You simply cannot imagine how beautiful it is here. I keep wishing you could see it sometime. This region is—I do believe—so unique that it really does look different every day. I've already told you that we live here at an altitude of 1,000 meters on a plateau of rolling hills that rises on one side to meet the Koralps— which, however, are far enough away so as not to seem oppressive (as is the case in villages that lie at the foot of high mountains). But to the right and left of this long outstretched mountain ridge the horizon extends ever farther: From here one can already see beyond the characteristic valleys of the southern Styrian Alps to the high mountain ridges in the distance (for instance the Bacher Mountains). Looking north, finally, there's a vista of the entire Styrian paradise, the plain around Graz and further northeastward all the way to the Hungarian border, and in clear weather all the way to the Wechsel range in Lower Austria. You can imagine, dear Herr Schönberg, what wonderful air there is in these free heights, what simply eternal freshness! One can practically see the oppressive mugginess that hovers over the plain, whereas here it's almost cold. It's twice as easy for me to live here as in Vienna, and I think this also affects my work. I've already finished *something* here, the first of the three orchestra pieces, which I'm calling *Präludium*. At present I'm copying the *March* I finished in Vienna into full score and then I have to finish the third piece, called *Reigen* and write that out in full score. There will be only three pieces in all, they are about as long as your Orchestra Pieces and longer.

Nothing came of Dr. Kalmus's plan to include one of my songs in the "modern song album": Wöss, who is the editor, turned it down. Reason: technical difficulties, pagination changes, etc., as he had already put everything together and the songs (Webern's too) would have been too difficult to include.—

And now, dear Herr Schönberg, I have to thank you once again: at your instigation van der Henst asked me for my sonata.[1] He wants to play it. I owe his interest and intention solely to you, which makes me very happy. And I hardly need to tell you that I also have you to thank for many wonderful hours up here, dear Herr Schönberg—when I read through the newly published music. But again and again I feel compelled to tell you how great my gratitude and my devotion are.

Your Alban Berg

1. The Dutch pianist Enrique van der Henst.

### Schoenberg to Berg (postcard)

Berlin-Südende, 18 August 1914

Dear Berg,

What's the matter with you? Why haven't I heard from you? Have you lost all interest in me?—I am quite well at the moment. I still haven't been called up.[1] Frau Mahler has arranged the matter of my money transfers, so I and my family will at least be protected from want, even if I do have to report for duty. Let me hear from you soon. Will you stay in Trahütten much longer?

My best to your wife. Warm regards

Schönberg

1. Germany and Austria had been at war with Russia, France, England, and the other Allied powers since the beginning of August.

### Berg to Schoenberg

Trahütten, 27 August 1914

I needn't tell you, dear, kind Herr Schönberg, how happy your card of the 18th made me (it arrived in Deutsch Landsberg yesterday, the 26th). My first personal word from you in a quarter of a year—and: taking me completely by surprise—and at a time, when I was cut off from all news of you and living in the greatest apprehension. But your words: "have I (I can scarcely write them down:) lost all interest in you?—" hurt me. However, I realize thereby that you haven't received my last letters to Murnau (I wrote from Vienna prior to my departure for here, and then from here on 2 and 11 August). A letter I had written to Stein asking for news of you was returned; Webern, to whom I wrote for the same purpose, still hasn't answered—so that I'm already quite anxious about him—. Finally—immediately after war broke out—I wrote a (registered) letter to Frau Mahler with regard to your financial affairs: no answer there, either. So you see, dear Herr Schönberg, I even have <u>ac</u>tual proof that my interest in you and your affairs hasn't diminished in the slightest. Indeed, it was reasonable for me to assume that <u>you</u>, dear Herr Schönberg—and the others, too—didn't want anything more to do <u>with me</u>. Now your dear card has reassured me most wonderfully. But—more important—it also gives me some reassurance regarding your financial situation. For that was my biggest worry when I considered the effects of this war. That even led me to forget my own (for I, too, have had to suffer financially—only for the duration of the war, I hope), and to forget about the possibility of being called up. As far as <u>that</u> goes, I believe that <u>you</u>, dear Herr Schönberg, can rest easy for the time being! To date Austria has called up everyone who <u>ever served</u> before (up to the age of 42), as well as those who haven't yet served but were <u>registered</u> this year. Unless preference is given to older years who have already served and younger ones who haven't served but seem fit, the next ones to be taken will be the men aged 21–37 who have never served and were declared unfit, which includes me. Only then men aged 37–42, in other words you, dear Herr Schönberg! (For as far as I know you have never served before.) That won't happen very soon. But if it does happen, will you be able to report to the consulate in Berlin(?!) Perhaps we'll see each other in Vienna after all, though, granted not for a performance. I told you of my fears in this regard in my last letter of the 24th, which you will probably have received by now. Also that for the time being I shall remain in Trahütten.

Many, many warm regards to you and your dear family—also from my wife—and again thanks for your card.

Your Berg

## Berg to Schoenberg

Trahütten, 8 September 1914

Dear Herr Schönberg,

Under separate cover I'm sending you a roll of music as registered printed matter. I have been told here that it is now the only possibility of sending anything to Germany safely. I'm sending you the Orchestra Pieces, dear Herr Schönberg, which I'm dedicating to you on the occasion of your birthday.

For four years it has been my secret but no less fervent wish to dedicate something to you. The things I composed under your supervision, dear Herr Schönberg, the sonata, songs and quartet, were ineligible from the start, having been received directly from you, as it were. Unfortunately my hope of writing something more autonomous that would nonetheless have the same caliber as the first things, and thus to have something to dedicate to you without angering you, eluded me for several years. Then your kind suggestion last spring, during the trip from Amsterdam to Berlin, gave me the courage to attempt a work I could dedicate to you without being ashamed. I cannot yet tell whether I succeeded in this or whether it remains merely an attempt. Should it be the latter, you, dear Herr Schönberg, must, with the fatherly kindness you have always shown me, take the good intention for the deed. I really did try to give my best, to follow all your suggestions and advice, whereby the unforgettable, indeed overwhelming experiences of the Amsterdam rehearsals and close study of your Orchestra Pieces proved infinitely helpful and continually sharpened my self-criticism. That, too, is the reason I haven't forced the completion of the 2nd of the 3 pieces, *Reigen*, in time for this self-imposed deadline, preferring to postpone it until a later time when I will, I hope, succeed in correcting the flaws that I don't yet see clearly. Another reason is that of late, due to the great, unavoidable agitation, I have been unable to proceed with the work as I had projected before war broke out. And so I am—once again—forced to apologize! Don't be angry with me, dear Herr Schönberg, for daring to dedicate something to you that isn't finished! But I hope to finish the missing 2nd piece very soon (it's a piece of dancelike character, 100 measures in length (by the way), in other words longer than the *Präludium* and shorter than the *March*) and to add it to the two pieces sent you.

At the moment I'm working on the piano reduction of the Chamber Symphony. For that purpose I shall stay here a while longer, for here I believe it will be easier to curb the incredible impatience and restlessness brought on by the war than if I were in Vienna. The urge "to be a part of it," the feeling of impotence at not being able to serve the fatherland, would make it impossible for me to work there.

Please accept my very, very warmest wishes for your birthday, dear Herr Schönberg, and many regards to you and your esteemed wife and the dear children,

from your Berg

### Schoenberg to Berg

Berlin-Südende, 20 September 1914

Dear Berg,

Many thanks for your birthday wishes and for the score.

Unfortunately I can't say anything about your work just yet. Although I have looked at it often, you yourself know how difficult it is to get an impression from such a complicated score and you will understand that I haven't had the peace of mind for it during this time.

I confidently expect that your intention was as good as your will and thank you for the deed.—

Are you really still in Trahütten? In your place I would find it intolerable to be so completely isolated while such momentous events are taking place. Surely you must be getting all your news 4–5 days late.

Warmest regards

Schönberg

### Berg to Schoenberg

Vienna, 26 September 1914

Many thanks, dear Herr Schönberg, for your letter. It was forwarded here yesterday, where I've been since the 25th. I'm glad my sending the score didn't disturb you; I myself know only too well that one would rather read maps than scores these days and that it requires the greatest effort to occupy oneself with music (or in general anything not related to the war). And you point out quite correctly that it would have been intolerable for you to be in my position, living in the kind of isolation where it takes 4–5 days for the latest news to arrive. Naturally I couldn't have borne that either! But I wasn't much worse off up there in Trahütten than in the cities. The Graz morning papers arrive in the morning, 10, 10:30 at the latest, those from Vienna and the Graz *Mittagsblatt* arrive in the afternoon. And I can assure you, dear Herr Schönberg, that reading the Graz papers, particularly the *Tagespost*, is a real relief after those filthy rags, the *Wiener Tagblatt* and *Neue Freie Presse*. The authentic telegrams are, of course, the same. Likewise the private reports, which the censors edit in the same way. Everything else—in the major papers—is pages and pages of: mood, observation, authoritative(!) judgments, prophecies, etc. Roda Roda is the war correspondent for the *Neue Freie Presse*. That says it all. And the dreadful thing about it is that one nonetheless reaches greedily for the papers every few hours because there's nothing else. The only other thing open to one is word of mouth—the equivalent of gossip. Especially in this city—which has completely lost its senses. You have no idea, dear Herr Schönberg, what kinds of things are produced here in that regard. Every day—according to rumor—generals get pensioned off; others shoot themselves. Russian airplanes are expected over Vienna, etc. The fact is (apart from the Brudermann affair,[1] which no doubt has become known in Germany, too), there is no truth to any of it and our lack of success in the north should be given no less coverage than the German successes in France. What's clumsy is all this secretiveness! For instance, I heard of the fall of Lemberg in Trahütten 2 days before people heard of it in Vienna (of course from a source I can't repeat in this letter). But maybe that's unavoidable, given the Viennese populace, which is now divided into "optimists" and "pessimists") also called alarmists). Nor can one read anything here about the present situation in the north. We have been informed by some of my wife's relatives from Galicia that our command post has been established in Biala (Bielitz), that the Russians are between Cracow and Przemysl,[2] and that the Carpathian passes are occupied by German artillery. And finally that, due to our extremely advantageous position at present, a great Austrian victory can be expected. (That certainly belongs to the genre of prophecy!) The fortification project under way all around Vienna (also at Rosenhügel and Knödel-hütte, etc.[3] with which you're probably familiar) can be interpreted more as relief work than as an intention to expose Vienna to a siege.—Just this minute extra editions were delivered, reporting an attempt by Russian divisions to break through over the Carpathians. But the "interpretation" following the telegram doesn't mark the battle lines I just indicated in this letter (between Cracow, Przemysl, and the Carpathians), but much farther north, on the San line,[4] from which I thought our troops had long since retreated. So what's true? Whom can one believe? This

1. Rudolf Ritter von Brudermann commanded the third Austro-Hungarian Army, which suffered heavy losses in the first battle of Lemberg (26–30 August); the city was recaptured in the second battle of Lemberg (1–10 September). Information on a Brudermann "affair" has not been located.
2. Biala (Bileko-Biala), Cracow, and Przemysl are all in southern Poland.
3. Districts in the southwest of Vienna.
4. The San is a tributary of the Wisla river.

uncertainty is as dreadful and agonizing as the events themselves. You will surely understand, dear Herr Schönberg, that under such circumstances I cannot imagine how I am to <u>work</u> in the near future. Indeed, it sometimes seems downright wicked to think of anything but the war. If I have forced myself to do so notwithstanding—first finishing the score I sent you, then resuming work on the reduction of the Chamber Symphony and resolved not to rest until I've finished it—that was and is so because of the supreme determination and purpose that have hardened within me since your reproaches in the spring, to accomplish the work before me <u>under all circumstances</u> and to let <u>nothing</u> deter me from my purpose. Granted, I get more restless by the day and at the moment can't imagine how I am to continue work on the reduction, whose technical difficulties would normally tempt me, and which at other times would allow me to revel in the mysteriously beautiful form of this symphony—in other words, how I am to return to the work with the requisite peace of mind. Thank heavens—I would almost say—there's not much doing with "lessons" this year. And my administrative work is so mindless that half a head would suffice.

What are you doing these days, dear Herr Schönberg? You probably aren't able to work much either! And the students? I'd very much like to know about Steuermann.[5] And Clark[6] and the people from the *Pierrot* ensemble. Are there any chances for *Pierot* performances? The one in Vienna? It would be better to say nothing about the concert life here. Instead of taking advantage of the perfect opportunity to shut it down entirely, it continues to vegetate: you can see the Konzertverein program in the *Neue Freie Presse* sent to you yesterday.[7] Naturally nothing of yours or Mahler's. Nedbal's novelties, apart from the inevitable Korngold (*Sinfonietta*), Mandl (*Hymnus*), Schmidt (II[nd] Symphony), are Fibich, Prohaska, Suk (his countrymen), Reger (Ballet Suite), Siklos(?), Franco de Venezia(?), and—as there are no longer any native composers (no Mahler performances either!!, instead, *Till Eulenspiegel*)——our beloved threesome: Debussy, Delius, Liadov.—

Many warm regards to you, dear Herr Schönberg, and your dear family

from your Berg

---

5. With the outbreak of the war Eduard Steuermann, whose family lived in Sambor in Galicia, had returned home.

6. The British Edward Clark applied for German citizenship and volunteered for military service; he was interned in Berlin for the duration of the war.

7. The 23 September clipping from the *Neue Freie Presse* contained the 1914/15 Konzertverein program, which was to include works by Bruckner, Wolf, Strauss, and Reger, as well as more standard fare.

*Schoenberg to Berg (postcard)*

Berlin-Südende [5 October 1914]

Dear Berg,

Many thanks for the newspapers. I would like detailed news from Vienna as often as possible.—Steuermann is said to be in Vienna, living either at IX, 10 Frankgasse or with a Frau Dr. Geyer, 80 Karl-Ludwigstrasse. Won't you please get in touch with him?—You mention a Brudermann affair that was discussed in the papers in Vienna. There was nothing about it here; would you care to tell me more about it. Or is it just gossip? In that case don't bother. I want to avoid that sort of thing, as I consider it pointless to get excited over nothing. But of course everything else interests me enormously.—It's absolutely disgusting that Nedbal is performing French, Russian, and English music. I think one should protest. Do so!

Warm regards

Schönberg

*Berg to Schoenberg (letterhead: J. Berg / VI., Linke Wienzeile 118)*

Vienna, 8 October 1914

Dear Herr Schönberg,

Your suggestion to Webern, to observe clouds and the sky, moved me very much, too.[1] Already this summer—though certainly without connecting it with the war— I had noticed some unbelievable formations and had even written to you about it once—probably in one of the lost letters to Murnau.[2] I particularly remember one afternoon in August, when a huge double rainbow with the most vibrant colors overspread the entire delicately-clouded eastern sky as well as the landscape (the broad plain below Trahütten) lying in radiant sunshine below— while **at the same time**—in the western sky, covered with pitch black rags of clouds, a terrible thunderstorm raged over the Koralps. I myself stood on a small hill amidst these events, which may have lasted perhaps an hour, until both—rainbow and thunderstorm— slowly dissipated.

I, too, have noticed the continuously beautiful weather this summer (no rain whatsoever—except for a few thunderstorms—from the end of July until mid-September); only I chose to associate it with the war in a more material way. After frequently observing the marked effects of *Wetterschiessen*,[3] I thought the millions of shots—fired throughout almost all of middle Europe for weeks at a time, along a front line hundreds of kilometers long—could have had some effect on the weather. To be sure, what I now see in the sky seems to have other, more profound reasons. The night sky a few days ago, for example, was quite singular. Clouds shaped liked rhomboids were arrayed in regular formation; something like this:

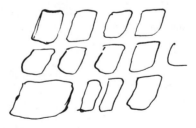

1. In a September letter to Webern, now lost, Schoenberg mentions having started a "wartime cloud diary" *(Kriegswolkentagebuch)*.

2. Probably the letter of 11 August.

3. A practice of diverting oncoming thunderstorms in the Alps.

The black night sky gleaming out between the clouds (illuminated by the moon) involuntarily reminded me of trenches. Another time there was a magnificent lunar rainbow. And the weather these past few days is such as I have never experienced, not even in April. At almost regularly spaced intervals of ½ to ¾ of an hour brightest sunshine in a deep blue, cloudless sky alternates with showers from black cloud masses that appear suddenly from nowhere. Very singular.—

Returned home I found your card, dear Herr Schönberg. Many thanks. Steuermann visited me a day after his return. He and his family have been in Vienna for about a week now. He had to leave his home, Sambor, south of Lemberg, which is occupied by the Russians now (though no doubt they'll soon be driven out). He has been through a lot. — Unfortunately I can't write anything about the affair I mentioned in my last letter, to which you referred. Just this, that it was settled a month ago and with it all of the unfavorable consequences for our side. It wasn't in the papers here, either, but everyone knew about it and it proved to be true—not gossip—which is why I suspected that you might have seen it in the German papers. But there's no longer any cause for alarm.

Similarly it's impossible for Webern to tell you all about Kraus,[4] dear Herr Schönberg. Have you heard about Altenberg's short essay: *Untergang des Franzosentums* [Decline of the French]?[5] He calls the French sham-romantics and heartless megalomaniacs in this earthly madhouse. He considers the Russians' insanity temporary and, given the right means, curable by the world psychologist, but that of the French to be the syphilis of false patriotism. Thus incurable. He sees some promise for a future cure in the war. That's about all he wrote. By the way there's another good story about him making the rounds. At the beginning of the war he was afraid that he, too, would be called up. To comfort him, Loos asked him whether he had ever seen a 60-year-old recruit, whereupon he exclaimed in tears: "No, but generals!!"

Several days ago Nedbal's final—revised(!!) program came out. The 3 (French, Russian, and English) were left out after all. Otherwise I would definitely have lodged a protest. Works by Reznicek, Weingartner, etc., were inserted in their stead.[6]

Weingartner is to perform a Mahler work (which one I don't know) in the Philharmonic concerts.[7]

I'm slowly continuing my work on the Chamber Symphony reduction. I find it excruciatingly difficult to make it easy to play. At present I'm completely reworking the Scherzo again. But though it's causing me a lot of trouble, I'm literally reveling in the beauties of the work itself, which become ever more apparent. Only now am I beginning to know and understand it. The way the individual sections are connected is mysteriously beautiful. The incredible power of the beginning of the 1st recapitulation (p. 15)! This A! There's not a theme in the world with the power of

---

4. Karl Kraus was an outspoken pacifist, which made him somewhat suspect among the Schoenberg circle. There are similar references in postcards from Webern to Schoenberg from this time.

5. Probably a newspaper editorial, as yet unidentified.

6. Emil Nikolaus von Reznicek's *Donna Diana* overture and Felix Weingartner's *Lustige Ouvertüre* and orchestral songs.

7. Mahler's Fourth Symphony.

this one note. In **that** harmonic context!

Likewise the entrance of the descending-fourths motive at the end of the Scherzo! (p. 26) But it doesn't end there!: the incredibly expressive theme beginning with the descending sixth A♭–C, the harmony: everything leading to f minor. And then entering upon this f minor, as if to postpone it (until the bass theme reaches the bass note F), the E♭-minor chord that itself, with great force—as if on its own—leads deceptively to F over the augmented ⁶₆ chord on the same scale step. But no respite before that loveliest of all themes experiences the same hesitation, postponement of the f minor ♩♪ and only then, after the strong outburst, finally, finally, to be released and glide into f minor ♫ !

Was there ever such a triad? I could listen to this passage for hours —And it's like that on every page! I only cited 2 passages here that caught my attention most recently. Otherwise it would be practically sacrilegious to speak of "lovely passages." This isn't a work like any other. It's a milestone in music, sufficient for an entire generation. One shouldn't even dare approach the later works until familiar with this one. Already I think I understand the Orchestra Pieces, already I fancy I'm slowly gaining an appreciation of all the most incredibly profound musical beauties of *Pierrot*, and already I'd like to immerse myself in *Glückliche Hand*, to study the *Seraphita* song and master it all, so as to experience in the short span of my life those things that still won't be completely understood in hundreds of years—that is, to experience it so that it becomes as much my own as the most intimate of experiences. Don't think it presumption or megalomania, dear Herr Schönberg. It is nothing but love (of course to some extent love is invariably presumptuous and megalomaniac!)

Accept my very warmest regards—also from my wife—to you and your worthy wife.

Your Berg

From military circles I hear that nothing could have been more welcome than a siege of Przemysl. The fort is said to be incredibly strong, indeed impregnable (as demonstrated now by the present bloody repulse of the attacks and the resultant events). But then, fortification artillery is supposed to be our greatest strength.—

## Berg to Schoenberg

Vienna, 27 November 1914

Dear Herr Schönberg,

I was called up for examination today and declared "unfit." I'm very disappointed and depressed, but would be even more so if I hadn't observed in the course of perhaps 100–150 examinations that very few are taken: easily no more than 5–10%. And practically only professionals. And only short men! They don't take the tall ones at all. Apparently they're not good for anything. As I think Balzac says somewhere, heart and head are too far apart in tall people.[1] So here, too, I've been

1. Berg may have been thinking of the passage in Balzac's *Seraphita*, where the character Wilfried, who has "raised himself above other men," is described as possessing a short neck and heart and head close together. This is, interestingly enough, a passage which Schoenberg retranslated in the margin of his own copy of the Balzac novel.

excluded and condemned to the role of an observer. That makes things even more difficult and unbearable. But I'm sure there's a reason for their not taking me. If only because they don't need many people, in other words because they feel strong enough against the enemy!

We haven't heard anything from you for a long time now, dear Herr Schönberg. Of course it's understandable that you have nothing to tell, but every few weeks it would be nice to know how you're doing. Perhaps you could send one of us a card again sometime, dear Herr Schönberg.

Warmest regards

from your grateful, devoted Berg

### Schoenberg to Berg (postcard)

Berlin-Südende, 8 December 1914

Dear Berg,

You want me to write more often, but you yourself write so infrequently!— However, I've long been meaning to thank you for sending the newspapers. The pages with casualty lists and military honors interest me, too, since I have some acquaintances at the front.—I've also been meaning to ask how much you have subscribed to the war bonds. I certainly hope you have given an amount commensurate with your circumstances.—What else is new?—I was very surprised that you are exempt from military service. I expect I'll be taken.

Warm regards

Schönberg

### Berg to Schoenberg

[in the Villach-Vienna train] 14 December 1914

Dear Herr Schönberg,

Back in Carinthia again for a few days.[1] I can't begin to tell you how these departures from reality affect me. Whenever I enter the Semmering region, burdened as I've been for months now with ceaseless and depressing thoughts of the horror, the infinite misery of these times— —and look out of the compartment window, what I see there, the unending peace of this unforgettably beautiful region, seems like a dream; indeed, to revel at the sight of the purity and delicateness seems forbidden and sinful to me, and when I return to reality after such abandonment to nature, when I turn my eyes away from the landscape, where the picture of transparent autumn hasn't quite given way yet to that of silent winter— —and pick up the newspaper and read that the frigate Scharnhorst <u>fought to the last minute, after which the entire company went down along with their admiral</u>[2]— — —then I feel

1. Berg had to travel to Villach several times that fall, as many of the farm workers from Berghof had been drafted and he had to find replacements.

2. Three large German destroyers, including the Scharnhorst, were sunk on 8 December 1914 in a battle with the English fleet off the Falkland islands.

I've awakened from my opiate dream, to which I would prefer to ascribe all emotions not related to the war, so as to excuse my carelessness and forgetfulness. And yet I often wish—so as just to get through this time, though I know it's an almost criminal ostrich policy—that I didn't know anything about it, that I could live deep in nature, better said high up in the otherworldly mountains—far from all knowledge of these dreadful, wretched events and their unavoidable but nauseating attendant phenomenon, the newspaper—and that I needn't return to this world until long after declaration of peace. You know, dear Herr Schönberg, that of course I couldn't really do it, but perhaps my thoughts of such an escape from life won't seem so wicked to you when I tell you that my unfitness for military service, pronounced at the "examination" and later confirmed in fact, was likewise a reason for such thoughts and vague wishes. I simply felt excluded, debased to the role of observer, and forced to stay away where I was of no use. Today, having overcome the rejection, I realize that it is of course my duty to live and persevere through this time, that this is a time of testing which no one may evade, not even those who cannot fight and suffer and those not personally drawn into the anguish. I said earlier that I had overcome the rejection inherent in my being declared unfit. That doesn't mean I'm glad I wasn't "taken." But resigned! Shortly after the examination I suffered a severe, if brief illness. An asthma attack, which broke out for no explicable reason and lasted for days (though I had been spared any attacks for years now), unmistakably demonstrated my unfitness. Thus my asthma, the propensity for which, because of its complete physical inexplicability and incurability, I've always regarded as a divine warning, was again merely a sign from above. And then the following occurred to me with unbelievable suddenness: I heard of a "successful"—I don't know whether it was German or Austrian—military ruse: in order to entice the Russians out of their trenches, a large bell, which on the previous night had been fastened to a tree close to the Russian trenches, was rung by a rope. The curious Russian heads that appeared—there were 25—presented excellent targets for the fatal bullets. It may have been curiosity—but if for one or the other it was forgetfulness of the situation at the sound of a bell reminding him of a past time and a beloved place—then what is here considered "successful" is beyond all measure horrible. And though until then I had considered it a matter of course that one must destroy the enemy—after all there is no other way than for one individual to destroy another individual (or more)——in that instant it suddenly occurred to me that only a short time earlier I faced the possibility of having to take aim at people, real people——and that—had I been declared fit at the examination—my spirit would surely have broken under this necessity of killing people. Or would it have been different—if I had really been placed in that position. Would I have felt differently under different circumstances? That certainly seems possible when I consider that none of this occured to me until I no longer had anything to do with it. And then there are always so many infinitely varied feelings within one. And how much more among all mankind. But what kind of consolation is it to point out that there are a billion degrees between the poet whom the war hounds first into madness and then death, and the simple peasant lad, who told me without the slightest expression of pain, almost with a bit of sensationalism, that of his 2 brothers in

Serbia, one had buried the other. Oh! I constantly pray to God that, since this torture cannot be mitigated and there's still no end in sight, many of the millions may endure it as easily as that peasant lad. Yes, I cling to such thoughts and thus keep hold of my 5 senses as best I can, otherwise I wouldn't even be able to write. (Work has become completely impossible of late anyway.) And yet I have an overwhelming need to share my thoughts with you, dear Herr Schönberg!—That I do so only in pencil and shaky handwriting is due to the train taking me back to Vienna. Outside, tempting pictures are gliding by again—but today, thank heavens—they no longer move me. We'll soon be in St. Michael, where they'll have the day's first newspaper. Farewell, dear, kind Herr Schönberg, as well as one can during this time.

Warmest regards to you and your dear family,

from your Berg

## Berg to Schoenberg

Vienna, 15 December 1914

Dear Herr Schönberg.

Returned home I found your card, and it's important to me above all to tell you why I couldn't contribute to the war bonds. I myself have no assets. The monthly sum given me by my mother and the small, irregular earnings from teaching barely suffice for my living expenses. Saving even so much as a single heller is therefore impossible for me (on the contrary, I'm paying off debts).—Nor does my mother have assets, i.e., capital. The rents from her houses go mostly toward paying off mortgages, taxes, and expenses for the upkeep of the houses. She needs what's left of the monthly and quarterly rents for her living expenses and to make monthly payments on the inheritance due her children. Taking out further mortgages on the houses is not only impossible at present, but impossible in any case, as they're mortgaged to the hilt.—

My wife's capital, the interest of which she spends without being able to save anything, is tied up in stocks. As a result of the war these have decreased so much in value, that if one were to convert them to cash for war bonds, her fortune and consequently her income would be reduced by more than a third, perhaps even by half. She couldn't bring herself to make this sacrifice, nor could she have persuaded her father, who manages her money, to do so. But her parents have subscribed a large sum for themselves and their children, which will—someday—be paid out to my wife and her siblings.—Naturally this state of affairs has not freed me from the agony of not being able to do anything for my fatherland here either. That was an added reason for my depression, for my feeling of being rejected by fate, which I told you about yesterday in the train.* But I believe I have done my duty and will continue to meet my responsibilities by continuing to give welfare assistance, which, if anything, actually exceeds my wife's and my circumstances.—

I always sent you the newspapers with the decorations and honors, dear Herr Schönberg. Webern had told me that you were interested in those. He had not mentioned the casualty lists, which is why one or the other was missing. Anyway, I suspect that the *Neue Freie Presse* is also incomplete in that respect, (<u>certainly</u> for the rank and file).

You are right, dear Herr Schönberg, I have written infrequently of late. But apart from my severe dejection, with which I didn't want to burden you, there was also my illness, my trips to Carinthia, and increased work and anxiety concerning my mother's houses. Then there's also something I've long been racking my brains over and about which I can write only the following in an open letter, namely that it concerns a new ballistics invention that would give us—should guns and cannon of this kind be manufactured soon (which would, however, require extensive technical and mathematical experiments)———that would, as I say, give us such an enormous advantage over our enemies that we could defeat any superior power. As soon as I have worked the thing out as far as my layman's abilities permit, I shall present it to the War Ministry.

Otherwise there's nothing "new." Something approximating a "concert life" really does exist here. I have no contact with it; one would only besmirch oneself: Weingartner premieres, performances of requiems and oratorios without rehearsals, Schalk, Luze, Spörr, symphonies by Schmidt[1]————a morass within which the whole horde skulks because it's gotten too hot for them out in the open.—

Many warmest regards and many thanks for your card.

Your Berg

*Maybe the present letter, which I shall send by registered mail, will arrive before the one I sent off yesterday from St. Michael.—

1. Berg is alluding to the Vienna premiere on 4 December 1914 of Felix Weingartner's opera *Kain und Abel* and a performance of Franz Schmidt's Second Symphony by the Vienna Philharmonic Orchestra under Weingartner on 29 November 1914. Among the many choral concerts with Requiems and oratorios were a 5 December performance of Beethoven's *Missa solemnis* under Schalk, a 17 December patriotic concert with participation by Martin Spörr, and a performance of the Verdi Requiem under Karl Luze scheduled for 16 January 1915.

# 1915

*Schoenberg to Berg*

Berlin-Südende, 2 January 1914 [1915]

Dear Berg,

Because your Christmas gift came so late, I returned "from my travels" and failed to thank you. I do so all the more warmly now as the atlas[1] (which, in view of my current state of mind, I had looked forward to with some apprehension) has given me great pleasure after all. It really is a magnificent book—so beautiful that, as with so many other valuable things, one hopes it will still be *valid* after the war—certainly it will continue to be valuable. And so I thank you very, very much.

Thank your wife, too, for her Christmas and New Year's greetings, which we return most warmly!

There's not much new to tell. At the moment my work is not going very well, but I very much hope to accomplish more in the new year. Two songs are finished, except for the full score.[2] First I'll resume proofreading the monodrama and will then send it to Stein, who is going to help me.[3] After that I want to compose.[4] Otherwise I'm occupied with various projects: bookbinding, wallpapering, carpentry, etc. That has resulted in some changes in my home, especially in my room, that would astound you. Maybe I'll photograph it sometime.

Somehow one has to kill time—since nowadays everything is being killed, it's high time for Father Time, too, "whom I knew when he was only 'so' big."[5]

Warmest regards

your Arnold Schönberg

---

1. *Andrees Allgemeiner Handatlas*, ed. by Professor A. Schobel, *Ausgabe für österreich-Ungarn*, 2nd ed. (Vienna, 1913). Markings in the atlas indicate that Schoenberg used it to chart the progress of the war.

2. The two songs on texts from Rilke's *Stundenbuch*, "Alle, welche dich suchen," completed 3 December 1914, and " Mach mich zum Wächter deiner Weiten," completed 1 January 1915, became the first and second of the Four Orchestra Songs, Op. 22.

3. Schoenberg was correcting proofs of the score of *Erwartung*, although the score was not published by U.E. until 1923.

4. Schoenberg was also working on a symphony. A text, *Totentanz der Prinzipien*, apparently intended for the third movement, was completed on 15 January, and on 18 January Schoenberg completed the related text, *Jakobsleiter*, the manuscript of which bears the notation "IVth Movement."

5. A paraphrase from Karl Kraus, whose lecture of 19 November 1914 opened with the words: "In dieser grossen Zeit, die ich noch gekannt habe, wie sie so klein war . . ." (In this momentous time, which I knew when it was only so big); the lecture was published in the *Fackel* XVI / 404 (5 December 1914), 1–19.

## Berg to Schoenberg

[Vienna] 6 January 1914 [1915]

Thank you very much and most warmly, dear Herr Schönberg, for your kind letter of the 3rd.[1] As for the delayed arrival of the atlas—it was sent off about the 18th—I can only imagine that it was held up by the censors. I also meant to tell you, Herr Schönberg, that an appendix to the present atlas will be published after the war with maps of the countries and regions affected by the war. Of course I shall get one myself—i.e., for you, Herr Schönberg.—

Besides the obligatory practical things, Christmas brought me more and lovelier things than I could have expected: the full score of *The Magic Flute* from my mother; all of Grimm's German myths and stories, Bismarck's *Memoirs*, and Feuerbach's *Vermächtnis* from my wife; Schopenhauer's *Letters* from Webern and the full score of three Mahler songs from Stein.

I was in Carinthia again after Christmas. This time it was very beautiful. Deep snow lay everywhere and it was the first time I truly realized the beauty—and purity of a snow landscape; I was there for days and spent hours driving through the snow in a sleigh. I would say that only now, having come to know the snow in its infinite expanse, do I truly understand what <u>purity</u> is. Everything else is only relatively pure. There's no barometer of impurity more sensitive or more reliable than snow. A single atom of dirt defaces the indescribable purity of an endless blanket of snow. Only then does one realize—how repulsive dirt is——and that man lives and breathes in a morass of filth (—in the city—) and merely deludes himself into thinking he can be pure.[2]—Just now I find it comparatively pleasant—because it "kills time"—to occupy myself rather more intensively with farming. Apart from that I also spend some time on "inventions." Even if the ones intended for military purposes can't be implemented (I assume you received the letter in which I wrote of that?), I have one for peacetime that can be implemented even more easily: a device making it possible to indicate—better said: record—the tempo of even the longest musical composition in every measure, down to the slightest variance and most precisely— and quite simply. A paper strip (like that on a Morse telegraph) running at uniform speed, on which the composer would conduct the entire work to himself by means of a lever. Naturally someone else could do it too, "taking dictation" from the conductor's beat in a real performance. The paper strip would need a grid, so that the intervals between lever marks could be easily read. Something like the following perhaps:

Paper strip:

The dots at (a) represent the individual beats of the measure, which the lever imprints on the graduated line (b), the dots (b) (possibly the result of a secondary lever) could

---

1. Actually Schoenberg's letter of 2 January (above).

2. Berg's comments about the snow are almost identical to a passage in his letter to his wife of 30 December 1914.

be indications of the first strong beat of the measure (downbeat). (h) is an extra staff for subsequent orientation (addition of the main melodic line, bar lines, or just tempo indication (according to the present example from $b_2$ on: *ritard.* until $b_4$; from $b_4$ on: *a tempo*))—I don't want to bore you, dear Herr Schönberg, with more details about this device and its advantages and the potential of further development.[3] Maybe you will consider the whole idea superfluous!—

Many warm, devoted regards

from your Berg

---

3. There is no evidence to suggest that Berg ever had his tempo machine built, nor have his notes and sketches for it been located.

## Berg to Schoenberg

Vienna, 27 January 1915

Dear Herr Schönberg.

Had I been found fit for service, I would have been called up in the next few days (1 February). This thought continues to haunt me. How different everything would be! How the passivity that has been tormenting me for months would then have been transformed into activity! As it is, though, everything I do is as under a cloud, a cloud that lifted only once with the news of your possible return to Vienna.[1] (But now we haven't heard anything more definite about that, either.) Life outside of oneself continues as usual. I tell you, dear Herr Schönberg, observing that is as horrible as the war is torturous. As if nothing had happened, as if unheard-of things weren't happening every hour, people here in Vienna live it up, there are premieres of operettas and burlesques "adapted to the times," every theater and movie house is overflowing, and truly—if it weren't for the inflation—there would be no reason to think of the war other than as a sensational event to titillate the imagination of newspaper readers. Again and again, when the sight of such godless activity fills me with new revulsion, I get the feeling that the war can't be over for a long time yet. For if it were what it has been described as: namely purifying, then it hasn't yet come anywhere close to fulfilling its purpose. Where filth lay, there it remains—just in a different guise! It seems it will never vanish from this earth, and the purifying power of these momentous events and times will never be felt by more than a few people, who are able to stop and reflect. All the others—as I once heard you say—get "ground in the dust" anyway.—

Many warmest regards, dear Herr Schönberg,

from your Berg

P.S. I keep forgetting to ask what I am to do with the piano reduction of the Chamber Symphony.[2] Should I send it to you? Or keep it here?—

1. With the outbreak of war, Schoenberg was considering the possibility of having to return to Vienna for military service.
2. Berg had completed his four-hand piano reduction of Schoenberg's Chamber Symphony at about this time; it was never published.

*Schoenberg to Berg*

Berlin-Südende, 1 February 1914 [1915]

Dear Berg,

My best thanks for your house-hunting efforts.[1] If you should see anything suitable in Hietzing, Hütteldorf, or Purkersdorf, please write. So far everything has been too expensive. I can't go over 2,400 kronen. But it can be an old cottage where one would install things oneself (bathroom, toilet, etc). On the other hand it must have at least 6–7 <u>rooms</u>, as well as servants' quarters and rooms one could turn into bathrooms or toilets. Also pantry, etc. I wouldn't mind attic rooms. What I'd really like to have is 3–4 large rooms upstairs, 3–4 large rooms downstairs (with adjoining rooms). Kitchen downstairs, or in a side room. It doesn't have to be a villa, anyway, that's not to be had at this price. But gas, electric light, water, plumbing: that's necessary. Have you considered Klosterneuburg, Weiding?—

I already mentioned the new arrangement of my room to you. A portion of it can be seen on the enclosed picture (on the drawing it's crosshatched:[2] No. 1 red, No. 2 blue, No. 3 green). Now I finally have a comfortable little study with an adjoining room that serves as a sitting room (that was my wife's idea). Of course I would be sorry to give that up now. But that's the way it is with us; no sooner do we feel comfortable in an apartment, then we move out. We haven't quite reached that stage yet. But we often think of moving. Sometimes we even think of going to Graz or Salzburg. It depends on whether we continue to feel comfortable here.

I thank you very much for your affectionate letter[3] and can assure you that I, too, would be very happy to be back with all of you again. What does Frau Mahler think of my idea?[4]

Let me hear from you soon. Many warm regards

Your Arnold Schönberg

I consider your invention of a "tempo notation device" very good. Particularly because I described exactly the same device to Jalowetz 2 years ago in Göhren. Incidentally: interesting that we should hit upon the same idea. Have the device built. I don't think it would cost more than 20–30 kronen. It involves a precise clockwork mechanism connected with a roll that turns and at the same time unrolls a strip at a given length per minute. This strip is gridded. And a spring (as in a barometer that indicates the day's air pressure) marks the various pulses of the measure. Very simple and surely not expensive. Any clockmaker should be able to do it for you!

I heard yesterday that Horwitz is living in Vienna. Have you heard from him? Has he contacted you? Was he taken at the military examination?[5]

1. Schoenberg's students had been enlisted to help find him a house; Hertzka, too, had promised to try to find him a rent-free apartment for the duration of the war.
2. The drawing has not been preserved.
3. Berg first responded to the possibility of Schoenberg's return to Vienna in a letter of 18 January.
4. Schoenberg wished to conduct a concert of classical works in Vienna, a project that required the backing of influential patrons. Alma Mahler had gone to Berlin in February to visit Walter Gropius, at which time Schoenberg mentioned the plan to her.
5. Karl Horwitz had returned to Vienna from Prague, where he had conducted at the Deutsches Landestheater since 1911. He, too, had been rejected for military service, as Berg tells Schoenberg in a letter of 17 February.

## Berg to Schoenberg

Vienna, 15 February 1915

As you could tell from one of my last letters, dear Herr Schönberg, my realization of how the world is dealing with the war has depressed me severely, and by now my belief that everything would be better and purer after the war has quite vanished. Now Karl Kraus's lecture the day before yesterday has reinforced that feeling.[1] He read many glosses from recent years and in the way he read them now, and in conjunction with the present situation, they often took on a completely new meaning, in any case appeared in a completely new light. And the "laughter" [*Lachen*] in the poorly-attended small hall of the Musikverein really often struck one like "a pool of blood" [*Blutlache.*][2] For that's how he justified the apparently lighthearted program in a preface preceding the glosses. In this preface he attacked the world in holy rage, the world upon which he has so often wished destruction, and of course he attacks it there where the life of the world is mirrored: in the newspaper. Above all he's outraged by the demands for relaxing censorship and he marvels that the papers don't recognize the censor's immeasurable forbearance in withholding perhaps: 2 or 3 truths, while permitting a hundred thousand lies (this, though the censors certainly wouldn't allow *him* even to reprint newspaper reports). And again he pleads with the censors (—in a tone, though, that already betrays resignation and the fact that he has given up hope—) to abolish newspapers now—or never!— Of the other excrescences of these times, to which people have already learned to accommodate themselves, I can recollect the renewed awakening of their ideals— above all that of the tourist industry. In Vienna there are plans for a figure carved in wood which, à la "Stock im Eisen,"[3] is to be covered with nails and erected to the eternal memory of these times. This "Schmock in Eisen,"[4] "shrouded by legend," will naturally boost the tourist industry of coming centuries. Not only is one permitted to pound a nail into the figure for one krone, but the names of the 500,000 donors, who wouldn't have a krone to spare for a blind soldier, are to be passed down to posterity.—

I hope this introduction will appear soon in an issue of the *Fackel*, so that I can send it to you, dear Herr Schönberg. I may have forgotten the most beautiful and important things and told you only the things I was able to understand and remember after one hearing.—

After the program, Kraus decided to read something more from the *Neue Freie Presse*. He juxtaposed a field report of the most terrible and heartrending events of a battle with the opening of a new Viennese café. I can't imagine a more outrageous

---

1. The program of Kraus's 13 February lecture, as well as the lecture's introduction, "Der Ernst der Zeit und die Satire der Vorzeit" were printed in the next issue of the *Fackel* XVI / 405 (23 February), 14–20.

2. Berg paraphrased the concluding sentence of Kraus' introduction, 20, when he speaks of laughter hitting the ground like a pool of blood, in German a play on the words *Lachen* (laughter) and *Lache* (pool).

3. The *Stock im Eisen* is a 16th-century tree trunk embedded with nails, located in Vienna's first district at the corner of Kärntnerstrasse and Stephansplatz; because its history is obscure many legends have grown around it and made it a favorite tourist attraction.

4. *Schmock*, originally an insulting Yiddish term for a fool, had at the turn of the century also acquired the meaning of an unscrupulous journalist, no doubt Kraus's intended target here.

document of our times! I left the lecture bitterly depressed. To be sure, I had already been deeply upset by another event that day: bidding Webern farewell.[5] Though the parting was made easier by his confidence that he would be home again in May once the war is over; but not only must I begin to miss him again, after having spent so many lovely hours and afternoons with him (most recently reveling jointly over the Chamber Symphony) . . . . . , the great uncertainty of his fate also weighs heavily on me.—

I shall send this letter registered. Not because I consider it important, but because I'm always afraid that my letters may not be reaching you, dear Herr Schönberg, and that you may think I'm not writing.—Many warmest regards to you, dear Herr Schönberg,

from your Berg

Also all the best to your esteemed wife and the dear children.

---

5. Webern had been inducted into the army earlier that month and had left Vienna to join a regiment headquartered in Klagenfurt.

*Berg to Schoenberg (letterhead: J. Berg / Wien VI., Linke Wienzeile 118, crossed out)*

[Vienna] 25 February 1915

I just received your card of the 21st, dear Herr Schönberg.[1]—Since the monthly installment is always sent directly by the bank (even the last one was sent by wire), the bank itself always deducts the fees from the fund automatically. As far as the fund is concerned: at the moment there is just one installment in the account (c. 500 kronen). That was due at the end of March and intended for April. As you were told last year, dear Herr Schönberg (I believe Webern did so on the occasion of the Orchestra Songs in Prague), the fund will continue until the end of 1915, in other words definitely through the months May to December 1915, in monthly installments of 500 kronen. Some money is still coming in, some is still outstanding at present, and the rest will certainly be raised. So, dear Herr Schönberg, you can count on these monthly installments with absolute certainty for the rest of this year. My thoughts and plans naturally extend beyond this year, but for now that is "speculation, wishful thinking."[2] Perhaps things will have changed so much by then (end of 1915) that you will be relieved of these worries, dear Herr Schönberg! Frau Mahler is going to do everything in her power to make you known for what you are: the greatest living conductor. The first step has apparently been taken. Immediately upon her return to Vienna she invited my wife and me and in her own magnificent way told us of her visits with you in Berlin. She was most delighted and enthusiastic about everything and immediately took steps to carry out your plan for a classical concert. I suggested the Philharmonic. And now today I found out (from my wife, who had been driving with her) that a large-scale benefit concert (under influential

---

1. In his 21 February postcard, Schoenberg asked for detailed and factual information on his Viennese financial accounts.
2. Schoenberg had implored Berg to stick to facts and not engage in "speculation; wishful thinking."

patronage of some sort) is to take place under your direction in the large hall of the Musikverein: Beethoven's IX$^{th}$ Symphony with the Philharmonic and the Opera Chorus. Frau Mahler has written to you in the matter, doubtless at much greater length than I, since of course I don't know details (rehearsals (chorus!!) (soloists?) etc.). In the 1$^{st}$ delirium of joy I wanted to telegraph all that to you. But no matter how long my telegram, I would probably have unsettled rather than surprised you, and then just when I had decided to write, your card came, which I can now answer right away. (You're probably not in the least interested in this background information, but at the prospect of seeing you in March—and on such a splendid occasion—I'm so overjoyed that I'm in danger of losing my reason!)

And now many, many warm regards

from your Berg

I shall get the 8 issues of the *Fackel* and send them to you soon. I hope you have received the most recent issue.[3]

---

3. Schoenberg asked Berg to order certain back issues of the *Fackel* for him. The most recent issue was number 405 of 23 February.

*Schoenberg to Berg (picture postcard: Zeppelin über Antwerpen)*

[Berlin-Südende, 14 March 1915]

Dear Berg,

2 requests: 1. please send the monthly installment immediately by express money order. 2. Ask Frau Mahler about the concert. I want to know where I stand.[1] Many thanks for the issues! Also for the letter regarding my *Einjährig* status.[2] I'll go to the consulate tomorrow to inquire. Do the same for me in Vienna. Surely you have some influential contacts to short-cut the bureaucratic procedure.[3] But I am Hungarian.[4]

Many warmest regards

Schönberg

1. Schoenberg follows this inquiry with a telegram of 17 March, but Berg, in both a telegram and a letter of 18 March 1915, was unable to give him any more information about the concert than Alma Mahler was willing to divulge.

2. In a letter of 11 March Berg advised Schoenberg to try to obtain the *Einjährig-Freiwilligen Recht*, a status normally granted to volunteers with higher educational degrees, which consisted of one year's service in a regiment of one's choice, with the possibility of rapid promotion to officer's rank. Since Schoenberg did not have such a degree and had never held an official position at an educational institution, he had to make a special application for the status, which was granted him on 31 May 1915.

3. Berg's parents-in-law had connections with the Austrian court, and Schoenberg was probably aware of the rumor that Helene Berg was an illegitimate daughter of the Emperor Franz Josef by Anna Novak Nahowski. In the letter of 18 March Berg responds to Schoenberg's reference, "I assume you were only joking about the 'influential contacts'?!".

4. Since Schoenberg's father, Samuel Schönberg, had been born in Hungary, his sons retained Hungarian citizenship. Berg informed Schoenberg on 19 March 1915 that he would therefore have to apply to the Hungarian Ministry of National Defense for the *Einjährig-Freiwilligen Recht*.

*Berg to Schoenberg*

[Vienna, 30 March 1915]

Dear Herr Schönberg,

Upon receiving your card of the 24th yesterday, I immediately visited Frau Mahler, who told me the following:[1] I. she had only just received the score; she had lent it to a German conductor (Bodanzky, I think). And therefore couldn't send it to you any earlier. She also has a complete, revised set of parts. These have been included with the revised Mahler score placed at your disposal.—II. Chorus and alto soloist still haven't been decided. But you are not to worry about that, dear Herr Schönberg. Presumably the chorus will be the 13-Linden Chorus, which has sung the IX[th] frequently. The Singverein can't. There are always great obstacles to overcome in arranging a concert like this, but we are to entrust that to Frau Mahler and her advisors. In any case it's all set except for chorus and alto soloist. As follows: The concert will take place 26 April (not 27th), the last rehearsal is 25 April. (IV.) More than 3 rehearsals are impossible. (III.) You yourself, dear Herr Schönberg, are to let her know about the choral and soloists' rehearsals. Likewise when you're thinking of coming to Vienna. In your next letter to Frau Mahler, I think you should state all your wishes in this regard. Perhaps on a separate sheet, which she can pass on to her advisors.[2] That sheet should (in my opinion) also include all the performance forces. Possibly no one has yet given that any thought and it might cause you problems later on. In addition to requiring 8 horns and 4 trumpets, Mahler also mentions "doubling forces" in some passages of the score. I believe this refers to the woodwinds (or just flutes?). Since the orchestra is to be combined from the Konzertverein and Tonkünstler Orchestras, it shouldn't be difficult to come up with such reinforcements. (In any case I, too, would like to interject a wish here *pro domo*: namely that I be permitted to attend the rehearsals. Höllering will have a say in the concert and might "make a fuss" again if a few people wish to attend rehearsals.[3] Perhaps you could avert this eventuality from the outset, dear Herr Schönberg! Joining me in this wish are, besides my wife, my Vienna friends and students, Linke, Steuermann, Polnauer, Schmid, etc.)

I can't begin to tell you, my dear Herr Schönberg, how very much I'm looking forward to your coming! Just see that you come very soon!! It has been such a long time since I last saw you. And the IX[th] under you! I'm already diligently studying the score. I'm amazed by Mahler's changes. In many passages I can't help thinking that it takes great courage to make such major changes in the work of one of the greatest! I'm very, very curious to hear your opinion.—And now many, many warm regards

from your Berg

Please give my best to your dear wife and Jalowetz and his wife.[4] We're very

---

1. In this response to Schoenberg's postcard of 24 March, Berg keys his answers to the Roman numerals of Schoenberg's questions.

2. Ludwig Karpath and Richard Specht.

3. Georg Höllering, manager of the Tonkünstler Orchestra, had tried to prevent Berg, Webern, Stein, and Königer from attending one of the final rehearsals of the March 1914 *Gurrelieder*, despite Schreker's express wish that they do so.

4. Over Easter the Schoenbergs visited the Jalowetzes in Stettin.

happy at the prospect of seeing your dear family again soon. Until then my wife sends all of you the warmest regards.

*Schoenberg to Berg (special delivery letter)*

[Berlin-Südende, 8 April 1915]

Dear Berg,

I have yet to be informed whether the concert will take place. Since you don't have a chorus yet, it's pretty unlikely you could get one in time to publicize the concert properly. I really should assume that nothing will come of it, nonetheless I'll have no peace until I've been told straight out. Besides, I'm much less enthusistic about it than at the beginning. At that time I was motivated by the thought that my military examination would soon be followed by my induction and before that, as a farewell as it were, I would have liked to conduct a classical work for the first time in my life. Today I am rather more indifferent to that sentimental reason and feel, instead, that the present time may not be ideal for such an undertaking. Particularly as the arrangers are doing it with an element of sensationalism and with the intention of furthering my career. Now it's not easy for me to cancel without hurting Frau Mahler's and Frau Lieser's feelings.[1] I'm sure they have gone to quite some trouble, and it's distressing to have worked for nothing.

You must try to understand (even apart from my personal reasons) that it is extremely unpleasant for me to remain so long in uncertainty. That was why I asked you to take over the correspondence and hoped to receive clear and frequent news from you. But since your letter dated 30 April [March], which arrived with the score, I haven't heard a word from you! I hope you haven't been putting off communicating important information until you get an answer from me. After all: How can I possibly schedule the rehearsals? Only you can do that! Surely it is obvious: in order that I accomplish everything as quickly as possible, but without having to rehearse much more than 6 hours a day: 1–2 times chorus alone, once with each soloist individually, 1–2 times with all the soloists together at the piano, and then everyone for the last orchestra rehearsal. But you can probably imagine that it's unpleasant to have to decide that in my present mood and without knowing whether the thing will even come off!

That's why I ask you for: plentiful, factual, and detailed information. One sentence on each point, clear and concise, and without regard to style, but comprehensive, so I know where I stand. And without forgetting anything! Surely by now you have learned from my letters how to handle such matters!

One more thing: You shouldn't be surprised that I always need the money so much earlier these days. It's becoming increasingly difficult to make ends meet; this month, in particular, I've had unusually heavy expenses: rent, tuition, schoolbooks, taxes, etc. It's getting to be too much for me.

---

1. Alma Mahler's friend, Lilly Lieser-Landau, was underwriting the cost of the Beethoven concert.

Incidentally: your telegram that you're sending 200 kronen came yesterday.[2] But by noon today the money still wasn't here! In the future, the bank must commission a local bank <u>by wire</u> to send me the money <u>by wire</u>.—By the way, I also wrote once about my military situation; didn't you get that letter?[3]

I'd like to know whether it could be arranged that I serve with an Austrian regiment. Webern advises me to choose heavy artillery (without a horse).[4] But I think that would require patronage. Do you have any connections or do you know someone who does? If I don't come to Vienna I will have to arrange it by letter. *

My military examination here will be in early May. If I'm taken, I'll probably be called up very soon.

Oh yes: one has to volunteer (where?) if one wants to choose one's regiment, right?

Please write soon and <u>fully</u>.

Warm regards,

Your Arnold Schönberg

N.B.: 1) the scoring is clear from Mahler's parts. It is: double (i.e., @4) <u>woodwinds</u>, 8 horns, extra trumpets, and many strings.[5]

2) I shall arrive in Vienna between the 17th and 20th;[6] for 10 or 6 days, depending on the rehearsal schedule.

* I have already sent the application for the *Einjährig-Freiwilligen Recht* to the Hungarian Ministry. No answer yet.

---

2. Schoenberg had telegraphed Berg on 6 April 1915, requesting immediate transfer of his monthly installment.

3. In his postcard to Berg, postmarked 24 March, Schoenberg had discussed the possibility, given influential patronage, of joining an Austrian regiment.

4. The artillery regiments were generally preferred because of their relative safety.

5. Berg responds to the question of scoring in a letter of 16 April. Because both the Tonkünstler and the Konzertverein Orchestras suffered severe manpower shortages during the war, they had pooled their resources as of the end of 1914 (they later merged to form today's Wiener Symphoniker). At this time, however, they did not even have six horns between them, as Berg writes, and auxiliary forces had to be engaged.

6. Schoenberg arrived in Vienna on the evening of 19 April.

*Berg to Schoenberg*

Vienna, 11 April 1915

Now for the answers to your other questions, dear Herr Schönberg, which I promised in yesterday's express letter:[1] On an Easter card sent to you in Stettin, I wrote that I myself have no connections and don't know of anyone who could establish contact with Prof. Redlich,[2]—and that I had turned to Loos. * And that he was in Semmering over Easter (of course, who wasn't!). He is back now, but

---

1. In an express letter of 10 April Berg explained at length that he had no influence on the course of the concert arrangements and therefore could not give Schoenberg any more information than he received from Alma Mahler or read in the papers.

2. Josef Redlich, a member of the Austrian Parliament.

doesn't know of a way to enable you, a Hungarian citizen, to serve in an Austrian regiment: But he will try. No news from him yet. Nor from Redlich, to whom I finally wrote, explaining the matter and what it is you wish. However, if you intend to volunteer during wartime, Herr Schönberg, and possess the *Einjährig* status (which is of course practically assured), then you can choose your regiment yourself. That doesn't happen—as far as I have been able to find out—until after one has been declared fit for service. Webern did it that way and I wrote to him yesterday that he should inform you immediately about the exact procedure. I will be able to find out a bit more, too, and will let you know. But I wouldn't recommend heavy artillery, dear Herr Schönberg. Should you be accepted and go through training, you would be putting your hearing at a great risk!—

Your remark: "You shouldn't be surprised that I always need the money so much earlier these days!" pained me deeply. I can only say, my dear Herr Schönberg: that I am repeatedly amazed at how you manage—during these times and under your present circumstances (no students, no conducting fees, no possibility of remunerative work)—how you manage to get by. Please excuse my meddling in your private affairs: but I perceive that to be yet another sign of great brilliance, here apparent in being economical and in the ability to accommodate oneself.—

I don't think I've forgotten anything you asked me. I can think of only one task I attended to but haven't yet told you about: my visit to Klosterneuburg-Weidling, which I didn't mention because it was totally unsuccessful. No sewerage, well water!— And no luck in any of my other househunts either, though I keep trying. More about that when you get here.—

Oh yes! Have you had your passport validated, Herr Schönberg? If you don't have a _new_ one, the _old_ one must definitely be validated and (I believe) a picture attached. Otherwise you can't travel to Vienna.—

Finally—it's noon now—I have more information about the concert: it will be on the 26th. Chorus is the Philharmonic (reinforced), which has sung it before and will "rehearse" it with a Schreker student.[3] 2–3 rehearsals will be allotted to you. I.e., 1 with orchestra and 1–2 without orchestra. The solo quartet is: Förstel, Kirchner,[4] Cankl,[5] and Raatz-Brockmann.[6] The first 3 are in Vienna: Kirchner is with the Berlin Court Opera and is serving here as an officer, but will get leave for this. Cankl is a former Vienna Court Opera singer, is said to be very musical. Raatz-Brockmann is in Berlin and has sung the bass part countless times. Including in yesterday's performance under Löwe. [*Berg gives Raatz-Brockmann's Berlin address.*]

I hope you, dear Herr Schönberg, agree to all this. Once you are here, much can still be arranged as you desire. I have—as I've often said—no influence and can only get the scanty facts for you indirectly.—**

I cannot understand the delay with the telegraph transfer of funds on the 7th. I thought telegraphic _postal_ transfer was the most direct means and don't understand why it should be faster through the *Deutsche Bank*. Nonetheless, tomorrow, when

3. Probably Paul Breisach, who studied with Schreker 1912–19.
4. The Austrian tenor Alexander Kirchner sang at the Berlin Court Opera 1915–35.
5. The alto Marie Cankl-Richter, daughter-in-law of the conductor Hans Richter.
6. The German baritone and concert singer Julius von Raatz-Brockmann lived in Berlin.

I hope to be able to transfer the remainder, I will do it as you suggested.—
And now, many warm regards

from your Berg

\* Loos told me that he has contacts everywhere. For instance, he succeeded in placing Kokoschka in a regiment of dragoons in which only aristocrats serve, all the way up to princes.

\*\* I shall also wire the information, so you won't be kept waiting too long.

## Berg to Schoenberg

Vienna, 30 April 1915

Dear Herr Schönberg,

The enclosed card just arrived. Emmy Heim's Schönberg-Mahler song recital was very good.[1] With a pleasant, expressive voice she sang "Traumleben," "Verlassen," "Die Aufgeregten," "Waldsonne," "Befreit," then, after an intermission the "Lied der Waldtaube" and after another intermission 5–6 Mahler songs. Your songs aroused the greatest interest and very enthusiastic response. Commensurate with her interpretive ability, Emmy Heim sang the easier, earlier songs better and they were therefore more successful. Thus the most successful was the Waldtaube, likewise "Waldsonne." The applause was also very strong after "Aufgeregten" and "Befreit."—Steuermann did a fine job accompanying. The hall was sold out and, despite a simultaneous *Elektra* with Strauss, Mildenburg, and Gutheil, was attended by the so-called "cream": Schnitzler, Loos, etc., naturally also Frau Mahler and Frau Lieser; but only a few critics, thank heavens.

I'm still living entirely in the memory of the lovely, unforgettable days of your stay here![2] Only they passed too quickly,—went by as if in a dream. But the memory of the (—forgive me: despite your misgivings—) incomparably beautiful performance of the IX[th] and *Egmont* Overture, and the thought of the many magnificent words I gleaned from your conversations and also at the rehearsals, that will stay with me as long as I live!

Many warmest thanks and regards to you, dear Herr Schönberg, and your esteemed wife, from us both.

Your Berg

---

1. Emmy Heim's recital, entitled "Schönberg und Jung-Wien," took place on 28 April. "Jung-Wien" was a label applied to the younger generation of Viennese artists around the turn of the century and by 1915 would already have acquired a certain retrospective flavor.

2. Schoenberg's concert had taken place as scheduled, with an open dress rehearsal on 25 April, followed by the actual performance on 26 April in the large hall of the Musikverein. The concert, held as a benefit in aid of needy musicians, was received indifferently by the critics and Schoenberg himself was dissatisfied with the performance.

## Schoenberg to Berg

Berlin-Südende, 1 May 1915

Dear Berg,

Please write by return post to tell me whether the *Egmont* score has been found and Frau Mahler has it back. I had actually asked you in my telegram[1] whether Frau Mahler <u>already has the score.</u> But in your telegram you didn't respond to that!!![2] Please do so now.

I. Enclosed I'm sending you a letter to M. P. Prof. Redlich. Please do the following:

    1. Address it

    2. Write to Redlich that you are sending him the letter because I don't have his address

    3. <u>Send it registered mail</u>

    4. If there's no reply in 3–4 days, telephone Prof. Redlich, or better yet: go see him.

Please do all this exactly as I have told you.

II. Further, I'm enclosing letters for <u>Kirchner, Cankl, Förstel.</u> I don't have their addresses and unfortunately didn't have any stamps, either; that's why I must ask you to take care of it. Read all the letters; I'd like you to know their contents.

We didn't talk much in Vienna. I needed sleep and you were dreaming. Next time I come to Vienna I'll have to get more sleep, but you'll have to be more awake. That'll be the right combination.—That reminds me: you and your wife plan to visit us in Berlin. I hope things will be livelier then. Well now: warmest regards and my best thanks; also for the trouble you took with the concert.

Your Arnold Schönberg

I'd also like to know as soon as possible when I can expect the next installment. Please wire Dr. Redlich's information to me.

My examination is 20 May.

The harmonium song[3] is for Förstel.

---

1. Dated 30 April 1915.
2. Berg's 30 April telegram has not been preserved, but is elaborated in an express postcard of 5 May 1915. His letter of 6 May (below) addresses again all the pertinent questions.
3. "Herzgewächse."

*Berg to Schoenberg (letterhead: J. Berg / Wien VI., Linke Wienzeile 118)*

Vienna, 6 May 1915

Dear Herr Schönberg.

Many sincere thanks for your kind letter of 1 May 1915.—I shall answer the 6 points of that letter:

I. *Egmont* score: In response to the inquiry in your letter I immediately (early yesterday) sent you particulars in an express card and I answered your letter that same evening, referring you to the express card that was on its way.[1] Thus it is apparent that if Frau Mahler asked you for the score again after, i.e., later than her telegram of early 30 April, then she did so despite my having long since told her that the score was at Frau Lieser's and that she would have it back shortly, as indeed

---

1. Schoenberg had meanwhile sent yet another telegram, dated 5 May, asking about the *Egmont* score. Berg sent him an express postcard on 5 May 1915; a letter from that evening has not been preserved.

was the case.[2] Besides, (as of midday, 30 April) Frau Mahler knew from me that it wasn't a score with Mahler's revisions.—

II. Military examination: I sent your letter to Redlich right away and just received his reply. Among other things he writes: . . . "I shall immediately do what I can and shall write directly to Schönberg about it. Incidentally, I hope Schönberg will be declared unfit at the examination. . . ."

III. Letters to Kirchner, Cankl, and Förstel (the last-named with Harmonium song enclosed) have been expedited.

IV. Transfer of funds. Unfortunately I cannot answer your question as to when you can expect the next payment. About four weeks ago, when you telephoned for the previous monthly installment, I sent you a registered express letter,[3] dear Herr Schönberg, telling you how things stood with the fund and that judging by recent experiences and Frau Mahler's information, the monthly installments would not be transferable until the beginning of every month. I explained it so thoroughly at the time that I need not repeat it. But I'd like to add the following: I would urgently recommend, dear Herr Schönberg, that you approach Frau Mahler directly in this matter—that is, bypass me or any other intermediary. It was she who initiated the campaign, most of the results of the campaign are thanks to her efforts and influence, and she has repeatedly given us (Webern and me) her word that the monthly installments are to continue until the end of 1915. Even recently. And she places a certain value in staying in direct communication with you in this matter, Herr Schönberg. I know that when you turned to us concerning the fund, dear Herr Schönberg—you did it to spare Frau Mahler any inconvenience; but I also know that she invariably resented our independent actions. Well, —as long as money was there I didn't care; the important thing was to have carried out your wishes. But now that there is no money and the next installment perhaps not coming in until the end of the month, I'm helpless in the face of her negligence. That word came from my pen inadvertently. But I'll let it stand; for Frau M. frequently passes over important things with truly irresponsible negligence. It's easy for her to raise the necessary money on time: one word or a letter to one of the many millionaires with whom she is closely befriended would suffice. But even for that she needs effective prodding and in this case that can come only from you, Herr Schönberg, if she is really to live up to what she promised. We—even Webern—can't accomplish anything. For the 2 reasons above, which I repeat:

1. because she considers our actions high–handed. I.e., doesn't consider us authorized to dispose over the fund.

2. because she wants to deal personally with you in this matter and her pride is hurt by the intervention of an intermediary.

But also for a third reason. Namely, that she doesn't think much of us, or possibly anything at all, and instead of respecting our ideas, wishes, indeed our most urgent

---

2. Once the score of the *Egmont* Overture had been returned to Lilly Lieser, Berg considered the matter settled, but Alma Mahler insisted on having the score returned to her by Helene Berg, to whom it had originally been entrusted; this did not occur until 2 May and further telegrams, telephone conversations, and letters document the continuing misunderstanding.

3. Berg had responded to Schoenberg's telegram of 6 April with an express letter of 7 April.

requests, is prone to reject them from the start.

But if you, Herr Schönberg, were to turn to her, for instance write to her that you require the monthly installment at a certain time, she would consider it an honor and a pleasant duty to fulfill your wish. Only I would recommend, Herr Schönberg, that you do so in plenty of time—better yet: ahead of time, and—if she's taking too long—that you not hesitate to remind her of your wishes.

I only decided to give you this advice, dear Herr Schönberg, after careful consideration and realizing that it would be welcome and important to you, too, that these financial matters be handled with absolute reliability and promptness. Of course I'm terribly upset that that is not possible through me or Webern (even if he were in Vienna), or through any intermediary. For thus I also rob myself of an opportunity of serving you a little in this matter. But that's not at issue here. Regardless of my own feelings, I simply had to make the suggestion so as to avoid future problems, which might easily occur if at some point I were unable to transfer the monthly installment to you as desired and also incapable of raising it in time. That would have been seen as further evidence of my "dreaming" instead of keeping an eye on the fund, and evidence that the statement I am about to make is not true. For I declare—thus making a leap to the last point in your letter—

(V.) that I'm not "dreaming." The following may have given rise to this impression:

1. my being busy with the concert arrangements
2. my silent demeanor.—But:

1.) The inadequacies of the concert arrangements did not result from my not paying attention, my not being "on top of things," but were due rather to the fact that from the start so many things had been neglected by others. Given my belated involvement—achieved only with great difficulty—it was impossible to make up for what had previously been botched. After all, many, indeed the most important things, were kept from me, others were reported incorrectly. (I needn't name names.) And given such mismanagement, no wonder things didn't run smoothly. If I nonetheless appeared calm throughout, that doesn't mean I wasn't taking the matter seriously enough or wasn't totally preoccupied with it (—often during rehearsals and during walks and meals together, too—), it means, rather, that I am accustomed to controlling my nervousness and my anxiety in a way that might give the impression of a dreamer — So, too:

2.) my continual silence doesn't prove that I don't listen when you talk, Herr Schönberg, or that I don't take a stand on what is said, that I'm not just as delighted if at some point my opinion coincides with yours, or just as glad another time to correct what I recognize as a false opinion, that I don't absorb the thousands of new impressions that grow out of your conversation with others with just as much temperament as those "wakeful" ones, who give easy expression to their enthusiasm, concurrence, and temperament. Rather, my silence is due to my fear, ever since Leipzig-Amsterdam,[4] of annoying you with so much as the slightest remark, Herr Schönberg, of displeasing you by emphasizing my presence; and, caught up as I am

4. Berg is referring to his presence at the rehearsals and performances of the *Gurrelieder* and the Op. 16 Orchestra Pieces, in Leipzig and Amsterdam in March 1914.

in this almost pathological self-consciousness, I become utterly thunderstruck the very moment I want to say something and at that point I make that confused, dreamy—indeed idiotic impression that so justifiably annoys you. That's why I wish so fervently—as others aren't even capable of wishing (—for what are the joyous needs of others compared to this longing of mine, crying for deliverance after years of torment—) to be able to be with you again for a longer period of time:

(VI.) My trip to Berlin now merely depends on the results of my follow-up examination, which will be sometime between 25 May and 15 June.—

And now many, many warm regards, dear Herr Schönberg, to you and your esteemed wife (also from my wife)

Your Alban Berg<br>7 May, 1915

Today I shall begin to read the 3<sup>rd</sup> set of proofs for Erwartung.[5]—

*[Berg includes a clipping from the New York Staatszeitung announcing a performance of Schoenberg's Verklärte Nacht by the Kneisel Quartet.]*

---

5. In a postcard of 17 May Berg informs Schoenberg of the errors in this last set of *Erwartung* proofs.

## Schoenberg to Berg (registered letter)

Berlin-Südende, 17 May 1915

Dear Berg,

I want the enclosed letter[1] to be shown to Frau Mahler in case she questions your right to deal with her in this matter. You don't necessarily have to read it to her or she'll complain again that you come to her with letters from me (not that I think there's anything wrong with that). But please be sure to use it if there's any chance of a misunderstanding! It would be best if you simply begin by talking about my wishes and then later let her read the letter. At this point I find it hard to believe that Frau Mahler should revenge herself on me because I didn't return the music myself; or because I didn't let the churlish letter she wrote me go unanswered.[2] Some time I'll send you a copy of this exchange so you can form your own opinion. Incidentally, Steuermann can tell you everything even more fully.—

Apparently Frau Lieser is angry with me, too. I can't imagine why: presumably by infection. I gave her a little manuscript and she never even thanked me.[3] Perhaps you can find out why *she's* sore at me!—By the way, I've been waiting in vain for a letter from you in explanation of your last telegram (regarding the concert fee)![4] I must know what's going on; we can't possibly leave it there. I can't expand my

1. See following letter.
2. Alma Mahler's undated letter to Schoenberg accuses him of having been negligent with Mahler's scores. In a detailed reply of 7 May Schoenberg defends his conscientiousness and integrity.
3. The manuscript has not been identified. Once their differences were settled, Frau Lieser wrote a letter of thanks on 26 May 1915.
4. Since the concert had not shown a profit Ludwig Karpath had arranged to pay Schoenberg by subsuming his fee among other concert expenses.

morals to fit Karpath's mold!—I'd also very much like to know what Frau Mahler told you in justification of her vehement letter. And whether my reply brought her to her senses. I'm very sorry I have to be on such bad terms with her now. But believe me: it's all Karpath's fault! If you sleep with dogs you wake up with fleas!—

You're angry that I accused you of dreaming! But I would like to make you still angrier. So angry that you jump up and bash me over the skull (of course it needn't be *my* skull, I'm not volunteering)! Yes: you should either have told Höllering that he's a low-down liar or the abbreviated version: boxed his ears. You mustn't put up with that. I've never put up with anything of the sort!

So please: wake up! I stand by what I said! Today more than ever it's important to be a man. Remember, in a few months you may have to wield a bayonet!

Of course I'd rather do other things, too. But if necessary one must be able to do that sort of thing, too.

I'm very pleased that you want to come to Berlin. I'll be very happy to discuss various such matters with you. Then other things will clear up quite naturally.

Incidentally you are quite wrong to accuse me of treating you differently since Leipzig. Maybe it's you who has changed! You need the kind of work where you'd have to slug it out. You should look for that kind! Look at me: I have never stopped fighting and that's why I'm always wide awake. Of course: for I must always be prepared for the nightly ambush of conspirators [*Nachtangriffe der Dunkelmänner*].

Now then: let me hear soon, and warmest regards to you and your wife from my wife and me.

Your Arnold Schönberg

*Schoenberg to Berg (enclosed with preceding registered letter)*
Berlin-Südende, 17 May 1915

Dear Berg,

What you tell me about the current state of the fund is very disturbing. After repeated assurances, I thought I could count on having my family provided for at least until the end of the year, when I'm called up.—Nevertheless it is out of the question that I turn directly to Frau Mahler. Apart from the fact that her extremely "peculiar" letter (as regards tone and content) have made me realize that she lacks the proper esteem for my person and achievements, after all (my reply seems to have increased the tension)—apart from that, I also refuse to do it because it **has been demanded of me!** It simply wasn't right that none of you took me seriously when I wrote: that I wish all who contribute to the fund to remain unknown to me. I wanted anonymous donors. I admitted it quite openly: because I wished to avoid the humiliating state of indebtedness to anyone.

However that may now be, I maintain: it's not my fault if, against my will, administration of the fund has remained mired in fractious human relations. I wanted to deal with a machine, which would, undisturbed and impersonally, fulfill the promised obligations. Furthermore: an obligation (even if it's not legally binding!) has been established through the various assurances, and therefore must be met.

That's why I ask you to visit Frau Mahler immediately and request that through you she give me clear answers to the following questions.

1. Whether I can count on regular monthly installments until the end of December of this year as promised?

2. Whether, should administering the fund be disagreeable to her with her current opinion of my merit, she would like to turn over the list of contributors and administration of the fund to you and Stein.

Please wire your reply. I must at least know where I stand.

Warm regards to you and your wife

Your Arnold Schönberg

*Berg to Schoenberg (express letter; letterhead: J. Berg / Wien VI., Linke Wienzeile 118)*

Vienna, 21 May 1915

Dear Herr Schönberg,

Steuermann's telegram the day before yesterday reassured and pleased me more than I can say. At least that anxiety—and it was one of the gravest in this anxious time—is off my mind! I touch on yet another one in answering your 2 letters of the 17th. Since it's impossible to give a decisive reply with Frau Mahler out of town just now and since I'm incapable of saying even a portion of what I have to say in a telegram, I shall write to you express.

*[Berg explains at length the central role Alma Mahler had assumed in the collection for the Schönberg Fund, many of whose contributors were enlisted solely through her mediation. Furthermore, Berg states that according to Alma Mahler the fund would end not at the end of the year, but in August, since the last four installments of 500 kronen had been subsumed in the 2,000 kronen Mahler stipend granted Schoenberg that summer.]*

Of course I feel terrible at having to go into such detail and because the fund doesn't function automatically as you desired and as we expected in the initial months of its existence. If it had depended on Webern and me alone and if war hadn't broken out, our and your expectations in this regard could have been fulfilled. But the war made it such more difficult to raise money and only Frau M.'s participation made the fund possible at all, though it also gave the machine that "personal" aura we would have liked to avoid. She is, after all, only a woman! Her behavior now is as unpleasant as her actions at the outset of the campaign were magnificent. Being a woman to the n[th] power, she combines to the highest degree cultivation of the good with the bad characteristics of a woman, thus the negative are just as prominent as the positive and as disturbing as the others are gratifying. But that's why one must measure all her words and deeds only with the yardstick of a woman and cannot take her more seriously than she really is. None of that business about the scores was seriously motivated, certainly not the motivations she presumably told you. I think I know what her motivations are and I'll tell you sometime—for your amusement. One can't write that sort of thing! In any case the "sanctity of Mahler's manuscripts" is just a pretty phrase, with which, following a change of mood, she wanted to entrap us. How holy Mahler's manuscripts—really—are to her is apparent from the fact that an unpublished, unprinted manuscript of a Mahler string quartet[1] (an early work) was **accidentally found** in the **orchestral parts** of *Coriolan* lent to Horwitz.[2] And that may not be an isolated incident. I can only tell you, dear Herr Schönberg: since having gained some insight into how these sacred relics are kept and knowing that the house is frequented by Spechts and Karpaths, Strzygowsky's,[3] and various other Beckmessers, I tremble for Mahler's manuscripts.

Therefore I beg you, dear Herr Schönberg, not to take Frau Mahler's actions too seriously. At bottom she knows—as far as a woman can comprehend it at all—**who you are** and she surely desires that these differences be cleared away. It's nothing but capriciousness, born of the moodiness of a woman used to dispensing favor and disfavor according to momentary caprice and whim. For love to turn to hate and hate to love, creatures like that need no greater reason than we need to decide between a light and dark tie. Maybe that is what Weininger calls the amorality of woman.[4] That would also explain everything else: the playful, unscrupulous ability of one and the same creature to adapt herself: to the morality of a Mahler and the immorality of a Karpath.—

Oh yes! Concert fee! It was Frau M.'s wish that I send you the telegram. Another situation where I knew nothing until it was too late to change anything. Nothing can be done about it now; exposure now would create unbelievable confusion and place Frau M. in a most embarrassing situation. But as it's an affair for which only those involved with it bear responsibility and not you, Herr Schönberg, who only *heard* of it (unnecessarily) as a fait accompli, I think it will be possible—as indeed it is necessary—to let the matter rest.— — —

As you point out very correctly, Frau Lieser's behavior can only be explained in terms of infection. Both women seem to be in a relationship of mutual dependency. Frau Lieser at any rate in one of moral dependency upon Frau M.— —

If Frau M. didn't answer your letter, then surely out of impotence. How can a woman's illogic stand up to a man's logic?! Since her churlishness didn't provoke churlishness in reply, which would have given her a weapon with which to trump the man . . . she has only one recourse: silence! Were she to speak, she would have to admit that you are right and that doesn't often happen with a woman, even when she has long since realized that she's in the wrong, and even if she's on ever so high an intellectual level.—

1. Possibly Mahler's incomplete A-minor Piano Quartet, first published in 1980.
2. Karl Horwitz had borrowed the parts to Beethoven's *Coriolan* Overture for a benefit concert he conducted in the large hall of the Musikverein on 31 March with the Tonkünstler Orchestra.
3. The Austrian art historian Josef Strzygowsky had been a friend of Gustav Mahler.
4. Through his book, *Geschlecht und Charakter* (Vienna, 1903), the Austrian psychologist Otto Weininger had exerted a tremendous influence on an entire generation of Viennese intellectuals. Many of Berg's remarks about Alma Mahler reflect his familiarity with Weininger's work, which postulated basic characterological differences between the sexes.

Incidentally: on only one occasion did I ever show <u>one card</u> of yours to Frau M. It contained urgent, purely factual questions about the concert that <u>only she</u> could answer. If she maintains that I am <u>"always coming to her with letters"</u> she's probably confusing me with Schreker, who as everyone knows, goes about peddling letters addressed to him.—

Proofreading for *Erwartung* is finished. Today Stein will send you the list of mistakes and questionable spots we found.

And now my thanks, dear Herr Schönberg, for your kind and friendly words at the conclusion of your letter and very, very warm regards to you and your esteemed wife from my wife and me.

Your Berg

## Berg to Schoenberg[1]

Vienna, 10 June 1915

Dear Herr Schönberg,

Stein told me that you had expected the monthly installment <u>earlier</u> and that I should immediately have <u>wired</u> you the money that was paid into the fund at the end of the month (May). To that I must respond as follows: In a registered letter of 7 April I wrote to you in great detail, dear Herr Schönberg, about the state of the fund and that Frau Mahler had told me she wouldn't be able to transfer the installments until the beginning of each month. I <u>repeated</u> that in a registered letter[2] <u>following</u> the Vienna concert (IX[th]), so as to save you problems that might arise in the future, should you wire for the money when I was not in a position to send it. At that time I also wrote that I had no right to administer the fund and that in case of urgent financial need it would be advisable to turn <u>directly</u> to Frau M. To your response that you could not or would not do this, I answered[3] that of course it would only be <u>in the event</u> that you needed the installment <u>earlier</u>. Whereupon you wired that we were not to pressure Frau M. in the financial matter and on 24 May you wrote "We must wait and see whether the June installment is sent punctually."[4] Nevertheless, I was uneasy as month's end approached; for although I had warned you frequently that you couldn't count on the money before the beginning of each month, I had to assume that there was a limit to this "wait and see." What would happen if Frau M. didn't remember it in time? Then you wouldn't even know to whom to turn with any hope of success. On my own I didn't dare send the partial sum that had been paid into the fund; I would, after all, be risking your reproaches: "Didn't I tell you, Berg, that we should wait. . . . etc." But I did want you to know that the fund contained something and that it would be possible (if

1. This letter is preceded by a flurry of cards and telegrams precipitated by the delayed arrival of the June installment of the Schoenberg fund.

2. Dated 6 / 7 May 1915.

3. Schoenberg's response is dated 17 May, Berg's reply is dated 25 May.

4. Schoenberg's telegram is dated 26 May, his 24 May instructions were on a postcard. Alma Mahler had visited the Schoenbergs on 25 May and although the question of the fund was not settled, she and Schoenberg were tentatively reconciled. In both his postcard and telegram Schoenberg instructed Berg to refrain from pressuring Alma Mahler.

you didn't want to wait) to withdraw at least 400 kronen.[5] Of course it was also possible that Frau M. had sent the payment from somewhere else and that my fear that you were being subjected to waiting in complete uncertainty was unfounded. In any case, dear Herr Schönberg, I wanted to give you the option of revising your 24 May order not to do anything! Which is exactly what you did in your telegram of the 31st:[6] namely that I transfer the partial sum immediately.

Fortunately Frau M. had returned to Vienna on the 31st. Upon her instructions—in other words before receipt of your telegram, which didn't arrive until that night—I was able—as I told you in a card[7]—to commission the Anglo Bank to wire the Deutsche Bank to transfer 500 kronen to you. Despite the fact that you had still not received this money by the 7th (even though the Deutsche Bank sent the Anglo Bank confirmation of a transfer to you on 1 June), I won't blame the Deutsche Bank (though it's due solely to their slovenly organization that you were placed in such a dreadful predicament, dear Herr Schönberg)—instead I will calmly characterize it as: my fate. That fate, which for years now has always made me appear disagreeable to you, if not through my own doing, then nevertheless in association with events that cause you annoyance. I remain unshaken in my firm belief in this fate, I could write a book on the subject; but even more interesting is the fact that it always involves a fateful number. The number 23! Without going into the many events in my life that have coincided with this number, I'll cite just a few of the more recent examples: I received your first telegram (to demand redress) on 4.6! [4 June] $(46 = 2 \times 23)$ The telegram bore the number Berlin-Südende 46 $(= 2 \times 23)$ $12 / 11$ $(12 + 11 = 23)$. The 2nd telegram bore the number $24 / 23$ and was sent off at $11:50$ $(1150 = 50 \times 23)$. Incidentally: Early in 1914, when beginning the campaign for the Schönberg fund, we (Webern and I) often met at Frau Mahler's, Pokoreygasse 23.—A delayed transfer of the monthly installment resulted in an unforgettably reproachful card from you. I should have transferred the money on 23 May 1914.—The first orchestra rehearsal of the IXth, instead of taking place in the evening as I had originally told you, took place in the afternoon of 23 April. Etc.

But never mind my destiny! What matters is the fund. I shall write to Frau Mahler in the next few days (Franzensbad, Hotel Holzer); shall point out once again the gravity of the situation. Above all point out how urgent it is that the money be deposited in the fund now, so that the next installments can be sent on time. But also to entreat her most urgently that she continue to help us (Stein and me): the fund simply must not end!—Despite your injunction not to pressure Frau Mahler, I can do so now that I was declared "fit" at the follow-up examination and will soon be called up* and it is crucial that I leave with this financial matter settled, or at least in responsible hands.—

I went to see Redlich the day before yesterday. He sends you many warm regards, dear Herr Schönberg, and was very understanding and appreciative, but couldn't give me much hope of fulfillment. It would have been possible earlier (about 4

5. Communicated in a letter of 30 May.
6. Actually dated 1 June.
7. Dated 1 June.

months ago). Earlier he would have been able to procure all sorts of favors for our friend,[8] indeed more than that, just as it would have been possible in your case. But now it is only possible through a great coincidence (contacts with a specific individual). Perhaps Redlich can manage to set up this contact. But we certainly can't count on it.—I shall contact Loos, too.—

Many warm regards, dear Herr Schönberg,

from your Berg

* The follow-up examinations proved necessary primarily due to Italy's intervention (declaration of war 23 May 1915).—I am to report to the Landstrasse Hauptstrasse Nr. 146

---

8. Berg is referring to Webern, who had been promoted several times and had just been transferred to Fronleiten near Bruck on the Mur; see footnote 8 of Berg's letter of 27 July 1915.

*Berg to Schoenberg (postcard)*

Vienna, 14 June 1915

Thank you very much, dear Herr Schönberg, for your card of 9 June.[1] There isn't much to say about my examination. I'm not surprised I was taken; indeed, I was surprised I wasn't taken the first time. Apart from my asthma, which can't be diagnosed—unless I happen to be having an attack—there's nothing wrong with me. And my physique?! My narrow chest! After seeing some of the figures at the examination, I immediately realized that I would be one of the approximately 30% to be taken. Linke and Horwitz were also taken. We won't be called up until 15 July, instead of 21 June as originally announced.* Steuermann already has to leave on 21 June. Since I must stay in Vienna as long as possible on account of the houses, I shall serve with the Deutschmeister,[2] to whom I was assigned anyway. (For my brother[3] was taken, too.) Of course I shall make use of my *Einjährig-Freiwilligen Recht*. (It's practically impossible to get assigned to any branch but that of infantry. Unless one has a horse![4])

Your conviction that the war won't last much longer makes me very happy. The present situation and the probable course of events seem to justify such confidence. But I wasn't really convinced until I saw your words. Many thanks! And many warm regards

from your Berg

* I just found out that it may be 21 June, after all.

---

1. Schoenberg wrote to Berg when he found out that Berg had passed his military follow-up examination.
2. Popular name for the Viennese infantry regiment "Hoch- und Deutschmeister," founded in 1695.
3. Charly Berg.
4. Ownership of horse was a prerequisite for service in the artillery.

*Schoenberg to Berg*

Berlin-Südende, 15 June 1915

Dear Berg,

I'm sorry to have to tell you that you're wrong, although you used almost two pages trying to prove that you were right:

I. Because I had initially written that you were to go to Frau Mahler with a letter from me and demand that she keep her promise, my subsequent telegram was worded: don't pressure Frau Mahler. II. If I wrote, "we must wait and see whether the June installment is sent punctually" that question was already 4/5 answered in the "affirmative" when 400 of the 500 kronen were deposited in the fund. I don't understand why you assumed that Frau Mahler might send the money directly to me since she had never done so before. III. It was obvious that I already needed the money by the 16th, as I had needed it by the 16th the previous month, too. IV. Instead of transferring the money to me, the Deutsche Bank should have "wired" it!

I believe I've shown that I'm right!

But maybe it's true that 23 is your unlucky number; if so then it was more mine this time. Incidentally, everyone has a number like that, but it doesn't necessarily have to be unlucky, it's simply one of the numbers that come into question. In connection with other numbers I'm sure it can have other and more favorable meanings. So you mustn't lose sleep over the fact that your induction involves so many 23's. After all, other numbers show up as well. Anyway: if nothing worse happens to you than happened with me, then it's not even so terrible. In any case, you must see that you become less dependent on these lucky and unlucky numbers by doing your best to ignore them!

So you'll be called up as early as July! We'll see each other before then, since we've been invited to spend our vacation with Frau Lieser and will arrive in Vienna around the 5th. I also plan to visit Webern.—I'm positive the war will be over before you get to the front!

Let me hear from you soon. Warm regards,

Your Arnold Schönberg


*Schoenberg to Berg (postcard)*

Berlin-Südende [17 June 1915]

Dear Berg,

You absolutely must get yourself a horse and join the artillery. After all, you must have relatives to whom you're worth that much! If they all pitched in together (though in this case it would also be possible alone) it wouldn't be so terribly expensive. It would probably cost at most 5–6,000 kronen! I know my wife and mother would do it for me! Show your military readiness by requisitioning this sum of money! A soldier has to know how to requisition, too.

Warm regards

Schönberg

## Berg to Schoenberg

Vienna, 20 June 1915

Thank you very much, dear Herr Schönberg, for your letter of the 15th. The news that you are coming to Vienna was an unbelievably joyous surprise for me. Not just for the purely selfish reason that I will see you again so soon, but also because Frau Lieser's invitation will presumably permit you and your dear family to enjoy a pleasant summer. I shall visit Frau Lieser right away. I'd like to know (— naturally without asking straight out—) whether the invitation applies to: her Hietzing house or the one in Semmering? That's not clear from your letters to Stein and me. Since my training will be in Vienna, I would naturally prefer that you spend your vacation in Vienna. But probably you would much prefer the Semmering. Anyway, the news made me tremendously happy and relieved me of a great anxiety.—

You are absolutely right, dear Herr Schönberg, in refusing to allow that a certain number—in my case the number 23—necessarily has to be an "unlucky" number. I myself have plenty of evidence that the number is also associated with good luck. It's just that in my letter before last I—once again—did not express myself clearly enough: I spoke of my fate during these last years in causing you so much inconvenience, and as evidence for my belief cited the fact that "my" number invariably appeared in connection with it. This number has always played a crucial role in my life and (since it seems as immutable and as unavoidable as the events it accompanies), I designated it as fateful, instead of just calling it significant. That it could also be a lucky number for me in connection with things related to you, was already apparent in the 1st performance of the *Gurrelieder*, which was a significant and joyous event in my life in more than one respect. Repeatedly scheduled and postponed in the 1912 / 1913 season, the performance finally took place 23 February 1913. So I didn't mean that the number 23 is an unlucky number for me, though it has recently been associated with events I needn't hesitate to designate as unlucky. Even if "nothing **happened**" to me, as you correctly point out, what I felt when you were plagued by such a series of aggravations—and what I feel now that I'm the one being blamed, is bad luck enough to overshadow every other event. Even that of my "induction," which by the way I only meant to describe as an unavoidable—not unlucky—phase of my life when I pointed out the peculiar convergence with the number 23. Nor do I—quite frankly—have any feelings of foreboding that harm might thereby result for me or others.

In any case your advice, that I become less dependent on these lucky and unlucky numbers, has finally allowed me to imagine the possibility of such freedom, the possibility of circumventing one's destiny, and thus also the belief that I can and will succeed in doing so.

Nevertheless, I must tell you briefly, dear Herr Schönberg—in this connection— about a book I had never heard of before that I came across by chance last summer—which seemed to confirm my old belief in the number 23. It comprises biological lectures by the well-known Berlin scholar Wilhelm Fliess: *Vom Leben und Tod*,[1] in which he espouses the belief that life and divisions in the lives of all living

---

1. The biologist Wilhelm Fliess's *Vom Leben und Tod* was first published in Vienna in 1909.

creatures proceed periodically, resulting in periods that are always divisible by 28 and 23. (As it happens, one year has $\underline{28^2 + 28 - 23} = 365$ days.) He proves this with
$$\phantom{xxxxxxxxxxxxxxxxxxx}4$$
extensive and absolutely amazing statistics for plants: (for instance a Clivia gets four shoots; they appear (to give just one example!) on

| | | | days |
|---|---|---|---|
| | 10/XI | 1901 | |
| | | | }28 |
| | 8/XII | — | |
| | | | }28 |
| | 5/1 | 1902 | |
| | | | }28 |
| | 2/II | 1902 then spontaneously a | |
| | | | }23 |
| bud appears on | 25/II | — | |
| | | | }23 |
| the blossom on | 20/III | — and the blossom falls off | |
| | | | }23 |
| spontaneously on | 12/IV | | |

in the case of animals (statistics from Brehm:[2]) ostrich female lays one egg

| | | | |
|---|---|---|---|
| on | 15/1 | 1857 | |
| | | | }368 = 16 × 23 days |
| the 2nd— | 18/II | 1858 | |

The same female starts incubating

| | | | |
|---|---|---|---|
| on | 2/VII | 57 | |
| | | | }253 = 11 × 23 days |
| and on | 12/III | 58 | |

Similar examples for horses, dogs, etc.) then also for humans, but not just for individuals, but also for birth and death dates, stages of life, periodicity of illness in whole families, generations, indeed nations; for the relationship of birth and death dates of a man and wife within individual families, royal lines, nations, etc.—— and the conclusion is that the woman's number is 28, that of the man 23. It's nearly impossible to choose the most convincing examples from the wealth of examples; it has to be read in context. If I weren't afraid of annoying you with the unreasonable suggestion that you read a statistical/scientific book, dear Herr Schönberg, I would ask whether I might send it to you. But of course I can do that when you come to Vienna. There may be a chance to do so, since I won't be inducted until the 15th (the date was postponed definitively from 21 June to 15 July) and you will be arriving around the 5th.

2. *Tierleben*, a standard six-volume reference work on the animal world, was written by the zoologist Alfred Brehm between 1864–69.

I'll write again before your arrival, Herr Schönberg. I hope Stein will soon have good news about Loos's efforts. Very many warm regards

from your Berg

P.S. It's finally raining. After about 6 weeks of drought! It reminded me of the dry and wonderfully beautiful Indian summer of 1914, about which I wrote at the time that I associated it with all the shooting. Don't you think, dear Herr Schönberg, that the enormous May offensive[3] (sometimes as many as 300,000 shots in 1– 2 days, east and west) is the reason it doesn't rain (just like *Wetterschiessen* in the Alps, where a dozen shots can drive away a thunderstorm). In any event the meteorologists are puzzled: The *Neue Freie Presse* writes: "that the weather maps show decidedly bad weather patterns, but, the unfavorable barometric pressure notwithstanding, we have only partial and temporary cloudiness and, aside from a few short, insignificant thundershowers, absolutely no precipitation."[4]—

---

3. During the joint German-Austrian offensive of May–September 1915, Austria succeeded in recapturing large areas of Galicia and Poland.

4. Berg quotes from the weather report of the war zone, "Das Wetter auf den Kriegsschauplätzen," from the 20 June edition of the *Neue Freie Presse.*

## Berg to Schoenberg

Vienna, 27 June 1915

Dear Herr Schönberg,

In response to your card of the 17th I have to say: It's impossible to join the artillery, since they don't accept anyone any more—not even with a horse! On the contrary, people are being transferred from artillery to infantry. But quite aside from the fact that it's impossible, I never really considered trying to lighten my military service that way and my wife has thankfully been spared having to raise the sum required for a horse. If it had been necessary she would naturally have done so; but I'm very glad the necessity and thus financial dependence on my wife and relatives, against which you once warned me, Herr Schönberg, has not occurred. After all, the sum of 5–6,000 kronen seems like a great deal to me, representing as it does more than ¾ of our yearly income. And I could certainly never have accepted it from my mother: because of the simultaneous induction of my brother, she is to a large extent forced to support his family (to which—as in the first 6 months of the war, when his company cut his salary—I naturally contribute). Surely supporting his family is more important than procuring dispensation for myself, particularly when I have the *Einjährigen-Recht* and he doesn't.—

Dear Herr Schönberg, you wrote Stein that Hertzka told you that Webern and I turned down an offer from the Tonkünstlerverein to grant you a stipend. Hertzka is distorting the facts again. The truth is: last winter when we recognized the necessity of channeling new sums into the "Schönberg Fund," and in order to avoid the very situation in which we find ourselves today, we remembered a promise Hertzka had made when the campaign started (January 1914). At that time he promised that in the event of great need he would see to it that the T[on] K[ünstler] V[erein] contribute a large sum. When we reminded him of this promise, he put us off (again!) until after the committee meeting of this fine organization, which was coming up. And then he really did call us in—via a pneumatic card to Webern—completely without warning, so that Webern couldn't even let me know and had to go alone. Hertzka then told him about the T.K.V.'s unbelievable proposal to give you, Herr Schönberg, a monthly stipend of 200 kronen as a loan. Repayment was to begin after the war, half in cash, the other half deducted from your royalties!! Naturally Webern was highly incensed at such effrontery, asked for time to think it over, and that same day arranged to see Frau Mahler, who shared his outrage and advised him to turn down that kind of "business proposition." Webern told me all about it that evening and I could only agree with his and Frau Mahler's decision. Next day Webern wrote to Hertzka that we, that is the "Schönberg Fund" regretfully declined the T.K.V.'s offer. We didn't tell you about it, Herr Schönberg: 1.) to spare you unnecessary aggravation; 2.) so as not to expose the anonymity of our campaign, which at that time was still intact.—

[Berg discusses the current arrangements of the Schönberg Fund, which was to run another five months, based on the Tonkünstlerverein loan of 200 kronen a month,[1] supplemented by funds to be raised by Stein and Berg.]

In case I don't get around to writing before your arrival, I'll go ahead and say it now: to a very happy reunion in Vienna. And many warm regards

from your Berg

---

1. The Tonkünstlerverein had initiated a fund for needy musicians in the fall of 1914. Emil Hertzka, as vice-president Tonkünstlerverein, was instrumental in obtaining the loan of 1,000 kronen for Schoenberg.

## Berg to Schoenberg

Trahütten, 27 July 1915[1]

Dear Herr Schönberg,

Stein wrote that Frau Lieser has offered you the apartment on Gloriettegasse.[2] So our old idea, the fervent wish we have cherished particularly this past ½ year, has come true. I simply can't wait to hear what you decide. I imagine you may have some reservations. But I'm certain that you will—conditionally, but nonetheless with satisfaction—accept the offer. If I had the right to advise you, Herr Schönberg, and there were so much as the slightest prospect that my advice would be heeded, I wouldn't limit myself to the expression of indescribable joy at the prospect of having you in Vienna again. But you can believe me, dear Herr Schönberg, that this joy is not purely egotistical.—

1. It can be assumed that Berg and Schoenberg met in Vienna between Schoenberg's arrival there on 5 July and Berg's departure on 12 July for Trahütten, where he remained until 13 August.

2. Schoenberg moved into Lilly Lieser's Hietzing apartment on 43 Gloriettegasse (just two blocks from Berg's apartment) at the beginning of September and remained there until the spring of 1918. In July 1915 he was staying with Lilly Lieser in her country home in Breitenstein in the Semmering region, where Erwin Stein visited him.

So you're in the Semmering now. Another hope come true. I would so much like to see you there. But 1. only if it wouldn't bother you to receive visitors—either because you wish to work—or are in need of quiet.

2. Without taking advantage of Frau Lieser's hospitality—if, for instance, I could sleep and take my meals at the local farmer's. I mean that I—and you, too, naturally—would feel uncomfortable if my coming to Breitenstein **obligated** Frau Lieser to invite me.

3. it still depends on whether the state of my health (frequent, all too frequent asthma attacks) will permit such a trip.

Anyway, I would like to ask you, dear Herr Schönberg, to let me know—perhaps through Stein—(i.e., if my visit wouldn't be a nuisance—) whether there is a place to sleep—for at least one night—at the local farmer's or in the vicinity. If I don't hear anything, I'll assume that you won't be in Breitenstein long enough for there to be a point to my visit and that I won't see you again until Vienna.

And from then on always, I hope!———

I finally managed to obtain a copy of the issue of *Zeit-Echo* with your song: "Alle welche dich suchen" . . . .[3] My God!, how beautiful! How beautiful it *surely* is!! For how can I possibly comprehend it yet! For the moment all I'm probably capable of is absorbing the overall impression of unbelievable grace. And beyond that merely to recognize the beauty of individual details. The beauty of the vocal line (low throughout); the overpowering expressivity of this flute melody

Then the bass entering 3 measures later (with the words: "ich will von dir keine Eitelkeit, die dich beweist"). And so on to the end of the song! I'm glad I finally have it—that I can enjoy it here amidst the purity of nature, far from all city filth. For nowhere else do I sense more clearly that the enjoyment of a work of art is the purest and most untroubled thing in existence. But nowhere can I find more of the inner peace needed to get to know a work of art (and to work oneself)—than here—far from all the petty influences and distractions of the city. I have always known this and have surely written this to you at least once, dear Herr Schönberg, if not repeatedly. I have noticed it again now while reading *Wilhelm Meister*. I had already read a good portion of it in Vienna without becoming as involved in it as I had expected. Only here did I recognize the beauty and grand design of the book. And that's when I found the passage "How will the man of the world with his distracted life maintain that inwardness in which the artist must live if he thinks of producing anything to perfection, and it should not be strange to anyone who wishes to take

---

3. Schoenberg's song on a text of Rainer Maria Rilke, "Alle, welche Dich suchen . . . ," Op. 22, No. 2, was published in Munich in *Zeit-Echo 1914–15. Ein Kriegs-Tagebuch der Künstler*, 14 (May 15), 206–9.

such an interest in the work as the artist wishes and hopes he will do."[4]—

If only my health were better! But I confidently hope my condition will have improved by the time I report for training. It seems a real blessing that my own military activity won't begin until now that everything looks so promising and hopeful, in other words when the will and eagerness "to do one's part" isn't clouded by misgivings. For, as things look now, I believe we can look forward to our victory with absolute certainty. If anything, our standing firm at Görz fills me with still greater confidence than our daily advances in Russia.[5] I believe we'll be seeing some extraordinary events down there. At any rate 1,900 pieces of armament were sent down from Skoda in the past few days.[6] Among them are said to be new cannon types that will play a special role.—

And now many warm regards and in hopes of seeing you soon!

Your Berg

(I assume you got my letter of the 15th?!)[7]

(How wonderful that your efforts on Webern's behalf were successful!)[8]

---

4. Johann Wolfgang Goethe's *Wilhelm Meister* (1829) is quoted here from the translation of R. O. Moon (London: G. T. Foulis, 1947), vol. I, 183. The underlinings are Berg's.

5. In the preceding weeks the Austrian forces at Görz (Gorizia), near Trieste, had repulsed two Italian offensives.

6. Skoda (Skotja Loka) was at this time in Austrian possession.

7. In his letter of 15 July Berg wrote that he would stay in Trahütten another two weeks and hoped to finish the third of his Three Orchestra Pieces, Op. 6.

8. It is possible that Schoenberg's efforts on Webern's behalf had been to prevent his being sent to the Carinthian front; instead Webern was transferred to Leoben, where he remained until the middle of December.

## Berg to Schoenberg (letter draft)[1]

Trahütten, 2 August 1915

Dear Herr Schönberg,

I just received Stein's card of the 31st. I'm terribly sorry I didn't know any earlier that you would be staying in Breitenstein until today; I could so easily have been there on one of the preceding days, or I could have arranged it so that I could join you on your trip to Vienna. As it was, though, I lost two days and I wouldn't be able to leave for Vienna until tomorrow morning and could then stay there as long as you, Herr Schönberg. I.e., could only see you on Wednesday, since (as I hear from Stein) you leave on Thursday. Naturally I would have done that, if an incident here in Trahütten hadn't required my presence. The most unbelievable thing happened: we—i.e., I and my wife's family, who have lived here for 23 years and are known to all the leading people of Trahütten and Deutsch Landsberg, as well as the most established farmers—were denounced on suspicion of being spies! The denunciation came from residents of that newly built "Hubertusheim," whose advertisement in the *Fremdenblatt* you showed me in Hietzing.* Grounds for the

1. The original of Berg's letter has not been preserved, and it is not clear whether Schoenberg actually received it; this draft is located in the Berg Archive of the Austrian National Library.

denunciation were: 1. a brightly burning alcohol lamp in our dining room (signals to the Koralps, the Carinthian border) 2. the Polish name, 3. my brother-in-law's conspicuous appearance (rather long blonde hair: disguised Russian <u>female</u> spy) 4. our aloof behavior toward the summer tourists here.—Constructing a charge of spying on the basis of these four items is the product of hysterical women and their like-minded husbands.—Naturally it is out of the question that one accept a thing like that lying down. I cannot say yet whether it will come to a lawsuit or just a confrontation and public apology. Yesterday I straightened out of a bit of gossip that had circulated among the hotel guests. But I couldn't get to the bottom of the matter, since everyone blamed someone else. In the meantime, however, in response to the denunciation that had been turned in, the <u>police</u> were here this morning and now is the moment to act and perhaps also the occasion for my first fisticuffs! If I were to leave Trahütten—before the matter has been settled—I would <u>at the very</u> <u>least</u> seem guilty of trying to <u>avoid</u> the matter. So—as you see, dear Herr Schön-berg—I am prevented by an unexpected but all the more valid task from traveling to Vienna tomorrow—and in this way of seeing you before your departure. This whole thing, then, is once again <u>fate</u>, which has robbed me of the happiness of spending at least one day with you. May God grant that your stay in Berlin is only temporary. Unfortunately Stein didn't write me one word about that. So I don't know <u>whether</u> and for when you have accepted Frau Lieser's invitation to live per-manently on Gloriettegasse.[2]—

I would also very much have liked, Herr Schönberg, to have personally presented you with the missing 2<sup>nd</sup> of the 3 Orchestra Pieces (dedicated to you last year). Now I have to do it through the post and, in order that you receive both letter and package while still in Vienna: express and registered.

I greet you, dear Herr Schönberg, and your dear family most warmly, wish you a most pleasant journey, and once again express my fervent hope to have you in Vienna soon for good.

Your Berg

My wife sends you and your wife her best.

\* The city's filth has made its way up here, too.—

---

2. In point of fact Schoenberg, because of a falling-out with Lilly Lieser, was reconsidering the offer of her Vienna apartment. In a letter to his wife of 14 August Berg relates Erwin Stein's descriptions of unpleasant scenes between Schoenberg and Lilly Lieser during Schoenberg's Semmering visit.

*Berg to Schoenberg (postcard)*

Vienna, 18 August 1915

Dear Herr Schönberg,

I've been in the service for 3 days now. I'm "stationed" on Winkelmannsstrasse (that is the street by the park in front of Schönbrunn). We are half a company of *Einjährig* volunteers, but are allowed to sleep at home. My training officers were themselves *Einjährig* volunteers, mostly fine, cultivated people who treat us very well. As far as I can judge (after 1 day of school, exercise on the Schmelz twice), duty is very interesting and stimulating and also suited to my physical capabilities. For the time being I left my wife in Trahütten. (Oh yes!: I'm with the Landwehr regiment No. 1, for which I volunteered.)

Many warm regards, dear Herr Schönberg, I hope you and your family are very well!

Your Berg

Chance has it that Linke is in my company, too. Many other teachers as well. Also actors, lawyers (3 conductors!!), etc.


*Berg to Schoenberg (draft letter!)*[1]

Vienna, 18 November 1915

Dear Herr Schönberg,

May I speak with you? This question—plea—is the result of weeks of pondering what to do about the untenable situation of knowing you to be terribly angry with me. It wasn't possible on my short trips from Bruck,[2] to visit you in your home unannounced, Herr Schönberg. I decided not to send an endless letter written in the hospital; though I could base my remarks therein on various indirect reports of the reasons for your anger with me, in the long run such countless efforts to defend oneself are pointless, since I lack your objection to <u>each</u> of my explanations, which would have placed the *[illegible]* contents in a completely different light—and because I would have spoken of so many other, even less important and *[illegible]* things, which were largely beside the point. Precisely the most important things are unknown or unclear to me. For that reason only one thing seems possible to me to alter my situation: a meeting. Won't you please grant me one, dear Herr Schönberg?

Of course I know that you are in great turmoil now due to your induction,[3] and that you have a great deal to do in that regard and that it is presumptuous of me to force my own problems on you. But in my plight I cannot turn to anyone but *you*, Herr Schönberg. For my last channels for news of you, even indirectly—Webern and Stein—are closed.[4] For that reason once again: Won't you grant me a meeting? One word from you is enough!: Because of my illness I am now in Vienna and presumably "free" for the immediate future: thus easy to reach at any time.

Greeting you warmly in unchanging esteem and gratitude

Your Berg

1. The original of Berg's letter has not been preserved; this draft is located in the Berg Archive.
2. Early in October Berg had been sent to the reserve officers' training camp at Bruck an der Leitha, but his health was not equal to the physical demands and in early November completely gave way. He was examined in hospital on 6 and 10 November, released from the company on the 16th, and thereupon sent back to Vienna.
3. On 3 November Schoenberg had received notice that he would be inducted into the service on 15 December.
4. The repercussions of Berg's falling-out with Schoenberg extended to other members of the Schoenberg circle. Webern and Berg became estranged that fall and were not reconciled until the fall of 1916.

## Schoenberg to Berg

Vienna, 20 November 1915

Dear Berg,

You could have taken the trouble to request a meeting before now.

Nevertheless, I'm ready to agree to it even now and shall expect you Sunday[1] morning at 11 o'clock.

Regards

Schönberg

---

1. 21 November

## Berg to Schoenberg

[Vienna, late November 1915]

Dear Herr Schönberg,

I think it would be better after all if I repeat what I wrote but decided not to send from Bruck Hospital, and supplement that with what has become clear to me only as a result of your explanations on Wednesday. To be sure, I will have to refer back so far and be so verbose that I must ask for your patience and that you read the letter only if you have spare time. For it grieves me to have to burden you with my affairs at a time when you yourself are facing that ultimate distraction, military service. But I believe I owe it both to you and myself to clarify what I call the "situation" that developed during the years you were away from Vienna and which I blame for my continually having vexed you with things that couldn't but diminish your interest and trust in me.

Since my condition took a turn for the worse and confines me to bed, I must unfortunately write in pencil.

The 1st time I noticed your dissatisfaction with me was during the Amsterdam trip. Later I found out the reason for your dissatisfaction by asking Stein and Webern. You had diagnosed an artistic "flagging" and "slackening off" in me at that time. On the basis of false and malicious reports from my sister and her girl friend, you had no choice but to think that this slackening was due to total dependence on my relatives and those of my wife. A dependence obligating me to daily card games and I don't know what all. Of course that was a lie. Perhaps there was a certain financial dependence on my relatives at that time, which led me to devote time to them and their affairs that would have been better spent devoted to composition. When I called to mind then what I had accomplished in that long stretch of time—apart from administrative work, apart from several trips (Munich (*Lied von der Erde*), Berlin, Prague (twice), Leipzig, Amsterdam, Berghof twice (fire)), apart from teaching 3 afternoons a week, various fund-raising campaigns, concert arrangements, reading the final proofs for the *Harmonielehre*, apart from publication of the "Arnold Schönberg" monograph (which, in fact, rested almost entirely on my shoulders), apart from all the work for *Gurrelieder* (: proofreading of score and parts, the 2 guides, the performance), apart from vocal scores for the 2 songs from the F$\sharp$-minor

Quartet, the partial 4-hand reduction of Mahler's VIII<sup>th</sup> Symphony, tranpositions of Strauss songs———nothing but my short Orchestra Songs and the even shorter Clarinet Pieces———when I called that to mind, I had to confess that it was a damned poor showing for 2½ years and that the principal cause must be poor use of my time. That led to my most earnest endeavor: to change. To do better!

First of all: To achieve complete independence from my wife's family. To limit dependence on my mother to the support due me as a result of my administrative work. No more involvement in family quarrels, complete withdrawal from gossip and the like.

Then: To change those many small things about me to which you rightfully object, like the illegible handwriting, rambling letter style, negligent dress, etc.

Finally I naturally took to heart your criticism of the insignificance and worthlessness of my new compositions and your objections to my piano reductions, and applied that to my subsequent work: the Orchestra Pieces and the Chamber Symphony.

The 3 Orchestra Pieces really did grow out of the most strenuous and sacred endeavor to compose character pieces in the manner you desired, of normal length, rich in thematic complexity, without striving for something "new" at all cost, and in this work to give of my best. Perhaps I could have achieved <u>more</u> if I weren't basically such a slow worker and if the war hadn't broken out, bringing with it an initial aversion to composing, as well as a practically doubled workload in connection with my mother's houses and Berghof. But I can't claim that. At any rate, I did what I could.

If I may trust Webern's and Steuermann's judgment, I believe I did well with the piano score of the Chamber Symphony, i.e., arranged something so that it is relatively easy to play and sounds good.

However, all my good intentions remained completely ineffective. What little I heard from you indicated that everything concerning me, even trivial matters, exasperated you. Finally, compelling reasons arose that, instead of raising your opinion of me, as I was constantly striving for, lowered it still further: I refer to the unfortunate fund affair and the preparations and arrangements for the concert in which you conducted the IX<sup>th</sup>.

I needn't repeat again how it happened that all the things I undertook in good conscience and with the best of intentions went partially or completely awry. No wonder I felt back then that a "fate" hung over me which, despite supreme efforts to <u>improve</u> myself and my conduct, repeatedly propelled me into disaster and caused you to think ever worse of me instead of better. Until finally you thought of me as a "heathen," someone totally unconscious of the duties of friendship, someone <u>against</u> rather than <u>for</u> you, indeed, someone who undertakes to do something for you only to insure himself immortality.[1] Of course this opinion of me also led to your treatment of me when you were in Vienna early this summer. I couldn't say anything that didn't exasperate you. In conversations it became apparent that you

---

1. Here and later in this letter Berg alludes to Schoenberg's accusation, made after the Beethoven concert, that he and Stein were cultivating Schoenberg's friendship only with an eye to posterity.

suspected me of things one really ascribes only to an enemy. For instance, that I conspired against you with Frau Mahler, who was behaving very tactlessly back then, or that in a letter I had thanked you ironically for well-meant advice, etc.[2] I was forced to conclude from all this that my entire personality was disagreeable and displeasing to you and that you would prefer, that at any rate it would spare you annoyance, if I stopped intruding. So I thought the most obvious solution would be: to rid you of my presence, since you were constantly surrounded by people anyway, and I remembered from the time of the performance of the IX[th] how tedious it had been for you to be constantly beleaguered. To be sure, this solution coincided with an earlier decision to spend a few additional weeks in Trahütten, a decision I had reached without danger of being egotistical, because I assumed you would be spending your summer in Semmering and surely it wouldn't have served any purpose if I sat around in Vienna all the while. Nothing came of my visit to Semmering—which I *had* planned and of which I wrote you and Stein in plenty of time—because I got no response, and that was renewed proof that my presence was not desired.—Realizing therefore, that I wasn't doing anyone a favor by staying, indeed that my presence was completely superfluous—in other words, without being particularly egotistical (for surely that involves not only suiting oneself, but inconveniencing someone else, which, by God, I did not suppose)——anyway, realizing that, I implemented the plan under the conditions described above, which were by now most excruciating to me personally. For there were of course other compelling reasons [for going to Trahütten], which I might perhaps have overcome or else explained plausibly to you, had I but assumed any interest on your part:

1. it was naturally to be expected that you'd be going to the Semmering sooner or later.

2. as a result of my induction the summer had already been decreased by half and I didn't want to deprive my wife of a rest in good air, which she very much needed at that time.

3. I wanted to finish the Orchestra Pieces:

    a.) because they should have been finished long ago

    b.) because I had explicitly promised them to you and

    c.) didn't know if in consequence of my military duty I would ever have a chance to finish them.

4. Finally the financial aspect. And here you don't think I could ever have difficulties that couldn't be easily overcome! But it is so nonetheless! To be sure, I have a steady income and in that regard can live free of anxiety. But that doesn't alter the fact that I can't spend more than that income without incurring debts that I have no means of repaying in the foreseeable future. Nor does my regular income justify the assumption that it allows me to save. As we already live beyond our means where housing and the like are concerned, and have often considered cutting back there to enable us for once to do something else (travel, a different summer vacation, etc.), we have no recourse other than to make sacrifices elsewhere. You

2. Schoenberg was offended by Berg's 27 June reply to his 17 June card, in which he had advised Berg to acquire a horse.

yourself know how rarely a chance comes along to make money. It's practically impossible for me to get money elsewhere, even the smallest sum. I have no acquaintances whom I could approach for something like that. That leaves the relatives: what my mother gives me for my administrative work is difficult enough for her as it is. To demand more would be tantamount to doing severe injury to her or my siblings. My wife's dowry is tied up and administered by her parents, therefore inaccessible to us, and it would be pure self-delusion to expect more from that quarter than occasional gifts for my wife in the form of clothes, etc., and the annual rent-free summer vacation.

These may be matters you don't quite comprehend, Herr Schönberg, but perhaps you'll believe me when I tell you that today I'm still paying off the extra expenses incurred during the Leipzig-Amsterdam trip; when I tell you that last summer (1914), when it became necessary for my wife to get treatment in Karlsbad in order to cure a long-standing illness, I could do no more than accompany her there and then leave her all alone for 4 weeks in a very modest room in an inexpensive pension because we couldn't afford so expensive a stay for both of us.—And that was before the war. This year, with inflation on top of it, having lost half of the customarily free summer as a result of my induction and indeed having had even greater expenses on a decreased income, the necessity of saving during at least a few weeks of the summer was particularly acute and, to anyone with a little insight into my situation, undeniable.

So I repeat: since I didn't have the slightest assurance that my presence was agreeable to you, and since in addition you were going to the Semmering sooner or later, I gave in to the above more or less compelling 4 reasons and spent several weeks in the country, without once suspecting that I might thereby be acting egotistically.

And the accuracy of my assumption appeared to be confirmed: my repeated and even rather urgent (maybe too urgent) inquiry whether it would disturb you if I came to Breitenstein remained unanswered. Again I had to assume that my presence was unwelcome. Finally, when it was almost too late, I heard that you were leaving for Berlin. Had I left immediately after getting this news from Stein, I would have been able to see you for only one day in Vienna. The spy affair in Trahütten prevented even that. I wrote you that, too, and at the same time sent you the completed score of the 3rd orchestra piece, in the belief that that at least would prove that I had been thinking of you continually and hoping to please you. No answer to that, either.—Whenever I wanted any news I had to go through Stein, whom I practically had to force to reply by sending him self-addressed postcards. In the meantime my wife had written to your wife how very much she was looking forward to seeing more of her in the fall, once you were settled back in Vienna. Your wife's silence confirmed my wife in the assumption that the remarks you supposedly made about her, which got back to her, did indeed reflect your and your wife's opinion of her and that there could not be anything like friendly feelings for her, but at best tolerance for her as my wife.

Please, Herr Schönberg, all of this, and everything else I shall write in this letter is absolutely real, not symbolic, and just as an example I would like to cite some more recent incidents, namely from last Wednesday, that demonstrate that you are absolutely bent on thinking the worst of me or of anything concerning me:

When you came to Vienna for the performance of the IX$^{th}$, i.e., at a time when I still felt confident of not displeasing you altogether, when I lived in the delusion of having done my duty as far as humanly possible and didn't yet have to fear that I might seem importunate, my first idea was naturally to invite you over, all the more because during your previous visit to Vienna I was of the opinion I had trangressed against my sense of hospitality with an unsuccessful dinner. Even then I was justifiably afraid that our company alone wouldn't be sufficient for you, so in order to honor you (for at that time nothing had occurred that might have led me to doubt Frau Mahler's absolute esteem for you—), we also invited Frau Mahler. That I swear! I fear you are now so convinced of my baseness that you can have no idea how insulting your interpretation of the invitation was. As well as being patently wrong, since we could have given a dinner in Frau Mahler's honor any time, and you must remember that I invited Frau Lieser solely at your own request, so that it is absolutely incomprehensible to me that you now claim we gave a dinner in Frau M.'s and Frau L.'s honor, to which we also invited you and your wife.— That automatically refutes your other reproach, that there was anything like "rating" in our manner towards your wife and Frau Mahler. Through correspondence and casual acquaintance, a friendship had quite naturally developed between my wife and Frau Mahler, in which it was absolutely inconsequential that Frau Mahler was the wife of Gustav Mahler. Frau Mahler could just as well have been the wife of some insignificant industrialist.

A further trait, admittedly trivial, but indicative! Coming away from the telephone Wednesday in a justifiable rage, after Stein had informed you of Bittner's crazy idea, you exclaimed, "I don't know what's gotten into Berg!"— —

Or: *Trara-Burg!* Amusing as this play on names is, I feel the sting and know that the sting is not intended for the place, which is anything but a *Burg* [castle] where life is *"trara"* [showy]—but just one of those impoverished little alpine villages (Trahütten, Glashütten, etc.), where I have spent several summers in a simple country house in close proximity to nature, working intensely almost all day— —
— —, that the sting could only be intended for me because I love the place and my tastes alone are enough to arouse your anger or derision.

Dear Herr Schönberg! I'm not telling you all this to rake up old stories or even to reproach you, which I would never have a right to do. But only to beg you to try to understand my situation a little. To try to understand what I've gone through these last 4 years when forced to see your affection slowly and inexorably ebb, even though I tried and tried to please you; when—while trying to correct one mistake— I always unwittingly committed another; when I finally had to recognize that you hated, or at least were annoyed by, everything I did or anything at all to do with me. And I was forced to conclude that you didn't want anything more to do with a person like me, which is, of course, understandable when I summarize the cited and uncited facts, a conclusion you yourself reached when you gave me to understand that I was risking the complete loss of your regard. "But what will that mean to you," you continued casually, "in 4–5 years, when the war's over, no one will be interested in my music anyway!"—clearly and for the 2<sup>nd</sup> time giving me to understand that I have only the meanest, lowest motives in trying to maintain or renew your friendship. In other words, not just to assure myself of immortality, but also to attach myself to your contemporary success and to accommodate my actions to that success: a second Paul Stefan!

Given this, can you wonder that I, who invariably tend to think I'm wrong anyway, invariably perceive everything I strive for with such profound yearning to be a failure—that I fell into a state of complete despair and helplessness, no longer able to trust my opinion at all, and that in the confused state of my senses, where everything seemed topsy-turvy, I neglected the simplest things, offended against the most basic social obligations. I can't explain it to you any other way: I was so stupid as not to dare offer you my help when you moved back to Vienna. That was not modesty; it was quite simply the fear that such a natural willingness to help (in which there can be absolutely no question of a "sacrifice") could be regarded as the attempt to edge closer to you à la Paul Stefan, to offer my services, make myself indispensable by exploiting your momentary situation. And due to the military training, which really took it out of me in every respect, I didn't have the peace of mind to recognize the gravity of my error until it was too late. I really thought I was doing the right thing by approaching you as unobtrusively as possible, in expectation of a word from you—you who have never hesitated to say what you think—.
. . . a word that would have made it easier for me to offer my services. If during those first days of your return you had remarked just once "when will we see each other again?" I would surely have found the courage to ask you, since you weren't yet set up for housekeeping, whether you would like to take your meals with us. Instead, however, you became cooler and cooler—something that today I understand and appreciate fully, but completely misunderstood at the time. More and more I lost the courage to approach you, until you finally made it clear that you would prefer not to see me. At the time it would never have occurred to me to place the blame on a renewed dereliction of duty on my part. Instead I considered it the long dreaded renunciation of your friendship, a catastrophe toward which I had been heading inexorably for years and which, after everything that had happened, had to happen, even without further cause.

Naturally today I see I was completely unjustified in that assumption. Likewise in the negligence and omissions, again simply the product of a vicious circle of false assumptions and conclusions. But what I did or neglected to do was not intentional, not due to egotism, but rather to complete confusion brought about by the inability to deal with the situation into which I had helplessly stumbled— —or, if you don't want to accept that— —to stupidity, which after all is pretty much the same thing.

I can only hope that you won't fear it would be a losing battle for you, that you won't entirely give up on me and will again accept me. At least your last request: that I should come see you again, justifies this hope of mine. God grant it won't be destroyed by my pouring my heart out in such a long letter.

Once I can assume that you have read this letter and that I won't have a relapse of my illness, I will take the liberty of asking when I can see you again, unless you prefer to let me know earlier. Since fate gone mad has not spared you induction after all, I could perhaps be of service to you with my military experiences, or could at least accompany you on the various errands.

Until then I greet you most warmly, dear Herr Schönberg.

Your Berg

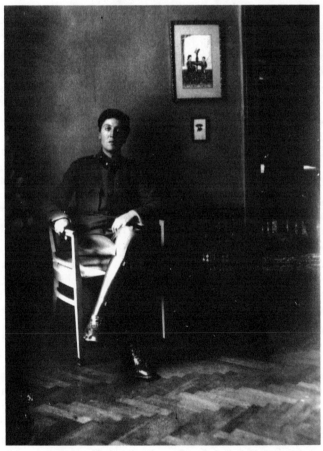

*Berg at home in his army uniform, early 1916*

# 1916-1925

The tensions in the relationship between Berg and Schoenberg were resolved only gradually and an easy footing was not reestablished until 1918. It is ironic that this period of estrangement coincided with the Schoenbergs' residence at 43 Gloriettegasse, just around the corner from the Berg's Trauttmansdorffgasse home. Proximity as much as any lingering resentment accounts for the sparce correspondence of these years, since it is clear from other sources that there were personal meetings and regular communication by telephone. With Schoenberg's move to Mödling in April 1918 (where he would remain until his 1926 move to Berlin), the telephone became a still more vital means of communication and questions that might earlier have given rise to extended epistolary ruminations were expedited in a matter of minutes.

No doubt communication during these years as well as the general conduct of daily life were made all the more difficult by the ever-present incursions of war. Both Berg and Schoenberg were in military service by the end of 1915. After his physical breakdown in November 1915 Berg had been transferred to guard duty in Vienna and in January 1916 he was assigned clerical duties in the War Ministry, a position he would hold until November 1918. Schoenberg, who was called up on 15 December 1915, received officers' training in Bruck an der Leitha from March to mid-May 1916 (when he, too, suffered a physical collapse) and thereafter served in Vienna. He was released from duty in October 1916, though he was called up again briefly in December 1917.

Even before the end of the war Schoenberg resumed his teaching and other musical activities. In September 1917 he began holding a twice-weekly composition seminar at the Schwarzwald School, which continued, with interruptions, through the academic year and was repeated the following year (1918–19). The seminar attracted a large number of students who became the core of a second generation of disciples. At the same time Schoenberg's relationship with his older student Berg, who often attended the seminar and kept in close touch, grew more cordial and finally culminated in Schoenberg's offer of the familiar Du form on 23 June 1918.

After the war the barriers erected in 1914 between nations and individuals gradually fell. In both Vienna and abroad, Schoenberg and his students assumed an active role in riviving cultural dialogue, most especially through Schoenberg's brainchild, the *Verein für musikalische Privataufführungen*, or Society for Private Musical Performances, officially founded in November 1918. The Verein focused the talents and interest of its members upon rehearsal and performance of a broad range of international contemporary music. By the time financial conditions forced its demise in 1922, the Verein had served as a model for a number of similar organizations in Austria, Germany, and Czechoslovakia.

The first post-war years were among Schoenberg's most productive and satisfying, for it was during this time that he developed his system for composition with twelve tones. Recognition of his contributions as a composer and pedagogue led to his appointment to hold a master class in the Prussian Academy of the Arts in Berlin. In January 1926 Schoenberg, now re-married to Gertrude Kolisch following the death of Mathilde Schoenberg in 1923, left Vienna for the third and last time.

It was only after the war that Alban Berg established his professional identity. He completed *Wozzeck* in 1922 and his Chamber Concerto in 1924 and both works, along with his earlier compositions, were soon published by Universal Edition. The 1923 performance of Berg's String Quartet, Op. 3, by the Havemann Quartet during the Salzburg International Chamber Music Festival first focused widespread attention upon Berg's music and the December 1925 Berlin premiere of *Wozzeck* catapulted him into international prominence.

*Schoenberg in his army uniform, 1916 (Arnold Schoenberg Institute 1222)*

# 1916

*Schoenberg to Berg*

[Vienna] 19 September 1916

Dear Berg,

I want to thank you most sincerely for the lovely birthday gift. I would have thanked you earlier if only I had had the time, and if I hadn't hoped to see you in the meantime. Actually, I have little time for reading, but have dipped into it frequently all the same. After all, once you have it, it's bound to arouse your interest, besides, it's finally time I took to heart your repeated "broad hints" about the beautiful letters other composers have written; whereas . . . !!!¹

But no! Of course that's <u>not meant seriously</u>! It's merely intended to express my wonderment that you are always giving me biographies or correspondences (it's terrible: all the rules of etiquette notwithstanding, I always look every gift horse in the mouth). I realize what you have in mind is not that I should learn from these letters or anything like that. Rather: you happen to like letters at the moment, so you assume it would be something for me as well; you've read the book and know that it is wonderful and now you'd like me to get to know this wonderful thing, too. I realize: the intention is very kind, meant in friendship. But what's the result: ultimately my library consists mainly of books that others have enjoyed; that others have wanted for themselves and that I never, or only in the last instance, would have considered acquiring myself. Invariably the ones I want are missing: my library never reflects my personality; (I'm not so concerned about that, but) it takes on a kind of hybrid personality smacking of an all-round education.

I'm sure you won't be angry with me for taking the opportunity to mention this. It's not meant unkindly. I just think it's better to tell you so that you'll remember it in the future.

When are you coming to see me? Let me hear from you.

Again, warmest thanks.

Your Arnold Schönberg

---

1. The volume Berg gave Schoenberg has not been identified.

# 1917

*Berg to Schoenberg*

Trahütten, 13 August 1917

I've been here for 10 days now, my dear Herr Schönberg.[1] During the first week I was still suffering terribly from the effects of years of confinement: asthma attacks of such severity that on one occasion I really thought I would not survive the night. But now it's much better and, as happens every summer I spend here, the desire to work is—at last—beginning to stir again: and I'm working again on the composition of the drama *Wozzeck* by Büchner, which I've been planning for more than 3 years.[2] Of course there is no chance for drafting out a larger section: In another week I lose my freedom again and the servitude in Vienna resumes, to last perhaps for years. But I can't find the peace I need for my work anyway, nor can I <u>will</u> it into existence: Several days ago I heard that one of my students, whose devotion and impressive gift for lighter music had been a great joy to me, died at the age of 20 from a case of pneumonia he had initially contracted at the front and then again as pilot officer in flights over the Alps.[3] (He is the second this year; a third has been in Russian captivity for over a year; a 4th, Adam, sustained leg wounds and frostbite and is probably ruined for life.)[4]—

The day before yesterday I received news from Vienna that the attic of my Vienna apartment as well as 4 other attics in the building were broken into and the contents of my luggage stolen. In any case my civilian clothes, which were stored there, were stolen, but I fear <u>other</u> things as well (a leather traveling case), whose presence or absence I cannot verify at this distance. I'll have to wait until I return to Vienna to "haggle" *[auszuschnapsen]* with the insurance company (to use a military term) how much they'll reimburse me for the serious loss I've sustained.

I'm dying to know how the plans for the American *Gurrelieder* are developing.[5]

1. Berg had been granted sick leave from the War Ministry 3–23 August.
2. Berg decided to compose an opera based on Georg Büchner's *Woyzeck* after seeing the 5 May 1914 Vienna premiere.
3. Karl Sluszanski died on 6 August 1917.
4. Theodor Adam returned to active service, but it is not known whether he survived the war.
5. Negotiations for an American premiere of the *Gurrelieder* had begun in the fall of 1916. On 26 July 1917 Berg received word that Breitkopf & Härtel was prepared to guarantee ten American performances at $500 each. However, Schoenberg's demands that the entire $5,000 be sent in advance, and that he conduct the premiere proved a serious obstacle. When America declared war on Austria-Hungary the project was shelved. The American *Gurrelieder* premiere did not take place until 8 April 1932 in Philadelphia under Leopold Stokowski.

My agitation in that regard,—leading me, immediately upon leaving Vienna on the 3$^{rd}$, to write a letter in the Wien-Graz express, which I hope you, dear Herr Schoenberg, have received,—has, if anything, increased. I will call you, dear Herr Schoenberg, as soon as I'm back in Vienna.

Until then all the best and regards to your esteemed wife,

from your Berg

I'll probably return home on the evening of the 23$^{rd}$.

*Schoenberg to Berg*

Vienna, 27 December 1917

Dear Berg,

Many thanks for the splendid Christmas gift.[1] I'm very pleased with it. Until now I knew very little by Poe. I've already looked into it a bit. I think I will find it very interesting. In any event, it seems to be <u>far more</u> than mere light reading. Incidentally, one shouldn't disparage light reading. Particularly if on occasion one really enjoys it, as I do.

So I thank you very much for your inspired choice.

I would enjoy a long visit with you sometime. And generally: more frequent visits. But how to arrange that. How can the "agitated ones" (I am thinking of my song on Keller's text)[2] overlook the deep chasms, the tragic conflicts, the insoluble problems that separate us?! It almost seems as if it would be easier to bring about world peace than to clear the air between us. Shouldn't one perhaps make a concerted effort to try to find a solution here once and for all? We took the first step a while ago, and none too soon; were each prepared to forget and forgive, and expected the same of the other. He who forgives doesn't give anything away; but he who can't forget, can't remember anything either: I would not forgive myself for that!

Another year will soon be over! Who knows how many more we'll have! Today more than ever it's time to think about such things.

In any event: my very best thanks.

And many New Year's wishes: for a better year than the last one was.

Warmest regards,

Your Arnold Schönberg

1. The six-volume German edition *Edgar Poe's Werke*, translated by Hedda Moeller-Bruck and Hedwig Lachmann (J. C. C. Brun Verlag, n.d.).
2. "Die Aufgeregten," Op. 3, No. 2, on a text by Gottfried Keller.

# 1918

*Berg to Schoenberg*

[Vienna] 24 June 1918

My dear, esteemed friend,

I must write to you today, for I was unable to find the words yesterday when you proposed we use *Du*.[1] I won't be able to find them now, either. But at least I must tell you that you have thereby given me the happiest day in years.

That day—with its many pleasures, great and small, and that one immense joy (—being together with you in the circle of your dear family and friends, the orchestra pieces, the beautiful photographs, the intimate conversation with a glass of splendid Rhine wine, the anonymous gift[2]— — — —the *Du*)—that day represents the climax of the ever-increasing riches you have bestowed upon me now for a month.

Deeply depressed [as I had been] by years of military service, yes, degraded to the point of self-loathing, there slowly arose within me—welcome in your dear home once again—a glimpse of real life, which found its magnificent fulfillment in the gift of those riches: working on the analysis of the Chamber Symphony, the increasingly beautiful "rehearsals," the unforgettable final performance[3] . . . . . all of which could only have been surpassed by yesterday's happiness.

For that I thank you, my dear friend!

I hope I will be able to visit you—in the course of this week. Until then the very warmest regards

from your Berg

1. During this time the Schoenbergs had a *jour fixe* for Sunday afternoon coffee, which Berg regularly attended. Those present at the 23 June gathering included the Weberns, Minna Webern's sister Maria Königer, and Eduard Steuermann and his sister Salka. Schoenberg, Webern, Steuermann, and Berg had played through Stein's eight-hand arrangement of Schoenberg's Orchestra Pieces, Op. 16. When the others left, Berg was invited to stay for dinner, after which Schoenberg offered him the familiar *Du* form of address.

2. As Berg tells his wife in a letter of 24 June 1918, Schoenberg gave him three photographs taken of himself in Prague. The Rhine wine was part of a large gift of food supplies that Schoenberg had received from the students of his Schwarzwald School composition seminar. The anonymous gift may be the 10,000 kronen that Schoenberg received following the 12 June performance of his Chamber Symphony (see footnote 3 below).

3. From 4 to 12 June Schoenberg held a series of ten open rehearsals of his Chamber Symphony, Op. 9, which found enthusiastic acclaim. This concept was subsequently developed into the Verein für musikalische Privataufführungen (Society for Private Musical Performances).

```
Konzertdirektion Hugo Heller, Wien, I., Bauernmarkt Nr. 3.

Karte Nr.                    Kleiner Musikvereinssaal

Zehn öffentliche Proben zur Kammersymphonie von
            Arnold Schönberg.

Giltig für die
1.—10. Probe                        1. Reihe

Die Daten der Proben werden rechtzeitig in der Zeitung
      und durch Plakate bekanntgegeben.
```

Ticket for the ten open rehearsals of the Chamber Symphony held by Schoenberg in June 1918

*Berg to Schoenberg*

Trahütten, 23 July 1918

Dear esteemed friend,

I've been here exactly a week now[1] and can report on life here in general and mine in particular. I am not quite well: my predisposition for asthma, which has intensified again in these last years—combined with the change of climate that is always dangerous in this regard—has brought on repeated asthma attacks of greater and lesser severity. Unfortunately this makes it difficult for the time being to take full advantage of my vacation: I have to avoid long hikes—which I used to take daily in peacetime—and constant shortness of breath even disturbs me while composing. After several unsuccessful attempts to write piano or chamber music, I finally returned to my old plan of composing *Wozzeck* and immediately found it quicker and easier to get back to work on that.[2] And after years of not working, that may be the main thing.

1. Berg's original four weeks' leave was extended and he remained in Trahütten until 31 August.

2. It is possible that Berg had been reviewing his early piano sonatas and sonata fragments (all of which precede the Sonata, Op. 1), for the beginning of the one of these sonatas was incorporated into the orchestral interlude before the final scene of *Wozzeck*. Berg's sketches for piano and chamber music are located in the Berg Archive. His early piano sonatas, edited by Rudolf Stephan, were published by Universal in 1985.

But the continuously changing atmospheric conditions here have also been unfavorable to my health. By now we have had every kind of weather: icy cold and fog as in late autumn, hot as in a summer on the plains, today the clearest, most pleasantly cool air with a strong west wind, and every now and then a few thunderstorms with hail (with stones the size of nuts and eggs) such as I myself have never experienced even in this region.

One can't call the food rationing situation particularly good; naturally compared to Vienna it is plentiful, since everyone gets 1–2 glasses of goat's milk a day, a little butter, and enough flour for bread and pastry. Vegetables moderately expensive but good. Meat cheap but almost impossible to get. Fat only available on the black market and through barter (for coffee, tea, and tobacco, for instance). Nor are prices much lower than in Vienna. The farmers are incredibly cunning and crafty. One has to trek far into the mountains to find a farm where one can get something at moderate prices (war prices all the same). And those, too, are special conditions that last only a few days or weeks: the second time one either gets nothing from their undoubted surplus or only at city black market prices.

Finally, smoking: vacation rations of 5 cigarettes a week.—

But all of this aside, I'm happy to be back here: to see my wife after a separation of six weeks—this time in the very best of health and looking better than she has in years—to live in this incomparably beautiful, open, free region, to be free, not to have to salute, and, at least for a couple of weeks, to be relieved of the tiresome worries of existence.

Only the fact that I can't visit you at least once a week and that I'm not up to date on all your plans and the details of your life often saddens me and arouses in me the longing for Mödling. I would so very much like some news of you and your activities. Are you working on the *Jakobsleiter*?[3] What about the founding of the "Verein"?[4] I have written to a few people to promote it.—How is your dear, esteemed wife? And the dear children? My wife and I greet you all many times and most sincerely; of course especially you, dear friend,

from your Berg

3. Schoenberg had resumed work on *Jakobsleiter* at the beginning of 1918.
4. Schoenberg's plans for a *Verein für musikalische Privataufführungen* (Society for Private Musical Performances) were taking shape during this time and the Verein was officially founded on 23 November. (See footnote 3 to Berg's letter of 24 June 1918 and pages 272–74).

*Berg to Schoenberg (typewritten letter)*

[Vienna] 27 September 1918

Dear esteemed friend,

It's unlikely I'll be able to come to Mödling this coming Sunday; our maid is arriving in the afternoon and I must pick her up. I would have liked to tell you about my meeting with Webern, though.[1] Unfortunately, I was also running too late on Tuesday to come to the seminar.[2] Therefore the most important points briefly in writing!

Webern cannot find an apartment in Vienna, so for the time being he is forced to live in Mödling again. But he doesn't want to stay there, rather, he is still hoping to obtain a position or to move to the little house in Styria. His reason for wanting to return to the theater is—as he firmly insists—purely financial. He interpreted your reply to the detailed letter in which he revealed all of his "feelings" on the matter as so curt a dismissal—and still regards it as such, despite my objections—that he saw no alternative but "to go into self-imposed exile." He firmly denies any other reasons for his action.

This was the substance of his explanation to me. Naturally there was a good deal of back and forth in the course of our discussion, which, however, left the fundamental issue unchanged.—

I'll call, dear friend, early Saturday or Sunday so we can at least have a little chat, and also hope to come to the seminar Tuesday evening. Until then the warmest regards

from your gratefully devoted Alban Berg

My wife finally returns—for good—early next week. Perhaps as early as Monday.

I hear from a reliable source that Bulgaria has already made peace with the Entente, something that will be made public in a day or two.[3] As a matter of fact, one can read it between the lines in today's newspaper reports and editorials. The Balkan train is supposed to start running tomorrow between Siebenbürgen and Constanța!

Again warmest regards!

1. After his discharge from military service at the end of December 1916 and another stint as conductor at the Deutsches Landestheater in Prague August 1917 to May 1918, Webern moved to Mödling to be near Schoenberg. However, by mid-September financial worries led him to consider a return to his position in Prague and he wrote to Schoenberg for advice. Schoenberg, exasperated with Webern's indecisiveness and upset that he would consider leaving just as the Verein was being formed, replied coolly, whereupon Webern broke off all contact. After a meeting with Webern on 23 September, Berg told his wife in a letter of the next day that he now considered Webern for the most part blameless. By the end of October Webern and Schoenberg had resolved their differences and Webern remained in Mödling.
2. On 18 September Schoenberg had resumed his twice-weekly seminar in harmony, counterpoint, instrumentation, and analysis at the Schwarzwald School in Vienna.
3. The treaty was signed on 28 September.

*Berg to Schoenberg*

Vienna, 30 November 1918
In bed

Dear esteemed friend.

I am forced to ask you to relieve me of my position as performance director.[1] My health suffered so severely during the 3½ years of military service that it will take months, perhaps years merely to become as healthy as I was before the war—which then, too, was the result of years of good care. I am told this not only by the doctors and all who know me well, but unfortunately also by my own awareness of the absolute inadequacy of my present physical condition. I am so run down that to accomplish what are actually nothing but the trivial incidental tasks of an active life, I have to summon the utmost willpower and, since I am ashamed of my condition: a good deal of dissimulation. So, for instance, a hurried errand in the city, repeatedly climbing 3–4 stories, standing in the street car for ½–¾ of an hour, etc., represent real exertion, and I must admit that in following conversations I actually have to dissemble to hide an exhaustion that others might interpret as indifference or lethargy. Don't think I have simply given in to these spells, which are occurring with ever-increasing frequency and have of late lasted entire days (I am not talking now about my present illness); (don't ask me to prove this)! But ultimately even narcotics, which I was forced to take in ever larger doses (black tea, black coffee, aspirin, Pyramidon, even atropine) fail me, careful husbanding of available strength fails me, as does self-hypnosis and a sense of duty, and I am left only with a longing for complete peace—or else, as happened just now—the whole sorry mechanism suddenly breaks down! To avoid such catastrophes and in order to continue to vegetate in apparent good health, I have in recent years—submitting to the constraints of military duty and avoiding even the slightest indulgence—led the monotonous life of a civil servant. But as I am not able, willing—or allowed to lead such a life today and in the future, now that a worthier activity again awaits me—lacking, on the other hand, the necessary strength—strength others take for granted (I am thinking above all of your enormous capacity, but also of the ease with which the young people in the seminar and in the leadership of the Verein meet the physical requirements of their tasks)—I must do everything in my power to regain such strength as quickly as possible. I will soon see how successful I am— given release from military service at last—and given the help of doctors and the closest possible adherence to their advice (rest cure, fattening(!) diet, avoidance of all narcotics, possible change of air, etc.). Of course I can't expect my asthma to be cured, since it has always been diagnosed as incurable; but I must restore my health to the point where attacks are mild and less frequent and, even when severe, do not seriously injure the system. In any case I must avoid everything that robs me of still further strength, that is, anything that demands more of me than I am able to accomplish easily.

1. In the newly formed Verein, of which Schoenberg was president, the function of the performance directors (*Vortragsmeister*), initially Webern, Steuermann, and Berg, was to supervise the rehearsal of new works.

A life thus defined and restricted prevents my devoting myself to a profession that, after all, demands full responsibility, precludes postponement or delegation of the accepted duties, and further requires dependability, independence, and being bound to time and place, etc., etc. It may have been possible to evade one or more of these obligations in the military, but not in an organization under your direction and one as dear to me as the other was despised. And that is the very reason I will not, indeed dare not expose you, the Verein, or myself, either, to the dangers of a possibly inevitable neglect of my assumed duties and have therefore virtually no choice but to resign before it's too late.

In view of the Verein's activities the present moment seems to me to be suitable, i.e., not too inconvenient; because

1) the final selection of the Verein's leadership has yet to take place (I suspect that it will take place at the general meeting)[2]

2) the duties I have undertaken are ending automatically, which obviates a transfer of these matters and consequently any major inconvenience to a committee member; and

3) the only new duty assigned to me is rehearsing *Don Quixote*, which—if it's all right with you—I would of course still like to carry out.[3]

In general—and I don't really have to say it—my resigning from the position of performance director naturally doesn't change anything—anything at **all** in my willingness to continue to serve you and everything concerning you—and also the Verein—to the best of my ability. That goes without saying! You couldn't possibly interpret my resignation any differently. In that case you would have to be really angry with me! And there's nothing I fear more! Only something as overpowering as my illness could lead me to "refuse you" anything at all.[4]—

As soon as I am able to leave the house again I will get in touch with you. For the time being just a short report:

None of the other composers who received letters has answered. Weigl sent his quartet.[5] I have written to Fürstner[6] about the 4–hand score of Mraczek's *Max and Moritz*.[7]

As you wished, I wrote Frau Mahler again with great urgency concerning her participation and publicity for the Verein. Also Frau Koller.[8]

As far as I can tell from a recent report, Kauder is in the process of founding a

2. The first general meeting, held on 6 December.

3. Four-hand piano performances of Richard Strauss's *Don Quixote* took place on 12 and 30 January and 16 March 1919 with Eduard Steuermann and Ernst Bachrich.

4. Schoenberg does not seem to have responded to Berg's request and Berg's next extant letter to Schoenberg, dated 23 December 1918, indicates that he continued to work for the Verein.

5. Karl Weigl's First String Quartet in E major was performed in the Verein by the Gottesmann Quartet on 23 February and 2 March 1919.

6. Otto Fürstner was the director of the Fürstner Verlag in Berlin.

7. The Czech composer Josef Gustav Mraczek wrote his symphonic burlesque *Max and Moritz* in 1912; the Verein gave a four-hand performance of the work with Olga Novakovic and Ernst Bachrich on 30 March 1919.

8. The painter Broncia Koller, whose son Rupert Koller married Anna Mahler in 1921.

quartet.[9] I told him to get in touch with Dr. Pisk.[10]

I have not been able to arrange the music subscription yet. If it's pressing, perhaps someone else could do that. Enclosed is a list of the scores presently available.[11]

With regard to the rehearsals for *Don Quixote*, I shall await Steuermann's call. Since he undertook to reach an agreement with Schmetterling[12] in the matter.

Wiener has signed up six new members.—

I hope your wife and Trude are better by now! The very best regards

from your gratefully devoted Berg

---

9. The Austrian violist and composer Hugo Kauder became the violist of the Quartett-Vereinigung whose members also included the violinists Mary Dickenson-Auner and Fritz Sedlak and the cellist Wilhelm Winkler.

10. Paul Pisk studied with Schoenberg 1916–19 and was the first secretary of the Verein. Kauder performed in two Verein concerts on 30 March and 6 June 1919.

11. The Verein had arranged to order scores needed for performance from the Viennese music store and publisher, Ludwig Doblinger. The list Berg enclosed included works by Bartók, Bittner, Debussy, Dukas, Finke, Janáček, Korngold, Marx, Novák, Pfitzner, Prohaska, Ravel, Reger, Schmidt, Schreker, Scott, Strauss, Stravinsky, and Szymanowski. All of the composers listed were performed by the Society, with the exception of Cyril Scott, Carl Prohaska, and Leoš Janáček.

12. Berg may mean the pianist Jan Smeterlin, who was at this time studying with Leopold Godowsky at the Vienna Academy. Smeterlin's name does not show up among the performers with the Verein.

---

# 1919

---

*Berg to Schoenberg*

[Berghof] 29 July 1919

Dear esteemed friend,

The days here are so monotonous that I actually hesitate to tell you about it. That is the only explanation—despite my daily wish to chat with you at least by letter—for letting weeks go by without writing since my last letters of 17 June and the 5th of this month.

For—it is easier to live such a life than it is to tell of it; especially when one has a particular reason for it, as I have, namely: to benefit both health and work.

My health has improved substantially; I have gained a good deal of weight and have also become stronger and tougher. Contributing factors, in addition to the good food, are my daily swims in the lake, rain or shine, and long walks. And in general not having to worry about life for the immediate future.

Work on *Wozzeck* is going slowly. Of the 3 acts with 5 scenes each, I have composed: the entire I$^{st}$ act (over 700 measures) and a lengthy scene from the II$^{nd}$ act (c. 200 measures). Perhaps I'll manage to finish the 2$^{nd}$ act here.

The balance of my daily routine includes: some country activities like fishing, driving the coach, riding, boating, repairs on the house and farm, and reading the paper. Finally, answering important letters.

Apropos letters, the Dresden people (Schulhoff, etc.) actually wish to "premiere" my 3 Orchestra Pieces—despite my warning.[1] Of course, they haven't seen the score yet. Kassowitz is copying out the parts and needs it just now. So who knows whether it will actually be performed. Anyway, I have serious doubts whether this series of 6 concerts is even going to take place, as well as misgvings about how. To judge by his driveling letters and long-winded, insipid compositions, Schulhoff doesn't make a good impression on me at all. Did he ever come to see you during his recent visit to Vienna?[2] I can't tell from his postcard. What do you think of him and of the entire venture? Do you think a performance, especially of *Pierrot*, possible in that setting? I am immersing myself completely in that work (the only score I brought with me to the country) and can't marvel enough at those depths that will remain unfathomable for decades to come. And these young people (I wanted to say Dresdeners, but they are from Prague, presumably from the Café Arco)[3] approach the work as if it were a composition by Schreker!

Schulhoff is also playing my sonata on a piano recital in this Dresden series. The 4 songs (the published ones) are to be included on the song recital.[4] He will likewise play the piano sonata in Prague in a recital of his own (5 November). Finally I hear that a Berlin piano virtuoso, Frau Dayas-Soendlin[5]—don't laugh!—will play the sonata again in October.

I haven't heard a word from the publisher Jatho in Berlin, who is supposedly so interested in your works and those of your students, and to whom I wrote some time ago about publishing my few things.[6] Here, too, I doubt whether anything will come of all these plans. Though it would be very nice if Webern's things and at least my quartet were to appear in print.

1. The Czech composer and pianist Erwin Schulhoff, who was later involved in the founding of the Prague *Verein für musikalische Privataufführungen*, was at this time planning a series of five or six *Fortschrittskonzerte* (Progressive Concerts) in Dresden, of which, however, only two actually took place, both in the first half of the 1919 / 20 concert season. Others in this Dresden group included the conductor Hermann Kutzschbach, the writer Theodor H. Däubler, the art historian Will Grohmann, and the artists Lazar Segall and Otto Dix.

2. Schulhoff was in Vienna in early July, but did not meet with Schoenberg.

3. The Café Arco in Prague was well known as a meeting place of radical young literati; Karl Kraus made the pretensions of its clientele a particular object of ridicule.

4. Schulhoff performed Berg's Piano Sonata,. Op. 1, in the first Dresden concert on 21 October 1919 and the Op. 2 songs in the second concert on 13 November 1919, along with works by Wellesz, Hauer, Erdmann, Scriabin, Loutsky, Schoenberg, and Schulhoff.

5. The American pianist Karin Elin Dayas-Soendlin, daughter of the pianist William Humphrey Dayas, settled in Berlin in 1914 and became known for her interpretations of contemporary music.

6. In the postwar period, a number of publishers began to take an active interest in new music, among them the Berlin firm of H. C. Jatho, who published several of Schulhoff's works. Schulhoff tried to interest Jatho in Berg and Webern, but though Berg sent the publisher his String Quartet, Op. 3, nothing came of it.

You too, dear friend, have probably received an invitation to participate in the *Musikblätter des Anbruch?*[7] I myself have agreed in principle. However, without committing myself in any way, since this is the music journal that was to have been founded by you,[8] and of course U.E. has once again given preference to the conventional and uninteresting, that is, the superfluous. But there might be an opportunity or even necessity to say something publicly on your behalf and then this organ (Hertzka's organ, great!) would be available.

Incidentally! Not long ago I received Hertzka's statement for the last half-year regarding the sale of about 200 copies of my Chamber Symphony guide @ 5 heller. On the other hand he charged me 11 kronen 10 for two Chamber Symphony and *Gurrelieder* guides *I* had ordered to give Rufer[9] and someone else in the Verein. Not itemized, as a precaution, but merely under the heading:

"shipment, see enclosed bill ................................................. 11.10."

As a precaution, however, the bill was not enclosed, but withheld, nor—in spite of my insistence—will it be sent to me. The whole matter is, thank God, a bagatelle and for that reason nothing to get upset about—laughable, if anything. But it does seem indicative to me.—

Now I've talked so much about myself. And yet questions about you and your loved ones come to my lips much more readily. Questions, for which the meager news I receive about you indirectly, is insufficient answer. How are you and yours faring during these horrible summer months? Thoughts of your physical well-being keep me from enjoying the fact that I myself am at present relieved of anxiety about subsistence. Not to mention other worries: cancelation of the 2 *Gurrelieder* performances,[10] other performances?

What about the American performance of the *Gurrelieder?* I have written concerning this to my brother, with whom I can once again correspond. Perhaps he can find out from the local representative of Breitkopf & Härtel. Should I write to him on your behalf? To date I have of course done so informally. Letters from there take about one month. I don't know how long they take from here.—

Despite our good living conditions, my wife suffers constantly from rheumatic pains, but otherwise she feels much better than in Vienna. She sends many regards and will write your dear wife soon.

Farewell, dear friend! All the best to you and yours,

from your Berg

---

7. In the fall of 1919 U.E. founded *Musikblätter des Anbruch*, a periodical devoted to contemporary music in general and U.E. works in particular. Schoenberg, too, was asked to join the *Anbruch* staff, but made demands that Universal considered unacceptable.

8. Schoenberg had discussed the idea of such a periodical with Hertzka as far back as 1911 and again in the early post-war months.

9. Josef Rufer studied with Zemlinsky and with Schoenberg in 1919–22.

10. *Gurrelieder* performances had been planned by the Konzertverein Orchestra. Instead there were two performances of the work the following summer with the Vienna Philharmonic under Schoenberg's direction.

# 1920

*Schoenberg to Berg (express letter in Josef Travnicek's hand)*

Vienna, 12 January 1920

By dictation, Travnicek[1]
(with the warmest regards)
Dear friend!

The publisher E. P. Tal & Co. wrote to me that as the first in a series of monographs about leading artists (Debussy, Reger, Marx, etc.) he intends to publish a book about me, about 10 folios in length (c. 160 pages), and would like me to suggest someone.[2]

I'm asking you first. He writes, however, that the work must be begun immediately, since the book is scheduled to come out in September. I assume, then, that it would have to go to press by the end of March (beginning of April) at the latest. Write immediately whether you have the time and inclination to do it or write directly to E. P. Tal & Co., Vienna VII, 4 Lindengasse, tel. 31044. I would be glad to advise you about a fee, etc.

Many warm regards

Schönberg

---

1. Josef Travnicek (later Trauneck) studied with Schoenberg 1918–22.

2. The first books published in the Tal series were studies on Schoenberg and Schreker, as well as Paul Stefan's *Neue Musik und Wien*.

*Berg to Schoenberg*

Berghof, 15 January 1920

Dear esteemed friend,

Letters take terribly long here, even express letters. I didn't receive yours until today. So forgive the delay.

It has only served to compound my despondency that I am **forced** to turn down your kind, flattering offer. It has long been my greatest wish—particularly of late, having enjoyed the *Pelleas* guide so much[1]—to be able to write something substan-

---

1. In December 1919 U.E. had commissioned Berg to write a guide for Schoenberg's *Pelleas und Melisande;* the guide was published in 1920.

tial about you, to devote time and all my energy to it and to do it in consultation with you. There is nothing I'd rather do—next to composing—than prepare guides, analyses, articles about you and your works, and piano reductions of your compositions. And now such a wonderful opportunity finally comes along—and I cannot seize it.

I'm so tied up here, so overburdened with work and worry (12–13 hours a day), that for now I cannot think of getting away and have absolutely no time (—not even an hour a day—) for myself and my own work.

It would take too long to go into details. In any case, my presence here—agonizing and injurious as it is to me spiritually, mentally—and physically—is absolutely necessary until we find a solution: leasing or selling.[2]

How long that will be I cannot tell you—or anyone, not even myself. I hope not long, for I simply wouldn't be able to endure it.

And now I must ask a favor of you: to relieve me of my responsibility to the Verein—naturally "with suspension of salary"—for an indefinite period.*

You can imagine how difficult this request and renewed refusal are for me, but— you *know* how I am once again driven by fate.

From my wife I hope to hear news of you and yours soon. I hope you are all well!

My greetings to you——in great haste—(because of the express train)——and in longstanding devotion and gratitude.

Your Alban

* I'm also sending an official request to the Verein!

---

2. Due to problems with the management of Berghof, Alban Berg took over direct administration of the property from his brother Charly on 1 January 1920. While Berg's mother initially hoped that he would assume permanent responsibility for Berghof, Berg finally decided to sell the property, a decision that caused a good deal of family dissension, particularly among the three brothers.

*Berg to Schoenberg*

Berghof, 21 February 1920

My dear esteemed friend,

For weeks now—no: for a month now I have been meaning to write you **every day**. Indeed, about 2 weeks ago I even began a long letter that was full of excuses and would have had to continue in the same vein. Excuses, first, because I let you down with the Verein, second, didn't undertake the monograph about you,[1] and third, write so infrequently.

1. From letters to his wife, who remained in Vienna during this time, it is evident that Berg was convinced of Schoenberg's displeasure with him. The situation at Berghof was increasingly frustrating after a tentative agreement for the sale of the property fell through at the beginning of February. On 1 February he wrote his wife that once the sale was concluded he planned to ask whether he could still undertake the monograph on Schoenberg. By the time Berg was free to take up the project, Egon Wellesz had been asked to write the book.

Having heard today that you are leaving on the 27th, my fear that a letter may no longer reach you is so great that I sit down tonight despite extreme exhaustion to send you at least a sign of life. I will save myself— — —and you— —all the above excuses and ask only one thing of you: <u>believe me</u>, I did not turn down work on the monograph about you rashly. The promptness with which I did so should not mislead you as to the thorough deliberation and <u>absolute</u> necessity of the refusal, still less as to my agony, truly bordering on contained fury and suppressed <u>desperation,</u> indeed, as to my <u>jealousy</u> in being <u>forced</u> to relinquish it to someone else. Believe me, dearest friend, as soon as I have the privilege of speaking with you, I will be able to convince you that—did I not want to be guilty of an irresponsible <u>failure,</u> thereby <u>damaging</u> the publisher and <u>above all</u> you—there was **no alternative** but to refuse immediately and irrevocably. Please <u>believe</u> me— —for the time being take my word for it.

This and everything else I hear from Vienna is only a source of most painful longing. All the more painful because it cannot be fulfilled. My God, how beautiful the last Verein concerts with chamber orchestra must have been.[2] How wonderful it would be to be able to go along to Prague[3] and at least <u>talk</u> with you about all that lies ahead for you in the near future: Mannheim, Amsterdam.[4] While here in my exile I can't even receive—or expect—reports detailed enough to allow me to revel in all these wonderful things in my thoughts.

On the evening of the 25th I shall try nevertheless.[5] Perhaps you will sense, my dear friend, how constantly and in most profound friendship I think of <u>you</u> and <u>everything</u> concerning you and emanating from you.

Your Berg

2. These two Verein concerts took place on Friday, 30 January (with Szymanowski's Romance for violin and piano, Op. 23, Webern's Five Pieces for Orchestra, Op. 10, in an arrangement conducted by Webern for violin, viola, cello, piano, and harmonium, and piano pieces by Erik Satie) and Friday, 6 February (with Ravel's second *Daphnis et Chloë* suite, arranged for piano four hands, an arrangement of Mahler's *Lieder eines fahrenden Gesellen* for flute, clarinet, two violins, viola, cello, contrabass, piano, and harmonium, conducted by Schoenberg, a repetition of the Satie pieces, seven songs by Mussorgsky, *The Nursery*, and a repetition of Szymanowski's Romance).

3. Zemlinsky had arranged for guest performances of the Vienna Verein in Prague, which took place on 7, 8, 13, and 14 March.

4. Schoenberg's extended concert trip was to take him from Mannheim, where opera director Wilhelm Furtwängler had invited him to conduct *Pelleas* on 3 March, via Berlin to Prague, where he led the four Verein concerts between 7 and 14 March, and finally to Amsterdam and Utrecht, where on 24 and 25 March he conducted performances of *Verklärte Nacht* and the first two of the Orchestra Pieces, Op. 16. Schoenberg returned to Vienna on 12 April.

5. In a special Verein concert on 25 February 1920 Schoenberg conducted an open rehearsal of the chamber orchestra version of his Orchestra Pieces, Op. 16, in the concert hall of the Schwarzwald School.

## Berg to Schoenberg (postcard)

Vienna, 8 May [1920]

On a postcard, so that it gets past the censors[1] more quickly, just the following news to reassure you, dear esteemed friend, about the presently deserted Verein:[2]

Since yesterday I've been working for the Verein again and can devote my time and energy to it,[3] so that presumably the coming concerts and the special general meeting can go smoothly and as you would wish.[4]

Many, many warm regards to you and your family. Best regards to Webern, too.

Your Berg

---

1. Postal censorship continued through the first postwar years.

2. Schoenberg and several of his students, including Webern, were in Amsterdam to attend the Mahler Festival (6–21 May). In addition to performances of all of Mahler's works, the festival featured contemporary chamber music, including Schoenberg's Piano Pieces, Op. 11, Nos. 1 and 2, and "Warnung" from Op. 6.

3. After the sale of Berghof Berg and his wife, who had joined him there at the end of February, were able to return to Vienna early in May.

4. There had been a Verein concert the evening before and two further concerts were scheduled during Schoenberg's absence, on 14 and 21 May, respectively; the general meeting was on 14 May.

## Berg to Schoenberg

Trahütten, 9 July 1920
Friday

My dear friend,

I am writing with pencil because I'm outside and, given the high humidity, paper and ink begin to "run" within minutes, which would make the letter still more illegible than my handwriting already makes it.

It was harder than ever to leave Vienna this time: thanks to the *Gurrelieder* and *Pelleas*,[1] and thanks to your and your dear wife's hospitality, the last weeks in Vienna were so wonderful, that we knew in advance that changing our location could only be a change for the worse. Further:

These are the last 2–3 months you will be in Vienna and in leaving I shall spend almost 2 months away from you, further:

There are so many things I would have liked to discuss with you, should have discussed with you—this, naturally in the course of frequent meetings and not in one or two hours—: the Verein, the Mahlerbund.[2] My own affairs: above all *Anbruch*,

---

1. The performances of *Gurrelieder* on 12 and 13 June 1920 at the Vienna State Opera under the auspices of the 1920 *Wiener Musik- und Theaterfest* had been an overwhelming success; Schoenberg conducted the Vienna Philharmonic Orchestra and the Singverein, with the soloists Berta Kiurina, Olga Bauer-Pilecka, Carl Oestvig, Josef von Manowarda, Hubert Leuer, and Wilhelm Klitsch as the speaker. These performances represented the realization of plans dating back to 1919 to perform the work under Schoenberg's direction. Also part of that year's summer festival was a performance of Schoenberg's *Pelleas und Melisande* under Alexander Zemlinsky on 2 June.

2. Mengelberg had first broached the subject of a Gustav Mahler League during the Mahler festival in Amsterdam the previous May; Schoenberg was appointed president and entrusted with drawing up the statutes.

the commission I received in a roundabout way to write a pamphlet about Zemlin-sky.[3]

I knew all that; and yet—suddenly tearing myself away after long hesitation—I left all the same: our inexpensive life up here, almost expense-free, makes it possible for me to save enough so as just to get by on my income from *Anbruch* and the Verein in the fall. That's one reason, the compelling one. The other I have already told you: I have the desire—I would almost call it a sense of obligation—to compose something after a break, virtually, of years: since 1914 I haven't finished a single composition. First the 5 wartime summers with their infrequent vacations. 1919 the first extended summer and now the 6–7 weeks this year, which I would certainly have "frittered away" in Vienna if, as I said, I hadn't torn myself away.

For so many responsibilities await me in the fall that I should actually be attend-ing to them already, which I would certainly have done in Vienna, whereas here they're only a secondary concern.

For example the Zemlinsky book. I have a terrific desire to do it and have a great many significant things to say about this music that has grown so dear to me. I'm also firmly determined to make this one of the first items in *Anbruch*. For it has to be said once and for all, that here, living inconspicuously, is one of the few masters, worth more than all the officially accredited "masters" Pfitzner, Schreker, and the whole German and Nordic lot.[4] Anyway, my article might be a good preliminary study for a monograph about Zemlinsky. But I am tormented by doubts whether I am well enough informed for this project. Certainly not with regard to the biogra-phy: that could be rectified. The works! How much I would have to learn first: for instance, I don't know *Sarema*[5] at all. Nor the "*Meerjungfrau*, symphonic poem."[6] And then there are the works of whose very existence I am probably ignorant. Finally there's the conductor and opera director. Right now, I think this chapter would be the most difficult for me.—By the way, Tal hasn't contacted me person-ally yet, just made indirect inquiries. In the end Wellesz will probably do it! At the thought that the book on you slipped away from me (also something I have my dear family to thank for!) I grow red with anger, shame, jealousy, injured pride.—

Yes! I also wish I could have stayed on in Vienna to see how you liked my Pfitzner article.[7] Of late I have had many misgivings about it. That is, I couldn't even look at it anymore, it was so repugnant to me. The beginning! It's all much

3. Through his connection with the editorial staff of *Anbruch* (on 24 June 1920 Berg had signed a contract with Universal Edition to serve as one of the editors) Berg had heard of a projected book on Zemlinsky, to be published by E. P. Tal & Co. The book never appeared.

4. Schreker, who was enjoying increasing successes as opera composer, had been named director of the Berlin Musikhochschule in March. It is nonetheless ironic to link him with Pfitzner, as Schreker (along with Schoenberg and Mahler) was one of the personalities indirectly attacked in Pfitzner's 1920 pamphlet, *Die neue Ästhetik der musikalischen Impotenz* (see footnote 7 below).

5. Zemlinsky's first opera, composed in 1895, premiered 10 October 1897 in Munich, and pub-lished in piano vocal score in 1899.

6. Actually *Seejungfrau*, a fantasy for orchestra that was premiered 25 January 1905, but never published.

7. Berg's "Die musikalische Impotenz der 'neuen Ästhetik' Hans Pfitzners," which appeared in *Anbruch* II / 11–12 (June 1920), 399–408, was his contribution to the exchange between Hans Pfitzner and the German critic Paul Bekker.

too mild! Instead of coming right out and saying: he's a fool, I speak of a "composer of Pfitzner's stature." Still, I was pursuing a strategy there. I wanted to have the fool emerge gradually from the essay as a whole: to begin at least with a degree of superficial respect (leaving it ambiguous whether it's meant seriously or ironically ("erudition!") and only slowly to strip him of all the attributes of which he is so proud: his Germanness, his style!, his musical learning, the logic of his book, finally, as trump card, his composition, which I expose and denounce with the same foolish "how beautiful—, how beautiful—, how beautiful!" that he used for the *Pastoral* Symphony.[8] And all of it dipped in the irony of the incredible stupidity of this "master."

That was my intention! I cannot judge whether I succeeded. The lengthy, but essential analysis of "Träumerei" seems to lose the thread (despite frequent repetition of the point of my criticism). That's why I would so much have liked to hear your opinion and in general to have witnessed the effect the article had on our circle. Perhaps Webern will write and let me know.[9]

Now I have talked enough about myself. Whereas the purpose of my letter was also to ask you about your affairs (which of course are to some extent mine, too): about the Verein, the Mahlerbund, your preparations for the Amsterdam concerts and courses[10]—the new edition of the Harmonielehre——and finally, most important: *Die Jakobsleiter*.

Not knowing about all these things is really a constant distress to me when I'm away from you. Even now this first week—and how much more over the entire summer——I dare not think how it will be in the months between October and April! Then I would lose even my capacity to enjoy the beauties of country life. And that's saying something; for—as far as my physical well-being goes—I only feel really well and happy here in the mountains. If only we: you and yours and my wife and I could just spend a summer together in such surroundings! But who knows what the future holds!

Many warm regards

from your Berg

Best wishes to your wife, Fräulein Trude, and Görgl!

8. In his pamphlet Pfitzner argued that all analysis is meaningless in the face of the profundity of a work such as Beethoven's Sixth Symphony. Berg's repeated exclamation "Wie schön!" in his discussion of Pfitzner's song "Nachts" (Op. 26, No. 2) is in imitation of Pfitzner's remarks on Schumann's "Träumerei."

9. In a letter of 14 July 1920 Webern tells Berg that Schoenberg liked his article. Berg, on the other hand, informs Schoenberg in a letter of 21 July of Alma Mahler's negative reaction. According to Berg Alma Mahler had written to Helene Berg: "all Pfitzner's quotations show him to be right. Nothing is more inexplicable than music. Above all melody.———Not A B C D. x y z. Does Alban really believe you can explain anything that way—anything at all———?"

10. Mengelberg had asked Schoenberg to conduct nine concerts of his own works with the Concertgebouw Orchestra during the 1920/21 season and to teach a composition course beginning in October, for which he was to be allowed two assistants of his own choosing. Schoenberg and his family left for Amsterdam at the end of September.

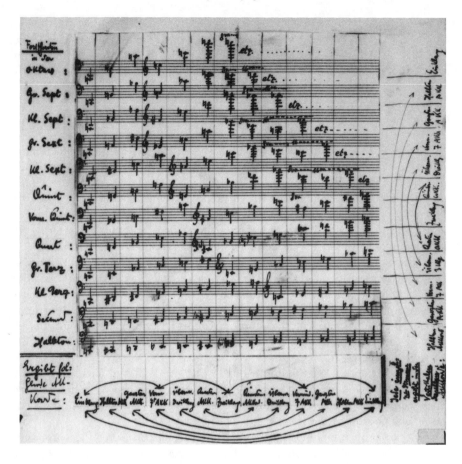

## Berg to Schoenberg

Trahütten, 27 July 1920

Dear friend,

I came upon the above oddity by chance. A theoretical trifle.[1]

At the moment I'm reading Walter Krug's *"Modern Music."* The ultimate enigma of your music has at last been solved. It comes from **Grieg**.[2]—

No more today! Many warm regards, my dear esteemed friend.

Your Berg

1. The chart shows what George Perle has called "Berg's master array of the interval cycles." See Perle's article in *The Musical Quarterly* LXIII / 1 (January, 1977), 1–30. Berg first made use of the relationships of his "theoretical trifle" in *Wozzeck*, Act II, scene 9.

2. Walter Krug devoted one chapter of his *Die neue Musik* (Rentsch in Erlenbach b. Zurich, 1920) to Schoenberg (57–69), where he wrote, among other things, that Schoenberg's earlier music developed not from Wagner, but from imitation of Schumann and even Grieg (p. 67). Berg's heavily annotated copy of Krug's book survives in his library.

*Berg to Schoenberg*

Trahütten, 14 August 1920

I shall copy this letter, as it contains things that are important to me; then if this gets lost, a distinct possibility given the postal conditions here, I can send you the copy!

Dear esteemed friend,

For a long time I have been meaning to tell you, or rather, "confess" the following.

You know that since the war ended, I have considered publishing something of my own. I don't have to tell you the general reasons for this. Now, however, there is a specific one as well. I am—as you also know—forced to establish a livelihood for myself. I don't get anything from my family since my return from Berghof; the interest on my wife's continually shrinking "fortune" is likewise almost nothing by today's standards. You can well imagine, then, how opportune—also from the standpoint of a livelihood—the combination of *Anbruch* and Verein is for me.*

And so—following the dictates of necessity and less those of my own inclination, which make a retiring life dedicated to composition and to writing about your works and on your behalf much more desirable———I have now thrown myself into the arms of the public and must seek there what is known by that revolting term, "a career" (synonymous with the living one earns in this way), and cannot afford to pass up any opportunity promoting such a "career." Since I also appear in my capacity as composer, that requires compositions. And these have wider significance only when they are performed and otherwise available. You, dear friend, have seen to a number of performances these past 2 years. So it remains to make these compositions available to those who are interested, who wish to orient themselves and possibly to perform something.

This possibility has not existed—outside my immediate sphere of activity—until now. (And the fact that a sonata of mine is "generally" known and doesn't displease people doesn't change anything.) But if I now pursue that possibility and publish something of my own, it is not due to ambition, but solely because I regard that as one way effectively to establish my public standing, which I have resolved to do, though again not for reasons of ambition.

I secured the means for this through the sale of a few old items from my household that I could easily spare and the sale of which, by a happy coincidence, brought a very good price by today's standards.

As the matter now stands, my publisher Haslinger (i.e., Schlesinger, Berlin) 1.) will, at his own expense, publish a new edition of the two out-of-print works, the sonata and songs,** and from now on I will receive a percentage share of this and subsequent editions.

2.) That I will have the quartet and clarinet pieces engraved at my own expense and the publisher—as he recently notified me—will publish both pieces; the proceeds of this edition, however—with the exception of the publisher's percentage share of every copy sold by him—accrue to me. (By the way, I won't sign the actual contract until I'm in Vienna; these are just the main points.)

I hope to recover a part of my outlay through the proceeds from sales, which accrue largely to me. If everything goes according to plan, 4 pieces of mine will be out by fall, a result I could not have obtained without this financial sacrifice, which really isn't one at all; these days, where one doesn't even have enough on the table or something in the oven, it doesn't matter if some old collection in a chest or picture on the wall is gone.—

And now, the reason I used the word "confession" at the outset (for surely you won't have any objection to publication in and of itself): because I did not—as you have so often advised me—wait for Hertzka!

I did it for the following reasons:

1.) I don't believe Hertzka will publish anything of mine any time soon, having neglected to do so for 10 years, despite your frequent advocacy to the point of quarreling with him, and even though at one time I offered to assume the engraving costs (of the sonata) myself and he has since then published every other Viennese beginner, be he ever so untalented and immature.[1]

But should he do it after all for any reason—which would be just as incomprehensible as his not publishing me until now—, publication couldn't be expected before spring (even if he still made the offer this winter). So for purposes of what I call a career, another full year—one season would be lost.

2.) For Hertzka the only reason to publish something after all could be if he wanted to take advantage of me in some other way, for example, if I were to come to him after a probationary period at *Anbruch* with the demand for a salary increase he could say, "I can't do that, for I can't increase the already high costs of *Anbruch*, which brings in no profits, but I will publish something of yours, for the time being as a supplement in *Anbruch*, Fleischmann[2] will write about it, and you and your name would be better served than if I raised your salary from 500 to 550 kronen."

A tidbit! Just as he waited for an occasion to publish Webern's works.[3] Namely, the *Gurrelieder* success at the Opera. Instead of increasing your royalties tenfold and publishing Webern's things years ago upon your recommendation.

3.) My position as editor of the U.E.-sponsored *Anbruch* makes it almost desirable (with regard to Hertzka and still more to the public) not to be connected with U.E. in any other way. Especially in public it might put me in an awkward position, the avoidance of which reminds me of your not dissimilar step in not performing anything of yours in the Verein.

4.) My having something appear now doesn't in the least prevent Hertzka from publishing me. He can either take over the published pieces from Haslinger, or me, as the case might be, or he could publish something else of mine.

---

The 2 new things (quartet and clarinet pieces) will turn out quite nicely. I have already read the 1st proofs and have, particularly in the quartet, where I still wrote sloppily and notated imprecisely, atoned for my sins. This took a good deal of time and again I've done less composing than I had expected (I still hope to get some-

1. After World War I Universal Edition began an ambitious publishing program that included a number of composers much younger than Berg himself. Above all, there were the works of Schreker students such as Karol Rathaus, Felix Petyrek, and Josef Rosenstock.

2. The music journalist Hugo Robert Fleischmann was a frequent contributor to *Anbruch*.

3. Hertzka had actually planned to begin publishing Webern's works in 1914, but due to the war Webern did not sign a contract with Universal until August 1920; the first works to be published were Opp. 1, 2, 3, and 6.

thing finished during these last 1–2 weeks). Copious correspondence for *Anbruch*, and related plans and drafts and reading have also cost much time and intellectual work without producing any appreciable results. The October issues—not to mention the later ones—have already caused me sleepless nights. Great project!—

I'm extremely anxious to find out what is new with you and your affairs. I heard from Webern that you have written piano pieces.[4] You cannot imagine how I long for them, though at present I'm still immersed in the score of *Glückliche Hand*, almost my only intellectual relaxation this summer.[5] But now I believe I'll soon feel comfortable even <u>there,</u> just as it should be; everything else is just nibbling.

A thousand greetings

from your Berg

Many regards to Mathilde. Helene sends all her love to you both.

**17 August.** The postman went on strike again, so the letter has been here 3 days.[6] If he comes tomorrow, the letter can leave from Deutsch-Landsberg on the 19th. And be in your hands a week after it was written. In the meantime I received a telegram from Stein, from which I gather that he accepted the position you offered him.[7] I'm supposed to send him Verein materials ("whatever isn't needed until September.") But that is impossible:

*[Berg cites as reasons the uncertain post, the scattered location of the materials, and Stein's own impending return to Vienna.]*

———

In any event I'll write to Stein immediately.—I'm <u>very</u> happy you engaged him. I believe he will be very suitable for the position of performance director, thanks to his musicality, but also to the convenient location of his apartment[8] and [his having] a telephone and other connections. I believe, indeed I'm convinced that I'll be able to work with him very well. Again I am looking forward to the coming season with great hopes (they were but slight after you and Webern left).[9]

Again, 1,000 greetings, dearest friend!

Your Berg

Sent 18 August, p.m.


\* For I live in hopes that Stein has taken the position you offered him with the Verein. At least I advised him to do so most urgently.

\*\* In doing so the publisher will add a number of revisions to the engraving plates that proved necessary in performances in the Verein and which I undertook according to Steuermann's specifications.

4. Schoenberg completed the first two of his Op. 23 piano pieces in July 1920.

5. Berg was studying Schoenberg's opera because of plans to perform the work in the Verein with a reduced orchestra.

6. As Berg had informed Schoenberg in a postcard of 6 July 1920, Trahütten received postal deliveries only three times a week, on Monday, Wednesday, and Friday.

7. Stein, who taught part-time in Frankfurt and Darmstadt, returned to Vienna to take over Webern's position as performance director.

8. In Vienna Stein most likely lived in his parents' home at 20 Kohlmarkt in Vienna's first district.

9. Schoenberg was planning his six-month trip to Amsterdam and Webern was leaving for Prague, where he held a position at the Deutsches Landestheater from the end of August until early October 1920.

*Berg to Schoenberg (letterhead: Musikblätter des Anbruch)*

Vienna, 1 September 1920
Midday

Dear esteemed friend,

After a 17-hour trip coupled with the most indescribable hardships, I reached Vienna late yesterday evening. In the night (after an interim of almost ¾ years), a terrible asthma attack. 1 o'clock the first injection (almost without effect), then until morning black coffee by the liter, 8 a.m. the 2$^{nd}$ injection (morphine), producing a dull half-sleep continually interrupted by recurrent shortness of breath. During one of these spells (I'm not sure: a "breathing spell" or the reverse), which is certain to be too short to establish a telephone connection (and in which I myself couldn't take part anyway, as I am lying down and can only stammer), I shall contact you in writing.

Naturally all the arrangements I had made for today have become impossible and must be postponed for at least 1–2 days. I planned to call you today at 8 o'clock and if possible arrange a meeting for this afternoon or tomorrow. 9 o'clock rendez-vous with Pisk (to discuss certain misgivings about *Anbruch*). 10 o'clock U.E., official assumption of all *Anbruch* responsibilities and finalizing the summer's pre-liminary work. 1 o'clock at my mother's, who is leaving this afternoon on "summer vacation." (2 weeks ago May Keller bought a cottage in Küb in the Semmering.) 2:30 with Waldheim regarding the engraving proofs for the compositions I'm pub-lishing.—The afternoon left open for you (possibly to attend a Verein meeting or rehearsal?). All of that has fallen through now. I had to send Kassowitz to: Pisk, U.E., and Waldheim, and have asked Pisk to come here this afternoon at an hour when I hope to be awake and alert, so I can at least attend to the most pressing matters. I hope he can come.

The cause of this particularly severe attack, aside from the direct results of the hardships of travel, was my weakened condition from overwork this summer. Besides composing, every 2$^{nd}$ or 3$^{rd}$ day spent entirely with correspondence: **above all** *Anbruch*, my publishing affairs (Waldheim and Haslinger, Vienna **and** Berlin), also the Ver-ein and letters to friends and relatives, 3.) proofreading (devil of a job!). Finally, during the last 1–2 weeks I wrote an article for *Anbruch*, a contribution to the theme "Schönberg and the Critics," in which I held forth at length on Korngold's latest feuilleton about your (atonal) music and on Bienenfeld's incredibly imperti-nent review of Walter Krug's *Die neue Musik*, in which she primarily discusses you.[1]

This scrawl has taken me more than 1½ hours and I have reached the end of my previously nonexistent strength. Many regards to your dear wife. All my love to you both—also from my completely despairing wife. She will call you at the 1$^{st}$ oppor-tunity.

Your Berg

1. Berg's "Wiener Musikkritik," written in response to Julius Korngold's "Nachlese zum Wiener Musikfest" (*Neue freie Presse* of 17 July 1920) and Elsa Bienenfeld's "Gegen die moderne Musik" (*Neues Wiener Journal* of 11 July 1920), did not appear in *Anbruch*, but was later given to Schoenberg. See Berg's letter of 9 September 1921.

## KONZERT

zu Ehren Maurice Ravels

**Samstag, den 23. Oktober 1920, nachm. 3 Uhr**

**im Kleinen Konzerthaussaal.**

## PROGRAMM:

| | |
|---|---|
| MAURICE RAVEL: | Gaspard de la nuit. Trois Poèmes pour Piano. (1. Ondine, 2. Le gibet, 3. Scarbo.) Herr Eduard Steuermann. |
| ARNOLD SCHÖNBERG: | Fünf Lieder aus Op. 15. Herr Helge Lindberg, Herr Eduard Steuermann |
| ARNOLD SCHÖNBERG: | Zwei neue Klavierstücke. Herr Eduard Steuermann. |
| ANTON WEBERN: | Vier Stücke für Geige und Klavier, Op. 7, Nr. 1. Herr Rudolf Kolisch, Herr Eduard Steuermann. |
| ALBAN BERG: | Vier Stücke für Klarinette und Klavier, Op. 5. Herr Karl Gaudriot (Staatsoper), Herr Eduard Steuermann. |
| MAURICE RAVEL: | Valses nobles et sentimentales pour deux pianos à quatre mains. Der Komponist und Herr Alfredo Casella. |
| ARNOLD SCHÖNBERG: | Jane Grey, eine Ballade aus Op. 12. Frau Olga Bauer-Pilecka (Staatsoper), Dr. Ernst Bachrich. |
| MAURICE RAVEL: | Streichquartett in F-dur. Das Feist-Quartett. |

*Program of the concert in honor of Maurice Ravel, October 1920*

*Berg to Schoenberg*

Parksanatorium [Vienna] 28 October 1920

Forgive my handwriting, I'm in bed!

Dear friend,

My intention of reporting to you on our first Verein activities on our own, including the Ravel concert, was thwarted by my renewed severe illness. On the day before the Ravel concert, I again suffered a frightful asthma attack and now am lying here in the sanatorium, facing another gradual convalescence.[1] The first undertaking since the onset of my illness is to be this letter to you, dear friend.—

How could this have happened to me again? Unquestionably I "overdid" it again recently. I have many students now (more about this later). The work for the Verein, which I normally would have been able to handle quite easily on the side, took on decidedly larger proportions as a result of the propaganda and Ravel concerts.[2]

1. During Schoenberg's stay in Holland, Berg had been given full administrative powers over programming, rehearsals, and the operation of the Verein. However on 22 October he suffered a serious relapse and reentered the Park Sanatorium for three weeks, from 23 October to 8 November.

2. Maurice Ravel was on a two-week visit to Vienna from 16 to 30 October for two concerts of his works on 22 and 25 October. A Verein concert held in his honor took place on 23 October 1920 and included *Gaspard de la nuit*, *Valses nobles et sentimentales* (two pianos), *Trois Poèmes de Stéphane Mallarmé*, and the String Quartet. The program also included Berg's Clarinet Pieces, Op. 5, five songs from Schoenberg's George Songs, Op. 15, the "Jane Grey" ballad from Op. 12, and two of the new Piano Pieces, Op. 23, as well as Webern's Four Pieces for Violin and Piano, Op. 7.

Understandably, the urgency of these matters pushed all thoughts of moderation aside. It's simply impossible to remain idle when one is needed and part of the success is dependent on one's participation. So it was that—right before the Ravel concert, whose success was so important to us all, there were countless extra meetings, rehearsals, arrangements with all attendant problems with which you are certainly familiar; seemingly insurmountable obstacles, delays, program changes, of which the serene, unproblematic course of the ensuing concert gives no inkling. But at least I can tell myself that I had no small part in the success of the Ravel concert and that my illness only struck after everything concerning the concert had been dealt with, all obstacles overcome, and it only remained to do the honors at the concert itself, which Stein took care of. I had often consulted with Ravel <u>beforehand</u>, had—representing you, as it were—invited him, taken note of his wishes. He wanted only to hear <u>your</u> music, which, in view of our previous repertoire, posed great difficulties. You can see from the program to what extent we were able to accomodate his wish. For a while we also tried to work up a 4-hand performance of your Chamber Symphony. 2–3 rehearsals did take place, which finally convinced us that the piece couldn't be prepared adequately in such a short time. Due to Ravel's own performance of his most recent work on 2 pianos with Casella,[3] which, as he told me, was intended to honor you and the Verein, and Freund's last-minute decision to sing,[4] the concert grew to a length of 3 hours with short intermissions and the undiminished interest of all present. I mention this because I was advised before the concert by a friend of Ravel's (Clémenceau)[5] to keep the evening as short as possible, as in Paris Ravel is notorious for leaving before the end of every concert. <u>So here it was just the opposite</u>. In other ways, too, this concert was sensational, as well as good publicity. We had submitted numerous newspaper notices. Next to the performance of your works, the names Ravel, Casella, Helge Lindberg,[6] and in general the entire affair proved an attraction. And if it still wasn't a particular financial success, that may have been due to the high prices of the festival tickets (100 kronen). After all, in wealthy social circles there isn't much interest for Ravel either; (his own 2 concerts were <u>very</u> poorly attended, despite the French embassy, etc.). <u>Artistically,</u> however, the success of our concert was very satisfying. Besides the Ravel entourage others said to be there included: Schnitzler, little Korngold, Szymanowski, Loos, Pless-Pischinger,[7] who by the way is conducting *Verklärte Nacht* on 13 November and, inexplicably, a handful of critics as well: Bach, Konta, Bienenfeld. No one admits to knowing how they got in.[8] Unfortu-

3. The Italian composer Alfredo Casella was in Vienna, where he and Ravel were Alma Mahler's house guests. Casella performed with Ravel in *Valse nobles et sentimentales*.

4. Marya Freund had accompanied Ravel from Paris in order to participate in the two Ravel concerts; she agreed to participate in the Verein concert with the three Mallarmé songs that she had already been scheduled to sing on Ravel's chamber music concert of 25 October.

5. The wealthy patron of the arts Paul Clémenceau, brother of Georges Clémenceau, was married to Sophie Scepes, who had been primarily responsible for arranging Ravel's Vienna visit.

6. The bass Helge Lindberg performed the Schoenberg George Songs, Op. 15.

7. The conductor Hans Pless (-Pischinger).

8. While the other critics adhered to Schoenberg's declared wish that Verein concerts not be covered by the press, Elsa Bienenfeld of the *Neues Wiener Journal* published not only a review of the Ravel concert but a critique of the Verein itself.

nately Puccini didn't come. In an interview he had expressed a strong desire to get to know your music and the Verein. I invited him by letter and had Rufer personally pick up his answer, which was unfortunately negative—since he already had another commitment at the time of the concert and actually wanted to hear your orchestral things.[9] Webern, Stein, Rufer, etc., will have told you about the rest of the concert, and about the quality of the performances. After all, I wasn't there. At the time my clarinet pieces were being played, my wife was bringing me to the sanatorium by auto. Incidentally, it was the 23rd. Apparently my pieces were so well received that Ravel is taking them back to Paris, where they are to be performed. I also hear there was a very good review of my songs in *Melos*.[10] Finally, the so-called Sak-Philharmonic (the 2nd Czech orchestra) wants to do my orchestra pieces in December.[11] I am telling you all this not out of vanity, but because I know what a warm interest you take in everything concerning me and because I don't wish to keep the few pleasant matters from you.

To continue about <u>myself</u> (I have so much to tell you). <u>Before</u> my illness I had had Dr. Schweinburg[12] do a <u>blood</u> test, which pointed conclusively to <u>bronchial</u> asthma (only secondarily to <u>nervous</u> asthma). But the doctors are all very much in the dark about how to treat this illness. On the advice of Dr. Schweinburg, a nose and throat specialist, and my family physician. I am going to try <u>calcium lactate</u> now, which I am to take daily for several months, and while here—after all, something effective has to be done—I have begun a course of treatment with atropine (as well as all the usual remedies). This treatment, which is used by Prof. Noorden,[13] is said to be very effective and should insure my being free of asthma for a long time to come. You can well imagine that this renewed sanatorium stay (I am to remain at least 2 weeks!) is catastrophic for me financially. Added to that the fear that my students may scatter. Certainly for now they are very devoted to me and visit me often, but in the end—if I should be sick too long! I have 6 students at present, of whom a Rumanian[14] and Wittenberg[15] each pay 1,000 kronen, the others together come to c. 1,000, so that I earn c. 3,000 kronen from teaching and 1,000 kronen from the Verein. (The 4 are Kassowitz, Watza,[16] Mahler[17] (from your course), and a 2nd Rumanian who is very talented: Saltar.)[18] Rufer and Greissle[19]

9. Giacomo Puccini was in Vienna at this time for a new production of *La Rondine* at the Volksoper on 7 October, as well as the Viennese first performances of his three one-act operas (*Il Tabarro, Suor Angelica,* and *Gianni Schicchi*) at the State Opera on 20 October. The interview with Puccini appeared in *Anbruch* II / 13 (second October issue, 1920), 549–50.

10. Hans Heinz Stuckenschmidt devoted one paragraph to Alban Berg's Songs, Op. 2, in his article "Neue Lieder," *Melos* I / 17 (16 October 1920), 395–6.

11. The Sak Philharmonic Orchestra, founded by the wealthy conductor Vladimir Vladislav Sak in 1919 and disbanded in 1921, did not perform Berg's Orchestra Pieces.

12. Fritz Schweinburg was a specialist in infectious diseases; he was also a member of the Verein.

13. Karl von Noorden was a renowned diabetes specialist.

14. Filip Herzcovics.

15. Franz Wittenberg.

16. Georg Watza.

17. Gustav Mahler's grandnephew Fritz Mahler studied with Schoenberg 1919–20, with Berg 1921–24, and with Webern 1923–24.

18. N. Saltar studied with Berg in 1920.

19. Felix Greissle studied with both Berg and Schoenberg. In 1922 he married Schoenberg's daughter Gertrud.

also approached me recently and I'll probably take them together. I take care of the Verein matters quite amicably with Stein (and Rufer and Sachs.)[20] We see each other regularly, above all we telephone several times a day—often for hours. Naturally this facilitates administration considerably. If it was nonetheless too much for me recently, that was because of the extraordinary pressure placed on everyone by the additional Verein activities. It should be more manageable again from now on. The program guide should appear soon; I only have to add the finishing touches. After a number of meetings with me, Sachs did very good preliminary work.

Artistically the 1st propaganda concert went very well,[21] (financially probably with a deficit of 4,000 kronen. Interest was strong, but the prices too steep.) The Romantic Suite sounded really terrific. If we could keep a chamber orchestra busy all the time, we'd be in the clear.

Of course after one hearing I don't have an opinion yet on your new piano pieces, just an unspeakably warm, intimate impression. I even seem to have understood the 2nd one a little. But how long until I am truly familiar with this music. I noticed that during the 5th Verein evening,[22] when Steuermann played your Op. 11. But then, the way he played it. It has never been played like that before, which is why it has never made such an overwhelming impression as this time. It was followed by the Reger C major Violin Sonata: a colossal and very incomprehensible work. Good performance. Then Petrushka.[23] VIth concert:[24] 3 piano pieces from *Am Kamin*, Op. 143, by Reger (Hartungen) and outstanding repeat performance of the above C major Violin Sonata by Reger. *En blanc et noir*, which unfortunately suffered from the pianos. VIIth evening.[25] Finally Vomáčka, solo violin suites by Reger, pieces for violin and piano by Reger, Suk pieces (Serkin).[26] That was the day before yesterday,[27] so naturally I wasn't there. But apparently it was very beautiful!

Steuermann is away at the moment, but he'll be back soon.[28] Stein and Rufer have already told you about the necessary postponement of the 2nd propaganda evening.[29]

My wife will write to your wife soon. Initially distracted by a variety of things, she is now entirely preoccupied with my illness and very anxious. Despite that she

---

20. Benno Sachs, a student of Schoenberg, was active in the Verein.

21. The first propaganda concert of the season, on 9 October, included Reger's *Eine Romantische Suite*, Op. 125 (in Reger's own arrangement for chamber orchestra), Béla Bartók's Piano Rhapsody, Op. 1 (in Bartók's two-piano arrangement), Schoenberg's Op. 23, Nos. 1 and 2 (first performance), and Debussy's Sonata for Flute, Viola, and Harp.

22. On 13 October.

23. Reger's Violin Sonata, Op. 22 was performed by Oskar Adler and Ida Hartungen, followed by a four-hand arrangement of *Petrushka* with Eduard Steuermann and Rudolf Serkin.

24. On 18 October.

25. The Ravel concert of 23 October.

26. The eighth Verein concert on 27 October featured Reger's A-minor Violin and Piano Suite, Op. 103a, Boleslav Vomáčka's Four Piano Pieces, Op. 4, Reger's A-minor Solo Violin Sonata, Op. 91, and Josef Suk's *Vom Mütterchen*, Op. 28, performed by the pianist Rudolf Serkin.

27. This seems to indicate that Berg either misdated this letter or wrote it over two days, 28 and 29 October.

28. Eduard Steuermann was on a concert tour in Dresden.

29. The second Verein propaganda concert, initially postponed until 21 December, was finally held on 20 January 1921.

is **madly** looking forward to *Pelleas* (Furtwängler, 3 and 4 November).[30] That too is denied me. Not to mention the wonderful things that may be happening in Amsterdam. You have probably already conducted. A thousand regards to you all,

from your Alban Berg

---

30. On 3 and 4 November 1920 Wilhelm Furtwängler conducted Schoenberg's *Pelleas und Melisande* and Brahms's First Symphony with the Vienna Philharmonic Orchestra.

## *Schoenberg to Berg*

Zandvoort, 12 November 1920

Dear friend,

I hear from Greissle(!!) that you are doing better and that you even want to resume teaching.[1] I'd like to take this opportunity, though, to warn you of renewed overexertion. Do no more than is good for you. As you see, you have nothing to gain by it.—I assume your wife has meanwhile received [my letter] answering your detailed one. I hope I responded to everything you asked.[2]—I don't have much news. My seminar isn't very well attended, though there were advertisements and posters. They say the Dutch are slow to make up their minds. I'm actually a little surprised. But nevertheless a seminar has materialized, which may not bring in much but still enough to enable me to hold it.—I'd like to know exactly why the four-hand performance of the Chamber Symphony was not done. Is the reduction usable? Easily playable? Whose reduction was used?[3] There is to be a performance of the Chamber Symphony here on the 29th (and earlier on the 20th in Utrecht).[4] I'd like this work to be a little better understood here than the orchestra pieces and have therefore requested that U.E. send "Berg-Guides." Maybe you can find out whether they have done so.—It appears that I won't be conducting for quite some time.—I hope some things will change—for the better—when Mengelberg returns, though he is still ill. The Concertgebouw seems to be in bad straits as a result of his absence. They have to use guest conductors who don't have the same appeal as Mengelberg. As a result my affairs too, but especially those of my students and of the Mahlerbund, have been completely neglected. I hope things will improve now.

I enjoy hearing plenty of news from Vienna. Tell everyone you see that they should write often. I don't get any newspapers; not that they're very informative anyway.—

---

1. In his reply of 17 November Berg tells Schoenberg that the loss of his two Rumanian students (Saltar and Herzcovics) has reduced his monthly teaching income from 3,000 to about 1,500 kronen. His remaining students were Greissle, Kassowitz, Mahler, Rufer, Watza, and Wittenberg.

2. In this letter to Helene Berg of 3 November 1920 Schoenberg expressed his concern for Berg's health and offered financial assistance. Berg gratefully declined that offer in his 17 November reply, since he had recently received 10,000 kronen each from Alma Mahler and his brother Hermann.

3. In his reply of 17 November 1920 Berg informs Schoenberg that the Chamber Symphony performance in the Verein, with Rudolf Serkin and Ernst Bachrich, had not taken place due to lack of sufficient rehearsal time; the reduction was Berg's own.

4. Performed by the Concertgebouw Sextet and members of the Concertgebouw Orchestra.

I meant to tell you; next time you do an analysis of one of my works (for example, II$^{nd}$ Quartet or Orchestra Pieces), excellent as the Chamber Symphony and *Pelleas* [guides] are, you shouldn't design them so that they are practically unintelligible without the score, but rather, so that they can be understood at a performance even without a score. In this respect the *Gurrelieder* guide is excellent,[5] even if there is a bit too much "scientific" text with $x^2$. $y^3 + ab$. $2[3Q^5 \pm (f \times I^2 \rightarrow \leftarrow \{ \nearrow + \times I^{b+a?!}$ ⌐⊐)—4fffsf]:26$^a$A. You won't take my joke amiss. But it lacks immediacy. If you could find a happy medium here: symbols that don't require so much memorization and can be deciphered more quickly, plus numerous examples, some analytic, which you do very well, and some just for reference, and in the text some differentiation between description and analysis, possibly with the latter in smaller print and <u>summarized</u> in <u>separate</u> paragraphs, and in combination with foldouts of musical examples, but in such a way that there are <u>several</u> in the booklet, every 6–8 pages or so, <u>printed on both sides</u> so that the front side can be used for the preceding and the reverse for the following pages, thereby achieving something still better at no great expense and without limiting yourself to so few examples. In a pamphlet of 20 pages you could have two tables, one double-sided. The first after about eight pages (for pages 3–8 and 9–15) and the 2$^{nd}$ at the end for the remainder.—What do you think of that?

—Early next year the Rebner Quartet will play one of my quartets here. I don't know which one. Maybe Hertzka will decide to publish analyses of them. If not, one could also consider a Dutch publisher. Should I ask one? Would it be legal? I think so. In any event the fee would be larger. Maybe Hertzka wouldn't even object. At any rate, you shouldn't always work for nothing.

Students are coming. So I must close. You mustn't be surprised that I write so infrequently. I write a great deal: to many people. So everyone gets less. People simply have to write to me more often than I do to them and without waiting for an answer.

Many warm regards to you and your wife from me and my family

Your Arnold Schönberg

---

5. As a matter of fact, Schoenberg withheld praise of the *Gurrelieder* guide until June 1918; in a letter to his wife of 10 June of that year Berg wrote that Schoenberg's belated endorsement pleased him so particularly because he was prouder of the guide than of any of his compositions.

## Schoenberg to His Students and Friends

Zandvoort, 6 December 1920

Dear friends,

I can't possibly write to each of you as often and in as much detail as you write to me. You must take into consideration that I correspond with 15 times more people than any one of you. But I am nonetheless very pleased with every letter I receive and will answer everything asked of me. Only not right away.—But what I have to report, to the extent that it is of general interest, I will do in this manner and send the letter alternately to one of you who, however, must then see to it that all for whom it is intended read it.

Well now: recently I have again been rather busy with rehearsals of two of my works; the I$^{st}$ String Quartet and the Chamber Symphony.

The String Quartet was played <u>really excellently</u> by the Budapest Quartet (a new group, not to be confused with the Hungarian Quartet "Waldbauer").[1] I think it may well be one of the best quartets I have ever heard. Incredibly diligent and serious. They rehearse at least as much as we do. Maybe even more. In this regard they are inferior to us in perhaps only 2 areas: I. that we may have a more highly developed musical background, taste, and culture (Mahler era!) and for that reason alone our musical insight, especially with regard to modern music, provides us with superior and more precise models because some of the most modern composers have helped develop it. II. that we have already gone beyond the latest interpretive ideal: to subordinate everything to a clearly articulated main voice, in that we now envisage a truly polyphonic performance ideal: to make each voice (based on a **conceptual** understanding of **all** voices) absolutely clear! That rests on the truly <u>polyphonic</u> approach characterizing our school. The other ideal, from a transitional period, stems from a homophonic approach in which there is not yet a pure, new polyphony. Of course that has been one way of making works of this style comprehensible to ears schooled in absolute homophony. But it is, after all, only an expedient. And our goal: to make everything audible, graduated according to significance, and at the same time obtain a "homogeneous" sound—this, our goal, will prove its real value all the more in homophonic music, where <u>all voices</u>, which remain voices even in homophonic garb, are thus brought to life. And the "homogeneous sound" that is attained notwithstanding, is *different* from the one based on the domination of a single voice.—This aside—and one cannot demand this new ideal, which is <u>ours</u>, from anyone else; only from us—the performance was perhaps the best I have heard to date. Even if Rosé in his energetic way shapes some features more clearly and—where they remain unclear to him—preserves an elegant bearing behind industrious technical display and the truly Viennese tone quality of his quartet always produces a "homogenous sound," here <u>everything</u> was played with conviction; even where the interpretive abilities didn't quite suffice and the conceptual understanding was different from mine. At the same time everything was really extraordinarily clear. I did achieve some of the above goals in 3 three-hour rehearsals, but I must say that sections such as the first development were excellent from the start; as I've never heard them done before. And what a tempo! I finally restored the basic tempo (in the printed edition it is wrong)  = over 100!.[2] That was terrific. The whole thing made an excellent impression. It was successful, very successful, in fact; [the success] was based, however, primarily on the "timbral effects": har-

---

1. The Budapest String Quartet performed Schoenberg's First String Quartet, Op. 7, on 17 November. Founded in 1917 by the Hungarians Emil Hauser, Imre Poganyi, Istvan Ipolyi, and Harry Son, the group in the course of the later Twenties and Thirties gradually evolved into the American-based Budapest Quartet, which was not disbanded until 1967. The renowned Waldbauer-Kerpely Quartet was in existence 1909–46.

2. The printed score of the first movement of Op. 7 reads "Nicht zu rasch" (Not too fast).

monics, pizzicato, *sul ponticello*, etc., and the Adagios. The audience here seems a long way from grasping the "symphonic" and melodic qualities. Insofar as it is "well-disposed," it responds only to "mood" and "poetry," while the modern-minded cling to the abstruse and only enjoy it if it remains unclear to them. The usual fate of my music.

That's why I was very anxious about the Chamber Symphony. I wasn't at the performance because Mengelberg is feuding with the conductor of the performance, Cornelis,[3] a former student of his, who supposedly plotted against him. Since a certain amount of effusive handshaking is unavoidable after a concert, I didn't want to close a friendship pact with Mengelberg's enemy in front of the entire audience, knowing that in his place I, too, would have taken it ill. So I sent word that I had lumbago. In any event the performance was not outstanding, although not bad. Nothing was entirely wrong or really unclear, though all the fast tempos were **much** too slow and hardly anything was absolutely clear. In general the musicians played well and apparently with interest, some even with enjoyment, and the conductor likewise. They are said to have held 15 rehearsals, but I believe my performance with 10 rehearsals was clearer. That was primarily because I was only invited to two (2!!) short rehearsals. I corrected a few things there, but to achieve half of what is at all necessary I would have had to conduct at least 3 × 3-hour rehearsals. Above all, they never played a real *p*, let alone a *pp* or *ppp*. Indeed, the oboe generally only played *mf* and the bassoon *mf–ff*. And then: all those emphasized beats:

For: especially in polyphonic music, staccatos can't be short or sharp enough. Only when of the utmost brevity do they remain clear and not distort the texture. The same is true of our *p>*. (piano-marcato-staccato) attack. I don't mean to say that this is the only way to make polyphony clear; but it is certainly a good one. At any rate I must say: today's fashion of emphasizing one voice by playing it strongly and everything else softly seems more and more intolerable to me. These days everyone does that completely mechanically, though at one time it may have been an interpretive expedient. I believe that must increasingly be done differently: Each voice must have life, be somewhat expressive, and that is only possible if the interpreter has a concept of the total sound. After all, if a composer heard that many voices and if these aren't ornamental, but part of the composition—where now one, now another of these voices has significant influence on the progress of the work—it must be possible at some point to realize it as the composer heard it. However, that requires: rehearsals!

Then there is the following to report:

Mengelberg is back, but my position still hasn't been defined. My agreement was really only with Mengelberg, and his illness prevented him from arranging things

---

3. Evert Cornelis was the assistant conductor of the Concertgebouw Orchestra 1908–19.

as would have been necessary. I hope he can still do it. As a result, unfortunately, many of the hopes I had: of summoning some of you here, have more or less fallen through. I'm completely innocent in the matter. Everything depends on Mengelberg here.—The Mahlerbund will be founded soon. I have come to the conclusion that my autocratic conception is not feasible here at the moment. I'm not giving up the plan entirely, but have concluded to try it as is for the present and if it doesn't work to extend an ultimatum.[4]

My seminars have not attracted many participants. I can give only one on "Elements of Form," which has 11 participants (@20–30 gulden). People here are accustomed to very low prices—in spite of inflation. So far I've had a few inquiries regarding lessons, but they all thought it too expensive. However, I'm not interested in giving the Dutch inexpensive instruction. Apparently they only want things from us cheap. As if our countries hadn't already given them enough bargains! That's not a very sympathetic trait here. Other things aren't at all bad.

I don't have time to work here. The trips to Amsterdam take two hours each way. Twice already I've had to go in morning and evening to avoid having to hang around Amsterdam for 6–8 hours; that made an 8 hour trip in all. That's annoying. Otherwise Zandvoort is very pretty. Especially the sea, where there have been a number of big storms in recent weeks. But to be honest, I much prefer a landscape such as the Gmündener-See. One has to be raised to the poetry of the sea if one is truly to feel it and I happen to have been raised to the poetry of our landscape. I am too old to talk myself into something. However, the sunsets are magnificent. That's something one can only see here. Naturally that's the "heavy brass" of the landscape here, but I don't have an ear yet for the subtler voices. Even though my ear is schooled to hear subtler voices.

What I've seen of the composers here (young men who've come to me) is very depressing. Everyone imitates Debussy and everything has a veneer of film music. They have no ability; to think of all the things they didn't learn! But they are artfully modern; that is, Debussy-ish.—One could accomplish a great deal here; and I must say: people know it and realize they are at a dead end and will never write music of any significance if they continue like this, and yet they can't help themselves because they lack the right teachers. All the same, our scores are much cheaper than the Romanic (Latin) ones and *they* aren't bad teachers either. I could accomplish a great deal here. But it would take years. A society like ours and teaching like mine might not bear fruit for perhaps 10 years. But then with certainty. In general people here are musical and love music. No doubt that is the German element. But the cinema and French influence ruin everything. It is to Mengelberg's credit that he has awakened appreciation for Mahler here. I cannot yet decide favorably whether it is purely musical or only poetic.

Otherwise one can live here quite well. Except for the enormous inflation (300–500%, and for some things, like toys and hardware, 1000%) there's nothing to stop one from living just as in peacetime. Autos are unaffordable. Heating—very nec-

---

4. Schoenberg and Mengelberg could not agree in their concepts for the organization of the Mahler League and the plan was never realized.

essary due to the humidity and the storms—is very expensive. Especially expensive are all those luxury items that begin to make for real comfort. But still, one doesn't feel that wretched envy that makes life in Austria so miserable even when one has enough money: at least that is a considerable relief.

I think I have written enough now. Nor can I think of anything else to report at the moment.

So: enough for today. Many, many warm regards to you all.

Your Arnold Schönberg

P.S. from the bands around the papers I see that you have subscribed to the *Neues Wiener Tagblatt* for me. But I don't want that. It's a waste of money. I don't need to read this paper every day. It must cost at least 2 kronen 50. I wanted you to send clippings that might interest me. If that isn't possible, it would still be cheaper to subscribe to the paper in Vienna and send it every ten days. That couldn't cost more than 60–80 kronen. Please tell me who paid for this.[5]

One of you is to to confirm the arrival of this letter immediately.

---

5. Berg, Stein, and Rudolf Kolisch had joined together to take out the subscription for the Schoenbergs. Berg assures Schoenberg in his reply of 12 December that the subscription cost only 80 kronen.

*Schoenberg to Berg (postcard)*

Zandvoort, 8 December 1920

Dear friend,

Yesterday I sent a letter to all my friends addressed to you. Without a word to you, as I had to close and had no time to write to you too.—I'm very glad you received an offer to write a book about me. Nor do the terms seem basically unfavorable to me. Translation rights are generally held by the publisher, but one can reserve the right to examine the artistic quality of the translation and must in any event share in the translation profits.[1]—That you wish to write only on the music is in accordance with my wishes. In my opinion: my biography as such is highly uninteresting and I consider the publication of any details embarrassing. A few place names, dates of composition, there's really nothing more to say. There certainly isn't much to say about positions, for instance. It would be interesting to outline my development through the music. I am convinced that you yourself will know what's right. I only ask myself whether this won't keep you from composing.—In any event: don't overexert yourself. And don't worry about your work for the Verein. Leave that to the Verein, whether it can survive or not does not depend on your salary. Warmest regards to your wife. Many regards from me and mine. We think of you often.

Your Arnold Schönberg

1. In a letter of 12 December 1920, Berg tells Schoenberg that he had signed the contract for the book on him, according to which the author would receive the same fee for the translation as for the original; the manuscript was due by 1 March 1921. The series in which the book was to be published never materialized.

*Berg to Schoenberg (letterhead of the Verein)*

Vienna, 26 [27] December 1920[1]

Dear esteemed friend,

This is our new stationery, we had it printed without an address because many of the Verein letters are written by me (and Stein).

Today I just want to wish you and your dear family all the best for the New Year and to take this opportunity to send you my new <u>score</u>, which appeared the day before Christmas.[2] At the same time I am sending the parts as registered printed matter. Please acknowledge their receipt when you have a chance!

I got some very nice books for Christmas: Kepler's *Harmony of the Universe* and a new Strindberg volume from his posthumous papers: *Socrates* (a drama). And other things. . . .

We will report about the Verein after Wednesday's meeting. Besides your Opus 11, today's concert will include Debussy's Violin Sonata and Mussorgsky's *Songs and Dances of Death* (Fleischer).[3] The next concert[4] will include a repetition of these songs and a 2-hand version of the Chamber Symphony played by Steuermann. He does it fabulously!!!! After that he's going to Dresden, so we will have to do without him in the near future.[5] As of January we will have the Schwarzwald hall. In the end the Railwaymen's Hall was no longer tenable.[6] Now we are simply trying to part amicably. On the 10th we perform Mahler's IVth with chamber orchestra and possibly the Romantic Suite,[7] on the 20th finally the IInd propaganda concert, with Mahler's IVth as yet the only certain thing on the program. <u>Planned</u> are: Orchestra Songs, Opus 8 (Oestvig), Celesta Song (Schumann, State Opera), Webern's first Orchestra Pieces.[8] But will it work?? We would so like to contact the quartet that played the D-minor Quartet in Amsterdam. Perhaps it would come to Vienna? We can't even find out if it was the Budapest (<u>Lener</u>) Quartet[9] or some <u>Berlin</u> Budapest Quartet? Please advise! (There isn't even anything in Hesse's German

1. Berg misdated this letter; see footnote 3.

2. This score of Berg's String Quartet, Op. 3, is now located at the Arnold Schoenberg Institute.

3. Since the concert that Berg describes took place on 27 December, it is probable that the dating of Berg's letter is incorrect. Eduard Steuermann performed the piano pieces and accompanied Arthur Fleischer in the Mussorgsky songs.

4. On 3 January 1921.

5. Steuermann was away from mid-January to 5 February.

6. Since the fall, the Verein concerts had been held in the concert hall of the Klub österreichischer Eisenbahnbeamter (Austrian Train Officials' Club) on 3 Nibelungengasse in Vienna's first district. In a letter of 17 November 1920 Berg informed Schoenberg that the hall had become too noisy; the last concert held there was on 27 December. The Schwarzwald Hall was located in the same district.

7. This concert brought the first book of Debussy's Preludes (performed by Bachrich) and Erwin Stein's chamber orchestra arrangement of Mahler's Fourth Symphony. Erwin Stein conducted, the soloist was Martha Fuchs.

8. The second propaganda concert on 20 January included Schoenberg's songs, Op. 8, Nos. 5 and 6 (Karl Fälbl, Ernst Bachrich), Op. 14 (premiere), and Op. 6, Nos. 1, 3, and 4 (the latter two sung by Erika Wagner, accompanied by Ernst Bachrich), and a repetition of Mahler's Fourth Symphony. Neither Karl Oestvig nor Elizabeth Schumann ever participated in the Verein concerts.

Webern's Orchestra Pieces, Op. 6, were first performed by the Verein in a version for chamber orchestra on 23 January 1921.

9. The Lener Quartet was founded by the Hungarian violinist Jenö Lener in 1917.

Music Calendar for the year 1921.*[10]

I work on the book about you every day; but it will require a good deal of preparation before anything more than notes are evident. It would actually be a subject for a work of many hundred pages. And it is difficult to summarize only the most important things and still be complete. I am concerned with setting straight all the nonsense about atonality, impressionism, and expressionism. I believe that will also coincide with your concerns. I have asked Eisler to speak with you about it to relieve you of having to report to me. Especially concerning the unusable term "atonality" and what one should use instead. Polytonal as you once suggested. . . . or: pantonal, as the writer Pannwitz once called it**[12] (incorporating all(?) tonality).—

Enough for today——and for this year. I wish you and your dear wife and Trude and Görgl—as on every day of the year—the very, very best for 1921.

Warmest regards to you all

from your truly devoted Alban Berg

The warmest and most affectionate wishes for the New Year to you all

from your Helene

*I asked once before: may Rosé play your quartet for us?[11]

**known for his book: *Der Geist der Tschechen*, wherein he supposedly writes beautifully about Mahler.

---

10. Hesse's *Deutscher Musiker Kalender* was an annual address book of musicians and musical organizations begun in 1878, which covered Germany and Austria in depth and the other European countries more briefly.

11. In a letter of 8 December 1920 Berg had first asked whether Schoenberg would allow the Rosé Quartet to perform the D-minor String Quartet in the Verein.

12. Rudolf Pannwitz, *Der Geist der Tschechen* (The Spirit of the Czechs) (Vienna, 1919).

# 1921

*Schoenberg to Berg (postcard)*

Zandvoort, 18 January 1921

Dear friend,

Above all my warmest thanks for the beautiful Christmas gift, the Voltaire.[1] I was as surprised as I was pleased. Had not expected that you would be able to surmount the difficulties of sending something here.—I am in the state I'm always in when I have some very distracting activities that don't take up all of my time: I find myself unable to start anything else and waste the extra time. On top of that, I just had these 2 concerts plus rehearsals,[2] and after the 2nd concert I was ill for several days, which is why I haven't written until now.—I haven't heard from any of you for a long time. You are probably angry that I haven't written. But you shouldn't be. Sometimes it's just impossible. And then I always have to write 10 letters or more to your 2 or 3. Or perhaps you write with greater facility than I, for whom it is a great effort. When I write a letter, I should be given the kind of credit that in my opinion is due a rich person when he gives something. For a generous man it is not an effort, but a pleasure. For a rich man it is a great effort and brings him no pleasure. That's why one should give him great credit for the effort.—Today or tomorrow I'll write another letter to you all. This time to Webern. Many warm regards to you and your wife

Your Arnold Schönberg

1. The two-volume edition of Voltaire's novels and stories, *Die Romane und Erzählungen* (Postdam: Gustav Kiepenhauer, 1920).

2. Schoenberg conducted a concert of his own works with the Concertgebouw Orchestra in Amsterdam on 6 January, which was repeated in the Hague on 8 January; on the program were *Pelleas und Melisande* and four of the Six Orchestral Songs, Op. 8 ("Natur," "Das Wappenschild," "Sehnsucht," and "Wenn Vöglein klagen"), with Hans Nachod as the soloist.

*Berg to Schoenberg*

Vienna, 21 January 1921
[*Berg writes the date:*] 21.1.21

Dear esteemed friend,

Enclosed the copy of the letter I sent you 5 days ago.[1] I'll send you the copy of my present letter at some point. Meanwhile the following has occurred: the tobacco arrived!!![2] You can imagine our joy!! A thousand thanks, dear friend. With this amount of tobacco, I'll be set for a long time!! In agreement with Webern and Stein, I arranged the distribution as follows, with each of us relinquishing 1 box because it was impossible to make a fair allocation of the remainder according to your instructions. Thus, Webern and I each took 5 boxes, Stein and Steuermann 2 each, Rankl, Rufer, Greissle, Steinbauer,[3] Travnicek and Kolisch 1 each = 20 boxes!

Yesterday was the II[nd] propaganda concert.[4] It went very well. Artistically as well as with respect to audience response. The Mahler symphony was really flawless. Due both to Stein's performance, which hadn't yet been quite up to the mark at the previous Verein concert (chamber concert in the Kammersaal),[5] as well as that of the soloists, who really pulled themselves together and gave their best, indeed better than that! The singer (Fuchs)[6] was very good, too. Much better than Palffy.[7] Your songs, sung by Wagner,[8] were very beautiful, as far as that is possible for such a 2nd-rate singer; the orchestral songs less so. Bachrich[9] was impossible. Nevertheless all the songs, since the spirit was right and they are in any case indestructible, were very effective and particularly "Vöglein klagen" and "Traumleben" were well-received. Next time they'll be even better. There wasn't enough time!

Public success was apparent in that the hall was sold out (as of 2 days before the performance) and was filled to the *rafters at* the performance. The gratifying thing about it is that many of the members who took their time ordering tickets got *none*. We had set low prices: members according to the categories 10, 20, 30 kronen, guests 20, 30, and 40 kronen, as well as standing room for the latter at 10 kronen, which, strangely enough, was the last to go. The whole thing was an experiment, from which we conclude—just as we concluded from last year's experience that prices at 30–100 kronen result in an empty hall—that next time we will set prices between c. 20–70 kronen, with no standing room. That way we should be able to break even; which was not the case this time (nor did we expect it), despite the fact that we took in over 8,000 kronen, and that's why we shall repeat the concert on the 23rd (Webern's Orchestra Pieces, Opus 6[10] (which you performed once), will be

1. This letter is written on the back of a carbon copy of a letter dated 16 January, in which Berg reported on the progress of his Schoenberg book and the Verein.
2. Shortly before Christmas 1920 Schoenberg had sent tobacco, which Berg was to share with Webern and others.
3. The Austrian composer and conductor Karl Rankl and the music theorist Othmar Steinbauer both studied with Schoenberg.
4. This 20 January concert, repeated on 23 January, brought two of Schoenberg's Op. 8 songs ("Voll jener Süsse," "Wenn Vöglein klagen"), performed by Karl Fälbl and Ernst Bachrich, the premiere of the two Op. 14 songs and three songs from Op. 6 ("Traumleben," "Verlassen," and "Mädchenlied"), sung by Erika Wagner, as well as Erwin Stein's chamber orchestra arrangement of Mahler's Fourth Symphony.
5. On 10 January.
6. Martha Fuchs was the featured soloist in Mahler's Fourth, which Stein conducted.
7. The mezzo-soprano Kamilla Palffy.
8. Erika Wagner, who later married the conductor Fritz Stiedry.
9. The pianist and composer Ernst Bachrich studied with Schoenberg 1916–19.
10. In an arrangement for chamber orchestra by Webern, who conducted.

inserted between your songs and Mahler's IV[th]. They are already going very well and sound wonderful).

Arranging the repeat performance was a real feat. Getting <u>20</u> people free. Obtaining tickets, newpaper announcements, programs, hall, the 5-string bass, bells, bass drum, etc., all in 2 days. And on the following Monday (24th) there is another Verein meeting at Schwarzwald. . . . . .

Oh yes! Your <u>D-minor</u> Quartet with Rosé![11] The performance really isn't good. Hasn't gotten better, either. In fact, probably worse than when Rosé played it in Vienna (during the war). Great success both times, though not without the inevitable opposition, especially at the actual subscription concert, which was, however, properly squelched.

I must close, my dearest friend, I'm frightfully busy, therefore the brevity. Again many, many thanks for the tobacco and a thousand regards to you all from Helene and me.

Your Berg

Another very important matter:

Kolisch requests remuneration. I would like to add that he definitely deserves it. He does an enormous amount of work for the Verein. Aside from the many, many sectional and ensemble rehearsals for the chamber orchestra, his frequent participation as soloist, and finally, his contributions amounting to those of a performance director (assisting Stein with the *Pierrot* rehearsal, for example). The <u>quality</u> of his contributions, especially in the chamber orchestra, is beyond question. I don't think remuneration such as Steuermann's can be considered here, since Kolisch is, after all, very much involved with <u>rehearsals,</u> etc. Naturally I leave the <u>amount</u> of remuneration to you, dear friend. I believe Kolisch envisages an amount of c. 1,500 kronen (as much as Stein or the Secretary). I don't think we can give him less than 1,000 kronen. Please let us have a decision soon. He would like the salary already for <u>January.</u> In part because of his family, who give him no peace about activities that don't earn him a <u>living.</u>

P.S. I had to open the letter again, since <u>your card</u> just arrived. A thousand thanks for your magnificent words about the rich and the generous man (the fact alone that you didn't say "poor man" is such an incredible linguistic and intellectual refinement). How can you think that we are angry and didn't write for that reason. It just happened; first the Christmas lethargy, then the postal strike, then the approaching chamber orchestra concerts, and finally, with regard to a few points of news, we were awaiting your answers to some <u>important</u> questions, which of course Deutsch or Eisler[12] could have taken care of, particularly the latter, who has not yet written a <u>single</u> line, though he has been gone for over 1 month and had promised and I had earnestly implored him, and though he can easily imagine how we thirst for every bit of news about you, your concerts and everything, everything concerning you. He was also supposed to let me know about your final position on

11. The Rosé Quartet performed Schoenberg's D-minor String Quartet on 11 January; Berg is comparing that performance to one on 25 March 1917.

12. Schoenberg had taken two of his Viennese students to Holland with him as assistants. The Austrian (later French) composer Max Deutsch studied with Schoenberg 1913–20; the German composer Hanns Eisler studied with him 1919–23.

the term atonal. I need that most urgently for my book about you. Possibly also concerning expressionism!—

Today, 22 January, I shall deliver the piano score of your quartet.[13] I think it turned out very well. Should the dedication "To my wife" be included? Thanks again for your dear card.

Your Berg

---

13. The piano vocal score of the third and fourth movements of Schoenberg's F♯-minor String Quartet, Op. 10, which Berg had finished in September 1912, was published in 1921, after Berg had once again reworked and simplified it.

## Schoenberg to Berg

Zandvoort, 25 January 1921

Dear friend,

I answered your questions on the copy of your letter.[1] Now for those in the letter of 21 January.—II[nd] propaganda concert. Too bad the choruses had to be dropped.[2] Was that necessary? You consider Frau Wagner only moderately good? And she's to do *Pierrot?*[3] I wanted Gutheil! That should have been possible! Too bad Bachrich accompanied. Couldn't you have waited for Steuermann?—Why are the receipts only 8,000 kronen with an audience of 400? That wasn't managed very well! Perhaps 70 kronen would again be too expensive for the most expensive seat; since you were successful with 20–40 you shouldn't go over 50–60 for the time being. How high was the overhead? How large the deficit? Will you make a profit with the repeat performance?—Kolisch. Agree to the salary. But: is it possible? Have the costs been calculated? His contribution should be remunerated like that of everyone else. But I think it might be better to give him good performance fees so he has an inducement to play. Guarantee him 3 concerts a month @3–400 kronen so that he can earn about the same or even more.

I share your opinion regarding "atonal." There is no such thing in music. You know my opinion about "labeling." Otherwise I would prefer "polytonal," as I myself wrote c. 4 months ago, hence independently of the Czech writer. "Expressionism," too, is just a name and only serves the same purpose that a trade name does for manufactured goods. "Globin," the superior shoe polish. What's the point of saying something basically unessential when what's essential is never recognized until 50 years later and then one realizes that it was basically the same old thing.

I am very eager to see the piano score of the II[nd] Quartet. If there is to be a title page such as for a complete piano score, the dedication could be included just as in the original.—Ask Hertzka whether he wouldn't like to do a 2-hand score of the first two movements as well. Then he could do 2 editions. A: the entire thing, B: the vocal movements for rehearsal purposes only. It really doesn't make much sense

1. Schoenberg's answers on the copy of Berg's 16 January letter concern, among other things, Berg's work on the reduction of Schoenberg's Op. 10 String Quartet, Berg's *Anbruch* activity, and Verein matters.
2. Unidentified.
3. A Verein performance of *Pierrot lunaire* took place 12 May.

to publish only those two movements.

I received Wellesz' book.[4] On the whole it is surprisingly good. A few inaccuracies should be corrected. The analyses, which really don't contribute anything, are the weakest feature. You must guard against that. Better to take a single example from each work and say something _**short**_ and characteristic about it. His thorough discussion of technical matters is good. He thereby avoids sentimentality and bombast. That way one can gradually make this or that point musically comprehensible to people. Especially if one gives them some insight into melody. What am I really getting at? I would be happy if in the forseeable future the surface qualities were understood.

Many warm regards to your dear wife, I hope she will be better soon! Likewise, regards to you from me and my wife.

Your Arnold Schönberg

---

4. _Arnold Schönberg_ (Vienna, 1921).

## Berg to Schoenberg

Vienna, 8 June 1921

Dearest esteemed friend.

I wanted to await the last Verein concert and last committee meeting before writing.[1] Now that, too, is over and I shall report to you on a separate sheet.

My wife left for Hofgastein early the day before yesterday. Now we'll be separated again for 3–4 weeks. That's not right. But it has to be!—

I heard the following story about Scherchen: after getting no response from him for months (despite an express letter, etc.) (he has an article of mine and a musical supplement for _Melos_), I suddenly got a letter from a coeditor whom I hardly know, asking me to submit something (article and musical supplement).[2] Upon my inquiring into the meaning of this, above all what had happened to Scherchen, I was told by this Fritz Windisch, who is now the sole editor of _Melos_, that Scherchen is no longer connected with _Melos_, that he had been quite irresponsible (financially and artistically) in his direction of _Melos_ and "for months had been embezzling editorial funds and immense quantities of expensive music", etc. Isn't it incredible?!—

Arthur Bodanzky of the Metropolitan Opera House[3] is in Vienna and was very eager, as Frau Bodanzky[4] and Frau Hartungen[5] told me, to visit you in Mödling.

1. The last Verein concert of the 1920–21 season, on 6 June, presented piano pieces by Satie, Stravinsky's _Piano-Rag Music_ (which was repeated at the end), Webern's Four Pieces for Violin and Piano, Op. 7 (performed by Rudolf Kolisch and Eduard Steuermann), and Busoni's Toccata for Piano (performed by Hilde Merinsky); Berg's Clarinet Pieces, Op. 5, were to have been on the program as well, but the clarinettist Karl Gaudriot did not show up for the performance.

2. Hermann Scherchen founded the music periodical _Melos_ in February 1920; as of May 1921 the editor was Fritz Windisch.

3. Arthur Bodanzky succeeded Alfred Hertz at the Metropolitan Opera in 1915.

4. Probably Bodanzky's mother.

5. The pianist Ida Hartungen had been married to Arthur Bodanzky and was closely affiliated with the Verein.

He was extremely sorry that it wasn't possible. He is traveling to Karlsbad in about a week, where he can be reached by letter ("Kapellmeister A.B. of the Metropolitan Opera House in New York in Karlsbad") and in August he is going to Zell am See and will be passing through Salzburg, where he will try to visit you. I believe he will be able to give you reliable information about American conditions. Frau Hartungen, with whom I spoke about this, told me that a single person needs $600 a month to live in New York. He, Bodanzky, lives very luxuriously and in great style. Apparently he earns $50,000 a year, of which he saves half. There is great excitement among the young people here, that is, the fairly young ones (of course the really young ones can't be considered) because he is looking for a principal solo rehearsal pianist and a choral director and has turned to us in the matter. Dr. Bachrich, Pisk, Deutsch, and Sachs all aspire to these positions. You will hear the outcome soon.

And now I want to thank you, my dearest friend, that due to your initiative and the energy with which you surmounted all obstacles, we were paid, and could be paid such a high summer salary by the Verein. Many thanks!!

I got a telegram from Erdmann[6] today with the news that he is playing my sonata in Donaueschingen[7] and requests a picture, biographical dates, and analysis of the sonata for that purpose. Since it comes from him and he has always behaved correctly towards me, I don't think I can refuse him. This is the same "court library" in Donaueschingen that once requested scores from me for its concerts (and shamelessly, from you as well), mentioning at the same time the patronage this venture enjoys (Busoni, Hausegger,[8] Nikisch,[9] Pauer,[10] Pfitzner, Schreker, chairman: Strauss)—naturally I turned the court library down at that time, as well as taking the same opportunity to write them a tart letter. (And included one of our brochures, as you advised me.) No response. And now this request of Erdmann's!—

You're probably enjoying beautiful weather now! Since yesterday we have had wonderfully clear, cool days even in Vienna, after a spell of indescribable heat. (Every afternoon my thermometer registered 38° R in the sun.)[11]

And now I'll get to work. I'm worried how it will go!

Many regards to your dear wife, also to Trude and Görgl. To you, all my love
from your Berg

*[Berg appends a three-page report on Verein events and plans.]*

6. The German pianist Eduard Erdmann specialized in contemporary music.

7. The first of the Donaueschingen contemporary music festivals took place 30 July–2 August 1921; this annual festival became a major forum for new music.

8. The Austrian composer and conductor Siegmund von Hausegger, director of the Munich Academy.

9. The German conductor Arthur Nikisch was the director of the Leipzig Gewandhaus Concerts from 1895 to his death in 1922.

10. The German pianist Max von Pauer, director of the Stuttgart Conservatory.

11. 38° Reaumur is 47.5° Centigrade and 117.5° Fahrenheit.

*Berg to Schoenberg*

Vienna, 28 June 1921

Dearest, most esteemed friend,

Completing the enclosed 2 lists, which I promised to send you in my last letter,[1] has taken so long that I was prevented from writing to you again. You can ascertain everything concerning the repertoire from the lists, which I ask that you save or give to Greissle for safekeeping.[2] I don't need to add anything. Greissle can answer the questionnaire on your behalf; so that you do not waste any of your precious time on such matters. I am so glad that you are so deeply immersed in your work, that you seem to have finished the *Harmonielehre*[3] and that the *Jakobsleiter* is next. It is wonderful, just knowing that there is someone who creates such things, someone almost like the dear Lord himself, who <u>watches over</u> one and all, and ultimately over the whole world, while as for oneself, one lives almost unconsciously, or at any rate without constant awareness!

Apropos getting work done, I have nothing favorable to report about <u>myself,</u> though I've been working steadily for c. 3 weeks now. It seems to me—and you will notice it even in the style of this letter—that I can't <u>write</u> any longer. Whenever I try to give shape to the extensive material I have for the book about you, for which I have recently gathered a great deal more, I make absolutely no headway. So that I see my grand summer plans: completing the book, composing a ballet,[4] and finishing *Wozzeck*, already frustrated at the outset. (Out of despair over this I wrote some dancelike music—inspired by our waltz concert[5] and your idea of a ballet.)

So I am rather depressed just now, compounded by the fact that it's unlikely anything will come of that little excursion to Mattsee. My brother's widow is expected in Vienna early in July.[6] I'll <u>have</u> to be here then. My wife, from whom I've not had very good news by letter and telephone, will also be returning to Vienna at that time—after completing her treatment. It has taken longer than we expected.—

I received a periodical from Paris (actually my publisher did) with a review of the clarinet pieces, which were performed at the Société Musicale Indépendante on 2 June 1921.[7]—

Just like <u>you,</u> dear friend, and Webern, I filled out a form—about a month ago—

1. These lists have not been located. They concerned a contract ledger Berg had set up for the purpose of planning the coming Verein season, with the signatures of prospective participants and an indication of the compositions they were prepared to play; in the Verein portion of his letter of 8 June 1921 Berg had promised to copy out the relevant information for Schoenberg.

2. As of 1 February Felix Greissle had succeeded Josef Rufer as Secretary of the Verein.

3. Schoenberg finished preparing the second edition of his 1911 *Harmonielehre* on 24 June, a project that involved expansion and revision of several chapters. Berg was again entrusted with the preparation of the index.

4. Among Schoenberg's plans for the coming Verein season was the idea for a ballet concert, for which Webern and Berg were to compose works. Berg's plan to do so was never carried out.

5. In a special Verein concert that Schoenberg conducted on 27 May, waltzes were performed in chamber orchestra arrangements by Schoenberg, Webern, and Berg; after the concert the composers' manuscripts were sold at auction.

6. Berg's oldest brother Hermann, who lived and worked in the United States since 1888, died on 22 February 1921 in Palm Beach, Florida; he was survived by his wife Alice Schäfer Berg.

7. Performed by Suzie Welty and J. Guyot; the concert was reviewed in the French periodical *Le Menestrel* LXXXIII / 23 (10 June 1921), 244.

that the American Relief Administration[8] sent us for the purpose of charitable distributions for intellectuals. Now I've recently received 2 huge packages (c. 40 kg) of groceries (e.g., 22 kg flour, bacon, fat, oil, milk, chocolate, rice (9 kg), salmon (10 cans), etc.). Distribution is probably alphabetical, so the shipment to you and Webern, which should contain a greater number of packages—corresponding to the larger number of family members—can still be expected.

Last week I spent a day in Küb with my family. I traveled there with Alma. She is doing very well. She is living relatively secluded—in Werfel's company,[9] to be sure—in Breitenstein.

30 June 1921. I had to interrupt this letter, too. In the meantime I met with Polnauer, who reported to us (Webern and me) about the Mattsee intermezzo.[10] I don't want to write anything about that in a letter that might go astray. But the parallels between events are absolutely amazing:

| 1911 | 1921 |
|---|---|
| Beginning of the Summer intensive work on the *Harmonielehre* | Beginning of the Summer intensive work on the *Harmonielehre*, II[nd] edition |
| Begun with severe toothache, tooth pulled! | same |
| Threatened in your own house (the insane engineer) | The Mattsee threats |
| Polnauer appears | Polnauer appears[11] |

Thank God the final consequence was avoided. And thank God everything else Polnauer reports from Mattsee is so gratifying that the present event seems almost comic compared to the tragic one 10 years ago.

I shall give the layout of the subject index a great deal of thought and present you with suggestions soon. But I can't get to it—i.e., begin the <u>work itself</u>—until <u>page proofs</u> of the new edition are available.

Excuse the smeared writing! The paper lay out in the open for a day and with the air so misty and humid, the ink runs.

And now many regards to all your loved ones. All the very best to them and you for the summer.

Your Berg

*[Berg appends a one-page questionnaire dealing with Verein matters.]*

8. This Quaker organization was sponsored by the Philadelphia publishing firm of Theodore Presser.

9. Alma Mahler had had a liaison with the writer Franz Werfel since 1918; they were married in 1929.

10. Schoenberg and his family were spending the summer in Mattsee near Salzburg. When an anti-Semitic placard was posted that suggested that all Jews leave the town, Schoenberg, who had converted to Protestantism in 1898, was outraged. Josef Polnauer had returned to Vienna on 29 June, after a short visit to Mattsee.

11. In a letter to his wife of 29 June 1921 Berg sets up a similar comparison, with, however, one further entry: "Flight (to Bavaria)——Flight to Mödling?"

*The Villa Josef in Traunkirchen (Private collection)*

*Schoenberg to Berg (picture postcard: Traunkirchen, Salzkammergut)*

Traunkirchen, 16 July 1921

Dearest friend,

We've been here since the 14th.[1] Toward the end it got very ugly in Mattsee. The people there seemed to despise me as much as if they knew my music. Nothing happened to us beyond that. But it's just as unpleasant outside one's profession as within it—only there one has to accept it. Perhaps here too? I wouldn't know why.— Now I want to continue working here. I had already written the first 10 pages of *Zusammenhang*.[2] I hope I can get back into it again soon.—What are you doing? Don't despair if writing is difficult at first: you've probably set yourself higher standards and now have to attain this level. I know how it is: it is a painful state, but one full of promise.

Many warm regards to you and your wife

Your Arnold Schönberg

1. Early in July Josef Rufer arranged for the Schoenbergs to move into the Villa Josef in Traunkirchen (also near Salzburg), which belonged to the Baroness Anka Löwenthal; the Schoenbergs had the entire house, a private beach, and a boat at their disposal.

2. Schoenberg's work on a book dealing with the topic of coherence *(Zusammenhang)* dated back to a 1917 plan for a four-volume work on the subjects of coherence, counterpoint, instrumentation, and form *(Zusammenhang, Kontrapunkt, Instrumentation, und Formenlehre).*

*Berg to Schoenberg*

Trahütten, 4 August 1921

Dear esteemed friend.

We've been here for 10 days now. After a completely wasted July—as regards work—I have taken up *Wozzeck* again here, so as to accomplish something on at least *one* of my many unfinished, planned projects.[1] God willing and if I can keep up the pace I've adopted, I will finish composition of the opera this month still* and then my head will be free for other things. Of course it won't be enough to assuage my conscience. Only completion of the book about you could do that— and at least finding a promising subject for a ballet. But I have accomplished nei- ther, and although work on *Woyzeck* is going well, I'm not really happy.

I work daily from 7–1. After the midday meal I rest a little (for I have to do something for my "health," too) and then either do a little more work (copying) or correspondence or the like. After tea a long walk. Evenings: III^rd *Blue Book*.[2]

[*Berg discusses alternative methods of handling the index to the second edition of the* Harmonielehre.]

I have therefore decided on the following method, which also coincides partly with your wishes: I will allow only one person to help me; but he will do a great deal. He is your former seminar student Fritz Mahler, who was my student this year and with whom I was quite satisfied as regards diligence, reliability, and pro- gress. What speaks for the selection of this young student (doctoral candidate in music) is that:

1. He himself has a burning desire to do the work.

2. He studied the entire *Harmonielehre* with me this year and thereby acquired a really extraordinary and most complete familiarity with your book—which he has also demonstrated to me. So he is just the man for the task of comparing the I^st and II^nd editions, besides having the very greatest theoretical interest in doing so (this is another reason for the 1^st argument).

3. I know him to be an incredibly reliable, almost pedantic worker; and I think pedantry is indispensible for such a job (at any rate it was my disposition toward pedantry that qualified me for the job in the first place).

4. I have already discussed the matter with Mahler and given him thorough instructions, so the 2 of us can begin working as soon as the page proofs are ready and we are assured that there will be no further changes in the page breaks (which would involve changes in the page numbers). For this reason I have asked U.E. to send a copy of the final page proofs both to me and to him when the time comes.

5. By a division of labor such as this I am in a position, so to speak, to inspire the work, to supervise it at all times, and finally to guarantee its accuracy; better said: to vouch for it personally.—

Is that all right with you, dear friend?

I wonder how you are, now that this Mattsee outrage is over. I hear that the place where you are now is absolutely wonderful. I hope you have recovered and found your way back to your interrupted work. And I hope it hasn't been too hot for you.

1. By this time Berg had finished two acts of *Wozzeck* and begun the third.
2. Strindberg's *Blue Book* is a collection of aphorisms, nature observations, and reminiscences.

Up here, where I am, it was very comfortable, actually more pleasantly summerlike than it has been in years, while at the same time we were reading newspaper reports of the most frightful heat. Now it seems to be—getting <u>cold</u> again up here.

Warmest regards to you all. Especially to you, my dear esteemed friend

from your Berg

My wife sends all the very best to you and Mathilde and Trude and Görgl.

* without orchestration, of course

*Schoenberg to Berg*

Traunkirchen, 9 August 1921

Dearest friend,

It seems you didn't get a letter of mine from Mattsee. I can't remember any more what I wrote. But it was in answer to questions in your last letter.

*[Schoenberg makes suggestions for Berg's work on the Harmonielehre index.]*

I still haven't read half of the I[st] proofs, but that's no problem because Hertzka hasn't sent any more.—Mattsee was a serious interruption. It robbed me of much valuable working time, as well as completely disrupting my momentum. But the situation here—beautiful as it is—isn't ideal either. I am constantly being interrupted (by <u>very, very dear</u> visitors). Individually and at a more appropriate time all would have been very welcome. I have enjoyed chatting with every one of them. But the net result is such a serious loss of time, such distraction of my interest, and such a complete disruption of my concentration, that I am very worried. It is the one- to two-day visits in particular that interrupt my work. If someone is here longer, my free time suffices for visiting. But I have to devote an entire day to every "short" guest (Karpath). Since we've been here we've had: Zemlinsky about 4 days, Travnicek 1, Polnauer 1, Travnicek with Ullmann[1] 1½, Prof. Rebner[2] from Frankfurt 3 days, Bachrich 1 day. Then Dr. Frischauf came today, his wife comes tomorrow;[3] my brother with his wife and child probably also tomorrow.[4] Scherchen, too, is expected. Then Rankl and Eisler. Finally Stein! If this continues there'll be no chance for any work at all! I will simply have to withdraw a little. Everyone will have to understand that.

And yet we would love to have you and your wife here. Isn't that at all possible?[5]

It is very gratifying to hear that you are making progress with *Wozzeck*. It would

---

1. The Austrian composer and conductor Viktor Ullmann studied with Schoenberg 1918–19; during the preceding 1920 / 21 season he had been one of the conductors under Zemlinsky at the Deutsches Landestheater in Prague.

2. The Austrian violinist Adolf Rebner was vacationing in Salzburg that summer.

3. The dermatologist Dr. Hermann Frischauf was married to Dr. Marie Pappenheim.

4. Heinrich Schönberg, a bass-baritone engaged at the Prague Deutsches Landestheater, his wife, Bertel Ott (daughter of the mayor of Salzburg), and their one child, Gitti (Brigitte) Schönberg.

5. Helene Berg's tentative plan early in July to visit the Schoenbergs from Hofgastein where she was then completing treatment was discouraged by Berg; in a letter to his wife of 2 July 1921 he listed six reasons against her going, primarily because he himself had neither the desire nor the time to go. The Bergs did visit the Schoenbergs in Traunkirchen for several days in mid-October.

be very interesting to see an opera of yours. Once you have finished it, I'm sure everything else will come more easily again too. Don't worry about it. As a rule that takes care of itself.

I'll close now. Many warm regards to you and your wife. Also from my wife

Your Arnold Schönberg

## Berg to Schoenberg

Trahütten, 24 August 1921

Dear esteemed friend,

The 1$^{st}$ of September is approaching and I will not be able to reach the goal I had set myself (to finish the composition of *Woyzeck* this summer). And therefore won't find the peace (of mind and heart) with which I would have liked to begin the coming season. An interruption of the composition—as experience has taught me every year now—means postponing by an entire year the completion of the opera and the chance of beginning something else. Indeed this interruption (it would be the 4$^{th}$ on this work!) might well mean that I will never muster the remaining bit of energy to complete a project that in some ways I have practically finished with, and would thus lose a work on which I have lavished so much time, effort, and love (I was almost going to say: "faith, hope, and charity").

Can the Verein, i.e., can you, dearest friend, whom as President of the Verein I hereby ask officially, grant me an extension of my summer vacation until the completion of my composition?

Speaking practically: I see it like this; that during the initial Verein period—thanks to your precise guidelines—Webern and Stein, the two performance directors, will be perfectly capable of running the Verein alone, with the administrative assistance of Dr. Sachs, whom you've been thinking of involving more, anyway, and the other officials in Vienna (I am assuming—as your wife wrote—that you will remain away from Vienna for a while longer).

Further: I will of course accept no remuneration for the period in which I deprive the Verein of my participation, which is all the more equitable as this time I'm not asking for leave due to reasons of health or family matters (in other words *force majeure*), but for purely personal reasons.

Since I have 2–3 scenes left to compose—I anticipate a leave of c. 2–3 weeks in length.

Finally, during a leave of this kind, I could of course be reached by letter and would always be available for matters relating to my area of competence that can be settled at this distance and in writing.—

I won't write anything else in this letter, since it is an official "request" belonging to "Verein correspondence," which can, of course be granted—in your name—by the secretary.

So it only remains for me: to ask that you grant this request and that you not take it ill—in the event you grant it—that I neglect my Verein responsibilities for a while.

Many warm regards

from your Alban Berg

### Schoenberg to Berg

Traunkirchen, 26 September [August] 1921

Dear friend!

Of course I agree to a leave. Don't worry about anything and stay away as long as necessary. The others will manage all right.

I shall write you a long letter soon. For today warm regards to you and your wife.

Your Arnold Schönberg

### Berg to Schoenberg

Trahütten, 9 September 1921

My dearest, esteemed friend,

How I wish I could spend your birthday with you, like all those who are hurrying to Traunkirchen or are already there. But as it is, I can only tell you in writing what a festive day your birthday is for me and how clear it is to me that one day it will be a festive day for the whole world: a day for the world—taking time out from the routine of everyday life—to reflect upon its higher, its very highest qualities. And to find it incomprehensible that there was a time when it <u>didn't even take notice</u> of it. Not even enough notice to make room for this birthday in a calendar of German musicians* for the year 1921, next to the death days of J. Rietz, Chabrier, and Kretschmer, and birthdays for A. E. Müller and Ed. v. Mihalovich, which are entered for this 13th of September!

We, your friends, have decided to forego our modest individual gifts and join together this time, so as to be able to give you a worthy gift.[1] I hope we have found the right thing. I can't say more, as my letter could come too early and spoil the <u>surprise.</u> Let me just say that what it represents is one of the few things that has always affected me very deeply—and always will—and means a great deal to you, too—I remember an hour, beautiful despite its deep sorrow, spent with you a few years ago!— —

In order to be with you on your birthday in person, at least in <u>some</u> form, I am sending you the essay I wrote a year ago,[2] which I have since withdrawn—recognizing the futility of wrangling with critics and recognizing the wordy, awkward style in which I had done so—perhaps the content may interest and entertain you

1. A collection of lithographs by Gustav Klimt.

2. Berg's "Schönberg und die Kritik" (Schoenberg and the Critics) had been rejected by *Anbruch* (as well as *Melos*). The article, first mentioned in a letter to Schoenberg of 1 September 1920, attacked music criticism in general and the critics Julius Korngold, Elsa Bienenfeld, and Max Kalbeck specifically. It was first published by Willi Reich in his 1963 Berg biography.

In his response to Berg's letter of 16 January 1921, telling of the rejection of his article by *Anbruch*, Schoenberg had written, ". . . I don't think it's a good idea for you to skirmish with journalists. It intensifies hate, but lessens contempt, thereby serving the journalists and injuring you! I'm quite practical. One would have to devote every single minute to the conflict with journalists. And you can see where that leads by looking at Kraus, of whom it has made a prisoner who cannot escape. Ultimately Kraus today is no longer master of his own time, nor can he select his themes according to his likes or dislikes, rather he has them forced upon him by attacks against which he has to defend himself." After rereading the article, however, Schoenberg, in a letter to Berg of 26 September 1921, wrote that he found it "very good and entertaining."

for a few minutes on your birthday. I hope so!

And now my most affectionate congratulations to you, my dearest friend, and many, many regards to you all

from your Berg

*[Berg adds a postscript regarding 3,000 kronen he was sent for Verein work; he writes that he intends to forward the sum to Webern, Stein, Greissle, and Sachs, who had taken over his duties.]*

\* Max Hesses Berlin

*Berg to Schoenberg (picture postcard: Frankfurt / Main, Opera House)*

Frankfurt[1] [19 December 1921]

Dearest friend,

Finally the most important events are over and we can report to you briefly: prior to a final decision (which appears fairly probable to us), Lert[2] wants to see the full score. As does Darmstadt, which, however, seems less promising. Steuermann's recitals both splendid.[3] Great success. We return home on Wednesday. 1,000 regards to you all!

Berg and
Steuermann

1. On 14 December Berg went to Frankfurt where Eduard Steuermann was to play an audition of *Wozzeck* at the Frankfurt Opera on 17 December; the next day, he played the work for the directors of the Darmstadt Opera.

2. The Austrian stage director Ernst Lert was director of the Frankfurt Opera 1920–23.

3. Steuermann played two concerts, on 15 and 16 December, in Darmstadt and Frankfurt respectively, in which he performed the Bach-Busoni Chromatic Fantasy and Fugue, Beethoven's Piano Sonata, Op. 111, Berg's Sonata, Op. 1, two Humoresques by Reger, and his own arrangement of Schoenberg's Chamber Symphony, Op. 9.

# 1922

*Berg to Schoenberg (postcard)*

Hofgastein in Salzburg, 2 June 1922

Dearest friend,

Arrived here yesterday evening[1] and send you and yours many regards. Also from Helene. She doesn't feel particularly well. But apparently that's only to be expected. I myself find it very strange to be thrust suddenly into a state of idleness. But with the help of the *Harmonielehre*, I will soon be acclimated again.

The last days in Vienna were pretty exhausting. But at least *Wozzeck* is <u>entirely</u> finished now. 2 identical, beautifully bound scores now exist. The reduction is largely finished, too, and awaits my revision in a couple of weeks.[2]

What do you say to Lert.[3] Of course his canceling is understandable, and given the current state of the theater, one can't even blame him!—

I am very pleased about your Holland trip.[4] Do you leave on the 6th already or not until the 8th? Is Mathilde going along? Give her our best. Helene would have written long ago if she hadn't been feeling so wretched. Mathilde must not be angry with her.

As soon as I'm finished with the *Harmonielehre* I will let you know and send the index. I am already looking forward to reading it.

Warmest regards, dear friend,

from your Berg

1. On 23 May Helene Berg had traveled to Hofgastein for treatment, where Berg joined her on 1 June.
2. Berg had completed the short score of *Wozzeck* in October 1921 and the orchestration in April 1922. The piano score was being prepared under Berg's supervision by his student Fritz Heinrich Klein.
3. In response to news that the full score of *Wozzeck* was now available Ernst Lert had written Berg that financial conditions prevented the Frankfurt Opera from producing the work at that time.
4. Schoenberg had planned to travel to Holland early in June to conduct the first Dutch performance of *Pierrot lunaire*. However, the performance did not take place until 9 December 1922.


*Berg to Schoenberg*

Hofgastein, 12 June 1922

Dearest friend,

I was very sorry to hear that as yet nothing has come of the *Pierrot* tour. All this time I thought you were in Holland, and though I have followed the currency inflation with anxiety: I was happy for you and those with you about the strength of the Dutch Guilders! I hope something will still come of it soon!—

We imagine the inflation in Vienna must be awful. Businessmen here are rather more naive: they raise their prices only <u>gradually,</u> so right now it is cheaper to live here than in Vienna. And I have to add: <u>better, too!</u> That's why we would rather like to extend our stay here. If only I felt better. Time and time again I have had whole nights—or even days of asthma. Also I am plagued by a disinclination to work, stemming both from that and from the uprooted feeling of being "abroad," and I yearn for my desk in Vienna——or even my upright piano in Trahütten.

My wife's treatment—if she doesn't rush it—will last another 10 days or so. So we'll probably stay another 1–2 weeks. I am undergoing the treatment, too. It was most urgently recommended to me. So, as long as I'm here, I, too, am taking advantage of the opportunity to do something "for my health." The baths in these warm thermal waters are very pleasant and seem to be good for my "nerves," which had been acting up of late.—

I will write separately about the enclosed indexes, dear friend. I would only like to say that I am enormously pleased with the new edition of the *Harmonielehre!* The addition of the guidelines[1] has added immensely to the book's clarity and practicality (for teachers and students). I can already tell that the guidelines will help <u>me</u> in teaching. Indeed, now that they're there, one wonders how one ever did without them. And yet it is obvious that they could only have been written after working through the old book <u>frequently</u> and <u>for years.</u> The other new additions are—I find nothing more fitting (at first I wanted to say "brilliant flights") than— jewels of mental and linguistic skill. I particularly like the way you introduce many a polemic point so gracefully—hidden, so subtle, and yet devastating. For example, the footnote on pp. 24 / 25 about the influence of Oriental music on modern styles; 118 / 19 about the lost war! Footnote p. 83, parallel fifths in modern music! Particularly the interpolations on p. 480, where you speak about the so-called revolution and don't even use phrases like Bolshevist music (because there will be others tomorrow), but simply talk about "the refuse of political vocabulary." Not to mention the footnote about atonalists, with its grandiose closing sentences.[2]

The linguistic creations, too, are fantastic (changing-note cambiata—*Aufkaschieren!*)[3] And such an infinite wealth of detail!

Aside from the guidelines, I find it enriching to have many <u>theoretical</u> questions that I myself had never quite understood cleared up at last. For instance, the <u>summary</u> of all the <u>cadences</u> (authentic, plagal, deceptive, etc., etc.), the summary of <u>all</u> the possible scales, p. 464. And in general all the summary material and what is

1. Schoenberg's revisions for the second edition of his *Harmonielehre* included four sets of guidelines giving succinct summaries of subject matter.

2. In these footnotes, which are actually long subjective asides, Schoenberg expands on various ideas in light of the intervening historical changes. The corresponding pages in Roy Carter's 1978 English translation are given in parentheses: 24 / 25 (423–25), 118 / 19 (425–26), 83 (68), 480 (401), 487–88 (432–33).

3. Schoenberg examines the linguistic development and meaning of words like changing note (*Wechselnote* and the Italian *cambiata* in a footnote on pages 221–23 (429–30); he discusses the origin of "*Aufkaschieren,*" (meaning to line or conceal with paper) in a new footnote on ornaments on 416 (344).

added about the methodology of teaching harmony (pp. 398–99).[4]

Oh! I can't wait for the book. Especially using it at last in teaching, when I can try out all the new things!

I have written this letter in terrible haste; hence the poor handwriting. I want it to get off by today's train, because of the index. Excuse the haste! And 1,000 regards

from your Berg

Also all my love to Mathilde! How is she? And the young couple[5] and the football champion?[6] Give all of them my best. Also from Helene!

[*Berg appends a three-page discussion concerning the indices for the* Harmonielehre.]

---

4. The resume of all possible keys begins on 464 (387–89), the discussion of principles of the harmonic system on 398–99 (328–29).

5. Schoenberg's daughter Gertrude and Felix Greissle had become engaged in September 1921 and were married 10 November 1921.

6. This is in reference to an incident in which Schoenberg's son Georg, playing outside in the garden, accidentally kicked a football through the window into the bowl of soup his mother was just serving to the visiting Francis Poulenc and Darius Milhaud.

## Berg to Schoenberg

Vienna, 17 July 1922

My dear friend,

I would so very much like to write you a long letter, but I haven't the time. So briefly at least the most important matters.

We just spent 5 days in Küb with my mother, and I took the opportunity to climb the Rax again, which was wonderful. The rest of the time I was revising my *(Wozzeck)* piano reduction (see below).

Helene is not at all well. If anything, the Gasteiner treatment hurt her more than it helped; once again she is in such constant pain that after her experience during this short summer visit to Küb, we are considering foregoing a further summer vacation. That is: for the time being I will send her to a clinic in Vienna where she will have access to all means of treatment, such as baths, massages, diet, etc., etc., better access than was the case, for example, in Gastein, where they leave everything to radium. Perhaps she will improve in a few weeks and then we'll see. So we'll stay in Vienna for the present. That's good for me, too, since the following has happened:

Wozzeck. I have notified several music periodicals of the completion of the opera and have already received a promise from some that the notice will be "placed." In addition, my sister's friend, May Keller, has agreed to have the piano score engraved. Her idea (and mine too) is as follows: a limited edition of the score available in the fall would enable me to distribute it to all eligible opera houses. Simultaneously, which is impossible when (as now) only 1 score is available, not to mention the risk of loss. In my opinion, that would offer my best chance for an acceptance (should there be any at all). Should this happen, a publisher would probably turn up as well, who would then take over the work for the sum put up by May Keller (i.e.,

1,000 Swiss franks). (100 copies cost about 5 million, today 1 frank is worth about 6,000 kronen.) Of course I won't give the score to a publisher now, but will simply have it printed for my own purposes. I think I am doing the right thing. At any rate I'll avoid the kind of nonsense I got myself into with my first published compositions. The annual statement (21–22 April) from <u>Haslinger (that is, Schlesinger)</u> credits me with the sale of

| | |
|---|---|
| 73 sonatas and 30 sets of songs | from these, since these works have been taken over by the publisher (though by contract the plates still belong to me) I receive 10% |
| Further, 10 scores and (?) <u>10</u> parts (@4) of the quartet and 33 clarinet pieces | from these, since these works are only handled by the publisher on <u>commission,</u> I receive 25% |
| | sum total 230 marks |

—I just got a letter from *Melos*-Windisch asking me to visit you to try to persuade you to write the article for the Salzburg Festival issue that he has repeatedly requested of you and you have rejected.* What's young Windisch thinking of! Certainly it would tempt me; but since you have turned it down and probably had good reasons for doing so, my presence would hardly persuade you to write something hastily now. If, however, you should write something <u>after all,</u> Webern, who is now with you, could assume the mission, <u>as it were,</u> and thereby <u>in effect</u> receive reimbursement for the "trip" (there and back) and the "expenses incurred."** His willingness to let an article of yours cost him something should not—I think—be passed up. Unfortunately <u>I</u> must do so! I cannot leave Helene alone just now. Nor do we have a maid at the moment.

So I'm using my stay in Vienna to finish the piano score with Klein[1] and prepare it for printing.

I'm taking great pains with it, but I hope that it will also be good and meet <u>your</u> standards.

I finally received the 2nd set of proofs of the index (*Harmonielehre*) and read them right away.

Have you heard that Josef Schmid got the position of 1st Kapellmeister in Graz?

Scherchen wants to perform my Orchestra Pieces.[2] Thank God the parts are already available!

I am very depressed that I haven't composed anything yet this summer and that there are no prospects for it in the near future either.

Your intention of working on *Jakobsleiter*, which you mentioned on your picture postcard, makes me so happy! Has anything come of it yet?

I send you and yours, dear, esteemed friend, a thousand regards; also from Helene.

Your Berg

1. Fritz Heinrich Klein studied with Schoenberg 1917–18 and with Berg from 1921.
2. Nothing came of this plan; Berg's Orchestra Pieces, Op. 6, were not premiered in their entirety until 1930.

Do you have the new *Fackel* yet? It also includes a gloss on the Korngold affair.[3]

\* *Melos* would pay travel expenses.

\*\* In this case I would send Webern the pertinent letter from *Melos*.

---

3. The *Fackel* XXIV / 595–600 (July 1922), 115–19 contained glosses on both Julius and Erich Wolfgang Korngold, whose *Tote Stadt* was then in the repertoire of the Vienna State Opera. Julius Korngold, always a staunch and public partisan of his son's music, had become increasingly critical of Richard Strauss's management of the Vienna State Opera, especially with regard to the repertoire and day-to-day performance quality and most particularly in connection with the production of *Tote Stadt*. There was a short flurry regarding the matter in the press, which Berg had first mentioned to Schoenberg in a postcard of 4 July 1922.

## Schoenberg to Berg

Traunkirchen, 20 July 1922

Dearest friend,

I consider it a <u>very good</u> idea that you have *Wozzeck* engraved yourself, although Zemlinsky\* (who is spending the summer in Bad-Aussee—couldn't you play *Wozzeck* for him?) thinks otherwise. But you mustn't expect that that will automatically insure a performance. (Zemlinsky, by the way, is more in favor of: playing it for people!) In any case it will take a long time until the printing costs are recovered! Of course Fräulein Keller—give my best to her and your sister—must understand that she is making what could be a <u>long-term</u> loan!—However, given these conditions, wouldn't an agreement with U.E. be possible? But would that be a good idea?

It is really very sad that Helene's health is so poor—however, it is a very inclement summer—at least so far.—<u>Windisch</u>—I have neither the time nor inclination to write articles. —After a short break I'm going to resume work on *Jakobsleiter*.

Many warm regards

Your Arnold Schönberg

\* who was here from 4 p.m. yesterday until 10 a.m. today

## Berg to Schoenberg

Trahütten, 28 July 1922

Dearest friend,

You'll be surprised to get a letter from here after all. I am, too! That is, surprised! It happened thus: the doctor in the clinic to which I wanted to bring Helene for a couple of weeks advised a course of treatment of at least 3–4 weeks. At the clinic itself. To my shame, I must admit that I was not able to persuade Helene to do this. "She doesn't want to lose the <u>entire</u> summer," "the fall would be soon enough for such a course of treatment," etc. In a word: once again we postponed what should have been done long ago and decided overnight to come here, having heard reports of a milk surplus here, of which Helene wanted to take advantage for her health (in fact, she is supposed to eat as many dairy products as possible and little meat). Besides, my presence is no longer required in Vienna, since I am far enough along in the *Wozzeck* matter to be able to take my time revising the 2ⁿᵈ and 3ʳᵈ acts and preparing them for engraving (the 1ˢᵗ act is already being engraved and the whole thing is to be finished in the fall(??)).

That's why I didn't get around to writing these last few days, dear friend, but I am making up for it first thing this morning (we arrived here yesterday evening).

1. The corrections you want in the index will be taken care of. Eliminating the dots makes me very happy.[1] I didn't quite have the courage to suggest it.

2. I am very nervous about playing *Wozzeck* for people. 1. I play too poorly, 2. I feel self-conscious about doing it in any case. It only makes sense when one can do it convincingly, indeed with the intention of convincing others of its "beauty." Doing this for my own work would embarrass me to such an extent, that I would do it even worse than I would anyway because of my awkwardness at the keyboard. Of course, Zemlinsky with his virtuosity overcomes such impediments with ease, although I'm not so sure his music wouldn't have found acceptance earlier if reductions had been available. Because, these don't prevent one from playing it oneself where it is expressly requested. Or do you think that once they see such a difficult score, the prospects of further interest dwindle to zero?! In any case, I don't have any particular expectations; I just want—as you yourself advised me—to leave nothing undone!

3. I spoke a good deal about you with Polnauer. He told me everything about Traunkirchen. Unfortunately—in addition to so much good news and the most wonderful news of all: your work on *Jakobsleiter*—thee was also something distressing (which Polnauer told me in confidence).[2] I won't write about it; except to say that I find it very reassuring that Webern is close by.[3]—

4. Dr. Ploderer[4] left for a 4-week stay in the country a few days ago. He wouldn't be suited for your problem anyway.[5] Practically speaking—he understands nothing at all about such matters. But I could recommend another lawyer to Polnauer, whose specialty is just such a copyright and performance rights affairs and who made a very agreeable and extremely competent impression on me. Anyway, he is someone who stands behind the artist in such cases. Polnauer will ask you whether he can discuss your problem with this Dr. Fischmann.[6]

---

1. In a letter of 18 July 1922 Schoenberg had indicated his annoyance with dots in the index linking entries with page numbers.

2. Josef Polnauer visited Schoenberg in Traunkirchen on 23 July. The distressing news was probably a family matter.

3. The Weberns arrived on 17 July to spend the summer in Traunkirchen in an apartment not far from the Villa Spaun; they remained until early September.

4. Rudolf Ploderer was a lawyer who specialized in estate management.

5. Schoenberg was having difficulties with the Gesellschaft der Autoren, Komponisten und Musikverleger in Wien (Society of Authors, Composers, and Music Publishers in Vienna, also known as AKM); he had resigned from the organization at the end of 1912, and according to its statutes, the AKM continued to owe him royalties for the next ten years. However, as of the end of 1922 performance royalties of the early Schoenberg works originally registered with the AKM were no longer being collected.

6. Schoenberg did indeed tell Polnauer to lay the matter before Dr. Leo Fischmann and he himself corresponded with the lawyer. It has not been determined how matters were finally resolved between Schoenberg and the AKM, but there were continuing difficulties in the following years.

5. Have you received the Verein brochures from Fräulein Klarfeld?[7] Some were also sent by registered letter to Dr. Cronheim.[8]

Many regards to you, my dear esteemed friend. Also to your loved ones. From Helene as well.

Your Berg

---

7. Pauline Klarfeld studied with Schoenberg 1917–19 and served as business secretary in the Verein.
8. Paul Cronheim was the business manager of the Amsterdam Concertgebouw.

## Berg to Schoenberg

Trahütten, 25 August 1922

My dear friend,

I've been meaning to write for a long time, but have been so uneasy the last couple of weeks that I put if off until I could finally see clearly in the matter causing the uneasiness. Now I do. The engravers had "left me hanging" for weeks. At last today I hear that—despite agreement and assurances—the engraving was delayed. However, the firm has now promised to begin the work with the greatest expeditiousness. Of course that's no comfort, because instead of being ready at the beginning of the season (as planned), the score won't be ready now until far into the actual season. And at a significantly higher cost to boot. Last, I could have postponed the work of revising Klein's reduction until I was back in Vienna (where it would have gone much faster in person than by written communication with Klein) and could have spent the summer composing. Consequently I feel that this most valuable time of the year has been wasted and am very depressed about it, too, which in turn appears to have a negative effect on my health; certainly there's no other way to explain my having been so unwell all this time. Certainly the living conditions themselves are the best imaginable. Uninterruptedly beautiful weather (all summer), very good food, cosiest surroundings, no family squabbling.

Helene's condition has remained more or less the same. That is: occasional slight relief due to regular sun bathing, interrupted by the now customary rheumatic spells. Although there hasn't been any worsening, one unfortunately can't speak of improvement either, so this coming fall she will have to submit to treatment in a Vienna clinic after all.

Once my piano score is out, I will resume work on my book about you. I feel an ever-increasing urge to do so. Not just desire, but also a clear feeling of reawakened ability to accomplish such a difficult task. I think about it a great deal and believe that I have finally hit on the right approach. To be sure, it will be quite different from what I began writing 2 years ago.

Many thanks, dearest friend, for the card from Alt-Aussee.[1] From that and the reports from Webern, and from Schmid, who visited me here, I see how you are

---

1. Schoenberg's picture postcard of 21 August was also signed by the various members of the Schoenberg, Zemlinsky, and Webern families.

doing and what kind of life you and your family are leading. Through Stein I am also informed about your immediate plans. But I hear nothing about *Jakobsleiter*. I would very, so <u>very much</u> like to know something about it!—Nor have I heard anything at all about the success of the *Gurrelieder* in Duisburg.[2]—No doubt you, too, have received the brochure for the flutist Alfons Lichtenstein in Berlin. He is giving 10 concerts, nothing but new compositions for the flute (30 works); including *Pierrot lunaire* on 21 November.[3]

Farewell, my dear friend, and many warm regards from us both. Also all our love to your loved ones.

Your Berg

---

2. On 22 July Schoenberg's *Gurrelieder* had been performed in Duisburg under the Duisburg music director Paul Scheinpflug.

3. The flutist Alfons Lichtenstein gave ten programs of contemporary flute music between September 1922 and April 1923. Among the composers represented were Eugene Goossens, Arnold Bax, Igor Stravinsky, Francis Poulenc, Arthur Bliss, Darius Milhaud, Arthur Honegger, Serge Prokofiev, Paul Hindemith, Georges Enesco, and Alfredo Casella.

*Berg to Schoenberg*[1]

Christmas, 1922
[Vienna, 24 December 1922]

You can well imagine, my dearest friend, that the rapid, almost harried completion of the *Wozzeck* piano score has absorbed all of my time these past two to three weeks. This, as well as my intention to surprise you, and the resulting impossibility of telling you the <u>real</u> reason why I have so disproportionately much proofreading to do that I still haven't found time for the chamber orchestra arrangement of my Orchestra Pieces[2]. . . . this is why I had to withdraw a bit of late. Added to that, my telephone—as of one week now—is completely dead.—Now—having relieved my conscience—I dare to hope that you, my dearest friend, will accept my Christmas greetings and the small gifts without anger.[3] Please give dear Mathilde and your dear children my warmest regards.

We will spend Christmas Eve with Helene's parents and the following day with my mother, who is alone in Vienna. On Tuesday (St. Stephen's Day) we will finally be able to follow our true inclination and—given your kind permission—spend the afternoon with you.

Then I will also ask your advice as to what I am now to do with the *Wozzeck* score.—I'm <u>writing</u> all this because our telephone doesn't work and probably won't be fixed before Christmas, so that neither now nor <u>before</u> Tuesday will I have a chance to speak to you in person. Forgive me for taking so much of your time on this lovely Christmas Eve, and a thousand affectionate regards from

Your Alban Berg

1. The original of this letter is located in the Arnold Schoenberg Institute.
2. Intended for a Verein performance, but never realized.
3. Among Berg's gifts was a copy of the piano score of *Wozzeck*.

# *1923*

*Berg to Schoenberg*

Vienna, 27 January 1923

My dearest friend,

Until now I couldn't find out your address. Now I see it on your 2 kind cards that just arrived.[1] Many thanks!

Your family is fine. Except that Felix has a bad cold. My wife saw yours yesterday afternoon at Frau Novakovic's.[2] Mathilde is coming to see us on Monday. And generally things in Vienna are just fine.

Werner Reinhart[3] ordered 2 copies of my piano score. Which pleased me very much. That is 40 francs–530,000 kronen. Your word is invariably effective. There have been practically no orders in response to my sales invitation (even at the low price of 150,000 kronen). Not even from Seligmann, Kaltenborn,[4] Jalowetz—not to mention poorer ones! Incidentally, the situation with the piano score has entered a new phase: the New York publisher Schirmer wants to publish modern things, and Alma, who was approached through an intermediary to secure such works or manuscripts for him, is sending over a piano reduction through this intermediary. In the belief that this publisher might be happy to acquire a work engraved cheaply in Europe ( = $500). Do you think it possible, anyway is there a point? As always you must—please—advise me! I won't undertake anything with Hertzka before then.[5]

Now here I've gone and pestered you again with my affairs, when I'm really thinking only of yours: I am completely immersed in *Erwartung*.[6] What a work!! What an infinite abundance of supremely wonderful music—supremely wonderful,

1. Two picture postcards from Copenhagen, both dated 24 January 1923. Paul August von Klenau, conductor of the Philharmonic Orchestra in Copenhagen 1920–26, invited Schoenberg to conduct his Chamber Symphony, Op. 9. The 30 January concert also included four of Schoenberg's Op. 6 songs and the song of the Waldtaube from *Gurrelieder* (with Marya Freund as soloist).

2. The pianist Olga Novakovic studied with Schoenberg 1918–21.

3. The wealthy Swiss businessman and amateur clarinettist Werner Reinhart, brother of Hans Reinhart, was an influential patron of the arts.

4. The German Walter Herbert Seligmann (also known as Walter Herbert) studied with Schoenberg 1919–22, as did Fritz Kaltenborn.

5. The New York publishing house G. Schirmer did not pursue the connection with Berg. Emil Hertzka, however, had expressed interest in acquiring *Wozzeck*, and Berg signed a contract with U.E. for both *Wozzeck* and his Orchestra Pieces, Op. 6, in April 1923.

6. Eduard Steuermann's piano reduction of *Erwartung* appeared that month with U.E.

*Benedikt F. Dolbin drawing of Arnold Schoenberg and Alban Berg with the Kolisch Quartet, 1923 (Reprinted with permission)*

if only because in <u>every</u> phase there is undreamt-of originality—and, most miraculous of all: this infinite abundance compressed into the smallest space and thus of a concentration without its equal in music—what am I saying: in the art of all times and all peoples.—One doesn't dare think of one's own "works." Otherwise—now that it's too late to condense these 3 acts of verbosity and loquaciousness into a single movement—one would become so despondent that he would like nothing better than to destroy this thing also called an opera.

Thank you, my dearest friend, for this beautiful creation!

Looking forward to seeing you, and with many warm regards from us both.

Your Berg

I'm sending quartet score and parts to Fräulein Gunna Breuning by the same post.[7]

7. In his card of 24 January 1921 Schoenberg had asked Berg to send score and parts of his String Quartet, Op. 3, to the Danish violinist Gunna Breuning, first violinist of the Breuning-Bache String Quartet.

*Berg to Schoenberg*

Berlin, 2 June 1923
Sommerstrasse 7

Dear esteemed friend,

The first rehearsal is over and it went very well and also provided an overview of the subsequent schedule.[1] First Webern rehearsed his Passacaglia; that went "like clockwork," so that after a scant 1¼ hours he had already made good progress and with just a <u>little</u> work in the coming rehearsals is sure to achieve a wonderfully clear performance.——My pieces came after the break: a read-through of the I$^{st}$ *(Präludium)* and then focusing on a few particularly difficult passages. So that it was already beginning to take shape. In any event I realized that all of it is certainly feasible: to be sure, given such a fabulous orchestra as this one. The most difficult phrases are played with a purity and unerring accuracy of pitch(!) that I would <u>never</u> have thought possible. Of course shading and working out individual parts is a lot of work. But, as I said, was already fairly successful in the I$^{st}$ piece.—The II$^{nd}$ piece, on the other hand and to my surprise, seemed <u>less</u> "securely" orchestrated after the 1$^{st}$ read-through. But here Webern hasn't begun to polish anything yet. There wasn't time. The III$^{rd}$ piece already sounded clear in the 1$^{st}$ read-through, but had to be cut off when the rehearsal ended.

The upshot is that probably only 2 pieces will be done. (I$^{st}$ and II$^{nd}$). So that at least their main <u>outline</u> will be **intelligible.** Because if they're <u>not,</u> there would no doubt be a scandal. I fear that <u>**as it is.**</u> For they really are still very unusual, "tame" as I thought them.—Well, we'll see. I'll give you a brief progress report of the coming rehearsals.[2]—

Our trip in the sleeping car was wonderful. We arrived in Berlin well rested, where we have fantastic accomodations: with the president of the Reichsrat: Löbe,[3] that is in a palace that is part of the Reichsrat building.—

Yesterday afternoon we attended a rehearsal of Mahler's 8$^{th}$ Symphony. It will be quite good. The orchestra is fantastic: the wind players (horns!!), the contrabass players. And how precisely they follow dynamic markings!! Quite automatically, out of pure respect for the parts (though these are poorly written). These instrumentalists are enthusiastic in a way we Viennese cannot even comprehend.

Otherwise we spend our time in the circle of various Viennese friends and acquaintances, which grows ever larger. The Rufers, Seligmann, Hertzka, naturally

---

1. Included in the programs of the Austrian Music Week, a festival organized by Heinrich Jalowetz and Paul Pella, was a 5 June concert of novelties with orchestral songs by Julius Bittner, Schoenberg's Chamber Symphony, Op. 9, in Eduard Steuermann's piano arrangement, the premiere of the first two of Berg's Orchestra Pieces, Op. 6, Webern's Passacaglia, Op. 1, and Zemlinsky's Maeterlinck Songs, Op. 13 (with the soloist Felicie Hüni-Mihacsek); Zemlinsky conducted his own work and Webern conducted the remainder of the program. In addition there were two performances of Mahler's Eighth Symphony, conducted by Paul Pella, and three performances of Schoenberg's *Gurrelieder* on 7, 8, and 9 June, conducted by Heinrich Jalowetz.

2. Following the second rehearsal Berg sent Schoenberg another report in a postcard postmarked 4 June 1923.

3. The German Social Democrat Paul Löbe was president of the Reichstag 1920–24 and 1925–32.

Jalowetz and the Pellas,[4] the Alters.[5] In restaurants and cafes as well; but so far everything we've eaten has been indescribably bad.

Life here is significantly cheaper than in Vienna.

The traffic is bewildering.

Forgive my handwriting, but I wanted to tell you so much and have so little time. Tonight is the 1st performance of the VIII[th].

Then finally the *Gurrelieder*, the first rehearsals of which are said to have gone splendidly. It is sure to be wonderful!

1,000 regards

from your Berg

Please give many regards to your loved ones, also from Helene!

I tried to telephone you Thursday to say adieu and ask about Greissle's concert. Unfortunately no one was home.

---

4. The Viennese conductor Paul Pella studied with Schoenberg in 1917 and was at this time beginning his career as a conductor.

5. Georg Alter was secretary of the Prague Verein für musikalische Privataufführungen.

*Berg to Schoenberg*

Berlin, 6 June 1923

Dearest friend,

The concert yesterday went splendidly. Program order: Bittner songs, Chamber Symphony. Intermission, Zemlinsky songs, Berg pieces, Passacaglia. The Bittner songs were the least successful. The Chamber Symphony made a colossal hit. Only then did the audience really become interested. Steuermann had a tremendous success and took countless bows. Zemlinsky enjoyed the greatest success of the evening. The audiences wouldn't stop applauding until the last song was repeated. But then, the performance really was fantastic.* Thus primed, the audience received my 2 pieces very calmly and, by all appearances, with warm interest. But then Webern had both audience and orchestra so completely under his spell that a performance resulted such as no one would have thought possible given so few rehearsals (3½ hours in all). I took several bows too, some with Webern and some alone. Finally, Webern was also immensely successful with his Passacaglia. The generally successful concert came to an end at 10:15.—

But how much happier we would have been over these successes if you, you and Mathilde, had been here. There really is great disappointment in Berlin's music circles that you aren't coming. Your sister[1] is sorry, too, we've already seen her several times. Other people there were: Ratz[2] and Fräulein Schlichter,[3] who came from Weimar, Kassowitz and his wife from Vienna, and Schmid, who came especially from Graz.

---

1. Schoenberg's sister Ottilie was married to the operetta librettist Oskar Felix.

2. Erwin Ratz studied with Schoenberg 1917–20.

3. Dolly Schlichter attended Schoenberg's Schwarzwald School seminar 1918–19.

Naturally Hertzka, Kalmus, and the whole music festival crowd. Also Anny Mahler[4] and correspondence-acquaintances from Berlin, Schreker, the Rufers, Fleischer (!),[5] etc., etc.

All of this notwithstanding, we long for Vienna. Everybody lives so far apart here that in order to meet, one has to spend hours and hours on the road or in restaurants (where the food is incredibly bad). Add to that the freezing cold here (our previous lodging even had steam heating) and, despite relatively low prices, the very, very large sums of money required for such a way of life. That's another reason we're already thinking so much about our return. We plan to leave Friday evening. And arrive in Vienna on Saturday, when I'll call you right away and Sunday afternoon we'll come out to see you.

This way, besides rehearsals, we'll hear only the I[st] *Gurrelieder* performance (Thursday), which we really regret. After all this time, I would love to spend days submerged in this music I love so passionately. But it's impossible. Also, having had to move with the resumption of the Reichsrat sessions, we were given very undesirable quarters: a little room somewhere in the West, where it is really difficult to spend more time than absolutely necessary.—But I'll tell you all this in person!

Enough for today. Today *Gurrelieder* rehearsals, in the evening *Schatzgräber*,[6] tomorrow the last rehearsal (the 10th) and in the evening the performance. Day after tomorrow tea with the Ambassador in the afternoon, departure in the evening.

A thousand warm regards from Helene and me to you both and to your dear ones.

Your Berg

*Zemlinsky rehearsed for 2 hours in the morning, so that in the last rehearsal there was barely time to read through my 2 pieces.

---

4. Anna Mahler was the daughter of Gustav and Alma Mahler.
5. Arthur Fleischer sang in many of the Verein concerts.
6. The Berlin State Opera performance of Schreker's opera was also part of the Austrian Music Week.

## Berg to Schoenberg

Trahütten, 12 July 1923

My dear esteemed friend,

I have been here over a week now, and as of a few days feel better again and am finally back at work, which, however, is going slowly: after all, I have composed practically nothing for almost 20 months; but something seems to be taking shape again. From the many plans growing out of my intention to write something for the Copenhagen wind group, as well as from much earlier plans, the following has finally emerged: a concerto for piano and violin with accompaniment of 10 winds (woodwind and brass).[1] Admittedly I have therewith distanced myself significantly, perhaps even completely from the opportunity to have Hagemann do it and I am

---

1. Berg's Chamber Concerto, ultimately scored for piano, violin, and 13 winds. In a letter of 29 March 1923 Berg had told his wife of Schoenberg's initial negative reaction to his plan to compose a chamber concerto with piano.

terribly sorry about that.[2] But for years the idea I've had—for a piano concerto (originally suggested by you, by the way) then for a double, triple, or even quadruple concerto (excuse my incurable elephantiasis!), moreover: first with large orchestra, then with chamber orchestra accompaniment—would give me no peace. So when the wind idea came up I wanted to accommodate the piano concerto idea at least to the extent of including piano and a few, then later a great many winds. But—as you know:—that was all wrong! Finally I found the solution I mentioned at the outset, which I hope to retain, particularly because it automatically eliminated the problems of a chamber orchestra accompaniment, which seem almost insoluble to me. Namely: 1. How does the piano of the chamber orchestra relate to the solo piano?

2. how does the solo violin relate to the solo string quintet of the chamber orchestra (especially 1st and 2nd violins)?

3. The harmonium as an orchestral instrument in this particular instance—— and in general?!

I admit that all of this can be solved. But—as you remarked so convincingly a while ago:—why select such awkward instrumentation from the outset? Aside from the fact that I am intrigued by it, the difficulties simply disappear with the 10-wind accompaniment. The fact that the work is getting off to a slow start (I have only finished c. 50 measures and it is to be a long three-part movement of symphonic character, perhaps 500 measures in length) is due not to the scoring, but—as I said—to an unpracticed hand.

Only initially I hope!—Too bad that once I've hit my stride I'll have to go to Salzburg. But the Havemann Quartet wants to rehearse with me two days before the concert in Salzburg (2 August), perhaps even somewhere in Bavaria after the 25th, and I know I mustn't let that opportunity pass.[3] I probably won't be able to take Helene along: the trip is very strenuous and she is still not as strong as we would like, though she is living only for her health. As soon as I know more about my plans, I will write to ask whether a short trip to Traunkirchen from Salzburg would be possible—without disturbing you. I have much to ask you and would like to know so much about you, things I cannot expect to have answered in a letter. Above all: how are you? And Mathilde and the young people down to the very youngest?[4] And what you are working on now and are you content?

13 July 1923.

And just now your letter came, dearest friend, showing me how much time you still have for me despite all that.[5] And what affectionate solicitude! How I thank

2. The Danish banker Paul Hagemann was director and flutist of the Copenhagen Wind Quartet. At Schoenberg's suggestion, he wrote to Berg requesting a work for his ensemble.

3. The Havemann Quartet performed Berg's String Quartet, Op. 3, on 3 August at the 1923 Salzburg Chamber Music Festival. Gustav Havemann, the quartet's founder and first violinist, taught at the Berlin Musikhochschule; the other members of the group were Georg Kniestädt, Hans Mahlke, and Adolf Steiner.

4. Gertrud and Felix Greissle's son Arnold was born on 9 April.

5. Schoenberg was on a committee charged with the distribution of funds from American to Austrian and German musicians suffering the effects of inflation. On 9 July, he wrote to Berg of his disappointment that the sum would be awarded in Austrian currency which was worth considerably less than its American equivalent. Eventually, Berg and Webern, along with other composers, received five dollars in the form of 6% gold bonds of the German Reich.

you for it! Believe me, that makes me happier than 10 times the sum from an anonymous source. And Helene too!

If I understand correctly, I am to sign the enclosed receipt and send it to Dr. Rösch?[6] If that is so, I ask you please to post it.

And now I'll close quickly—since the postman is waiting. All our love to you and yours

from your Berg

The very best regards and thanks also from Helene. She will soon write Mathilde a long letter.

(260 Chamber Symphony guides were sold the 1st half-year.—)

_____

6. The German composer and lawyer Friedrich Rösch, who was on the committee for the distribution of the above-mentioned funds.


## Berg to Schoenberg (picture postcard: Salzburg from the Kapuzinerberg)

Hallein, 3 August 1923

Dearest friend,

Although the performance of the George Songs was not very good (too colorless, for one thing), it made an enormous impression notwithstanding, the performers took many bows.[1] It did me such good to be able to sit back and listen to this music again.

The performance of my quartet was fantastic, I'm so sorry you didn't hear it! I believe that you, too, would have been very pleased with the performance.

Auf Wiedersehen,

Your Berg

_____

1. The 3 August concert with Berg's String Quartet, Op. 3, also included Schoenberg's Op. 15 George Songs, performed by Martha Winternitz-Dorda and Friedrich Wührer, and Bartók's Second Violin Sonata, performed by Alma Moodie and Manfred Gurlitt.


## Berg to Schoenberg

Trahütten, 2 September 1923

[on a cover sheet:]           WARNING
Completely uninteresting letter!
Please do not read until you have time!

My dear esteemed friend,

We are very worried about Mathilde.[1] Since my visit in Traunkirchen[2] we have

_____

1. Mathilde Schoenberg had cancer of the kidneys. On 20 September 1923 she was brought to Auersperg Hospital in Vienna, where she died on 18 October, the 22nd anniversary of her wedding day.

2. The Schoenbergs had again spent the summer in the Villa Spaun in Traunkirchen, where Berg and Paul Hagemann had visited them 8–9 August, following the Salzburg Festival concert.

heard nothing about her condition, and though we tell each other that your dear wife naturally has no inclination to write letters and that you don't have time for it, your silence nonetheless makes us very uneasy. We now hope to hear something about Mathilde and all of you from Greissle, to whom I wrote 12 days ago. Perhaps you will be so kind as to encourage him to write me a short letter. Surely he has a great many other things to tell as well, something—as you well know—I can't say for myself. Otherwise I would have written more often. As it is, however, my monotonous reports are invariably restricted to the following: I work in the morning, but not very diligently or successfully: of the single-movement, three-part concerto, the first part, a scherzo-like variation movement, is finished. It has over 200 measures, but measures that contain a great deal: 6/4 meter. There's much contrapuntal work in it, without, however, weighing down the generally light mood. Or so I fancy!

The 2ⁿᵈ movement will be an Adagio. The third a summary of the first 2: a sonata movement.

If only I can get a lot written here! The consistently beautiful weather lures me outside more than is good for my work. Again I am as taken with the beauty of the countryside as ever. Indeed, more so, and despite my liking the Salzkammergut region so enormously! It is the big, big sky that so appeals to me here. The view to the north and east stretches over 80 km, up to the northern Styrian mountains (near Bruck) and eastwards straight through all of Styria, right up to the mountains of the Hungarian border. The south and west—similarly spacious—are bordered by the Yugoslavian and Carinthian Alps. However, what is essential for me is not this so-called panorama, but rather the diversity of the sky above it. It is not at all uncommon here, for example, to see on the plain below a giant wall of black clouds containing a terrible—but thankfully distant—thunderstorm with an uninterrupted series of lightning bolts like a river delta. While in front of that there arises from the plan a rainbow like a giant column of fire, which soon spans the entire eastern sky. Right next to it a second, and both in such intense colors that—were one to see it painted—one would think it impossible. Then further to the right one sees very clearly sheets of rain streaming out of clouds onto the distant hills; still further to the right the sky brightens: against the pale blue spring sky, little pink clouds, lit by the setting sun, which itself stands directly above the Koralps, sending immense radial strands of light into the western sky as in a picture by Greco, while—still further to the right, up out of the deep valley hollows swirl thick clouds of fog: the last vestiges of an earlier thunderstorm perhaps, which in the meantime has withdrawn to the eastern plain, there—the circle closes—to burst. And all of this happens within minutes, that is, simultaneously—and is, of course—constantly evolving—continually taking on different forms.

A quarter of an hour later—the sun is gone—and the sky has changed so much— yes, changed on the whole into a no less richly contrasting opposite, that—to give you an idea of it—I would have to begin to describe it anew.

But—what have I gotten myself into?! I intended to write a reasonable, matter of fact letter and suddenly see myself in the middle of a school essay with the likely title: "Summer Evening in the Mountains." My only excuse: these are my only experiences here besides work and I discuss this with you just as I do the other events in my life. Sorry! I hope that reading this letter didn't interrupt your work. I will use the ajoining half page as a warning to precede my silly drivel.

Yes—your work. If only I knew more about it! Everything you have discovered in the area of 12-tone music and now apply so sovereignly occupies my imagination constantly.[3] I can't wait for the appearance of your first composition in this style!—

Farewell my dearest, esteemed friend. All my love to you and yours, also from Helene.

Your Berg

---

3. Schoenberg officially introduced close friends and students to his concept of twelve-tone composition on 17 February of that year, at which time Erwin Stein took notes that he later published in the article "Neue Formprinzipien." It is not known whether Berg was present at that meeting. Schoenberg's first completed composition in this system was the Prelude of the Suite for Piano, Op. 25 (composed July 1920); at this time he was working primarily on the Wind Quintet, Op. 26, which he completed 26 July of the following year.


## Berg to Schoenberg (postcard)

Vienna, 14 November 1923

Dearest friend,

I haven't written for a long time. Helene's departure was imminent.[1] Now she postponed it again until early next week, for the following reason: Kleiber is coming to Vienna and asked Hertzka to tell me to play Wozzeck for him.[2] That will be Saturday afternoon at Hertzka's. I have asked Dr. Bachrich to assist me. So we are practicing the piano score partly together, partly alone. I will let you know the results of the "audition" right away. Until then I send you my warmest regards, dearest friend, also on Helene's behalf.

Your Berg

1. Helene was planning to leave for a sanatorium in Parsch near Salzburg.
2. The Austrian conductor Erich Kleiber was General Music Director of the Berlin State Opera 1923–35. Berg's audition with Kleiber took place on 17 November.

# 1924

*Berg to Schoenberg*

Vienna, 25 March 1924

My dear friend,

The enclosed clipping may interest you. If anything, it makes the situation more confusing than it already was. Anyway, I entered *Wozzeck.—*

*[The clipping, from the* Neues Wiener Tagblatt *of 22 March 1924, announced the competition for a Cultural Prize of the City of Vienna, consisting of a cash prizes to be awarded for exceptional works of music, literature, and art on 1 May of each year.[1] The 1924 jury members for music were Josef Marx, Richard Strauss, and Julius Bittner.]*

I wonder how you are? We think of you daily and <u>often during</u> each day and we're glad you are in <u>Italy</u> during these first spring days,[2] which hardly seems so here; for here it's as dreadful as ever. Wet and foggy weather. Nonetheless we, Helene and I, have resigned ourselves to <u>not</u> making the trip to Venice. Helene (especially again of late) is just not well enough to endure 2 nights in a train in the space of one week, or even a part of what such a trip would entail. And I couldn't bring myself to go <u>alone;</u> especially as I've already been in Venice twice and she never has. Besides, we are planning 2 expensive trips shortly: Prague *Erwartung*[3] and Frankfurt the *Wozzeck Bruchstücke.*[4] After years of longing, I simply <u>cannot</u> deny myself the former; I suppose I <u>have to</u> attend the latter; I can't risk having Scherchen botch those couple of scenes, thereby destroying the last changes of

1. Both Berg and Webern, as well as Carl Prohaska, Franz Schmidt, Max Springer, and Karl Weigl were awarded the prize in May of that year.

2. On 19 March Schoenberg traveled to Italy for the Italian *Pierrot lunaire* tour arranged by Alfredo Casella, whose Concerto per due violini, viola e violoncello, Op. 40 (premiered at the first concert in Rome) preceded *Pierrot lunaire*. Schoenberg conducted the performances of *Pierrot* on 28 and 29 March in Rome, 30 March in Naples, 1 April in Florence, 3, 4, and 6 April in Venice, Padua and Turin, and 7 and 8 April in Milan. The performers were Erika Wagner, Eduard Steuermann, the French flutist Louis Francois Fleury, the clarinettist Henri Delacroix, and the members of the Brussels-based Pro Arte Quartet (Alphonse Onnou, Laurent Halleux, Germain Prevost, and Robert Maas).

3. The premier of Schoenberg's monodrama *Erwartung* took place on 6 June in the Deutsches Opernhaus in Prague under Alexander Zemlinsky, directed by Louis Labor, and with Marie Gutheil-Schoder as soloist.

4. Hermann Scherchen had suggested that Berg prepare excerpts from *Wozzeck* for concert performance. These *Bruchstücke* were premiered at the International Music Festival in Frankfurt on 15 June, where they were a sensation.

getting the whole opera performed. We are definitely counting on these 2 impera-
tive trips; counting in the truest sense of the word: that is, saving.

Aside from that, some incredible things are getting performed in Frankfurt: Rathaus
II[nd] Symphony,[5] Hába quarter-tone choruses and a sixth-tone quartet(!),[6] Keussler,[7]
Pfitzner (*Columbus* chorus),[8] Petyrek,[9] Schoeck,[10] etc., names I've never heard of.
Krenek too, incidentally: premiere of *Sprung über den Schatten*.[11]

As of a few weeks I've resumed work on my concerto. And—thank God—it's
going quite well. I would like to finish it in one stretch, and that's what I keep
telling myself when I'm depressed about not making the Venice trip: I say to myself:
"At least the work won't be interrupted" . . . But it is poor consolation. Another
consolation is your Serenade. I am immensely looking forward to all the rehearsals!
The preparations (enthusiastically carried out by Dr. Schwarzmann) are proceeding
slowly but steadily.[12]

Please give many regards to Frau Wagner and the Steuermanns. Also to the
Casellas and the 2 gentlemen from the Pro Arte Quartet.

And most affectionate regards to you from Helene and me!

Your Berg

Is it very presumptuous to ask for news of rehearsals and performance of *Pierrot*?
Perhaps Steuermann can let me know in telegram style! Please ask him!

---

5. The Polish composer Karol Rathaus was a student of Franz Schreker (1914–22). His Second
Symphony, Op. 7 (1923), was premiered in Frankfurt on 15 June 1924.

6. The Czech composer Alois Hába, also a Schreker student, was at this time teaching at the
National Conservatory in Prague. His quarter-tone choruses and quartet were performed in Frankfurt
on 10 June 1924.

7. The German composer, conductor, and musicologist Gerhard von Keussler was at this time
director of the Prague Singverein. His oratorio *Zebaoth* was premiered in Frankfurt on 13 June 1924.

8. Pfitzner's choral work *Columbus* (1905), on a text by Schiller, was performed in Frankfurt on a
14 June 1924 concert that also included Schoenberg's *Friede auf Erden* and works by Alexander Menitz,
Felix Petyrek, Richard Strauss, and Othmar Schoeck.

9. The Austrian pianist and composer Felix Petyrek studied with Schreker in Vienna. His *Irrende
Seelen* was performed in Frankfurt on 14 June 1924.

10. The Swiss composer Othmar Schoeck was particularly known for his songs; his "Ghaselen" were
performed in Frankfurt on 14 June 1921.

11. Ernst Krenek studied with Schreker 1916–22. His comic opera *Der Sprung über den Schatten*,
composed 1923, was premiered in Frankfurt 9 June 1924.

12. Schoenberg's Serenade, Op. 24, was privately premiered in Vienna on 2 May in the home of the
arts patron Dr. Norbert Schwarzmann. The official premiere took place on 20 July of that year, during
the Donaueschingen festival.

*Schoenberg to Berg (printed thank-you letter)*

Mödling, [1] October 1924

To all who on various occasions during these last weeks have bestowed friendship, sent congratulations, presented gifts, given happiness, and demonstrated kind-

ness to me and mine: my most heartfelt thanks![1]

I would have liked to have written each individually. Not so as to ration the thanks according to its component parts. But rather to match appropriately, to seek equivalency. For I have received much and varied happiness during these days.

But unfortunately I am forced to take the conventional route: to say the same thank-you to all at once. An equally hearty one, to be sure.

I can assure you, though, that while addressing these I shall think of the wishes and cordiality of each individual and send a work of thanks in my thoughts. Maybe it, too, will arrive!

My heartfelt thanks!

October 1924

ARNOLD Schönberg

Mödling, Bernhardgasse 6

[*in Schoenberg's hand:*] Many heartfelt thanks, dear Helene and dear Alban, for all your love and for the beautiful gifts.

Your Arnold Schönberg

1. Schoenberg's fiftieth birthday was celebrated with various festivities and performances. On the evening of 12 September, his intimate friends gathered for a supper party in Mödling at which they presented him with a leather-bound album containing photographs and brief autobiographies of most of his students up to that time. On the following day, Schoenberg's birthday was officially honored by a ceremony at City Hall, with the mayor Karl Seitz presiding, that included a performance of Schoenberg's *Friede auf Erden* under Felix Greissle; later the Woodwind Quintet, Op. 26, was premiered by an ensemble consisting of younger members of the Vienna Philharmonic Orchestra.

*Arnold Schoenberg and Emil Hertzka, Vienna, 1925 (Arnold Schoenberg Institute 1294)*

# 1925

*Schoenberg to Berg (picture postcard: Nice—La Jetée-Promenade.
Les Mouettes)*

Beaulieu-sur-Mer, 4 February 1925

Dear friends,

You'll be surprised at our being here.[1] We left quite suddenly. We found a pension here where we can live more cheaply than in Vienna. At the moment we are still living rather more expensively. It is absolutely beautiful here. We want to stay as long as possible, at least another 10 days. I'm eager for news of you.

Warm regards

Arnold Schönberg

Warmest regards to your wife and you

Gertrud Schönberg

---

1. Schoenberg married Rudolf Kolisch's sister Gertrud Kolisch on 28 August 1924. In January 1925 they traveled to Venice for their honeymoon, from where they went on to Milan and then San Remo and Nice.

*Berg to Schoenberg (open letter)*

9 February 1925

Dear esteemed friend, Arnold Schönberg!

Composition of this concerto, which I dedicated to you on your fiftieth birthday, was finished only today, on my fortieth.[1] Overdue though it is, I ask that you nonetheless accept it kindly; all the more so as—dedicated to you since its inception—it is also a small monument to a friendship now numbering 20 years: in a musical motto preceding the first movement three themes (or rather motives), which play an important role in the melodic development of the piece, contain the letters of your name as well as Anton Webern's and mine, so far as musical notation permits. *

---

1. Berg dedicated his Chamber Concerto to Schoenberg in this open letter, published in the February 1925 issue of *Pult und Taktstock*.

That in itself already suggests a trinity of events, and as a matter of fact—for it concerns your birthday, after all, and all good things that I wish for you come in threes—it also applies to the work as a whole:

The three parts of my concerto, which are joined in one movement, are characterized by the following three headings, or rather tempo indications:

I. Thema scherzoso con Variazioni;

II. Adagio;

III. Rondo ritmico con Introduzione (Cadenza).

In exploitation of the trinity of available instrumental genres (keyboard, string, and wind instruments) each part [of the work] is associated with a particular sonoral quality, in that sometimes the piano (I), then again the violin (II), and finally in the Finale both solo instruments are juxtaposed against the accompanying wind ensemble.**

This [wind ensemble] (which together with piano and violin comprises a chamber orchestra of fifteen, a sacred number for this type of scoring ever since your Opus 9) consists of: piccolo, large flute, oboe, English horn, E♭, A, and bass clarinets, bassoon, contrabassoon; two horns, trumpets, and trombone.

Formally, too, the trinity or multiples thereof keep recurring.

Thus in the first movement the sixfold return of the same basic idea [*Grundgedanke*]. This idea, a tripartite variation theme of 30 measures presented in the exposition by the wind ensemble, is initially repeated (1<sup>st</sup> recapitulation), i.e. varied for the first time by the piano alone exploiting its virtuosic potential. Variation 2 presents the melody of the "theme" in inversion; variation 3 in retrograde;[2] variation 4 in retrograde inversion (whereby these 3 middle variations can be regarded as a quasi-development section of this "first movement sonata form"), whereas the last variation returns to the basic shape [*Grundgestalt*] of the theme. Because this occurs by means of a stretto between piano and wind ensemble (—these are canons in which the voice that enters later tries to pass the one that entered first and indeed achieves this and leaves the other far behind—), this last variation (or recapitulation) takes on a entirely new dimension corresponding to its simultaneous structural function as a coda. Which really needn't be stressed particularly, since each of these thematic transformations obviously takes on its own character, even though—and this I consider important—the Scherzo character of the first part generally predominates and must be adhered to during performance. The formal structure of the Adagio, too, is based on the "da capo song form": $A_1$–B–$A_2$, where the $A_2$ is the inversion of $A_1$. The return of the first half of the movement, comprising 120 measures, occurs in retrograde, either as free presentation of the thematic material spooling back, or, for instance during the entire middle part (B), in exact mirror image.

The third movement, finally, is a combination of the two preceding ones (see table). Due to the resultant return of the variation movement—though enriched through simultaneous return of the Adagio—the overall formal structure of the concerto is likewise tripartite.

2. Actually the second variation presents the retrograde, the third the inversion of the theme.

On the whole the union of movements I and II results in the following three types of combinations:

1. Free contrapuntal treatment of the corresponding parts.

2. The consecutive juxtaposition of literal repetitions of individual phrases and passages, in other words a quasi-duet, and

3. the precise transfer of entire passages from both movements.

The attempt to bring all of these disparate components and characters together (—consider, esteemed friend: on the one hand a basically scherzoso variation movement of c. 9 minutes duration, on the other a broad, lyrical, expansive Adagio lasting a quarter of an hour!—), in other words the attempt to create out of *that* a new movement with its own individual character resulted in the form of the "Rondo ritmico."***

Three rhythmic forms: one primary and one subsidiary rhythmic idea as well as one that is likewise a motive are applied to the melody of the *Haupt-* and *Neben-stimmen*, admittedly in the most diverse variants (extended and shortened, augmented and diminished, in stretto and in retrograde, in all conceivable forms of metric displacement and transformation, etc., etc.) and thus and through the rondo-like return, thematic unity is achieved that is by no means inferior to the traditional rondo form, and that—to borrow one of your *termini technici*—assures comparative "accessibility" of the musical events.

It was in a scene of my opera *Wozzeck* that I first demonstrated that this device of giving a rhythmic idea such a constructively important role works.[3] But that it is also possible to achieve an extensive kind of thematic transformation on the basis of a rhythmic idea, as I attempted in the present rondo, was revealed to me by a passage in your Serenade, where in the last movement—to be sure, with entirely different motivation—a number of motives and themes from preceding movements are joined with rhythmic ideas not initially associated with them; and vice versa. And when I learn from Felix Greissle's article on the formal structure of your wind quintet (*Anbruch*, February issue, 1925), which I only just saw, that in the last movement "the theme always returns with the same rhythm, but each time composed of pitches from a different row," that strikes me as further justification for such rhythmic construction.

Another device for giving the finale of my concerto its independence (despite the dependence of all of its pitches on those of the first two movements) was in choice of meter: Whereas the variations were in triple meter throughout and an even-numbered meter predominates in the Adagio, the rondo is characterized by continual fluctuation between all conceivable even and uneven, divisible and undivisible metric forms, thus emphasizing even in the metric aspect the trinity of events.

This [trinity] is apparent also in the harmonic aspect, where next to long stretches of completely suspended tonality there are also individual shorter passages of tonal character that correspond to the regulations established by yourself in the "Composition with 12 notes." If I mention, finally, that divisibility by three also applies to the number of measures in the *entire* work as well as within sections, I'm sure

---

3. *Wozzeck*, Act III, scene 3.

that—to the extent I make this public knowledge—my reputation as mathematician will rise in squared proportion to the demise of my reputation as composer.

But seriously: If in this analysis I discussed almost entirely matters relating to the trinity, that is: first, because they are the very events that would be overlooked by everyone (in favor of musical events). Second, because it is much easier for an author to speak of such structural matters than of the inner processes, though this concerto is surely not poorer in that regard than any other piece of music. I tell you, dearest friend, if anyone realized how much friendship, love, and a world of human-emotional associations I spirited into these three movements, the proponents of program music—if indeed there are still such—would be delighted and the "linearists" and "physiologists," the "contrapuntists" and "formalists" would come down on me, incensed at such "romantic" inclinations, if I hadn't at the same time divulged that they too, if so inclined, could find satisfaction.

For it was my intention with this dedication to present you on your birthday with "all good things," and a "concerto" is precisely the art form in which not only the soloists (including the conductor!) are given the opportunity to display their virtuosity and brilliance, but for once the composer, too. Years ago, dear friend, you even advised me to compose one—and with chamber orchestra accompaniment at that—little suspecting (or did you?) that, as always, your advice anticipated a time when—as is true everywhere today—precisely this art form would be infused with new life. So that in presenting it to you, as a token moreover of the initially mentioned threefold anniversary, I hope I have found one of those "better opportunities" of which you say prophetically in your *Harmonielehre*:

"And so perhaps this activity, too, will eventually return to me."[4]

Your Alban Berg

*namely A–D–S–C–H–B–E–G–, A–E–B–E–, and A–B–A–B–E–G.

**In the case of <u>separate performance</u> of Parts I or II individual conclusions have been prepared for the variation movement (for piano and wind ensemble) as well as for the Adagio (violin and wind ensemble) to replace the elision between movements that is otherwise intended.

***duration of this movement (with repeat) is also about 15 minutes. Overall duration therefore circa 39 minutes.

---

4. Berg quotes the concluding sentence of the foreword to Schoenberg's 1911 *Harmonielehre* (quoted here in Roy Carter's 1978 translation). Schoenberg had declared that the principal task of a teacher is to rouse his students and that the resulting activity (*Bewegung*) eventually accrues back to the teacher.

*Berg to Schoenberg*[1]

Trahütten, [c. 13 ] September 1925

If, dear, esteemed friend, this year for your birthday—in spite of your antipathy for letter editions—I again present you with a volume of "letters," there are various reasons:[2] 1.) because they are Strindberg's; 2.) because they are not private letters but communications and disclosures almost exclusively providing revelations about the last 20 years of his creativity, and this in a concise and summarized form not to be found anywhere else in Strindberg's writings 3.) because this edition also contains several previously unpublished articles and essays of Strindberg's 4.) because the letters present an absolutely complete picture of his activities in his "modern theater" (how very like—even to the details of organization—your activities with the Verein für musikalische Privataufführungen!) 5.) because one gets to know Strindberg as letter writer. 6.) because I myself liked it all so enormously that I can't believe you, too, wouldn't get some pleasure out of it. Finally because the volume—even unread—will complete your otherwise complete collected edition of Strindberg's works. So please be so kind as to accept this, dear friend, along with my and Helene's most affectionate regards.—

We have come up here now—for the 2^{nd} time in 2 weeks—and apparently: this time we will be able to stay, i.e., recuperate for a couple of weeks. I am in particular need of it, for I haven't been really well for months now, and of late am completely run down. Helene too, of course. And perhaps I can find the serenity (inner) to compose again. For that, too, has come to a standstill.[3]

Casting a glance into your new score[4] a while back was immeasurably exciting. How long will it be before I understand this music as thoroughly as I fancy, for example, that I understand *Pierrot*. For the present I am slowly familiarizing myself with your *Opera* 23–26, the only scores I have up here with me. But [to think] what you have achieved in the meantime?! Who could possibly keep pace with you, that is follow your footsteps, except those who outlive you by decades. Isn't *that* how I am to interpret the dedication "to the little boy Arnold"??[5]

I hope your birthday, which we unfortunately have to celebrate far away from you, will be very enjoyable and happy; our very affectionate regards to you and your dear wife from us both.

Your Berg

---

1. The original of this letter is located in the Arnold Schoenberg Institute.
2. This letter accompanied a volume of Strindberg letters to his German translator, Emil Schering: *Briefe an Emil Schering* (Munich: Georg Müller, 1914).
3. Sometime in September Berg had begun composing his *Lyric Suite* for string quartet.
4. Schoenberg's Quintet for Flute, Oboe, Clarinet, Bassoon, and Horn, Op. 26.
5. Schoenberg's young grandson Arnold Greissle.

## Berg to Schoenberg

Vienna, 19 November 1925

Dearest, esteemed friend,

Just back from Berlin,[1] I hear to my greatest dismay of your operation.[2] We are with you always in our anxious thoughts, hope you have a very, very speedy recovery and send you—and your dear wife—the most affectionate regards

Alban and Helene Berg

Perhaps these lovely little stories[3] will make the period of convalescence pass a little more quickly.

1. Berg went to Berlin on 13 November for the first rehearsals of *Wozzeck*.

2. Schoenberg developed acute appendicitis in November and was operated on at the Crown Prince Rudolf Hospital in Vienna.

3. Franz Kafka's collection of short stories, *Ein Landarzt. Kleine Erzählungen*. (Munich: Kurt Wolff Verlag, 1919).

## Schoenberg to Berg (telegram)

Vienna, 13 December 1925

Hope for premiere success.[1] Heartily wish all the best. Sorry not to be there. Most warmly

Schönberg

1. *Wozzeck* was premiered in Berlin on 14 December under Erich Kleiber, with Leo Schützendorf, Sigrid Johanson, and Fritz Soot in the principal roles; the director was Franz Ludwig Hörth, with the sets designed by Panos Aravantinos.

*Set design by Panos Aravantinos for* Wozzeck, *Act I, Scene 2 in the Berlin production, December 1925 (Alban Berg Stiftung)*

# Staats-Theater
## Opernhaus

---

Berlin, Montag, den 14. Dezember 1925

### 14. Karten-Reservesatz.
#### (Außer Abonnement.)

## Uraufführung:

### Georg Büchners

# Wozzeck

Oper in drei Akten (15 Szenen) von **Alban Berg.**
Musikalische Leitung: General-Musikdirektor Erich Kleiber.
In Szene gesetzt von Franz Ludwig Hörth.

---

| | |
|---|---|
| Wozzeck | Leo Schützendorf |
| Tambourmajor | Fritz Soot |
| Andres | Gerhard Witting |
| Hauptmann | Waldemar Henke |
| Doktor | Martin Abendroth |
| 1. Handwerksbursch | Ernst Osterkamp |
| 2. Handwerksbursch | Alfred Borchardt |
| Der Narr | Marcel Noë |

---

| | |
|---|---|
| Marie | Sigrid Johanson |
| Margret | Jessyka Koettrik |
| Mariens Knabe | Ruth Iris Witting |
| Soldat | Leonhard Kern |

Soldaten und Burschen, Mägde und Dirnen, Kinder.

---

Gesamtausstattung: P.-Aravantinos.

---

Technische Einrichtung: Georg Linnebach.

---

Nach dem 2. Akt findet eine längere Pause statt.

### Kein Vorspiel.

---

**Den Besuchern der heutigen Vorstellung wird das neu
erschienene Heft der „Blätter der Staatsoper"
unentgeltlich verabfolgt.**

---

*Program for the premiere of* Wozzeck *at the Berlin State Opera, 14 December 1925*

# 1926-1935

Berg's astonishing international career following the premiere of *Wozzeck* subtly altered his relationship with Schoenberg, for the student had attained a level of popular success and acclaim his teacher had never enjoyed. The letters from these last years while fewer in number, are clearly an exchange between equals, though Berg dutifully retains all the formulae of obeisance. His new-found self-confidence is, however, evident in a growing independence from Schoenberg's influence.

Personal contact between the two men became increasingly rare during this last decade of their friendship. Schoenberg taught in Berlin during most of the academic year and spent his substantial vacation time in southern climes. He visited Vienna only rarely before his 1933 emigration, the last time being in February of that year. Together with his young wife, Schoenberg, now an establishment figure, led a life that was notably more stylish and outgoing, and at the same time freer from financial worries than ever before. At the same time, his preoccupation with moral and religious questions is reflected in his work on the opera *Moses und Aron* and his reconversion to Judaism in 1933. During these same years Berg traveled quite extensively in connection with performances of his music, particularly *Wozzeck,* and his jury duties with music organizations such as the Allgemeiner Deutscher Musikverein (ADMV) and the International Society for Contemporary Music (ISCM). On several occasions he visited the Schoenbergs in Berlin, but plans for a vacation together never materialized.

When Adolf Hitler was named Chancellor of Germany on 30 January 1933 the Schoenbergs' days in Berlin were numbered. In May they left Berlin for Paris and that fall continued on to America. After one season in New York and Boston Schoenberg and his family found a permanent home in Los Angeles. His correspondence with old friends became sporadic during the American years, due partly to the sudden geographical and psychological dislocation and partly to his own time-consuming efforts to establish himself in a foreign land.

For his part, Berg felt increasingly isolated from events in his native land and in the music world. As performances of his works declined his means of existence became precarious, and his emotional and physical health suffered. During his last two years Berg and his wife lived primarily in the seclusion of the Waldhaus, their property on the Wörthersee. Here he continued to work on *Lulu* and wrote the violin concerto, his last completed composition.

# 1926

*Schoenberg to Berg (postcard)*

[Berlin-]Charlottenburg, 11 January 1926

Dear friend,

We saw *Wozzeck* the day after we arrived.[1] It made a very good impression on me. Can't say, of course, that I know the work well yet. But I could recognize it and with repeated hearings (they say it's becoming a hit; been in the papers so often!), I'll certainly be able to get an overview. Unfortunately the performance isn't particularly good. Not even the orchestra, which stumbles over many a phrase and difficulty. The singers sing very little and exaggerate all the more. An orgy of temperament. As regards the staging, I find the black and white sets extremely irritating. One goes absolutely blind—physiologically speaking, when in almost every scene $\%_{10}$ of the stage is kept pitch black and $\frac{1}{10}$ bathed in glaring, brilliant light. Too bad I don't have the piano score here yet. I would have liked to check some things. But it will be here in a few days along with my scores. I'm not sure whether on first impression after one hearing I'm justified in saying that there are some things I don't find good, things that I'd like to discuss with you in detail. I refer to the fact that almost every scene builds to a great orchestral *fff*. I'm not sure whether a change here might not be necessary or possible.—Incidentally, the orchestra is often much too loud. But: on the whole it is very impressive and there's no doubt I *can* be proud of such a student. Many warm regards to you and Helene.

Your Arnold Schönberg[2]

---

1. The Schoenbergs moved to Berlin on 6 January. The Berlin State Opera scheduled twelve *Wozzeck* performances in the 1925 / 26 season. Schoenberg heard the fourth performance on 7 January, with the original cast.
2. Gertrud Schoenberg also adds a note to the Bergs in this card.

*Berg to Schoenberg*

[Vienna] 21 January 1926

Thank you so *very* much, my dearest friend, for your kind words about my opera. That you were favorably impressed after only one hearing and that you really didn't need to feel ashamed of me (as a student) makes me very happy and relieves me of an anxiety that has burdened me for more than half a decade. I'm also overjoyed that you intend to hear the work a few more times to get to know it <u>better</u>. Thanks, a thousand thanks!

I hear from Frau *Dozent* Kolisch[1] and U.E. that you and your dear wife are well and have spent pleasant days in Berlin. I always knew you would: now that it has come to pass, I'm all the happier. Easy as it is to play off Berlin against Vienna, one continually—I think—has to admit the justification anew. As I see it, complete winter hibernation has set in <u>here</u>. Even the performance of a big oratorio by <u>Suter</u> (the only concert event) and the coming premiere of *Andrea Chenier* at the State Opera doesn't change that.[2] In this environment, our life glides along uneventfully; but I hope to give it more meaning soon. I don't really believe that the *Wozzeck* premieres in Breslau and Prague are still possible <u>this</u> season.[3] Zurich, thank God, backed down from a performance of my concerto:[4] so that I may be able to leave for the country as early as spring (May) for what I hope will be months of uninterrupted work.

We, Helene and I, send our very best and most affectionate regards to you and your dear wife, whom we thank for her kind words in your letter.

Your Alban Berg

---

1. The mother of Rudolf and Gertrud Kolisch.

2. The Swiss composer Hermann Suter's choral work *Le Laudi di San Francesco d'Assisi*, Op. 25, was performed in Vienna on 20 January 1926 under Wilhelm Furtwängler. The premiere of the new production of Umberto Giordano's opera *Andrea Chenier* took place on 28 January 1926.

3. The Prague production of *Wozzeck* took place the following season; the Breslau plans were not realized.

4. Berg's Chamber Concerto was not premiered until 20 March 1927 in Berlin under Hermann Scherchen; the second performance, also under Scherchen, took place in Zurich on 25 March 1927.


## Berg to Schoenberg

Vienna, 13 March 1926

Dearest friend,

I haven't written for quite a while; partly because we heard from one another (indirectly) through my sister's visit, partly because preparations for today's Workers' Symphony concert with my *Wozzeck Bruchstücke* under Jalowetz have taken much of my time.

You were so very kind as to ask my sister about my material well-being, so I would like to tell you that thanks to the opera royalties, I am now doing better financially. I.e., I feel at least somewhat secure now that Hertzka is giving me 600 schillings a month on the strength of those receipts.[1]

To be sure, I'm not earning <u>anything else</u>: the first half season in 15 years in which I don't have <u>a single</u> [student] (not even a nonpaying one)! And still I can't compose; it is impossible in Vienna, which is why I want to leave for the country as soon as possible.

The past few days of orchestral rehearsals under Jalowetz were very exciting and

---

1. Berg signed a contract with U.E. for *Wozzeck* and the Orchestra Pieces, Op. 6, on 13 April 1923; he was not offered a general contract until May 1927. His monthly advance from U.E. was balanced against income from his works, a customary arrangement between publisher and composer.

very instructive with regard to instrumentation (Jalowetz devoted almost 2½ of the 3 orchestral rehearsals entirely to the *Wozzeck* Pieces, the remainder to Beethoven: Piano Concerto in E♭ major and the III$^{rd}$ *Leonore*: the performance should be very good, the orchestra was extremely willing, even interested, and with the exception of a couple of deficiencies (: lack of discipline, bad clarinetists, mediocre horns) has great qualities.) Actually the lessons I was able to draw from these rehearsals are negative. That is, the experience has taught me that with regard to <u>dynamics</u> there is no <u>certainty</u> in orchestrating; that it doesn't work without <u>adjustment</u> to each individual set of spatial conditions. Aside from the relationship between the strings and the winds, which in <u>Vienna</u> produced precisely <u>opposite</u> results to those in Berlin, other dynamic variables—the result of seating plan, location of the orchestra: whether in a theater or on a concert stage, rehearsals in different <u>halls</u> (Konzerthaus or Musikvereinsaal)—are such that I really don't know any longer how one should set dynamics. For example, here I had to take out dynamic revisions added especially for Prague.[2] I also gained some interesting vocal insights. Given a real singing voice, these apparently unsingable melodies are singable after all: at any rate (without being a <u>really great</u> singer) the singer here (Frau Achsel from the State Opera[3]) sings the <u>lyric</u> *pp* ♭○    just as beautifully as the high dramatic *f* ♮ .

Her low G ♮ , and everything in between, sounds just as good when she sings as when she speaks; furthermore, she learned the entire part, which has easier passages along with musically very difficult ones, in 8–10 days of study, even though she doesn't have absolute pitch. She already sang it perfectly at the <u>first</u> orchestral rehearsal.

Of course Jalowetz is really fantastic and the orchestra is very enthusiastic about him.

But those are mere rays of brightness in the darkness of this musical winter. Today's concert, for example, will open with brass fanfares by Notre-Dame-Schmidt, who will conduct them himself.[4] You can't imagine, dear friend, the dilettantism of this composition or that of an *Idylle* by Marx, which Cremens Klauss [sic] recently programmed before an absolutely scandalous performance of Mahler's VII$^{th}$.[5] Or the kind of thing Dirk Fock, here justifiably nicknamed "Refuse of the Netherlands," commits as conductor.[6] Enough of that; I would rather tell you how happy it made me to hear all the lovely and wonderful things my sister related about you and your Berlin life—how much we worry, on the other hand, that you may still

2. Alexander Zemlinsky conducted the *Wozzeck Bruchstücke* in Prague on 20 May 1924 with Tilly de Garmo as soloist.

3. The German dramatic soprano Wanda Achsel-Clemens sang at the Vienna State Opera 1923–39.

4. The Austrian composer Franz Schmidt had enormous success with his first opera *Notre Dame* (1914). The 13 March Vienna Philharmonic concert opened with fanfares from Schmidt's second opera, *Fredigundis* (1922).

5. On 4 March Clemens Krauss conducted a Vienna Philharmonic concert with Josef Marx's *Idylle—Concertino über die pastorale Quart* (1925) and Mahler's Seventh Symphony. Berg's misspelling of Krauss's name is deliberate.

6. The Dutch conductor and composer Dirk Fock directed the Vienna Konzertverein 1924–27.

be suffering from the effects of your appendectomy. I hope that has finally improved now.—

We send you and your dear wife our most affectionate regards

Your Berg

Your cufflink is ready; Hertzka will bring it to you around the 26th.—

We enjoy your radio very much. Yesterday we heard the <u>complete</u> *Meistersinger* from the State Opera.—

*Berg to Schoenberg*

Trahütten, 30 May 1926

Oh, how happy your "Foreword"[1] made me, dearest esteemed friend. You really have finished off Krenek with this, and with him half—what am I saying—⁹/₁₀ of the U.E. catalogue![2] And it pleased me not only because of Krenek's article in the almanac,[*3] but also because—out of an impulse to educate myself: to become familiar with some modern operas, for a change—I took a pretty close look, with the greatest imaginable objectivity, at Krenek's *Orpheus and Euridike*[4] and was extremely doubtful whether what this Ernest [*Ernst*] means to say with his music is really said in earnest [*im Ernst*]. In any case, only very, very little can be <u>taken</u> in earnest (nota bene, I didn't enjoy other aspects of my opera review very much either. <u>Szymanowski</u>, for example: I've absolutely never seen anything so over-loaded and monotonous. If one combined the thickest Reger with the sultriest Schreker and poured over this an uninterrupted stream of mush from the latest Strauss operas, the incidental by-product would no doubt be the sound to which Szymanowski unremittingly aspires <u>from the 1st to last page</u> of *King Hagith*(?).[5]—Reznicek: completely impossible; that's the sort of thing Specht wrote one of his dithyrambic biog-

1. Schoenberg's *Three Satires for Mixed Chorus*, Op. 28, entitled "Am Scheideweg" (At the Crossroad) (originally "Tonal oder atonal"), "Vielseitigkeit" (Many-sidedness), and "Der neue Klassizismus" (New Classicism), were published in 1926. In his original foreword, Schoenberg derides those contemporary composers who seek the middle of the road, as well as those who cultivate "isms."

2. In a postcard of 6 June Schoenberg sent Berg a short addition to the forword, making it clear that he was not attacking the entire U.E. catalog, but only the incompetents (*Nichtskönner*); this addendum was included in the complete edition of Schoenberg's works. In a letter of 27 June Berg writes that he is reassured by Schoenberg's qualification, "as one movement of my second quartet-in-progress represents an attempt to write strictest 12-tone music with a strong <u>tonal</u> feeling; at any rate, that was possible."

3. Krenek's article, "Musik in der Gegenwart," (Music in the Present) was published in the 1926 Universal Edition Yearbook 25 *Jahre Neue Musik*, which celebrated the publishing firm's 25th anniversary with a series of essays on the general theme of what the next 25 years would bring. In his article, Krenek discusses the fragmentation of the contemporary public and its corollary, the divergence between serious and light music, and finally the theater's potential for effecting a new, more broadly based synthesis. Schoenberg contributed the introductory essay to the yearbook, an article entitled "Gesinnung oder Erkenntnis?" (Opinion or Insight?) and Berg contributed the article "Verbindliche Antwort auf eine unverbindliche Rundfrage" (Binding Answer to a Non-Binding Inquiry).

4. Krenek's opera *Orpheus und Eurydike* was premiered later that year in Kassel.

5. Berg is confusing Polish composer Karol Szymanowski's first opera *Hagith* (composed 1913 and premiered 1922 in Warsaw) with *King Roger* (composed 1918–24, and premiered 19 June 1926 in Warsaw).

raphies about![6]—Gál:[7] quite nice and respectable, but—something I've never encountered in all of modern music: a Zemlinsky imitation!—Finally <u>Prokofiev</u>, whom Bruno Walter praised highly in a Vienna interview and played off against me, who (that is <u>I</u>) doesn't satisfy his musical hunger.** Well; if he likes Prokofiev so much, he can't be very hungry. I consider *The Love for Three Oranges* very engaging, flowing music, but it certainly can't be ranked much above salon music! Even if it's only that of a Bolshevist salon.—) Excuse my excursus from the main theme, your "foreword," which I also found indescribably beautiful from a linguistic standpoint.

On the other hand—I must admit to my shame—I still haven't figured out the canon for Bernard Shaw, though I have spent hours on it.[8] If I understand it correctly it is a <u>6</u>-voice canon. The entrances are always at the sign 'S.' but at which intervals? Does V mean dominant? or a fifth <u>below</u> (subdominant)? Are the entrances as follows?:

<u>I</u>[st] soprano (tonic)
    II[nd] Soprano (illegible): (I or V?)
  Alto (a fifth below)
    <u>I</u>[st] Tenor (an octave below soprano I)
      II[nd] Tenor (a twelfth below)
        <u>Bass</u> (2 octaves below)

Of course I'll keep trying. Perhaps I will hit on it yet. It would be very painful to me if I—"had so little honor!"[9] Yes, the <u>text</u> of this canon! It is a prime example of how, <u>without compromising himself</u>, one truly great man honors someone of whom it is questionable whether he is a great man at all. I swear that not one of the many poets and writers in this portfolio could have accomplished the like!

To continue with the linguistic theme: naturally I purchased your "texts" long ago and have read them with the utmost enthusiasm.[10] Especially the "Requiem,"[11] which had previously been <u>unknown</u> to me. There are sentences there—aside from the grandeur of the entire concept—, that are surely among the most sublime in

---

6. Richard Specht, *E. N. von Reznicek, eine vorläufige Studie* (Leipzig, 1923). The Austrian composer Emil Nikolaus von Reznicek was best known for his operas *Donna Diana* (1894), *Ritter Blaubart* (1920), and *Holofernes* (1923).

7. The Austrian composer Hans Gál had enjoyed considerable success with his opera *Die heilige Ente* (1923). HIs *Das Lied der Nacht* was premiered in 1926.

8. Schoenberg appended three canons in C major to his Op. 28 *Satires* to demonstrate the twelve-tone system's possibilities for the seven diatonic notes; the third of these canons is dedicated to Bernard Shaw on the occasion of his seventieth birthday. In the six-voice G. B. Shaw canon the first soprano begins on the tonic, the alto enters a fifth below (which Schoenberg indicates with a '5'), the second soprano enters at the unison, followed by the first tenor at the fifth below, and finally the second tenor an octave below, followed by the bass at the fifth below that. The canon was also published in *Bernard Shaw zum 70. Geburtstage* (Berlin, 1926), edited by S. Fischer and S. Trebitsch, a collection that included contributions from 105 German authors, artists, and intellectuals.

9. Schoenberg's text begins with the words "Wer Ehr erweist, / muss selbst davon besitzen;" (he who pays honor / must himself possess it).

10. U.E. published the texts of Schoenberg's dramatic and oratorio compositions in 1926.

11. Begun in 1919 and completed soon after Mathilde Schoenberg's death, this text was never set to music.

the German language. For example the verse:

> Dem Herrn sind 1000 Tage wie ein Tag.
> Solch einen, so oft sie einander verlieren
> Schenkt er Liebenden,
> sich wieder zu sehn,
> sich immer wieder zu finden.[12]

and the way it interweaves and grows in intensity from line to line; the way it sounds (the many i's) as if it were the most precise rhymed poetry, whereas it actually possesses the absolute freedom of most exquisite prose.

To say nothing of the 3 words: "which is difficult" after the line: "If one can die." Only an aside! But unsurpassable in its clarity and power — — — —

How long before the professionals, the poets and writers, realize what stylistic wonders lie hidden here?!

Slowly, very slowly I am beginning to understand the quintet. Not long ago I played through it with Webern (the reduction is very good![13] With one small exception: the missing rests, which greatly impede fluent reading), I enjoyed it tremendously and since then have felt deep regret that I can't be in Zurich.[14] I'm sure that Webern will do it quite particularly well. I imagine he wishes you could be there! Unfortunately I must make do with the thought of it and with closer study of the score—the only score I brought along. In the meantime you have finished another big work[15] and have us all agog with anticipation. I congratulate you—and us— with a sincere friend's heart and musician's mind!

If, dearest friend, I may also add some superficial news, it is that—overestimating Wozzeck royalties—we have had our Viennese apartment renovated a bit. After 15 years. And I have finally had all my unbound scores and books bound. Everything turned out very beautifully and I am particularly pleased with your various volumes, which were especially well and tastefully bound.—

Before coming up here we spent some time in Küb with my mother. Helene, who is actually not at all well (the same old complaints with which you're familiar), was to have a rest from household chores and I, a small climatic transition to this all too raw Trahütten mountain air. And now we are here, where I immediately continued work on my quartet, which I want to finish before we have to leave (in the middle of the summer: July?) that is, make room for other members of the family. That—and because I had absolutely no students in Vienna—was the reason for our early departure for the country, which, on the other hand, is sad for me: because I will not be able to see you when you come to Vienna (I assume: at the end of June)! So I can't even say (which would have made me so happy:) "Auf Wiedersehen!", but only send my regards. but I do that with the greatest warmth

12. To the Lord 1,000 years are as a day. One such [day], as often as they lose one another, he grants to lovers to see each other again, to find each other again and again.

13. The piano score of Schoenberg's Wind Quintet, Op. 26, was prepared by Felix Greissle.

14. Webern had been invited to that year's ISCM festival in Zurich to conduct both the premiere of his Five Pieces for Orchestra, Op. 10, on 23 June, and a performance of Schoenberg's Quintet, Op. 26, on 19 June.

15. Schoenberg had completed his suite, Op. 29, on 1 May 1926.

and affection for both of you from both of us!

Your Alban Berg

\* How did you like <u>my</u> article in the almanac? I'd like to know!
\*\* music makes him feel (I quote) "like a butterfly without a stomach."—

### Berg to Schoenberg

Trahütten, 13 July 1926

My dearest esteemed friend,

I just heard from Stein, who, thank heavens, also told me some other things about you, that you are in Vienna. I hadn't known that earlier, but didn't suppose you were in Berlin any longer, which is why I hadn't dared send something off at random—that explains my long silence.

We are unhappy not to be in Vienna, too, now that you are there, and fear that once <u>we</u> are back, you will be somewhere in the country. We're not staying here much longer: in 1–2 weeks, perhaps earlier, we must leave to make room for other family members. That's why I'm working with great haste, even nervousness, and also differently than usual. On several movements at once; merely sketching some things to outline as much of the <u>whole</u> as I can, and postponing the completion for Vienna, where I never *can* do any real <u>composing</u>. It will be, as I believe I once told you, a suite for string quartet, that is, 6 movements of a rather more lyrical character: Allegretto, Andante, Allegro, Adagio, Presto, Largo. I definitely hope to have it finished by the fall. On the enclosed sheet of staff paper I have taken the liberty of making a note of my experiences with "composition with 12 notes" in this project (as well as earlier). Gradually, even I am becoming adept in this method of composing, and that is very reassuring. For it would have pained me dreadfully if it had been denied me to express myself musically <u>this way</u>. And I *know*, aside from personal ambition (and idealism), that from now on, long after the residual tootling of the I.G.f.l.M. (i. A.)[1] (forgive the crude joke!) has died away, no one will **be able** to compose in **any other way**. Without even using the <u>most sublime</u> as a point of comparison: you or Mahler or the classics, one need only hear in succession the famous *Pacific* or *Till Eulenspiegel*, to see clearly what this <u>international</u> music is all about.[2] Webern's experiences in Zurich must have been very instructive in this regard and I literally thirst to hear everything about the "festival" and <u>your</u> relationship with the I.G.f.n.M.[3] Indeed everything concerning you and your Berlin expe-

1. The Internationale Gesellschaft für Neue Musik, or I.G. f.n.M. (International Society for Contemporary Music, or ISCM) had been founded in the summer of 1922, following the Salzburg Chamber Music Festival. Berg's facetious respelling, I.G.f.l.M.i.A. (leck' mich im Arsch) stands for International Society for Kiss My Ass. Berg frequently used this variant.

2. The Swiss composer Arthur Honegger's *Pacific 231* (1923) and Richard Strauss's symphonic poem *Till Eulenspiegels lustige Streiche*, Op. 28, (1895). The relative merits of an "international" as opposed to a specifically "national" style of music were debated with particular vehemence during the Twenties and Thirties.

3. Schoenberg, whose interaction over the years with the ISCM was fraught with tension, was at this time upset that Webern and not he had been asked to conduct his Wind Quintet, Op. 26, at the Zurich festival.

riences—and your works (Oh! *Jakobsleiter*!!)—and last but not least, your still unsatisfactory health![4] I have to summon all my powers of concentration to remain at work and not suddenly to cut short this summer stay (what with the lousy weather to boot) so as to be in Vienna at a time when this normally godforsaken city isn't forsaken by God after all.

Helene, too, is very, very sorry, that now she may miss seeing you and your dear wife. She sends both of you her most affectionate regards, in which I join her.

All our love and affection

from your Berg

1 enclosure

### Composition with 12 Notes

For my first attempts I chose the row discovered by Klein, which contains not only all 12 notes but all 12 [sic] <u>intervals</u>*[5] (while composing I naturally didn't bother to follow the <u>interval</u> succession) It is:

Its symmetry has advantages, as well as disadvantages. Among other things, rows of fourths and fifths can be derived from it:

hence by axis rotation the C major and G♭ major chords

with their scale segments and resultant tonal tendency towards A minor and E♭ minor, that is, F and B [major]. But this symmetry also has a serious disadvantage. For the <u>second</u> half is the mirror image of the <u>first</u> half transposed down a diminished fifth, as you can see from the following:

4. Apparently Schoenberg was still suffering from aftereffects of his appendectomy.

5. Fritz Heinrich Klein had identified this row in the foreword to his Variations, Op. 14, published in 1924. Berg used the same row in his second Theodor Storm song, "Schliesse mir die Augen beide," which precedes its subsequent use in the *Lyric Suite*, the subject of this analysis.

from which it follows that this row has no independent retrograde form. As a matter of fact, the retrograde is the original row R transposed down a diminished fifth:

which with appropriate transposition is equivalent to the row

(see above left) [*first example*]

For that reason (I didn't notice this until I began working) I decided in my next efforts to alter the row as follows:

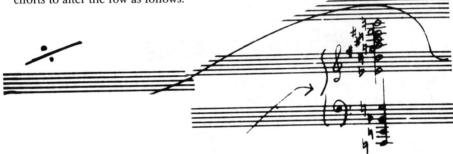

and while I was composing, the first four notes proved to be a particularly important motive. In order to retain this succession of 4 notes (better said, 4-note group (Gr)) in the transpositions and inversions [of the row] as well, rather like an ostinato, I searched for exact transformations and found that this group of notes (reordered, to be sure) is contained in only 3 other forms of this row, making in all 4 (plus retrograde = B) forms at my disposal.

(the only inversion form in which the group Gr occurs.) Aside from the 4-note group (F E C F♯, i.e., E F F♯ C, E F C F♯ and C F♯ F E) I thereby obtained what remained: four 8-note rows, which, when I attached them to the end of Gr., proved quite diverse. Thus:

All of these, of course, with their retrograde forms. But otherwise, as I said, there are no transpositions to other scale degrees.—

Further, I gained the following from the row and its inversion: partitioning in

$7 + 5$ —————  which in addition

to the chromatic scale, yielded the following motive   and its inversion

as well as a characteristic rhythm along with its complement. Thus

Nobody in the world—excuse me, only you, dearest friend, can imagine the difficulties I encountered in working out the possible 4-voice canons (there are 17) in these 4 forms (RI, II, III, and U). That's why the slow progress. That's also why—and so as not to despair—occasional backsliding into my accustomed free style.

*This row, just like the chord derived from it,

which likewise contains all 12 notes and all 12 intervals (along with its inversion and a third form achieved by rotating the axis) is the only one of its kind.![6] thus, an interesting theoretical phenomenon.—

6. This row is actually but one of 1,928 rows with such all-interval properties. See Stefan Bauer-Mengelberg and Melvin Ferentz, "On Eleven-Interval Twelve-Tone Rows," *Perspectives of New Music* III / 2 (Spring / Summer, 1965) 93–103.

## Berg to Schoenberg

[Vienna] For the 13th of September 1926

My dearest friend,

I had intended to use this handmade paper to congratulate Shaw on his 70th birthday. But though I did not do so and use it instead to wish you, dear friend, from the bottom of my heart, everything loving and good and beautiful on your 52nd, you mustn't take ill this substitution of Schönberg for Shaw Berg has committed, all the more as the number 52 is somehow connected with

$$5 + 2 = 7$$
$$(: \qquad 10 \times 7 = \quad ) \quad 70.$$
$$5 \times 2 = 10$$

Seriously, though—and you will no doubt recognize the seriousness behind the play on words and numbers—I wanted to say that all the 50-, 100-, and 1,000-year anniversaries of all living and dead poets and writers don't mean as much to me as each and every birthday of yours, without whose birth I, too, or at least that part of me worthy of having been born, would never have come into being!

I'm very pleased at the thought of your vacation in my beloved Carinthia. Perhaps you can visit the Ossiachersee nearby, where years ago I spent 15–20 summers (in Berghof).[1]

Any day now the house in Trahütten will be free again, so after spending all of August in Vienna we will go up there for another 1–2 weeks. I must write the last (6th) movement of my quartet suite (the first 5 are finished) and unfortunately that's impossible in Vienna. You will probably be in Vienna by the time we return, or soon thereafter (as I hear from Frau Dr. Kolisch) and then I'll finally, finally be able to see you again. I look forward to that more than I can say. With affectionate regards to you and your wife

Your Alban Berg

[Helene Berg:] and likewise from Helene, who joins in Alban's wishes for your birthday with all her heart!

1. During August and September the Schoenbergs spent several weeks with Franz and Maria Schreker in Pörtschach on the Wörthersee, about 25km from the Ossiachersee.


## Schoenberg to Berg (picture postcard: Pörtschach, bathing beach)

[Lienz-Klagenfurt] 19 September 1926

Dear friends,

Warmest thanks for the beautiful gift and the birthday wishes! I was very pleased! I am already very curious about your new quartet.—I haven't worked on anything this summer, but have made a good recovery.[1] My asthma is almost gone. I hope you and your wife are well, too.

Many warm regards to you both.

Your Arnold Schönberg

1. For reasons of health Schoenberg extended his vacation in Carinthia into early October. Berg saw Schoenberg in Vienna on 9 October for the first time in almost a year.

*Berg to Schoenberg*

Hotel Imperial [Prague] 10 November 1926

Yesterday I was only able to write you a brief card, my dearest friend.[1] Today I have a bit more time (a day off (before the premiere tomorrow) for the soloists and orchestra) and can report to you in greater detail. I have the very best impression of this theater. I find the diligence, the stamina, the good will, indeed the most devoted enthusiasm of everyone, above all Ostrčil,[2] so surprising and gratifying that I am completely overwhelmed. I am only sorry I didn't come much earlier. Then I would have been able to achieve a perfect performance in every respect. Since the willingness to meet every one of my wishes is boundless. In this short time I have achieved everything that was still possible. The orchestra is **very good** in all sections, woodwinds as well as strings, extremely pure in intonation and careful to play everything as it is in the score. But then Ostrčil held 30 rehearsals, of which 10 were sectional, 15 full orchestra, and 5 ensemble rehearsals. So there really isn't a single unplayable measure and everything so astonishingly accurate (no wrong notes, which amazes me all the more as the theater produced both score and parts itself.)

Best of all, however, wherever there is singing, it is **sung** throughout, often beautifully and with beautiful voices. So my resignation since the Berlin performance, namely that in most cases I had demanded something impossible of the voice, has been fully dispelled. To be sure, I have thoroughly 1st-rate singers (and not as in Berlin, where vocal raw material was concerned, 2nd- or 3rd-rate). Given the amazing musicality of the Czechs I don't even need to say that they all sing with complete accuracy. Granted, their preparations at the piano couldn't have been better. At the first rehearsal I heard here, one conductor, Maixner,[3] played the entire opera with all the soloists under Ostrčil's direction so completely, note for note, that this alone would have given any listener a complete picture of the entire score. As for Ostrčil himself, he is certainly no fiery spirit, let alone a conducting composer. But since he really plays everything in the score correctly—everything at least has body, even though the musical soul may sometimes be lacking. I am not as satisfied with the staging, which lacks even the most commonplace routine, not to mention any real spirit. But at least everything works. I'm least satisfied by the sets, of which one can only say that (aside from a somewhat dadaistic touch) they follow customary practice (or rather: customary malpractice). Nevertheless, I have no other wish than that you see the performance here, or what is more to the point in this case, **hear it**.

And it occurs to me: couldn't you make a stop here on your way to Berlin?! For example, toward the end of the month, when Ostrčil is doing your 5 Orchestra Pieces (and *Das Lied von der Erde*) on the 28th with the Czech Philharmonic.— Perhaps that could be combined with a *Wojzeck* performance on the day before or

---

1. Berg, in Prague for the Czech first performance of *Wozzeck* on 11 November, had sent an enthusiastic picture postcard, dated 9 November, following the dress rehearsal.

2. The Prague *Wozzeck* production was conducted by Otakar Ostrčil, director of the Prague National Opera 1920–35. The Prague production included Václav Novák as Wozzeck and Marie Veselá as Marie, stage direction by Ferdinand Pujman and sets by Vlatislav Hofman. The performance was sung in Czech, after a translation by Jiří Mařánek.

3. Vincent Maixner was an assistant conductor at the Prague National Opera.

after!! I'm sure Ostrčil would do that. Which reminds me that I don't want to leave unmentioned that one of his first questions was: "Is Maestro Schönberg coming?" and that he still hopes he'll be able to do *Wozzeck* for you. In fact, his enormous regard for you and that of all the musicians I've met so far is such as only befits the "greatest living" [composer] (that's how they speak of you here).

Tonight we are invited to Zemlinsky's. I dedicated my last quartet to him and he was very pleased (though he hasn't seen it yet).[4] All the more as he was really hurt that the Czechs and not he will do *Wozzeck*. Which of course I understand only too well, now that I have some insight into the way both theaters are run.—

Don't think, dearest friend, even when I write uninterruptedly about myself, that I'm not uninterruptedly thinking about what must be your sole preoccupation now, the illness of your poor dear wife. Believe me (despite the bustle of the premiere) we too (Helene and I) are deeply concerned and long for news (I hope very, very good news) of her condition. I have asked Stein to write me briefly about it.—

I hope to speak to you Monday—at least by telephone—since we are leaving on Sunday. Until then and with all our love and best wishes to you both.

Your Alban Berg

The II$^{nd}$ *Wozzeck* performance is Saturday 13 October, the III$^{rd}$ is Tuesday the 16th.

---

4. Berg completed the *Lyric Suite* early in October before his return to Vienna from Trahütten; the fourth movement included a musical quotation from Zemlinsky's *Lyric Symphony*.

## Berg to Schoenberg

Vienna, 13 December 1926

Dearest esteemed friend,

In exactly one month Kolisch plans to premiere my new quartet.[1] However, I have not yet finished the clean copy, and the parts, too, are still being prepared; everything is so crowded together these last weeks that I am under more pressure than ever before. **That** is the only reason I haven't written yet, my dearest friend, and why I must unfortunately keep it brief today, too.

My health is so-so, but Helene's is worse than ever. I'm at my wits' end. She is beginning a radium treatment now (in the form of baths) and bromide. But will it help??—

You will probably read about the further fate of *Wozzeck* in Prague in the next issue of *Anbruch*.[2] The affair continues to arouse public interest; every day I receive newspapers with reports about the matter, interviews, protests, etc., etc., though I must say that since everyone who matters is on my side, everything—except for the fact that there still hasn't been another performance of the opera—has been gratify-

---

1. The Wiener Streichquartett (or Kolisch Quartet) with Rudolf Kolisch, Felix Khuner, Marcel Dick, and Joachim Stutschewsky gave the *Lyric Suite* its premiere on 8 January 1927.
2. *Wozzeck* was withdrawn after only three performances in Prague due to political and anti-Semitic opposition (although Berg was not Jewish). In the December 1926 issue of *Anbruch* (VIII / 10), Paul Stefan wrote a review of the Prague premiere (416–417), and H[ans] H[einsheimer] (417–420) detailed the widespread support for the work in Prague's musical community.

ing. Incidentally, the latest news is that the lifting of the ban on W. performances is imminent.

Vienna's musical life is lousier than ever. The choice of Dirk Fock's successor = Reichwein says it all.[3] I heard Honegger's *King David* in a miserable performance under Klenau.[4] This oratorio consists entirely of short pieces that are generated by breaking off long pieces at some point soon after they are begun. When that has happened some 20 times, any initial interest one might have had in this string of character pieces of the most diverse styles gives way to a tedium that no amount of "modernity" can overcome.

However, the performance of Webern's Ist String Quartet the day before yesterday with Kolisch in the International Society, was really beautiful.[5] It was presented so convincingly and with such beautiful sound that it couldn't fail to be a great success for Webern (despite the small audience).

The performances of Wiesengrund's[6] incredibly difficult quartet was a *coup de main* for the Kolisch Quartet, which learned it in 1 week and performed it quite clearly. I find Wiesengrund's work very good and I believe it would also meet with your approval, should you ever hear it. In any event, in its seriousness, its brevity, and above all in the absolute purity of its entire style it is worthy of being grouped with the Schönberg school (and nowhere else!).

A Butting quartet next to it, for instance, seems like something impure.

I found Milhaud's endless Jewish songs very tedious. Pijper isn't even worth discussing.—

My extreme lack of time is due to a great deal of correspondence and unfortunately also to social-professional obligations. But as soon as I have finished the quartet I will write to you at greater length and more coherently. Forgive the fact that that isn't the case in this letter.

with affectionate regards

Your Alban Berg

All our love to you both! I hope you are both well!

3. Leopold Reichwein conducted the Konzertverein concerts 1927–35.

4. The Viennese first performance of Arthur Honegger's oratorio *Le Roi David* (1921) was given on 3 December by the Konzertverein Orchestra and Chorus, conducted by Paul Klenau; the concert also included Hugo Wolf's *Der Feuerreiter* and Liszt's *Die Glocken des Strassburger Münster*.

5. Webern's String Quartet, Op. 5, was performed by the Wiener Streichquartett on 10 December 1926. Also on the program were Willem Pijper's Second Violin and Piano Sonata, Darius Milhaud's *Poèmes Juifs*, the first Viennese performance of seven pieces from the Little Pieces for String Quarter, Op. 26, by Max Butting, and the premiere of Theodor Wiesengrund-Adorno's Two Movements for String Quartet.

6. The German aesthetician and composer Theodor Wiesengrund-Adorno studied composition with Berg in 1925.

# 1927

*Berg to Schoenberg*

Vienna, 10 January 1927

Dearest friend,

Our most affectionate thanks to you and your dear wife for your kind note.[1] We are extremely sorry about your apartment-hunting woes and hope that you'll soon be relieved of these worries by suddenly finding an especially suitable apartment.[2]

Due to rehearsals with the Kolisch Quartet (there must have been about a dozen!), the last few days have been both very agitated and very wonderful for me. I found it exciting and thrilling to see how the piece, which didn't sound like music at all during the first rehearsals, slowly took shape and began to sound like something, until suddenly, in the last rehearsals, the whole thing was there before us as intended and in the performance reached a level that, considering the limited rehearsal time, no one, not even Kolisch or I, had anticipated for a first time (that is, for a premiere). It was also thanks to this completely natural, sovereign performance that it was such a great success: from the 2nd movement on there was applause after every movement. Now my only hope is that you will get to know the quartet! (Duration 30–35 minutes).

The concert was unusually successful in other ways, too, governed as it was by a performance style based entirely on the rehearsal methods you established.[3] One could see that in the incredible, well-rehearsed performance of Beethoven's E♭-major Trio, which excited the most enthusiastic amazement. The performance of Webern's songs by the young singer (who began her career awhile ago with my *Bruchstücke**) was absolutely outstanding and aroused truly genuine, heartfelt applause. The songs were repeated. Finally, Bach's 4-piano concerto: a short but

1. Both Arnold and Gertrud Schoenberg wrote to the Bergs on 6 January 1927 to thank them for their Christmas gifts, which included among other things the full score of *Wozzeck*.

2. Since their arrival in Berlin the Schoenbergs had lived in the Pension Bavaria on Steinplatz; they moved to another set of furnished rooms later that year, but did not find an apartment of their own until 1928.

3. The remainder of the program on the 8 January concert in which the *Lyric Suite* was premiered comprised Beethoven's Piano Trio, Op. 70, No. 2, the premiere of Webern's Op. 12 songs, performed by Co van Genus, and Bach's Concerto in A minor for Four Pianos, BMV 1065, based on Vivaldi's Op. 3, No. 10. The piano soloists were Eduard and Hilde Steuermann, Josefa Rosanska, and Leopold Münzer.

wonderful piece with unexpected contrasts and moods. In other words, just the thing for Webern, whose conducting was really thrilling.

Then afterwards we all went to the Café Museum, where we wrote to you and where—as in the next few days—all our thoughts and discussions focused on the next concert; for it will be a Schönberg evening![4] Unfortunately without the quintet arrangement;[5] but we are already madly looking forward to hearing *Pierrot* again.

After that Vienna can sink back into the mud that is raining incessantly from the heavens.— —

Helene is not well; actually she gets worse and worse and we wander from one doctor to the next.

My own health is quite good. In the next few days I shall prepare my Quartet for engraving; then I hope to get back to composing a bit: songs. There's not much chance of an opera at the moment, much as every play entices me to compose it.[6] I was also particularly taken with Bronnen's *Rheinische Rebellen*.[7] But it is a difficult decision to commit oneself to such a thing for years!

Have you seen *Grabmal des unbekannten Soldaten* in Berlin?[8] I would very much recommend that you both see it: I consider it one of the most significant war plays, moreover, it's real theater and full of poetry. For a time I was very tempted to compose it. What do you think?—

I hope to discuss all this with you in Berlin sometime soon. If *Wozzeck* actually is done there again, we would certainly like to hear it again. All the more as a trip to Leningrad for this purpose is completely up in the air. The theater there isn't doing anything and has answered evasively in response to my direct inquiry.—

And now our most affectionate regards to you and your dear wife!

Your Alban Berg

A Freudian slip making the rounds here: Klenau, asked at U.E. how the *School for Scandal* premiere was, replied: "Oh, it was a great flopcess—sorry, success."[9]—

* and who sang the F#-minor Quartet surprisingly well for the first time at a read-through not long ago with the Kolisch Quartet.—

---

4. This concert, scheduled for 13 January, included Schoenberg's Piano Pieces, Op. 23, and *Pierrot lunaire* under Erwin Stein, with Erika Wagner as soloist.

5. Probably the unpublished arrangement of Schoenberg's Wind Quintet, Op. 26, for cello (or bassoon) and piano by Felix Greissle.

6. Berg was considering a number of opera texts at this time and shortly thereafter decided to set Gerhart Hauptmann's *Und Pippa tanzt*.

7. For Christmas Schoenberg had given Berg the two dramas by Arnolt Bronnen, *Rheinische Rebellen* (1925) and *Katalaunische Schlacht* (1924).

8. Paul Raynal's antiwar drama *Le Tombeau sous l'Arc de Triomphe* (1924) was translated into German in 1926 as *Das Grabmal des unbekannten Soldaten* (translated into English as *The Unknown Warrior*). Berthold Viertel's production of the play at the Volksbühne (Theater am Schiffbauerdamm) was given more than 150 performances between 1 September 1926 and 16 January 1927; Berg must have seen one of the last performances.

9. Paul von Klenau's opera *Die Lasterschule* was premiered at the Frankfurt Opera on 26 December 1926. Klenau may have been thinking of the colloquial expression for "fiasco," *Reinfall* or *Durchfall*, when he said *Erfallg* instead of *Erfolg*.

## Berg to Schoenberg

Vienna, 25 January 1927

My dearest friend,

Though I have scarcely time to think of anything not related to business—I'm filled with a kind of homesickness for Berlin. That's how wonderful that week in Berlin was![1] Let me thank you once more from the bottom of my heart for all your loving kindness to us during that time. And for that which you granted us at a time when we didn't yet know each other: for *Pelleas*.[2] It is truly music that echoes within one week after week, as if one had heard the last note 5 minutes earlier. Gradually the <u>world</u> will also come to feel it. Some of the reviews I saw (especially Jarnach's,[3] a composer, strangely enough, whom I've always admired far more than others of equal prominence) are also beginning to reflect this realization.

As I mentioned above, I am at present very preoccupied with my affairs, but since these also concern performances, they are at any rate agreeable. In addition, the U.E. accounts turned out better than I had feared. Right now I owe them only 1,300 schillings, which, with just one or two more performance at the Kroll Opera in February, would almost be <u>paid off</u>.

<u>My</u> share of the <u>scores</u> sold amounts to c. 1,000 schillings, of the <u>parts</u> rental (which, however, already includes those sent to the Petersburg opera house) c. 2,000 schillings and of performance royalties in Berlin (1925 / 26) and Prague: over 5,000 schillings.—

And now, in closing, a big favor; I forgot to ask you for the address or the letter of the English girl who might want to study with me.[4] Would you be so kind as to put the letter in the enclosed envelope?! Many thanks in advance and all our love and best wishes to you and your dear wife!

Your Alban Berg

1. Alban and Helene Berg visited Berlin 13–22 January. They saw the revival of the *Wozzeck* production on 15 January (staged at the Kroll Opera due to renovations in the State Opera) and heard Schoenberg deliver a lectured in the Academy on 20 January, "Probleme der Harmonie," which was later reworked for publication as "Problems of Harmony" in the American periodical *Modern Music* XI (May–June 1934), 167–87.

2. Schoenberg's *Pelleas und Melisande*, completed February 1903, before Berg and Schoenberg had met, was performed in Berlin on 21 January under Erich Kleiber.

3. The German composer and Busoni student Philipp Jarnach was music critic for the Berlin newspaper *Börsen–Courier*. His review of the 21 January *Pelleas* concert appeared in the *Börsen–Courier* on 23 January 1927 and was reprinted in *Anbruch* IX / 3 (March 1927), 135.

4. Schoenberg had mediated the connection with an American—not English—theory student, Elizabeth Amelia Cook, who eventually studied with Berg during 1927.

## Berg to Schoenberg (letter fragment)

Vienna, 16 February 1927

My dearest friend,

Many thanks for your second note about Miss Cook.[1] She has meanwhile come

1. Schoenberg had appended another note to a letter from Elizabeth Cook of 28 January 1927.

to Vienna and will take harmony with me for the present, no easy task in English. But she pays very well: 250 schillings (for 2 lessons a week). I am very, very grateful to you for this!

Perhaps you have heard of my so-called appointment as professor at the Vienna Music Academy (through director Springer).[2] The news was reported with a big splash one day——in the *Stunde*,[3] and the foreign papers reprinted it. **I myself,** however, know absolutely nothing about it and since there has been nothing to confirm the report, I don't put much stock in it. Indeed, I believe: if there ever was any truth to it, it has been completely nullified by the premature announcement; certainly my appointment could never have been dear to Springer's heart; rather, a cheap headline from which he'll be easily dissuaded now that opponents of the idea know of it!

But another bit of good news: on 29 March (during the Beethoven Festival[4]), the Vienna chapter (i.e., Bach-Breitner[5]) of the International Society for Contemporary Music is sponsoring a chamber concert in which Webern will perform my "double concerto" with Steuermann and Kolisch.[6] Webern is allowed 15 rehearsals with 13 members of the Philharmonic (young people, not the esteemed *Regierungsräte*, professors, etc.[7]), so that we have a month of intensive rehearsals ahead of us. However, I have to spend about a week of that time (19–26 March) in Zurich, where Reinhart was so extremely kind as to invite Helene and me because Scherchen is doing my Chamber Concerto there on the 25th (with Swiss soloists) and prior to that in Winterthur. But Reinhart's plan to perform my concerto in Berlin with Scherchen and the same 2 soloists on 19 March will not be realized.[8] Aside from the fact that I am absolutely set against tossing off such a difficult work—moreover, before such an important audience as in Berlin, and thus anticipating the Frankfurt performance (with Scherchen, Steuermann, and Kolisch)[9], . . . . I still nurse the

2. The German composer and journalist Max Springer became the director of the Vienna Music Academy in 1927. Berg was never officially offered the position.

3. The Viennese periodical *Die Stunde*, 8 February 1927.

4. A festival commemorating the hundredth anniversary of Beethoven's death was held in Vienna 26–31 March.

5. David Josef Bach was vice-president of the Vienna chapter of the ISCM. Hugo Breitner was the financial manager of the city of Vienna, which was co-sponsoring the festival.

6. The Viennese first performance of Berg's Chamber Concerto took place on 31 March, under the auspices of the Vienna chapter of the ISCM; the work was conducted by Webern after thirteen rehearsals. Also on the program were Beethoven's Rondino for Winds, and songs by Beethoven and Carl Prohaska (who had died on 27 March).

7. Senior members of the Vienna Philharmonic often carried titles such as Government Councillor, and the Vienna Academy routinely drew the senior Professors of its instrumental teaching faculty from the orchestra's ranks.

8. Hermann Scherchen did in fact premiere the Chamber Concerto in Berlin on 19 March with Stefi Geyer and Walter Frey as the violin and piano soloists. The wind players were drawn from the Berlin Philharmonic Orchestra. Also on the program was the first Berlin performance of Webern's Five Pieces for Orchestra, Op. 10, and Schoenberg's Chamber Symphony , Op. 9. The same soloists gave the first Swiss performance of the work with members of the Winterthur Stadtorchester in Zurich on 25 March (there was no performance in Winterthur, where Scherchen merely rehearsed the work 11–14 March); also on that program were the first movement of Ernst Krenek's Third Symphony, Op. 16, and Max Butting's Chamber Symphony for Thirteen Solo Instruments, Op. 25. Helene and Alban Berg were Werner Reinhart's guests 20–26 March.

9. On 2 July 1927.

quiet but genuine hope of a performance led by you, my dearest friend, a prospect that the violinist Frenkel (with whom I spoke here in Vienna) gave me reason—however slight, to anticipate.[10] On the basis of the performance rights (for Berlin) that Frenkel acquired from U.E. a while ago, U.E. can and must reject Werner Reinhart's Berlin performance request on legal and contractual grounds. Which, as I said (between us), is fine with me.

By the way, Scherchen tells me you attended his first Berlin concert (financed by Reinhart) a few days ago and it would interest me immensely to know what you, dear friend, thought of the performance.[11]

Furthermore, I can report that the "Donaueschingen" people (this year in Baden-Baden) are going to do my quartet suite (for the first time before a larger audience). I let them have it on condition that the performance is by the Kolisch Quartet. Unfortunately they don't have a cellist right now: Stutchewsky (here I have to agree with Kolisch: thank heavens!) finally quit.[12]—

There was a Loos lecture here yesterday: "The Birth of Form." Loos, who got a frenetic reception, isn't doing so badly in Paris.[13] He presently has: 3 buildings and holds regular lectures at the Sorbonne, which are enthusiastically received. He looks very good and is in the best of spirits.

Unfortunately I cannot say the same for myself (despite many gratifying artistic events): Helene's condition gets worse every day and we are more and more perplexed. As for her throat, apparently an operation is unavoidable. Prof. Denk[14] is in favor of it and it is only a question of [The conclusion of this letter is missing.]

---

10. Nothing came of the plan for a performance of the work with the Polish violinist Stefan Frenkel under Schoenberg. Berg mentioned the possibility again in a letter of 24 February, whereupon Schoenberg told him in a telegram of 26 February that it would be impossible.

11. In the first of his Berlin Chamber Concerts on 11 February Scherchen conducted works by Beethoven, Reger, Stravinsky, and Honegger; it is not known whether Schoenberg attended.

12. That year's Donaueschingen Chamber Music Festival presented a performance of Berg's Lyric Suite on 16 July by the reorganized Kolisch Quartet. The cellist Benar Heifetz had joined the group in April and the violist Eugen Lehner replaced Marcel Dick in May.

13. Adolf Loos was active in Paris 1922–28. His lecture was entitled "Die Geburt der Form."

14. Professor Wolfgang Denk, an oncologist, was one of the Bergs' family doctors.


## Berg to Schoenberg

Vienna, 11 May 1927

Dearest, most esteemed friend,

The day before yesterday I received your Suite, sent by U.E.;[1] I'm not sure: whether due to your standing order or by your special request? Anyway, I thank you most, most warmly. I thank you as one who feels greatly enriched. For enrichment is always the first thing I feel when—almost trembling with joyous excitement—I take a new work of yours into my hands. Unfortunately I've been unable even to get a rough idea of the score these past couple of days (I'll tell you the compelling reason for this in a moment). Anyway (despite C transpositions), I find it incredibly

---

1. U.E. published Schoenberg's Suite, Op. 29, earlier that year.

difficult to read such extremely concentrated music.* At the piano it would take months of study to get to know this Suite as well as, say, the Serenade, which, when I pick it up today, as I often do, seems like a dear old acquaintance. So you can imagine, dear friend, how I wish and hope that my familiarity with this work could be facilitated by something like 20 rehearsals under your direction.

I think I will learn to understand the "variations" most readily. At least for now I find easier access to the timbral wonders, in which this 3rd movement is so rich, than to the rhythmic wonders of the 2nd movement or the polyphonic wonders of the last. But the "overture," too, which seems somewhat more accessible to me, at least in the rather accompanimental piano style (am I right?), is of such dizzying richness that I feel like a beggar in comparison (I am right about that!)

(By the way, quite by chance I noticed a couple of engraving errors: page 59, measure 185, piano right hand lacks a   .—Page 60, measure 189 piano right hand, first note 16th instead of 8th.—)

---

We've had a difficult time of it these past few weeks; that's another reason I haven't written since Easter. Soon thereafter we had decided to have Helene's throat operated on. The swelling of the thyroid gland had increased to such an extent, especially inwardly, making breathing difficult, that the cyst had to be removed. So Helene was operated on c. 10–12 days ago by Prof. Hans Lorenz in the Sanatorium der Kaufmannschaft, remained there only five days, but will require nursing care for another 2–3 weeks. It was quite a major operation and really took its toll on Helene. But already today I believe I can report that the operation was successful. The wound has healed well and she is slowly regaining mobility in her neck. And the horrible aftereffects of anesthesia, which lasted for days, have worn off.

You can imagine, my dear friend, that next to this really all-consuming experience everything else takes second place. So that during that entire time I really didn't make any headway in my own affairs or work. Only now has my quartet suite been sent off to press, the parts off to be engraved. So I hope to be able to send you the score soon.

I still hope to get to the Wozzeck premiere in Petersburg toward the end of the month[2] and right after that to Trahütten to my work, which has lain idle for more than half a year.

How are you, my dearest friend, and your dear wife? I would be very, very happy to hear directly from you sometime. But I can imagine you have trouble just attending to all your professional correspondence; (it's almost getting too much for me, too!) So I should not and will not be so presumptuous as to intensify the wish for a couple of lines from you to a request. Anyway, I hope to hear more soon from Rudi, who is coming to see you in a week (for your students' concert).

And now all our love and best wishes to you and your dear wife!

Your Alban Berg

*the many string harmonics also make reading difficult for me

---

2. Berg left Vienna on the 66-hour trip to St. Petersburg (now Leningrad) on 8 June to attend the performance of Wozzeck on 13 June 1927.

## Schoenberg to Berg

Charlottenburg, 12 May 1927

Dearest Berg,

At first I was very alarmed when I heard of your wife's operation. But since it is happily over now, congratulations are in order! That's as good as a birthday!

Was it really necessary?—Well, I'm sure it was for the best!

And now let's hope for: a speedy and complete recovery!

However: I advise you to go to a warm place, at least at first. How about: Pörtschach? Or: Berghof on the Ossiachersee? I believe that would be more suitable for convalescence than Trahütten!

Now I must thank you for your kind letter about my Suite, which reminds me that apparently I haven't written to you for quite a while. Soon after your last stay in Berlin I looked at your Chamber Concerto several times and after the performance[1] I found that suddenly I, too, could read it quite easily and was very impressed by it. It is certainly a <u>very beautiful piece</u> and I'm very sorry that I couldn't hear Webern's performance of it. It would be perfect if Webern could do it here, too!

My warmest regards to you and your wife. And again: a quick and complete recovery!

Your Arnold Schönberg

*[Appended to this letter is a note of sympathy from Gertrud Schoenberg to Helene Berg.]*

---

1. Schoenberg heard the 19 March performance of Berg's Chamber Concerto in Berlin.

## Berg to Schoenberg

Vienna, 16 May 1927

My dearest friend,

A thousand thanks for your so very dear words. You can imagine how happy your opinion of my Chamber Concerto makes me. I am very apprehensive about the performance in Frankfurt <u>under Scherchen</u>;[1] yes, if only <u>Webern</u> could do it! But long before the performances in Berlin and Zurich, I was practically forced into having it performed in a concert of the <u>German</u> section* and in the end had to abide by it in order to avoid a still greater danger: the danger of the Chamber Concerto being performed by the conductors of the <u>Vienna</u> chapter: <u>Heger</u>[2]—or—Klenau, both of whom were willing to travel there <u>without remuneration</u>, which would have been fine with the Vienna chapter, since it doesn't have a cent. So if it weren't for Kolisch and Steuermann, who will surely rescue what can be rescued, I would look on the Frankfurt concert with great misgivings. All the more do I look

1. On 2 July, during the fifth ISCM festival in Frankfurt (29 June–4 July), Berg's Chamber Concerto was performed under Scherchen with Rudolf Kolisch and Eduard Steuermann as soloists. Also on the program were string quartets by Conrad Beck and Vladimir Vogel (both performed by the Amar-Hindemith String Quartet), and Kaminski's Magnificat.

2. The German conductor Robert Heger joined the Vienna State Opera in 1925 and also directed the concerts of the Gesellschaft der Musikfreunde.

forward to the Baden-Baden performance of my quartet suite by the newly organized Kolisch Quartet. In the next few days Kolisch will tell you in greater detail than I can about his very advantageous 3-year contract with a concert agent.[3] I was pleased to agree to the stipulation of exclusive performance rights for my quartet suite for the 27 / 28 season and have had Hertzka see to it today. I hope very, very much that you'll be able to hear the newly rehearsed interpretation of this, my 2nd quartet, as early as June.

If only I could be there! But I **must** get to work, so it's off to the country.

And the country will probably be Trahütten again for now. First, because of my work. 2. Because Helene doesn't want to go to a lake due to her rheumatic pains, which are worse there. 3. Because I, on the other hand, don't want to go anywhere where it is hot with no water for swimming. 4. If we're going to the mountains anyway, where it's somewhat cooler, Trahüutten, where we're at home, is the obvious choice. . . .

However, since we can only stay there until 31 July, we plan to do something else in August and will perhaps after all arrange a 4–6 week stay at one of the Carinthian lakes I love so dearly.

Helene's a little better now; today she went out for the first time: a few steps to her parents' garden. She thanks you and your wife warmly for your kind words and greets you most affectionately.

I am slowly making progress with your "Suite." I have approached it from the "row," and my spontaneous recognition of this "row of six thirds" immediately explained much that had remained puzzling while merely reading it.[4]

I hope to hear a good deal from Rudi when he returns from Berlin, and in the meantime send you and your dear wife many regards!

Your Berg

*which is paying for everything!

---

3. The Viennese agency Internationale Theater- und Musikeragentur (ITHMA).

4. In the third movement of Schoenberg's Suite, Op. 29, the tonal elements implicit in the row (B, G, F♯, B♭, D, B, C, A, A♭, E, F, D♭) are exploited.

## Schoenberg to Berg (note)

Berlin, 13 October 1927

We just heard your quartet played on the radio by Rudio [sic].[1] As well as a very enthusiastic lecture by Kastner.[2] We were very impressed although one heard little of the *ppp*! In any case: very beautiful!

Many regards

1. The Berlin broadcast performance of Berg's *Lyric Suite* by the Wiener Streichquartett (Kolisch Quartet) took place on the afternoon of 13 October 1927.

2. The Berlin critic Rudolf Kastner wrote for the *Berliner Morgenpost* and gave regular introductions to radio progams of new music.

Schönberg
*[Schoenberg adds a typed message informing of his new address on 4 / IV Kantstrasse in the Berlin district of Charlottenburg.]*[3]

---

3. The Schoenbergs had taken three furnished rooms with board.

## Schoenberg to Berg (picture postcard: Cannes—Hotel Californie / Le Port et le Suquet)

Cannes, 26 December 1927

Dear friends,

Warmest thanks for the Christmas greetings, to which we return our <u>warmest New Year's wishes</u>. Paris was very beautiful, but incredibly exhausting.[1] <u>I was dead</u> tired. But you are right that it is too bad you didn't come here and I am glad that you agree now.—The performances were quite good, though not exactly what all of you are accustomed to from me. Not so finely balanced, not so carefully worked out, not so secure. Excellent reception. We shall stay here until c. 10 January. Then on to London.[2] Happy New Year. Most warmly

Your Arnold Schönberg
*[Gertrud Schoenberg adds a short note inviting the Bergs to join them in London.]*

1. Schoenberg and his wife were invited to Paris by the Société Musicale Indépendante for two concerts, including the 15 December premiere of the Suite, Op. 29, which Schoenberg rehearsed and directed. In a letter to Winfried Zillig of 1 December 1948 Schoenberg recounted how Adolf Loos had taken him to countless restaurants, and that as a result he had been too exhausted to prepare the performance adequately. The second concert in Schoenberg's honor included *Pierrot lunaire*, the four songs of Op. 6 (of which "Traumleben" had to be repeated), and the Song of the Waldtaube from the *Gurrelieder*; the soloist was Marya Freund, accompanied by Steuermann. Further, Schoenberg gave a lecture at the Music Academy entitled "Wissen und Erkenntnis" (Knowledge and Understanding). From Paris the Schoenbergs traveled on to Cannes where they spent Christmas and New Year.

2. On 14 January the Schoenbergs went to London, where Schoenberg conducted the *Gurrelieder* on 27 January 1928 in Queen's Hall.

# 1928

*Schoenberg to Berg (printed address card)*

Berlin-Charlottenburg, 3 February [March] 1928

Dear friend,

Warmest thanks for your last two letters. I am really very sorry I didn't hear what you describe so beautifully.—A letter of yours seems to have gone astray, for I didn't know you had gone to Italy to see Hauptmann.[1]—I very much concur with your plan to compose *Pippa tanzt*. Tell me more about your plans. I hope you'll remember that it is about twice as long as it should be!! I must warn you about that in particular. But I'm sure it will be very, very easy to cut.—I am absolutely <u>against</u> any work of mine being performed by the I.G.B.f.N.M. (International Swindler's Gang [*Gaunerbande*]), as Herr Dent's action has yet to be atoned for. I <u>forbid</u> any performance of my work by this Society.[2]—I'm curious as to what you'll write from Paris. Is your wife going along?[3] How is she? Many regards to your wife and you.

Your Arnold Schönberg

Also from my wife

*[Schoenberg's printed card announced his new address: Berlin-Charlottenburg / Nussbaum-Allee 17.]*

1. In January Alma Mahler invited the Bergs to spend a week with her in Portofino. On that occasion Berg met Gerhart Hauptmann in Rapallo to discuss the opera rights to *Und Pippa tanzt* (1905); Berg had been considering that play since January 1926 and early compositional sketches for it exist.

2. Schoenberg resigned from the International Society for Contemporary Music in June 1926, in reaction to an incident at the 1925 festival in Venice, in which he had conducted the premiere of his Serenade, Op. 24; there had been an unpleasant exchange of words with Edward J. Dent, president of the ISCM, when Schoenberg exceeded the rehearsal time allotted him.

3. Berg and his wife traveled to Paris for a private concert on 22 March in which Berg accompanied the soprano Ruzena Herlinger in his Four Songs, Op. 2, and Marie's Cradle Song from *Wozzeck*; the program also included the first French performance of the *Lyric Suite* by the Kolisch Quartet.

*Berg to Schoenberg (typwritten letter)*

Vienna, 30 March 1928

My dearest friend,

I meant to answer your dear card before my departure. But I didn't get around to it, what with all the travel preparations and rehearsals (more of this later); it was even more impossible in Paris and Zurich and only today, one day after my return, have I found time to thank you for your kind note.

Naturally, I'll have to make great cuts in Hauptmann's drama to suit my purpose, indeed, I even intend to combine the 3rd and 4th (last) acts, thereby somewhat alleviating the weakness of precisely that portion of the drama. I hope I'll succeed!

The rehearsals mentioned above, besides the ones with Frau Herlinger[1] (Op. 2 songs and the lullaby from *Wozzeck*), also included some with Frau Heim, who sang the same songs wonderfully and with enormous success in Prague (with Steuermann at the piano).[2] Then the old sonata with Fräulein Rosanska, who played it in Budapest, Prague, Amsterdam, etc.[3] Furthermore, I had rehearsals with the State Opera singer Achsel, who sang the old songs I had just orchestrated on the Vienna radio.[4] Klenau conducted, but it didn't amount to much, since he held only one three-quarter-hour rehearsal for these 5 songs. Nevertheless they were well received.

One hour after that radio performance we boarded the sleeping car for Paris. It was—how can it be anything else in that city—magnificent there. And the concert went very well, too. Frau Herlinger sang with surprising accuracy and, since I myself accompanied on the piano (!),[5] the songs were interpreted as I wished. I don't suppose I need add a single word of praise or of highest admiration for Kolisch's achievement, who will soon have publicly performed my *Lyric Suite* 20 times this season. Kolisch's success and that of his colleagues was naturally quite phenomenal; they performed in Paris on several other occasions and may soon be invited to give a big public concert.

Unfortunately we had to go to Zurich directly after my concert.[6] But we saw a great deal of Paris during those 5 days and thoroughly savored the life there.

Zurich was the greatest imaginable contrast: the city, the people, the life. . . . The jury meetings of the I.G.f.n.M. were very exhausting. Since there will be only 3 chamber music concerts this year, it wasn't easy to choose equitably among the many countries that fancy themselves musically productive. All the same, I succeeded in seeing that Austria will be well represented. Namely with Webern's trio and Zemlinsky's latest quartet.[7] Apparently not all of the gentlemen of the jury

---

1. Berg probably met the Czech-Austrian soprano Ruzena Herlinger through his activities with the Vienna section of the ISCM.

2. The soprano Emmy Heim performed Berg's Op. 2 songs in Prague on 13 April.

3. The pianist Josefa Rosanska, who later married Rudolf Kolisch, included Berg's Sonata on a tour that included concerts in Budapest (7 March), Prague (10 March), Amsterdam (14 March), and London (15 March).

4. Berg had orchestrated the first five of his Seven Early Songs. Wanda Achsel-Clemens performed them on an 18 March 1928 Vienna radio concert of the Vienna Symphony Orchestra under Paul von Klenau. Also on the program were Debussy's *Iberia*, Weber's Konzertstück, and Beethoven's Fifth Symphony.

5. This is one of the very few occasions on which Berg performed in public.

6. While Helene Berg returned directly from Paris to Vienna, Berg traveled on to Zurich, where he met the other members of that year's ISCM music selection committeed (Volkmar Andreae, Alfredo Casella, Philipp Jarnach, and Karel Boleslav Jirák) to decide on the 1928 festival program in Siena.

7. Webern's String Trio, Op. 20 was published the previous fall and premiered on 16 January 1928 in Vienna by Rudolf Kolisch, Eugen Lehner, and Benar Heifetz. These same musicians performed the trio on 13 September at the sixth ISCM festival in Siena.

Zemlinsky's Third String Quartet, Op. 19 (composed 1924), was performed in Siena by the Kolisch Quartet on 11 September 1928.

were aware that Zemlinsky's quartet writing isn't much worse than that of, say, Bridge, that his powers of invention aren't that much poorer than, say, Bloch, and that he is scarcely less modern than, say, Alfano—and that it is a scandal of the first order that until now he has never been performed by the I.G.f.n.M. I am all the happier that I carried the point and my satisfaction will be even greater after the performance in Siena: for in the case of the 12 other composers selected for this concert (Tommasini, Hába, Hindemith, Ravel, Bridge, Tiessen, De Falla, Blum (a Swiss), Martinů, Prokofiev, Alfano, Bloch), for the most part they're twelve to a dozen.[8] The fact that no work of yours may be performed was not only sincerely regretted by all, but also regarded as an irreplaceable loss for the coming music festival.

Enough of myself and my activities! Directly after my return I was very happy to hear news of the Breslau performance of *Glückliche Hand*.[9] How I wish I could see that again sometime! Only then, I'm sure, would I perceive many hitherto unsuspected details.

And how I wish I could see you again! You have an apartment now and I'm sure it's wonderful; when shall I set foot in it. But I mustn't allow myself even to wish to travel again; after all, I have to compose *sometime*.

A thousand regards to you and your dear wife from us both! In love and devotion
Your Berg

---

8. The following works were selected for performance at the Siena ISCM festival: the Third String Quartet (1926) by the English composer Frank Bridge, the Piano Quintet (1923 / 24) by the Swiss composer Ernest Bloch, the Cello Sonata (1925) by the Italian composer Franco Alfano, the Second String Quartet (1926) by the Italian composer Vincenzo Tommasini, the Duo Sonata for Piano and Violin, Op. 35 (1925), by the German composer Heinz Tiessen, the Harpsichord Concerto (1923–26) by the Spanish composer Manuel de Falla, an Octet (*Musik für 8 Instrumente*, 1927) by the Swiss composer and conductor Robert Blum, and the Second String Quartet (1925) by the Czech composer Bohuslav Martinů.

9. Schoenberg's *Die glückliche Hand* had been performed in Breslau under General-Intendant Josef Turnau on 24 March (the first performance since its Vienna premiere in 1924). The performance, which was conducted by Fritz Cortolezis and directed by Herbert Graf, satisfied Schoenberg.

*Berg to Schoenberg (typewritten letter)*

Vienna, 10 April 1928

A thousand thanks, my dearest friend, for your kind intention to allow me to participate in your project as a proponent.[1] But I must take advantage of your permission "not to feel compelled" and tell you that I don't dare join in. At the moment I cannot take the risk that Hertzka—in reaction to this project—might take a businessman's attitude and suspend or reduce my monthly 600 schillings, an annuity representing my sole income (the few student fees don't count), for which the current returns from my works are no equivalent. (Already I owe—even if only on paper and not morally—about 6,000 schillings on this annuity, which has only been running for 2¼ years.) It is quite a different matter for you, of course: the

1. In response to rumors that Emil Hertzka might be retiring from Universal Edition, Schoenberg and Schreker, mistrustful of Hertzka's possible successors, sought to form an U.E. authors' association to protect their interests. Schoenberg invited Berg to join them in a letter of 4 April 1928.

whole world, and that includes Hertzka, knows that all of U.E.'s expenses on your behalf will be returned a hundredfold, if not next year, then at any rate in the foreseeable future. Schreker, too, can afford to dictate—though for a different reason, namely: on the basis of his 1,000 stage performances.[2] But I, with my two dozen *Wozzeck* performances and the prospect (not even assured) of another acceptance in——Oldenburg, depend on Hertzka's personal goodwill if I am not to endanger the continuation of my full annuity for the next few years (until I finish another opera). For my contract, which runs until 1932, doesn't offer the slightest security in this regard.

I don't need to tell you how difficult this refusal is for me, and how well I know that if you are indeed angry with me in consequence, my pleading with you not to be won't have any effect. I venture this plea nonetheless. . . .

I spoke with Bittner at length about the matter. He considers founding such an organization—particularly with regard to a change of U.E. management—very necessary, but believes it would still be possible when the time came and that it would be easy to organize such a group overnight. For now, however, feeling personally very close to Hertzka as he does, he himself prefers to refrain from such a step, since it would doubtless hurt Hertzka's feelings. Alma Mahler is not in Vienna. I shall send a copy of the two printed items to her in Venice right away and assume that either you or I will hear by return post—one might expect: a <u>positive</u> response.

"Among another" I shall likewise inform Webern.

———————————————————————————————

Your kind inquiry as to our well-being sounds as if you hadn't heard from me in a long time. Didn't you get the letter I wrote about 8–10 days ago? I gave full details about Paris (where it was wonderful) and Zurich (where it was awful) and about the jury meeting there of the I.G.f.l.M.i.A.,[3] the results of which satisfied me in only one respect, that (in addition to Webern's trio) I was also able to prevail with Zemlinsky's III[rd] String Quartet for Austria. I hope that letter did not go astray too!

In the meantime there has been nothing new, save for continuing negotiations with S. Fischer-Berlin for *Pippa*. Hauptmann continues to insist on his 50% share of the royalties, another 20% of the libretto and 5% of the music. Agreeing to these extraordinarily oppressive conditions is very hard for me (and for Hertzka). So I spent this Easter less "happy" than helpless. I hope that you and your dear wife and also her dear mother, all of whom we greet warmly, enjoyed the holidays! And I hope—I ask you once again—that you're not angry with

Your Alban Berg

———————

2. By this time the operas of Franz Schreker, then the most successful Austrian opera composer, had been given approximately 1,000 performances in well over 100 productions throughout Germany, Austria, Switzerland, Czechoslovakia, Sweden, and Russia.

3. See footnote 1 to Berg's letter of 13 July 1926.

*Berg to Schoenberg (typewritten letter)*

Vienna, 26 April 1928

Dear, most esteemed friend,

Since my last letter, in which I unfortunately had to disappoint you, there has been nothing new save for the performance of "Herzgewächse."[1] But that was quite an event! We **reveled** in the sounds we had, until now, only <u>dimly imagined.</u> It is wonderful: upon 1st hearing, <u>each</u> of your works has an unprecedented impact on <u>every</u> listener—even if it is 20 years old, like this one. Whether it's the *Gurrelieder* or the last quartet—or the *Friede auf Erden* chorus or the Serenade—or whether it will be the Four Songs, Op. 22, or *Jakobsleiter* . . . . .

The performance was fantastic in every respect. There were moments, as with the words: *"Sinnbildhaft ist seiner Blumen Zier"* and the entire closing section of the song, in which one actually forgot to breathe—not just I, but—I would maintain—everyone in the hall. This was felt—even more—during the second performance of the song—the repetition resulting not from pedagogical considerations, but having actually been <u>demanded</u> by the audience, who wouldn't stop applauding. It was, by the way, <u>jam-packed</u>, in fact these Kolisch-Steuermann concerts are increasingly successful and widely considered the only concerts in Vienna worthy of being taken seriously. Encouraged by the wonderful results with the really unique Bach performance which followed—a small string ensemble under Webern's direction with Steuermann, Kolisch, and Wangler as soloists—we very much hope to be able to incorporate such small orchestral concerts into next year's subscription series as well. Of course, that was always your idea—<u>one</u> of your ideas, which invariably bear you out in the end.

As for us, neither of us is quite well: Helene's system reacts to all the globe's earthquakes and spring floods; and I'm suffering again from those annoying intestinal pains. We already think often of leaving for the country; consequently I'm thinking of my new work with the apprehension I feel before every new project. It will probably be *Pippa*, though Hauptmann's oppressive conditions (including 50% share of the royalties) don't make the work seem very advisable—from the "practical" standpoint.[2] I now have a completed piano and orchestral score, including parts, of the Seven Early Songs (1907)—you know, the ones Klenau performed on the radio—and they will probably appear in the course of the summer. Likewise the score of the three pieces for string orchestra from the *Lyric Suite*.[3]

Incidentally, Kleiber wants to premiere the latter (this year still?) in Berlin.[4]

A few days from now Kraus will give a first reading of his still unpublished play: *Die Unbesieglichen* [sic]. Featuring Barkassy and police chief Wacker.[5] No doubt you have read in the German papers about the suit Kraus lost against police chief

1. Webern had conducted the premiere of Schoenberg's *Herzgewächse*, Op. 20, on 17 April, under the auspices of the Kolisch-Steuermann concerts. The soprano Marianne Rau-Höglauer was the soloist, accompanied by Hanny Haumer (harp), Erna Gál (harmonium), Steuermann (celesta), Fritz Wangler (flute), and the members of the Kolisch Quartet. Also on the program were Mozart's Flute Quartet, K. 285, Debussy's Sonata for Harp, Flute, and Viola, and Bach's Concerto in A minor for Flute, Violin, and Piano, BWV 1044, with Franz Wangler, Rudolf Kolisch, and Eduard Steuermann.

2. As a result of the exorbitant demands made by Hauptmann and his publisher, as well as their refusal to grant exclusive composition rights to work, Berg eventually decided against the project.

3. Berg had prepared a string orchestra arrangement of the second, third, and fourth movements of the *Lyric Suite* for a chamber orchestra series being published by U.E., which also included arrangements of Schoenberg's *Verklärte Nacht* and the Second String Quartet, Op. 10.

4. Nothing came of this plan; the *Lyric Suite* pieces were premiered by Jascha Horenstein in Berlin on 31 January 1929.

5. Karl Kraus's postwar drama *Die Unüberwindlichen* (The Indomitable) was given its premiere at the Berlin Volksbühne on 20 October 1929, but was canceled after several performances as a result of

Schober (to be sure, Schober declared that his insults (directed solely at Kraus, of course) were <u>not</u> intended for him, which is all Kraus wanted to achieve anyway).

My recent refusal of your kind invitation to join the U.E. Authors' Association really doesn't entitle me to ask how the matter stands. But I must tell you that of course I'm immensely curious and genuinely interested in how the project has developed. No doubt you have heard from Webern and Alma Mahler in the meantime.[6]

And now, farewell, my dearest friend, and most affectionate regards to you and your dear wife—and her dear mother—from both of us.

Your Berg

I just received word that Wiesengrund had a serious auto accident. He is in the hospital with a concussion, a deep head wound, and severe bruises—though apparently out of danger.

---

intercession from the Austrian Embassy in Berlin. In the play, the character Barkassy is editor of the journal *Die Pfeife*; the police chief Wacker in the drama is a caricature of the Vienna police chief Johann Schober, who later became Chancellor of Austria. The feud between Kraus and Schober is well documented in the pages of *Die Fackel*; Kraus had published a public appeal for Schober's resignation on 7 September 1927, following the bloody riots on 15 and 16 July, in which Schober had ordered his men to open fire on the rioters, an order that left 88 dead and hundreds wounded.

6. Schoenberg wrote to Hertzka in the matter on 12 April, to which Hertzka responded 25 April that he did not consider the precaution necessary, as he had no intention of resigning.

## Berg to Schoenberg

Trahütten, 9 July 1928

Dearest, most esteemed friend,

We were <u>tremendously</u> pleased by your card.[1] Here we thought you were long since somewhere in the south, but we couldn't find out your whereabouts and I didn't dare write to the Wiedener Hauptstrasse address.[2] That's the only reason for my long silence. But I certainly thought of you every day! Looking back: to the wonderful reunion with you in June and looking forward (always the case when I work): to what you will think of a new composition of mine . . .

Yes, I'm working. But it's going very slowly and with difficulty.[3] No doubt that's because of the almost two-year break from composing, the considerable difficulty of organizing an entire opera around a "single row," and finally, my extremely curtailed working capacity due to renewed severe asthma attacks. Of course it was to be expected that—no sooner arrived up here—I would be beset by respiratory problems. But it's unusually protracted this year. My sensitivity to drastic contrasts is becoming increasingly evident with the passing years. This sensitivity (<u>character-istic</u> of my personality), which in <u>psychological</u> matters I believe I have completely

1. The Schoenbergs saw the Bergs during a visit to Vienna in mid-June. On 11 July 1928 they sent the Bergs a picture postcard from Roquebrune-Cap Martin on the French Riviera, encouraging them to join them there.

2. Rudolf Kolisch's address in Vienna, where the Schoenbergs stayed during their June visit.

3. By this time Berg had turned to Wedekind's Lulu dramas, the two plays *Erdgeist* (1895) and *Die Büchse der Pandora* (1904), but he did not begin negotiations for the opera rights until the fall of that year. Berg must have discussed his new plans with Schoenberg during their June meetings.

in hand and can control to the point of making a thick-skinned impression, indeed, one of spiritual banality . . . this sensitivity I find impossible to master in <u>physical</u> matters. My body just doesn't accept contrasts between city and country air, between high altitudes and the plains, and it rebels against the middle European assumption that one can, within a few months and without effect, cope with temperature changes of 40 degrees or more. But maybe the whole thing has more pathological [sic] than organic causes![4] Increasingly I believe that there are none but mental illnesses.

But be that as it may: you are obviously both <u>quite right</u> that a stay in the south would do us good and for now we console ourselves with the thought that we may be able to consider such a s<sup>t</sup> y for the fall or winter, since something simply <u>must</u> be done to build up my resistance again. For the present it will have to be Trahütten* and (as of 1 August) Berghof.[6] If only for financial reasons! A look at my U.E. accounts for the I<sup>st</sup> half year of 1928 would bring greater conviction of the validity of the financial consideration than an arithmetic comparison between the costs of a summer stay in the south (if one doesn't live there!) and that of life in the Alps (where I'm practically at home). During the past 6 months with no theater royalties, I earned . . . 1,300 schillings from sales and parts rental.

On the basis of the monthly "advances," a sum of almost 8,000 schillings stands "to my debit" and if nothing comes of *Wozzeck* again this year, it could easily swell to 10,000 schillings by the end of the year, a fact Hertzka might not pass over without drawing some consequences. . . .

But though I have no good news of myself, at least there is good news of Helene, who is, thank heavens, quite well. This year we are alone in Trahütten (without family), so Helene can enjoy the exceptionally beautiful summer quite peacefully, which will at least be good for her "nerves." She will write to your dear wife very soon and for now greets you both warmly; and from me: all my love and best wishes to you both.

Your Berg

*whose usually harsh climate actually seems "well tempered" <u>this</u> summer (on the average 16 degrees, i.e., room temperature in the winter), while there have been reports of extreme heat (45 degrees) on the plain[5]

---

4. Berg no doubt meant "psychological" rather than "pathological."

5. Berg's temperature indications are in Centigrade; the Fahrenheit equivalent of 16° C is 55° F, that of 45° C is 113° F; clearly Berg is referring to the temperature in the sun.

6. The Berghof property had been resold in 1928 to Erich and Louise Loewe. From that time on until 1932 Alban and Helene Berg spent portions of their summers there, renting a small cottage called the "Denishube."

*Berg to Schoenberg (two picture postcards: Heiliges Gestade am Ossiachersee)*

Berghof, 18 August [1928]

We arrived here, my dearest esteemed friend, after over 2 weeks' delay.[1] And

---

1. The Bergs chose to remain longer in Trahütten because Helene's sister and her family were coming two weeks later than originally planned.

found everything in good order. We have a very comfortable little house near the lake entirely to ourselves (electric light, telephone, running water). I can work on a rented upright <u>without disturbing anyone</u> and without myself being disturbed, and we are close enough to Berghof and its very kind present owners, as well as to the other lake hotels (by bus and motorboat), so as not to feel isolated in the wilderness. Climate, now that the worst heat seems to have passed, also very pleasant; the lake, my giant bathtub, absolutely magnificent. All this—not to mention the "cable car"[2]— is of course ideally suited to distract one *completely* from work. But I hope to pick it up again soon, for it's making slow enough progress as it is. I want to stay here a long time. But I have to be in Vienna on 6 November (when <u>Heger</u> performs my 7 Early Songs for the 1<sup>st</sup> time in the Gesellschaft Concerts).[3]—Berlin extended the *Wozzeck* contract again for this season (28 / 29). Otherwise I don't hear anything at all about any *Wozzeck* performances.—The Allgemeiner Deutscher Musikverein invited me to join the music selection committee.[4] Since three opera premieres are planned for 1929, I am even interested and accepted.—

Enough about <u>myself</u>! How much rather would I discuss matters exclusively concerning <u>you</u> in my letters, dearest friend, if only I knew something about them. I mean those of the last 2 months. May I ask for a little card with news of your health, your work, and other plans? Or maybe your dear wife will write again sometime! We send our very best regards to you both!

Your Berg

---

2. Installed at the northwestern end of the Ossiachersee in 1928.

3. Robert Heger conducted the Vienna Symphony Orchestra in the premiere of the orchestrated version of the complete Seven Early Songs on 6 November 1928 with the soloist Claire Born.

4. Prior to the organization of the International Society for Contemporary Music in 1922, the Allgemeiner Deutscher Musikverein (ADMV), founded in 1860 by Franz Liszt, among others, was the principal forum for new music in Germany. The program selection committee of the ADMV met in Duisburg in the fall of 1928 in preparation for the 59<sup>th</sup> annual ADMV Music Festival, to take place in Duisburg 2–7 July 1929.

*Berg to Schoenberg (3 picture postcards: Ossiachersee Carinthia; Mood on the Ossiachersee; The Cable Car on the Ossiachersee)*

Berghof, 1 September 1928

My dearest, most esteemed friend.

I was enormously pleased to receive your letter with so much news about you and your recent work and life. A thousand thanks!

My heartfelt congratulations on your new work.[1] The thought of it is—as always— deeply exciting, until it changes, with my first glance at the score, into that joy that belongs to the purest and most unspoiled emotions life has to offer, a joy that <u>only grows</u> with study and from performance to performance.—If only a <u>first</u> performance were already scheduled! But I'm still thirsting in vain for one of the Suite

---

1. Schoenberg finished the composition of his Variations for Orchestra, Op. 31, at the end of August; the orchestration was completed the following month.

and the Choruses[2] and am at times beset by the fear that in this short life I won't become as familiar with your later works as I believe I am with the first half.—

Your interest in my new opera also makes me happy, and I take your suggestions no less seriously than those you gave me 20 years ago. I believe I am following them in that I'm not restricting myself to a single row, but have from the outset derived from it a number of other forms (scale forms, chromatic, fourth and third forms, progressions of triads and tetrachords, etc., etc., etc.), which I then interpret (each one) as an independent row and treat as such (with all of its inversions and retrograde forms). Always retaining the right,—in case that doesn't suffice: to construct a new row, as I did in my *Lyric Suite*, where the row underwent small changes with each pair of movements (through the reordering of a few pitches), which at least back then was very stimulating while working.

But such decisions need not be made for a long time yet: although I have already composed over 300 measures, that's a mere beginning for an opera of over 3,000 measures. And to think of what fate may have in store for these plans of mine—despite the most rigorous planning—in the course of the years of work ahead!

Next to my work, my greatest pleasure is life in the water (at all temperatures). Because my heart is much too small and rather disqualifies me from other forms of physical exercise, swimming and floating in the water are most compatible with my physique. I would like to keep it up in the winter, too, and do something for my health in addition to satisfying my insatiable longing for sports (which I can only dull by passionately following the "sports news"). How I wish I could play tennis (not to mention soccer), but my heart simply couldn't do what my muscles accomplish with ease, and I must refrain from it (just like mountain climbing). But now there's a substitute for the latter in the cable car, a better "substitute" than most, as the picture on the reverse shows.)[3]

When will I see you again, dearest friend?! Soon, I hope, in Berlin. On 28 October I have to attend a jury meeting in Duisburg. Perhaps I can travel through Berlin and stay there a day in order to see you. Yes, that would be nice!!! But before then you will certainly hear again often

from your Berg

All our love to you and your wife!

---

2. Opp. 27 and 28, respectively.
3. Berg wrote this letter on three picture postcards, see descriptive titles above.

*Schoenberg to Berg (typewritten letter to his friends)*
[Roquebrune, 22 September 1928]

### UNIVERSAL ARTRUD-JOURNAL

| Volume 1 | Number 1 |
| --- | --- |

Roquebrune-Cap Martin, Pavillon Sevigne, 22 September 1928

Annual Subscription, incl. home delivery: 1,000 Aus. kr.

To our readers:

In response to a frequently expressed wish, we have resolved upon the publication of this newspaper and believe that we are correct in assuming that it meets a broad demand. Not least, we expect from this measure an increase in the tourist trade, which now lays such great stress on hot and cold running water, and from which, of course, we must live.

We believe we have expressed ourselves clearly enough and now proceed to our further business—in a word: enough nonsense!

———

Report from the Public Health Office: in response to the question "How's it going?" we can answer for the editors in good conscience, "Fine thanks, and you?"

The Registration Office of Roquebrune reports: the tourist trade still has not entirely subsided. For some time now the Sch[önbergs] have been the only guests here (almost, editor's note). Apparently they plan to stay at least another two weeks. At any rate there is nothing to indicate that conditions may improve. Although the weather (as reported by the resort commission) isn't nearly as stable as in the summer (but no longer so unbearably hot, either, editor's note); although the management of the pension is actually changing hands in the next few days; and although, as we hear, hordes of Berlin students are already awaiting their duly esteemed teacher with duly prescribed longing; despite all that there is no indication yet that the Sch.'s will be vacating the place.

XXXXXXXXXXXXXXXXXXXXXXXXXXXXXXXXXXXXX

SPORTS NEWS. At a club tournament which took place in Monte Carlo two weeks ago, AS and TS achieved some decent results, not sufficient, however, despite a large handicap, to earn them the prize (10, I repeat, ten French francs). On the other hand, AS's improvement was generally acknowledged. It must be said that he no longer hinders the ball from going where it (that is, the ball) wants to go. While TS had something to boast about; in that she managed to defeat precisely her most unsympathetic opponents. One expects further notable achievements from the young couple.

SPORTS ACCIDENT: During training, AS recently sustained an injury, subsequently named the eyeball [*Augenball*], in which a ball he was very well capable of hitting bounced into his eye through no fault but his own. Though he had recovered sufficiently after a few hours to be able to continue playing, he had to cancel his participation in this week's tournament.

MEDICAL NEWS. The well-known composer AS has been diagnosed with an outbreak of Meschugennensis Sporticae Senilia. For the time being nothing can be done but to await further developments of the illness. That means: one has to let him talk about his sports successes: after all, one needn't listen.

374

FROM THE HOUSING MARKET: Wanted: no apartment! However, to give up: an apartment in the remotest quarter of Berlin; 6 marks 50 from the center of town; uncomfortable to the n$^{th}$ degree; bound up with housekeeping worries; servant question unavoidable. . . . Oh well: it is better to live in a hotel after all. Every place is like home [*Kein eigener Herd ist Goldeswert*.].[1] Editor's note. As we have heard, there is a chance the Artruds will be so lucky as to rid themselves of their apartment and move into a hotel. We are also told that it still depends on whether the bidder on their present apartment will pay enough.

OOOOOOOOOOOOOOOOOOOOOOOOOOOOOOOOOOOOO

FROM THE ANIMAL MARKET xxxxxxxxxxxxxxxxxxxxxx. The wire-haired fox terrier, appropriately named Witz [joke] and notorious after his 40-meter fall from a high cliff as well as through various other equally costly stunts, has finally attained the appearance befitting his pedigree. That is owing to an English lady who instructed TS in the art of trimming. Otherwise he is fine. His proverbial amiability toward strangers of all races seems so conducive to international peace that a plan is underway to propose that the League of Nations in Geneva organize the coming reconciliation of all nations around him.

. . . . . . . . . . . . . . . . . . . . . . . . . . . . .

THEATER NEWS: Nonperformances of *Erwartung* and *Glückliche Hand* are being planned by the court theaters of Berlin, Vienna, Munich, Dresden, Stuttgart, and Karlsruhe, as well as the city theaters of Leipzig, Hamburg, Frankfurt, Halle (not to be omitted) and all others (for more information see the theater directory for Germany and Austria: where *Anschluss* [unification] has already been effected.)

CULTURAL NEWS: The well-known tennis beginner AS has just, that is, on 21 September, successfully completed the full score of a quarter-hour-long work, Variations for Orchestra. Both opponents and friends of his music are of the opinion that this work will be just as beautiful as all his others. The premiere will take place in Berlin at the beginning of December under Furtwängler in the Philharmonic concerts.

The following premieres have not yet been scheduled. Probably the East Crainian will be first, then the South West Thuringian; further, several western German provinces will apparently give simultaneous premieres in their respective spheres of influence on a day as yet to be determined. Additional information will be publicized in numerous notices ad nauseam.

MOOD: As you see, not entirely listless!

CONCERT NEWS: In the course of the season, countless performances of *Pierrot lunaire* are to take place under the direction of the composer on 5 March 1928 between 8–9 o'clock in Nuremberg. Many further notices will follow.

In Response to Queries from various sides: the news published in a Viennese paper

---

1. A play on the expression, *Eigener Herd ist Goldes Wert* (there's no place like home).

that I am writing an opera *Philemon and Baucis* is, as is scarcely obvious, a joke.[2] The funny thing about it is principally that it can't possibly be serious. Besides, it's very easy to recognize the kind of joke that appeals to the Viennese mind, which simply wouldn't concern itself with me without a small barb of spite.

Arnold Schönberg

EXPRESSION OF THANKS: to all who gave me such joy on my $n^{th}$ birthday, I say my most fervent thanks in this no longer uncommon fashion.
[*handwritten:*] Warmest regards, Trude

Dearest Friend,

Many thanks for the magnificent birthday gift, for the wishes and the loving skill with which you are able to time it to exactly the right day! How do you do it? You will gather from this journal why I haven't written for so long; I have been working steadily and also plan to write the text of a cantata here.[3] I hope I'll be successful! Many affectionate regards to your wife and you. Also from my wife

Your Arnold Schönberg

---

2. In a birthday greeting to Schoenberg dated 10 September Berg had enclosed a newspaper report from the 6 September 1928 edition of *Der Tag* that Schoenberg was composing a comic opera *Philemon and Baucis*. As a matter of fact, Schoenberg was working on the comic opera *Von heute auf morgen*, on a text by Gertrud Schoenberg under the pseudonym Max Blonda.

3. Probably the first draft of the text of *Moses und Aron* (originally conceived as an oratorio), which was completed on 16 October.

*Berg to Schoenberg (typewritten letter)*

Vienna, 6 November 1928
afternoon

My dearest, most esteemed friend,

The thought of you working so intensely in Roquebrune is such a joy to me that it almost compensates for my great disappointment at not having seen you in Berlin. But I must say, it was a great sorrow when I had to conclude, after repeated attempts to reach you, that you had not yet returned to Berlin. First I called you: repair work on the telephone cable prevented my getting through. Whereupon I asked at the Akademie der Künste. Although I could halfway assume from the answer that you were not yet in Berlin, I wanted to make certain you hadn't perhaps arrived the day before, so I drove to your home, which I only found, however, after taking a botany exam. But it certainly is beautiful there and though I found the house quite abandoned, at least I know how you lived (this, in case you really do move and I can no longer visit you there).

On my way to Duisburg, where the jury of the ADMV met on the $28^{th}$, I made this detour to Berlin, where I wanted to combine the useful with the enjoyable: it was only useful: a discussion with Frau Wedekind about the *Lulu* libretto.[1] The enjoyable, seeing and speaking with you for at least a few hours, didn't come to

---

1. Berg met with Frank Wedekind's widow, the actress Mathilde (Tilly) Newes, to discuss composition rights for *Lulu*.

pass. Rather, I succeeded in combining the unenjoyable with the useless: quite incognito in the IV[th] gallery of the State Opera and without anyone in the theater knowing of it,[*] I attended this year's reprise of *Wozzeck*, which coincidentally fell exactly on the 26th, i.e., the day, or rather evening, of my 24-hour stay.

The meeting in Duisburg, which was very stormy, resulted in the following program:

I. Evening: Kick-Schmidt (a Schillings epigone) *Tullia*,[2] a terrible old rind of an historical opera.

II. *Die glückliche Hand* and a comic opera by a certain Gropp: *George Dandin* after Moliere,[3] quite a young musician, but very talented and modern in orientation in our sense of the word.

III. Braunfels: a short new opera of "dancelike" character and a ballet *Salambo* by Tiessen.[4]

IV. Evening. The Duisburger opera house itself will contribute: *Maschinist Hopkins* by the Viennese Brand, of whom you will have heard (from Stein, with whom he studies, and from Hertzka, who considers the work very promising).[5]

V. Szymanowski: *King Roger*.[6] Very boring and superfluous.

VI. Either a Strauss or Reznicek.[7]

The opera house in Duisburg is certainly in a position to produce your opera worthily. But the main requirement seems to me (I heard the Szymanowski premiere there) that you yourself take charge of <u>everything</u> (stage direction and orchestra). Recognizing this, we strongly advised the theater to invite you to do so, which has probably been done in the meantime.

Dealing with these c. 50 operas took a frightful amount of time. Never again! In the course of September and October I had to look through about 300 kilograms of operas: full scores, piano scores, and librettos. It was like cleaning a sewer! The sad thing about it was that it slowly but surely wrenched me completely out of my own work, so that I didn't get as far as I had a right to expect during my nearly four-month-long summer. But the odious work was also the reason for my having postponed—for my having had to postpone from day to day—answering your letter of 22 September (with the Artrud Journal), which <u>made us incredibly happy</u>; for it was precisely then that these huge packages of scores were being sent to me across the lake, to torture me day—and <u>night</u>. That lasted until the middle of October, when we returned to Vienna, where, after 4 months' absence from Vienna, I had <u>so</u>

2. Paul Kick-Schmidt studied composition at the Cologne Conservatory. *Tullia*, based on an episode in Roman history, was his fifth opera.

3. Hellmut Gropp, a student of Philipp Jarnach at the Cologne Musikhochschule, wrote this comic opera in 1927–28.

4. No work by Walter Braunfels was performed at the 1929 festival, but it may be that the still unfinished opera *Galatea* (completed in 1929 and premiered on 26 January 1930 in Cologne) was under consideration. Heinz Tiessen's dance drama *Salambo*, Op. 34, was premiered in Duisburg on 21 February 1929.

5. The Austrian composer Max Brand had also studied composition with Franz Schreker; his *Zeitoper, Maschinist Hopkins*, enjoyed tremendous success and numerous productions following its 13 April 1929 Duisburg premiere. The work was published by U.E.

6. Berg had attended the first German performance of Karol Szymanowski's *King Roger*, Op. 46, in Duisburg on 28 October 1928.

7. No work by either Richard Strauss or Emil Nikolaus von Reznicek was presented at the Duisburg festival.

much to do (things concerning U.E., correspondence, etc.) that again I didn't get around to thanking you, my dearest friend, and replying fully to your so very kind and delightful letter. And then came travel preparations as well as my expectation of telling you in person in Berlin everything I should have told you long ago in a letter. After my return, there were preparations for the concert of the Gesellschaft der Musikfreunde, in which Heger will perform my 7 Early Songs (of which Klenau did a partial performance in the radio a while ago). The performance is this evening and to judge by the rehearsals it should be pretty good: Claire Born from the State Opera is the soloist.

I'm taking advantage of a one- or two-hour lull that suddenly came up before the concert to write this letter. I'll follow it soon with a second, in which I'll tell you about the performance and about the Webern concert on the 11th and 12th with *Friede auf Erden* and Mahler's II[nd] Symphony.[8] Judging by the rehearsals with Webern that I've heard so far, the performance of your chorus will be wonderful. We are looking forward to it enormously!!

But what happiness yesterday evening at 9 o'clock to hear the Vienna radio broadcast of *Pierrot*.[9] Although I only have a small crystal radio set, which is connected to the bedpost and gets but weak reception, I heard timbral nuances there, and differentiation of a kind I had never heard before, which allowed an almost dizzying clarity. During this hour at the receiver with the score before us, Helene and I were swept away as we hadn't been for a long time.

In thinking of your works, I now switch from the past to the future: the oratorio, the text of which you are writing.[10] Forgive the word "text"; I know it is a work of poetry! I cannot describe the feeling with which I look forward to it; for what are words like curiosity, joy, expectation, longing, interest compared to this sensation, which even today is coupled with a racing heart, when I but think of the moment when I will be allowed to hold this new work of yours in my hands!

Farewell for today, my dearest friend, our warmest regards to you and your dear wife, and don't be angry that I haven't written for such a long time, more particularly that I didn't answer your letter for six weeks.

Your Alban Berg

I hope you received my card from Berlin.[11]

*Only after the performance did I look up a very surprised Kleiber.

---

8. With the Singverein and Freie Typographia Chorus, both of which Webern was directing at this time.

9. The 5 November radio performance of *Pierrot lunaire* was directed by Erwin Stein and featured Erika Wagner, Rudolf Kolisch, Benar Heifetz, Franz Wangler, Victor Polatschek, and Eduard Steuermann.

10. Schoenberg began composing *Moses und Aron* later that month.

11. Berg sent a picture postcard from Berlin on 25 October, expressing his disappointment at not having been able to see Schoenberg.

*Berg to Schoenberg (typewritten letter)*

Vienna, 7 December 1928

My dearest friend,

I postponed the letter I had promised you so long ago until I could be sure of its reaching you in Roquebrune or Berlin.[1] Only today have I learned that you didn't go to Berlin for the premiere of your Variations after all, in other words, that you stayed in Roquebrune.[2] How right you are! Specifically (after all, how good can a two-rehearsal performance of a new Schönberg be!) and generally: because you are working!

I haven't even told you yet how wonderful the performance of your *Friede auf Erden* chorus was; Webern accomplished a miracle of rehearsing and Stein brought about a fantastic performance.[3] I say: a performance and thereby mean the second (which you didn't hear in the radio), for only then was he sufficiently relaxed to shape this magnificent material. But there was colossal jubilation from the entire audience both times. For me personally it was a festive event. This work (despite Scherchen's fabulous a capella performances[4]) has only now become a real part of my aural world; I would almost say: Now I no longer need the score. The orchestral accompaniment is a chapter unto itself.[5] It never makes the impression of a performance aid, nor does it turn the a capella chorus into a "chorus with orchestra." It's almost mysterious, the way that is achieved. Now and then one or another of the voices mixes with the brilliance of some solo wind, thereby transporting the given passage even further into the poetic realm—so that one would no longer want to do without it. (Oh! If only you would also write a textbook on instrumentation!!!)

However, a melancholy shadow lay over these 2 Worker Symphony concerts because of Webern's cancelation and our great anxiety on his behalf, anxiety which had actually been consuming us for weeks—already before and especially afterwards. Thank God, there is now no longer any cause. I have received good news from Semmering, where he'll receive medical attention at a spa until early January at Herlinger's very kind and generous invitation.[6] So we can definitely expect his full recovery soon. We are seeking to address our concern for his financial situation with a campaign to raise at least a couple of thousand schillings for him, which is

---

1. Schoenberg had obtained a six-month leave from the Prussian Academy and remained in Roquebrune until early February 1929.

2. Furtwängler's premiere on 2 December of Schoenberg's Variations, Op. 31, with the Berlin Philharmonic Orchestra caused a scandal.

3. The exertion of the preceding weeks proved too much for Webern and at the last minute Erwin Stein had to conduct both concerts with Schoenberg's *Friede auf Erden* and Mahler's Second Symphony (11 and 12 November), the first of which was broadcast.

4. Hermann Scherchen performed the work a capella on 24 June 1923 during the Frankfurt festival.

5. Webern, too, had decided to use the orchestral accompaniment Schreker had asked Schoenberg to provide for the 1911 Vienna premiere of *Friede auf Erden*. Clearly Schoenberg had long since accepted the necessity for performing the work with accompaniment; on the occasion of the 1923 a capella performance Schoenberg, in a letter to Scherchen of 23 June, referred to his original concept as an "illusion for mixed chorus."

6. After Webern was forced to cancel his participation in the two concerts 11 and 12 November, his doctors prescribed a rest cure. David Josef Bach and Ruzena Herlinger made the necessary financial arrangements for Webern to be admitted to the Kurhaus Semmering, where he stayed 1–20 December.

being carried out quite discreetly within the "Society for Contemporary Music."[7] Let's hope it succeeds! The performance of my 7 Early Songs in a Gesellschaft concert under Heger went pretty well. He went to great trouble, also followed my advice. I was also quite satisfied with the singer, Claire Born. It was quite successful; of course there was no reason for a failure, after all the songs are more than 20 years old.

To date the Kolisch subscription concerts have been wonderful. The way they play the classics completely by memory has caused a great sensation.

The 300th Kraus lecture in the jam-packed large hall of the Konzerthaus was really terrific, indeed more wonderful than any I've ever experienced.[8] This—and even more so—the performance of your chorus have been the only artistic events that have recently made life bearable in this godforsaken city. And what haven't we experienced! The Schubert week.[9] Naturally my faint hope that in his honor at least one chord in the dozens of concerts be played correctly was dashed. But that was nothing compared to what was <u>spoken</u> by our dignitaries. Then the Loos affair! You can tell what sorry circumstances they were from the fact that the so-called "sentence" was considered a favorable outcome.[10]

And now the Furtwängler-Schalk affair.[11] What sorry circumstance these are, too, can be seen from the fact that one would have welcomed a Furtwängler (-Heger) administration with open arms (although personally I wasn't at all convinced by the Rheingold performance, with its attempt to interpret Wagner as chamber music.)

Enough about our beautiful Vienna! We ourselves, Helene and I, are pretty well and already looking forward to the warmer weather. We greet you most affectionately.

All our love

from your Berg

When will we get another ARTRUD JOURNAL? We're all longing for it!

7. The response to the collection taken up for Webern was widespread and included a contribution by Schoenberg.

8. Portions of Karl Kraus's lecture were published in the next Fackel XXX / 800–805 (February 1929).

9. In honor of the 100th anniversary of Schubert's death, the Austrian Cultural Ministry sponsored a Schubert week 17–25 November.

10. On 5 September Adolf Loos was arrested in Vienna and charged with child molestation; four days later he was released on 20,000 schillings bail. The case came to trial on 30 November and on 4 December Loos was given a probationary sentence of four months' imprisonment, which he never served.

11. Franz Schalk submitted his resignation as director of the Vienna State Opera that previous summer, but continued to hold the position while a successor was sought. Wilhelm Furtwängler, who had recently conducted new productions of Rheingold and Figaro, appeared the most likely candidate, though he did not have Schalk's support. He nearly signed a contract, but backed out at the last minute, citing his obligation to the Berlin Philharmonic Orchestra.

# 1929

*Berg to Schoenberg (typewritten letter)*

Vienna, 19 January 1929

Dearest, most esteemed friend,

The *Gurrelieder* performances are over and turned out better than could have been expected on the basis of the (3) rehearsals.[1] The power of this immortal work of art ultimately so enraptured and inspired all participants (even the conductor), that the performance—as invariably happens with this work—was a truly great event and left an almost unbearably deep impression. Some details, too, succeeded so well that even you would have approved. But this was probably only thanks to the soloists, whom I found much better than in earlier performances. Patzak (Waldemar),[2] simply fantastic: a musician through and through and with a very beautiful voice that is extremely pleasing in all ranges and perhaps only in the highest range lacks that certain tenorial power. Peltenburg,[3] on a high level of vocal and performance artistry, was also excellent and—were she ever to study this part with you (or Webern), could become a first-class Tove. Likewise Anday (Waldtaube)![4] Manowarda (Bauer) quite solid![5] Klitsch fantastic: the best of them all! Preuss (Narr) the worst![6] The choruses . . . well! We have been spoiled by Webern's Workers' Chorus! It was simply the current Viennese performance style. Enormously effective, notwithstanding! The Lehrer A-Capella Chorus, which supplied half the men, was in fact very beautiful vocally and brought out the more difficult choral parts very nicely. It was apparent that the orchestra really pulled itself together yesterday for the performance. And Klenau? Well, when one considers what it means, given the present Vienna music scene to bring off such a performance, one should probably characterize his activity as gratifying and meritorious. And from this standpoint I was able to sign our telegram yesterday in good conscience.[7] After all, we were all so elated,

1. The performances of Schoenberg's *Gurrelieder* on 17 and 18 January in the large hall of the Konzerthaus were with the Vienna Symphony Orchestra, conducted by Paul von Klenau. The performance on 18 January was broadcast.
2. The Austrian lyric tenor Julius Patzak was engaged at the Bavarian State Opera in Munich 1928–45.
3. The Dutch soprano Mia Peltenburg.
4. The soprano Rosette Anday had been a member of the Vienna State Opera since 1921.
5. The German bass-baritone Josef von Manowarda sang at the Vienna State Opera 1919–35.
6. The tenor Arthur Preuss sang at the Vienna Volksoper.
7. A telegram dated 19 January 1929 was signed by Alma Mahler, Paul Klenau, and others.

after finally hearing this heavenly music again! We remained at Alma's late into the night, Peltenburg sang all the Tove songs—with Klenau at the piano, where he is much more at home than in front of an orchestra—and we thought of you with the deepest and most genuine enthusiasm, dearest friend, to whom, full of gratitude, I now send the very, very warmest regards.

Your Alban Berg

Helene too, whom the *Gurrelieder* once again made <u>truly</u> happy, sends you many thanks and regards. We also send all our love to your dear wife!

### Berg to Schoenberg (typewritten letter)

Vienna, 17 January [February] 1929

My dearest, best, most esteemed friend.

If I reply only briefly to your wonderful, dear, dear letter it is because: I'm <u>terribly</u> busy just now—and shall <u>see</u> you shortly. For we're coming to Berlin at the end of the month, where I will accompany my Early Songs in the radio on the 27th.[1] After that it's off to Oldenburg, where I'll give a lecture on 3 March and attend the first performance of *Wozzeck* on the 5th.[2] (Due to preparations for the lecture—a sort of introduction to my opera—and practicing the accompaniment I'll be incredibly busy in the next few days and must restrict myself to essentials in this letter.)

We hope to see you, if not as soon as the end of February, then for sure in March, on our way back from Oldenburg (probably around the 7th)!

I have missed you in Berlin for the second time now, as I told you in a card from there two weeks ago that apparently went astray. I was invited to the performance of the 3 Lyric String Pieces and we were in Berlin for 38 hours (for 2 rehearsals and the performance).[3] Exactly as long as we spent in the trains, since the first one (on the trip there) had an accident at Regensburg.[4] (No doubt you read about the horrible nighttime collision that resulted in four deaths and numerous injuries), so that instead of 14 hours it took 24. But we weren't hurt at all, unless one takes the psychological effects of a sort of train-psychosis into account.

But this time, our <u>third</u> advance on Berlin, we hope to find you there at last! In any case, I shall telephone both times.

Now to answer just the most important questions of your letter: At the time submissions were being sent to the Allgemeiner Deutsche Musikverein, *Die glück-*

---

1. With Lisa Frank.

2. The Oldenburg *Wozzeck* production proved that the opera could be managed by a smaller opera house (Erwin Stein undertook a slight orchestral reduction for this performance). This was the first time Berg gave his introductory *Wozzeck* lecture, which he gave at many subsequent performances; the lecture was first published in its entirety by Redlich.

3. The premiere of the Three Movements for String Orchestra from the *Lyric Suite* took place on 31 January on a Philharmonic concert under Jascha Horenstein. Other works on the program included the Berlioz *Roman Carnival* Overture, Mozart's *Coronation* Concerto, K. 537 (with Magda Tagliaferro), and Beethoven's *Eroica* Symphony.

4. At 1:50 am on 30 January, the train in which Berg and his wife were traveling ran into a freight train near the station at Sünching outside of Regensburg. The accident caused a six-hour delay.

*liche Hand* was requested by the Verein itself and thereupon presented to the jury, which unanimously agreed that it be "unconditionally accepted for performance"* and at the jury meeting, in which the entire music committee participated, it was scheduled without any debate—the only work accepted without debate.

Regarding the performance of your Orchestra Variations, I heard—strangely enough—only good, indeed excellent reports in Berlin, and on the basis of numerous reports, I now have the impression that the performance was a really good one. But how is that possible with three rehearsals, even if (as you say) they really were twice the usual length! *Only*, I imagine, if once again it is one of those simply indestructible works! I read your inquiry concerning the Vienna *Gurrelieder* performance in the *Tag*.[5] I didn't answer because I only spoke with Vienna radio listeners, who praised the broadcast highly. But I have heard that the foreign broadcasts were apparently very bad. Cause: cannot be determined!

After the fact we are terribly distressed to hear about your wife's illness at Christmas, but at the same time very happy that she is once again in good health! Please give her our very best regards.

I most confidently hope I'll soon be able to talk with you at length about everything else, about the many points in your wonderful letter concerning both you and myself—and am madly looking forward to that. You can't believe, or rather: You must be aware that your long letter telling of your enormous productivity and with its wealth of interesting news, stirred me to the very core!!! Thank you, a thousand times thank you, my dear, good friend! And: *Auf Wiedersehen*!

With most affectionate regards, also from Helene

Your Alban Berg

*On the review sheets given each juror for every work there were the following 3 decision categories: Unconditionally rejected. Conditionally recommended and Unconditionally accepted for performance. As well as a "reason."

---

5. Schoenberg's letter inquiring about the nature of the technical disturbances he had heard during the broadcast was published in *Der Tag* on 25 January 1929.

*Berg to Schoenberg (letterhead: Europahof-Dresden)*

Dresden, Sunday, 10 March 1929

My dearest friend,

We just want to thank you and your dear wife once again for devoting a few hours to us on the very day of your return[1]—such beautiful hours for us—and for entertaining us so kindly and well. Being together with you was really the highpoint of my "tour!"

---

1. On their way to a planned 11 March performance of the Chamber Concerto in Dresden, Alban and Helene Berg stopped in Berlin, where on 7 March there was a reunion with the Schoenbergs.

I'd rather not talk about the situation here; we (Horenstein[2] and I) would almost have preferred to cancel my Chamber Concerto altogether. Finally we agreed to perform just the first two movements (with the endings composed especially for that purpose). But the way they're being performed! This fellow Aron!!![3] Not to mention the violinist!!!!![4]

Horenstein does what he can; but what can he do in 4 rehearsals, when—besides these 2 Chamber Concerto movements—he is also doing the Chamber Symphony*—and a piano concerto by Stravinsky.

I'll send you a report directly after the concert.[5] Tuesday night (12 March) we'll be back in Vienna.

All our love to you and your dear wife!

Your Alban Berg

*Yours, of course; there is no other!

---

2. The Russian conductor and Schreker student Jascha Horenstein was principal conductor at the Düsseldorf Stadttheater 1928–30.

3. The pianist Paul Aron was active in Dresden. A series of contemporary music concerts he initiated there in 1919, had reached 50 concerts by 1929.

4. Francis Köne.

5. In the end Berg's Chamber Concerto was replaced by a Concert Suite for Piano and String Quartet by Milhaud. The final concert program also included Schoenberg's Chamber Symphony, Stravinsky's Piano Concerto, and a concert aria by Ernst Krenek.

*Schoenberg to Berg (typewritten letter)*

Charlottenburg, 21 March 1929

Dear friend,

Many thanks for your letters from Leipzig.

If you want to read the libretto of my opera and the oratorio, get in touch with Trudi, to whom I've lent a copy of each for awhile. Webern will read it too, maybe Stein as well, but no one else. And the last person must then send it back to me.

How are you?

I have a lot to do, much of it, as always in Berlin, unimportant!

Many warm regards from our house to yours,

Your Arnold Schönberg

*Berg to Schoenberg (typewritten letter)*

Vienna, 4 April 1929

Dearest friend,

I have probably never picked up a libretto with such suspense, indeed excitement, as *Von heute auf morgen*. An excitement, however, that while reading was soon transformed into a downright pleasant, relaxed mood. You've really hit the mark there, dearest friend! It is just what an opera composer could wish for, or should wish for if he isn't a theatrical symphonist: a <u>libretto!</u> No more, no less. But that is a great deal, indeed everything!

Over and beyond your happy choice in selecting this text, I believe I can perceive the influence of your own hand, a truly *"glückliche Hand,"* in—besides the basic idea of the piece—a great many other things as well. Indeed, there are even sentences whose cadence is so much your own that they could only be by you or someone so close to you, that they are really by you, even if entirely by another.[1]

Beyond this attempt of mine at a fairly objective judgment, there is naturally a subjective interest in my capacity as my own librettist, if I may call myself that on the basis of the fact that I am transforming an enormous drama like *Lulu* into a libretto. And there I was struck above all, indeed fascinated, by the librettist's absolutely brilliant solution for texting the ensembles towards the end of the opera. I refer to the passages where two or more characters—as in the old opera—are given the same text (with only the pronouns altered). Only <u>thus</u> is intelligibility possible—even in ensembles—and thus the action—despite closed forms (which otherwise tend to retard things)—need never stand still.

In other ways, too, it strikes me that in this libretto the <u>clarity</u> of <u>action</u>, without which theater isn't theater, is achieved <u>solely by what happens on the stage</u> and by <u>the way</u> it happens. <u>So much so</u> that I even fancy I have an inkling of the accompanying music. In saying that, however, I only meant to indicate something about the strength of the text, not about my imaginative powers, which must certainly fail in the face of such <u>unheard</u> music, music, that is, that until now only you have heard, and that I'll only understand entirely when I have known it for years.

It is with the same feeling of intuitive awe, still far removed from real "understanding," that I stand before your *Moses und Aron.* Today I can only say that my experience of this poetic work—and it is that in the highest sense of the word—is so powerful that I must call it—even without the music—a very, very great composition, one of the half-dozen immortal oratorios! I don't feel entitled to say more; though I ventured to congratulate you on the happy choice of V*on heute auf morgen,* here, where you speak of what takes place "from eternity to eternity,"[2] it is for others to fall silent and listen in reverence!

Infinite thanks, dearest and noblest friend!

In eternally devoted love, your Alban Berg

Tomorrow I shall give Stein the two texts to read and pass on. As I write this sentence, it occurs to me that I haven't even thanked you for the trust you've placed in me in allowing me to see these texts. Allow me, dearest friend, to make up for that now and believe me when I assure you that I know how to value such trust!

---

1. Most likely Gertrud Schoenberg's authorship of V*on heute auf morgen* was something of an open secret even then.

2. The quotation, "from eternity to eternity" ("von Ewigkeit zu Ewigkeit"), is probably drawn from an early draft of the text of *Moses and Aron.*

*Berg to Schoenberg*

[Vienna] 16 April 1929

My dearest friend,

That was an evening of rare beauty last night![1] And it is a great pity that you weren't there. Right up to the last minute we expected that you might suddenly appear.

What was characteristic of the performance of both the sextet and *Pierrot* was: 1. beauty of tone, 2. clarity, 3. exacting rehearsal.

Re 1. It was really surprising how much attention was paid to beauty of tone: the individual instruments were never strained, the ensemble sonority was never less than elegant. Especially remarkable was the beauty of the flute (much more beautiful than Wangler's, for instance). Also the clarinet, fantastic! Strings not bad, especially the viola (= violin)!

Re 2. Particularly in the sextet: not a single measure that wasn't entirely clear, the main voice always dominant, every chord intelligible, every rhythm precise.

Re 3. One had the feeling that it was completely out of the question that anything go wrong, indeed even that an error was possible. Even in *Pierrot*, which Schmidt—as far as this can be claimed for him at all: conducted with sovereignty—that is, in command of the situation.

Of course—and now for the qualifications: this "having command of the situation" is naturally circumscribed by his artistic limitations. In some pieces, for example, he just beat time (but, since well-rehearsed and balanced: [they were] never chaotic!). Whereas others, especially the grotesque, humorous, and lighter ones—above all the entire 3$^{rd}$ part—were really fantastic. These also suited the speaker much better than, for example, those of the 2$^{nd}$ part, which she was not up to either vocally or emotionally. Also she sang a bit too much now and again.

The——Schorsch Songs (as "Professor" Ender called them!)[2] were surprisingly successful, also in the suppleness of the interpretation! Whereas the performance of the sextet in particular had something academic about it, through which the work took on a somewhat professionally cool veneer. But of course only I and our kind perceived that. The audience reacted with truly—uncommon enthusiasm! And after each work!

Naturally there were many professors, government and court councillors in the audience, gentlemen from the Ministry of Education, including Schmitz.[3] It was generally considered a "red letter day for the Academy." And it was, too—indeed, one for Vienna, I would contend.—

The previous evening your: *Friede auf Erden* and Mahler's II$^{nd}$.[4] And here, in

---

1. On 15 April a student concert at the Vienna Music Academy presented Schoenberg's sextet, *Verklärte Nacht*, six of the George Songs, Op. 15, sung by Anastasia Woynikowa and accompanied by Hubert Kessler, and *Pierrot lunaire*, conducted by the composer Franz Schmidt; the speaker in *Pierrot* was Hilde Kretschmayr.

2. Hans Enders, who taught voice at the Academy for Church Music in Vienna, apparently used the French pronunciation of the surname of poet Stefan George.

3. Probably the Austrian politician Richard Schmitz, a member of the Ministry of Education.

4. Webern conducted this concert in the Konzerthaus (on both 7 and 14 April) with the Freie Typographia Chorus, the Singverein, the Vienna Symphony Orchestra, and the soloists Ruzena Herlinger and Jella Braun-Fernwald.

my opinion—an unsurpassable pinnacle of <u>interpretive art</u> was attained. After the performance a week ago one would have thought that that had already been <u>attained</u> and that this repeat performance could be at best—only a <u>repeat performance</u>. Indeed, could only be a <u>let-down</u> after the performance that <u>Webern</u>, the **chorus**—and even the _**orchestra**_ (you wouldn't have recognized it!) attained by straining to the utmost. But nothing of the kind! These outermost limits were surpassed yet again!—Especially in the performance of your chorus. I can only say that you—if you knew <u>how</u> it sounded and <u>that</u> you (and we, too!) may never again hear such a perfect performance of it—that you would very much regret having missed it. Don't think, dear friend, that I am pronouncing superlatives, they are inadequate praise; I would have to go into detail now, only then could I give a resume that would halfway do justice to this evening.

I have heard the chorus 4 times now this season—and my admiration and passionate love for this miraculous work I have known so long has grown each time— —attaining a level yesterday where I believed I could no longer bear the sheer sublime ecstasy. . . . . . . . . . . .

Thank you, thank you, my dearest, dearest friend!

Your Alban Berg

_Berg to Schoenberg (typewritten letter)_

Vienna, 7 May 1929

Dearest friend,

Your telegram made me incredibly happy—as well as the fact that you went to the concert at all.[1] Because these songs are so closely bound up with my studies with you, they mean more to me than they are really worth. And the fact that I succeeded in orchestrating these piano songs so that <u>you</u> think they sound good, brings that past even closer! For that I thank you a thousand times!

Thank heavens the season is coming to an end. In about 2 weeks we are leaving for the country (first to Carinthia). I _must_ compose again. I shall probably interrupt my work on _Lulu_ in order to carry out a very enticing "commission." Frau Herlinger has requested a lengthy concert aria from me, for which she will give me 5,000 schillings.[2] 2 years of exclusive performance rights. The matter will be decided in the next few days. Recently—aside from the usual unfruitful Vienna activity—I have been very busy with revisions and the like. To prevent singers and conductors in future _Wozzeck_ performances from doing their own arbitrary "arranging," I have added "ossias" to all the vocal parts where it might be necessary.

I also revised the 3 Orchestra Pieces: Schüler in Oldenburg, who will be able to rehearse them adequately and is competent to do so, will perform them next season; <u>that</u>, and Hertzka's intention to produce usable parts, motivated me to do this.[3]

---

1. Schoenberg had sent an enthusiastic telegram on the occasion of a 3 May performance of Berg's Seven Early Songs by Claire Born and the Berlin Staatskapelle under Erich Kleiber.

2. Berg began working on the commission later that month; he himself chose the text for _Der Wein_, which is drawn from Baudelaire's _Les Fleurs du mal_ in a German translation by Stefan George.

3. Until this time only the first two movements of Berg's Three Orchestral Pieces, Op. 6, had been performed (by Webern in 1923).

Schreker was here yesterday and conducted his five radio pieces in the Vienna Radio, which aren't at all bad. On the other hand, the excerpts from the *Singende Teufel*[4]—at least for my taste—didn't meet even my lowest expectations. Unfortunately it wasn't until I was there in the studio that I found out you were conducting the *Gurrelieder* in Leipzig at the same time.[5] I would a million times rather have heard that!

Our most affectionate regards to you and your dear wife.

Your Alban Berg

My health is quite good. Helene's—as always—only marginal. She is currently undergoing a diathermy treatment.

My hope of seeing you in Berlin before the summer has unfortunately come to nothing: the invitation to the State Opera concert came too late. I would very much have liked to come for the rehearsals; but not just to take a bow!

---

4. On his Ravag (Austrian Radio) concert of 6 May, Franz Schreker conducted five of the six pieces from his *Kleine Suite* (1928), a commission by the Breslau radio, as well as orchestral excerpts from his latest opera, *Der singende Teufel* (1928).

5. On 6 May Alfred Szendrei, not Schoenberg, conducted the *Gurrelieder* in Leipzig's Albethalle.

*Berg to Schoenberg (typewritten letter)*

Trahütten, 26 August 1929

My dearest, most esteemed friend,

I hope this letter reaches you, though, despite various attempts, I cannot find out where you actually are. Most likely Berlin, which is why I'm sending it there.

We have been here since the beginning of the month, after spending the first part of the summer at the Ossiachersee, from where I also wrote. Though I've been diligent, so far I have only composed the aria commissioned by Frau Herlinger. It is a work of about 15 minutes' duration (over 200 measures) and I have, thank heavens, finished everything (full score, study score, etc.).[1] Now I plan to return to *Lulu* and shall stay here at least until the end of September for just that purpose. In the meantime, after very lengthy negotiations, an extremely favorable contract has been reached with Wedekind's heirs.[2]

So much for my work. My health is not as good here as in Carinthia; again I have several weeks of asthma behind me: but one can get used to anything! Helene is, for the most part, quite well.

But. . . . how are you and your dear wife? Couldn't you decide to send your Vienna friends another report. Believe me: I am greatly distressed at not having heard from you for so long! Not even indirectly! Not even Rudi, whom I implored for news, writes to me. And yet I well understand that I shouldn't expect letters from you. You certainly have more important things to do.

---

1. Berg completed composition of the concert aria *Der Wein* on 23 July and the orchestration one month later.

2. The contract was signed on 26 July 1929.

But I console myself with the hope of possibly seeing you this winter in Berlin. Various performances in Germany during the coming season will no doubt take me through Berlin frequently and I hope to have more luck this year than last, when I missed you three times.

You probably won't come to Vienna!

Did you read the latest *Fackel* with the letter that Steuermann wrote to Karl Kraus (also on Kolisch's and my behalf) concerning the Pisk Offenbach review?[3] That, too, was a rather time-consuming matter this summer.

I was very pleased by the enormous success and <u>beautiful</u> performance of *Glückliche Hand* in Duisburg.[4] So there was a point to my horrible jury activity last summer and I was <u>publicly</u> vindicated for having stated as the reason why your work should be "unconditionally accepted for performance" (this and 2 other possibilities: "conditionally accepted" and "unconditionally rejected" were the categories on the questionnaire) that it was the obligation of an organization whose title bears the words: "general" [*allgemein*], "German," and "music."

And now the premiere of your <u>new</u> opera is just around the corner.[5] My God, how I would love to be there for that, including the final rehearsals! I will certainly *hear* it this season, my trips to Germany will also have to see to that. But when???

Most affectionate regards to you and your dear wife from us and don't be angry if I ask you once more to see that we hear a bit about you and your present life.

Your Alban Berg

---

3. On seven evenings, 3–10 June, Karl Kraus, accompanied by the pianist Georg Knepler, had given readings of eight lesser-known Jacques Offenbach operettas. Paul Pisk, once a Schoenberg pupil, wrote a review for the *Arbeiter Zeitung* criticizing Kraus for slighting the music in favor of the satiric texts and their applicability to contemporary life. Kraus wrote a lengthy response to Pisk's criticism and Eduard Steuermann wrote to Kraus saying that he, as well as Kolisch and Berg dissociated themselves from Pisk's position and praised Kraus for his understanding of true musical values. The Pisk article, Kraus's response, and Steuermann's letter were all published in the *Fackel* XXXI / 811–819 (August 1929), 75–93.

4. The performance of Schoenberg's *Die glückliche Hand* on 3 July at the 59th ADMV Music Festival in Duisburg (2–7 July 1929) was so successful that a second performance was scheduled for 8 July. Paul Drach conducted the performance and Wilhelm Trieloff sang the baritone solo.

5. The Frankfurt premiere of Schoenberg's *Von heute auf morgen* was to take place on 1 February 1930.

## Berg to Schoenberg

In the train, 5 December 1929

My dearest friend,

Since our return from the country I have been so busy that I really didn't have time to write at length. I'm taking the occasion of our trip to Essen (where Schulz-Dornburg will do the "Rhineland-<u>World</u>-Premiere" of *Wozzeck* and I will give a lecture) to do so in the train.[1] That explains the shaky pencil writing, which I hope you'll excuse.

The main event recently: the performance of your Bach and folksong arrange-

1. The Essen *Wozzeck* premiere took place on 12 December. The German conductor Rudolf Schulz-Dornburg was artistic adviser and opera director in Essen 1927–32.

ments![2] The 2 choral arrangements alone were a wonder of sound, let alone the Prelude. If I hadn't had the score in front of me I wouldn't have been able to tell how some passages were accomplished. So simple and yet so new, so absolutely unheard of; so homogeneous and at the same time multifaceted and varied in every measure, giving one the impression of a gigantic heavenly orchestrion[3] with stops never played before. And that wasn't just my impression, but that of everyone in the hall. Everyone was completely bowled over. . . .

I won't—waste—words (for that's what it would be) on the beauty of your 2 choral songs. (I suppress the belittling word "arrangements") or on the thoroughly enigmatic way it (this beauty) was achieved; tears of deepest emotion that these miracles of the human heart and spirit stirred in me—and not just in me—spoke more than words.

We also enjoyed the very successful broadcast of *Verklärte Nacht* with the Philharmonic—(albeit!) under Nilius.[4]

Otherwise it is better not to comment on Vienna's musical life. But no; one word about the Vienna Opera: From what I have seen so far—the new production of *Meistersinger*[5]—one certainly gets the impression they're trying with some degree of success to counteract in the orchestra and on stage the worst effects of years of carelessness. I cannot yet judge the extent to which—with regard to the music— that will benefit my premiere (presumably in February).[6] But so far—at least outwardly—they (especially Krauss and Wallerstein) have been eager to comply with my wishes. For instance by calling upon Zillig,[7] who was in Vienna for 4 days (naturally at the invitation of the State Opera) to play the opera for all those participating in *Wozzeck*. And what a job he did!!!: except for the 4-hand passages (in which I assisted him) he played every note of the reduction and sang and spoke all the roles) as if it were Puccini. They were all dumbfounded and simply gaped! Especially the 4 rehearsal pianists, who, though vocal rehearsals have already begun, didn't seem to have the faintest idea.—He really is a splendid fellow, this Zillig! Also as composer! He showed me a "Serenade" for 9 instruments[8] that seemed quite

2. On 10 and 11 November Webern conducted the premiere of two Schoenberg works on a Worker's Symphony Concert with the Singverein: the orchestral transcription of Bach's Organ Prelude and Fugue in E♭ major (1928) and two of the three arrangements of German folksongs for mixed chorus a cappella (1929) ("Herzlieblich Lieb, durch Scheiden" and "Schein uns, du liebe Sonne"). The concert, which was in celebration of the annual Republic day, also included Brahms's "Beherzigung," Hanns Eisler's two choruses "Naturbetrachtung" and "Auf den Strassen zu singen," and Mahler's First Symphony. After the concert Berg sent Schoenberg a congratulatory telegram dated 11 November 1929.

3. The Orchestrion, invented in 1851, was one of many mechanical orchestra devices developed during the eighteenth and nineteenth centuries.

4. Rudolf Nilius conducted the Vienna Symphony Orchestra. Also on the program were songs by Mahler, Marx, Wolf, and Johann Strauss, and orchestra works by Schreker, Schubert, and Korngold.

5. The new production of Wagner's *Die Meistersinger* at the Vienna State Opera, which premiered on 30 September, was conducted by Clemens Krauss and directed by Lothar Wallerstein, with Wilhelm Rode as Hans Sachs.

6. The Vienna State Opera production of Berg's *Wozzeck* eventually took place on 30 March 1930, and was conducted by Clemens Krauss and directed by Lothar Wallerstein.

7. The German conductor and composer Winfried Zillig had studied with Schoenberg and was solo coach and conductor at the Düsseldorf Opera 1928–32.

8. Zillig's 1929 Serenade was premiered in a concert of Schoenberg's students at the Prussian Academy in Berlin on 20 May 1930.

outstanding to me! Outstanding in its own right,—outstanding in that it reveals in all respects <u>what</u> he has <u>learned</u> from you and your works and now <u>masters</u> himself.— — — — —

Having mentioned this piano performance in the Vienna Opera and other conferences there, I have already cited some of the reasons why I've had so little time until now.

Furthermore, I'm also very busy in connection with other coming premieres. Above all, letters. In fact correspondence in general!!! Then there's the fact that the *Wozzeck* parts (which we've needed for months) only appeared in print <u>a few days ago</u>, resulting in endless proofreading for me (and my students). That was likewise the case with the (newly written) parts for the aria and the 3 Orchestra Pieces, which Schüler in Oldenburg is performing for the first time in their <u>entirety</u> and with my revisions. Then I was quite ill for a week, before that a week in Venice (for the 1st time at Casa Mahler, from where we also wrote to you)[9] and finally, of course, I have lessons to give, the lecture to prepare, and a little "authoring," then rehearsals and practicing the piano (not long ago I accompanied Stella Eisner in my Early Songs—at the Austrian Club).[10]— — — —so that during the last 2 months I really didn't have the time or peace of mind for a letter to you, my dearest friend.

Having found it <u>now</u>—I have written practically only of <u>myself</u>. But after all I don't want to be so presumptuous as to ask <u>you</u> 1,000 questions about yourself and your life. Thank heavens I heard some things from Reich,[11] Scherchen, and Zillig, and I hope soon to hear much, much more from Webern, who will see you <u>soon</u>.[12] I'll certainly get to Berlin <u>sometime</u> this season—perhaps even see you at your Frankfurt premiere!

Both of us greet you and your wife most affectionately!

Your Berg

---

9. Alma Mahler bought a villa in Venice in 1922, thereafter named Casa Mahler. A card or letter to Schoenberg from Casa Mahler has not been located.

10. The modern chamber music concert on 27 November at the Austrian Club featured works by Berg, Hans Gál, Egon Kornauth, Krenek, Ernst Toch, and Karl Weigl.

11. The Austrian writer and later biographer of Berg, Willi Reich, began music theory and composition studies with Berg in 1928. Reich worked as a music critic in Vienna 1924–37.

12. Webern had been invited to conduct a radio concert in Berlin on 18 December; during his stay there he was Schoenberg's guest.

## Schoenberg to Berg

[Berlin-]Charlottenburg, 5 December 1929

Dear friend,

I've been meaning to write you a long letter for three, five, seven, God knows how many months, but rather than put it off any longer I prefer instead to tell you this in a short letter, which I'm writing during a break of sheer exhaustion, though I really don't even deserve that: there is still so much work to do.

I cannot write, much less tell you how much work, trouble, worry, and aggravation I've had recently.[1] By the time I have a chance to do so, I hope to have forgotten 120% of it.

But I must and would like to thank you very much for the beautiful birthday gift. It really is touching that you invariably remember, and pitiful that I invariably forget your (and Webern's) birthday no matter how hard I try to remember! Although I realized just recently that both of you have also had your fortieth by now, which I didn't even celebrate. No doubt because I still think of you in this regard as the young people you were 25 years ago and it still hasn't sunk in that that relationship has after all long since changed.

I am very happy about the many coming performances of *Wozzeck*. You, too, have had to wait a long time!—I'd like to know how the one in Vienna turns out.

My opera might well have been produced in Vienna this year, too, if—ah, if only!—Krauss had accepted it. But after a very amiable letter, which I answered in kind, I haven't heard another word from him.[2] In other words he doesn't like it: but that's nothing new. That's what's good about it! That is just what he should expect: that is precisely where one must begin! Or doesn't he like the text? Also a mistake; one should have more faith in me than in oneself: if I liked it, it is good and, most important: the opera is good. Surely it would be a sad state if I couldn't take any text and write the kind of opera in which one sees and hears only what I intend and becomes blind and deaf to all else.[3]

Write to me soon. Especially about the course of the rehearsals. A piece of advice: rehearse with the singers <u>yourself</u> and see to it that they sing <u>beautifully</u>. Not dramatically, not reciting, not attempting to move heaven and earth, but singing. For opera, too, is a <u>kind</u> of concert.

Many, many warmest regards, also to your wife, also from my wife.

Your Arnold Schönberg

---

1. Schoenberg decided to publish V*on heute auf morgen* in collaboration with a young businessman turned publisher, Benno Balan, after Universal Edition proved hesitant, Schott and Adolf Fürstner turned the opera down, and an offer from Bote & Bock was not financially satisfactory to him. The arrangement with Balan was to prove far more unsatisfactory and very costly to Schoenberg.

2. In response to a letter announcing the publication of V*on heute auf morgen*, which Schoenberg sent to a number of opera directors, Clemens Krauss had written back on 30 August, expressing interest. However, though a score and libretto were sent, Krauss did not pursue the matter and on 22 October Schoenberg demanded the return of his score.

3. Here Schoenberg employed an untranslatable play on the figure of speech *"dass einem alles Hören und Sehen vergeht"* (literally that one loses hearing and sight), meaning that one's head is reeling.

*Berg to Schoenberg (picture postcard: Essen, Stadttheater)*

[Essen, 10 December 1929]

Dearest, best friend,

Your dear, dear letter is a ray of light in the hectic days I'm experiencing here, where I must do my utmost to see that *Wozzeck* isn't staged as the "Two-Penny

Opera by C. Neher <u>based on</u> Büchner and Berg."[1] Thank God it is well rehearsed musically and the <u>singers</u> are almost all magnificent. The lecture in the opera house (with orchestra and singers) went very well. Still better and more effective was an open discussion with the entire faculty of the Folkwang School, where I spoke for 1½ hours about the "Viennese School":[2] 90% of this being about you and your position in "New Music," 12-tone rows, etc. The half a hundred musicians heard things they had never before imagined.

1,000 regards and more from Vienna!

Your Berg

No doubt you received my long letter—posted in Linz—from before the trip. Again 1,000 thanks for yours!

1. The Essen production of Berg's *Wozzeck* was under Rudolf Schulz-Dornburg and directed by Wolf Völker, with Heinrich Blasel as Wozzeck and Dodie van Rhyn as Marie. Berg's joke about *Wozzeck* as *Zweigroschenoper* is an allusion to the sets by Caspar Neher, who was known for his close association with Kurt Weill and Bertholt Brecht; their highly successful collaboration in the *Dreigroschenoper* (1928) was then enjoying tremendous popularity.

2. Berg's lecture was on 8 December. The Folkwang School in Essen was established by Schulz-Dornburg, who was also its first director.

*Photomat portrait of Alban and Helene Berg sent to Schoenberg for New Year 1930. On the reverse, Berg wrote "taken in Essen after the dress rehearsal of Wozzeck where we 'just kind of looked at one another'." (Library of Congress)*

# 1930

*Berg to Schoenberg (typewritten letter)*

Vienna, 1 March 1930

My dearest friend,

I've been meaning to write for a long time. But my by now chronic lack of time repeatedly prevented it; and then I wanted to await two things before writing—and thanking you: attending the Frankfurt performance of your opera[1]—and official word about my nomination to membership in the Prussian Academy.[2] Neither has occurred, but I'm writing anyway.

Yes, unfortunately nothing came of my hope of seeing your opera in Frankfurt on 20 March [February], although I had arranged with Steinberg to travel there between the dress rehearsal of *Wozzeck* on the morning of the 20th and the premiere on the evening of the 21st. There simply wasn't enough **time** between the conclusion of the dress rehearsal and the beginning of your opera: the express train from Aachen to Frankfurt does, after all, take 5–6 hours. Having to miss this cast a pall on my otherwise untroubled Aachen stay. The performance there under Pella, who is quite fantastic, was excellent in every way (in contrast to Essen under Schulz-Dornburg, excuse me: schulz-dornburg in essen, which they don't capitalize, though they Gorge themselves [*Fressen*] there pretty well nonetheless).[3]

And naturally the radio broadcast of your opera from Berlin to Vienna was no substitute for what I missed in Frankfurt![4] Unfortunately it must be said that all bass instruments were inaudible in the broadcast unless they were playing *f*. And though it is easy in the case of tonal or otherwise familiar music to compensate for the bass consciously (or unconsciously) in one's inner ear, I missed it all the more here. It was therefore an incomplete experience, but I still got a great deal out of it, particularly as regards the overall disposition of tempos and voices, which, curiously enough, could be heard quite wonderfully, and I especially liked both Hinnenberg

---

1. *Von heute auf morgen* was premiered in Frankfurt on 1 February, conducted by Hans Wilhelm (later known as William) Steinberg and directed by Herbert Graf. Berg was unable to attend.

2. The Prussian Academy of the Arts was an advisory council to the Prussian State. External membership was honorary. Berg was first nominated by Schoenberg and Schreker in January 1929. They renominated him on 8 January 1930 and Berg was accepted as a member on 23 January. Schoenberg had been a member since 1927.

3. The Aachen Stadttheater performance under Paul Pella took place on 21 February. The Essen opera director Rudolf Schulz-Dornburg was in the habit of signing his name in lowercase letters. Berg's remark is a play on the literal meaning of the word *Essen*, "to eat," and the word *Fressen*, "to gorge."

4. On 27 February a performance of *Von heute auf morgen* under Schoenberg's direction was broadcast in the Berlin radio program "Funkstunde."

and the baritone.[5] That's why—along with my unfortunately still superficial knowledge of the score—I already have an approximate impression of the work, which is—I would like to have it said from an artistic and human standpoint: a <u>gratifying</u> one!

Since the publisher sent me a piano score in addition to the music I had immediately <u>ordered</u> (full score and libretto), I assume the former was sent at your request; for that, I thank you most sincerely.

But I must thank you for something else, too. The nomination to membership in the Prussian Academy was not only a great joy for me and Helene, but also an enormous surprise. I fancy I'm not off the mark in assuming that it is owing above all to your initiative, and—as I said—I would have thanked you long ago, if I hadn't still been waiting for <u>official</u> notification from the Prussian Academy. Of course I should also write to thank the Academy itself; but I really do have to receive an official nomination first. If that doesn't come soon (it has been almost 3–4 weeks!), I shall express my thanks on the basis of the newspaper reports, after all, I can't just accept it <u>without responding</u>! Anyway, we were very happy about it; if only because of Vienna, which continues to ignore us, Webern and me. Many, many thanks, my dear good friend!

Speaking of Vienna, there is increasing evidence of opposition to the *Wozzeck* premiere (set for 29 March).[6] In the forefront Liebstöckl[7] and *Das Neue Wiener Journal*, which (as usual) has printed the most outrageous lies;[8] in the background no doubt Schalk, too, who still hopes to get Schneiderhan's position, that is, become *General-Intrigant* [General Intriguer] of the State Theaters.[9]

Starting next week, I will participate in the rehearsals at the Vienna Opera. But before that are the rehearsals of your Op. 29 Suite, which are already underway,[10] and I'm looking forward to them like mad. I'll tell you about it after the performance. Today I can attend a rehearsal for the first time. I'm immensely excited!

Otherwise we are not very well; Helene is in bed with the flu and I cannot recover from the flu I had at Christmas—the week-long rest in the resort town of Aachen, notwithstanding.

Now farewell, my dearest, most esteemed friend; our warmest regards to you and your dear wife!

<u>Your</u> Alban Berg

5. The soprano Margot Hinnenberg-Lefebre later married the music journalist Hans Heinz Stuckenschmidt. The baritone Gerhard Pechner was engaged at the Deutsches Opernhaus in Berlin.

6. The Vienna State Opera production of *Wozzeck*, premiered on 30 March 1930, was conducted by Clemens Krauss and directed by Lothar Wallerstein, with sets by Oskar Strnad; the principal soloists were Josef Manowarda (Wozzeck) and Rose Pauly (Marie).

7. The Viennese music critic Hans Liebstöckl wrote for the Vienna *Sonn-und Montagzeitung*.

8. The *Neues Wiener Journal* published various articles criticizing the time and expense involved in mounting *Wozzeck*, including a 22 February report in the section "Hinter den Kulissen." In the latter, a joke is told of one Burgtheater employee asking a colleague from the State Opera how he was, to which the State Opera employee replied, "Hoffentlich sind wir bald überm Berg" [mountain] (a pun on a colloquial expression, here meaning "hopefully we'll soon have it [i.e., Berg] behind us").

9. The industrialist and art patron Franz Schneiderhan was *General Intendant* of the Vienna State Opera from 1926 until the end of 1932. Franz Schalk was at this time serving at the State Opera only as a guest conductor. *General Intrigant* is a play on the title *General Intendant*, or General Director.

10. Webern was preparing Schoenberg's Suite, Op. 29, for its first Vienna performance on 5 March.

*Berg to Schoenberg*

[Vienna] 14 March 1930

My dearest, best friend,

Thank you for your kind telegram.[1] An official notification from the Academy of the Arts has meanwhile arrived, which I answered by return post. Thanks again!!!

I would like to write much, much more, especially about your Suite, which, thanks to the rehearsals, I know quite well—and not only on paper, as is unfortunately the case with your latest works, but from hearing it in all its vitality! The sound of it is so fabulous that it makes a compelling and coherent impression even on those who cannot follow the melodic-thematic development; that was evident from the overwhelming success (about which I wired you).[2] I believe one can predict a relatively quick triumph for this work—like that of *Pierrot*.

Just briefly today, dearest friend: I am extremely pressed for time, am at the Vienna Opera almost all day.

They really are taking pains to stage a good performance of *Wozzeck* there. Nevertheless I am naturally experiencing all the customary ups and downs of the last weeks preceding a premiere (30.3.30)—aggravated by the fact that it is—in Vienna.

We send you and your dear wife our very warmest regards.

Your Alban Berg

1. Schoenberg's telegram, dated 12 March, advised Berg to await official notification before responding to his selection to the Prussian Academy.
2. In the second Kolisch-Steuermann concert of the season on 5 March Webern conducted Schoenberg's Suite, Op. 29; the program further included Bach's Brandenburg Concerto No. 3 and Schoenberg's First String Quartet, Op. 7. Berg sent Schoenberg a congratulatory telegram on 6 March.

*Schoenberg to Berg*

Baden-Baden,[1] 10 April 1930

Dearest friend,

My wife was bedridden for almost six weeks. An intestinal problem, still unexplained, and now she has been sent here to recover, which has already had favorable results. After a year of most exhausting work I, too, badly need a rest and am diligently playing tennis instead of working as I had planned.—Just before my departure (and this is the main reason for my letter) Schreker called me and asked that I sound you out on something. I had to refuse, as I had done him a similar favor once before (Frau Gutheil),[2] which compromised me when, after receiving an acceptance, he let the matter drop. I have to preface my inquiry with this so as not again to arouse hopes that might not be fulfilled and I must tell you that you, too, must be prepared for that if Schreker *does* make an offer. For they make it easy

1. The Schoenbergs spent part of April and May in the Sanatorium Allee-Kurhaus in Baden-Baden, before returning to Berlin.
2. Schoenberg wrote to Marie Gutheil-Schoder on 29 May 1926 to tell her that he had suggested her for a teaching position in Berlin.

on themselves here: they ask several people in a <u>nonbinding</u> way; but they don't make a final decision until all the acceptances are in and only then is the approval of the ministry sought!!! Anyway, the question will be: whether you would accept a position teaching composition at the Hochschule für Musik.[3] Salary, 8–900 marks a month; teaching subsidiary subjects as well (you would have to insist on substantial vacation time—and discuss it with me!)—If you were to ask my advice: yes! definitely: yes! You could breathe freely here. And it does offer considerable security. True, the salary is not high and won't permit great extravagances, but one can get by on it very well. You would **definitely** have to get a guarantee for an apartment. Preferably by asking that the Ministry 1. pay your moving costs; 2. pay the security or mortgage fee, as well as 3. an initial monthly subsidy of 2–300 marks until you find an apartment.

But I must also tell you: when I refused to mediate, Schreker said he would do it himself since he's coming to Vienna anyway. But he might not do it after all. I'm telling you so that you have time to consider. Otherwise a matter like this can catch one unprepared. I do hope Schreker asks you. I would be overjoyed to have you in Berlin. <u>N.B.</u> you do realize that such inquiries must be kept confidential and that you must not tell <u>anyone</u>.

Briefly, I still want to congratulate you with all my heart on the success of your opera. I was extraordinarily pleased.—I just received an invitation from Düsseldorf: but a day too late.[4] My post wasn't forwarded until <u>today</u>, though I've been away since the 6th! Perhaps—if my wife had been well—I might have come. As it was: she didn't feel particularly well the day before yesterday.—How is your wife? Does she join you on all these big trips? We haven't heard from her in a long time!

Finally, to close: my *Begleitungsmusik zu einer Lichtspielszene* for small orchestra is appearing shortly with Heinrichshofen, and with Bote & Bock: a cycle, six men's choruses.[5] But I don't know yet what I'll write next. Preferably an opera; I do have plans, even for my own libretto, and have also thought of Werfel, whose novel (your gift—did I ever thank you for it? Anyway, I do so now!) I liked very much.[6] Do you think he would do something <u>in collaboration</u> with me. In the case of my first opera I also worked along throughout.[7] But perhaps I'll do *Mose und Aaron*.[8]—Now: many warmest regards to your wife and yourself. Also from my wife.

Your Arnold Schönberg

3. Schreker had offered a position to Berg once before, in January 1925, but Berg had declined.
4. Schoenberg had been invited to attend the 10 April Düsseldorf performance of *Wozzeck*.
5. Schoenberg's *Begleitungsmusik zu einer Lichtspielszene*, Op. 34, composed between 15 October 1929 and 14 January 1930, appeared with the Magdeburg publishing house Heinrichshofen and was to be premiered on 6 November of that year in a symphony concert of the Kroll Opera under the direction of Otto Klemperer. Schoenberg's Sechs Stücke für Männerchor a cappella, Op. 35, composed between 16 June 1929 and 9 March 1930 on texts by Schoenberg, were published by Bote & Bock in Berlin.
6. The Werfel novel has not been identified, although H. H. Stuckenschmidt speculates in *Schönberg. Leben-Umwelt-Werk* (Zurich, 1974) 305 that it may have been *Der Abituriententag* (1928).
7. The text of *Erwartung* was written by Marie Pappenheim in close collaboration with Schoenberg.
8. Here Schoenberg deleted the final "s" in Moses to avoid a title with 13 letters (his superstition about that number is well documented); he later decided to delete instead one "a" from "Aaron."

## Berg to Schoenberg

On the Düsseldorf-Oldenburg trip, 11 April 1930

My dearest friend,

We are returning from Düsseldorf, where the *Wozzeck* premiere took place yesterday.[1] It was a <u>very lovely</u> performance—and I can say, notwithstanding the well-rehearsed <u>Vienna</u> performance, in the preparations for which I participated for weeks, that I didn't really <u>recognize</u> my opera again until I arrived <u>here</u>, where I heard just 3 preliminary rehearsals! Horenstein is a musician <u>in our sense of the word</u>, just as his <u>complete</u> allegiance is *<u>only</u>* to us, as was apparent in a speech he gave after the premiere at a banquet sponsored by the <u>city</u>, where he invoked the "sacred names of Gustav Mahler and Arnold Schönberg."

We did indeed experience wonderful things here, but it all paled beside the tremendous, unspeakable joy that literally sent shivers through me when I caught sight of the words you dedicated to me in the opera program.[2] Oh my dear, good friend! That is <u>too</u> beautiful, I blush with pride——and modesty, just thinking of it. And while writing this, I reddened twice over. . . . and Helene, who is sitting across from me, saw it——and now she too has blushed. . . . . . and that's the reason for this declaration, which really isn't and never has been necessary: living up to that and only that which you expressed in such wonderful words shall be my lifelong "endeavor," "until the last hour." ————————

Tonight we'll be in Oldenburg, where tomorrow I'll attend rehearsals of the 3 Orchestra Pieces, I'm already very excited at the prospect. The performance is on Monday, then homeward at last, for the Lübeck *Wozzeck* premiere has been postponed.[3] The conductor is seriously ill and the *Intendant* asked me to recommend a young conductor to him who is <u>free</u> and could finish rehearsing the opera in 3–4 weeks. I recommended—more to help the <u>man</u> than the <u>cause</u>—: Josef Schmid.[4] Maybe he'll succeed, then it would be a springboard for the poor fellow!—But I am well aware that the whole thing is a gamble.—

The engineer seems to have gone mad, so furiously is the train racing through these boring plains. Lurching and shaking so much that I must stop writing. Excuse the handwriting. But I was afraid I wouldn't find time to write to you in Oldenburg and wanted to tell you as soon as possible—also on Helene's behalf—what I repeat here: Thanks, a thousand thanks, infinite thanks!

All our love to you both!

Your Berg

---

1. The Düsseldorf premiere of *Wozzeck* on 10 April was conducted by Jascha Horenstein and directed by Friedrich Schramm, with sets by Hein Heckroth; the soloists included Berthold Pütz (Wozzeck) and Hanna Gorina (Marie).

2. Schoenberg wrote his *Bekenntnis* (Testimonial) to Berg for the Düsseldorf Opera program booklet, *Die Theaterwelt* V / 10 (10 April 1930), 1. Here Schoenberg speaks of his respect and affection for both Berg and Webern and states that the subjective ties of friendship are reinforced by the objective judgment of the artist.

3. The premiere of a *Wozzeck* production at the Lübeck Stadttheater eventually took place on 13 May 1930. Karl Mannstädt was the conductor who became ill, Dr. Otto Liebscher was the Intendant.

4. At this time Josef Schmid was working part time as a copyist for U.E.

*Schoenberg to Berg (letterhead: Sanatorium Allee-Kurhaus / Dr. B.
Hahn—Dr. K.H. v. Noorden / Baden-Baden)*

Baden-Baden, 17 April 1930

Dear friend,

Many thanks for your dear letter, which crossed with the one I wrote to Vienna.
I was very interested in what you intimated about the Viennese performance. I'd
like to hear more. And is Horenstein really so good?—You recommended Schmid
to conduct *Wozzeck*; I hope he can stand up to the test. Of course it's very nice that
you want to help him, but are you sure he would be good for your opera? I don't
want to say anything against Schmid, who is no doubt a very serious musician; the
fact that Zemlinsky doesn't think much of him doesn't mean anything, since there
are very few people of whom he thinks well. I just wondered, since Zillig is asking
me to put in a word for him with Krauss (Vienna) (apparently he is under consideration for a choral conducting position), whether you might not be better served
with Zillig and whether it might not be better to help someone who has a chance
of making it, while Schmid may already have given up all hopes and would only
be facing fresh disappointments.—In my opinion: if Schmid can't come, consider
Zillig <u>first and foremost</u>. He can conduct and is very conscientious.

I have nothing else to report today. It is not yet certain whether I will conduct in
London on 13 May (*Erwartung*), for they have offered far too little rehearsal time.
I expect the decision today.[1]

Have you read that *Erwartung* and *Glückliche Hand* are to be done in Berlin on
7 June?[2] Maybe that would be a chance to see each other.

My wife isn't much better. But there is some progress.

Enough for today: many affectionate regards to your wife and yourself, also from
my wife.

Your Arnold Schönberg

---

1. The planned 13 May performance of *Erwartung* in London was eventually postponed until 9
January 1931.

2. A performance of *Erwartung*, under Alexander Zemlinsky, and *Die glückliche Hand*, under Otto
Klemperer, took place in the Kroll Opera in Berlin on 7 June.

*Berg to Schoenberg*

Vienna, Easter Monday [21 April] 1930

My dearest, best friend,

Never before have I left two such important letters unanswered for so long. But—
returning from Oldenburg I had a long radio talk to prepare for the day after tomorrow ("What is atonal?" in the form of a dialogue).[1] And I am using the first and
only break in this work in order finally to write to you. Above all: how can I thank
you with words for the letter in which you wrote in such detail about the Berlin

1. Berg's radio talk, "Was ist atonal?", was first published by Willi Reich in 23—*Eine Wiener Musik-
zeitschrift* 26 / 27 (8 June 1936), 3–4.

offer and gave me such thoughtful advice? You have heaped so many signs of kindness and friendship on me recently, that I continually ask myself how I deserve it and what I must do to show myself worthy of it. Today, next to assurances of my ever-growing friendship and my adoration of your art, which have lasted over a quarter century—I can only thank you; thank you and thank you again and again! And Helene joins me in this.

And now to the most important matter: you can imagine how profoundly affected we are, indeed overwhelmed by the possibility of an appointment in Berlin. And yet—though we no longer talk of anything else, we have not decided yet whether I should accept the appointment if I receive an official offer (Schreker was in Vienna in the meantime, but was unable to reach me). You yourself have made the arguments in favor of it with such thoughtfulness, and I can only add my full endorsement to everything, but we feel that the prospect of living near you again, and for years to come at that, is one of the most enticing reasons for accepting the offer.

The argument against it is my dreadfully slow work pace and the necessity of finally finishing something again, which I hope to achieve by from now on working on Lulu not only in the coming summers, but also in the winter and—starting with the coming season (1930 / 31)—by our going south for a few months—i.e., above all getting away from Vienna. And I cannot deny that my health, which has been less than optimal for months, makes me unfit for a workload that combines a career with composing. Although I don't suffer from any actual illness, I haven't felt at all well for a long time and—despite utmost care (and, for example, total alcoholic abstinence for a quarter year now)—can't seem to get better. So that Helene in particular even fears my having to face such new and demanding tasks.

Despite these misgivings, however, this is not yet a firm decision and we're glad there's still time to consider it. In any case, I will let you know immediately if I hear from Schreker—or other official channels.

24 April 1930

I couldn't continue writing on Monday, after all. But now that yesterday's lecture is successfully behind me (I mainly went after Korngold![2]), I have some time again.

We are very concerned about your dear wife's illness; please give her our regards and tell her that we fervently wish her a speedy convalescence and a complete recovery!

We also very much hope that your indisposition is merely passing and that you get a thorough rest in Baden-Baden. After all—we, your Vienna friends, speak of it often—you have accomplished an incredible amount. And already you're talking about new compositions! In particular I can't get over the fact that you have written a score to a film scene. Was it composed for a particular film? Or is it something for general use (in the sense, say, of a comedy overture)? You can imagine how much I, too—personally as a composer—am preoccupied with the question of silent and talking films.

From what I know of Werfel (and I know him well) I'm convinced he would

2. Though he does not refer to Julius Korngold by name, Berg addresses the fact that the term "atonal," first used by journalists in a pejorative sense, had become an umbrella word for everything that set "new" music apart from traditional music.

consider it a great pleasure and honor to work with you and that he would be able to do your bidding with a minimum of friction since you always know exactly what you want. He is presently in the Semmering (Breitenstein, Haus Mahler). Should I mention something to him about it?—

I cannot be as pleased with the Vienna success as might have been expected, since I find it inexplicable on the basis of what the audience is being offered musically. Or am I too close to the performance, having been involved with it for weeks beforehand, deadened to the good things and now just aware of the bad? I'm at a loss! Anyway—I repeat—Horenstein's interpretation satisfied me 1,000 times more.

In the "Lübeck Wozzeck" matter I naturally thought of Zillig, first thing as a matter of fact. But he couldn't have taken those 3–4 weeks off; we discussed it in Oldenburg. On the other hand, both Horenstein and Johannes Schüler were willing to take over in Lübeck and would have gotten time off from their Intendants. But all this proved unnecessary (Schmid's application as well) when the Lübeck Intendant ended up engaging a certain Leschetitzky from Braunschweig,[3] surely the worst possible decision.

Of course I spent a good deal of time with Zillig, whom I really like very much. In fact, everything was very enjoyable in Oldenburg. J. Schüler's performance of my Orchestra Pieces was absolutely fantastic (after 4½ full three-hour rehearsals, to be sure) and I very much wish you could have been there! And how especially wonderful it would have been for Helene and me if you had come to Düsseldorf!

One consolation though! I'll see you in Berlin on 7 June. I'll certainly be there for that! I can't wait. Perhaps Helene will come, too (she always joins me on these trips to Germany). Then we can finally talk with one another at length, my dearest friend, and I can get the kind of news that simply isn't possible in letters!

If only these foreign broadcasts were better! How I wish I could hear the one on 5 May (London)! Tomorrow (besides Palestrina, Strauss, etc.) Schalk is doing your Friede auf Erden.[4] That Opera Chorus concert will also be broadcast. I shall give you a brief report. Until then I send you and your dear wife a thousand regards (also on Helene's behalf) and thank you again with all my heart.

Your Berg

---

3. Following his successful Wozzeck performance, the conductor Ludwig Leschetitzky was appointed to the position of principal conductor at the Lübeck opera.

4. On 25 April, in a concert that included Palestrina's Pope Marcellus Mass, Strauss's sixteen-voice Hymn, Brahms's Fest- und Gedenksprüche, and two Bach motets. In addition Professor Franz Schütz premiered four little organ preludes and fugues by Franz Schmidt.

### Berg to Schoenberg

Vienna, 18 May 1930

Finally, my dearest friend, a sign of life from me again.

From the enclosed letter to Schreker (I received his written offer 2 weeks ago) you will see that I have turned it down after all. Believe me, best friend, it wasn't an easy decision for me—even today I am not so sure I haven't made a monstrous mistake! No doubt it will seem so to you: but please don't be angry with me!— — — —

Since my return from Düsseldorf I have been so terribly busy that I could't write any earlier; in addition to the many, many pointless tasks, which in city life rob one of ¾ of one's time, there were also some more meaningful ones: on 23 April a radio talk in dialogue form, which went very well and on 15 May my lecture: "The Atonal Opera" in the Kulturbund,[1] which was so well attended that more than 100 people had to be turned away. In both lectures I found very opportune occasions to "go after" old Korngold, who is up to his old tricks more than ever!

In the meantime simultaneous first performances of Wozzeck took place (13 May) in Lübeck and Königsberg. And to all appearances very successfully, so that I am finally reassured that it's possible without me, too, and that in the future I won't have to concern myself any more with Wozzeck (as I did for so many weeks and months this season), but can devote myself instead entirely to Lulu.

I hope I still can compose; these long interruptions always induce agonizing doubts in me. How wonderful in your case! Another work finished: The Lichtspielbegleitmusik [sic]. I already own it, of course, and am—after just brief study—thrilled. Of course it is a complete work of art even without film; but wouldn't it be wonderful if it could be heard synchronically (or whatever it's called!) with a film created by you. If you were interested, it would surely be feasible in Berlin!

Incidentally: I have long been absolutely convinced of a great future for the talking film (also in connection with our music). Speaking of which, have you seen the latest Jannings film: The Blue Angel?[2] If not, be sure to go see it! — — — — — —

Are you still in Baden-Baden? And has your dear wife quite recovered? I sincerely hope so!—I imagine you'll be needed in Berlin soon for rehearsals of Glückliche Hand and Erwartung. How I look forward to that! Concerning the date: 7 June will be splendid for me; for the aria will be premiered in Königsberg on 5 June[3] and Wozzeck is scheduled for the 6th. Then I'll finally see you again after exactly five quarter-years (7 March 1929)![4] Until then all our love to you and your dear wife.

Your Alban Berg

---

1. Berg's talk, "Die atonale Oper," was a version of his Wozzeck lecture.

2. The film Der blaue Engel (1929) was directed by Josef von Sternberg and starred Emil Jannings and Marlene Dietrich.

3. Berg's concert aria Der Wein was premiered at the 60th ADMV Music Festival in Königsberg on 4 June 1930 by the soprano Ruzena Herlinger.

4. Berg had last seen Schoenberg in March 1929 when he stopped in Berlin on his way to the planned Dresden performance of his Chamber Concerto.

*Berg to Schoenberg (typewritten letter)*

Berghof, 22 July 1930

Dearest friend,

A thousand thanks for your dear card! We have been here now for 12 days and of course my first intention was to write to you. Only briefly, though, since I was afraid it might not reach you. For I had previously written to your new Berlin address, which I got from Webern while still in Vienna, requesting that my letter

*Arnold and Gertrud Schoenberg vacationing in Lugano-Besso, July 1930 (Arnold Schoenberg Institute 321)*

be forwarded, for which I included an international stamp. Apparently this was not done; however, my request for your vacation address has just been answered by your card[1] and now I can finally write the longer letter I had promised.

Of course I wanted to write immediately upon our return from Berlin. Those two days were so wonderful for us. To see you again at last, to be able to speak with you! And then the evening at the opera! Not a day passes that I don't think of it and feel a surge of emotion. For myself, I would say that only now (Prague and Vienna notwithstanding[2]) has this immeasurably beautiful music, this undreamt-of new theatrical experience, become truly my own. Of course I am well aware of the flaws in these performances, something I didn't, for instance, recognize so clearly at the Vienna performance of *Glückliche Hand*. Anyway, I thank you most sincerely and a thousand times—as I planned to long ago—for the joy and happiness that you and your work and the reunion with your dear wife gave us.

"As I planned to long ago": that I didn't write for so long despite my intention, is, of course, due solely to lack of time these past four weeks in Vienna! Upon returning home from performances of one's own works (Königsberg), there is always so much to do, as well as an accumulation of so much left undone during the long absence. Then there are the end-of-the-season theater contracts and preparations for an extended absence from my desk in Vienna. And my remaining time, indeed most of it, was entirely taken up with the purchase of a car and the driving exam.

1. Schoenberg sent a picture postcard from Lugano on 15 July, informing Berg of his new address in Berlin (3 Nürnberger Platz); the Schoenbergs had moved to this large five-room apartment on 1 July and were to remain at that address until they left Germany in 1933.

2. Schoenberg's *Erwartung* was performed in Prague in June 1924, *Die glückliche Hand* in Vienna in October 1924.

Thank heavens I passed easily and I could be driving all through beautiful Carinthia now . . . if only I had the car. For it turned out, long after the sale, that the kind of car I wanted and of which I saw a great many in Berlin, couldn't be obtained in all of Europe. So I had to start all over again and finally hit on the solution by ordering an English Ford, which is on its way now and should be here by the end of the month. Only then will we begin to enjoy our stay here; for the present we are rather cut off from the world and from all means of transportation. Though that may be good for my work. I immediately began working on *Lulu* here—after a 10-month break—and got back into it rather quickly. However, having told you that, I have told you everything about myself worth telling. Helene is feeling fine here; her nerves get calmer by the day. It was cold here at first; you can't imagine how cold, even if you thought it was chilly in Lugano. I hope that your weather is as beautiful as ours is now—that your dear wife recovers thoroughly and that you too, dearest friend, will for once relax completely after your so very productive season!

Our most affectionate regards!

Your Berg

I am eager to see your new home and don't mourn for the old one with its 4 thirteens: 9 Charlottenburg and 17 Nussbaumallee: $9 + 17 = 26$, Nussbaumallee has 13 letters, not to mention the telephone number 2266! I much prefer 4466, which contains my number (23)!

*Schoenberg to Berg (postcard)*

Lugano, 25 July 1930

Dearest friend,

Funny that I, who can't stand postcards, should write you one! But now I've already penned in my address, so let it be. In the morning it is my habit, before beginning to work, to doodle, draw, or carve something. That way I slowly begin to concentrate on my work. I'm trying to compose *Moses und Aron* and am presently paring down the libretto a bit. It is to be a stage work, a dramatic oratorio or the like.—I hope I'll make some progress with it. If only I can stay away from Berlin long enough!—I received both your letters, the first one after my card from Lugano, which you obviously acknowledge.—We've had a few days of bad weather here, thunderstorms and persistent drizzle. But now it's lovely again.—Unfortunately I can't play tennis, since there aren't many players here and none who plays badly enough for me. For a good player won't play with me.—Why don't you tell me more about your work? Can't I even get a look at the libretto?—I could only "glance" at your aria, as we were very busy moving. Do you hear from Webern?—We are both fine and I am glad that you and your wife are well.—

Many affectionate regards to you both, also from my wife.

Your Arnold Schönberg

*Berg to Schoenberg (typewritten letter)*

Berghof, 7 August 1930

My dearest friend,

Your lovely photos gave us enormous pleasure. The sight of you made us almost homesick, but also very happy because you both look so well and rested. I hope both of you will be able to remain away from Berlin for a long time to come and that you can continue with *Moses und Aron*. Your plan for this opera strikes me as particularly exciting: the concept alone is fantastic. What a work that's going to be! Once again something that in an instant will void everything that might possibly bear a <u>superficial</u> similarity.

Regarding my new opera, I can only tell you that I'm still working on the I$^{st}$ act. Aside from the composition, the 12-tone style of which still doesn't permit me to work quickly, the libretto slows me down a lot, too. Because finalizing the text goes hand in hand with composing. Since I have to cut $^4/_5$ of the Wedekind original, selection of the remaining fifth is torture enough. How much worse when I try to make the text fit the musical forms (large and small) without destroying Wedekind's idiosyncratic language! That's why I could send you only the "text" of what I have composed so far; but I would rather wait until the whole thing is finalized.

Despite my preoccupation with detail, the main outline of the libretto as an opera has of course been entirely clear to me for a long time. This applies to the musical as well dramaturgic proportions. Particularly the succession of scenes, which is, briefly, as follows:

| | | The Two Dramas | The Opera |
|---|---|---|---|
| **Earth Spirit** | Act I | Painter's studio, in which Dr. Goll, Lulu's husband, has a heart attack. | |
| | Act II | Home of Lulu and her 2$^{nd}$ husband, the painter, who commits suicide | Act I — 3 scenes |
| | Act III | Theater dressing room of Lulu the dancer, to whom Schön promises marriage. | |
| **Pandora's Box** | Act IV | Home of Schön, who is murdered by Lulu. She herself is arrested. | Act II — 1 scene separated by a long orchestral interlude |
| | | After a 10-year [sic 1-year] imprisonment, freed by Alwa (Schön's son) and Geschwitz, Lulu returns again to | |
| | Act I | Schön's home (same scene as before). She becomes Alwa's lover. | |
| | Act II | Casino in Paris. Lulu must escape | Act III — 2 scenes |
| | Act III | In the Attic in London | |

From the braces (left and right) you can see how what is separated in Wedekind—after all there are two plays—is deliberately fused (by my II$^{nd}$ act).[1] The orchestral interlude, which in my version bridges the gap between the last act of *Erdgeist* and the first of *Büchse der Pandora*, is also the focal point for the whole tragedy and—after the ascent of the opening acts (or scenes)—the descent in the following scenes marks the beginning of the retrograde. (Incidentally: the 4 men who visit Lulu in her attic room are to be portrayed in the opera by the same singers who fall victim to her in the first half of the opera. In reverse order, however.)

That, I believe, is the most interesting dramaturgical aspect I can tell you. Are you sufficiently familiar with the play to be able to understand it without having Wedekind's text at hand. It is only because I feared that might not be the case that I included (in red) the otherwise ludicrous plot summary, with its few purely superficial reference points.[2]— — — — —

Aside from this, my work—and even that's no longer news—there's no news to tell. Still without a car! Weather constant: one day it rains, the next is indescribably beautiful, then lousy again. And it has been like that since we got here!

Helene and I send you, my dearest friend, and your dear wife our warmest regards.

Your Alban Berg

*[referring to a paper tear:]*
Excuse the tear—it was the typewriter's fault!

---

1. Wedekind himself had originally conceived of the two plays as one and he occasionally produced them as such with his Munich Künstlertheater; Berg may even have been present at one such performance in Vienna on 27 May 1913.
2. Berg's plot descriptions are typed with red ribbon.


*Schoenberg to Berg (typewritten letter)*[1]

[Lugano] 9 August 1930

Dear friend,

Above all I congratulate you most cordially on your new car and hope that it gives you much pleasure. Next, many thanks for telling me about your adaptation of *Erdgeist* and *Büchse der Pandora*. Your arrangement is certainly very good: that much is already apparent. I am very eager to see it in its completed state, but can fully comprehend your point of view in not wanting to show it before that stage. Unfortunately, the impressions of a third person seeing an unbuilt house are usually so irrelevant that it's hard to understand how artists of earlier times could discuss unbuilt houses with their friends, though one sometimes wishes it were possible.

That's why I also understand (your allusion, the second now, is evidently meant to warn me) that you are still apprehensive about my *Moses und Aron*; I assume because you've discovered a similarity with some other work on the same subject; with something that, as you write, "might possibly bear a superficial similarity." You're obviously thinking of Strindberg. I already looked at the play[2] a year ago

---

1. The original of this letter is located in the Pierrepont Morgan Library.
2. Schoenberg is referring to the first play of Strindberg's posthumous historical trilogy *Moses, Sokrates, Christus*, which appeared in Emil Schering's German translation in 1922.

with that in mind. There is in fact a certain similarity, insofar as we both employ certain reminiscences of biblical language, indeed, use many literal quotations. However, in addition to other improvements, I am at this very moment deleting those reminiscences. Not because of the similarity with Strindberg; that wouldn't matter: but because I'm of the opinion that since the language of the Bible is medieval German, obscure to us, it can at most be used for color; and I don't need that. I cannot suppose, considering your thoroughness and the confidence you surely have in my creativity, that you have found any similarity beyond that. For the moment I can't remember what ideas Strindberg presents. But mine, my main idea, as well as the many, many explicitly stated and symbolically represented subsidiary ideas, all that is such an integral part of my own personality that Strindberg couldn't possibly have presented anything bearing even a superficial similarity. You would certainly have realized that upon rereading it, especially if—and this, as you know, is indispensible with my work—you had examined every word, every sentence from various angles. Today I scarcely remember what is mine, what is still mine: but one thing you must grant me (I insist on that): everything I have ever written bears a certain intrinsic similarity with myself.

I have already finished the first scene. Have sketched out a good deal and hope to pick up a faster pace soon. I hope to produce a respectable and definitive libretto soon. Then you shall see it. Meanwhile: many warm regards to your wife and you, also from my wife

Your Arnold Schönberg

*Berg to Schoenberg (typewritten letter)*

Berghof, 13 August 1930

My dearest friend,

I am quite dismayed about the misunderstanding between us, arising out of my remark about "superficial similarity." Not for an instant did I intend to compare its content with that of any other work, let alone entertain apprehensions on that score. My remark referred solely to your designation "dramatic oratorio or the like," which admits the possibility of a purely superficial comparison with stage works in which a synthesis of the oratorio-like with the operatic is likewise attempted, but all of these, be they new works or old (including staged Handel performances), shrivel to nothing the moment your work is <u>conceived</u> and exists—to exist for ever. Just as in the case of your other works, whose "superficial similarity"—whether in the choice of the symphonic poem form *(Pelleas)* or the old suite forms, or in the choice of a libretto set in the mundane present *(Von heute auf morgen)* etc., etc. . . . in short: whose "superficial similarity" <u>nevertheless</u> allows of no comparison other than the one, that measured against your work, all other symphonic poems and all other "suites" and all other *"Zeitoper"* are worthless.

In any case, I didn't so much intend to stress the idea of similarity as to affirm once again that despite any potential for purely superficial comparison, the one will be an immortal work of art, whereas the other is—and always has been—rubbish.

You mention yet another allusion, an earlier one, with which I "evidently meant to warn" you about *Moses und Aron*. I'm completely mystified what that could have been and it's downright incomprehensible, since I wouldn't have forgotten such blasphemy had it ever occurred to me. How can you imagine that I would dare to "warn" you in matters that concern what is supremely sacred to me: your work. (No more than it would occur to me to advise you in <u>that</u> regard.* I would have to be a megalomaniac, what am I saying: an absolute idiot!

Notwithstanding the danger of being taken for one, I almost rejoice in this misunderstanding; since it gave me your wonderful thoughts on superficial similarity and your wonderful words on the topic, as well as the heartwarming and inspiring news of your intense work on *Moses und Aron* and of your progress with this work, which—always—brings me—such perfect joy.

> Most affectionately, your Alban Berg

All our love to you both from Helene and myself!

*which would in any case be conceivable only in matters of lesser importance (in that I might, for instance, recommend that you unhesitatingly entrust your works to a Johannes Schüler or a Ladwig,[1] but would warn you against a Schulz-Dornburg).

---

1. The German conductor Werner Ladwig had been General Music Director and Opera Director in Königsberg since 1928.

## Schoenberg to Berg

Lugano, 12 September 1930

Dearest friend,

Above all, congratulations on your car. Good luck and much joy with it! It looks fantastic.[1] I am amazed at your skill in making such a long journey on your first trip!

Next: many sincere thanks for your birthday wishes and the gift you announced, which embarrasses me very much since I always (truly!) <u>forget</u> [yours] (invariably at the time, no matter how often I think of it at "the wrong time").

And now in particular to your canon.[2] After looking at the enclosed sheet you'll be able to appreciate the great joy and great service you've done me. Herr Turnau,[3] who scheduled my opera only four times despite 7 curtain calls at the last performance, who didn't want me there before the final rehearsals, who didn't spend any money on my work and who talked the stage director into all sorts of foolishness that I had the greatest difficulty preventing at the last minute, this Herr Turnau wants me to send congratulations to the Frankfurt theater, to this opera house, where I had a row with a singer and the biggest scandal of my life with the orchestra

1. In his birthday greetings of 10 September 1930 Berg sent two photos of his new car.

2. In his 10 September letter Berg had enclosed a four-voice canon he composed for the *Festschrift* of the Frankfurt Opera House, which was celebrating its fiftieth year; the canon was based on the row of Schoenberg's comic opera *Von heute auf morgen* and in his text Berg concludes with the words: "*von heute auf morgen / in aller Ewigkeit.*" (from today to tomorrow / for all eternity).

3. Josef Turnau was the *Intendant* of the Frankfurt Opera who had arranged to premiere Schoenberg's *Von heute auf morgen*.

and where no one greeted me at the dress rehearsal.[4] You'll see a few facetious drafts on the original letter.[5] But I simply didn't answer. And now you have done so: and truly: <u>splendidly</u>! When did you suddenly develop such skills? Obviously: one can never demand enough of oneself! One can always do more than one thought possible just a short time earlier. It really is amazingly well said and so unequivocal. Musically extremely polished and it should sound good.

Now I wish you good luck on your work.

I myself have had to be idle for a week. I was rather worn out, though I haven't accomplished <u>nearly</u> as much as I had hoped. Scarcely 400 measures. Finished, however, in full score (without transpositions), since I want to publish it as it stands: at most c. 8–15 staves, even with chorus. But still reworking the text holds me up extraordinarily often. For I retain very little of what was there originally and usually change it just before, but also during composition.

Now once again: sincerest thanks and many regards, also to your wife; also from my wife

Your Arnold Schönberg

4. On the day before the premiere of V*on heute auf Morgen* Schoenberg sued the Frankfurt Opera for providing insufficient orchestral rehearsal time. Details of the suit are related in Peter Gradenwitz, "Max Kowalski (1882–1956)," *Bulletin des Leo Baeck Instituts* 58 (1981). There is an interesting allusion to the affair in a letter from Kurt Weill to UE, in which Weill writes: ". . . I fear the gentlemen [at the Frankfurt Opera] will use the same tactics with me as with Schönberg; it is well known they didn't consult him during rehearsals and at the dress rehearsal they ushered him out when he tried to state his view." (letter of 28 September 1930).

5. Schoenberg enclosed Turnau's letter to him of 23 August, on which he had jotted various epigrammatic trial responses.

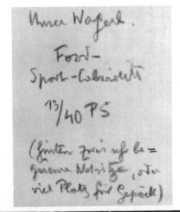

*The photographs of his new car that Berg sent to Schoenberg on 10 September 1930 (Library of Congress)*

*Schoenberg to Berg*[1]

Berlin, 28 November 1930
[envelope, Berlin, 30 November 1930]

Dear friend,

I liked your aria very much.[2] A wonderfully beautiful piece; excellently constructed, very beautifully written for the voice, magnificent sound—I am very satisfied and the only reason I don't say that I am proud of you is because the first line of the biography, printed on the opposite page, almost robs me of that right.[3]—I know very well that you have nothing to do with it and don't intend to disclaim me; and I know myself that my teaching is better today than when you were my student. But: who wrote that? It is really outrageous and can't even make the claim of not wanting to hurt you. For today, where you yourself are a master, no one can think ill of you for once having been a student.

Certainly it is more comical than aggravating. But why should I, who otherwise adorn myself only with my own and never with borrowed plumes, not be allowed to embelish myself with two students?

Again and nevertheless: I am very proud of you.

Many affectionate regards

Arnold Schönberg

1. The original of this letter has not been located. This translation follows Willi Reich's published transcription in "Ein unbekannter Brief von Arnold Schönberg an Alban Berg," *Österreichische Musik-zeitschrift* XIV / 1 (January 1959), 10.

2. On 28 November Erich Kleiber conducted a performance of Berg's *Der Wein* in a concert of the Berlin Staatskapelle.

3. The program did not mention the fact that Berg had studied with Schoenberg.

*Berg to Schoenberg*

Vienna, 4 December 1930

Dearest, best friend,

Your words of approval about my aria have made me unbelievably happy! My joy is only clouded by aggravation over that stupid biographical note. I'm almost ashamed to mention that I am absolutely innocent in the matter; also that—even in public—I never miss an opportunity of proudly asserting that you are the teacher of my life. Be it in interviews or in the *Wozzeck* lecture, which I have now given before hundreds, even thousands of listeners, and where I mention, "that I wanted to pay homage to you, my teacher with the Chamber Symphony scoring of the middle, the most central scene of my opera." Thank heavens, the world does not know differently and now as ever—thank heavens!—calls me (for instance, in the most recent review of the aria in the Berlin *Lokalzeiger*): "Schönberg student." And everyone who knows me even slightly knows that I will remain so until the end of my life. And this: despite such a stupid biographical reference, for which I can only find the following explanation:

For years one has read in "Riemann" that I (nota bene: "a composer of futuristic tendencies") "remained autodidact until the age of 15,"[1] which is idiotic in itself,

1. Berg is quoting from the article on him in the 1922 edition of Hugo Riemann's *Musik Lexikon*, 11th ed., which states that until the age of 19 (not as Berg says, 15) he was self-taught.

because back then, before I came to you (at the age of 20), I hadn't bothered with study at all, but simply bungled at "composing" until I found out from you that one can also <u>learn</u> something . . .

This "autodidactism" [*Autodaxie* [sic]], which never existed, was apparently accepted blindly by the author of the program notes—and blindly elaborated ("later joined A. S.") without necessarily being meant tendentiously, but simply concocted with journalistic freedom, thus becoming, like everything journalistic, imprecise, false, indeed absurd. *[Berg cites several additional errors in the program.]* <u>Nowhere in the entire</u> program can one find the name of the person <u>responsible</u> for this permanently enshrined nonsense; nor do I think it possible to "correct" such a thing. But perhaps an effective sort of defense against such an unusual situation will occur to me; in that case I won't pass up the opportunity. But maybe I'll be coming to Berlin soon and then I'll look into the matter <u>on the spot</u>. For it is possible—again because of the *Wozzeck* lecture—that sometime before Christmas I'll have to go to Braunschweig for the premiere there . . . That wouldn't be far from Berlin . . . and it would be too tempting to visit you! Maybe it will work out; I'm still awaiting the date.

And now thank you again for your dear note, which made me so happy and please accept our most affectionate regards to you both! But most particularly to you

from your Alban Berg

*Berg to Schoenberg*
Vienna, 27 December 1930

My dearest friend,

Things must be jinxed: you are doing *Erwartung* in London on the 9th and I don't arrive there until the 11th, after my <u>own</u> premiere in Braunschweig on the 9th.[1] So it's quite out of the question that I hear *Erwartung* and I don't imagine there is much chance of still seeing you in London either. I will be in London a couple of hours on the 11th; but will you still be there? I shall arrive in the morning, and in the course of the day must travel on to Cambridge where the jury meetings begin the next day.

Possibly we'll meet on the high seas in the night (of the 10th to 11th) — — — —

However: I have written my exact arrival time to Clark;[2] perhaps you will be staying in England longer <u>after all</u>. Cambridge isn't far from London! And I could still see you and not just have to imagine you somewhere on the North Sea. . . . .

We send our warmest regards to you and your dear wife!

Your Alban Berg

And a Happy New Year, my dearest friend, to you and yours from us both!

1. Schoenberg wrote to Berg on 22 December that he was conducting a BBC performance of *Erwartung* with Margot Hinnenberg-Lefebre on 9 January. Berg was serving on the ISCM jury, which was to meet in Cambridge later that month.

2. Edward Clark, who arranged the Schoenberg concert, worked for the BBC.

# 1931

*Berg to Schoenberg*

Vienna, 13 February 1931

My dearest friend,

I haven't written since my return from London. The reason: aside from extensive professional correspondence and other business and family matters:* my illness. On 1 January I came down with an unusually bad case of flu, which forced me to cancel Braunschweig and from which I had <u>scarcely</u> recovered by the time I left for Cambridge. Thanks to the wonderful English climate, I recovered there and might have returned home in good health, if during the crossing to Ostend I hadn't been caught in the storms then raging and become terribly seasick. The result: a severe gallbladder attack with the most excruciating colic (lasting for weeks), from which I recovered only very slowly. Now I am quite well again.

The trip was quite adventurous in other respects, too; on the way there I had to pull the emergency brake near Wels to bring the Vienna / Paris express to a stop because (through no fault of my own) I had ended up in the wrong part of the train . . . —But I was nonetheless very glad I made the trip and got to know both London (relatively well) and Cambridge (inside and out). Of course the professional task at hand was very depressing since I, alone against 4, sometimes 5 opponents (a Frenchman, an Italian, a Belgian, and a Pole (+ an Englishman)), was able to accomplish practically nothing worthwhile, as you can see from the concert programs of the Oxford Music Festival.[2]

Thank heavens at least Webern will be heard!

I haven't heard from you for a long time, my dearest friend; not even indirectly. I would be very, very pleased to know what you've been doing and experiencing lately. I haven't given up hope yet of traveling through Berlin <u>this</u> season in order to see you there; there are still a few more German opera houses to tap in the next 2–3 months.— —

I finally own your male choruses! And—thanks to their simplified legibility[3]—I already know them much better than your recent scores and consequently enjoy

---

1. Helene Berg's family home.

2. Berg's colleagues on the ISCM jury, which was under the chairmanship of the Englishman Edward Dent, were the Frenchman Charles Koechlin, the Italian Alfredo Casella, the Belgian Desire Defauw and the Pole Gregor Fitelberg. Adrian Boult served in an advisory capacity. The program for the ISCM festival, to take place in Oxford 22–28 July, included works by Webern (his Symphony, Op. 21), Otto Jokl, Paul Hindemith, and Erwin Schulhoff.

3. The score of Schoenberg's Six Pieces for Men's Chorus, Op. 35, published by Bote & Bock, had all transposing instruments sounding as written.

them even more, if that is possible. How wonderfully beautiful and how wonderfully new they are! And yet behind the absolute, eternal values of this opus there seems to be something timely as well: just as in the magnificent texts[4] (especially in II, III, and V and VI) you reflect upon today's communal ideas [*Gemeinschafts-ideen*] (in such a way that they also become those of tomorrow and of all times). . . . it also appears that you (you who have always shown the younger generation [the way]) for once wished to <u>show</u> something <u>after the fact</u>, thereby demonstrating that the simple forms generally associated with low "communal music" can also <u>lay claim</u> to the highest standards of artistry and skill, and that their level need not be so debased as to make them suited to be sung only by children or on the street.[5]—

Less satisfactory than my pleasure in studying this new composition was my reaction to hearing your Bach Prelude and Fugue.[6] Kleiber plays the 1st half on Ultraphon with $\quad$ = 76 (instead of 108), though he later picks up the tempo somewhat. But that distorts the whole thing. However: one can <u>hear</u> almost everything (I followed it with the score) and it seems generally well rehearsed. Finally I helped myself out by playing the first part in G major, the 2nd in F major. What a shame that <u>you</u> aren't making these records!—

How is your dear wife? Give her our best. Helene is quite well, but she has a

---

4. Schoenberg had written the texts for this work.

5. During the later 1920s, many composers sought to reestablish a link with a broader audience through music intended for practical use or community performance. The term *Gemeinschaftsmusik* became a catch phrase for this type of composition.

6. Schoenberg's arrangement of Bach's Prelude and Fugue in E♭ Major.

*The ISCM jury at Professor E. J. Dent's home in Cambridge. From left to right: Casella (at the piano), Koechlin, Boult, Berg, Dent, Fitelberg, and DePauw*

great many worries concerning her people.[7] She, too, sends you her very best. All my love and best wishes, best friend!

Your Berg

*I finally succeeded in selling the family villa on Maxinggasse;[1] at a relatively good price, too.

---

7. Helene Berg's brother Franz suffered from schizophrenia. In a letter of 10 September 1930, Berg told Schoenberg of a crisis when the young man "made a sacrifice" by cutting off the end of the little finger of his left hand; for a time he was in an institution in Rekawinkel, near Vienna, but a more permanent arrangement had to be found.

## Berg to Schoenberg

[Berghof] 6 August 1931

My dearest friend,

We have been here exactly 2 months now and that's how long it has been since I last wrote to you. Again that's a <u>longer</u> interruption than I had intended and I must apologize: initially I did my best to avoid distractions from composing and later all manner of time-consuming matters of a different nature arose, which I'll tell you about later. Unfortunately the latter <u>severely</u> disrupted my work, which had been going well after the first few weeks. I'm finally to the point where, in addition to various rather disjunct sections, one act is as good as finished (though not orchestrated, which I won't do until the very end of the <u>entire</u> composition). The principal difficulty remains shaping the text, finalization of which goes hand in hand with composing, indeed the text often has to be directly fitted into the music. Just now, for example, I was held up by the end of Act I, where <u>musically</u> it became necessary to round out the act with the development and last recapitulation of a large sonata form, whose exposition and first recapitulation had occurred much earlier and now had to be recalled from considerations of <u>textual</u> and <u>dramatic</u> as well as <u>musical</u> development. But I think I succeeded and that will have to console me for my slow progress. After all, I can't simply treat the whole thing as a rush job for Philadelphia, which is what U.E. and Stokowski would like![1] For now I have given both of them* hopes for a "world premiere" in the 1932/33 season. And I'll try to <u>meet</u> that deadline too, which is why I shall stay away from Vienna in the <u>fall and winter</u> as well, especially as there's really nothing to keep me there any longer. (Again no efforts were made to recruit either Webern or myself during Hofrat Sr-Wiener's reform of the Vienna <u>Musikhochschule</u>.[2] On the contrary: an interpellation in Parliament as to why they were "letting me go" (as if I had ever been <u>asked</u>!) remained unanswered. This just as an aside!)

But meanwhile we intend to stay here, where we both feel very well, physically, too. Apparently last spring's severe <u>gallstone</u> attack is not going to recur. Aside from

---

1. After Leopold Stokowski premiered *Wozzeck* in the United States on 19 March 1931, he began negotiating first performance rights to *Lulu*.
2. In 1930 *Hofrat* Karl Wiener was appointed chairman of a commission charged with reorganizing the Vienna Musikhochschule and Musikakademie, which had existed as separate entities since 1925. They were reunited in 1931 and Wiener served as director until his retirement at the end of 1932. The prefix "Sr" before Wiener's name probably stands for a derogatory term such as *Swiener* or *Schwiener* (dialect derivation of pig).

work we go driving a couple of hours every day and now that Helene, too, has passed her driver's test and can drive—quite well, at that—I'm no longer just <u>chauffeur</u> like last year, but can continue to reflect on my work as we drive—something I formerly did on <u>walks.</u> And during the evenings in our remote seclusion we turn to the 5-tube radio set that Siemens & Halske placed at my disposal. I get excellent reception for all of Europe and it's great fun searching for and tuning in the various stations. A few weeks ago this machine provided me with a particularly great, festive pleasure when I was able to hear parts of your Variations——and **your dear voice** (which Frankfurt had recorded on disk from your lecture in the spring).[3] Helene, who sat there just as excited as I, told me afterwards that while straining to hear your voice I looked like the poster: "His Master's Voice."[4] to which I could only reply: "I should hope so!"—

Unfortunately there have also been less pleasant events recently; those "time-consuming" matters I mentioned at the outset. I believe you know that my mother-in-law, who died recently, had sold her house in Hietzing.[5] And on rather good terms, too. Though with <u>installment payments</u> over a period of years on a large outstanding low-interest mortgage. Now it turns out the buyer couldn't pay the July installment on account of the German Reichsmark disaster[6] (he's one of Vienna's largest publishers, Erika Wagner's brother-in-law)[7] and that's causing me (as the only man in the family) a great deal of worry and aggravation—particularly since my wife's siblings had been counting on these installments.

The second thing that interrupted my work was the fact that I had to go to Salzburg where I had a rendezvous with the directors of the Philadelphia Opera. Also present were the stage director Wymetal, Jr.,[8] who doesn't seem very trustworthy, and the conductor Levin,[9] Stokowski's very likable assistant. Apart from that, though, we more or less fled Salzburg after a 3-hour stay, for the <u>first</u> people I caught sight of were those notables, Knepler[10] and Salten,[11] after which I looked neither to the left nor right to avoid further encounters in this encampment of "artists." Since we had made this little "business trip" in our little car, we proceeded to combine it with a trip via Bavaria (Königssee), Tyrol, and various high Tauern passes, and

3. On 24 March 1931 the Frankfurt Radio produced a performance of Schoenberg's Variations, Op. 31, conducted by Hans Rosbaud, on which Schoenberg had given a lecture-analysis two days earlier. Portions of the lecture-analysis were recorded by the Frankfurt Radio, along with Rosbaud's performance. The lecture has been published in Arnold Schoenberg *Gesammelte Schriften*, 255–71, on the basis of a manuscript bearing the date 28.2.[1931]. Schoenberg himself translated two portions into English for use in his 1934 Boston lectures. For a published English translation, see "The Orchestral Variations, Op. 31. A radio talk," *The Score* 27 (July 1960), 27–41.

4. The well-known trademark of the Gramophone Company was a painting by Francis Barraud entitled "His Master's Voice" (1899) depicting a fox terrier listening to a phonograph.

5. Anna Novak Nahowski died on 21 March 1931.

6. The German Reichsmark crisis was another repercussion of the American Wall Street crash. In Germany the bankruptcy of a large textile concern in June led to the serious weakening of the Darmstadt Bank and to a crisis affecting the entire German financial system.

7. Leo Schiedrowitz.

8. Wilhelm Wymetal, Jr., was the director of the American *Wozzeck* production in Philadelphia.

9. The American Sylvan Levin was Stokowski's assistant and conductor of the Philadelphia Orchestra Chorus.

10. Probably Hugo Knepler, the owner of the Viennese concert agency Albert Gutmann.

11. Possibly the Austrian writer Felix Salten (pen name for Siegmund Salzmann) is best known for his children's book *Bambi* (1923).

returned here yesterday safe and sound, where I'll finally get back to work.

But I've said enough now—indeed, too much—about myself. If I haven't mentioned you and your dear wife, that is only because it would have been nothing but questions. And because asking them would be tantamount to asking you to write about yourself, about your life and your plans and ———— your present work. I would just love to know much more of your doings. Since I didn't get to Berlin at all last season I have felt more out of touch with you than ever this year. But can I really expect you to write me a long letter??? Perhaps just a word as to whether you have been affected by the German disaster. I'm very worried about that! I hope my anxiety is unfounded and that you are both quite, quite well in every respect! Our warmest regards to you both.

Your Alban Berg

*U.E. and Philadelphia

*Schoenberg to Berg (typewritten letter)*

Territet-Montreux[1], 8 August 1931

Dearest friend,

I'm very glad to have heard from you again at last. [*Schoenberg adds a footnote defending his use of the lower case for the familiar* Du *form, normally capitalized in correspondence.*] I had often remarked upon it and wondered, since you had promised in your last letter to write more fully. Above all I must say: I'm disappointed that you didn't extend your journey just a few hours and visit us here. After all, you were quite close to the Swiss border.[2] Didn't it even occur to you? What a shame! We'd have been so pleased!—Next: sorry I haven't inquired about your gallstone attack until now, although I often thought of it. It's reassuring that it turned out to be the random consequence of some "excess" or other serious dietary problem. You've been on the road so much and it's easy to pick something up.—Something else I forgot which I've been meaning to tell you: about your contribution to the Loos book.[3] I must say I was really impressed and very proud of my friends (I liked Webern's contribution very much, too).—So you too have finished an opera act: so have I. It's almost 1,000 measures long. But I also already have 250 of the second act and am taking a small rest (rest indeed: during this rest I think I've continued to work at least several hours every day) devoted to revising the second act. I think it will be pretty good. Curiously enough, I work in exactly the same way: the final text is finished only during composition, indeed, sometimes not until afterwards. That works extremely well. Naturally, and you, too, must have experienced this, that's only possible if one already has a very precise overall concept, and the art lies not only in keeping this vision continually alive, but in further strengthening, enriching, and expanding it while working out the details! That should be recommended to all opera composers. Not that it would do much good! I'm going to do my best to finish the opera before returning to Berlin. It isn't going as quickly as I

1. The Schoenbergs were in Territet-Montreux from May until September.

2. The travel route Berg gave in his letter of 6 August was underlined in red, probably by Schoenberg.

3. A *Festschrift* had been compiled for Adolf Loos's sixtieth birthday on 10 December 1931 (*Adolf Loos Festschrift zum 60. Geburtstag*, Vienna, 1930), which included contributions by Schoenberg, Webern, and a nine-line double acrostic by Berg, in which the initial letters spelled "Adolf Loos" and the last letters spelled "Alban Berg."

had hoped in the beginning, when I counted on a daily <u>average</u> of 20 measures. My pace is much slower than that, although I was able to count on 25 measures a day in my previous opera. Principal cause: the libretto and the choruses. Just writing out the choral parts is such an effort and waste of time, even working out the 4–6 voice counterpoint is nothing by comparison. Then too, it has taken much more time than I expected to write out the entire full score as I go along, which is certainly time consuming. But it has the advantage that I'll be completely finished when the last note is composed. I'm afraid of only one thing: that by then I'll have forgotten everything I've written. As it is, I hardly recognize what I composed last year. And if it weren't for a kind of unconscious memory, which instinctively leads me back to the original train of musical and dramatic thought, I'd have no idea how the entire thing could have any organic coherence.

I am very interested in what you write about Stokowski and your mutual plans. All the more as I had thought of him, too, and had sent him word to this effect through Adolph Weiss, who was here several weeks ago. I don't know whether the message was delivered or not; at any rate: there has been no answer yet. But it doesn't really matter, since this time I'm bound and determined to take as long as necessary to secure a performance that will represent the work accurately.

You're absolutely right in wanting to avoid Vienna. But where will you go when it gets cold? Are you considering the south? How about the Dalmatian coast?

It really is almost inconceivable that again neither you nor Webern has been approached about a professorship at the Vienna Academy. But believe me: you needn't regret it; one day they'll be the ones to regret it!

I'm glad you heard Rosbaud's radio performance and his rebroadcast of my lecture. I heard it, too, quite by chance(!!). He really did it very nicely and with enthusiasm. Very touching, the way you describe your listening experience. It really is surprising to hear one's own voice, but I wasn't at all enamored of mine.—Yes, radio is a wonderful thing; but turning it off remains the greatest pleasure: when in an instant one can shake off the nightmare of these horrible, dreadful sounds and free one's ears again—that is deliverance not paid for too dearly with the preceding agony.

Thank the Lord, the mark crisis hasn't affected me yet. At the very moment it began, two students turned up, a Swiss and an American. With that I'll probably manage to survive the embargo for the time being. The American, however, has already quit, he returned to America because his mother-in-law suffered a stroke. But he had paid for a month and that was very welcome.

Now I've told you a great deal and hope you will write again soon. It is a great and marvelous surprise that your wife has learned too drive. Certainly you both seem to enjoy it. Give her my best. I take it she's finally in good health! Many affectionate regards, also from my wife,

Your Arnold Schönberg

## Berg to Schoenberg (typewritten letter)

Berghof, 27 August 1931

Dearest, best friend,

Your dear, dear letter made me extremely happy and I would have preferred to answer right away, but I was making a frantic effort at that stage of my "work," which was going very well just then, to put off everything for later, even a letter to you (though I'd much rather write that than music).

When we made our Salzburg trip we naturally thought of the possibility of combining it with one to see you in Switzerland. But the distances are very great, even for a motorist. From Kitzbühl, the place where we were closest to you, it is almost 700 km to Montreux. And since I don't like to drive more than 3 to 400 km a day (especially when these include tricky passes and completely unfamiliar roads), the driving time alone would have extended our three-day Salzburg trip by four days. And that was something I dared neither grant myself nor take from my work. For although I remain determined to work through the winter (far from Vienna: more about this later!), I already know there will be interruptions. For instance, Brussels and the "French" Wozzeck (I'll definitely skip the other opera houses), then there's the dentist in Vienna: a loose, but otherwise sound upper incisor has become so loose over the summer that it will have to come out sooner or later. After all, I can't very well go around with a gaping hole like that. Especially on the French Riviera, where we plan to go after our stay in Carinthia. Surely it is warm there a few months longer than here, and since it is supposed to be relatively inexpensive to live there (we're thinking of a small cottage somewhere off the beaten track where we can cook for ourselves) we have decided upon it. You know the area so well: can you perhaps suggest something? If not, we'd simply drive down there, find a hotel and look around. They say it's very easy to find something.

Since you'll probably be in touch with Stokowski about your new opera, I'd like to tell you something about my experience with the Americans: when the Curtis Institute acquired Wozzeck (both for its school and the Grand Opera Company associated with it),[1] it purchased all the parts for this purpose and paid U.E. 2,500 dollars (from which I, in consideration of the fact that performance royalties are quite low—80 to 100 dollars per performance—got 1,000 dollars instead of my quarter share of royalties; the American representative of U.E. received, if it's true: c. 600 dollars). Artistically, to the extent that they understand it, no effort was spared: Stokowski's achievement and that of the singers, but especially that of the orchestra, was impressive. The sets, on the other hand! à la Caligari film![2] And I fear that (with the exception of some brilliantly solved technical problems) everything else about the staging was inferior. Anyway, the stage director Wymetal, whom I met in Salzburg, made a very lightweight impression on me and I shudder to think that he is to stage Lulu. Obviously all the external trappings associated with such an "American premiere" ("sensational" buildup, publicity,* transfer of the entire production to New York in November, etc. etc.) can't be compared with European dimensions. EVERYTHING, however, that was done for the work (from artistic and logistical standpoints) was done without the slightest consideration, to say nothing of consultation with or even participation of the author: beginning with

1. The American Wozzeck premiere in Philadelphia on 19 March 1931 was a joint project of the Philadelphia Grand Opera, the Philadelphia Orchestra, and the Curtis Institute; Ivan Ivantzhoff sang Wozzeck and Anne Roselle sang Marie, and the sets were by Robert Edmond Jones. The Philadelphia Wozzeck production was given at the New York Metropolitan Opera on 24 November 1931.

2. Berg is alluding to the expressionistic film decor in Robert Wiene's Das Kabinett des Dr. Caligari (1920).

LEOPOLD
STOKOWSKI
CONDUCTING
PHILADELPHIA GRAND OPERA

*The cover of the program booklet for the New York performance of* Wozzeck *on 24 November 1931*

the cover of the program booklet, where over the figure of a dandy ("Wozzeck in the *Wunderbar*") there loomed only the giant letters: Stokowski . . . . . right up to the half-hour radio broadcast of the second act, which, since the act is longer than half an hour, broke off in the middle of a measure.—

Much as I appreciate Stokowski (from recordings) and know that he stands head and shoulders above the European conducting giants, it is also clear to me that he is consumed with boundless vanity. As when he prohibited curtain calls at the premiere, so that the inevitable premiere applause went exclusively to him, who for this performance had had a podium built so high above the orchestra that he obscured half the stage . . . . . . and therefore he naturally does not welcome the interference or even presence of the composer. And the whole opera company, which sees him as a God, thinks the same way. The leading personalities of this institute (among them, Mrs. Curtis-Bok, one of the richest women in America)[3] were quite taken aback when Hertzka (who was over there) suggested they invite me to the premiere of *Lulu*. And yet they are the ones who have done everything to acquire this "World Premiere Performance" (which really isn't mine to give since I promised it to Kleiber long ago).

But I'm not worrying about it at this point, since I can't even see an end yet to the work on *Lulu*; I'm only telling you this in such detail because you may soon find yourself in a similar situation with your new opera and I can imagine that unlimited influence is more important to you than anything else and that you will want to secure it for yourself in time.

I am very happy that you liked my contribution to the Loos book. I found it incredibly difficult to follow the constraints of the given initial and final letters of

3. Mrs. Mary Louise Curtis-Bok, daughter of the magazine and newspaper publisher Cyrus H. K. Curtis, was a well-known patron of the arts and founder of the Curtis Institute of Music in Phildelphia in 1924, of which she was the president until her death. She contributed $40,000 toward the *Wozzeck* production.

each verse line, while adhering strictly to the distich meter, especially when you bear in mind that (aside from foreign words and names) there are only circa[4] two, three words that end on a. *[Berg responds to Schoenberg's opinion on lower and upper case Du.]*

I just received a letter from Ernst Schoen[5] (Frankfurt) wherein he writes:

> Since I am considering publishing the lecture you broadcast (on *Wozzeck*, on the occasion of the premiere there[6]) along with that of Arnold Schönberg, I take the liberty of politely asking whether you would consent to this and under what circumstances. Arnold Schönberg has already given us his permission.**

Since I can't imagine how he proposes to do this publication (if only because of the many musical examples that illustrate the lecture) and since (AS ALWAYS) I would like to act in conformity with you, I'd very much like to know—if you wouldn't mind—under what conditions you gave your permission for the publication. Is this request very presumptuous? I'm afraid it is. But this is really a case where I might do the wrong thing unless I discussed it with you![7]

And now farewell, my dearest friend. Again many, many thanks for your letter, which really made me enormously happy, and all our love to you and your dear wife!

Your Alban Berg

Even if I didn't respond to that part of your letter: I practically devoured (with greedy eyes) the news of your work.

Thanks also for that, dearest friend!

*[concerning a paper tear on page 1:]*
(SORRY! The typewriter did that!)

*for example, special trains from New York, Washington, etc., with giant placards in the stations, and on the locomotives and cars bearing the words: WOZ-ZECK TRAIN.

**It would naturally be appealing if for Schoen Berg does something that Schönberg also does.

---

4. Berg underlined the ending letter "a" (in two words, *etwa* and *da*) in allusion to the ending letter "a" needed to spell his own name in the double acrostic for Adolf Loos.

5. Director of the Frankfurt radio.

6. The Frankfurt production of *Wozzeck* was premiered on 19 April 1931 under Hans Wilhelm Steinberg.

7. Schoen had first written Berg concerning the publication of his lecture on 22 August 1931, to which Berg replied on 9 September. Schoenberg responded to Berg's question (repeated in a birthday letter of 10 September) in a postcard dated 12 September 1931, telling him that he had agreed with Schoen in principle but knew no details. Nothing came of the plan.

## Schoenberg to Berg (postcard)

Territet-Montreux, 12 September 1931

Dearest friend,

My cough was bothering me so much recently that I had to call a doctor, who strongly recommended I spend a winter in the south.[1] What if we were to go to the same place. Since we both have work to do and I play tennis and you go driving, I certainly wouldn't disturb you! But I think (at least for me): we would be good company for one another in our free time!—I have been prescribed a dry, warm climate (Biskra, Ajaccio, Rouck). But I just got a letter from Gerhard[2] in which among other things he describes living conditions in Spain (Catalonia, Barcelona, where it is apparently absolutely calm).[3] Life there is supposed to be extraordinarily cheap (hotel 10 schillings a day). And it is beautiful there.—What do you think; wouldn't you both like to go there, too?—I don't insist on Spain if we can agree on something else. But I think it would work out particularly well and I have often thought of it. Answer me soon so that I won't have to decide beforehand.—Many sincere thanks for your kind birthday greetings. I'm amazed that you are always able to remember it, while nothing works for me.

So: maybe we'll see each other! Many warmest regards

Your Arnold Schönberg

---

1. Schoenberg's renewed request for extension of his contractual 6-month vacation was to cause friction with the Prussian Academy.

2. The Spanish composer Roberto Gerhard studied with Schoenberg in Vienna and Berlin 1923–28; at this time he taught at the Ecola Normal de la Generalitat in Barcelona.

3. Spain had only recently been declared a republic.

*Berg to Schoenberg (two picture postcards: landscape photos: Dolomites, Grödner-Joch, 2,200 m)*

[Berghof] 19 September 1931

Dearest best friend,

How wonderful! I had no idea you could take time off during the Berlin winter; otherwise I would have thought of the idea myself. Please choose the place <u>yourself</u> where we should go. The main thing is that it's <u>warm</u> (and that is probably even <u>more</u> the case in the regions you mentioned than on the French Riviera, which we only selected, despite the not very hospitable winter, because we are not so well informed about other places).

Please be so kind as to let me know when you have decided and know something more definite. We will be here until the 28th and after that, until our trip to Leipzig[1]— thank God, only a short time—in Vienna, where, as I read in the *Neues Wiener Journal*, in the newly renovated and in all likelihood ruined Café Museum, "composers, performing artists, and critics: Dr. Julius Korngold, Alban Berg, Bella Paalen,[2] and her colleague Hadrabova,[3] sit together in perfect harmony. . . . ."[4]

Oh! How we look forward to getting away from this Vienna, from this Café Museum (with the emphasis on the word "Café")* and to be together with you somewhere in Spain or Corsica. . . .

1. Berg attended the final rehearsals and Leipzig premiere of *Wozzeck* on 11 October.

2. The alto Bella Paalen was a member of the Vienna State Opera 1906–37.

3. The soprano Eva Hadrabova was a member of the Vienna State Opera 1928–36.

4. M.Z., "Künstler hinter Spiegelscheiben" (Artists Behind Plate Glass), *Neues Wiener Journal* of 17 September 1931.

Please: keep me informed; of course I will let you know my whereabouts and plans at all times. Until then, our most affectionate regards to you both!

Your Berg

*Vienna seen as nothing *but* a museum of cafés

## Berg to Schoenberg

Vienna, 20 October 1931

Dearest best friend,

Returned home, I find your very dear card from Barcelona waiting for me—unfortunately also a letter I sent you a while back.[*1] "Unfortunately" because you must have thought I had left you in the dark about my current plans. However, I hope you received my Leipzig card.[2]—

Yes, when will we join you? I found an enormous number of time-consuming matters here (family related), which have to be attended to. Then: two days after my return (days with nothing but aggravation) I was again overcome by a severe gallstone attack (after almost half a year). Now the treatments must begin all over again. In addition, I am presently ill with the flu as well.

So that settles things for the next few weeks. You can imagine our irritation: the memory of my work, which was going so well—indeed: even the memory has almost vanished; this morning it was 0° (zero degrees [Centigrade]), and added to that, these despised Viennese surroundings! Instead of being in the sunny south now: partly at work and partly in your dear company, of which we've been deprived for so long.

The only consolation: we have, of course, not given up hope that it will still be possible this winter; after all, the winter is long.

It was quite nice in Leipzig:[3] the wonderful orchestra (which Brecher,[4] who is very impressive, has kept in hand through years of work) was ultimately really very beautiful (from the dress rehearsal on). And since the voices, too, were very beautiful and in the end even the stage direction came off without a hitch, I could be quite satisfied. Also with the audience response.

Zurich too (Kolisko!) went quite well.[5]

It was a very great disappointment to me that the performance of your *Lichtspielmusik* was canceled:[6] it would have been so important for me to become acquainted with the orchestration of your latest works; I had so very much looked forward to the rehearsals and performance under Webern.

1. The Schoenbergs sent an undated picture postcard from Barcelona, whose blurred postmark reads October 1931; they arrived in Barcelona earlier that month and moved into a small villa overlooking the Mediterranean. Berg's returned letter was probably the one dated 1 October.
2. A picture postcard from Leipzig, dated 11 October 1931, the day of the Leipzig performance of *Wozzeck*.
3. The Leipzig production was conducted by Wilhelm Schleuning and directed by Walter Brügmann; the soloists included Karl August Neumann as Wozzeck and Ella Flesch as Marie.
4. The German opera conductor Gustav Brecher was General Music Director of the Leipzig Opera 1924–33.
5. The 17 October *Wozzeck* production in the Zurich Stadttheater was conducted by Robert Kolisko.
6. On 18 October Webern was to have conducted a radio program that included Schoenberg's *Begleitungsmusik zu einer Lichtspielszene*, Op. 34, but the concert was canceled due to Webern's illness.

As soon as my situation has changed somewhat, I'll write again. Until then we send you both a thousand regards!

Your Berg

I will keep Gerhard's letter to you for the time being.[7]

*which I enclose

---

7. Roberto Gerhard had written a detailed letter to Schoenberg on 20 September, which Schoenberg enclosed in his letter to Berg of 24 September.

## Schoenberg to Berg[1]

Barcelona, 23 October 1931

Dearest friend,

It's a real shame that you've done this to yourself. You could have been here by now and would have been further along in your work! You shouldn't—don't be angry if I take the liberty of meddling, my wife will be very upset with me for it. But who is to advise you but I, who knows from personal experience what it means to be interrupted?—you shouldn't let anything or anybody keep you from your work and should strive for only one thing: to do everything in your power for your health, the one superfluous thing one shouldn't neglect.

Yes: I, too, have to abstain entirely from cognac and alcohol. And you know what I say: "Smoking is work, a 'must'; drinking is a pleasure, a 'may.' " But I may not, and believe that if you have to worry about gallbladder attacks, there are things you continue to do from which you should abstain!!

So there: a sermon from the old professor!

---

So: you really want to come here? That would be very nice! What kind of accommodations do you want?

We have an unfurnished house: five small rooms, a small villa = 150 pesetas, that is 100 schillings a month. Rented furniture = 100 pesetas a month. We had to buy all the kitchen supplies. And linen (sheets, table cloths; utensils—you should bring all that along!!) We figure on 300 pesetas a month for the entire house: i.e., 200 schillings! We need 15 pesetas a day for food. Add heating and light to that. You certainly can't find anything cheaper on the Riviera. We have our maid along. It is very practical.

If you would like us to find you something, tell us exactly what you want. Then you can come, live a couple of days in the hotel and choose.

I won't write anything else today, since I assume we'll see each other soon.

If you like, have Trudi give you the libretto (⅔) of *Moses und Aron* and send it to me when you've read it. But don't show it to anyone else. Especially not to Herr Reich, who is a big blabbermouth and already has several indiscretions on his conscience for which I'd gladly give him 25 lashes.* Many affectionate regards, also to your wife, also from my wife.

Your Arnold Schönberg

*I'm just afraid he'd give the papers a false report: that I boxed his ears

---

1. The original of this letter is located in the Pierrepont Morgan Library.

## Schoenberg to Berg (postcard)

Barcelona [17 November 1931]

Dearest friend,

I have long wanted to thank you for the encyclopedia,[1] but just can't get around to writing a letter. So for now accept this card with my best thanks. The encyclopedia is something I have splendid use for. I often need something like that on my trips! So: many thanks.!—Now what's up: are you coming?—What's wrong with Webern?[2] Is he really so ill. Or is it basically just the result of aggravation and excitement?—I am working a lot and making slow but steady progress: I have already finished almost 900 measures of Act II and hope it won't be more than another 300: for that I'll need 5–6 weeks at my present pace (full score and libretto!). Have you already read my libretto? My health is somewhat better. But it gets worse every time the weather does! I hope it will soon be warm.—

Many affectionate regards

Your Arnold Schönberg

But when it's nice we have a good deal of sun.

---

1. Berg sent Schoenberg a *Konversationslexikon* on india paper.
2. Webern wrote to Schoenberg on 13 November, describing both his illness and a controversy that had arisen over the programming of a sacred cantata (Bach's Cantata No. 106, *Actus Tragicus*) on the Socialist-oriented Worker's Symphony concert. Webern, after conducting the last rehearsal on 31 October, became too ill to conduct the performance, which was taken over at the last minute by Erwin Leuchter and Oswald Kabasta.

## Berg to Schoenberg

Vienna, 10 December 1931

Dearest friend,

I haven't written for so long because I felt downright embarrassed at having nothing but negative news for you. However, I am <u>even more</u> embarrassed now at having left your dear card unanswered so long, so I will overcome the first shame to give you after all——nothing but negative news:

I know absolutely nothing about our coming—or in general about our trip south. The Brussels *Wozzeck* performance was postponed until January, so I've not only lost December, but have to wait until January now before I can get away. In the meantime there have been all kinds of things to detain me, such as a trip to Zurich I had to make*[1] because there is a possibility that the *Wozzeck* production there may be done as a guest performance in Geneva at the next League of Nations meeting.[2] (Incidentally: <u>Kolisko</u> managed to bring off a surprisingly good performance).

Then I recently had to go to <u>Munich</u> as a juror of the ADMV (the Music festival

---

1. Berg traveled to Winterthur, where he was the guest of Werner Reinhart, to attend a 15 November performance of *Wozzeck* in Zurich under Robert Kolisko. On 18 November he attended a concert conducted by the Swiss conductor Ernest Ansermet, whom he also consulted about his setting of the original French text of *Der Wein*.
2. This did not come to pass.

is in Graz this year).[3]

And in addition to that, Vienna's so-called cultural life: from the horrors of innumerable Schalk memorial events[4]—in which my only participation was to turn down invitations with suitably acerbic letters—to a very nice reunion with Gerhart Hauptmann, who was in Vienna recently on the occasion of an outstanding performance of *Fuhrmann Henschel*.[5]

I'd rather not talk about what lies between.—

II. I still haven't read your new libretto. Greissle promised it to me long ago and I am expecting it any day—any day for weeks now. I am very excited at the prospect. I'd like to say: my only consolation during this unproductive period is that this work is being written, indeed, that perhaps at this very moment Act II is finished or close to it. What you must be feeling!!! And that you are in such a location, with such a climate, that too is consolation for me here in a Vienna drowned in snow and mud!

III. As you know, Webern is presently in Berlin and the jury meeting of the ISCM (which will hold its festival in Vienna this year), from which you will gather that he is fairly well again.[6] Unfortunately I'm not in a position to give you an accurate description of his illness. It would be easier [to give you] an idea of his symptoms, which were similar to the others we have often observed in Webern's life. No doubt there is something physically wrong (small intestine); but I, who can't help believing that "there are only mental illnesses," continue to suspect (I tell you this in strict confidence:) that here too the decisive factor is psychological. Of course it goes much deeper, that is: it has much deeper causes than the aggravation and excitement of the last Worker Symphony Concert. Webern could have coped with it easily if it hadn't been for the fact that again (these last months) he has been so consumed with the idea that he "is not a conductor," but a composer, that already he canceled various engagements for the summer and fall (Salzburg, London, Vienna Radio concert, an American concert in Vienna).[7] Of course there was always some justification (too few rehearsals, a disagreeable soloist, lack of time, and the like), since he isn't a career conductor and therefore can and must reject everything a career like that includes.

But how can one help him???!

For despite **many** really wonderful successes recently as a composer, he will always

3. The ADMV music selection committee met on 20 December in Munich, but illness prevented Berg from attending. The 61st Music Festival of the ADMV was to take place 10–14 June in Zurich, not, as originally planned, in Graz. The Schoenberg circle was represented on the festival program by songs by the Berg student Hans Erich Apostel.

4. Franz Schalk died on 3 September.

5. A new production of Gerhart Hauptmann's play *Fuhrmann Henschel* had opened in the Volkstheater on 12 December 1931, with Emil Jannings in the title role.

6. Following this collapse on 31 October, Webern spent two weeks in a sanatorium, after which he left for Berlin for the ISCM selection committee meeting; the tenth ISCM festival was to take place in Vienna 16–22 June 1932.

7. Among Webern's canceled conducting engagements was a popular concert in London for the BBC on 20 July (which would have allowed him to attend the ISCM festival performance of his Symphony, Op. 21, one week later); Webern turned this down ostensibly for financial reasons. He was also slated to conduct a concert of American music on 15 November, but the concert, featuring works by Carl Ruggles, Charles Ives, Aaron Copland, Alejandro Caturla, Henry Cowell, Wallingford Riegger, Carlos Chavez, and Adolph Weiss, was rescheduled for 21 February 1932.

need help![8]

I hope we'll finally make it to Barcelona, where we can discuss this at length; naturally this situation with Webern affects me very, very deeply and I often wish I had your advice in the matter.—AS IN ALL THINGS!

And now we send you both a thousand regards.

Your Berg

Please drop me a line again sometime.

*I spoke at length about you, dearest friend, with Ansermet, who also happened to be there!

---

8. Webern had a number of important performances in 1931, although these were by no means all successful. His string Quartet, Op. 22, was premiered by the Kolisch Quartet in the first all-Webern concert on 13 April 1931 in Vienna; on 8 May Webern conducted a concert in London that included Schoenberg's *Begleitungsmusik zu einer Lichtspielszene*, Op. 34, and his own Five Movements for String Quartet, Op. 5, in a string orchestra arrangement. His Symphony, Op. 21, had received poor reviews after the Berlin performance under Otto Klemperer on 10 April, but was given a more successful performance under Scherchen at the ISCM festival in London on 27 July.


*Berg to Schoenberg*

Vienna, 23 December 1931

My dearest friend,

Yesterday I finally got your manuscript and hastened to read and read it again today, and am sending it to you now posthaste, although I'm very sorry I can't read it a few more times.

It is so wonderful! What glorious thoughts, what supreme wisdom! And the organization! The wonderfully suspenseful, yet forthright style of Act I! Not to mention Act II. My God, what have we in store for us there! Just reading the stage directions is an unparalleled dramatic sensation. Truly: unparalleled! But what will the music be like!!! And to think, it already exists! One can't fathom it, can't even get close to imagining it . . .

The only sad thing, that the manuscript breaks off on page 34, indeed, in the middle of a word that I can't even complete with certainty: should it be *Ge-danken* [thoughts]?

Be that as it may: my thoughts during these holidays will be with your work and thus with you, my dearest friend! A thousand thanks

from your Berg

# 1932

*Berg to Schoenberg (typewritten letter)*

Vienna, 16 January 1932

Dearest friend,

I must write to you today in my capacity as member of the executive committee of the Vienna chapter of the ISCM. It concerns your refusal to allow a performance of your *Lichtspielmusik* at the Vienna Music Festival.[1]

Your refusal has greatly upset the Vienna chapter, particularly its president, Dr. Bach. Having to cancel your work, which is included in all the published programs, is regarded—particularly by Dr. Bach—as an international disgrace, for that fraction of the press hostile to the ISCM would inevitably seize on the fact of your refusal. In order to avoid that it was decided at yesterday's executive committee meeting (7 to 2: WEBERN, BERG), that it was necessary to write to you once more, so besides this letter of mine you can expect to receive 2–3 others regarding this matter.

Well, I won't pester you with it for long. I don't need to tell you that I would naturally have been very happy if performances of your works were to take place at this music festival. All the more so as for years I tried unsuccessfully to accomplish just that when I was a juror myself. You will remember that you always made your permission contingent upon Dent[2] being persuaded to apologize to you. I informed Webern of this before he went to Berlin for the jury meetings, and when he succeeded in this respect—in a way that was tantamount to Dent's moral annihilation—I really thought the matter resolved and considered it the solution of (for us chapter members) an untenable situation. I was as pleased then,—as I now regret that it didn't succeed.

Of course I am well aware, dearest friend, that my regret cannot and will not change your mind; even if Dent's expected letter of apology does arrive; I have read the six irrefutable points in your letter to Webern, and at our committee meeting yesterday I continually emphasized the futility of attempting to change your mind. If I write notwithstanding, it is due solely to my membership in this Vienna chapter, which really had the best intentions this time, but certainly finds itself in a very awkward situation now.

1. For an explanation of Schoenberg's anger with the ISCM, see footnote 2 to Berg's letter of 3 February 1928. An extensive correspondence—primarily between Webern and Schoenberg—developed in 1932 regarding the performance of a Schoenberg work under the auspices of the ISCM.
2. The English musicologist Edward Dent was the first president of the ISCM, 1923–38.

Enough of that! I kept meaning to write of late, but am embarrassed at repeatedly having to tell you that I still can't get away from Vienna: next week the Philharmonic is doing my 3 String Pieces from the *Lyric Suite* (Clemens Krauss)[3] and the Brussels premiere of *Wozzeck* takes place (finally) at the end of February. In the meantime—especially during the entire Christmas holidays—we've been ill with this and that and so have lost weeks of time even in that respect.

How are you both? I hear that you were ill, too; I hope you have completely recovered! But I have heard nothing else of you for a long time, dearest friend; the most recent was a card in late November. Please write me another such card sometime about your work, your health and about your dear wife and how you like it in Barcelona. I hope you've received my various letters and packages[4] (most recently your libretto).

And if you do drop me a line, please tell me that you're not angry with me for pestering you with this tiresome chapter matter. In any event you'll give Dr. Bach your final decision, who is also writing to you today.

Now our most affectionate regards to you and your wife!

Your Alban Berg

---

3. On a Philharmonic concert of 23 and 24 January; also on the program were Strauss's *Don Juan* and Bruckner's Eighth Symphony.

4. For Christmas Berg had sent Schoenberg an undated card as well as several books and a score of *Der Wein*, which had appeared in November.

*Schoenberg to Berg (letter, partially typewritten)*

Barcelona, 19 January 1932

Dearest friend,

You are absolutely right: it really is shameful that not only did I not thank you for your marvelous gift, but that I also left you in uncertainty as to whether I had received it. It would surprise me if you could muster the restraint not to think the worst of me. To be honest, I would be very indignant.

And yet: I can be excused to some extent. Particularly because I was ill again and had to give up smoking. Furthermore, I haven't made any real progress in my work for more than a month. I seem to be a bit overworked and that makes me very ill-tempered. Nonetheless I have not been idle recently and that's the damnable thing. Instead of resting completely for 2 or 3 weeks, I worked on other things: above all I have reworked the text of the conclusion of Act II several times (it is pretty definitive now so long as the vocal writing doesn't create new requirements), then there were articles that turned out badly, countless "diary pages" (theoretical, personal, etc.), and finally a few canons, of which I'll send you one sometime. At least for now my health is better. I have gotten terribly fat; since I don't smoke I'm always hungry! But I hope I've reached the climax (if one can speak of a stomach in those terms) and at any rate I want to slim down again now. Maybe then the work will go better too.

Now about those presents: first I must say that I was most pleased with the full score of your *Wein*: (it is a wine I drink with my eyes:[1] a <u>fabulous score to look at</u>). I look into it often and already know many passages quite well. A very beautiful piece!—

*[typewritten:]*

Your letter regarding the ISCM matter just came. I must say first of all: it is a mistake to think I would accept an apology from Herr Dent. He has already sent me one (thoroughly inadequate, by the way!!) and I explained then that I do not accept it. But I believe I also said (and if I didn't do it then, I do so now; anyway let it be said—once more—here:) I would consider a reconciliation only if Herr Dent were hounded out of the executive committee in ridicule and disgrace: even then, however, I would also set conditions to the remaining members of the committee.

As you can see I do not expect a reconciliation, nor do I desire one.

I ask that you make the relevant portions of this letter known to the ISCM. Very likely I won't answer either of the announced letters: my position is known; nothing should have been undertaken without asking me first. *[handwritten margin note:]* Why is the situation supposed to be so unfavorable for the Vienna chapter? They can cancel my work without a word and schedule another! Nobody would give a hoot.

$$- - - + + +OOO+ + +OOO+ + +OOO+ + + - - -$$

Now back to your *Wein* [literally, "wine"] (N.B. for a long time I've wanted to answer it with a Spanish champagne that is <u>very good</u> and dirt cheap; but I fear Austrian customs; there has been rather a stiff duty on everything we've sent so far. And it would be annoying to think one paid more for it there than here, which is quite possible with champagne.) Once again: I find the arrangement and instrumental disposition of this score of such extraordinary clarity that I want to emphasize this impression as something quite exceptional. I really know very few modern scores (mine included) of which I could say the same. I find the thematic ideas equally significant. Incidentally: what is the meaning of the retrograde repetition at rehearsal number 142?

I'm really extraordinarily pleased with the piece!

*[Schoenberg inquires regarding the production of the score of* Der Wein, *which was photo-reproduced rather than printed.]*

I would also like to thank you for the wonderful books and, but no, I must overcome the dilemma—I already own the principal work you gave me[2] and since I know how very expensive it is and how distressed you would be to have such a valuable gift lose its meaning in this way, and since, on the other hand, it is always awkward to mention it, I have put off my thank-you letter through abreaction or suppression or some other such psychoanalytically expressible means: now it's out. I very much regret that you give me such valuable gifts that I lack the talent and

---

1. Schoenberg is quoting from the first of the *Pierrot lunaire* melodramas, "Mondestrunken": "Den Wein, den man mit Augen trinkt."

2. As becomes clear from Berg's reply of 16 February, this was a history of the Jews, probably the three-volume edition of Dr. H. Graetz's *Geschichte der Juden*, entitled *Volkstümliche Geschichte der Juden*, first published in 1888.

imagination to reciprocate. It must be because I am never in a position to give you or Webern Christmas or birthday gifts. For I'm certainly not shabby or stingy. I really do lack the talent for giving. My wife thinks so, too, and it is probably true. It irritates me but I can't do anything about it. An illness for which there is no cure. Even given a larger income, nothing would occur to me that might—as I <u>imagine</u> it!!—give pleasure to someone else: and that is probably the reason!

The book about the Jesuits[3] is very interesting and is confirmation of a number of things I had already thought myself. Beyond that, however, it gives one a very vivid historical picture and I find that very valuable.

I have known for a long time that you wouldn't come here; let us say since about mid-October. I had very much looked forward to your being here. But I am most sorry that now, perhaps because of me (unconsciously handicapped by the thought that you really wanted to come here), you haven't gone anywhere. But I had the best intentions, and can never say more or ever say better on my behalf.

I received the libretto and was very happy with your response. I would like to have shown you two stages of the project: for after you read the 2$^{nd}$ act I revised it a few more times and you would certainly be amazed how sweeping these changes are (though in keeping with the central idea). But I would have had to copy out a large portion and unfortunately I didn't do that: now it is too late, because the repeated changes have eradicated all intermediate stages.—Do you think that Krauss can do your *Lyric Suite*? From what I've seen, it is extraordinarily difficult for the strings: is he even aware of that? He is also supposed to do my Chamber Symphony this year: or has it already been done? However, since I did it with the Philharmonic recently he can't ruin it completely.[4]—

I would be interested in your impression of the <u>Golden Calf</u> scene, with which I had a great deal "in mind." It will probably run to a good 25 minutes. But I think there's enough going on so that the audience will get its money's worth, even if it understands absolutely nothing of all I meant to say. But: is it at all intelligible? I would very much like to know—if you can remember.

It is true that we were ill. But we're both better now.

Well! I have blathered on like an old woman and have no idea what this letter will look like. So for now: Many affectionate regards to your wife and you, also from my wife

Your Arnold Schönberg

*[Schoenberg adds a postscript regarding upper- or lower-case* Du.*]*

---

3. Rene Fülöp-Miller's three-volume *Macht und Geheimnis der Jesuiten* (Grethlein & Co.: Leipzig, 1929).

4. Krauss did not perform Schoenberg's Chamber Symphony during the 1931/32 season.

*Berg to Schoenberg (letter with landscape photograph)*

Hofgastein, 16 February 1932

My dearest, dearest friend,

Your long letter (of 19 January) made me deliriously happy. Believe me: no

Christmas gift, however practical, valuable, or thoughtfully selected could have made me as happy as this letter of yours. In the time since I wrote the *Wein* aria, there couldn't have been anything more beautiful than your praise of the score. That has been no more than 2½ years; but consider that it has taken almost 25 to get from my first score, which met with your devastating criticism (I was supposed to orchestrate a Beethoven sonata movement[1] and the results were atrocious!) to this last one, which has won the highest acclaim there is: yours.

The return of the retrograde repetition after the II[nd] song is supposed to correspond to the return from the realm of this song to that of the III[rd] song, which is the same as that of the first. If I had the aria here I could demonstrate this with the text.

[*Berg responds to Schoenberg's questions regarding the production of the score of Der Wein.*]

Yes, we have finally buried our Barcelona plan. You are so right: because we always had this months-long sojourn in Barcelona in mind we never even considered the kind of shorter absences from Vienna that would have been possible now and again, and as a result we didn't get away at all. That is to say: until now. But even this isn't the answer. I've been alone a good portion of the few weeks I've spent here; Helene had to return to Vienna on account of her brother. That, too, is a persistent cause for our immobility: complications of her mother's estate, who died almost a year ago, the sale of the family house and part of the Trahütten property, moving, etc., etc., repeatedly require our presence in Vienna. Helene is there even now. We came here 4 weeks ago at the invitation of dear friends who have a spa hotel here. Gladly: because there was just enough time between the Vienna Philharmonic Concert and Brussels, 2. because the wonderful baths couldn't hurt us, 3. because I certainly don't wish to be in Vienna, and 4. because it made it possible for me to work. 5. because it is wonderful here, particularly now: granted, instead of 20° of warmth as in Barcelona, here there is 20° of cold: but during the day the temperature climbs to such an extent that by midday the thermometer often reads 30–40° in the sun (which shines for hours upon this snowy landscape from a deep blue cloudless sky).

I have also managed to do some work. Unfortunately I don't have a piano and the baths and walks are very fatiguing, so the work didn't go as well as I had a right to expect after the long interruption. But I have decided a good deal more concerning the text and musical disposition, and hope to be able to continue from there in March. Now I have to go to Brussels, where the first French performance of *Wozzeck* takes place on the 29th and the Chamber Concerto on 1 March.[2] The Pro Arte people did the latter last year and are repeating it this year at their 10th anniversary

---

1. Probably the last movement of Beethoven's Piano Sonata, Op. 10, No. 3, for which a version for string quartet exists among exercises Berg prepared under Schoenberg.

2. The *Wozzeck* production at the Theatre de la Monnaie in Brussels was conducted by Corneil de Thoran.
   The Chamber concerto was performed by the Pro Arte Orchestra under Arthur Prevost, with Godelieve Mathys (violin) and Paul Collaer (piano); the program also included works by Darius Milhaud, Henri Saugeut, and Igor Stravinsky.

concert; I'll have my fill of rehearsals to conduct or attend during these 8–10 days.— The 3 String Orchestra Pieces *(Lyric Suite)* went relatively well in the Vienna Philharmonic concert. There were 3–4 rehearsals, the orchestra made an enormous effort, and some things were surprisingly successful. Of course Clemens Krauss's interpretive ability is very limited. And even when he devotes diligence and enthusiasm to something, it doesn't help much. For next season's programs, instead of your planned Chamber Symphony, he is now airing the idea of doing the Orchestra Pieces (Peters), which I personally consider very sensible: I rather believe there's a better chance that he bring off an acceptable performance of the orchestra pieces than of the Chamber Symphony, of which one can expect a level of perfection these days that probably eludes Clemens Krauss in any music.

Imagine my bad luck: I couldn't hear (or just barely) your *Lichtspielmusik*.[3] the Vienna station is too weak for a morning broadcast from Vienna to come through clearly. Even though there is an excellent radio here (Telefunken 1932 from Siemens Halske) (recently, for instance, I had excellent reception for my Chamber Concerto from Prague).[4]—

I wonder how much further along you are on your opera since you last wrote (a month or so ago)! How I'd love to see the changes in the text of Act II! All the more as I was only able to see the libretto so briefly. That's why I got only a vague idea of the philosophical background, what was "meant," for example, with the golden Calf scene. Particularly because when I read it the first time I mainly had the purely theatrical in mind. And from this standpoint I must say that it will be the strongest half hour the operatic stage (indeed any stage) has ever known. I'm sure I'm not wrong there! But you, whose mind conceived the entire eternity of this half hour, probably know that best yourself!—

Apropos the *History of the Jews* I gave you: if it doesn't complicate matters too much and you don't have any other use for it, I would gladly take it back, I would like to own it myself: it wouldn't be necessary to "exchange" it and I would be very happy to send you something you don't already have. If it is not too much trouble, send me the book as printed matter or tell me what you plan to do with it. I'll be back in Vienna in early March.—

What are your plans for the near future? Are you staying in Barcelona much longer? This is probably the most beautiful time there. Oh! how we wish we could be there: I can't bear to think of it!

I hope you are both quite, quite well! Give your wife my warmest regards. All my love to you, and again my heartfelt thanks for your letter and the lovely picture!

Your Berg

---

3. In a Vienna radio concert on Sunday, 31 January, Webern conducted the Vienna Symphony Orchestra in performances of Schoenberg's *Begleitungsmusik*, Op. 34, and Brahms's Serenade in D major.

4. Berg's Chamber Concerto was broadcast from Prague on 1 February 1932 in the last season concert of the Society for New Music; the conductor was Otakar Jeremiáš and the soloists were Dr. Václav Holzknecht (piano) and Frantisek Daniel (violin). Also on the program was Berg's Piano Sonata.

*Berg to Schoenberg*

Berghof, 26 August 1932

My dearest friend,

I haven't written for over two months. And now I ought first to try and explain how such a long break could come about. But even if I succeeded with such an explanation (many pages in length), that wouldn't excuse the lapse; so I had better admit right away that all apologetic explanations aside, my not having written even once these past 2 summer months, my not having found: one or two hours to write to you about myself, is inexcusable. So just this request, which is dictated by the sincerest and most ardent hope: Forgive me! And the assurance (surely superfluous) that—as always—I think of you, my dearest, most esteemed friend, every day and often during each day: your photograph (my favorite picture of you) hangs above my desk; your Orchestra Variations, *Von heute auf morgen*, and the *Lichtspielmusik* lie on the piano and wherever I can, in letters and conversations (the latter with Kolisch, Stein, Heinsheimer, Director Winter[1]) I try to obtain news of you, and sorry as I am to think of you in Berlin's heated atmosphere,[2] I (and Helene too) nonetheless delight in the knowledge of your life with the sweet little baby.[3] This new happiness may have lit up your life in an entirely new way and I ponder constantly how I could make a little side trip to Berlin in the fall to spend a few days near this child and its dear parents. I mean: solely for this purpose and not in connection with concerts, rehearsals, meetings, etc.—

Perhaps I can grant myself that indulgence in the fall. For the time being I want to stay put here. Again I haven't accomplished as much (on my opera, where I am still in Act II) as I had initially hoped. In June* the work was going really well— then came the Vienna Music Festival, which was quite beautiful in many ways; the most beautiful were the 10 minutes of your *Lichtspielmusik* (Webern did a wonderful job!).[4] But then July and August were so hectic that it was very difficult to retain the proper concentration for work, and then only with frequent interruptions. My mentally ill brother-in-law, who was in Trahütten, again caused us a good deal of trouble. We drove back and forth between Trahütten and Berghof any number of times (no mean driving feat either, since it involves "clambering" over almost impassible Alpine passes each way). Whenever I was in Trahütten I got asthma, so finally Helene stayed there alone several times until I would bring her back across the Alps a few days later! (At present Helene is alone in Vienna, likewise on account of her brother and I'll be glad today when she has covered—all alone—the 360 km

1. After Emil Hertzka's death in May, Hugo Winter, Alfred Kalmus, and Hans Heinsheimer were made co-directors of U.E.

2. The National Socialists became Germany's second-largest party after the elections of September 1930. In order to combat rising unemployment and political and economic instability, the German Chancellor circumvented the Reichstag with a series of emergency decrees. With the summer elections of 1932 the Nazi Party won 37% of the vote and Adolf Hitler became a serious candidate for the chancellorship.

3. Nuria, their first child, was born on 7 May 1932 in Barcelona.

4. Schoenberg finally consented to the performance of *Friede auf Erden* and the *Begleitungsmusik* in a special concert of the Workers' Symphony Orchestra during the time of—but separate from—the ISCM festival. Also on the 21 June program were Berg's *Der Wein* (first Vienna performance) and Mahler's Second Symphony, all conducted by Webern; the concert was an unqualified success.

of the trip: I shall meet her in Klagenfurt.)

Finally I was ill for a week, too: during a walk along the country road I was attacked by a raging-swarm of wasps, who left me in a sorry condition (I had about 20–30 stings on my head, throat, neck, arms, legs): I even had to stay in bed a few days.

But there have been pleasant distractions, too. The whole area was full of acquaintances. Friends and acquaintances, some of whom one wants to see, some of whom one must see, were staying (some briefly, others longer) at each of the 3–4 Carinthian lakes. I'll mention some names:

Millstädtersee: Kolisch (and quartet), the Steuermanns,[5] the Gielens,[4] the Viertels,[7] Reich, the pianist Süsskind[8] (and for the fun of it I'll mention, "Frau Herschel," whom I naturally did not see),[9] Stein.

Wörthersee: Krenek, Intendant Ebert,[10] General Music Director Böhm (Hamburg),[11] Heinsheimer.

Fackersee: Prof. Strzygowsky

Ossiachersee: Director Winter (U.E.), Kapellmeister Ormandy (Minneapolis) and wife: Steffy Goldner (harp).[12]

Still planning to visit us on their trips through Villach: Alma Mahler, the Grafs (Frankfurt),[13] Scherchen.

. . . not to mention other Vienna acquaintances whom you don't know and whose names wouldn't mean anything to you.

Even though I always defer these encounters, some of which are **extremely** dear to me,** to the afternoon: they still represent some degree of distraction. Back when I wrote *Wozzeck* or the *Lyric Suite* in Trahütten, I really worked all day. Mornings at the piano, afternoons during long walks. Well! I hope to be able to concentrate again, even here, once the "season" is over and my family affairs have been settled.— — —

My account has turned into a confession. Even something of a "general confession"; for from what I've told you about my life these past 2 months, it may also sound like an attempt to excuse my 2 months' lapse in writing: whenever I decided to write a letter, there were always so many business letters to answer that the few one would enjoy writing, as well as the one I would have liked to write most, the one to you, remained unwritten.

5. Eduard Steuermann was married to the pianist Hilde Merinsky.

6. The German stage director Josef Gielen, father of the conductor Michael Gielen, was director at the Staatliches Schauspielhaus in Dresden from 1923 until 1934; his wife, Rosa, was Eduard Steuermann's sister.

7. The German poet and stage director Berthold Viertel was married to the actress Salome (Salka) Steuermann, Eduard Steuermann's sister.

8. The Czech conductor Hans Walter Süsskind (later known as Walter Susskind), began his career as a concert pianist; he had played Berg's Sonata in Prague the previous February.

9. Possibly the pianist Helene Herschel, who studied with Schoenberg 1917–20 and occasionally performed Berg's Piano Sonata.

10. The stage director Carl Ebert, director of the Berlin Städtische Oper 1931–33.

11. The young Austrian conductor Karl Böhm was General Music Director in Hamburg 1931–34.

12. The Hungarian conductor Euguen Ormandy emigrated to the U.S. in 1921. In 1922 he married the Hungarian harpist Steffy Goldner.

13. Herbert Graf, son of the critic Max Graf, directed the Frankfurt *Wozzeck* production the previous year. His wife was Lieselotte Austerlitz.

I repeat what I said at the outset of this epistle: forgive me!
And please believe in the unchanging devotion, friendship and love

of your Berg

Please give my best to your gracious wife.


*when we were here before; I wrote to you at the time.—
** particularly with Kolisch, whom I've seen frequently (in Millstadt and Velden):
he looks marvelous and feels great!


### Berg to Schoenberg

Berghof, 10 September 1932

My dearest friend,

I am sending you a three-volume novel[1] today, which represents a small token for your birthday. I consider this book to be more than mere "entertainment"; especially the chapters of volume III, dealing with the "Decline of Values"! The author is a schoolmate of mine, who only began writing 3–4 years ago and became "famous" overnight; he admires you enormously and once asked me to tell you of his admiration sometime. I'll take this wonderful opportunity of your birthday. All the very, very best from us!

Since I last wrote (about 2 weeks ago) something terrible happened here: a bottle of denatured alcohol exploded due to the carelessness of our maid[2] and Helene, who was standing right there, was badly injured. Severe burns over her entire face I$^{st}$ degree, thank God. Singed hair and eyelashes, swelling and infection of eyes, lips, etc.

Her right hand (with which she tore the burning apron from the maid, thus saving her from being burned) is even worse: partially II$^{nd}$ degree. It will be weeks, maybe months, before she has fully recovered and the last traces have vanished from her face.

You can imagine what she—(and I) have been through. . . . .

Farewell, dearest friend, and again accept our most affectionate wishes.

Your Alban Berg

All our love also to your dear wife.

---

1. Hermann Broch's *Die Schlafwandler* (1931–2).
2. Anna Lenz, a native of Trahtten, was a long-time employee of the Bergs and before that of the Nahowski family.


### Schoenberg to Berg (typewritten letter)

Berlin, 23 September 1932

Dearest friend,

I was dreadfully shocked by your wife's misfortune. To sacrifice oneself for the stupidity and carelessness of another! For surely it happened when the girl poured alcohol into a burning flame or something of the sort! We were paralyzed, my wife and I, when we read your letter. How fortunate that her facial injuries were not as severe. But the pain must have been terrible. Please let me know soon about your wife's condition and give her, from my wife and myself, our very best wishes for a quick and complete recovery and our hope that she regain her old pleasing appearance!!

I would also like to thank you very much for the beautiful birthday gift. Though I haven't had a chance to read it yet, your choice and your recommendation make me curious. Again many thanks and for myself I hope I'll finally have a suitable inspiration in time for your birthday, so I needn't always be the embarrassed recipient.

Apparently I haven't written for a very long time. I believe the main reason may have been my disappointment that all my encouragement did not suffice to persuade you to join us in Barcelona. After your initial assent I was very happy at the prospect, but then having to back away from it little by little unintentionally slackened communication between us. But it wasn't just that, but also my depression, no doubt related to my life in Berlin, which robs me of all pleasure in my work. More and more I am forced to concern myself here with the question whether and to what extent it is wise to count myself in this camp or that, whether it depends upon my volition, determination, inclination, or whether it is coercion. Naturally, even without the nationalist hints of the last few years, I know exactly where I belong. It's just that it's not as easy to switch places as one would imagine.—

*[handwritten:]*

—(typed letters are so hard to finish.—begun on the 23rd, I am continuing today—on the 26th(!))—

Of course I know exactly where I belong. It has been hammered into me so loud and so long that I would have had to be deaf, even before now, not to have understood the message. And the time for any regret on my part is long gone. Today it is with pride that I call myself a Jew; however, I am aware of the difficulties of really being one.[1]—

But enough of that: it is certain to come up again some other time.—

Only it's a pity that it seriously dulls my desire to work. Recently I have begun to sift through and organize my "literary output" (finished and unfinished). I figure it will amount to 1500 printed pages—perhaps more! That's 4–5 rather large volumes—in addition to the *Harmonielehre* and the volume already in print. I plan to publish part of it now—(much of it would be possible only after my death and that of others)—but no doubt it will be difficult, particularly today, to find a publisher with enough money (for such a solid investment). For I will only turn it over for a substantial down payment.—

Now I'm off to play tennis with Rudi. My wife and I find it is our greatest pleasure.—Write again soon. I will start writing more frequently again, too.

Again many best wishes for your wife's recovery; also—from my wife—and many warm regards

from your Arnold Schönberg

Why did you send your letter to the Academy????

---

1. Schoenberg's reassessment of his Jewishness was not of recent date but goes well back into the early twenties; in a letter to Wassily Kandinsky of 19 April 1923, for instance, he wrote of having been forced to realize what he will not again forget, namely "That I am not a German, not a European, indeed perhaps hardly a human being (in any case Europeans prefer the worst of their race to me), but rather, that I am a Jew."

## Berg to Schoenberg

Vienna, 13 December 1932

My dearest friend,

Now I'm settled in Vienna again for the next 3–5 months. The last 2 months have been a constant back and forth between Vienna, Graz, and Klagenfurt; in between I was also in Brünn[1] for a *Wozzeck* premiere (quite well done by a very young conductor, a former Horenstein rehearsal pianist)[2] we finally sold all of Trahütten and now actually own a little house on the Wörthersee. We are very happy with it: the house is so solid one could also live there in the winter; the lot is relatively large (12,000 square meters = over two *Joch*[3]), so we are undisturbed by neighbors. Because it lies on the so-called shady side [of the lake],

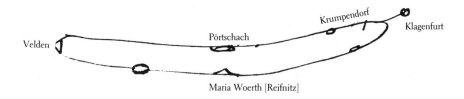

Maria Woerth [Reifnitz]

that is, not along the rail lines, not along the highway, I am far enough away from the tourist spots and nonetheless in a civilized area, which was not the case at Berghof, let alone Trahütten. Yet I am *right on* the lake, something I always wanted, on a *very* decent (but not very busy) country road, which will do my Ford good,* and quite secluded withall from everything that might disturb me in my work. The only problem is that it must also serve as the summer home for my "ward," Helene's brother.

We plan to go there early in the spring and make it habitable as soon as possible, so that I can resume composing. Since Helene's accident I have accomplished scarcely anything worth mentioning; but now I hope to have my head clear again for work. Helen's condition has improved surprisingly fast in the last 3–4 weeks and today, after 3½ months, it seems like a miracle to me (and to everyone who was there at the time and saw for so long the devastation wrought by the catastrophe)!

Forgive me for speaking only of myself. But I do so because that which is dearest to me: speaking of you, can only take the form of questions:

How are you and your dear wife and the little one?

Are you very busy? Students?

Do you find time to compose?

How much longer will you stay in Berlin?

What are your plans after that?

Are you still coming to Vienna to give a lecture in the "Kulturbund"?[4]

1. Now Brno.
2. The Brno production of *Wozzeck* on 6 December at the Deutsches Theater was conducted by Otto Ackermann.
3. One *Joch*, an antiquated Austrian surface measure, is equivalent to about 120 yards square. 12,000 square meters are approximately 3 acres.
4. Schoenberg had been invited to speak at the Vienna Kulturbund on 15 February.

WHEN?

And <u>what</u> will you talk about?

And <u>will</u> you be able to spend any time in Vienna, or even want to?

Oh, that would be lovely! I <u>must</u> see you again sometime: when I heard your chorus "Verbundenheit" the day before yesterday (for the first time):[5] I was truly heartsick with longing for you. To be sure, <u>this</u> is the kind of music that even one <u>not</u> so bound to you as <u>I</u> would be filled with deep melancholy at the sound of those mysterious triads. I say: mysterious because the <u>tone</u> of the music defies any attempt to define it <u>analytically</u>. "Bless you". . . . .

. . . and a thousand regards from us!

Your Alban Berg

All our love to your wife!

*which I have "garaged" for the winter with a light heart; for a car <u>in the city in the winter</u> without a chauffeur is just a burden.

---

5. Erwin Stein conducted "Verbundenheit," the sixth of the Pieces for Men's Chorus a cappella, Op. 35, in a concert of the Freie Typographia on 11 December.

*The Berg's summer home, the Waldhaus, on the Wörthersee (Archiv der Universal Edition, AG)*

# 1933

*Berg to Schoenberg*

Vienna, 25 January 1933

My dearest friend,

Believe me: for years I haven't been as happy as I was these last few days.[1] I thank you—and your dear wife sincerely and a thousand times—and ask you sincerely and a thousand times (if I don't see you again for a long time: say for a season or so) to allow me to make similar visits in the future. Of course I always knew it, but now I am more sure of it than ever: <u>I need that to live</u>! Now and again I need to be allowed to breathe the air of your study, which seems to me like the inside of a giant brain filled to bursting, to stand at your desk and to savor the other joys of your lovely home: your dear wife's warm, natural hospitality, the sight of the sweetest child in the world, whose very existence I regard as an immense <u>enrichment—of my life</u>.

To thank you for that, for <u>all of that</u>, but also for the wonderful binding machine, which really gives me a great deal of pleasure, is the principal motive for today's hasty letter.

Next: I trust your health is already much improved. I was so happy to be able to note the progress of your recovery on Monday and I hope that the telegram from the Academy, that you "were prevented from attending the election meeting" (I thereupon gave my vote to Hindemith, as advised) isn't to mean, God forbid, that you're feeling worse again.[2] Finally: enclosed the list of those invited to the banquet, which you will please approve and/or supplement.[3] Please send it right back to me: then, having copied it and added addresses, I shall send it to Dr. Jacobi.[4] She wants to know again whether your lecture will include <u>piano examples</u>. (She would particularly <u>enjoy</u> that!)

---

1. On 21 January Berg traveled to Berlin for a two-day visit with the Schoenbergs.

2. Due to ill health Schoenberg was unable to attend the meeting of the Prussian Academy of the Arts on 26 January, during which new members were elected. Schoenberg asked Heinz Tiessen to nominate Webern, who was, however, not voted in. Berg, also absent from the meeting, was represented by Paul Juon.

3. A banquet-reunion was planned for the evening preceding Schoenberg's 15 February lecture at the Kulturbund in Vienna. The list Berg enclosed is in the Berg Archive.

4. Jolande Jacobi was the executive secretary of the Austrian section of the European Kulturbund, an organization founded after World War I to foster inter-European cultural exchange.

Invitations to the informal dinner after the lecture (to be paid for by the individual) are, as usual, automatically extended to the members of the Kulturbund as well as to friends and acquaintances of the lecturer, which is why I need the approved list.

Again, many affectionate thanks to you and your dear wife! Get well soon and have a nice trip! And all our love to you all!

Your Berg

1 enclosure

## Schoenberg to Berg (card)

Berlin, 29 January 1933

Dearest friend,

Warmest thanks for your dear letter! It was a great pleasure for me at long last to be able to discuss things again; two (unfortunately only two) very beautiful days.— I still haven't been out and don't know yet whether I'll be able to travel to London.[1]—Maybe I'll just do what I can. Possibly Cologne (10th), Frankfurt (12th), and 13th–15th Vienna (on the 16th I may have to be in Brünn).[2]—Thank you for the list, I have added a few question marks. I fear that particularly on that last evening I won't be able to speak with anyone I like! And who knows when I'll be in Vienna again!—Are you very upset that I referred my old schoolmates to you without asking you first. But 1. I don't know anyone else; 2. you have Frau Schloss[3] at your disposal; and 3. and most particularly, I am hoping that your diplomatic skills succeed in keeping the reunion to a warm and cordial minimum that will allow me more time with those dear to me; and: you yourself told me about your disappointment of a similar reunion!—I, too, find this cultural evening a bother. It would have been nicer if only about 14–15 really close friends could have been together!

But what is one to do?

I must get back to work: the lecture and studying my Variations.

Many warmest regards, also to your dear wife

Your Arnold Schönberg

1. Schoenberg's planned trip to conduct a radio concert on 8 February was indeed canceled.

2. On 12 February Schoenberg gave a lecture on the Frankfurt Radio, in celebration of Brahms' 100th birthday, "Brahms, der Fortschrittliche" (revised and translated in 1947 as "Brahms the Progressive" and included in Schoenberg's collection of essays *Style and Idea*). He repeated his lecture in Cologne on the 10th and in Brno on the 16th. On 15 February Schoenberg spoke in the Konzerthaus, sponsored by the Kulturbund, on "Neue und Veraltete Musik, oder Stil und Gedanke," a lecture he had first given in Prague on 22 October 1930; it was first published in English in *Style and Idea* (New York, 1950), ed. Dika Newlin, under the title "New Music, Outmoded Music, Style and Idea." This was to be Schoenberg's last visit to his native city and the last occasion on which Berg and Schoenberg met.

3. Presumably related to Berg's student Julius Schloss.

*Berg to Schoenberg (typewritten letter)*

Vienna, 8 March 1933

My dearest friend,

I have just returned from Munich, where the jury meetings of the Allgemeiner Deutscher Musikverein took place.[1] Again the results were very meager from our point of view. Aside from Webern's old Orchestra Pieces (the six of Op. 6), I can really endorse only the acceptance of a string quartet by a certain Schacht, whom, to judge by the overall structure of his very appealing score, I take to be a direct student of yours.[2] Am I right? Otherwise the unavoidables, for example, Pfitzner, Braunfels, Reznicek, Franckenstein,[3] Wolfurt,[4] Lechthaler,[5] and consorts.

So I was rather depressed on my return from Munich, where Carnival, which was in full swing (oblivious to all Reichstag and other fires of the world[6]:) understandably had not cheered me. All the more do I prefer to think back to the days of your Vienna stay: that really was a series of holidays and—I'm not afraid to say it:— holy hours, for which I'd like to thank you after the fact with thousand affectionate words of gratitude.

And even though my concept of *Pelleas* differs from the way Scherchen did it,[7] my joy in the indescribable glory of the music is still somehow connected to the memory of those unforgettable "Schönberg days." When I say: "my concept differs" I refer mainly to the question of tempo. In <u>that</u> regard Scherchen is certainly very self-willed, not to say self-indulgent. To give just one example: he takes the Adagio (36) so fast from the outset that later, it <u>practically</u> turns into an Allegro, in which hardly one main voice, not to mention subsidiary ones, can be distinguished, but only a climactic buildup (though an intoxicating one played with thrilling vitality). On the other hand, the *"Gehende Bewegung"* of figure 59 becomes a decided Largo in which one can hardly follow the chorale, but which, on the other hand, brought out the indescribable <u>sonic</u> beauty of the passage more effectively than I had ever heard it before. That seems to be his forte anyway—especially with significant works—

1. Berg was in Munich from 26 February to 1 March. This was to be the last year of Berg's participation in events sponsored by the ADMV, which in early May of that year aked him to resign, on the grounds that he represented music not condoned by the state. The organization was itself disbanded four years later by the Minister of Propaganda, Joseph Goebbels.

2. Peter Schacht studied with Schoenberg at the Prussian Academy 1927–33; he was killed in World War II.

3. The German conductor and composer Clemens von Franckenstein was Generalintendant of the Munich Opera 1924–34.

4. The German composer and journalist Kurt von Wolfurt was secretary of the music division of the Prussian Academy of the Arts 1923–45.

5. The Austrian church composer Josef Lechthaler taught at the Vienna Academy 1924–38 and again after 1945.

6. On 27 February the German Reichstag (parliament) building in Berlin was set on fire, ostensibly by Marinus van der Lubbe, a Dutch Communist. The Nazis exploited the event to outlaw the Communist Party and issue another emergency decree that transformed Germany into a police state. The state of crisis was maintained until general elections in March, which gave the Nazis enough of a working majority in the Reichstag to pass the Enabling Bill that effectually annulled the constitution.

7. On 17 February Hermann Scherchen conducted a concert of *Pelleas und Melisande* with the Vienna Symphony Orchestra. Also on the program were Stravinsky's *Les Noces* and Hauer's *Wandlungen*.

that despite failing in the most important aspects, he achieves tremendous effects, as demonstrated by the colossal Viennese success, through exaggerated emphasis of less important details. In this he is similar, in my opinion, to the director Reinhardt[8]— and strangely enough, also in his ability to make weak pieces unexpectedly effective, as demonstrated, for example, with Hauer's very, very problematic music.

But the *Pelleas* performance was of the greatest importance for me for other reasons, too: just when I was discussing the work in my lecture series "on your music"[9] and though I had studied it thoroughly once (I still have the manuscript of a much more detailed guide, which U.E. didn't print because it was too long),[10] I discovered an abundance of new and wonderful things. And this is now happening with every opus I analyze, so that giving these lectures has become a real pleasure. In all there are three times four two-hour sessions: I. up to the F♯-minor Quartet, which I just got to (naturally including Opp. 12, 13, and 14), II. Opp. 11, 15, 16, 17, etc., up to and including 22, and III. Opp. 23 to 35.

By the end of April, beginning of May I will have concluded these lectures and then hope to be able to move to Carinthia. But until then I still have over 260 scores to look through for the Hertzka competition.[11] I shudder!

Have you heard that Webern's Mali is gravely ill:[12] in addition to her kidney stone problem she also has a serious case of septicemia. The past few days have been very critical, but they hope the worst is over.

Bittner's condition, however, is quite hopeless, his other foot will be amputated today.[13] I will keep you informed of the results of this life-threatening operation.

How are you, my dearest friend? Have you finally recovered from your flu? And how was Blunzi[14] when you got back? Please give us a word about her when you can: I really long for that child! We hope your dear wife is in the best of health!

In closing may I add, better said: repeat one more request: can and would you lend us (Webern and me) your Brahms lecture. We would read it right away and send it straight back. And not show it to anyone else if you don't want us to.

And now, farewell, dearest friend, and our very warmest regards to both of you!

Your Berg

I just heard that at the last minute they didn't operate on Bittner after all; they hope it can be avoided for the time being.

---

8. Max Reinhardt.

9. Berg's was holding these lecture-analyses privately in his home.

10. The manuscript of Berg's original *Pelleas* guide is located in the Berg Archive. His shortened thematic analysis was published by U.E. in 1920.

11. The Emil Hertzka Memorial Prize was to be awarded annually to a young composer of promise. The prize was first awarded in May 1933; the panel of judges included Berg, Webern, Krenek, Franz Schmidt, Erwin Stein, and Egon Wellesz, who decided to divide the prize of 2,500 schillings among five composers: Roberto Gerhard, Norbert von Hannenheim (both Schoenberg students), the Berg student Julius Schloss, the Webern student Ludwig Zenk, and the Pisk student Leopold Spinner.

12. Webern's oldest daughter Amalie (Mali) suffered from a recurrent kidney problem that necessitated various operations in the following years.

13. Julius Bittner began showing the first symptoms of diabetes in 1925, and by 1931 some of his toes had been amputated; the other leg was amputated later in 1933.

14. Nuria Schoenberg's nickname.

*Schoenberg to Berg (postcard)*

Berlin [20 April 1933]

Dearest friend,

Above all I return your Easter greetings and wishes most heartily and ask that you also pass them on to your wife.[1] I did indeed receive your letter with the news about your course. It would interest me very, very much to know what you are saying. I know the thoroughness and resourcefulness you are capable of devoting to such analyses. I would have liked to write to you about that, too; for I'm very pleased that you are able to take time for such things. And it is very flattering for me that you study my works in such detail. I wish I could do that, too: that is, repay you in kind.—I plan to begin my vacation soon, for the cold, unpleasant weather is again beginning to affect my catarrh adversely. Probably we'll go to Spain again. It is still very uncertain whether I'll go to Florence for the Music Congress.[2] What for? To listen to lectures on things that don't interest me? I myself haven't been asked to say anything. I'm needed as audience.—My 1st String Quartet will be played there later.[3] But in Turin there was apparently unrest during a performance of it, though a good deal of applause at the end as well. In any event it is indicative of the audience's attitude there toward my music, which could probably be equated with their attitude toward German music. Will anything of yours be performed?—Write to me again soon. Many warmest regards

Your Arnold Schönberg

---

1. Berg sent Easter greetings in a picture postcard from Vienna, postmarked 15 April 1932.

2. An International Music Congress took place in Florence 30 April to 4 May in conjunction with the first Maggio Musicale; a number of lecture-discussions were scheduled in addition to musical events. Though no work of his was performed, Berg attended and was pleased at the reception given him by his colleagues; Schoenberg did not attend.

3. Schoenberg's First String Quartet, Op. 7, was performed at the third chamber music concert of the Florence Congress by the Kolisch Quartet; also on the program were a quartet by Vito Frazzi and Béla Bartók's Third String Quartet. During this first Italian tour, the Quartet also performed Schoenberg's First String Quartet in Milan and Turin.

*Schoenberg to Berg (picture postcard: Paris-Place de l'Opéra)*

Paris [20 May 1933]

Dear friend,

I have begun this year's vacation.[1] The first leg brought us as far as Paris; perhaps we'll go on to Spain next if something comes of my concerts there: a question of money! As long as I have my salary it's all right.[2] I hope to find a publisher for my

1. On 16 May Rudolf Kolisch sent Schoenberg a telegram from Florence, cryptically advising a change of climate for his asthma. The Schoenbergs thereupon left Berlin the following day and traveled to Paris. In a letter of 18 May to the Prussian Academy Schoenberg explained his abrupt departure as motivated by an urgent publishing matter, after which he resigned himself to awaiting further developments.

2. On 7 April the new German government under Adolf Hitler passed a law designed to restructure the German bureaucracy (*Gesetz zur Wiederherstellung des Berufbeamtentums*), one of whose purposes was to remove Jews and functionaries identified with the policies of the Weimar Republic from official positions. Schoenberg and Schreker were among the first affected. Although his contract with the Academy had been renewed for another five years in 1930, Schoenberg was given an official "leave of absence" on 23 May 1933.

drama[3] and for the cello concerto,[4] perhaps for *Moses und Aron* as well. But that isn't so easy nowadays. What are you up to? Are you already in Carinthia? Or will you go to Italy?—I'd like to have you both here!

Many warmest regards, also to your wife, also from my wife

Your Arnold Schönberg

Give Stein my regards!

---

3. The text for *Der biblische Weg*, the first version of which had been written in June 1926, the second in July 1927.

4. Schoenberg's Cello Concerto after Georg Matthias Monn's Harpsichord Concerto, Op. 6, No. 7, begun in November 1932 and completed the following January.

## Schoenberg to Berg (postcard)

Arcachon[1] [? August 1933]

Dear friend,

I only want to tell you quickly that I received both of your letters, but that I most certainly wrote to you once before from Arcachon.—There has been nothing new since my letter to Webern.[2] One waits, but nothing happens.—I am trying to finish a Concerto for String Quartet and Orchestra after a Handel Concerto Grosso.[3] It's very tedious work. I need about 4–5 times as long as I had thought and about 8–10 times as long as I have at my disposal. But in the end it will be a very good piece and that won't be Handel's doing, if I do say so. I liked the piece better in the beginning.—I hope you are working and are both well.—At the moment everything is going well with me.

Many warmest regards

Your Arnold Schoenberg[4]

Oh yes: I was able to get money again from Berlin this month after all; not much, but it's enough.

---

1. The Schoenbergs moved to the resort town of Arcachon at the end of July. They returned to the Paris in September.

2. In a 4 August letter to Webern Schoenberg discussed his situation and his plans to participate actively in the Jewish cause, which he considered more important than his own art. Berg made a copy of the letter.

3. Early in May Schoenberg had begun his "free transcription" for string quartet and orchestra of Handel's Concerto Grosso, Op. 6, No. 7.

4. After July 1933 Schoenberg chose to spell his name without the *Umlaut*; see footnote 1 to his letter of 16 October.

## Schoenberg to Berg

Arcachon, 17 September 1933

Dearest friend,

Many sincere thanks for the fantastic books. They are extremely interesting, one especially (which I am now reading pretty much straight through) is something everyone should have read. Then one would have to reconsider some things. Although even without that it would be possible to act differently.—But of course it's only theoretical.—I am also very interested in the other books. Especially the small Palestrina book. The third, I fear, may be by a Jewish Spengler.[1] But perhaps one can pick up some factual information about interesting, mysterious times.

Again: many <u>heartfelt</u> thanks!

———

You don't mention your work. Have you made good progress? Stuckenschmidt writes[2] that the Berlin *Intendant* Tietjen[3] told him that he definitely wants to do your new opera! You should see to it!

So far I haven't had a chance even to think about *Moses und Aron*. Because until yesterday I was working on the String Quartet Concerto. And as soon as I begin working again (tomorrow or the day after; I can't stand loafing longer than that; though even the loafing is heavily interspersed with letter writing), I'll take up the revision of my drama *Der biblische Weg*. I won't be able to think of *Moses und Aron* until after that—if I get to it at all. It is strange that all my larger works (beginning with *Gurrelieder*) have been in danger of remaining torsos: *Jakobsleiter*, *Der biblische Weg*, *Moses und Aron*, the counterpoint book, and the other theoretical works. Will I finish it? At the moment the requisite interest is directed elsewhere. Besides, I have accepted an offer by the "Malkin Conservatory" in Boston to go there as a composition teacher in October, provided a minimum sum is guaranteed through student registrations.[4] I don't think anything will come of it. It will probably be decided in the next 2–3 weeks.—

I still haven't heard anything from the Academy: whether I'm to be relieved of my duties. I almost fear (i.e., I doubt; others fear) that I'll be required to return and go on teaching. But then they'd have to lift the ban on teaching! That would be an awkward dilemma for me, but it would be regulated by the stipulations of my contract, which are not unfavorable.[5]

In case I have the Handel concerto printed (I wrote it on photoprint paper) I'll send you a copy as "author-publisher." My dealings with "The Oxford University Press" in London have fallen through.[6] The incompetence of those people as demonstrated on this occasion was enough to place a Hertzka in the most shining light.

———

1. Possibly Fr. Muckle's, *Der Geist der jüdischen Kultur und das Abendland* (Vienna-Leipzig-Munich, 1923), in a copy of which Schoenberg had written on page 234: "This is pure swindle (just like Spengler, Chamberlain, Riemann and this breed of scholar) . . ." (Arnold Schoenberg Institute) The other books sent by Berg have not been identified.

2. Hans Heinz Stuckenschmidt, the music critic for the *Berliner Zeitung am Mittag*. He had become associated with the Schoenberg circle in 1923, when he and Josef Rufer organized a performance group in Hamburg modelled on Schoenberg's Verein für musikalische Privataufführungen.

3. The German conductor and opera director Heinz Tietjen was Intendant of Berlin's Städtische Oper 1925–27; 1927–45 he was Generalintendant of all the Prussian State Theaters.

4. The American cellist Joseph Malkin, who was founding a music conservatory in Boston, offered Schoenberg a position teaching composition; his telegram to confirm Schoenberg's acceptance reached Schoenberg in Arcachon on 6 September, along with a copy of the contract.

5. In a long letter to Webern of 18 June 1933, Schoenberg indicated that he was aware of the finality of his departure from Germany, though he mentioned that influential personalities were working to find a solution to his Berlin situation. However, on 20 September 1933 his forced "leave of absence" was changed to outright dismissal. Although Schoenberg's contract ran until October 1935, his salary was paid only until October 1933, despite his strenuous protestations.

6. After lengthy negotiations concerning publication of the arrangement of the Handel Concerto Grosso Schoenberg considered the sum finally offered him too small and retracted his work.

At the very least they are blackmailers and cutthroats, if not swindlers!

So now you have a complete report. Unfortunately I still have another 6–8 long letters to write and will have to repeat myself often enough. I shall have to write another Schoenberg-Journal.

Many warmest regards from our house to yours. A picture of Nuria we intended to send wasn't ready in time.—

Your Arnold Schoenberg

We shall stay here another 2 weeks. Address in an emergency: Universal Edition

## Schoenberg to Berg (typewritten letter)

Paris, 16 October 1933

Dear friend,

It wasn't until 1 October that my going to America became the kind of certainty I could believe in myself. Everything that appeared in the newspapers both before and since was founded on fantasy, just as are the purported ceremonies and the presence of "*tout* Paris" at my so-called return to the Jewish faith. (*Tout* Paris was, besides the rabbi and myself: my wife and a Dr. Marianoff, with whom all these dreadful tales probably originated.)[1] As you have surely observed, my return to the Jewish faith took place long ago and is even discernible in the published portions of my work ("Du sollst nicht . . . du musst[2] . . .") [Not, you should, [but] you must] and in *Moses und Aron*, which you've known about since 1928, but which goes back at least another five years; most especially in my drama *Der biblische Weg*, which was also conceived in 1922 or '23 at the latest, though not finished until '26–'27.—In the past few days I have often thought of writing a "Schoenberg"-Journal again and sending copies to my closest 25–30 friends, who are scattered throughout the world. It is hard to write everyone the same things fully and still answer all the questions. I mention that because I suspect you may be upset at first finding out about Boston from the papers. But you can see that you wouldn't have known it any earlier, even if I had written you myself, particularly because I didn't immediately know when we'd be leaving, a number of incidental questions still had to be settled, and other complications intervened. Even now there is still a great deal to settle, and countless difficulties to overcome, which continue to arise. But we're setting sail on the 25th, and leaving Paris on the 24th. We hope to be there on the first.

What you tell me about U.E. is very unfortunate.[3] I'd like to make a suggestion

1. Schoenberg, who was born a Jew, had converted to Protestantism on 21 March 1898. He returned to his original faith in Paris (see document on p. 447).

2. The title of the second of the Four Pieces for Mixed Chorus, Op. 27.

3. During the preceding years Universal suffered a number of reversals and with shrinking demand for new music (much of which was now banned in Germany) the firm's financial dilemma was becoming acute. Although Berg's contract expired in May 1932, he initially continued to receive his monthly 1,000 schillings, but that sum was reduced to 700 schillings in June 1933 and ceased altogether in October (at which point Berg's deficit with U.E. had reached about 5,000 schillings). This was probably the state of affairs when Berg wrote to Schoenberg. Eventually a still lower monthly stipend of 500 schillings was reinstated, but as German and Austrian performances of his works and thus royalties continued to dwindle he became all the more eager to explore concert possibilities abroad.

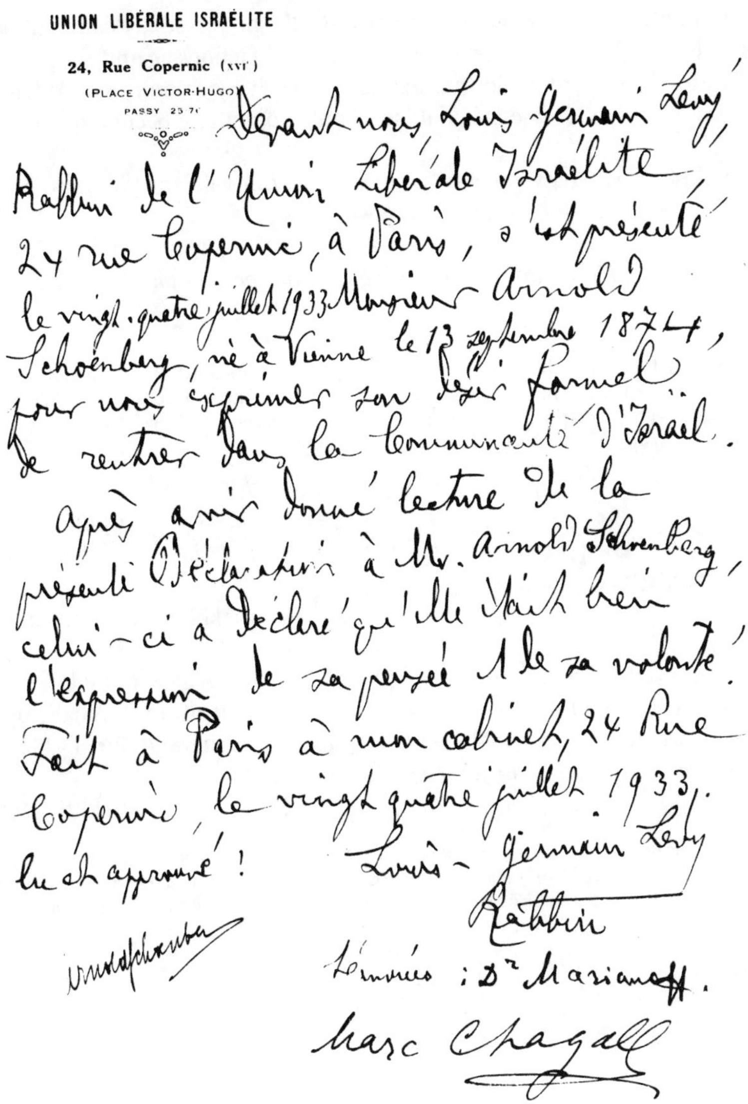

UNION LIBÉRALE ISRAÉLITE

24, Rue Copernic (XVIᵉ)
(PLACE VICTOR-HUGO)
PASSY 23 71

*[handwritten document in French]*

Devant nous, Louis Germain Lévy, Rabbin de l'Union Libérale Israélite 24 rue Copernic, à Paris, s'est présenté le vingt-quatre juillet 1933 Monsieur Arnold Schoenberg, né à Vienne le 13 septembre 1874, pour nous exprimer son désir formel de rentrer dans la communauté d'Israël.

Après avoir donné lecture de la présente Déclaration à M. Arnold Schoenberg, celui-ci a déclaré qu'elle était bien l'expression de sa pensée et de sa volonté. Fait à Paris à mon cabinet, 24 Rue Copernic, le vingt quatre juillet 1933.

lu et approuvé!

Louis-Germain Lévy
Rabbin

Témoins: Dr Marianoff.

Marc Chagall

*Document attesting to Schoenberg's return to Judaism in Paris on 24 July 1933, witnessed by a Doctor Marianoff and the painter Marc Chagall (Arnold Schoenberg Institute 2282)*

to you: perhaps U.E. would be prepared to join forces with a second publisher. I imagine one could find a wealthy publishing house willing to advance the necessary funds if U.E. gave them a share of the profits! Suggest it! I would also like to know if I can do anything for you in America: to the extent, of course, that I have the power to do so. For who knows how uninfluential, how disregarded, how disdained I may be there. I hope it won't be as in Holland, where I had scarcely arrived before public opinion was entirely against me because all who feared my competition had immediately mobilized the press and other powerful factions against me.

Didn't Stokowski want to do the premiere; what has come of that? What other possibilities are there. Please think about it <u>until</u> something occurs to you and let me know.

I must close now. Many affectionate regards to your wife and you, also from my wife, and many thanks for your very kind wishes.

Your Arnold Schoenberg

[*handwritten note in the margin regarding the first paragraph:*] Werfel is to read this![4]

---

4. Franz Werfel, Jewish by birth, had come very close to converting to Catholicsm and even at this time remained ambivalent in his identification with his Jewish heritage. Later that year Werfel began his collaboration with Max Reinhardt and Kurt Weill on a biblical epic for New York, eventually called *Der Weg der Verheissung* (The Eternal Road).

## Schoenberg to Berg (picture postcard: St. Mary's of the Assumption Church, Brookline, Mass.)

Brookline, 21 November 1933

Dear Berg,

You have owed me a reply for so long that I was already beginning to fear—no, I'm not seriously afraid of that; but I can certainly say it in jest![1] What's up with you? Soon—when I have time—I'll write a lengthy "Schoenberg-Journal"—for today just my address and many warmest regards

Your Arnold Schoenberg

---

1. Schoenberg had considered the possibility that Berg and Webern had undergone a change of political heart and had sought information from others in the old Vienna circle; there is an undated letter from this period from Erwin Stein, reassuring Schoenberg that both Berg and Webern were unchanged in their loyalties.

## Berg to Schoenberg (typewritten letter)

"Waldhaus," 6 December 1933

My dearest friend,

Your card from Brookline of 21 November, which just came, made me immensely happy and gives me the impetus for a long overdue reply to your letter of 16 October, which you are quite right in demanding.—First I'll tell you why there has been such a great delay (not—to enter into your jest—because I'm composing orchestral variations on the Horst Wessel Song[1]):

---

1. Horst Wessel, a young SA member killed in a clash with communists, was commemorated in the so-called "Horst-Wessel-Lied" (based on a well-known German folk melody), which became a battle hymn for the Nazi movement.

In a letter to Webern on 1 January 1934 Schoenberg confessed his depression and despair over the fact that neither Webern nor Berg had written to him since early October, but that he had recently received Berg's answer to his direct question, which completely reassured him.

At the very moment your letter came, with the kind offer to do something for me in America, various plans were going through my head concerning my livelihood and America. So nothing would have been more obvious than to come right out with it in response to your letter. But I felt a certain hesitancy in doing that at that point: you were about to leave for the U.S.A. and I can imagine how preoccupied you were with other things! It would have seemed to me unspeakably self-seeking to have asked you to think about <u>my</u> affairs and plans in America, when (aside from the travel preparations) you must have had more than enough plans of your <u>own</u> for over there—you weren't, after all, going as a tourist.

On the other hand, I couldn't bring myself just to say in response to your extremely kind offer that there wasn't anything you could do for me in America. And so, vacillating between a yes and a no, I decided to remain silent for the time being, which is how your dear long letter remained unanswered until today, except for the short receipt-confirmation-picture-postcard (!) [*Erhaltsbestätigungsansichtskarte*], that I wrote together with Webern, who was visiting me here at the time, and that I hope you received prior to your departure from Paris.

But though I haven't written these past 6–7 weeks, my thoughts have been with you constantly! Beginning with the alarming news (thank God later clarified) of the French train disaster on the day of your departure;[2] then with word I received from Vienna about your safe arrival, etc., right up to a few days ago, when I got a look at the issue of *Musical America* with the dear, dear picture of the three of you and the report of your reception in the U.S.A.,[3] the teaching offers, and the coming celebrations and concerts.

Knowing all this and at the same time imagining how happy you and your dear wife must have been and will be, and assuming that after all the European suffering you will finally be able to breathe feely again, fills us with as much happiness as if we had experienced it ourselves. Indeed, since it is so contrary to the way <u>we</u> are presently living, it seems like the necessary complement, and this is the only thing that allows me to bear my own experience of current world events.

For we are still in this dreary place, surrounded for almost two months now by ice and snow and, aside from my steady work on *Lulu*, encumbered by the petty, pettiest cares of such a life, such as (just to mention a few examples that may illustrate the obvious contrasts between your life and ours:) which farmer has the drier firewood in stock and for how much longer, or whether the water pipe will freeze tonight or whether to take a small auto trip through the winter landscape in order to enjoy the rare bliss of a bathtub (in Klagenfurt or Villach), etc., etc.—This said, and repeating that despite everything I would rather be here than in Vienna because this is the only way I can find the concentration for composing, you won't be surprised at my designation for this self-imposed exile: concentration camp.[4]

Back to facts: since I last wrote fully, U.E. has declared itself willing to give me 500 schillings a month until spring, which relieves me of the worst worries, but not

2. On 25 October the Cherbourg-Paris express derailed, killing 35 people.
3. *Musical America* LIII/17 (10 November, 1933), 3.
4. By the end of 1933 the German government had begun erecting internment camps (called concentration camps even then) to detain political opponents of the regime. Berg was no doubt aware of the implication of his term *Konzentrationslager*.

of the worry of incurring ever larger debts with U.E.[5] Of course that was why I was for a time considering America-related plans. Precisely the plans I hesitated telling you about a month ago so as not to burden you.

I was wondering, for example, whether one couldn't perhaps find an American sponsor who is willing to let the dedication of *Lulu* cost him something. Naturally I thought first of Misses [sic] Coolidge, who, as you yourself know best, has collected such (chamber music) dedications from almost all living composers, and for whom it might be tempting to be able for once to call a full-length stage work her own—and remunerate it accordingly.[6]

Another idea was that I offer to sell the autograph score of *Wozzeck* to a rich manuscript collector in America and receive for these three stout volumes a tidy sum from which I could live for a year without going further into debt. However, I was always fully aware of the dubiousness of these plans since they presuppose a "*Ruhm*" [fame] that I may have had three seasons ago, but that in the meantime has perhaps long since evaporated (like that without an "h") [rum].

I no longer hesitate to tell you about it, dearest friend, because now that you will have gained great insight into American conditions, knowing of these ideas can't burden you as they might have if I had approached you while you were still in Europe. Today, without having to give it much thought and without being terribly distracted from your own affairs, you'll know immediately whether my ideas make any sense or whether there are other possibilities easier to implement—or——none at all! Ultimately that wouldn't be a catastrophe either. I am assured of a 1934/35 premiere at two major opera houses where I can exercise some influence. And even if the one in Berlin is by then no longer advisable, I would still have the one in Vienna.* And I can hold out at least that long. If only spring were already here: everything is easier and more beautiful in the spring!

Enough, more than enough about <u>myself.</u> My only desire now is that the "Schoenberg-Journal" you announced may arrive very soon. Wherever you send it, it will circulate quickly among all those for whom it is intended. How I look forward to it!

And now farewell, my dearest, best friend; all the best for you in America, which is envied for having you

by your Bergs

P.S. Where is this "Brookline"? Near Boston? It certainly can't be identical with the New York suburb Brooklyn. And—has Massachusetts gone "wet"?[7]—

---

* Apropos: the telegraphic request for the world premiere of *Lulu* that Stokowski sent after the Philadelphia *Wozzeck* premiere, has since become meaningless, as he's not interested in the drama (by Wedekind).

---

5. On 11 October Berg had written to Yella Hertzka (Emil Hertzka's widow and a part-owner of Universal Edition) outlining his financial needs until the completion of *Lulu*, which he projected would be in six to ten months.

6. In 1925 the American patron of the arts Elizabeth Sprague Coolidge created a foundation in her name at the Library of Congress. In 1927 Schoenberg had composed his Third String Quartet, Op. 30, on commission from her.

7. Prohibition was repealed in the United States on 5 December 1933.

# 1934

*Schoenberg to Berg (picture postcard: The Colonial Room, the Park Central, 55th Street at Seventh Ave., New York City)*

[New York, 27 March 1934]

Dear friend,

Engel in Washington, who offered you a commission for a quartet and made an offer for your score, has just written that he still hasn't received an answer from you![1] What's the matter?

Warmest regards

Arnold Schoenberg

---

1. On Berg's behalf Schoenberg approached Elizabeth Sprague Coolidge and Carl Engel, head of the music division of the Library of Congress, about purchasing the autograph score of *Wozzeck* for the Library of Congress. The score, which by contract belonged to U.E., was finally sold in June 1934 and Berg and U.E. divided the purchase price of $1,140 (at that time equivalent to 6000 Austrian schillings).

Engel offered Berg $1,000 to write a string quartet for a Library of Congress chamber music festival planned for April 1935. Berg turned down the commission for lack of time.

*Schoenberg to Berg (postcard)*

Chautauqua,[1] 16 August 1934

Dear friend—

It's faster to write a postcard, sorry. I can't believe I didn't let you know my address here. Apparently my picture postcard went astray. We've been here since 12 July and so far I haven't done anything except recover from the frightful New York season. This is a truly unique place. For the past 60 years, professors and students have been coming here from all over America to spend 5–10 weeks together, there are lectures, lessons, courses, concerts, and theater. This year there were only 5 weeks, due to the depression, but we're staying at least another 5 weeks since we can get by here very comfortably on 80–100 dollars a months and are living in a very nice little cottage. I intend to work now: Act III *Moses und Aron* and possibly

---

1. After their first American season in Boston and New York, where they had moved on 25 March, the Schoenbergs were invited to spend the summer from June to 15 September in Chautauqua, New York. Established in 1874, the Chautauqua Institution sponsored annual summer programs with lectures and courses by eminent academicians, artists, and musicians and performances by a summer orchestra and opera company.

"The musical Idea, Logic, Technique and Art of Presentation," for the preparation of which in June alone I wrote almost 200 octavo sheets and did a number of analyses.[2] So far I have no prospects at all for the winter, it is therefore not impossible that we'll spend it in some small town in the south, where I would like to recuperate further.—Weiss and his wife[3] were here during the time he played in the orchestra. We had a good time together, played a lot of tennis and my wife won the "World" Championship "of Chautauqua" (a joke) in ping-pong, whereas in tennis we were both thrown out in the first round. I was also thrown out in ping-pong—I guess I just don't have a very winning personality.—We trembled with you during the dark days, but were reassured by the news.[4]

Many warmest regards from us all, also to your wife

Your Arnold Schoenberg

---

2. Schoenberg does not seem to have continued work on the planned book, *Der musikalische Gedanke, die Logik, Technik und Kunst einer Darstellung* (the manuscript of which is located at the Arnold Schoenberg Institute).

3. Schoenberg's former student Adolph Weiss, a bassoonist, and his wife Mary Weiss.

4. On 12 February there had been a worker's uprising in various cities throughout Austria, which led to more than one thousand casualties. The Nazi assassination of the Austrian Chancellor Engelbert Dollfuss on 25 July was a further consequence of the unrest.

## Berg to Schoenberg

"Waldhaus," 28 August 1934

My dearest friend,

I know that to my (—to Alwa's) question: "may I come in?" (the first words in the opera *Lulu* after the curtain rises) you would reply with Schoen: "Come right in!" and that I would then put into my embrace all the feelings that move me on this 13 September. But the fact that I can do so only from afar is <u>one</u> thing that grieves me on this day. The <u>other</u>—everything a result of these dreadful times—is that I can't come to you with a <u>real present</u>, but only with a <u>dedication</u>. Please accept it, not only as a product of years of work most devoutly consecrated to you, but also as an outward document: the whole world—the German world, too—is to recognize in the dedication that this German opera—like all my works—is indigenous to the realm of that most German of music, which will bear your name for all eternity.

A <u>third</u> cause for sorrow: that I cannot lay the score of the <u>entire</u> opera at your feet, but only a copy of the beginning.[1] But alas, alas, I am prevented by the contract I signed in 1930, which contains the clause: "The autograph of the work remains in the possession of the publisher as its property."

The other things I have to tell you on this day I have said more worthily and gracefully elswhere than is possible in this letter,[2] which is only intended to accom-

---

1. Berg's dedicatory copy of the *Lulu* prologue is located in the British Library.

2. Universal Edition published a Schoenberg *Festschrift* in September 1934, with contributions by Schoenberg's students and friends, including Oskar Adler, David Joseph Bach, Alois Hába, Heinrich Jalowetz, Josef Polnauer, Darius Milhaud, Erwin Stein, Alexander Zemlinsky, etc. Berg was represented with the anagram "Glaube, Hoffnung und Liebe."

pany the package and I won't even attempt to express the birthday wishes spanning the entire spectrum of my emotional being. I know that—even when unspoken— you understand that they have been spoken for life and will therefore accept them graciously

from your Berg

I am also having a more than 300 page-long *Fackel* sent to you from Vienna: "Warum die Fackel nicht erscheint?".[3] It—a bit of the old world—will surely interest you.

---

3. The last regular issue of the *Fackel* was published at the end of December 1932 (XXXIV/885– 887). Except for a reprint of Karl Kraus' funeral oration for Adolf Loos in October 1933 (XXXV/808) there was nothing until 23 July 1934, when a sixteen-page *Fackel* (Nr. 889) appeared with commentaries on Kraus's long silence reprinted from a variety of sources. At the same time Kraus announced that the next *Fackel* would appear in a few days. It was this issue from the end of July (XXXVI/890–905), which bore the title "Why the *Fackel* hasn't appeared?" that Berg sent Schoenberg. Kraus answers the question epigrammatically: "Mir fällt zu Hitler nichts ein" (Nothing occurs to me regarding Hitler), as well as at length. Shaken by the political events, he admits the hopelessness of fighting the existing world order. The next *Fackel* did not appear until April 1935 and from then until his death on 12 June 1936 (the last issue of the journal appeared in February 1936) Kraus restricted himself to discussions of literature, theater, and culture generally.

*Schoenberg to those who congratulated him on his sixtieth birthday (typewritten general letter)*

Hollywood[1] November 1934

On my fiftieth birthday many people felt moved or obliged to declare themselves for or even with me; on my sixtieth many of these same people felt freed from the bothersome constraint, while others, under the constraints of a Nordic point of view, managed to achieve the same, though possibly unwelcome freedom; on my seventieth—that's as far into the future as I'm prepared to consider—the circle of those who will not regret my first birthday will perhaps be smaller still; but I hope that by then only volunteers will approach me, and of these only such who recognize fulfillment in my preliminary achievements.

I have known for a long time that I won't live to experience a wider understanding of my work and my much-acclaimed perseverance is an exigency based on the desire to experience it after all. I have set my goal high enough to assure that those who resist and even those who oppose me will of necessity reach that point at some time. Even parallel lines meet—as mathematics assures us—at such points, if one only has the patience to wait.

Perhaps it is now generally expected that the comforts offered me in a new world are rich compensation for a loss for which I had prepared myself in the course of more than a decade. To be sure, I have effected the break with the old world, but not without feeling it to my very core, for I wasn't prepared that it would leave me both homeless and speechless, so that to everyone but my old friends I can express

---

1. Schoenberg's move to California was largely due to the adverse climatic conditions on the East Coast. The family moved to Pasadena on 15 September, then to Hollywood on 1 October.

it only in English; to the extent they are interested. On the other hand one really lives better here than the Good Lord in France, for He would certainly have a harder time getting a work permit there than here. I am universally esteemed here as one of the most important modern composers; along with Stravinsky,[2] Tansman,[3] Sessions,[4] Sibelius, Gershwin,[5] Copland,[6] etc. . . . etc. . . . etc. So I can certainly count on the fact that it won't be any different on my seventieth birthday than I predicted above.

Nevertheless I am very determined to experience it. For if, next to my personal happiness, only those friends remain who give me so much joy, each of whom makes me proud through the strength, spirit, intelligence, originality, and learning with which he expresses why he believes in me: then I may already congratulate myself.

That I can be proud of having such friends determines the measure of my thanks. But only in music would I be able to express how heartfelt those thanks are.

Warmest regards
Arnold Schoenberg

2. Igor Stravinsky, who was still living in France, was at this time planning his second American tour (1935), during which he would conduct performances of his works with a number of major American orchestras.

3. The Polish-French composer Alexander Tansman was active in Paris, except for the years 1941–46, when he lived in the U.S.

4. The American composer Roger Sessions.

5. George Gershwin was to become a friend of Schoenberg's during the first years of Schoenberg's stay in California. Berg had met Gershwin in Vienna in the spring of 1928 and had entertained him in his home with a special performance by the Kolisch Quartet of his Lyric Suite.

6. The American composer Aaron Copland.

*Schoenberg to Berg (typewritten general letter)*

Hollywood, [25] November 1934

Above all I must explain why I have taken so long to thank you for the many good wishes for my sixtieth birthday. First, however, I was able to enjoy everything enormously and was completely content, even though we spent the day without any ceremony, without any visitors. Trude and Nuria the first well-wishers, then the many telegrams, letters, and the fantastic *Festschrift*: all that made me much happier than public celebrations ever could. Although I shall never forget how moved I was years ago by the Vienna ceremonies and the speech by the ill-fated Mayor Karl Seitz,[1] a man estimable above all party loyalties, whom today I would have liked to have given a sign of my thanks.

By 13 September we had already packed a portion of our luggage. Some time earlier we had come to the conclusion that it would be best for me to go to Hollywood, i.e., California, and this decision became final in the last weeks of August.

1. The Mayor of Vienna 1923–34, Karl Seitz, had given a speech honoring Schoenberg on his 50th birthday (1924). Following the uprising of February 1934, Seitz and other Social Democratic leaders were jailed.

I will now give a short overview of my first year in America, which ended 31 October.

I cannot deny that it surpassed in disappointments, aggravation, and illness almost everything in my previous experience. Of course our first disappointment came in Paris, when there was no response to the news that I had to leave Berlin and when we faced with considerable anxiety the prospect of a very distressing winter in France. By that time I no longer harbored those expectations of mountains of gold, which an American engagement would once have aroused in me. However: by the time the Malkin Conservatory offered me somewhat less than a quarter of what I considered minimum compensation for my Berlin salary,[2] I was sufficiently weary to accept this lone offer after only a few hours of reflection. To mention only the more important events, the next great disappointment was when I discovered that through an oversight I had agreed to teach for the same salary not only in Boston, but in New York as well: a subsequent condition, whose pitfalls I had overlooked. These weekly trips were the principal cause of my illness. Then: on the trip from Washington to Boston I asked Malkin what the Conservatory's orchestra was like, only to find a small music school in Boston with perhaps 5–6 classrooms. The school had set all its hopes on me, but had published announcements much too late and, moreover, charged fees more than double those attainable during the depression; further, it stood in a crossfire of intrigues stemming from professional jealousy and artistic enmity, so that all told I had 12–14 students in Boston and New York, some of them complete beginners. There were agreeable aspects. The League of Composers organized a concert (only chamber music though) and a very large reception with purportedly 2,000 people present, where I must have shaken 500 hands and the patrons' committee allegedly included everybody in New York (in any way) interested in art.[3] Soon thereafter there was a second, similarly frenetic reception, but I can't remember who sponsored it.

I enjoyed the actual teaching. Even the more advanced students had a very meager background, but I had two really gifted students and several fairly gifted ones. Besides, in the last few months I had stored up so much new material within me that I was able to tell the students a great deal that was completely new to them and surprised them immensely.—In Boston I gave a concert with the resident symphony orchestra, which is extraordinarily good.[4] I also met Polatschek there.[5] The permanent conductor is Serge Koussevitzky,[6] formerly a touring contrabass player,

2. Schoenberg's calculation is difficult to fathom, as his Berlin salary had been about 18,000 marks annually, at that time roughly equivalent to $4,500, and the Malkin salary had been $4,800. Schoenberg may have been thinking of the two-years' salary that he lost through cancelation of his Berlin contract.

3. On 11 November 1933 the League of Composers sponsored a performance of the Chamber Symphony, Op. 9, and held a reception in Schoenberg's honor, at which he gave a short speech.

4. Schoenberg's conducting engagement with the Boston Symphony Orchestra in a concert of his own works had originally been scheduled for 11, 12, and 13 January 1933, but was canceled at the last minute due to Schoenberg's illness. The concert finally took place on 16 March; Schoenberg conducted his *Pelleas und Melisande*.

5. The Austrian clarinettist Viktor Polatschek, who at this time played in the Boston Symphony Orchestra, had been a member of the Vienna Philharmonic and a frequent participant in Verein concerts.

6. The Russian-American conductor and composer Serge Koussevitzky emigrated to the United States in 1924, where he succeeded Monteux as conductor of the Boston Symphony Orchestra.

who hasn't played a <u>single</u> note of mine in ten years, which is how long he has been there. It is my firm conviction that he is so uneducated that he can't even read a score. At any rate, orchestra musicians told me that he has hired two pianists who play every new piece four-hand for him, over and over, until he has learned it. Furthermore, he doesn't conduct all the rehearsals himself but has the concertmaster lead the preliminary rehearsals while he sits in what he imagines to be a dark corner and conducts along. As everywhere else there are many charlatans here too. On the occasion of my first attempt to conduct in Boston, on Friday, 12 January, after conducting a quasi dress rehearsal in Cambridge (a small city adjacent to Boston), I had a coughing fit in the elevator of our apartment at 2:30 in the afternoon and as a consequence pulled something that caused such terrible pains in my back and chest that I couldn't move, even though I was bandaged. I had already been ill as of the beginning of December, when the weather turned bad, but was always able to get by, with some obviously harmful medicines, so as halfway to fulfill my duties. For the climate there is very harsh, and was especially so this winter. The temperature can drop 60 or more degrees Fahrenheit within 12–24 hours, that is 34 degrees Celsius. Then in March, when these temperature plunges occurred repeatedly, I had a dreadful asthma attack, intensified this time by an irritation of the heart. (The doctor had given me *Jod* [iodine] for the cough even though I told him not to; since it's called iodine here, we didn't realize it: Iodine checks the illness without curing it, which is why it soon flares up again. But aside from that, it upset my stomach to such an extent that for at least two months I couldn't eat anything but weak tea, ham, and toast. And that weakened my heart.) I had to take it very easy in April, May, and June, and recovered quickly over the summer in Chautauqua, but not enough that I could have risked a second winter in the New York area. My contract with Malkin had run out at the end of May, and although there was general interest in me (general, except among conductors) and I was in demand as a teacher (to date I've had to turn down no fewer than five offers), there was none that offered me security or wasn't in New York or Chicago, where I couldn't possibly live.—

I was astounded, on the other hand, at least in the beginning, by the attitude of the conductors, with the exception of Stock in Chicago.[7] Eggs are even cheaper here than opinions on art, which is how a lot of it gets on people's faces, where they tend to wear it.[8] The cultural leaders, but especially the conductors, seem to have a particularly large quantity, since it is after all their responsibility, for which they could be called to account: it remains obscure what else they could be called upon for. At best they have done *Verklärte Nacht* or one of my Bach arrangements, but most of them haven't done a single note. On the other hand, Stravinsky, Ravel, Respighi, among various others, are played frequently. It is not terribly different from the situation in Europe: here, too, I have a very great number of—what should I call them?, you can't really call them followers, for they are almost all future

7. Frederick A. Stock, principal conductor of the Chicago Symphony Orchestra.

8. This is an approximation of Schoenberg's untranslatable phrase "Butter ist hier noch billiger, als Kunsturteile und es kommt daher eine grosse Menge auf dem Kopf, wo man sie auch infolgedessen hat."

defectors [*Abfall*], but there are some among them who won't become [defectors] until the opportunity is right. That notwithstanding, I can say that interest in me is only just awakening. The younger people all support me very strongly, and in general the opinion is that I am "the coming thing." But not for people like Walter and Klemperer.[9] Naturally Klemperer plays Stravinsky and Hindemith here, but not a single note of mine, with the exception of my Bach arrangements. And Walter always was (I must take the precaution of requesting that my remarks be kept strictly confidential so as to prevent their becoming public or even getting into the papers. Today I couldn't win the battle against those forces on such terms: but I will certainly fight it to the end on other terms!)—anyway, Walter is a great conductor (in private, however, he always was a repulsive pig and I get nauseated just thinking about him: so I do my best to avoid that).

Los Angeles is a *tabula rasa* where my music is concerned (Hollywood is something like a Floridsdorf[10] or Mödling of Los Angeles, with the distinction that those wonderful films are produced here, whose extremely curious plots and wonderful sounds—as everyone knows—I love so well). Here and there someone has made an effort with my music (Goossens,[11] Rodzinski,[12] Slonimsky,[13] but with no other result than that the audience hardened in its aversion to new music. Like everywhere else, the conductors are at fault. For example, the Philharmonic Orchestra in San Francisco hasn't played a single note in 25 years: take note of the name Alfred Hertz!![14] All these gentlemen, from sergeant [*Feldwebel*] on down (and there's nowhere but down from there) call themselves conservatives, which I have interpreted as follows: they don't have anything to guard, to conserve but their own incompetence, ignorance, and cowardice: but they guard those so that no one will detect them.—That is the reason I have refused to conduct concerts here and in San Francisco, for I wish to lead the guilty to their just punishment. I have made many enemies that way, but I don't believe I have to fear them since on the other hand I also have many friends. Namely as a teacher. Unfortunately I can't get a decent fee, only ⅓ to ⅖ of my New York price,[15] but I already have a course with 10 students, as well as a few private students so that I'm sure when people find out I'm teaching, some better-paying ones will start coming and I'll be able to survive here quite well. For six weeks this summer I shall teach at the local Southern California University for two hours daily (with the exception of Saturday and Sunday). Here, too, the pay is not princely, nonetheless it will see me through the 3 summer months.—They also want me in New York now. We were hardly here a

9. Bruno Walter was now active primarily in Austria and Holland, though he made annual guest appearances with the New York Philharmonic Orchestra 1932–36. Otto Klemperer emigrated to the United States in April 1933 and was the director of the Los Angeles Philharmonic Orchestra 1933–39.

10. A workers' district to the northeast of the city on the far side of the Danube.

11. The English conductor and composer Eugene Goossens was conductor of the Cincinnati Symphony Orchestra 1931–46.

12. The Polish-American conductor Artur Rodzinski took over the Cleveland Orchestra in 1933.

13. The Russian musicologist and composer Nicolas Slonimsky emigrated to the United States in 1923; his conducting activities concentrated primarily on contemporary music. On 23 July 1933 he had conducted Schoenberg's *Begleitungsmusik*, Op. 34, with the Los Angeles Philharmonic.

14. The German conductor Alfred Hertz, conductor of the San Francisco Symphony Orchestra until 1929.

15. Schoenberg's fee for lessons in New York was $30.

week when I got an offer from the Juilliard School of Music, the largest and wealthiest American music school, which unfortunately I had to turn down, for we can't risk the winter in New York. But the director Hutcheson,[16] whom I met in Chautauqua, a very good pianist and musician and a very dear fellow, wants me for the year following and I can only hope that by then I am healthy enough to be able to accept it. For that would be a very favorable position in every respect, as all the good and important things here are automatically connected with such jobs. But I'll be very satisfied even if we stay here. Today, 25 November, I am sitting here writing by an open window and my room is full of sunshine. I have written so much about myself now and want to add that my wife and Nuria also feel very comfortable here. We have a very nice little house, furnished, not too large, and with many comforts practically unknown in Europe, which are customary here. As soon as we can get our furniture, which is still in Paris because the German government isn't willing to pay my remaining 22 months' salary, we will probably rent an unfurnished house, which is cheaper yet; then we'll try to live farther out in the hills, where it is both less humid and sunnier. Until now I haven't done any more work on my opera, but am writing a suite for String Orchestra, tonal, a piece for school orchestras.[17] I am writing it at the suggestion of a musician at New York University,[18] who directs a school orchestra there and tells me a great many encouraging things about the American school orchestras, of which there are hundreds. That convinced me that that's where the fight against this infamous conservatism must begin. And so this piece will actually be a model for the advances that are possible within tonality if one is a real musician and knows one's craft: a real preparation not only in the harmonic, but also melodic, contrapuntal, and technical sense. I am quite convinced it will be a valuable contribution in the battle against cowardly and unproductive forces.

Many warmest regards to all my friends<br>Arnold Schoenberg

5860 Canyon Cove
Hollywood, Cal.

16. The Australian pianist Ernest Hutcheson became Dean of the Julliard School of Music in New York in 1927.

17. Schoenberg's *Suite in the Old Style* for string orchestra was begun in Chautauqua and completed 26 December 1934. It was given its premiere on 18 May 1935 by the Los Angeles Philharmonic under Otto Klemperer.

18. Schoenberg met New York University professor Martin Bernstein in Chautauqua, where Bernstein had played double bass in the Symphony Orchestra.

*Berg to Schoenberg (postcard)*[1]

[Vienna] 27 December 1934

Dearest friend,

Your long mimeographed letter just arrived in Vienna. It took three weeks to get here and you are probably worried about its whereabouts, which is why I <u>confirm</u> its arrival by <u>return post</u>. Today <u>just this</u>, in haste, along with my heartfelt thanks for this wonderful "document!"

I wrote to you c. 2 weeks ago for Christmas and the New Year and very much fear that my letter, too, took as long as your "III$^{rd}$ class matter" did, in other words arrived late.[2] Forgive me, dearest friend! The parcel with the *Symphonische Stücke aus Lulu* I had promised was sent off as soon as it was printed. I mention this since I didn't find out until afterwards that U.E. neglected to send this printed matter registered, and I am consequently slightly anxious about its whereabouts. I assume that everything else: letters from September and November[3] and the manuscript of the *Lulu*-Prologue, reached you on time.

As soon as I have more time (I'm still working on the full score of the opera!), I shall answer your mimeographed letter fully. Until then I greet you with the most sincere devotion and affection.

Your Berg

All my love (also from my wife) to the three of you!

1. The present translation is based on the transcription in Josef Rufer's article, "Dokumente einer Freundschaft," *Melos* 1955 (hereafter Rufer 1955).

2. Berg's letter has not been located, but that Schoenberg received it is verified by his response of 2 January 1935.

3. In his Schoenberg biography H. H. Stuckenschmidt mentions a pessimistic Berg letter of 4 November 1934, but its present whereabouts are unknown. The September letter to which Berg refers is his birthday greeting of 28 August 1934.

# 1935

*Schoenberg to Berg*[1]

Hollywood, 2 January 1935

Dearest Friend,

In the meantime my "Journal," which I sent off a few weeks ago, together with my thank-you note (to almost 100 people), has caught you up on my activities. But I've owed you a thank-you for your birthday present so long, that I really ought to be very ashamed, if I weren't excused by the constant drain on my energies, which is often very exhausting. But if I am now to find adequate thanks for that wonderful present, this most recent dedication of a large and significant work, I can only say: I hope I won't disappoint you all—you who grant me so much trust and give me so much credit—and I hope my enemies, who have now buried me for good, aren't right: I would regret it for your sake! (But I'm not always this pessimistic and, to be honest, when I'm really depressed over the confidence with which they walk over my corpse I only need to glance into my scores and yours to be convinced that only we are capable of such things: if nothing else at least the meticulousness with which it is worked out, which calls to mind our good models.)

I have already read through the prologue several times now and have been repeatedly struck by the originality and richness of this piece. I am absolutely convinced that your second opera will meet the standards that your first not only promised but achieved. And I hope the time will soon come where it can be performed again! I haven't read anything here in the *Los Angeles Times* about events in Germany, but have meanwhile been fully informed in person by some Viennese friends. At any rate, I was very pleased at your Berlin success, which, as I heard, was apparently even marked by a demonstration.[2] But what does the future hold? What will become of Hindemith? I hear he had to give up his position at the Academy. Will he be permitted to leave Germany?[3]

1. This translation is based on a photocopy in the Prussian State Library; the original is in private possession.

2. The 30 November 1934 premiere of Berg's Symphonic Pieces from *Lulu* unleashed a virulent press campaign against both the conductor, Erich Kleiber, and the work. Four days after the concert Kleiber resigned as General Music Director of the Berlin State Opera and left Germany in January 1935. Berg's music was not heard again in Germany until after 1945.

3. Since the National Socialist takeover, Hindemith's works had gradually been disappearing from the concert repertoire, though his Symphony from *Mathis der Maler* had been successfully premiered

It has occurred to me that perhaps we, for instance: you, Webern, Krenek, Hindemith, perhaps also Zillig, Hannenheim, and other Germans,[4] could join together to form a defensive alliance [Schutzbündnis]. Of course I don't know whether we could accomplish much unless other threatened members of the intellectual community, such as scientists, researchers, inventors, painters, poets, etc. joined us. But yesterday I drafted a short outline for the formation of a "Defensive Cultural Alliance" [Schutzbund für geistige Cultur], and if you could ask around a bit in Vienna to see if there is any interest, I would develop it further and send it to you. What I have in mind is that each person would have to contribute ½ to one percent of his earnings to a war chest. Perhaps some things can be achieved with money. I myself will try to enlist the interest of people here, which doesn't seem impossible, since, through avoiding all political overtones, I intend to include everyone, whether threatened from the left or the right, from the front or from behind. For it seems that everything is at stake! In all countries! Just like after the suppression of the French Revolution, when it took another 50 years for the victory of liberalism. Apparently we are to experience something similar!

I have to close now; I'm tired. I've spent all day working on an article in English attacking Casella, who once again, though without naming me, wrote spiteful things about me.[5]

So: again many sincere thanks and many affectionate greetings and all good wishes for the New Year.

Your Arnold Schoenberg

I was very worried about your illness. But perhaps you don't know that I underwent something similar; my heart was undermined by iodine and by the fact that the doctors let me drink whiskey, which I did with great pleasure and to excess, though it was very injurious.

Many sincere thanks also to your dear wife for her congratulations and many regards; also from my wife.

You'll be getting a picture of Nuria soon.

---

on 12 March 1934 by the Berlin Philharmonic under Furtwängler. On 25 November 1934 Furtwängler spoke up for Hindemith in his article "Der Fall Hindemith" in the Deutsche Allgemeine Zeitung, to which Joseph Goebbels responded negatively in a 7 December speech. Hindemith did not resign his Berlin Musikhochschule position and leave Germany until March 1937.

4. Ernst Krenek had by this time moved back to his native Vienna and become closely associated with Berg and other members of the Schoenberg circle. Winfried Zillig was principal conductor of the Düsseldorf Opera 1932–37. The Austrian composer Norbert von Hannenheim had been Schoenberg's student in Berlin 1929–31.

5. In his article "Modern Music in Modern Italy," Modern Music XII (November–December 1934) 19–22, Casella declared Italian music and audiences to be largely independent of European influence, particularly that extreme variety of chromaticism, atonality. Schoenberg's response, "Fascism is no Article of Exportation," remained unpublished during his lifetime; the title was drawn from one of Mussolini's well-known maxims, an indication that Schoenberg considered Casella's standpoint politically tainted. Differences of opinion between Schoenberg and Casella date back to Casella's article, "Harmony, Counterpoint, etc." (published in Pro Musica, March–June 1926, 31–35), in which Casella assigned Schoenberg, along with Wagner and Scriabin, to that nineteenth-century romanticism being combatted by contemporary developments of twentieth-century new music.

## Schoenberg to Berg (letter copy)[1]

Hollywood, 22 January 1935

Dearest Friend,

This is the poem I began, which initially put me in an optimistic mood that promised to overcome even the difficulties of meter and rhyme:

> Die mir die Mitwelt geraubt,
> Rühren mir jetzt an die Nachwelt,
> Die ich mir sicher geglaubt.
> Dem, der auf sie seine Sach stellt,
> Sollte, die keinem gehört,
> Dienen solange als Zuflucht,
> Widerspruchslos, ungestört,
> Als noch im Kampfe er Ruh sucht,[2]

But my optimism soon evaporated and I had to give up my plan to say that posterity will not be able to deny us, you, Webern and me, what is our due. I can still believe it often enough, but can no longer say it. There is at present so much revoltingly wrong with the world that I have the urgent need of your, my friends', firm faith in order to put up resistance.

But now on your fiftieth birthday I wish you the continued strength and health so necessary for our battle—you, who alone in our cause, managed to win general recognition. It is our common cause, we three stand and fall together, and were it not sympathy, friendship, and recognition of the True and Good, our community of destiny alone would insure our mutual loyalty. The thanks that I owe and offer you and Webern for this will convince you of the sincerity of my wishes: be happy; we have a share in your happiness; in every sense!

The canon and the recording,[3] neither turned out quite as well as I wished and I am convinced that in at most one week I would have been able to write something much better. But I hope you infer from both the central purpose: the wish to give you small, possibly even great pleasure.

Your Arnold Schoenberg

---

1. This translation is based on a copy located in the Library of Congress.

2. Those who robbed me of my present/would now rob me of the posterity/of which I had been certain./Posterity, belonging to no one/undisturbed, beyond conflict,/should serve as a sanctuary/to him who trusts to it/and seeks rest in the midst of battle.

3. The original letter accompanied both a canon based on motives from Berg's *Lulu* (published in *Arnold Schoenberg Gesammelte Werke: Chorwerke* I/V Reihe A, Band 18, 184) and a recording (apparently lost) of birthday greetings from Schoenberg.

## Berg to Schoenberg[1]

[Vienna] 30 January 1935

You can't imagine, dearest friend, how happy, how overjoyed your letter of 2 January (which I received c. a week ago) made me—and—how it reassured me. For (as regards the letter) I had already been very anxious about your long silence

---

1. This translation is based on the transcription in Rufer 1955.

and had——in hours, days, and weeks of paranoia, entertained the most terrible thoughts. . . .

Thank God—and thanks and praise unto you as well: all of that has now been erased and I am entirely absorbed in the thoughts aroused by your letter. Above all concerning the formation of a "defensive alliance." You have no idea—but no: that's just it—you sense how very important it is for us Austrians as well. Our Art, which is regarded as alien—and thereby our material existence—is just as threatened as elsewhere, where "cultural bolshevism" is "under attack," and one thinks and talks of little else than how best to defend oneself against this attitude. Unfortunately we are very handicapped by the fact that at the moment it is practically impossible without being interpreted politically by our opponents, which of course is precisely what we do not want (or ever wanted). It is all the more necessary for those of us who are "threatened" to establish that kind of unpolitical intellectual common front. We shall discuss it here very thoroughly and since Rudi is—thank God—going over, he will be able to report to you in person.[2]

In the meantime you will have heard about related cultural events in central Europe:—— Only Kleiber refused to stay and is moving to—Salzburg.[3] But compared with events at the Vienna opera: one could write entire novels on the subject——but prefers to make jokes instead, some of which, however, are really great. Rudi will tell you about that at length, too, and not just in jest (jesting that is really bitter earnest).

Otherwise I'm still sweating over my opera score and will have to sweat over it for a long time yet. Meanwhile the *Symphonic Pieces* from it are "going" quite well: Prague (Talich) and Geneva (Ansermet) have already done them;[4] I heard the latter on the radio (with poor reception). The Italian radio (Turin) is to do it sometime soon. Then Rotterdam, Brussels (Kleiber), London (Boult) and . . . Koussevitzky.[5] As far as the Boston performance is concerned, you can imagine how I fear for it after reading your "journal." Of course you have meanwhile received the score and will understand that fear. I am less worried about the coming *Wozzeck* performance at Covent Garden, since I am already familiar with the musical performance from the radio[6] and will discuss the staging in detail) with the director Dr. Ehrhardt,[7] who is here at the moment. I hope I will be invited——if only to get away from the culturally stifling atmosphere here. That would be the end of April. Upon our return we would then move to Carinthia as soon as we can, for we miss it practically

2. Rudolf Kolisch was on a concert tour that included the United States, where he saw the Schoenbergs; he did not emigrate to the United States until 1940.

3. After his resignation from the Berlin State Opera Erich Kleiber traveled extensively and in the years 1936–49 conducted most frequently in Argentina.

4. Berg's symphonic *Lulu* Pieces were performed in Prague (under Václav Talich) on 9 January, in Geneva (under Ernest Ansermet) on 16 January.

5. Further performances took place in Brussels (under Erich Kleiber) on 22 February, in London (under Adrian Boult) on 20 March, and in Boston (under Serge Koussevitzky) on 22 March; the performances in Turin and Rotterdam have not been documented.

6. On 14 March 1934 *Wozzeck* had been given a very successful performance under Adrian Boult on one of the BBC's Symphony Concerts at Queen's Hall; Berg was able to hear the broadcast.

7. The German stage director Otto Ehrhardt, at this time guest director at Covent Garden. The plan for a staged *Wozzeck* performance, set for 30 April 1935, did not materialize.

every day.

To think that you two don't know our "Waldhaus"! And indeed that you never even saw our Ford, which is showing signs of becoming old and dilapidated. And in general: how little we know about one another these days. Despite letters and "journals" . . . the most important things remain almost unsaid. [*Rufer's transcription ends here.*]

## Berg to Schoenberg[1]

[Vienna] 9 February 1935

My dearest, best, kindest friend,

I didn't think it was still possible to be as happy as I was (and have been ever since) when early this morning: on my birthday—precisely to the minute—your congratulations arrived. I don't know what I am most pleased with: your so very dear letter, the wonderful poem, the ingenious canon with its affectionate words and [*Lulu*] references (even including the *Erdgeist*—fourths!!!)———or with the recording: when we heard your dear, beloved voice, both of us: Helene and I, burst into tears: it was as if, after a long, long separation, you had entered the room . . .

My dearest friend, we embrace and thank you a thousand times—today I can do no more than stammer these words: I will write you a longer letter soon.

Helene, too, thanks you with deepest affection.

Your Berg

All our love also to your dear wife.

---

1. This translation is based on the transcription in Rufer 1955. There is no indication whether the transcription is complete.

## Berg to Schoenberg[1]

[Vienna] 11 March 1935

My dearest friend,

What a lovely evening that was yesterday: the *Gurrelieder* Part I, from London (BBC, Clark). Listening to these dear, beloved, wonderful sounds one could gauge again how happy one had once been. And what dreary times these are, in which we have lived for almost two years now. Even if there are certain signs—at least in Austria—that things will recover from the low point of the Marx[2] and Weingartner[3] era, we are filled with the same pessimism as you, and at heart more depressed than ever before. This (as far as I myself am concerned) despite many very gratifying

---

1. This translation is based on the partial transcription in Rufer 1955.

2. Joseph Marx joined the faculty of the Vienna Music Academy in 1914. As director of that institution 1922–25, he initiated the formation of a separate Musikhochschule, whose rector he was 1925–27. See footnote 2 to Berg's letter of 6 August 1931.

3. Felix Weingartner, who had been director of the Vienna Court Opera 1908–11, held that position again 1935–36.

*Alban Berg's studio at Trauttmansdorffgasse 27, Vienna (Library of Congress)*

things brought me by my "fiftieth": by way of celebrations,[4] congratulations, gifts, "appreciations" in newspapers and periodicals. However, none of that, my dearest friend, gave me nearly as much joy as <u>yours</u>. The canon, your reservations notwithstanding, is really "successful"; I wrote it out for myself in a two-hand version and when played thus continuously, it sounds wonderful. And as far as your poem is concerned: I think that even without an optimistic close it results in a wonderful, fully rounded epigram. And the way its sense, its thought is expressed—! there is no one who could match those eight lines, not even someone who is a "poet" by profession.—And what a contrast to the pithy poetry: the natural prose of your recorded speech.

When will your Handel and Monn concertos appear? And the tonal suite?[5] I long for them.

[. . .][6]

4. Berg's 50th birthday was honored by the Vienna Section of the ISCM with a celebration in the small hall of the Musikverein on 9 February.

5. Schoenberg's Monn and Handel arrangements as well as his tonal *Suite in the Old Style* for string orchestra were published by G. Schirmer in New York in 1935.

6. According to Stuckenschmidt (*Schönberg*, 366), Berg further describes how he listened to Schoenberg's recording together with the members of the Kolisch Quartet, Paul von Klenau, Anna Mahler, and Willi Reich and his wife.

*Berg to Schoenberg*[1]

"Waldhaus," 28 August 1935

My dearest friend,

Will this letter arrive by 13 September? I tried to work it out, but it's really very questionable. However: whether before or after, . . . . . you know that on this day I think with special affection of that—which I wish for you all year and shall continue to wish for you in the decades to come.

From your last letter to Webern[2] I believe I can infer that for the immediate future your life—and that of your family—is regulated to your satisfaction——thus pleasant and secure; and to know this with certainty would be enormously reassuring. I also hope that you are now completely well again. And since (according to Viennese newspapers) *Moses und Aaron* [sic] is to receive its world premiere, I assume that you have been working on that. Or can it be that you are already finished with it? If so: where will this work be published? Will we be able to see it or must we, as with your last 3 works, continue to long for it in vain?!—

I myself can report that as of two weeks ago the violin concerto is completely finished.[3] It is in two parts. Each part with two movements: I a) Andante (Präludium) b) Allegretto (Scherzo) II a) Allegro (cadenza) b) Adagio (chorale setting). I chose a very advantageous row for the entire piece (since D major and similar "violin concerto" keys were of course out of the question), namely:

which coincidentally corresponded with the chorale beginning of Bach's "Es ist genug"

My expectation that "upon accomplishing the task" [*nach getaner Arbeit*],[4] which chained me to my desk almost constantly these incomparably beautiful two to three summer months, I would then be able to take it easy the remainder of the summer, unfortunately did not come to pass. As a result of an insect sting I developed a hideous boil—in the middle of my spine—which has tormented me for 2 weeks now and will probably last again as long. That's why I won't be able to go to the International Music Festival in Prague (for political reasons Karlsbad canceled practically at the last minute![5]), and will therefore miss your work yet again, which I

1. This translation was based on a facsimile reproduction of the original in Rufer 1955.

2. Webern visited Berg on 19 August.

3. Earlier that year Berg met the American violinist Louis Krasner, who commissioned a violin concerto from him. Berg finished composition of the work on 12 July, and the orchestration on 11 August.

4. *Nach getaner Arbeit ist gut ruh'n*, a well-known German proverb, meaning that a rest is satisfying after a task has been accomplished.

5. The ISCM Music Festival scheduled for Karlsbad had been canceled when right-wing political groups threatened a disruptive protest. The festival was held in Prague 1–8 September.

had been looking forward to so very much. Also Webern's and my pieces. But I hope to hear it on the radio (2 September) (my own on 6 September; Webern's work, because it is a chamber music concert, will not be broadcast.)[6]

Otherwise there has been much illness in our circle, even death. Just to mention U.E., several weeks ago director Winter's wife and Stein's father both died on the same day. (Shortly before that, Heinsheimer's father and uncle.) And poor Stein has been seriously ill for a terribly long time now.[7] I assume you have heard of it. It looked very, very serious; the appendectomy came almost too late; that explains the complications that have already lasted 4–5 weeks now. But Stein ought to be out of danger by now, and back home.—

We shall be here for the next 2–3 months. I finally want to finish orchestrating *Lulu*. And until then I also have to earn a living. What I'll do then—time will tell. In any event—apart from the question of material existence—we both fear . . . . . . . the cold. Thank heavens you are at least spared that!

We send our warmest regards and once again our most affectionate congratulations to you (also on Helene's behalf)

from your Berg

6. Schoenberg's Variations, Op. 31, were performed and broadcast by the Prague Radio Symphony under Jalowetz on 2 September. On 6 September Jalowetz led a performance of Webern's Concerto, Op. 24, and on the 7th Georg Szell conducted the Czech Philharmonic in a performance of Berg's *Lulu* Suite with Julia Nessy as the soloist.

7. Stein had a burst appendix that summer, which became infected; he spent six weeks in the hospital and recovered only slowly.


*Berg to Schoenberg*[1]

[Vienna] 30 November 1935

[. . .]

For <u>myself</u> I can only say that during these two two-hour interludes[2] I once again felt, after months, that it is also possible to be happy in this life. Helene felt the same.

Oh, how I would like to go through this miraculous work again together with you, page by page, to tell you all the new and beautiful things I've discovered in the score!

We had a similar experience a few days earlier with the George Songs, which were beautifully performed by Julia Nessy and Steuermann.[3] This, too (despite being held in the inner Hagenbund Hall, which was, by the way, very well attended), was an absolutely frenetic success.

1. This translation is based on the partial transcription in Rufer 1955.

2. Bruno Walter performed Schoenberg's *Gurrelieder* in the Konzerthaus on 28 and 29 November and Berg heard the broadcast of the second performance.

3. On 21 November the Vienna section of the ISCM sponsored a concert that featured the Viennese first performance of Krenek's *Symphonische Musik für neun Instrumente*, the premiere of songs by Webern's student Ludwig Zenk, the premiere of Josef Matthias Hauer's Piano Quintet, Op. 69, the first Viennese performance of Webern's Concerto, Op. 24, and Schoenberg's George Songs, Op. 15.

*One of the last photographs of Alban Berg, taken in late 1935*

In this way my return to the city (after a 6-month absence), which I had almost <u>dreaded</u>, included some beautiful aspects after all, and I consequently have an easier time accepting everything else that life in Vienna brings with it. Even the imminent performance of my *Lulu* Pieces (11 December), which inspires me with nothing but dread: the Gesellschaft der Musikfreunde and Ravag are going to do these pieces with Kabasta in the large hall of the Musikverein.[4]—I will be there for the last rehearsals and am curious to know what this music sounds like. Until now there have been 11 performances elsewhere and (with the exception of 2 poor radio

4. The performance of Berg's *Lulu* pieces was conducted by Oswald Kabasta with Lillie Claus as the soloist. This was to be the last concert Berg ever attended.

broadcasts) I still haven't heard a single one. For this season the following are planned: Amsterdam, Zurich, Stockholm, Helsingfors, and possibly Philadelphia (Stokowski?), Karlsbad, Cleveland (?), Copenhagen??

I would be very satisfied with this; and also with the fact that I have something new in the meantime: the Violin Concerto, of which you will have heard (I wrote to you a while ago about the "commission" from the Boston violinist Krasner). Nonetheless, I am not well. Not well financially, as I am not able to maintain my present way of life with the Waldhaus (and yet can't make up my mind to sell the Waldhaus, where I've gotten more work done in 2 years than in the previous 10). Not well as regards my health, since for months now I keep getting boils (at present again, too, therefore my recumbent position!). It first began shortly after completion of the concerto with a frightful boil resulting from an insect sting, which immediately destroyed any possibility of recuperating in the fall, something I very much needed after the summer's work and the preceding *Lulu* years. Finally I am not well emotionally either, which won't surprise you at all in someone who suddenly discovers that he isn't considered a native in his fatherland and is thus completely homeless, all the more since such things cannot be experienced without effects of profound and lasting human disillusionment.

But it isn't appropriate that I tell this to you of all people, who has experienced the same on such a gigantic scale as to make my experiences appear miniscule by comparison. After all, I live in my homeland and can speak my mother tongue.

I would so much like to know more about you, dearest friend and of your loved ones and your life and your work! Thank God I was able to hear a few things from Greissle and Görgl. But alas they also told me of your renewed illness. Get well very very soon and all our love to the three of you!

Your Berg

## Helene Berg to Arnold and Gertrud Schoenberg[1]

Rudolfs Hospital [Vienna] 17 December 1935

My dear friends!

You will have been surprised not to have received a Christmas greeting from us and not even to get our New Year's wishes in time. But we have gone through hard times lately: Alban's months-long illness caused by the boil, of which he wrote you, took a turn for the worse soon after our return here, and developed into a dreadful furunculosis; after 3–4 weeks of home remedies an almost constant fever of 40° set in, which forced him to go to hospital, where he has been operated on several times. Today he received a blood transfusion and now we hope it will gradually improve——but when! You can imagine that he wasn't able to deal with correspondence during this time; having these last 3 years devoted himself full time to his work—correspondence and reading, he is now laid low, totally listless, tortured

---

1. The original of this letter is in private possession; this translation is based on a copy that was kindly made available to the editors by the Alban Berg Stiftung in Vienna in cooperation with the Prussian State Library in Berlin.

by fever and by pain that has resisted all treatment.

But it is for both of us a heartfelt need to give you, you dear friends, at least a sign of life at this time—and we wish the 3 of you all the very, very best for the New Year and greet you most affectionately.

Alban and Helene

I assume that you yourself well (!) remember Crown Prince Rudolf's Hospital.[2]

2. In 1925 Schoenberg had undergone his appendectomy in the same hospital.

# 1936

Hollywood, 1 January 1936

Dear Helene,

I still cannot believe that my dear Alban is gone. I still talk to him in my thoughts, as before, and imagine his answers, and it still seems to me as if he were only as far away as Europe is from America. And I can imagine your pain, since I know how affectionately the two of you always lived together. It is terrible, that he had to die so young, particularly from the human, but also from the artistic standpoint.

Just now, when he had gained renewed artistic recognition with his *Lulu* Suite, which would surely have led to a performance of the entire opera very soon—and though that will probably happen soon now, it would have been recompense for what he had to go through in Germany and Austria. For here in America he is highly respected. I realized that not only from the numerous obituaries, so full of esteem, but also from the sympathy that has been shown to me, who has always——. And you can see to what extent the public sympathizes from the fact that a radio program broadcast all over America brought a dramatized scene from his life, in which he himself, the conductor Richard Lert, and I were cast as characters. . . . I'm convinced that the consciousness of your duty to collect everything that can aid his posthumous reputation and that concerns him—and this concern with everything that brought his work to life—will help you to bear the pain.

One can do no more: than mourn for the dead and make oneself strong, so that one has the strength to mourn for him as he deserves!

Am I to tell you of my sympathy—but I think you can imagine it.

But I do have one request: please write and tell me in detail how it all came about.[1] Did he suffer much? Was he conscious? Was it really a fatal illness or a fateful accident?

A thousand heartfelt regards

Your Arnold Schoenberg

I must add the following:

When I read in a New York paper that the orchestration of *Lulu* is not finished

---

1. In addition to Helene's reply of 14 January 1936 Schoenberg received more detailed reports from, among others, Webern and Stein.

and that Krenek or someone else is to do it, I had the spontaneous idea to ask you whether I should do it. But then my wife reminded me that this would surely harm the work, given the present situation in Germany. But if Alban happened to express the wish that I orchestrate the rest, and if you yourself consider it the best solution, then I would naturally be at your disposal. Of course in all other respects, too, artistic, personal or financial. I hope that Klemperer will perform the *Lulu* Pieces here, presumably at the memorial concert. I've also persuaded Maurice Zam[2] to give a recital where he'll perform the sonata and give a talk about it. Perhaps I can arrange something myself too. Again most warmly

Arnold Schoenberg

2. The pianist Maurice Zam, active in California.

## *Helene Berg to Schoenberg*[1]

Vienna, 14 January 1936

Most esteemed friend!

I thank you for your dear letter and your wonderful friendship that extends beyond death itself. I still cannot believe that Alban has gone for ever, but when such a moment of realization comes I feel as if I were plunging into an abyss. Alban suffered so dreadfully and his death was hard. On the day I wrote to you he spoke so warmly of you and pressed me to hurry. He retained consciousness until the end and his death struggle was frightful. More than 4 hours. I constantly see his desperate face before me and those sad eyes! I constantly ask myself: why not me?

That into this desperation of mine you, esteemed friend, have sent your wonderful suggestion to take over the completion of orchestrating the last act of *Lulu*—that was the 1st ray of light in my darkness! How can I thank you! I know that Alban would be happy that *Lulu* is to become something whole and that it is possible to disregard prejudice and politics where a work of art is concerned![2]

I thank you with all my heart.

All the very best to you and your dear wife.

Your Helene

1. The original of this letter is in private possession. This translation is based on a copy that was kindly made available to the editors by the Alban Berg Stiftung in Vienna in cooperation with the Prussian State Library in Berlin.

2. Schoenberg did not complete the third act. For a detailed account of the reasons which led Schoenberg to reconsider his offer see George Perle, *The Operas of Alban Berg*, Vol. II, *Lulu* (Berkeley, 1985), pp. 235–36 and 282–87.

The orchestration of the third act of *Lulu* was reconstructed by Friedrich Cerha from Berg's short score and the first complete performance of *Lulu* took place in 1979.

# Index of Proper Names

*Musical works are indexed under composers. Other composers. Other written works of Berg and Schoenberg are also indexed under their names.*

Aachen, 394–95
*Abituriententag, Der* (Werfel), 397n
Academy for Church Music, 386n
Achsel-Clemens, Wanda (1886–1977), 344, 366
Ackermann, Otto (1909–60), 437n
Adam, Theodor, 195n, 266
Adler, Alfred 1870–1937), 186n
Adler, Guido (1855–1941), 33n, 80n
Adler, Oskar (1875–1955), 291n, 452n
*Adolf Loos Festschrift zum 60. Geburtstag*, 416n, 419–20
Adorno, Theodor, *see* Wiesengrund-Adorno, Theodor
Akademie der Künste (Berlin), *see* Prussian Academy of the Arts
Akademischer Gesangverein, 95
Akademischer Verband für Literatur und Musik, 68n, 71–75, 77, 79, 82, 84, 86, 88n, 89n, 93n, 96, 110, 121n, 122n, 124n, 125–26, 130n, 131–32, 140, 142n, 163, 166n, 168, 169n, 170, 175, 181n, 184n, 185
*Alban Berg* (Reich), ixn, 312n
*Alban Berg: The Man and His Music* (Redlich), ixn
Albert, Eugen d' (1864–1932), *Tiefland*, 114n
Albert, Viktor, 168n, 174n, 175
Albert Hall (Leipzig), 183n, 388n
Alfano, Franco (1876–1954), 367
  Cello Sonata, 367n
"Alle, welche dich suchen" (Rilke), 225n, 252
*Allgemeine Deutscher Musik-Zeitung*, 42n
Allgemeiner Deutscher Musikverein (ADMV), 341, 372, 376, 382–83, 424–25, 441
Allgemeiner Deutscher Musikverein (ADMV) Music Festival, 372n, 389n, 402n, 425n
*Also sprach Zarathustra* (Nietzsche), 8n

Alt-Aussee, 320
Altenberg, Peter (1859–1919), 74, 145, 168–70, 173–74, 219
  *Neues Altes*, 75n
  *Semmering 1912*, 168n, 173n, 287
  *Untergang des Franzosentums*, 219
Alter, Georg, 324–25
American Relief Administration, 306–7
Amsterdam, 126, 132, 137, 181, 187, 201–2, 203n, 204, 207, 214, 239–40, 256, 259, 279, 280n, 282, 286n, 292, 296, 298, 300n, 366
Amsterdam Concertgebouw Orchestra, 116n, 132n, 181n, 282n, 292, 295n, 300n
*Anbruch*, see *Musikblätter des Anbruch*
Anday, Rosette, 381
Andersen, Robin Chr., 66n,
Andreae, Volkmar, 366n
*Andrees Allgemeiner Handatlas* (Schobel), 225n
Anglo Bank (Vienna), 245
*Anschluss*, 375
Ansermet, Ernest (1883–1969), 424n
Ansorge, Conrad (1862–1930), 68n, 112, 178n
Apostel, Hans Erich (1901–72), 425n
Aravantinos, Panos (1886–1930), 339n
*Arbeiterzeitung* (Vienna), 51–52, 168, 206, 389n
Arbter, Alfred (1877–1936), 115
Arcachon, 444
Arnold, Robert Franz (1872–1938), 109n
*Arnold Schoenberg Gesammelte Schriften*, 415n
Arnold Schoenberg Institute, 298n
*Arnold Schoenberg zum 60. Geburtstag, 13. September 1934*, 125n
*Arnold Schöenberg* (1912), 19, 31, 75n, 78–79, 114, 256
*Arnold Schönberg* (Wellesz), 304n

473